The American City

The American City
What Works, What Doesn't

Alexander Garvin

McGraw-Hill
New York San Francisco Washington, D.C. Auckland Bogotá
Caracas Lisbon London Madrid Mexico City Milan
Montreal New Delhi San Juan Singapore
Sydney Tokyo Toronto

Library of Congress Cataloging-in-Publication Data

Garvin, Alexander.
The American city : what works, what doesn't / Alexander Garvin.
p. cm.
Includes index.
ISBN 0-07-022919-8
1. City planning—United States—Case studies. I. Title.
NA9105.G37 1995
711′.4′0973—dc20
95-30375
CIP

2 3 4 5 6 7 8 9 0 KGP/KGP 9 0 0 9 8 7 6

ISBN 0-07-022919-8

The sponsoring editor for this book was Joel Stein, the editing supervisor was Ruth W. Mannino, and the production supervisor was Pamela Pelton. It was designed and set in Minion by Silvers Design.

Printed and bound by Quebecor/Kingsport Press.

• For My Students •

Contents

Preface

Most books approach the city from one perspective (housing, zoning, historic preservation, etc.), one discipline (history, politics, law, finance, architecture, etc.), or one city (Chicago, Boston, San Francisco, etc.). Instead, *The American City: What Works, What Doesn't* presents a comprehensive, multidisciplinary review of the many attempts to fix the American city (everything from parks to shopping centers, mortgage insurance to planned new towns): what has worked, what hasn't, and why.

The book covers two centuries of activity in cities from one end of the continent to the other. More than 250 projects and programs in 100 cities are analyzed. In all cases they are projects that I have personally visited, usually many times. Because most readers will be unfamiliar with many of the places that are discussed, the text is supplemented with nearly 500 illustrations, most photographs taken during my visits.

The text examines six ingredients of project success (i.e., market, location, design, financing, entrepreneurship, and time) and discusses the ways in which those ingredients affect its outcome. Since I do not believe that project success necessarily results in any improvement to the surrounding city (indeed, some have made things worse), I also redefine successful city planning as public action that generates a desirable, widespread, and sustained private market reaction. Thus, the programs and projects discussed in the book are always examined in terms of the private market reaction they have generated. Because it is impossible to judge project impact until some years after it has been completed, I have made 1990 the cut-off point.

The book presents the logic behind a wide range of strategies for municipal improvement, the initial project or program (some dating back to the nineteenth century) that launched the strategy, the classic cases of its application, and finally a framework for predicting whether that strategy will or will not succeed. It also examines how successful that strategy has been in generating the desired private-market reaction and what legislation, if any, is needed to improve its performance. The reason for this structure is to convince the reader that we have been fixing American cities for two centuries and can identify what will work and what won't.

In addition to the many secondary sources acknowledged in the footnotes, I have included information from a number of primary sources that have not until now appeared in any book, as well as observations that are at variance with often-repeated accounts of particular projects or programs. These differences should be of particular interest to specialists in the field and in some cases will cause them to revise long-held beliefs.

My purpose in presenting new information about classic programs and projects and fresh material on some that have never before been examined within a historical context is not to be original, nor to mention interesting innovations, but to evaluate the success or failure of specific strategies for fixing the American city and to recommend further action.

I hope my readers will come to believe, as I do, that we know how to fix the American city. More important, I hope that whenever their communities are considering any of the strategies presented, they will return to this book to read about what worked, what didn't, and why. Most important, I hope that this book will inspire them to get involved personally and take an active role in improving the American city.

Alexander Garvin, 1995

Acknowledgments

The number of people who have contributed to this book far exceeds the space available to thank them. They include students who have introduced me to their hometowns, friends and acquaintances who have taken me around their cities, librarians and archivists who have shown me documents that I didn't know existed, public officials who have shared stories and fugitive documents about programs and cities all over America. I thank them all.

In particular, I thank my parents, who always loyally provided support and good counsel, and my brother, George, whose enthusiasm is a constant inspiration.

Everybody is indebted to his teachers. Three in particular have influenced the contents of this book. To this day I think about the ideas that I first encountered in Vincent Scully's lectures on American architecture. Christopher Tunnard insisted that I consider the broad cultural underpinnings of American city planning. Dennis Durden persuaded me always to go out and see for myself before deciding whether something worked.

Yale University has nurtured my intellectual development for almost four decades, first while I was an undergraduate, then while I was a graduate student, and finally during the 28 years I have taught there. It has provided the best and brightest students to question my observations, talented teaching assistants to make sure I was clear and convincing in conveying my ideas, and generous colleagues with whom to discuss the widest range of subjects. I have found all sorts of unexpected treasures in its extraordinary library. For all of this, I am forever indebted to everybody at Yale (past and present) and to a series of deans (Georges May, Horace Taft, Sidney Altman, the late Martin Griffin, Howard Lamar, Donald Kagan, Donald Engleman, and Richard Broadhead) who provided support even when they were without conventional explanations for my presence at Yale.

My partners, Irwin Leimas, Fred Roth, Robert Haskell, and Alvin Schein have provided me with countless lessons in the day-to-day operation of a business. Thanks to them and to my father I understand how real estate works and am able to explain how and why public action can succeed or fail in generating any private-market reaction.

Donald Elliott and Edward Robin are responsible for bringing me into New York City government. I continue to regard their achievements as the truest demonstration of the role that city planners can and should play in government. During the 10 years I spent as a full-time "bureaucrat," I came to know hundreds of dedicated men and women who worked hard and effectively to make New York City a better place in which to live and work. I was inspired by the leadership of Roger Starr, John Zuccotti, Nathan Leventhal, and the late Robert Wagner, Jr. (who also helped me with the text of this book). I learned how government gets things done by watching such talented individuals as Jack Toby, David McGregor, Joseph Christian, Jolie Hammer, Victor Marrero, Joe Tenga, Robert Milward, Martha Davis, Barry Light, Charles Cuneo, Russell McCubbin, Henry Lanier, Barbara Leeds, Michael Lappin, Jean Lerman, Linda Einhorn, John Skelly, Chris Hooke, Tupper Thomas, Jesse Taylor, Robert Jacobson, and

Marilyn Gelber. Thanks to Joseph Rose, I am now back in government encountering a whole new generation of talented people who are working hard to make government effective. These dedicated civil servants helped me to grasp the meaning and possibilities of effective public action.

Without the help and encouragement of my friends this book would never have been written. Many do not even know the ways in which they helped to transform me into a writer. Among those who played a critical role are Alan and Leslie Beller, Eugenie Ladner Birch, Iris and Paul Brest, David and Susan Brownlee, Van Burger, Sherwin Goldman, Catherine Welsh Howe, Robert and Hannah Kaiser, Robert Kimball, Richard Kumro, Michael Larson, Lance and Carol Leibman, John Meigs, Nick Monroe, Richard Peiser, Michael Piore, Alec and Drika Purves, Keith Rogal, Daniel and Joanna Rose, David Rose and Gail Gremse, Richard Singer, Megan Tourlis, Tappy and Robin Wilder, and Rodney Yoder.

Con Howe, David Lahm, Bethami Probst, and Scott Stone made significant contributions to the text. Their suggestions helped me to clarify my thinking and increase the persuasiveness of my arguments. The FIND/SVP information service answered my questions when nobody else could. Chris Koon provided original drawings. The extraordinary book cover is the work of Sandra Baker. Arthur Klebanoff provided invaluable advice and is responsible for finding my publisher. The editorial team at McGraw-Hill—Joel Stein, Wendy Lochner, and especially Ruth Mannino—were of great assistance. The design team of Scott and Caryl Silvers transformed the text and illustrations into a beautiful volume. I cannot imagine working with more generous or supportive collaborators.

Last and most important are my two friends, Ted Volckhausen and Rick Henderson, who read every word of every version of every chapter. They patiently corrected spelling, grammar, punctuation—even footnotes. More important, they challenged ideas that were unclear or poorly explained, they questioned the logic of my theories, and they were always there to provide encouragement. I can never thank them enough. My major regret is that Rick died before I could give him his well-earned copy of this book.

Alexander Garvin, 1995

The American City

Chicago, 1892 *(Negative no. ICHi-03211; courtesy of Chicago Historical Society)* **and 1984** *(Alexander Garvin).*

Pittsburgh, 1936 *(Courtesy of Carnegie Library of Pittsburgh)* **and 1984** *(Alexander Garvin).*

Portland, 1974 *(Negative no. OrHi 76725; courtesy of Oregon Historical Society)* **and 1991** (Alexander Garvin).

1

A Realistic Approach to City and Suburban Planning

There is agreement neither on what to do to improve our cities and suburbs nor on how to get the job done. Some believe the answers are a matter of money; others believe they involve politics, or racial and ethnic conflict, or some other factor. One thing most people share, though, is disillusionment with urban planning as a way of fixing the American city.

This disillusionment with urban planning is far from justified. There are dozens of projects that are triumphs of American city planning:

- Chicago would not have 23 miles of continuous park land along Lake Michigan if this land had not been included in the city's comprehensive plan of 1909.
- The glorious antebellum sections of Charleston, South Carolina, would not have survived if the city had not adopted zoning in 1931.
- Pittsburgh would not rank third in the nation as a major corporate headquarters center if it had not virtually rebuilt its downtown during the 1940s and 1950s.
- Portland, Oregon, would not be a lively retail and employment center if during the 1970s and 1980s it had not enriched its pedestrian environment, built a light-rail system, and reclaimed its riverfront.

Such triumphs are easy to overlook. Once a problem is solved it disappears and is forgotten. Even local excitement over a successful project rarely spills over into national publications other than those with a narrow group of readers (preservationists, environmentalists, realtors, lawyers, architects, bankers, or some other group that is intimately involved with specific sets of city problems).

Many people are disillusioned with urban planning because so many of its promises are not kept. Usually these promises are made in good faith by city planners who believe that their job is to establish municipal goals and provide blueprints for a better city. Too often the efforts of these planners end without much consideration of how they will obtain political support for their proposals, who will execute them, or where the money to finance them will come from.

Charleston, 1991. *(Alexander Garvin)*

Pittsburgh, 1983. Property owners responded to public redevelopment of the Golden Triangle by erecting so many new buildings that they more than doubled the city's inventory of office space.

Disillusionment with urban planning also develops when physical improvements fail to solve deep-seated social problems. This is not the fault of urban planning. After all, fixing cities does not fix people. The disillusionment is the product of false expectations. Crime, delinquency, and poverty are afflictions of city residents, not of the cities themselves. Such problems can be found in suburban and rural areas as well.

We need more realistic expectations of what urban planning can accomplish. While it cannot change human nature and is therefore not a panacea for all urban ills, it surely can improve a city's physical plant and consequently affect the safety, utility, attractiveness, and character of city life. When Chicago began creating its waterfront parks, for example, large sections of the shoreline of Lake Michigan were being used as railyards and garbage dumps. Simply removing these uses reduced hazards and made neighboring property more attractive.

We also need a better understanding of how effective planning is translated into a better quality of life. It is not accomplished by planners operating in a vacuum. By themselves, urban planners cannot accomplish very much. Improving cities requires the active participation of property owners, bankers, developers, architects, lawyers, contractors, and all sorts of people involved with real estate. It also requires the sanction of community groups, civic organizations, elected and appointed public officials, and municipal employees. Together they provide the financial and political means of bringing plans to fruition. Without them even the best plans will remain irrelevant dreams.

Finally, the planning profession itself needs to improve its understanding of the way physical changes to a city can achieve a more smoothly functioning environment, a healthier economy, and a better quality of life. For example, the restoration of Charleston's historic district generated substantial tourist spending, just as the reconstruction of the bridges and highways leading into downtown Pittsburgh reduced the cost of doing business and initiated an era of major corporate investment. These and other successful planning strategies are too frequently ignored in the search for more innovative prescriptions.

At its best, planning alters the very character of city life. During the 1970s and 1980s, Portland completely reorganized vehicular and pedestrian circulation. The business district was encircled by a ring road that greatly improved motor vehicle accessibility. A light-rail system provided transit service from the suburbs. Pedestrian precincts were established by transforming the old downtown highway into a riverfront park, by eliminating private motor vehicles from two downtown streets and repaving them as transitways, and by acquiring several downtown blocks and converting them into new public parks. As a result, Portland became a safer, more convenient, more beautiful city. It also became a more attractive destination for the city's rapidly growing metropolitan region, drawing tens of thousands of additional weekday shoppers and weekend visitors.

Despite many remarkable successes, American city planning has been plagued with continuing mistakes. These mistakes were and are avoidable. More than three decades have passed since Jane Jacobs in her pioneering book, *The Death and Life of Great American Cities,* observed that we had spent billions of dollars for

> *Housing projects that are truly marvels of dullness and regimentation.... Civic centers that are avoided by everyone but bums, who have fewer choices of loitering places than others. Commercial centers that are lack-luster imitations of standardized suburban chain-store shopping. Promenades that go from no place to nowhere and have no promenaders. Expressways that eviscerate great cities. This is not the rebuilding of cities. This is the sacking of cities.*[1]

Three decades and hundreds of billions of dollars later, her criticisms still ring true. Most cities continue to lack housing, civic and commercial centers, places to congregate and promenade, and traffic arteries. In too many cases, the attempt to remedy the situation constituted further "sacking of cities." These attempts may have been financially and politically feasible. However, they failed because they were conceived without proper consideration as to whether they would benefit the surrounding city.

Defining the Planning Process

Much of the nation's unsuccessful urban planning arises from the erroneous belief that project success equals urban planning success. Highways that are filled with automobiles, housing projects that are fully rented, and civic centers with plenty of busy bureaucrats may be successful on their own terms. The cities around them, however, may be completely unaffected. Worse, they may be in even greater trouble than they were prior to these projects.

Only when a project also has beneficial impact on the surrounding community can it be considered successful planning. Thus, urban planning should be defined as *public action that will produce a sustained and widespread private market reaction.* That is precisely what has occurred wherever urban planning has been successful.

- When Chicago transformed its lake shore into a continuous park and drive, the real estate industry responded by spending billions to make it a setting for tens of thousands of new apartments.
- When Charleston preserved its "old and historic" district, it retained an extraordinary physical asset that, decades later, would attract a growing population and provide the basis of a thriving economy.
- When Pittsburgh cleared its downtown of the clutter of railyards and warehouses; reduced air and water pollution; and built new highways, bridges, and downtown garages, businesses responded by rebuilding half the central business district.
- When Portland invested in a riverfront park, a light-rail system, and pedestrianized streets, the private sector responded by erecting office buildings, retail stores, hotels, and apartment houses.

The scope of urban planning must be broadened. Over the past few decades, the areas of public concern and therefore of public action have expanded both substantively and geographically. Outraged citizens have demanded action to protect the natural environment, to preserve the national heritage, to provide a range of services that had never before been considered a public responsibility, and to deal with territory outside local political jurisdictions. The country should be deeply grateful to these activists for insisting that government fill important vacuums.

Pittsburgh, 1937. Downtown traffic congestion prior to redevelopment. *(Courtesy of Carnegie Library of Pittsburgh)*

Too often, we have responded to their legitimate demands by creating a set of protected special interests that are excluded from competition with other equally legitimate public concerns. As a result, large geographic areas are removed from active use without consideration of the social consequences. Buildings are declared landmarks without reference to economic impact. Services are provided to socially impaired individuals without any thought of the effect on the surrounding community. The situation can be rectified simply by including these new areas of public concern within the scope of city planning and simultaneously including a far broader range of participants in the planning process.

The broad definition of urban planning suggested above highlights the fact that planning is about *change:* preventing undesirable change and encouraging desirable change. It may involve a tax incentive, a zoning regulation, or some other technical prescription, but only as a mechanism for instigating change. The important element is change itself. Planners obtain changes in safety, utility, and attractiveness of city life through strategic public investment, regulation, and incentives for private action.

Strategic Public Investment

Nineteenth-century planning was particularly enamored of strategic government investment. Just think of the many loca-

Portland, 1990. Tri-Met light-rail system. *(Alexander Garvin)*

tions that were made more attractive for development by installing water mains, sewer pipes, or transit lines prior to development.

A more recent example is federal subsidization of the interstate highway system. It vastly increased the amount of land within commuting distance of cities and, in the process, increased the attractiveness of suburban locations. Developers eagerly purchased the newly accessible land and built houses, shopping malls, and office parks. In the process millions of consumers were given the opportunity of owning a house in the country, close to shopping facilities and sometimes also near their jobs.

There were adverse impacts as well. The interstate highway system, for example, attracted motorists away from traditional urban arterials, thereby reducing demand in the retail establishments that had previously catered to the large market of automobile-oriented consumers. For decades after the highways were built, cities were plagued with blighted retail streets, unable to replace the customers that previously had filled their no longer active stores.

The difference between routine capital spending and strategically planned investments lies in using these expenditures to spark further investment by private businesses, financial institutions, property owners, and developers. The revitalization of downtown Portland, Oregon, during the 1970s and 1980s provides a vivid demonstration of the effectiveness of such strategic capital investment. During this period the city rebuilt the streets and sidewalks of two parallel avenues, transforming them into handsome red-brick pedestrian transitways lined with bus shelters, artwork, fountains, and new street furniture. Portland also established a 27-stop light-rail system that starts downtown, moves along two parallel streets that cross the two transitways, and extends 15 miles into the suburbs. Eventually the city purchased the block where the pedestrian transitways and the light-rail system cross for a new public square.[2]

All this public investment transformed the area into the most convenient spot in downtown Portland—perfect for retail shopping. The response from the private sector was both predictable and impressive. Nordstrom's built a new store facing the square. The Rouse Company acquired the nearby Olds & King department store and converted it into "The Galleria," a 75-foot-high atrium surrounded by a variety of restaurants, cafés, and retail stores. Saks Fifth Avenue, like Nordstrom's, opened a department store. The block next to Saks was rebuilt as Pioneer Place, a multistory, air-conditioned atrium with shops, restaurants, and tourist-oriented retail outlets. Few cities have been as effective in using capital expenditures to spur private investment or in obtaining the accompanying increase in retail sales, employment, and taxes.

Regulation

Regulation is most often used to alter the size and character of the market and the design of the physical environment. Perhaps the single most effective example occurred during the 1930s when the federal government restructured the banking system and in the process dramatically altered the housing market. Prior to that time few banks provided mortgage loans that covered more than half the cost of a house. These loans were extended for relatively short periods of time (two to five years) and involved little or no amortization.

The *National Housing Act* of 1934, which created the Federal Housing Administration (FHA), changed all that. It regulated the rate of interest and the terms of every mortgage that it insured. By 1938, a house could be bought for a cash down payment equal to 10 percent of the purchase price. The other 90 percent came in the form of a 25-year, self-amortizing, FHA-insured mortgage loan. These new mortgage lending practices greatly increased the number of people who could afford a down payment on a house as well as monthly debt service payments on a mortgage, and thereby also increased the size of the market for single-family houses. That

Portland, 1990. One of two parallel pedestrianized streets. *(Alexander Garvin)*

Portland, 1990. Pioneer Courthouse Square built at the intersection of the light-rail system and the city's two pedestrianized streets. *(Alexander Garvin)*

is one of several reasons that the proportion of American households that owned their home increased from 44 percent in 1940 to 64 percent in 1990.

Not only did the FHA alter the size of the market, it also determined the design of the product. In order to be eligible for FHA mortgage insurance a house had to conform to published minimum property standards that included structure, materials, and room sizes. The effect of these regulations was to guarantee a minimum standard of quality on a national scale.

Regulation also can be used to alter the character of an entire area. This process usually begins with an attempt to prevent hazardous conditions. Local governments, for example, are usually interested in providing sufficient open land to permit natural drainage of rain and snow, to prevent waste from percolating through the ground to contaminate the water supply, and to ensure privacy. One way of achieving these objectives is to require a minimum lot size for any development (e.g., no more than one house per acre). The end result is the landscape of one-family houses on large lots that can be found throughout the nation.

As with strategic government investment, a regulation such as mandating minimum lot sizes also can produce an adverse impact. Since the amount of land in any community is finite, whenever a minimum lot size is adopted the future supply of house sites is reduced. This reciprocal relationship between the degree of regulation and the size of the market for the resulting product is inevitable. It was poignantly explained by Jacob Riis, who, in 1901, was already lamenting that the minimum construction requirements of "tenement house reform...tended to make it impossible for anyone [not able] to pay $75 to live on Manhattan Island."[3]

Zoning regulations can be used to exclude the intrusive development incompatible with desired land-use patterns. By eliminating the possibility of such undesirable change, it reduces the risk of future problems (e.g., traffic, pollution, and noise) and thereby increases the attractiveness of investing in real estate. Santa Barbara, California, and Santa Fe, New Mexico, demonstrate how land-use regulation can stimulate real estate activity by reducing the risk of developing property.[4]

Civic leaders in both cities were eager to spur economic growth and decided to do so by encouraging investment in tourist-oriented facilities. Not only did they need something with which to attract the growing tourist market, but they needed to induce the real estate industry to build the necessary facilities.

At the beginning of the twentieth century, when this effort began, both communities were dusty, wooden towns so typical of those seen in western movies. They decided to reshape themselves to conform to a specific heritage. Santa Barbara chose a

Portland, 1990. Shopping facilities built by private developers once the public transit and pedestrian system had been completed. *(Alexander Garvin)*

Santa Fe, 1868. Palace of Governors prior to remodeling in the "New-Old Santa Fe Style." *(Negative no. 45819; courtesy of Museum of New Mexico)*

Santa Fe, 1989. Palace of Governors after remodeling in the "New-Old Santa Fe Style." *(Alexander Garvin)*

Mediterranean image, while Santa Fe selected a Pueblo Indian one. Both adopted building laws that required property owners to develop in compliance with the image that had been selected.

By mandating design requirements, each city increased its tourist appeal. More important, since property owners were assured of compatible neighboring buildings, the risk of failure was reduced and the likelihood of capturing the customers who had been attracted by the area's charming heritage was increased. It would be difficult to create a more auspicious climate for a tourist-based economy.

Santa Barbara, 1880. Aerial view of the city when it was a typical wooden western town. *(Courtesy of Santa Barbara Historical Society)*

Incentives

Although the use of incentives is becoming more popular, the approach has been around a long time. One of the oldest examples is the incentive for people to own their homes. During the Civil War, Congress allowed taxpayers to deduct interest payments and local taxes from the income that formed the basis of federal tax payments. The same deduction of mortgage interest and taxes was reintroduced in 1913, when the federal income tax was adopted.

There can be no serious change either in cities or suburbs without a favorable investment climate. In many instances government need only guarantee two things: intelligent spending on capital improvements and regulatory policies that provide stability and encourage market demand. Only when investment and regulation are insufficient to do the job should incentives come into play.

New York City faced such a situation during the mid-1970s. The city's fiscal crisis precluded most capital spending. Political gridlock prevented serious regulatory reform. At the same time the rate of housing deterioration and abandonment had reached alarming proportions. The city administration had to develop a strategy that would prevent further deterioration.[5] One technique seemed most likely to succeed: incentives that were sufficiently generous to induce private investment in the existing housing stock. Consequently, the Housing and Development Administration proposed to revise the city's little-known J-51 Program. It provided a 12-year exemption from any increase in real estate tax assessment due to physical improvements and a deduction from annual real estate tax payments of a portion of the cost of those improvements.[6]

The problem with the earlier J-51 Program was that it did not apply to three-quarters of the city's housing stock. Existing apartments that were not subject to rent control (because they were in structures that had been built after 1947, or had experienced a change in occupancy after 1971, or were owner-occupied) could not obtain these benefits unless they became subject to rent control. Nonresidential structures that had been converted to residential use were completely ineligible. Without J-51 benefits, any major investment in improvements resulted in punishment—a major increase in the real estate tax assessment. This was especially burdensome to the 770,000 apartments then subject to rent stabilization, New York City's second rent regulatory system.[7]

During 1976, the Beame Administration persuaded the state legislature and the New York City Council to smash the

Santa Barbara, 1988. Aerial view of the city after it had been altered to conform with the Hispano-Mediterranean esthetic required by local zoning. *(Alexander Garvin)*

rent control barrier by extending eligibility to rent-stabilized apartments. J-51 benefits were also provided for cooperative and condominium apartments in newly rehabilitated residential structures and to rental apartments in buildings converted from nonresidential to residential use, provided that they would become subject to some form of rent regulation.

These tax incentives completely altered the climate for investment in existing buildings. Banks increased their lending for housing rehabilitation, building owners increased their investments in building improvements, and developers began purchasing vacant structures for conversion to residential use. In fiscal 1977–1978, the first year in which the full impact of these incentives could be measured, more than 48,000 apartments were granted J-51 benefits.

J-51 provided an incentive that was sufficiently attractive to induce major investment in housing rehabilitation. However, there was another reason that so many property owners chose to apply for benefits. The administration of the program was made user-friendly. Until 1975 the program operated subject to unpublished regulations. Specific improvements that were eligible for benefits and the maximum allowable expenditures for those improvements were listed on a typed schedule that was kept by the individual responsible for reviewing applications. Applicants had to file 26 separate forms. Program procedures were known to a few well-connected lawyers and developers, but had never been made public.[8]

Within months of enactment of the revised J-51 Program, the administration published official regulations, made public a printed schedule of all allowable costs, and reduced the required filing to three one-page forms. Even unsophisticated property owners and poorly informed mortgage officers were now able to calculate probable J-51 benefits. As a result of these efforts, hundreds of property owners who had always had an aversion to government agencies were willing to seek the assistance they needed. In the process tens of millions of dollars were invested in improving the existing housing stock, demonstrating that properly conceived incentives can generate a desirable, sustained, and widespread market reaction.[9]

A New Approach to Urban Planning

We need a new approach to urban planning that explicitly deals with both *public action* and the probable *private market reaction.* Such change-oriented planning requires general acceptance of the idea that while urban planners are in the change business, it is others who will make that change: civic leaders, interest groups, community organizations, property owners, developers, bankers, lawyers, architects, engineers, elected and appointed public officials—the list is endless.

Being entirely dependent on these other players, urban planners must concentrate on increasing the chances that everybody else's agenda will be successful. They may choose to do so by targeting public investment in infrastructure and community facilities, or by shaping the regulatory system, or by introducing incentives that will encourage market activity. But whatever they select, their role must be to initiate and shepherd often controversial expenditures and legislation. More important, the public will be able to hold them accountable by evaluating the cost effectiveness of the private market reaction to their programs.

Only when this approach to urban planning takes hold will we get beyond the technical studies, needs analyses, and visions of the good city that currently masquerade as urban planning and get on with the business of fixing the American city.

Notes

1. Jane Jacobs, *The Death and Life of Great American Cities,* Random House, New York, 1961, p. 4.
2. A more detailed discussion of downtown redevelopment in Portland can be found in Chapters 7 and 18.
3. Jacob Riis, in a letter probably to Dr. Jane Robbins, October 10, 1891, quoted by Roy Lubove in *The Progressives and the Slums,* University of Pittsburgh Press, Pittsburgh, 1962, p. 181.
4. A more detailed discussion of regulation in Santa Barbara and Santa Fe can be found in Chapter 17.
5. The author, at that time deputy commissioner of housing in charge of J-51 and all other housing rehabilitation programs, proposed this strategy.
6. A more detailed discussion of J-51 can be found in Chapters 10 and 17.
7. New York City regulates rents pursuant to two programs: rent control and rent stabilization. In 1975, 642,000 of New York City's 2,719,000 housing units were rent controlled. Lawrence Bloomberg (with Helen Lamale), *The Rental Housing Situation in New York City 1975,* Housing & Development Administration, New York, January 1976.
8. The author was responsible for J-51 during the period in which these changes were made.
9. During the past 15 years many user-friendly characteristics of the program were eliminated. As a result, few property owners now apply for J-51 benefits without the assistance of a lawyer or expediter who specializes in agency processing.

2

Ingredients of Success

San Francisco, 1992. Ghirardelli Square. *(Alexander Garvin)*

There is no formula that guarantees a desirable private market reaction in response to public action. However, there are six ingredients that must be intelligently dealt with for any project to succeed. They are: market, location, design, financing, entrepreneurship, and time.

The need to consider these ingredients may seem obvious. Unfortunately, the proliferation of still-born projects reveals how little they are understood. Otherwise, why would there be housing for which there is no *market,* commercial centers that are in the wrong *location,* civic centers for which *financing* is not available, places whose *design* makes them unpleasant and unsafe areas in which to congregate, economic development projects whose completion is beyond the *entrepreneurship* of the responsible public agency, and public works whose *time* has passed but are still under way.

If any of these six ingredients is absent or if they are not combined in a mutually reinforcing fashion, the project will fail. Even when all the ingredients are properly combined, they may be insufficient to guarantee project success because city planners, unlike chefs, cannot keep unexpected ingredients from getting into the pot. Nevertheless, an intelligent mix of market, location, design, financing, entrepreneurship, and time is the key to success. Thus, an understanding of how these elements operate and interact will increase the likelihood of favorable results.

Market

The existence of a market for any urban planning prescription is primary, for without it there is no reason even to consider action. The word "market" is not synonymous with population. It means a specific population's desire for something and its ability and willingness to pay for it in the face of available alternatives. Nor is market synonymous with "need." Too often what one person calls a need is really a preference for what other people ought to have.

To be successful, an urban planning prescription must reflect both market demand and supply. The demand side requires a user population with enough money to purchase what it desires and the willingness to spend it. That means sufficient users to cover both capital cost and operating expenses. If it requires private action, there will have to be user charges; if it is a public project, the electorate will have to be willing to pay the necessary taxes.

The role that demand plays in determining the success of an urban planning prescription is illustrated by two neighborhood revitalization programs adopted for Savannah, Georgia. Both tried to preserve some of the nation's most attractive nineteenth-century buildings that, prior to these programs, had been vacant or dilapidated. The first neighborhood revitalization program began during the late 1960s and successfully revived the relatively small Pulaski Ward. It was followed by a second, similar effort that failed to restore the city's much larger Victorian District.[1]

In both instances, concerned citizens established nonprofit institutions to salvage threatened historic structures. The mechanism they employed was a revolving fund that provided money to purchase vacant or deteriorating buildings. The fund was reimbursed from the proceeds of the resale of these buildings to responsible owners who agreed to restore and maintain them.

Savannah, 1975. The Pulaski Ward Historic District that was successfully revived through the use of a revolving fund. *(Alexander Garvin)*

Savannah, 1990. Vacant and dilapidated buildings in the Historic Victorian District, 15 years after the initiation of two revolving funds that failed to spur widespread neighborhood rehabilitation. *(Alexander Garvin)*

The 15-acre Pulaski Ward, initially settled in the 1840s, surrounds one of Savannah's charming original squares. In 1964, when the Historic Savannah Foundation chose it as a target area, Pulaski Ward had become a dilapidated neighborhood with many vacant (albeit historic) structures. Over the next 18 months, Historic Savannah acquired and resold 54 buildings, generating more than $1.5 million in privately financed renovation. Subsequently another dozen buildings were acquired and rehabilitated privately. Eventually owners renovated every building in the ward and even began filling in vacant lots with small-scale new construction.

The effort to revitalize Pulaski Ward was so successful that in the mid-1970s, preservationists decided to try the same strategy in the 150 blocks that make up Savannah's Victorian District. This time two separate revolving funds were set up. Federal subsidies were obtained to reduce the cost of rehabilitation to a level that was affordable for the area's low-income population. By 1990 more than 300 housing units had been rehabilitated and another 40 units built.

These efforts did not spark widespread investment in the area, which in 1992 remained riddled with vacant and deteriorating structures. Failure became inevitable when federal subsidy programs were curtailed during the early 1980s. Those who had conceived this preservation strategy based it on subsidies without which the area's low–income residents would be unable to afford debt service on a mortgage (covering the cost of acquisition and rehabilitation). Thus, when the federal government terminated its programs there was no way to pay for further renovation of the area's vacant but dilapidated buildings.

The revolving fund was successful in Pulaski Ward because there had been enough households who desired and could afford to live in charming, restored residences on the edge of downtown Savannah. All that had been necessary to tap that market was an initial investment in some of the area's vacant buildings. The same prescription failed in the Victorian District because without subsidies there was an insufficient market for the renovation of its no-less-charming historic structures.

Market demand is not just a matter of affordability. It also involves alternatives that are currently available or may become available soon. Will they be cheaper, more convenient, or more attractive? Too often, completed projects fail because planners pay insufficient attention to probable competition.

Competition doomed the redevelopment of downtown New Haven, Connecticut. During the 1950s, the business district faced the usual symptoms of decline: accelerating physical deterioration, decreasing retail sales, and a diminishing tax base. The city's consultants proposed rebuilding its ostensibly obsolete physical plant and using federal urban renewal funds to pay for it. Their plan called for clearing a major portion of the central business district and creating Chapel Square: two department stores, an air-conditioned shopping mall, an office building, a hotel, and a parking garage. Since no substantial increase in demand for office space had been identified, Chapel Square was conceived as a predominantly retail center.[2]

In the late 1960s, not long after completion, one of the department stores closed. The shopping mall attracted few customers until the mid-1980s, when a new city administration provided substantial subsidies and brought in the Rouse Company to renovate and remarket the project. In 1993 the second department store closed.

What went wrong? The diagnosis was faulty. New Haven was not in trouble because of an obsolete physical plant. It was in trouble because suburban competitors were doing a better job supplying the same market. Restructuring the business district to accommodate unnecessary new retail structures could never be much help.

Location

Location consists of two elements: a site's inherent characteristics and its proximity to other locations. Site characteristics alone may be sufficient to make it attractive. A spectacular view is an example. Another is an architecturally distinctive housing stock, such as the one that made renovation particularly inviting in the historic districts of Savannah.

Site conditions can also ruin an otherwise desirable location. During the first half of the twentieth century, air pollution in downtown Pittsburgh was so serious that street lights often remained on 24 hours a day. Raw sewage polluted both river fronts. Daytime traffic congestion seriously restricted

New Haven, c. 1960. Aerial view of the Church Street Urban Renewal Project with a model of the Chapel Square Mall superimposed. *(From L. Redstone, The New Downtowns, McGraw-Hill, New York, 1976)*

TABLE 2.1
DISTANCE MEASURED IN TRAVELING TIME
(SWITZERLAND: 1951)[4]

Conveyance	Miles traveled in 30 minutes
Pedestrian	1.2
Trolley	5.3
Bicycle	5.6
Bus	6.2
Train (local)	7.8
Automobile	8.7
Subway	9.6
Train (express)	12.7

both circulation and business activity. In order to alter these inhibiting site conditions, the city obtained state legislation that allowed it to regulate air and water pollution, rebuild its highways and bridges, create more than 5000 parking spaces, and clear away the tangle of downtown railyards, dilapidated warehouses, and obsolete manufacturing lofts. Once these site conditions were eliminated, property owners invested hundreds of millions in redevelopment. Within a couple of decades, more than half of the business district had been rebuilt.[3]

Proximity involves both time and space. The temporal dimension is shaped by technology and can be understood in terms of available means of conveyance (Table 2.1). During the eighteenth century, when people were concerned with walking distances, cities had to be compact and densely built up. By the end of the twentieth century, when distance is measured in driving time, the resultant landscape is "spread city."

The spatial dimension of proximity involves interdependence with neighboring areas. An obvious example is the relationship between movie theaters, parking facilities, and eating places. On a larger scale, nineteenth-century warehouse and manufacturing districts often developed in close proximity to waterfront areas through which they received and shipped goods and materials.

Even before the end of World War II, most mercantile districts, especially in port cities and railroad towns, had begun a slow and steady decline. There was no longer the same need for large, multistory warehouses and manufacturing structures near the traffic-congested waterfront. Now merchandise could be stored in large prepackaged containers that were lifted by crane and shipped by truck along an increasingly convenient highway system. Containerports needed too much upland open space to be easily located along already built-up city waterfronts. Instead, they were being established along vacant shorefronts, nearer to major highways. Production was easier and cheaper in single-story, suburban factories that could provide extended horizontal production lines, easy parking for employees, and even easier highway access for

Pittsburgh, 1947. The rail yards, warehouses, and lofts that were cleared to create the Golden Triangle.
(Courtesy of Carnegie Library of Pittsburgh)

trucks. Technological change had transformed proximity to the waterfront from an asset into a liability.

Recognition of changing demand for different locations is often quite slow. Most city officials only became aware of the decreasing importance of waterfront shipping from declining tax collections and increasing building vacancies. Recognition of the opportunities provided by declining but still attractive waterfront locations became apparent only after the success of Ghirardelli Square in San Francisco.[5]

This project, conceived in 1962, converted into an urban marketplace 2.5 acres of factory and warehouse structures that had once housed a chocolate company. The design (by architects Wurster, Bernardi & Emmons Inc. and landscape architects Lawrence Halprin & Associates) established a charming combination of fashionable retail stores and restaurants in a physical setting redolent of old San Francisco. Ghirardelli Square became an instant tourist attraction. More important, it became an inspiration for similar projects in the surrounding Fisherman's Wharf section of San Francisco and throughout the country.

The imitators of Ghirardelli Square soon discovered that financial success was not guaranteed by rehabilitation and adaptive reuse of older structures, nor by creation of an urban marketplace with the imagery of a bygone era. River Quay in Kansas City, Missouri, is a particularly vivid example.[6]

In 1973, inspired by the success of Ghirardelli Square, enterprising planners decided to transform River Quay, the run down district of bars, rooming houses, cheap hotels, and dilapidated buildings along Delaware Street that had been the birthplace of Kansas City, into an "old town" marketplace. Their plan called for rehabilitated buildings, restored "historic" street fronts, and decorative sidewalks with new street trees. At first these improvements brought restaurants, shops, and artists' studios. But it soon became clear that the market they attracted was too small. Retailers moved away or went out of business and the area reverted to its former vacant and dilapidated condition.[7]

At exactly the same time, Westport, another decaying commercial section of Kansas City, was transformed into a

San Francisco, 1992. The Ghirardelli Chocolate Factory was transformed into a tourist marketplace. *(Alexander Garvin)*

thriving urban marketplace. Westport was an intersection lined with dilapidated storefronts that in the nineteenth century had been a busy departure point for wagon caravans going west. Eventually it was overshadowed by the port of Kansas City, 3½ miles north, and annexed. From then on, Westport had slowly declined until a developer acquired several of its rundown stores. He restored the façades, reconstructed the interior retail space, and installed new street furniture and decorative paving. The new "Westport Square" easily attracted the middle-class clientele from surrounding residential areas.

Like Ghirardelli Square, both Westport Square and River Quay renovated decaying, multistory commercial structures and recreated gussied up images of nineteenth-century mercantile America. The prescription failed at River Quay because it was applied to the wrong location. The bulk of Kansas City's population lived several miles inland. It was unwilling to drive to River Quay when there were more attractive alternatives (including Westport Square) closer to home. Daytime office workers were unwilling to travel a half mile from the business district, crossing a depressed multilane interstate highway, to get to River Quay. Without these cus-

Kansas City, 1981. River Quay was largely abandoned 6 years after it was transformed into an "old town" marketplace. *(Alexander Garvin)*

Kansas City, 1994. Westport Square was still thriving two decades after it was transformed into an "old town" marketplace. *(Alexander Garvin)*

tomers, there was no way all the stores, restaurants, and entertainment spots could survive.

Design

The most misunderstood of the six ingredients of success is design. Too often, it is thought of as decoration that can be applied after the important decisions have been made. In fact, design is the physical manifestation of any prescription and, therefore, is integral to its success or failure from the time of inception.

Design is not just a matter of architectural style. Styles go in and out of fashion; successful planning has to survive for decades. Other more enduring aspects of design are more important. They include the arrangement of project components, the relative size of those components, and their character. Each element affects a project's utility, cost, and attractiveness. When they are organized in a mutually supportive manner, the result is an identifiable destination that provides an auspicious place for the activities occurring there. When arranged to fit the right combination of market, location, financing, entrepreneurship, and time, the result is a successful project.

The components of New Haven's Chapel Square, for example, are assembled in a manner that reduces utility to retail shoppers and, therefore, retail sales. Its two-story shopping mall, instead of being placed between the two department stores, is at one end of the scheme. The five-story parking garage is next to and provides direct access to the two department stores, but not to the shopping mall. As a result, none of the mall's retail facilities profits from purchases made by customers stopping in on their way to another intended destination.

If Chapel Square illustrates how the inept arrangement of the components of a design can exacerbate already poor market conditions, Ghirardelli Square illustrates how it can enhance a potentially wonderful location. At Ghirardelli Square the components are terraced in a manner that increases the utility of the site, reduces costs, and attracts customers. On this steeply sloping site, parking is fitted in under several levels of shopping without taking up otherwise rentable floor area. At the higher end of the site, the parking structure provides the foundation for retail stores. In the middle, its roof provides an outdoor pedestrian level in which retail shoppers can freely circulate among the stores. Only at the lowest end of the site is parking fully underground.

By including in the design formerly obsolete buildings (especially the factory building that now includes a display about the chocolate company that was its initial occupant) and by reserving for public use spots with panoramic views of the waterfront, the design attracts additional tourists. It is a profitable combination of utility, economy, and picturesque features. Today this arrangement seems obvious, but when Ghirardelli Square was conceived, nothing like it had ever been designed.

Dimensions have to be correct from the beginning. For example, traffic engineers suggest a width of 12 feet for every lane of traffic. That may not be enough on busy streets where trucks keep stopping to unload merchandise. Similarly, build-

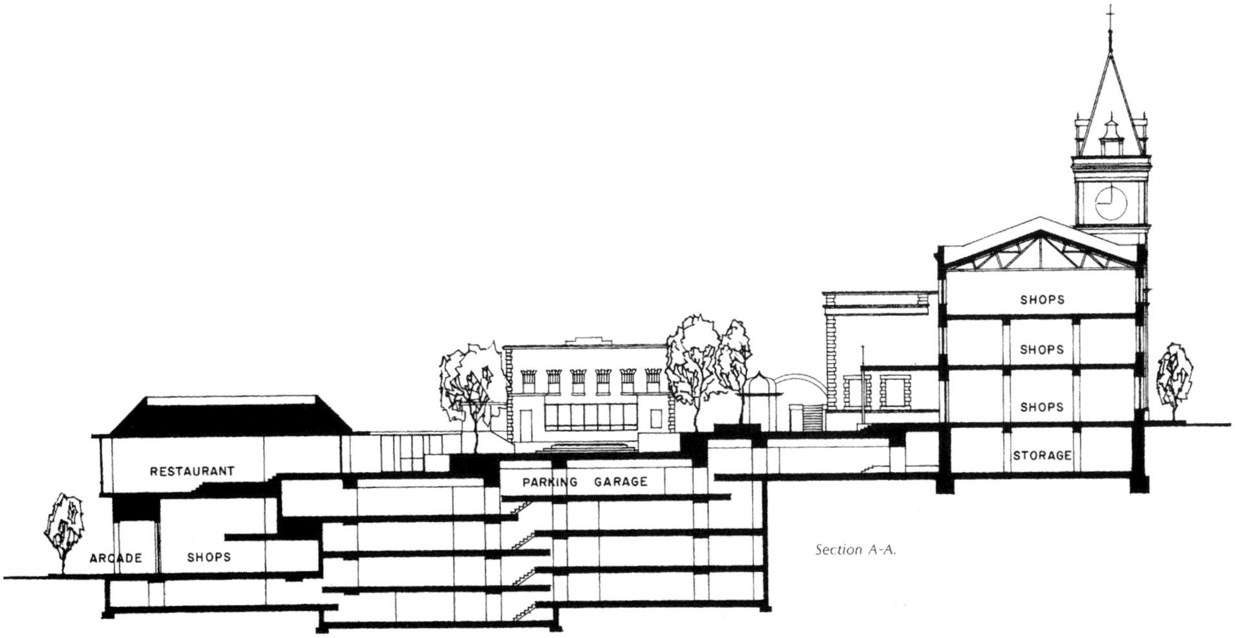

San Francisco, 1991. Ghirardelli Square—section drawing showing the arrangement of parking, pedestrian levels, shops, and restaurants. *(From L. Redstone, New Dimensions in Shopping Centers, McGraw-Hill, New York, 1973)*

San Francisco, 1991. View of the harbor from one of the restaurants at Ghirardelli Square. *(Alexander Garvin)*

ing codes mandate a minimum height for every habitable room (usually 8 feet). How much higher should one build? The answer should vary with the type and floor area of each room. But, whether the product is a traffic artery or a residence, the quality of the results will depend on dimensional appropriateness.

Character is the product of style, color, materials, and scale. The attractiveness of Charleston's historic district is largely a matter of architectural style. The red-brick paving highlights at Westport Square identify it as a distinctive retail destination among the ordinary sidewalks in that part of Kansas City. Similarly, the painted wood and brick buildings of Savannah's Pulaski Ward or Victorian District provide qualities that are not available in the city's post–World War II suburban subdivisions.

The importance of scale to the success of a design is often misunderstood. This is a particular problem in the case of public open space. Park enthusiasts are happy to get any public open space the society is willing to acquire. Budget-conscious public officials, on the other hand, seek to minimize expenditures on what they consider "frills" in order to devote resources to "serious priorities," such as police protection, sanitation, or education. Too often this results in parks that are too big or too small or include more facilities than the municipality is willing to maintain or too few to attract the surrounding population. The contrast between Kansas City's park system and that of Minneapolis is a revealing one.

In 1890 Kansas City decided it needed additional public open space. It hired George Kessler, a 28-year-old German-

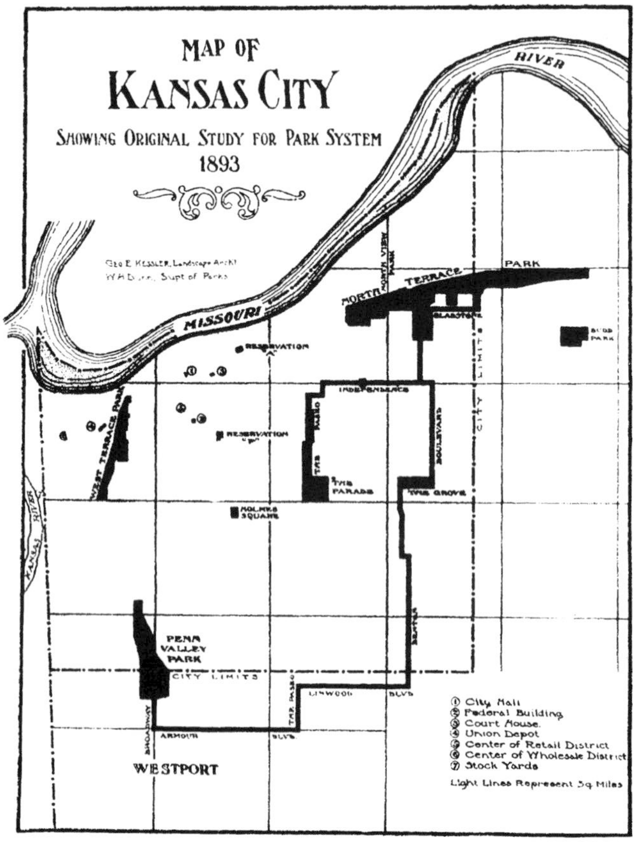

Kansas City, 1893. George E. Kessler's proposal for a park system. *(Courtesy of Missouri Valley Special Collections, Kansas City Public Library, Kansas City, Missouri)*

Kansas City, 1989. Linwood Boulevard nearly a century after it became a "parkway." *(Alexander Garvin)*

trained landscape architect to make recommendations.[8] Three years later it adopted his proposal for a new park and parkway system. Kessler's plan consisted of three intermediate-size parks tied together by "parkways." While the three initial parks had spectacular views, the primary reason for their inclusion was that their steep slopes precluded easy development. Consequently, they were relatively inexpensive to acquire. The parkways that were intended to tie them together into a coherent citywide park system were really tree-lined sections of the Kansas City street grid. Like the three intermediate-size parks, they reflected the park board's unwillingness to spend much money on property acquisition or to engage in controversial land condemnation.[9]

The park system's initial effect was to attract expensive residences to the lots bordering its tree-lined rights-of-way. This initial success, along with the opportunity of making relatively inexpensive and noncontroversial purchases of less developed land, further from downtown Kansas City, led the park board to consider extending the system. Under pressure from developers like Jesse Clyde Nichols, who was then laying out the Country Club District, the board decided on a further series of broader, more generously landscaped parkways. These newer parkways became the focus of the handsome new residential communities, created by the developers who had lobbied for more generous public open space. They also supplanted Kessler's older "parkway" neighborhoods, hastening their demise.

By the 1980s many of the earliest sections of the Kansas City park system were lined with vacant and abandoned buildings. One reason for the abandonment of these older neighborhoods was that Kansas City, like many American cities, experienced the outward movement of residents who could afford suburban homes in areas with plenty of open space. Had the initial sections of Kessler's park system been better designed, this trend might have been retarded.

The Minneapolis park system did retard suburban migration. Begun in 1883 by landscape architect Horace W. S.

Minneapolis, 1932. Lake Harriet, Lake Calhoun, and Lake of the Isles after becoming part of the city's park system. *(From T. Wirth, Minneapolis Park System, Minneapolis Board of Park Commissioners, 1945)*

Minneapolis, 1993. Recreation in the park surrounding Lake Calhoun. *(Alexander Garvin)*

Cleveland, the Minneapolis park system was specifically designed to keep the city from becoming "a dreary and monotonous series of ordinary dwellings." Large areas of undeveloped land were acquired and landscaped as neighborhood parks. Marshes were dredged to create spectacular lakes for summer boating, swimming, and fishing, and winter ice skating. Broad, generously landscaped linear parkways were added to connect the 153 large parks and 23 lakes. The result was an extraordinary 6380-acre park system.[10]

The parks and parkways of Minneapolis were sufficiently widespread to affect virtually every neighborhood and were ample enough to become major elements within those neighborhoods. The city's elected park commissioners also made sure there were sufficient funds to create the widest variety of facilities and to maintain them once they had been created. As a result every section of the city is supplied with beautifully landscaped, well-maintained, public open space that also has increased the desirability of adjacent land sufficiently that it has never lost its attractiveness. The city's extraordinary park system helped Minneapolis to withstand the allure of a move to the suburbs. In contrast, Kessler's initial Kansas City parks and parkways were just too skimpy.

Financing

Every prescription for fixing cities requires financing. When this involves public action, as is the case with parks, the financing comes from taxes. Among the reasons that Minneapolis has the best designed and best maintained park system in America is that its elected Park and Recreation Board can levy taxes and issue bonds. As a result it has money to pay for acquisition, design, development, program delivery, and maintenance. Elsewhere, whenever cities face a period of budget stringency, they transfer money from the parks to other "more pressing priorities."

Financing is equally important when a planning proposal requires private sector activity. Privately financed projects need *capital* to cover start-up costs, a short-term *development loan* to pay expenses until it is operational, and a *permanent mortgage* to replace the other two when the project is complete and tenanted. The obvious place to obtain financing is a bank. Banks lend their depositors' money to developers whose projects pay a large enough return to keep depositors happy and contribute toward covering the costs of bank operations. In other words, developers pay banks for the use of their money. The price will depend on its assessment of the risk involved. If the deal looks too risky, the bank will not lend a penny.

Most banks will not lend enough to cover project cost. The rest of the money, the *equity* investment, usually comes from the developer and from investors who have confidence in the venture. Investors know that the bank has not lent enough money to complete the project. They know that if the venture fails, the bank may recoup its investment but they may not. They also know how much the bank is getting for its money. Consequently, developers have to pay investors a higher price for equity funds than they are paying for bank money. Developers will put up their own money if bank mortgages and investor equity do not cover all development costs. Typically, if something goes wrong and the investment has to be liquidated, the bank mortgage will be repaid first, then the equity investors, and finally the developer. Since the developer is taking the greatest risk, he or she will not go into the venture unless the return is better than that of the bank and the equity investors.

In other words, money is obtained at different prices, depending on risk and availability. Mortgage money is usually the least expensive. Equity money is more expensive. The developer's money is the most expensive. The greater the proportion of project costs that comes from other sources (the greater the *leverage* of the developer's cash investment), the more attractive the venture will appear to be to the developer. Government can increase the likelihood of project success by creating an investment climate in which bank financing is readily available and developers maximize leverage.

Congress has consistently tried to ensure adequate financing for housing construction by increasing the safety of residential mortgages. During the Great Depression, it restructured the banking industry and established mortgage insurance programs that eventually led to construction of millions of suburban houses. Title I of the Housing Act of 1949 (popularly known as the urban renewal program) provided two-thirds of the money needed to subsidize planning, start-up costs, property acquisition, demolition, and relocation for federally approved urban renewal projects. Local governments had to pay the remaining one-third. In 1954 Congress added federal insurance on mortgages for new or rehabilitated housing in urban renewal areas. This was followed by a series of mortgage-subsidy programs that reduced housing costs to a level that was affordable for low- and moderate-income families.

These programs reduced the cost of money and assured older cities of the financing needed to pay for major neighborhood reconstruction. Some cities (in particular, Philadelphia, New Haven, and New York) used the money for more than just wholesale clearance. They recognized that deteriorating neighborhoods also could be revived by cutting away scattered pockets of blight. Philadelphia's Washington Square East Urban Renewal Project (better known as Society Hill) is one of the earliest and most successful examples. The money to pay for planning, property acquisition, clearance, and site preparation came from the urban renewal program. Banks provided mortgage money for housing construction and rehabilitation because it was federally insured. Payments to cover ongoing operations came from the middle-income residents of the new and renovated housing. Where necessary financing was supplemented with further federal subsidies.[11]

The revitalization of Society Hill was planned in the mid-1950s by Edmund Bacon, executive director of the

Philadelphia, 1993. The revitalization of Society Hill involved preserving and renovating eighteenth- and nineteenth-century row houses and selectively replacing vacant lots and nonconforming lands uses with new residential buildings. *(Alexander Garvin)*

Philadelphia City Planning Commission. He proposed selective clearance of only those structures that were beyond repair or that were incompatible with the rest of the neighborhood. These sites were to be filled in either with residential buildings sensitively fitted in between their older neighbors or with small "greenway" parks intended as both landscaped pedestrian paths and as small-scale recreation areas.

It was a perfect strategy for Society Hill. The bulk of the area's buildings were charming eighteenth- and nineteenth-century red-brick row houses. Once the blighting influence of neighboring properties had been eliminated, these row houses became extremely attractive to middle-class residents who wanted to live downtown. By 1970, owners had rehabilitated more than 600 of Society Hill's historic structures, property values had more than doubled, and the population had increased by a third.

More than a decade after the Society Hill project was under way, New York City adopted a similar strategy. Known as the "vest pocket redevelopment" program, it was launched by Mayor John Lindsay a few months after his election in 1965. The idea was to use local (rather than federal) funds to acquire vacant lots and dilapidated buildings. These sites would then be resold to developers who would receive federally subsidized mortgages either to rehabilitate salvageable abandoned structures or to build new apartment buildings, in both cases incurring little or no relocation.

In the Mott Haven section of the Bronx, these new and rehabilitated structures were to be the first phase of a much more ambitious community-renewal effort that included a second, third, and fourth round of housing, parks and playlots, schools, repaved streets and sidewalks, street trees, and a variety of other community facilities. From the start, most Mott Haven residents had been poor. They lived in walk-up tenements built to accommodate the overflow of immigrants from Manhattan. Over the years, little or no money had been spent on necessary repairs and maintenance, so that most of the buildings were seriously run down. Proper restoration now required substantial capital investment. Owners could not recoup such investments by increasing rents because residents could not afford to pay more rent and, where they could, were prevented from doing so by rent control.[12]

Realizing that private financing was not available, planners put their trust in the federal government. They made the vest-pocket redevelopment of Mott Haven a first phase of the recently enacted Model Cities Program, thereby becoming part of what promised to be an extraordinary demonstration of national financial commitment to the renewal of 150 "model" neighborhoods. City-funded early acquisition of property in Mott Haven was supposed to provide a relocation resource for residents that would be displaced by later Model Cities projects.

The construction on the first sites in Mott Haven had just started when President Nixon unilaterally declared a moratorium on all federal housing assistance. Neither financial institutions nor developers could continue without federal subsidies. As a result, the first stage of Mott Haven's "vest pocket redevelopment" also became its last stage.

The Bronx, 1978. In Mott Haven selective filling in of vacant lots and dilapidated buildings with new residential buildings failed to revitalize surrounding areas because financing for further development was not available. *(Alexander Garvin)*

Vest-pocket redevelopment was able to trigger private reinvestment in Society Hill because there was enough money to remove pockets of blight and to subsidize a few strategically located construction and rehabilitation projects. No further subsidies were needed because, once initial housing rehabilitation and new construction proved successful, banks had evidence of a growing market and readily provided mortgage financing to other property owners. The same prescription failed to work in Mott Haven because it was dependent on continuing public subsidies for nearly every property. Since residents were too poor to pay for building improvements and the federal government had terminated its subsidy programs, banks withdrew the necessary mortgage financing. At that time the city government, experiencing one of its most serious fiscal crises, was neither willing nor able to replace federal commitments. As a result, nothing further could take place.

Entrepreneurship

No prescription is self-implementing. Each requires talented public and private entrepreneurs. Without them a perfectly appropriate prescription will not get off the ground. Entrepreneurs conceive projects, often when others are unaware that there are any opportunities available. They assemble and coordinate the various players who will execute whatever needs to be done. Without the extra drive that entrepreneurs supply, these other players would be overwhelmed by the uncertainties of the marketplace.

Entrepreneurs do not appear automatically whenever there is unfulfilled demand for something. They have to believe that the risk of failure is minimal and the rewards that come with success are generous. Unless such favorable conditions are prevalent, entrepreneurs will exploit other, more attractive opportunities.

Public projects often fail because public officials ignore the role of entrepreneurship. They mistakenly believe that once a project has been assigned to a government agency, its role is purely administrative. In fact, public entrepreneurs are needed to assemble, coordinate, and inspire all the participants in the development process. Edmund Bacon performed that role in Society Hill. He successfully combined the activities of the bankers, bureaucrats, property owners, developers, architects, engineers, contractors, and countless other actors needed for the revitalization of the neighborhood. He also maintained public approval and bureaucratic momentum despite the uncertainty of acquiescence by property owners. He obtained timely approval by federal agencies and mortgage commitments from financial institutions. He stimulated developer interest in the project and political acceptance by Philadelphia's disparate civic and community groups. He sought and discovered opportunities for participation, funding, and implementation by previously uninvolved public agencies, nonprofit organizations, and private developers. Most important, Bacon implemented a strategy that had never been tried before: eliminating scattered pockets of blight, filling the resulting holes in the fabric of the neighborhood with new housing and parks.

While it is easier to understand the role of an entrepreneur in the private sector, it is essentially the same as that performed by public officials like Edmund Bacon. The role includes coordinating a plethora of participants, dealing with uncertainty, recognizing available opportunities that have not yet been exploited, and frequently accomplishing things in ways that have never been tried before. The difference between private and public entrepreneurial activity is only in the form of payment. The private entrepreneur is paid in hard currency; the public entrepreneur, in power. The sort of people capable of getting things done, however, will have to be extremely well paid in their respective coin.

In many cases private and public entrepreneurs work side by side. This is especially true in urban renewal projects like Society Hill where implementation is dependent on individual property owners and developers. When it enacted the Housing Act of 1949, Congress hoped to attract private developers into the business of redeveloping federally approved urban renewal areas by sharply reducing the risk of failure. This was accomplished by requiring the clearance of any blighted property that might affect the area. Local officials had to prepare a redevelopment plan that provided developers and financial institutions with certainty as to the future of every property within the area. Most important, Congress provided the subsidies needed to reduce land prices and site development costs to a marketable level.

Despite this reduced level of risk, few of the early renewal projects went into construction very quickly. Developers either were not willing to acquire approved urban renewal sites or, if they did acquire them, were unable to persuade financial institutions to provide the necessary financing. As a result, most cities initially generated government subsidized clearance but were unable to find the proper combination of developer and financing to get very much built.

Not just developers, but banks and insurance companies were afraid of investing in officially designated "blighted areas." Without institutional financing, developers would have had to invest substantial amounts of equity capital. Initially, neither lenders nor equity investors perceived a return commensurate with their risk.

In 1954 Congress made the changes that were needed to interest private entrepreneurs in carrying out approved redevelopment projects. The vehicle it chose was federal mortgage insurance that covered up to 95 percent of the cost of new and rehabilitated housing in urban renewal areas. Since financing now could be insured, banks were ready to issue mortgages on most approved urban renewal projects. For the first time, risk was minimal, equity capital requirements extremely low, and profits entirely a matter of entrepreneurial skill. Naturally, all sorts of businesspeople were eager to get involved.

Detroit's Gratiot Urban Renewal Project (better known as Lafayette Park) illustrates the importance of this entrepreneurial element to any redevelopment effort. The project was initially conceived in 1946. At that time two out of three dwellings in this 129-acre residential neighborhood were considered substandard. They lacked running water, central heating, private baths, indoor toilets, or some other feature considered necessary to the health, comfort, and safety of its residents. The best way to eliminate such "slums" was thought to be clearance and redevelopment.[13]

Before the project could proceed, however, Lafayette Park had to overcome community opposition, then a taxpayer's suit, then the high cost of acquisition. In 1952, when the site was put up for auction, there were no bidders. The following year a developer finally agreed to buy the site but had to withdraw because he was unable to obtain construction financing.

The project languished until 1955, when Herbert Greenwald, a successful Chicago developer, succeeded in assembling a development package that could be financed. Greenwald, his partners, and his architect, Mies van der Rohe, had been responsible for a series of glass apartment towers that revolutionized residential development in Chicago. He brought this successful team to Detroit where they began building one of America's most beautiful residential redevelopment projects. It was conceived as a 78-acre self-contained neighborhood (in the jargon of the period: a superblock) entirely closed to through traffic, containing many of the elements of a healthy community (an elementary school, a small shopping center, a clubhouse, and swimming pool), all organized around a 19-acre park. Within the superblock they proposed to build 2000 apartments in six towers surrounded by clusters of one- and two-story row houses.

Detroit, 1989. The redevelopment of Lafayette Park was stalled for more than a decade until Congress provided banks with mortgage insurance in urban renewal areas, thereby creating a financial climate that attracted entrepreneurs to areas that had been officially designated as slums. *(Alexander Garvin)*

In 1959, a year after the first residents moved into Lafayette Park, Greenwald died in a plane crash. His firm dropped out of the project. Redevelopment was continued by others who lacked his vision and know-how. Consequently, they produced the same mediocre buildings and inadequate public spaces that characterized most federal urban renewal projects.

Since the Greenwald-Mies portion of Lafayette Park was completed, Detroit has lost more than 40 percent of its population and experienced one of the nation's worst rates of housing deterioration and abandonment. But the Greenwald-Mies portion of the renewal project has remained fully occupied, integrated racially and ethnically, and consistently well-maintained. That is a record unmatched by most other housing redevelopment projects in Detroit or anywhere else.

Time

There are three time sequences that affect success. The first is relatively brief: the period during which a person passes through an area. The second takes into account what will occur 24 hours a day, 7 days a week. The third may take decades, during which political and financial climates will certainly change many times.

Developers of retail shopping facilities are perhaps the most skilled in predicting a person's activity pattern within an area. They have to be skilled in dealing with this brief time period because their tenants' profits are dependent on transient customer activity and their own profits are dependent on tenant success.

At Ghirardelli Square, for example, visitors come by foot or motor vehicle. In either case, when they arrive they are quickly faced with a wide variety of attractions. Passing from one to the next, these visitors invariably stop to look at or purchase something. The result is plenty of activity, a high volume of sales, and therefore high rents per square foot.

The movements of a single individual, on the other hand, are irrelevant in planning for a 24-hour day and a 7-day week. Such planning requires providing a suitable environment for a wide variety of users on a continuing basis. Thus, the crucial questions are who is likely to be in an area over a 7-day period, what will they want to do, how many people are needed to support those activities, and in what ways should the environment be organized to accommodate satisfactorily those people and activities.

At Lafayette Park, Mies, Greenwald, and their associates provided a simple but effective answer to these questions. Rather than a housing project that was devoid of people during substantial periods of the week, they created a self-contained superblock that included a school, convenience shopping, recreation facilities, and substantial open spaces. Thus, the project that emerged provides residents of every age with a suitable living environment every day of the year.[14]

Jane Jacobs calls for districts with a "diversity of uses that give each other constant mutual support both economically and socially."[15] But her reasoning is far more complex and time-sensitive than that of the planners of Lafayette Park. Rather than complete neighborhood units, she recommends districts that contain apartment houses with residents who leave for work every day, office buildings with daytime workers, performance halls that accommodate primarily nighttime customers, as well as bars, restaurants, retail stores, and all manner of service establishments. Together they constitute a district that is alive with people 24 hours a day, 7 days a week. Such a district surrounds and includes New York's Lincoln Center. It attracts people for different purposes at different times of the day, 52 weeks a year.

Successful planning also requires a strategy that will remain appropriate over long periods of time. Of all the strategies for fixing urban/suburban America, the planned "new community" is among the most sensitive to long-term cycles. During the decades required to plan, build, and market a new community, it will experience continually changing economic conditions, political trends, migration patterns, and consumer demand. Because of these inevitably changing market pressures, cash flow can vary substantially from year to year. However, to survive to completion, every planned new community must continue making debt-service payments on a massive, front-loaded investment in land, streets, sidewalks, sewers, water mains, and all the required infrastructure and community facilities. This requires access to plenty of capital and investors who are willing to wait for years before seeing profits.

Radburn, New Jersey, perhaps the best designed and most influential planned community in America, was never completed because it could not ride out these pressures. Radburn was developed by the City Housing Corporation, a limited-dividend company expressly created to demonstrate the efficacy of developing carefully planned new communities. In 1927, it purchased 1350 acres in Fair Lawn, New Jersey, 10 miles from the George Washington Bridge, where it intended to create "a new town for the motor age" with a projected population of 25,000.[16]

Clarence Stein and Henry Wright, Radburn's architects, devised a unique plan in which you drove to your home, parked, and entered the rear of the house. The house itself was turned around so that it faced a private yard that fronted on a landscaped pedestrian walk. These pedestrian walks opened onto beautifully landscaped common open spaces, large enough for children to play ball. They were, in turn, connected by an underpass to Radburn's school, swimming pool, and community facilities.

Radburn quickly became famous among city planners. Photographs of its underpass were printed in books and articles all over the world. Architects and planners, particularly in Europe, began copying what they called "the Radburn idea." Ironically, while giving new life to the idea of building planned new communities, Radburn itself failed. During the

Radburn, 1993. The city planning profession's most revered underpass. *(Alexander Garvin)*

Depression, few families could afford to purchase a new house. Sales were insufficient for the City Housing Corporation to service the debt it had incurred to pay for land, infrastructure, and community facilities. Its financial backers were not willing to continue the venture without receiving a return on their investment. So, in 1935, after completing about 300 houses, the City Housing Corporation declared bankruptcy. Nevertheless, more than half a century since its financial collapse, Radburn remains one of the world's most beautiful and important planned new communities.

Other planned communities, like Palos Verdes Estates, California, succeeded because they could withstand constantly changing market conditions. Palos Verdes Estates occupies one of the country's loveliest sites: a hilly peninsula jutting into the Pacific Ocean, 23 miles southwest of downtown Los Angeles. This beautiful landscape is enhanced by an extraordinary

Palos Verdes Estates, 1979. The streets and houses of this planned community are fitted to the topography. *(From R. Cameron, Above Los Angeles, Cameron & Company, San Francisco, 1978)*

town design by Frederick Law Olmsted, Jr. and Charles Cheney. Its streets, carefully fitted into the spectacular promontory, were laid out to provide building sites with even more spectacular views. Because of this sensitive planning, Palos Verdes' quasi-Mediterranean buildings seem to have been there for centuries. In fact, Palos Verdes Estates is a splendid twentieth-century oasis in the urban congestion and suburban sprawl of Los Angeles County.[17]

The site that was to become Palos Verdes Estates was first sold for development in 1913. Its buyer could not finance the purchase price and had to be bailed out by a syndicate controlled by the president of a New York bank. It was resurrected by another developer in 1921, only to fall apart again. Finally, in 1923, the syndicate that had purchased the property more than a decade earlier initiated development of a 3200-acre planned community. Within 2 years it had built and paid for 20 miles of landscaped boulevards and avenues, 60 miles of water mains, a shopping plaza, a country club and golf course, a public school, and 2500 prepared home sites.

The economic downturn of the late 1920s reduced demand for building sites and Palos Verdes Estates had to be refinanced for a third time. Then, during the late 1930s, the community faced another financial hurdle: unpaid county taxes. This was overcome with state legislation that allowed Palos Verdes Estates to become an incorporated city with an independent park and recreation district, thereby eliminating further county tax payments on community-owned public open space. From that point on, there were no further financial difficulties.

By 1980, Palos Verdes Estates had a population of more than 14,000 and was assessed for tax purposes at over $800 million. The project had taken a decade to get started and several decades more to come to fruition. However, because its developers had not sought immediate profits and had the resources to patiently withstand a series of reverses, Palos Verdes Estates was successfully carried through to completion.

Palos Verdes Estates did not succeed *only* because it was able to withstand the vagaries of time. All six ingredients of success played a part. It was able to attract the rapidly expanding market provided by the Los Angeles metropolitan region. It had a location with spectacular site characteristics near downtown Los Angeles, a location that became even more convenient as additional traffic arteries spread through the region. Olmsted and Cheney's design, which exploited the topography and views, only reinforced the attractiveness of the location to its expanding market. Its developer, a bank president, was able to obtain the necessary financing. He also had the vision and entrepreneurial skills needed to see the project past its critical early years and carry it forward to the point at which its future was assured. Without any one of these ingredients, the results would have been less than satisfactory.

Manipulating the Ingredients of Success to Obtain Desirable Private-Market Reaction

Palos Verdes Estates and Ghirardelli Square are real estate ventures that may be evaluated in terms of their profitability. City and suburban planning, on the other hand, must be evaluated in terms of the cost-effectiveness of the induced private-market reaction. That reaction is determined by the same ingredients that determine the community impact of profit-motivated projects.

While private developers rarely seek to generate and sustain a widespread private-market reaction, some of their projects make profound changes to surrounding communities. Ghirardelli Square, for example, altered the character of Fisherman's Wharf and shifted a substantial amount of San Francisco's tourism to the waterfront. It was able to sustain this widespread private-market reaction because, unlike Palos Verdes Estates, the ingredients of project success were manipulated in a manner that fostered the spillover of its customers into the surrounding area.

The only way to ensure that market demand will spill over into the surrounding area is to plan *not* to satisfy that market within the project. Then there will be a reason for people to go elsewhere. The 71 stores and restaurants that first opened at Ghirardelli Square could never satisfy all the demands of the customers who were attracted to the San Francisco waterfront. Nor was Ghirardelli Square conceived as a retail facility that would supply everything of interest to its visitors. In fact, its developers hoped to attract customers headed to other Fisherman's Wharf destinations.

Unlike the developers of Ghirardelli Square, the developers of Palos Verdes Estates hoped to absorb market demand without interaction with customers in competing areas. They consciously tried to satisfy consumer needs within Palos Verdes so that there would be no reason to go elsewhere. During the 1920s, when sales first began, the plains to the northeast were largely undeveloped and remained so for the next two decades during which the project succeeded in capturing the lion's share of the market. Only after World War II when the project had sold out and millions of people had moved into nearby sections of suburban Los Angeles County, did the spillover of that market result in increased prices for Palos Verdes property.

For a project to generate a sustained market reaction in surrounding areas, it must exploit linkages to those areas. The San Francisco cable car that goes to the waterfront terminates a few hundred feet from Ghirardelli Square. Customers have to pass other retailers on their way from the cable car to Ghirardelli Square, often making purchases along the way. The same linkage applies to automobile-oriented visitors. The project cannot fit all who come by car into its 300 spaces.

Consequently, many of these customers park nearby and also walk past other retailers on the way to their eventual destination.

Palos Verdes Estates is located in a manner that minimized linkages with surrounding communities. Because it is built on a hilly peninsula extending into the Pacific Ocean, there is nothing to influence on the ocean side. In an attempt to compensate for this isolation, the project included a school, a country club and golf course, a charming retail complex inspired by Italian piazzas, and beachfront recreation facilities. During the early years residents left Palos Verdes when they drove to work and spent most of the rest of their time away from home at facilities provided within the community. Consequently, this growing body of consumers had little impact on the rest of Los Angeles County.

Ghirardelli Square is designed both to profit from and to encourage maximum contact with neighboring attractions. It can be entered on foot from any of its four bounding streets and by car on three sides. Palos Verdes, on the other hand, is designed in a way that separates residents from surrounding areas and minimizes market spillover. Its designers chose to make the project initially accessible only along three widely separated routes.[18] Residents have to drive along one of these routes to get anywhere outside Palos Verdes Estates, usually bypassing nearby areas and continuing on to major shopping and entertainment centers 10 or 15 minutes away.

Private real estate ventures like Ghirardelli Square and Palos Verdes do not provide financing or entrepreneurs for other projects. At best, they demonstrate the potential of further real estate activity, perhaps attracting other developers and reducing the wariness of previously skeptical lending institutions.

Government programs, on the other hand, can manipulate financing and entrepreneurship in a manner that affects market activity. The renewal program for Society Hill, for example, included mortgage insurance for banks that financed rehabilitation and new construction. Because mortgage-insurance provisions also reduced cash equity to as little as 5 percent of project cost, home owners and developers were more likely to afford the equity payments needed to acquire, renovate, and build. Equally important, by eliminating all incompatible land uses from the area, the program also reduced the risk of failure, thereby attracting people who would not otherwise have been willing to get involved.

The only period of time during which a project can affect surrounding market activity is the period during which it is in operation. Its impact, however, is particularly important when it supplies neighboring businesses with additional customers during slack periods. The increased consumer spending may support neighboring businesses whose market would not otherwise be large enough. For example, the customers that Ghirardelli Square attracts during the day, at night, and on weekends bring enough spillover business to be of real help to shops and restaurants in less convenient waterfront locations.

The Role of Government

Government can play a major role in fostering desirable interaction between proposed real estate developments and their neighbors. By subsidizing housing construction in Society Hill, the city government increased the number of customers in walking distance of the downtown stores and restaurants. The additional consumer traffic allowed shops and restaurants to remain in operation for longer hours, and in the process increased the safety and attractiveness of downtown streets during the early evening. Some cities have enacted zoning ordinances that allow parking requirements to be satisfied at off-site locations. This increases pedestrian traffic between those parking facilities and the consumer's ultimate destination. Other cities offer a bonus of additional rentable space to developers who provide suitably designed open space, thereby

Palos Verdes Estates, 1925. Early development at Palos Verdes was far from the nearest settlements in Los Angeles County. *(Courtesy of the National Park Service, Frederick Law Olmsted National Historic Site)*

increasing pedestrian traffic to and from more congested nearby locations.

These examples involve the use of *investment* (housing subsidies), *regulation* (parking requirements), or *incentives* (a zoning bonus) to alter four of the ingredients of success (market, location, design, time of operation). Success in generating further market activity may also require the other two ingredients: financing and entrepreneurship. When Detroit finally launched Lafayette Park, mortgage insurance became available within the boundaries of the urban renewal area. Since insured mortgages were not available for surrounding areas, owners and developers in those areas found it difficult to raise money to improve their property. As a result, Lafayette Park was unable to generate the desirable, widespread, and sustained private market reaction that could be expected from the construction of hundreds of new apartments.

While private real estate ventures may be more likely to succeed when they interact with surrounding areas, publicly assisted projects are increasingly dependent on that interaction for their very existence. Think of the cities that want a plentiful supply of electricity but are unwilling to permit a power plant within their boundaries, or the neighborhoods that want clean streets but bitterly resist a sanitation garage in their neighborhood, or the homeowners who want a convenient school for their children but oppose locating it across the street. Public projects of this sort are regularly defeated by citizens who do not want them in their backyard and have little confidence that anything will mitigate their negative impact.

We can overcome citizen opposition and ensure project feasibility if we stop thinking solely in terms of individual projects. Instead, we must make decisions that are *also* based on the probability of a desired private-market reaction. Then the public dialogue will shift from consideration of the project itself to the ways in which its market, location, design, financing, entrepreneurs, and times of operation will benefit the surrounding community. More important, we will increase financial and political feasibility while simultaneously increasing the likelihood of the desirable, sustained, and widespread market reaction that is characteristic of good city and suburban planning.

Notes

1. A more detailed discussion of historical preservation in Savannah's Pulaski Square and Victorian District can be found in Chapters 12 and 17.
2. A more detailed discussion of downtown redevelopment in New Haven can be found in Chapter 6.
3. A more detailed discussion of downtown redevelopment in Pittsburgh can be found in Chapter 6.
4. This table is derived from Ernst Egli, *Climate and Town Districts, Consequences and Demands,* Verlag fur Architectur, Zurich, 1951, p. 49.
5. A more detailed discussion of Ghirardelli Square can be found in Chapter 5.
6. Historical and statistical material on Kansas City's River Quay and Westport Square is derived from Carla C. Sabala (editor), *Kansas City Today,* Urban Land Institute, Washington, D.C., 1974; Patricia Cleary Miller, *Westport: Missouri's Port of Many Returns,* Lowell Press, Kansas City, 1983, pp. 104–105; and George Ehrlich, *Kansas City Missouri—An Architectural History 1826–1976,* Historic Kansas City Foundation, Kansas City, 1979.
7. During the later 1980s the city successfully expanded nearby City Market, which attracts thousands of shoppers on Saturdays and Sundays. Despite all the additional traffic that passes through River Quay to get to City Market, in October 1994, only 5 of the 20 storefronts along Delaware Street between Third and Fifth Streets were occupied.
8. A more detailed discussion of Kansas City's park system can be found in Chapter 3.
9. Swope Park was an 1896 gift of 1350 acres unanticipated by Kessler.
10. A more detailed discussion of the Minneapolis Park System can be found in Chapter 3.
11. A more detailed discussion of Society Hill can be found in Chapter 11.
12. A more detailed discussion of New York City's Vest-Pocket Redevelopment Program can be found in Chapter 11.
13. A more detailed discussion of Lafayette Park can be found in Chapter 11.
14. When Herbert Greenwald died, half the apartments that had been initially planned for were completed or under way. In the absence of the rest of the project, it is impossible to evaluate fully the success of its planning.
15. Jane Jacobs, *The Death and Life of Great American Cities,* Random House, New York, 1961, p. 14.
16. A more detailed discussion of Radburn can be found in Chapter 13.
17. A more detailed discussion of Palos Verdes Estates can be found in Chapter 15.
18. The design provided access from the Pacific Coast Highway via Palos Verdes Boulevard, from Hawthorne Avenue via Palos Verdes Drive, and from Long Beach via Paseo del Mar.

3

Parks and Playgrounds

Minneapolis, 1992. Minnehana Parkway. *(Alexander Garvin)*

Traditionally, parks are either conceived as restorative (an idyllic counterpoint to the congestion of the city) or therapeutic (a place to relieve the tension of urban living). There is great wisdom in these traditional conceptions of park and playground. But parks and playgrounds are more than just places for city dwellers to relieve their tensions through communion with nature or in active, organized play. In most cities, parks and playgrounds take up large amounts of land. For that reason alone, they have a major impact on the development and character of every city.

The idea that parks can spur the improvement of the surrounding city has at times provided an equally compelling rationale for public investment. While this strategic approach to investment in parks has taken different forms depending on the city, it usually has been for one of three purposes: initiating urbanization at specific locations, altering land use patterns in surrounding locations, or establishing a comprehensive system that could shape the very character of city life.

To achieve these purposes, the quantity and quality of public investment has to be adequate to alter private-market conditions for neighboring properties. Only then will property owners react in the desired fashion. In St. Louis, for example, the combination of 1293-acre Forest Park and a trolley system that connected it with the city's Missouri River landings three miles away increased demand for residences in the surrounding area. In San Antonio, transforming an unsightly riverbed into a park created a tourist attraction that could be exploited by neighboring property owners. In Minneapolis, a superbly designed and maintained 6380-acre system of parks, parkways, playgrounds, athletic fields, jogging trails, bicycles, paths, lakes, and swimming pools created living conditions that were attractive enough for the city to retain a sizable middle-class population at a time when other cities were losing that market to the suburbs.

It has been many years since parks were thought of as central to the planning of cities. Their very existence has eliminated pressure for additional park development and made it possible for other issues to dominate the urban planning agenda. Nor is there the same certainty that existed during the nineteenth century that exposure to nature or active recreation can alleviate the effects of slums and poverty. Nevertheless, public open space remains an effective tool for shaping the American city.

Today, as never before, conditions are ripe for parks to reenter the urban planning agenda. This opportunity exists because so much inner-city land that was once actively used now lies fallow and can be reused for intelligently planned parks, because so much suburban land has been developed without adequate public open space that there is now a huge suburban constituency to support park development, and because so much undeveloped land is now subject to recently enacted legislation intended to protect the environment.

Nature as Restorative

The twenty-third Psalm suggests that green pastures restore health and still waters restore the soul. Ralph Waldo Emerson, writing in 1836, asserts that:

> *To the body and mind which have been cramped by noxious work or company, nature is medicinal and restores their tone. The tradesman, the attorney comes out of the din and craft of the street and sees the sky and the woods, and is a man again. In their eternal calm, he finds himself.*[1]

Even our word for paradise comes from garden, "pairidaeza" an old Persian word for garden. Living in paradise is a universal goal. It is not surprising that the remains of gardens can be found at most excavations of ancient civilizations.

In Europe, the nobility surrounded their residences with elaborate gardens as a way of having the restorative powers of nature near at hand. The design of these gardens for the aristocracy became high art in eighteenth-century England. Nature was not permitted to grow wild. It was transformed into living versions of Arcadian landscape paintings by the French seventeenth-century painter Claude Lorrain. The premier practitioner of this emerging eighteenth-century art of landscape design was an English gardener known as "Capability" Brown.[2] In designing the grounds of such estates as Blenheim, Petworth, and Sherborne, Brown evolved an approach that stripped the landscape of discordant blemishes and exploited the natural beauty of pure landscape—pure landscape as filtered through the images of Claude Lorrain.[3]

The pre-Revolutionary American landscape, unlike that of England, contained few sophisticated large gardens. A town might have a common or a few small squares. But, with a continent of wilderness just beyond the edge of town, there was little demand for large open spaces. Even in the more populous cities of Europe, public parks were almost unknown during the eighteenth century. The large parks of London, Paris, and Vienna were royal estates that in some cases, like London's Hyde and Richmond Parks, were open to the public.

The first truly *public park* was Birkenhead Park, Liverpool, England. Sir Joseph Paxton, who designed Birkenhead Park in 1843, created a 125-acre landscape inspired by Capability Brown's gardens for the aristocracy. Like them, it had areas of meadow, clumps of trees, serpentine lakes, and pedestrian paths weaving through the landscape to create different views. To these Paxton added circumferential carriage roads for pleasure driving, a single transverse street, and boundary roads for town traffic outside the park. Birkenhead Park inspired similar efforts throughout England. However, its most important influence was on Frederick Law Olmsted, who, in 1852 and 1859, published his observations on Birkenhead Park in *Walks and Talks of an American Farmer in England,* an account of his 13-week tour of Europe. What impressed him was that

> *In democratic America there was nothing to be thought comparable with this People's Garden.... Winding paths,*

over acres and acres, with a constant varying surface, where on all sides were growing every variety of shrubs and flowers.... A party of boys in one part, and a party of gentlemen in another, were playing cricket. Beyond this was a large meadow with groups of young trees, under which...girls and women with children were playing...I was glad to observe that the privileges of the garden were enjoyed about equally by all classes.[4]

When Olmsted visited Birkenhead Park, he was an unsuccessful farmer, who was trying his hand at journalism. He would go on to design many of the nation's first large city parks and to become the country's premier landscape architect and arguably its most talented urban planner (see Chapters 13 and 15).

Central Park, New York City

By the middle of the nineteenth century vast tides of immigrants were pouring into America's cities. The more congested these cities became, the more the public demanded parks. The first American city to respond to this demand was New York.[5] In 1850, when the city's population had reached 654,000, public clamor for parks spilled over into the mayoral election campaign. The following year the newly elected mayor, Ambrose Kingsland, obtained approval from the State

Manhattan, 1863. Aerial view of Central Park soon after it was opened for public use. *(Courtesy of the Museum of the City of New York, J. Clarence Davies Collection)*

Manhattan, 1994. Central Park, where Olmsted intended people to escape from the hustle and bustle of the city. *(Alexander Garvin)*

Legislature for the creation of a major public park. As he put it,

> *There are thousands who pass the day of rest among the idle and dissolute in porter houses or in places more objectionable, who would rejoice in being able to breathe pure air in such a place, while they ride and drive through its avenues free from...noise, dust, and confusion.*[6]

In 1857, after much discussion the Commissioners for the new Central Park decided to hold a design competition. Thirty-five designs were submitted. A proposal entitled "Greensward" by Frederick Law Olmsted and his architect partner Calvert Vaux won the competition.

Olmsted and Vaux's design, inspired by Paxton's Birkenhead Park, was an even more brilliant adaptation of English eighteenth-century garden design. Like the gardens created for an aristocratic elite, the new Central Park established for an entire city population, was to be a work of art. More than 2500 men were employed over more than 10 years transforming 843 acres of rough, largely undeveloped land into Olmsted and Vaux's populist vision of Arcadia. Tons of earth were excavated and moved to soften and improve the landscape; acres of land were dredged to create artificial lakes; miles of sewer and water mains were buried to artificially drain the park and supply it with water; tens of thousands of trees, shrubs, and flowers were planted to create the illusion of an Arcadian pleasure ground; and miles of gently curving paths and roads were introduced to permit easy access and circulation by the tens of thousands of pedestrians, horses, and vehicles that were expected to use the new park every day. The result appeared to be just another picturesque English garden with rolling lawns, serpentine lakes, clumps of trees, and meandering paths designed for the leisurely delight of the elite. In fact it was a tough public park designed for active use in the rapidly growing city of New York.

When Olmsted and Vaux submitted their design, the bulk of the city's population lay miles to the south. Nevertheless, they understood that Central Park had to accommodate tens of thousands of users every day. For it to do this, they designed a unique circulation system that made a series of very different places of recreation accessible to masses of people. Coming by carriage (or today by car), one entered at selected spots along the park's perimeter and rode along a beautifully landscaped roadway that encircled the park. Millions of people have enjoyed this pleasant drive either in the flesh or at the movies. Coming on foot, one entered at different spots and strolled to one's destination. There was also a separate bridle path for horseback riding. These three routes seldom intersect. When they do, there is often a pedestrian underpass that minimizes the chance of accidents.

Since Central Park extends north-south for $2^1/_2$ miles, dividing the east and west sides of Manhattan, there is a need for traffic arteries connecting them. To accommodate this traffic Olmsted and Vaux designed four crosstown roads that traverse the park, providing through-traffic routes never intersected by circulation within the park. Nowhere within Central

Manhattan, 1994. Central Park is still actively used by hundreds of thousands of New Yorkers a century and a half after completion. *(Alexander Garvin)*

Park is one ever aware that the transverse roadways exist because they are depressed and thereby separated from all other traffic and because they are cleverly masked by slopes, shrubbery, and trees. This allows other traffic on the carriageways and paths to pass over the transverse roads without noticing the vehicles below.

The other difference between an eighteenth-century English estate garden and Central Park is that Olmsted and Vaux designed a wide variety of settings for mass recreation. Among them are meadows for ball-playing, slopes for sledding, lakes for boating and ice-skating, a rustic ramble for wandering, a mall for promenading, and a variety of playing grounds. Today, on a typical weekend, at least 250,000 people can be found using the park.

Once New York City created Central Park, citizens in almost every other city pressed for something similar. The ensuing demand for public parks is exemplified by a *Minneapolis Tribune* editorial printed in 1880:

> *Public parks have come to be recognized as institutions essential to the health as well as the happiness of thickly settled communities. Children suffer from privations, pine, and sicken and fall into untimely graves because [they are] cut off from the healthful provision of God's light and the pure atmosphere that circulates among the trees and through broad expanses. To keep down the death rate, and to be rid of wasting disease, a plentiful supply of parks is needed in every large town.*[7]

Similar editorials appeared in every city. Fairmount Park in Philadelphia, Rock Creek Park in Washington, D.C., Forest Park in St. Louis, Golden Gate Park in San Francisco, and City Park in Denver are only a few of the more famous results.

Recreation as Therapy

At the time our notion that public parks would cure disease was taking shape, a second idea was gaining acceptance: that recreation would divert the city dweller from a life of crime. It is beautifully expressed by Jane Addams, the guiding spirit of Chicago's Hull House. She wrote that "To fail to provide for the recreation of youth, is not only to deprive all of them of their natural form of expression, but is certainly to subject some of them to the overwhelming temptation of illicit and soul-destroying pleasures."[8]

The formulation of Addams' philosophy coincided with the rise of organized sports and was derived from the notion that city dwellers, who no longer engaged in physical activities such as farming and hunting, needed an outlet for their accumulated tensions and, thus, required a place for physical exercise.

In the 1820s physical education became part of the curriculum of Harvard and Yale. Gymnastic societies, patterned after German "turnvereins," were founded in most big cities. New field sports such as football and baseball became popular. But, since there were no public parks, there were no public playing fields. It was not until 1871 that ball fields were includ-

Manhattan, c. 1889. Jacob Riis's photograph of the slum known as "Mulberry Bend." *(Courtesy of the Museum of the City of New York, Jacob A. Riis Collection)*

ed in a public park. It was then that Olmsted and Vaux, for the first time, made playing fields a central feature of the design of Chicago's new Washington Park.

Municipal playgrounds as we know them today did not exist. In 1872, Brookline, Massachusetts, became the first city to vote funds for the establishment of playgrounds. Hull House, Jane Addams' pioneering settlement house, began experimenting with playgrounds as early as 1884. However, it was not until the New York State legislature enacted the Small Parks Act in 1887, that the provision of public playgrounds, already a part of the agenda for municipal reform, became an accepted as a legitimate function of government.

The Small Parks Act established the principle that local government could condemn privately owned land for the purpose of creating public playgrounds. Legislation was only the first step. Next came the demonstration that playgrounds were effective in the battle with delinquency, crime, and slums. Mulberry Bend Park (today Columbus Park) on Manhattan's

Manhattan, c. 1900. Jacob Riis's photograph of Columbus Park, which replaced "Mulberry Bend." *(Courtesy of the Museum of the City of New York, Jacob A. Riis Collection)*

squalid Lower East Side was the first park to result from the legislation.

Jacob Riis, one of the major figures behind both the legislation and the park, wrote books and articles to demonstrate the case for public playgrounds. His writings remain a most eloquent argument for their creation. In discussing Mulberry Bend Park, he wrote,

> *I do not believe that there was a week in all the twenty years I had to do with... [Mulberry Bend], as a police reporter, in which I was not called to record there a stabbing or shooting affair, some act of violence. It is now five years since the Bend became a park and the police reporter has not had business there during that time; not once has a shot been fired or a knife been drawn.*[9]

Boston, 1886. Charlesbank prior to becoming a public park (currently Storrow Memorial Drive and Embankment Road). *(Courtesy of the Boston Public Library, Print Department)*

Charlesbank, Boston

When the new playground at Mulberry Bend opened in 1897, play equipment was only just being invented. Just as Frederick Law Olmsted provided the paradigm for the park as a restorative Arcadia, he also provided the paradigm for the playground as recreation therapy. In the late 1880s, he presented his first designs for Charlesbank, a 10-acre site along Boston's Charles River opposite Massachusetts General Hospital. Like Mulberry Bend Park, it was intended as a nostrum for the slums, in this case Boston's West End. Among reasons for the new playground enumerated by Olmsted were providing open-air facilities for an increasingly sedentary population and reducing the death rate from cholera among the children of the West End slums.[10]

The final plan for Charlesbank, completed in 1892, included a riverfront promenade, a playground for little girls with sandboxes, swings, and ladders, a small women's outdoor gymnastic area with a tenth-of-a-mile running track and small

Boston, 1889. Charlesbank men's gymnasium (replaced by Storrow Memorial Drive and Embankment Road). *(Courtesy of the Boston Public Library, Print Department)*

areas for jumping and shot putting, and a somewhat larger men's outdoor gymnastic field with a sixth-of-a-mile running track, a trapeze, flying rings, horizontal bars, and areas for shot putting, pole vaulting, and jumping. Olmsted consulted recreation experts in designing Charlesbank as did the Department of Parks in administering it. For the design of the men's playground, Olmsted used equipment designed by Professor Dudley Sargent of Harvard. For the supervision of the children's and women's playground, the Department of Parks used staff trained by the Massachusetts Emergency and Hygiene Association.[11]

Now that generations of children and adults have grown up thinking of sandboxes, swings, slides, running tracks, and playing fields as common fixtures of the urban landscape, it is hard to imagine how revolutionary Olmsted's design for Charlesbank was. Its success is not hard to imagine. In its first year of operation daily attendance at the women's and children's gymnastic field averaged 840.[12]

By 1898 Boston had approved legislation calling for one playground to be established in each of the city's wards. Chicago followed suit in 1903, the year of Olmsted's death, authorizing a bond issue of $1 million for the creation of "small parks or pleasure grounds not more than 10 acres each" and hired Olmsted's firm, now managed by his sons, to design them. Within two years, Chicago had 10 new playgrounds and San Francisco three. The increasing proliferation of playgrounds led, in 1906, to the establishment of the Playground Association of America.

Today, Charlesbank has been replaced by urban arterials. However, its importance cannot be eradicated. Olmsted's pioneering efforts at providing facilities for urban recreation influenced the creation of tens of thousands of American playgrounds with swings, slides, seesaws, and sandboxes.

Standardization and Mass Production

Olmsted supplied the paradigm for both the park and the playground. Reformers made them part of the public agenda. Now government had to standardize the product and make it generally available. What was the proper number and location for parks and playgrounds? Committees, organizations, and agencies studied the problem. Experts differed. Some proposed a standard of 30 square feet per child. Others proposed setting aside 10 acres per 1000 for playgrounds and 40 acres per 1000 for large parks. Eventually parks advocates settled on a standard of 10 acres for every 1000 people.[13]

Accordingly, cities prepared master plans measuring current population, estimating the probable growth in population, cataloguing current park acreage, tracing each facility's service radius, projecting the deficit in public open space, and proposing projects to fill the gaps (Table 3.1). San Francisco, in 1942, established guidelines for the distances between libraries, schools, and recreation places. Philadelphia, in 1968, even published a document entitled *Comprehensive Plan for Swimming Pools,* which advocated pools serving from 20,000 to 30,000 people in every neighborhood.[14]

TABLE 3.1

APPRPOPRIATE DISTANCES APART, IN MILES, OF PARKS AND PLAYGROUNDS [15]

Facility	Chicago	Denver	Minneapolis
Playground	1/4	1/2	1/4 – 1/2
Neighborhood Park	3/8	1/2	—
Playfield	—	1 1/2	1/2 – 1
Community Park	3/4	—	—
District Park	2 1/2 – 3	3	3
Regional Park	—	10	30

Since most standards failed to take into account differences in scale, the National Park Service in 1938 recommended distinguishing among communities of different size, by proposing differential standards for park acreage (Table 3.2). The irony of recommending more park acreage for communities that were less densely settled and, therefore, had more private open space, apparently eluded these single-function planners.

In 1943, the American Society of Planning Officials (ASPO) proposed lowering the standard to 10 acres for every 3000 city residents in cities with populations above 1,000,000, because higher standards were not attainable in more densely populated areas. The absurdity of this numbers game eluded them, too. At a standard of 10 acres per 1000 population, Manhattan at its peak population of 2,331,542 in 1910, would have required 23,315 acres of park, more than the island's entire 14,870 acres. Even at ASPO's lower standard of 10 acres per 3000, half of Manhattan would have to have been set aside for parkland.

The standards may have been helpful in determining how many facilities were necessary, what they should consist of, and where they should be located. However, they were more important as information for park administrators to use in competing with other agencies that advocated other, often more pressing demands for scarce budget allocations. The statistics thus became a tool in balancing the public's desire for recreation facilities with politically achievable levels of funding. Of course, they also became a justification for maintaining and enhancing growing park-department bureaucracies.

TABLE 3.2

NATIONAL PARK SERVICE ACREAGE STANDARDS (1938) [16]

City population	Park acreage per number of people
More than 10,000	10 acres/1000
5000 – 8000	10 acres/750
2500 – 5000	10 acres/600
1000 – 2500	10 acres/500
Less than 1000	10 acres/400

While park advocates and urban planners were trying to arrive at equitable standards, city officials were grappling with the problems of acquiring land for recreation, financing the acquisition and construction of facilities, and insuring they were adequately maintained. They knew, as New York City Parks Commissioner Robert Moses explained, that there is "no such thing as a fixed percentage of park area to population....Sensible, practical people know that [it] depends upon the actual problems of the city in question."[17]

Moses acquired and developed more city parks and playgrounds than any municipal official in any American city at any time. While he was parks commissioner, between 1934 and 1960, he added 20,673 acres to the park system, including 17 miles of public beach, 218 tennis courts, 3 zoos, and 658 playgrounds. The location of these depended on the availability of funds, not on population within the service radius of the facility. For example, when federal relief workers were available, Moses employed them to create golf courses, swimming pools, and playgrounds in existing parks. While building bridges, tunnels, and highways, Moses usually condemned more land than absolutely necessary and transformed the excess into parkland. As anyone who has visited the Brooklyn Heights Esplanade, Shea Stadium in Queens, Manhattan's Henry Hudson Parkway, or any of these "nonpark" projects will tell you, what Moses created in the wake of his other public works makes major park projects in other cities appear insignificant.[18]

Moses was able to produce this vast inventory of facilities by standardizing their design. He used the same benches, swings, slides, seesaws, sandboxes, comfort stations, and sycamore trees over and over again. He used the same cheap, sturdy materials (asphalt, concrete, brick, slate, and wood) in every situation. Parks projects built simultaneously in other cities used similar materials and similar designs. The bureaucracies in those cities also had to standardize their product. The only difference was in Moses' phenomenal ability to get things done.

Midcourse Correction

During the 1960s, when parks and playgrounds had become permanent fixtures of the cityscape, it was easy to undervalue the park bureaucracies that had continued to produce and maintain standardized parks and playgrounds for half a century. People no longer believed, as had Jacob Riis, Jane Addams, and the reformers of a previous century, that parks would eliminate crime, delinquency, and contagious diseases.

The Bronx, 1990. Playground equipment installed by Robert Moses at Orchard Beach. *(Alexander Garvin)*

The Bronx, 1969. Vest-pocket park on Bryant Avenue soon after it opened. *(Alexander Garvin)*

The Bronx, 1971. Vest-pocket park on Bryant Avenue in disrepair after less than two years in operation. *(Alexander Garvin)*

A new wave of reformers demanded more effective public open space. They had had enough of the "swing, slide, sandbox stereotype." Now that parks and playgrounds were abundant, critics could label them "dreary 'people-proofed'" yards which fail "to offer any sort of relief valve for the overwhelming sense of frustration in the youth of a neighborhood."[19]

The redefinition of our image of park and playground began in scattered projects around the country but took its clearest shape in New York City. In 1966, the newly elected mayor, John Lindsay, and his newly appointed parks commissioner, Thomas P. F. Hoving, embarked on a program of creating what they called "vest pocket" parks. As Hoving explained, it was time to get rid of "the black-topped, link-fenced asphalt prison, that standard architecture that has made the W.P.A. style the longest art style of the 20th Century."[20] The idea was to work with community groups to select vacant lots and underutilized properties, easily accessible to toddlers, teenagers, and the elderly. Then the most talented designers would be hired to create exciting new play environments.

Robert Moses knew all the problems Lindsay would encounter. Except for design, the mayor's plan was not very different from the one Moses had implemented in the 1930s. Moses issued a nine-page analysis, calling it a grab bag of good ideas (for which there was not any money) and many poor ones (that had been tried and discarded). Given predictable levels of funding and staffing, Moses felt vandalism could not be controlled nor ordinary maintenance paid for. By the 1970s it had become clear that he was right. New York City had neither the money nor the personnel to keep its capital plan in a decent state of repair.[21]

Hoving's ideas, like those of Moses before him, were not new. Park enthusiasts and community activists across the country had been calling for new parks policies, experimenting with abandoned lots in slum areas, and scheduling rock concerts and other events more attractive to young people who otherwise preferred the livelier activities of city streets. Nor was the design of the "vest pocket" park original. Paul Friedberg, Lawrence Halprin, and other talented designers were already at work on more inventive forms of play equipment and playground design.

Hoving ignored Moses. He hired creative designers and succeeded in scattering vest-pocket parks in poverty areas. Within months many were in poor condition. The Parks Department could not keep up with ordinary repairs or provide necessary personnel for supervision. Benches were missing slats, paving blocks were gone, play equipment was broken, and graffiti disfigured the avant-garde designs.

The Lindsay Administration wanted both the new "vest pocket" and the older traditional parks to attract people no longer using the city's public open space. So it used them as settings for celebrations, festivals, and performances which Hoving called "Happenings." Holiday picnics, dances, outdoor movies, kite-flying, band concerts, and many of the other "Happenings" had been going on in parks for years. What was different was that now these events took place almost every day, attracted throngs of young adults who had never before thought of parks as a setting for popular culture, and resulted in a level of deterioration (crumbling pavement, ravaged lawns, eroded soil, exposed roots, etc.) for which no provision had been made. Neither funds nor personnel were sufficient to deal with the wear and tear. More important, no plans existed for regular, ongoing park rehabilitation.

Hoving never had to face the sad results of his program. Within a year of becoming parks commissioner he became director of the Metropolitan Museum of Art. By the time Mayor Lindsay left office the devastation was so serious that people were calling for a program of playground restoration and 10-year master plans specifying a regular cycle of rehabilitation for the city's major large parks. In the wake of the clamor for restoration, civic leaders established the Central Park Conservancy, which raised money and developed plans for the park's rehabilitation. Simultaneously, the recently elected Koch administration dramatically increased capital spending for park restoration.

In 1979 Elizabeth Barlow Rogers became the first Central Park Administrator. Under her inspired leadership the effects of years of abuse are being methodically eliminated and the park restored. A similar effort initiated by Tupper Thomas is under way in Brooklyn's Prospect Park. Many of Moses' playgrounds are being rebuilt. But, in New York and elsewhere, much more remains to be done.[22]

The reform effort of the 1960s may have had the flaw of ignoring maintenance and assuming unlimited budget allocations. However, it made several successful changes to our approach to public open space. It established once and for all that public open space was for daily use by large masses of people and that budget and personnel allocations for maintenance and restoration had to be sufficient to accommodate such use. It also introduced the idea that recreation facilities were not unchanging artifacts, but had to be adapted to the needs of contemporary users. Finally, it buried forever the "swing, slide, and sandbox stereotype" and replaced it with the idea that play equipment had to grab a child's imagination and encourage adventure and exploration.

The Adventure Playground

From the start, city parks and playgrounds attracted only a portion of the population. This was as true of Olmsted's greenswards as it was of Moses' playgrounds or Lindsay's "vest pocket" parks. In the wake of the city riots during the 1960s, an alternative was taking hold: the "adventure playground." As Robert Nichols, its most persuasive proponent, explained,

> *Big city playgrounds... do not work: so long as vast numbers of kids desert them for the street; so long as the functionaries who service them are behind a wall, isolated from the community; so long as there are insurmountable vandalism and maintenance problems; so long as the communities around them do not reach out their hands and help them because they have no stake in them.*[23]

Nichols believed that if you provide "an ever-changing and exciting environment, where children design, build and plan activities"[24] the entire community would respond. His ideas were based on work that had been going on in Europe for nearly 20 years.

After World War II, social workers in Scandinavia and England noticed that some children avoided carefully designed public open space preferring to play in the rubble of bombed-out sections of the city. They scavenged for broken beams, torn cloth, smashed tin cans, or other refuse that their imagination could transform into buildings, tools, weapons, or anything else their fantasies required. Accordingly, social workers began experimenting with playgrounds in which found materials could be built into fantasy playgrounds or used to destroy the ones that they had only recently erected. These experimental facilities, called "adventure playgrounds," were eagerly adopted by antiestablishment activists who were looking for an alternative to parks and playgrounds that failed to attract city kids.

Nichols and other activists proposed that the city should fund play leaders hired from the communities in which adventure playgrounds could be created. Each play leader would be trained in basic construction techniques and given a budget for tools and materials that could not be scrounged from the neighborhood. Vacant lots would be selected by neighborhood residents as sites for adventure playgrounds. Then, local kids supervised by the play leader would create and/or demolish whatever they desired.

The first adventure playgrounds that Nichols inspired were created in the poorest sections of Manhattan's Lower East Side. The kids who worked on them loved them. However, there were problems from the beginning. The lots became settings for gang turf wars. Broken bottles and other litter would appear after the kids had left. Not surprisingly, some kids were not satisfied with the impermanence of what they built. The structures that they wanted to maintain over longer periods of time were impossible to protect from other kids who were resentful and cynical about any program at all. Without a permanent organization (bureaucracy), at the end of the summer when the play leaders left, the playgrounds fell apart.

If adventure playgrounds were proposed for private property, the owners were not willing to carry the burden of insurance, which the city would not pay for. If they were proposed for city property, the government frequently refused to risk costly lawsuits. Instead, officials suggested that community leaders transform them into more conventional and less risky temporary playlots. In any case, those impermanent adventure playgrounds that were built were too easily later displaced by other land uses, such as housing, schools, or day-care centers.

Today, visitors to the Lower East Side and other poverty areas still come upon adventure playgrounds. These sloppy and awkward facilities continue to inspire neighborhood activists, poverty workers, and the kids they serve. Unlike more conventional facilities, though, they are personnel-intensive, require high ongoing levels of funding, and are not easily susceptible to standardization, mass production, or institutionalization. Thus, the adventure playground remains an intriguing but minor countercurrent to the mainstream use of public open space.

Manhattan, 1887. The vacant lots on Central Park West, south of 72d Street indicate that even three decades after Central Park was completed, the huge crowds that used the park came from great distances. *(Collection of the New-York Historical Society)*

Parks as a Strategic Public Investment

Writing in 1861, Olmsted predicted: "the town will have enclosed the Central Park....No longer an open suburb, our ground will have around it a continuous high wall of brick, stone, and marble." To evaluate its effectiveness, he suggested: "Let us consider, therefore, what will at that time be satisfactory, for it is then that the design will be judged."[25]

A continuous wall of brick, stone, and marble residences has been in place around Central Park for over a century and the residents of New York City have answered in exactly the same manner from the start. They use the park just as

Manhattan, 1898. Nineteenth-century strollers at the Central Park Mall. *(From Greater New York Illustrated, Rand McNally & Co., Skokie, Illinois, 1898)*

Manhattan, 1992. Twentieth-century strollers at the Central Park Mall. *(Alexander Garvin)*

Manhattan, 1898. Sheep's Meadow, Central Park. *(From Greater New York Illustrated, Rand McNally & Co., Skokie, Illinois, 1898)*

Manhattan, 1992. The Sheep's Meadow in Central Park as it is used at the end of the twentieth century. *(Alexander Garvin)*

Olmsted and Vaux envisaged. The intensity of that utilization only underscores their reply. On a typical weekend, more than a quarter of a million people go to the park.

The reasons for this phenomenal success are the same as those for other projects. The market, location, and design of Central Park are an extraordinary match. Hundreds of thousands of people live and work within a few minutes' walk of the park. Olmsted and Vaux created a facility that was carefully designed to accommodate them. Moreover, the park has been able to flourish because it has so often been managed by individuals of entrepreneurial capacity, including Olmsted (superintendent of Central Park 1857–1862 and superintendent or landscape architect 1866–1878), Moses (commissioner of parks 1934–1960), Rogers (administrator of Central Park 1979–present), and the talented civil servants whom they attracted. Central Park's problems have occurred during periods in which either adequate financing was not provided or political support was temporarily strong enough to permit intrusive additional facilities to be erected or to allow park-damaging activities to take place. The recently created Central Park Conservancy should help insulate the park from the problems created by momentary political fashion and financial stringency.

Many vest-pocket parks and most adventure playgrounds, on the other hand, were built to meet the requirements of a population that was in place when they were conceived but, in many cases, has moved on. The result is a mismatch of market, location, and design. This is perfectly appropriate as long as society is willing to discard facilities when market changes render them obsolete. Most cities, however, are unwilling to tie up land and make capital expenditures for periods of such short duration. Even if they are prepared to invest in disposable parks, the financial and entrepreneurial requirements are beyond their capacity. It is unlikely that these facilities will ever be able to compete with other government functions for the necessary operating funds or with other activities for sufficient operating, maintenance, and supervisory personnel with the necessary entrepreneurial skills.

Manhattan, 1894. Nineteenth-century boating in Central Park. *(Courtesy of the Library of Congress, J. S. Johnson Collection)*

Manhattan, 1969. Twentieth-century boating in Central Park. *(Alexander Garvin)*

The best argument for additional spending on parks is that, as was the case with Central Park, the money will stimulate widespread and sustained private investment. Simple retention of open space in its natural state, however, is not enough. Only when local governments establish programs and institutions that will make this land available for active public use and deploy the land in a manner that reshapes surrounding settlement patterns will we begin to exploit its potential as a tool for fixing the American city.

Paris and London

Strategic capital spending on landscaped public open space is responsible for some of the world's most admired urban open spaces: the squares, parks, and boulevards of London and Paris. The money for these facilities initially came from the aristocracy and the crown and later from local governments. It was spent for the specific purpose of attracting a market (the growing populations of these cities) and generating further real estate development.

Among the first such investments were those made by the kings of France. Starting with Henri IV, each new king opened an unimproved section of Paris for development by laying out public squares. These "places royales" were geometrically regular in shape (i.e., circle, square, rectangle, and triangle) and were accented at the center with a sculpture of the monarch who was responsible for its creation. Builders were required to maintain a uniform facade design behind which they could build as they pleased. Henri IV, starting in 1604, used the Place des Vosges to promote development of the Marais; Louis XIV created the Place Vendôme in 1677 and the Place des Victoires in 1684 to spur development of the second Arrondissement; Louis XV fashioned the Place de la Concorde to encourage development north and west of the Tuileries.[26]

A similar approach was taken by the English aristocracy, whose income was in large measure earned by leasing land on their large estates. Many estates required development to proceed according to predetermined plans that included landscaped squares, initially set aside for the exclusive use of the occupants of surrounding buildings. This altered the character of the remaining property sufficiently to stimulate additional interest in its development.[27]

Once a plan had been decided upon, the estates offered long-term ground leases (usually for 99 years) on the lots around the squares. The lessees were profit-motivated developers, who built townhouses for sale or rent, and families, who built for their own use. At the end of the lease the estate either renegotiated the deal or took possession of both the land and the buildings that had been erected on it. Then it re-leased the property. In both cases it usually obtained substantially higher rents. This additional revenue reflected the additional attractiveness of a location that by then included both well-established, landscaped squares and the substantial buildings that surrounded them.

London, 1974. Lonsdale Square was initially developed between 1838 and 1842 for use by the residents of buildings surrounding what was then privately owned open space. *(Alexander Garvin)*

Covent Garden, laid out in 1630 by architect Inigo Jones for the Earl of Bedford, was the first of these London squares. It was followed by Leicester Square in 1635, St. James Square in 1684, and Grosvenor Square in 1695. By the eighteenth century the landscaped square had become the accepted device for marketing estate property, a device that during the nineteenth century was primarily responsible for the development of Bloomsbury, Belgravia, and Islington. But it was an approach that was only possible at locations that included substantial amounts of undeveloped land close to already built-up areas with growing populations ready to settle nearby.

Once large territories had been developed, an entirely different set of problems emerged. By the start of the nineteenth century, London and Paris had become large, congested cities. The central sections of both cities had to accommodate rapidly increasing populations and expanding economies. Once again, public open space was used as a mechanism for accommodating growth; in this case, by providing a framework around which to reconstruct existing city districts. Although the process of reconstruction was different in each city, the situation was the same. Its most valuable locations had been built up in a manner that no longer satisfied the city's needs. Individual parcels might be rebuilt, but growth was so rapid and market pressure so intense that entire districts needed to be redesigned.

In London, the process of reconstruction was initiated in 1811 when the Prince Regent, anticipating the expiration of the lease on his 543-acre Marylebone Estate, engaged architect-developer Sir John Nash to propose a scheme for its redevelopment. Nash's plan consisted of three parts: refashioning the district around the existing royal garden, known as St. James Park, creating a new district on the Marylebone Estate encircling a relandscaped "Regent's Park," and connecting the

London, 1972. Regent's Park was conceived as an amenity that would increase the value of the rest of the Prince Regent's Marylebone Estate and induce residential development surrounding the park. *(Alexander Garvin)*

two park districts with a broad new artery to be called "Regent Street." Thereafter, the 2-mile stretch between the two parks could be rebuilt by individual property owners to meet market requirements.[28]

The land around St. James and Regent's Parks was bound to be prime territory for development. Without the new Regent Street, however, the scheme would have been far less successful. Prior to its creation, central London had three major east-west arteries (Oxford Street, Picadilly, and the Strand). Regent Street not only connected the parks but also provided, for the first time, a major north-south thoroughfare that connected these east-west arteries, thereby dramatically increasing accessibility to the entire district.

Nash's design concept for the land around the parks was intended to increase its already extraordinary marketability by creating a setting that gave the occupants of the surrounding buildings the illusion of nobility and great wealth. Opposite the park, Nash designed monumental residential structures, which the English call terraces. From within the park these terraces appear to be sumptuous palaces rather than the middle-class residences they in fact are. From terrace windows, the park appears to be the resident's own landscaped estate. By creating these twin illusions, the design transformed a large amount of crown property into fashionable sites that could command high rents and attract further development to less attractive adjacent land.

Successful as the squares and parks of London were, they did not provide the most influential evidence that strategic investment in public parks could spur the improvement of surrounding areas. That evidence was provided by the parks that Baron Georges Eugène Haussmann created in Paris. Haussmann was a public administrator who had worked in various parts of France before being appointed Prefect of the Seine (Paris) in 1853 by Emperor Napoleon III. In the 16 years during which he occupied that position, Haussmann transformed Paris from a congested jumble of buildings into a modern metropolis with large parks and broad landscaped boulevards (see Chapter 18).

Like Nash, Haussmann worked for the crown. Like Nash, he refashioned two large royal gardens into public parks (the Bois de Boulogne and the Bois de Vincennes), connected them to the rest of the city with new avenues, and rebuilt much of the city in between. However, the scale of his work dwarfed anything Nash dared dream about.

In 1850 Paris possessed only 47 acres of public park (one acre per 5000 inhabitants). The open-space system Haussmann and Adolphe Alphand, his engineer and landscape architect, established included two large regional parks (the Bois de Boulogne and the Bois de Vincennes), three district parks (the Parc Monceau, Les Buttes Chaumont, and the Parc de Montsouris), about 40 public gardens or squares (ranging in size from a quarter of an acre to more than six acres), 90 miles of tree-lined boulevards, and the landscaped quais that lined the Seine River. When Haussmann left office the park system included 4500 acres of parkland (one acre per 390 inhabitants).[29]

Each of the facilities Haussmann created was intended to stimulate development in the surrounding area. Avenue Foch (originally known as the Avenue de l'Impératrice in honor of Napoleon III's wife) provides an excellent illustration of Haussmann's approach. Ostensibly, the avenue was created to connect the Place de l'Etoile with the Bois de Boulogne. Its heroic width (460 feet from property line to property line) is far more than this job requires. As a result, the avenue is more than a heavily traveled traffic artery. It is really two linear extensions of the Bois de Boulogne that run alongside a central roadway. These linear parks are, in turn, flanked by boundary roads that service the buildings fronting on this extraordinary boulevard. Good vehicular access, however, is only one reason that Avenue Foch became the location of choice for some of the most elaborate mansions in Paris. The major reason is that the landscaped islands flanking the mon-

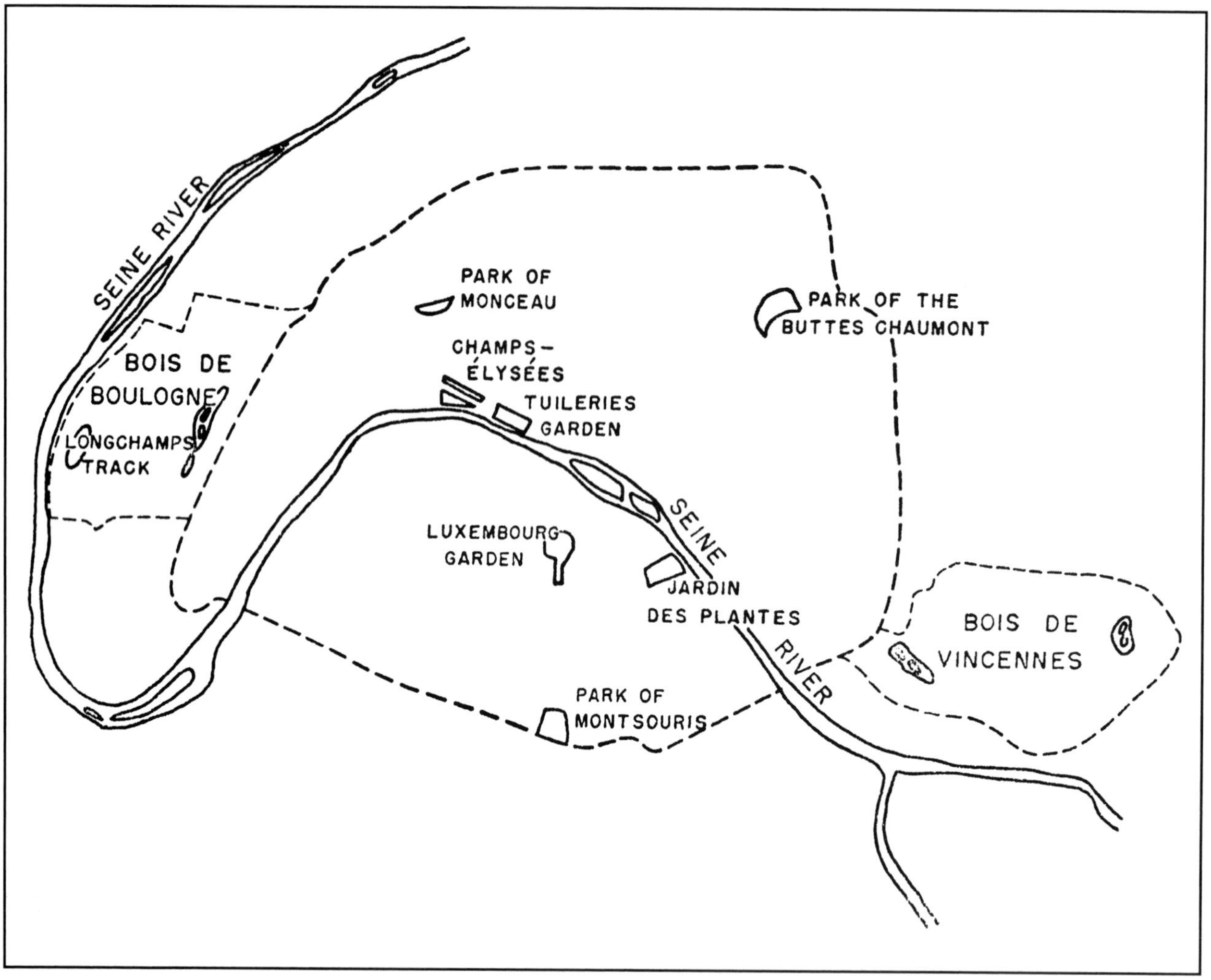

Paris, 1870. Haussmann's park system consisted of two large regional parks, three major neighborhood parks, large tree-lined boulevards, and scattered landscaped public squares. *(From D. H. Pinkney, Napoleon III and the Rebuilding of Paris: copyright 1972 by Princeton University Press, reproduced by permission)*

umental central roadway are wide enough for residents to have the illusion of living opposite a park.[30]

Importing European Models

Some of the conditions that made the boulevards, parks, and squares of London and Paris so successful were similar to those in nineteenth-century American cities. Burgeoning populations provided a rapidly growing market. Facilities could be located on open territory very close to that market. However, neither the European conception of public open space, nor the mechanisms for its establishment and maintenance were applicable to the United States. In Europe, parks were thought of as an integral component of the urban environment; in America, they were meant to stand in contrast to the city and provide a refuge from its noise, dirt, and confusion. In Europe, open space was specifically designed to meet the demands of surrounding building occupants; in America, parks were intended for widespread and active public use.

The techniques used to create squares and parks of London and Paris were not transferable to the United States because they were based on completely different notions of property ownership and government responsibility. Property development in substantial sections of London is based on the interrelationship between fee owners and their lessees, both of whom were financially dependent on the quality of commonly held open space. In America, most property owners avoid responsibility for nearby open space.

Haussmann's approach to project development also was inextricably linked to development of surrounding land. The Prefecture of the Seine, however, did not maintain continuing ownership of the property adjacent to its parks. It prepared district development plans, acquired the necessary land, and, once the project was under way, it sold the now more valuable edges to developers. In the case of the Bois de Boulogne,

Haussmann spent 14.3 million francs developing the park and sold excess land for 10 million francs. The investment in the Bois paid off handsomely because land that had previously been worth considerably less, could command a new, higher price based on the existence of the park. To put it another way, property owners, who gained from the presence of a park, paid for that benefit.

The district development procedures that Haussmann employed were no more applicable to the United States than those of London's great estates. In nineteenth-century America, government acquisition of land for the purpose of selling it at a profit might have been quite effective. But state constitutions and the prevailing view of the role of government made it impossible to condemn privately owned property for resale at a profit. The biggest difference, though, was that no American city administration had the power of the great estates of London or of Napoleon III's prefectures. In the United States, park agencies were accountable to local legislatures, mayoral administrations, and voters who intentionally restricted their powers. Political considerations forced these agencies to make expenditures whose short-term benefits had to be immediately obvious to the electorate. In Europe, from the very beginning the institutions that were responsible for park development conceived of them as long-term investments that would produce continually increasing benefits for future generations.

One device, however, was transferable to the United States: a development plan with plenty of open space set aside for use by area residents. Such plans could reduce uncertainty about the future of the area, reassure potential investors, simplify the subdivision process, and allow lots to be put on the market in response to changes in market conditions.

Rather than develop such plans, most American cities simply mimicked European precedents. Most city plans included an initial public open space from which their designers expected the city to expand. New Orleans' Place d'Armes (today Jackson Square), the Boston Common, and the New Haven Green are some of the more famous examples. Until the latter nineteenth century, however, little attention was paid to the role that public open space could play in shaping overall city development. The lovely parks of New Orleans, Boston, and New Haven came centuries later, when they did indeed affect urbanization.[31]

Philadelphia and Savannah were different. They provided public open space in a more systematic fashion. The 1683 plan for Philadelphia, by William Penn and Thomas Holme, provided an open space pattern (four 8-acre squares and a 10-acre central square) that its designers thought would determine the future character of the city. These five squares did shape development patterns within their immediate surroundings. However, the meager 42 acres they provided were insufficient to have any serious impact on the city as a whole.[32]

Only one major American city, Savannah, began with a plan that had the critical mass of open space that was necessary to affect the character of city life. James Oglethorpe's 1733 design is based on a system of wards, each consisting of eight blocks and each of which is centered around a public square. Unfortunately, once the first 26 wards were completed, the design was discarded.[33]

The results were similar in cities where the private land development included common open space. In New York City, a developer created Hudson Square, between Hudson and Varick Streets in lower Manhattan. As the locus of development moved uptown, however, Hudson Square was replaced with a railroad freight depot. The city's other developer-created square, Gramercy Park, survived.

In Boston, privately developed squares fared no better. Charles Bullfinch's Tontine Crescent, designed around a crescent-shaped open space, was demolished in 1858, to make way for some stone warehouses. Pemberton Square, another privately developed open space, was eliminated during the 1960s to make way for a new office building in an urban renewal area. The destruction and disfigurement of the districts around these squares was possible because there was no entity responsible for any continuing relationship between the buildings and the open spaces they surrounded. Nor was any entity responsible for creating additional public open space in the immediate vicinity. Unlike the great estates of London, the initial developers neither retained ownership of the land nor any interest in what happened after they were through, while property owners were at liberty to replace buildings at will.

Using Parks to Initiate Urbanization

American park advocates used the examples of Paris and London to buttress their argument that public open space could be an effective device for shaping the surrounding city. However, their principal argument had little to do with the quality of life in those cities. It was financial. They argued that as land values surrounding parks increased, owners either would develop their properties in a manner that justified that increased value or they would sell to somebody who would. Initially, real estate tax collections would increase as a result of the increase in land assessment, and later, as a result of development.

Park advocates during the last century were more sensitive to this thinking than we are today. In 1883, Horace William Shaler Cleveland, the initial designer of the Minneapolis park system, argued for its creation saying:

> *In the ten years succeeding the commencement of work on Central Park in New York the increased valuation of taxable property in the wards immediately surrounding it was no less than $54,000,000, affording a surplus, after paying interest on all the city bonds issued for the purchase and construction of the park, of $3,000,000—a sum sufficient, if used as a sinking fund, to pay the entire principal and interest of the cost of the park in less time than was required for its construction.*[34]

His point was that at first the increased taxes could be used to pay for park acquisition and development. Later they could pay for other municipal activities. For this reason, park advocates insisted that parks not only did not cost a penny; they earned the city increased taxes with which to pay for additional services.

Others argued that investing in parks would relieve congestion. As newcomers in increasing numbers squeezed into already crowded areas, established city residents sought more comfortable surroundings. Property owners in outlying undeveloped areas seeking to profit from their land investments favored park development as a way of attracting this market. Businesses trying to find downtown locations for commerce, warehousing, and manufacturing favored creation of new parks just beyond developed portions of the city as a way of releasing built-up land for their reuse. Political machines saw park development as a source of jobs for unemployed voters and patronage for party members.

Cities everywhere wanted to outperform New York City. Park advocates reasoned that if their parks were more impressive than the new Central Park, their city would surpass New York in prestige and become America's premier city.

Together, these nineteenth-century park enthusiasts became a powerful coalition of social reformers, businesspeople, political bosses, and ordinary laborers that succeeded in creating thousands of acres of public open space. They understood what we have forgotten, that parks are more than patches of green or accumulations of recreation equipment and that they must be created with an eye to their impact on the city as a whole. The parks that this coalition supported were created during a time of phenomenal population growth and coincided with the establishment of mass-transit systems that made accessible vast new territories. When a city chose to create a large park in the midst of all this activity, nearby property owners no longer faced the possibility of incompatible construction on what was now parkland. Consequently, the value of that property increased. The intense development that followed the establishment of Prospect Park in Brooklyn, Forest Park in St. Louis, and other similar large parks was the natural market reaction to this increase in property values. It did not accompany the establishment of Griffith Park in Los Angeles, or parks like it, because building conditions in the surrounding area were not favorable and because other locations were in greater demand.

Prospect Park, Brooklyn

The independent City of Brooklyn was one of the first municipalities to use a new park to spark real estate activity in undeveloped territory. In response to its request for authority to cre-

Brooklyn, 1990. View entering Prospect Park through Endale Arch. *(Alexander Garvin)*

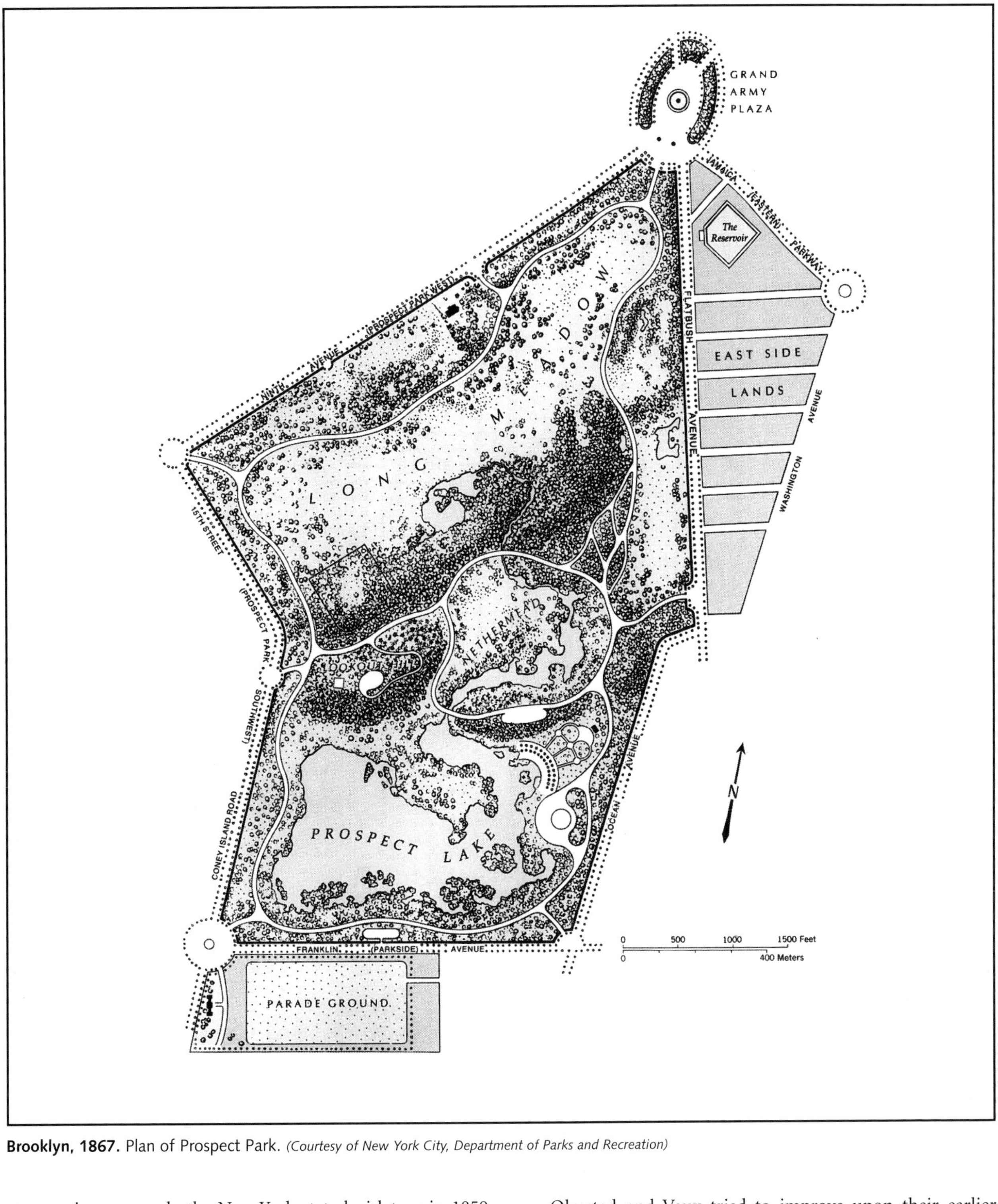

Brooklyn, 1867. Plan of Prospect Park. *(Courtesy of New York City, Department of Parks and Recreation)*

ate a major new park, the New York state legislature in 1859 authorized creation of a park commission similar to the one it had authorized for Central Park in neighboring New York City. The commissioners for the new Brooklyn park hired Olmsted and Vaux who, in 1866, completed the design of a 526-acre park designed to satisfy the needs of a city that in 1870 would have a population of 420,000, making it the third largest city in the United States, exceeded only by New York and Philadelphia.

Olmsted and Vaux tried to improve upon their earlier design across the river by creating an even lovelier landscape and further reducing the possibility of intrusions from the surrounding city. Their proposal included sweeping meadows, wooded hills, and an artificial lake. As in Central Park, the circumferential vehicular carriageway, bridle path, and pedestrian path are separate. The landscape is artificially built up even more dramatically along the periphery to eliminate views of

Brooklyn, 1990. Children playing on the Longmeadow in Prospect Park. *(Alexander Garvin)*

the surrounding city. Originally, conifers planted along the periphery of the park excluded any glimpse of the surrounding city, even during the winter when the leaves had dropped. Eventually, the conifers died and only began to be replaced in the late 1980s.[35]

Approaching Prospect Park from Grand Army Plaza, one walks toward a landscaped berm, passes through an underpass that tunnels beneath it, and, like Dorothy opening the door of her black-and-white house to wander into Technicolor Oz, enters into a gorgeous landscape devoid of any trace of the city, its smells, its noise, or its vehicles. Visitors who take this route experience a magical "feeling of relief" from "the cramped, confined" city and gain what Olmsted called "a sense of enlarged freedom."[36]

The only irreparable damage to the design is the result of the park's attractiveness. By the 1920s, its surroundings had become so popular that developers tore down some of the houses facing the park and built the handful of apartment

Brooklyn, 1967. Eastern Parkway. *(Alexander Garvin)*

towers that are now visible from the Long Meadow. They are the only intrusions that shatter Olmsted and Vaux's carefully designed separation of city and country.

Olmsted and Vaux also proposed three parkways, inspired by Haussmann's Avenue Foch: one leading to Prospect Park from Fort Hamilton at the Narrows (Ft. Hamilton Parkway), the second from the Atlantic Ocean at Coney Island (Ocean Parkway), and the third from Queens County (Eastern Parkway). Like Haussmann's boulevard, these parkways were to consist of a central roadway for through traffic, two flanking, landscaped, linear islands, and two service roads with sidewalks providing access to the buildings fronting on the boulevard. But they were much narrower and far less grandiose. In Paris the flanking landscaped islands were wide enough to be real parks; in Brooklyn they were paved walkways lined with benches and rows of trees. Nevertheless, Ocean and Eastern Parkways were sufficiently broad and alluring to attract quality buildings. They also provided an excellent setting for convivial chatter while promenading, sitting on benches, and walking the dog.

Olmsted predicted that Prospect Park and the parkways leading to it would spur development because

> *advance in value will be found to be largely dependent on the advantages of having near a residence, a place where…driving, riding, and walking can be conveniently pursued in association with pleasant people, and without the liability of encountering the unpleasant sights and sounds…in the common streets.*[37]

He was right. Developers responded to his park and parkways by building single-family homes in Flatbush (south of Prospect Park), row houses in Park Slope (north and west of the Park), and apartment houses along Ocean and Eastern Parkways (south and east of the Park). In fact, by the 1890s Park Slope had supplanted Brooklyn Heights as the location of choice for many of the city's wealthiest residents. Market reaction was intense because these facilities had little competition. There were no other landscaped parks or boulevards of their size and convenience, or with anything like their facilities anywhere in Brooklyn.[38]

During the 1950s and 1960s, many residents of the neighborhoods around Prospect Park and Ocean and Eastern Parkways left for the suburbs. Though they were quickly replaced by new residents, the buildings themselves began to deteriorate. When neighborhood decline was reversed during the 1970s and 1980s, public open space once again influenced the market reaction. Market activity and price increases began with buildings that lined Prospect Park and Ocean and Eastern Parkways (see Chapter 12).

Forest Park, St. Louis

Forest Park in St. Louis sparked the same initial market reaction that was experienced around Central and Prospect Parks. Unlike them, however, it was not as carefully tailored to the needs of a growing population and failed to anticipate future uses.[39]

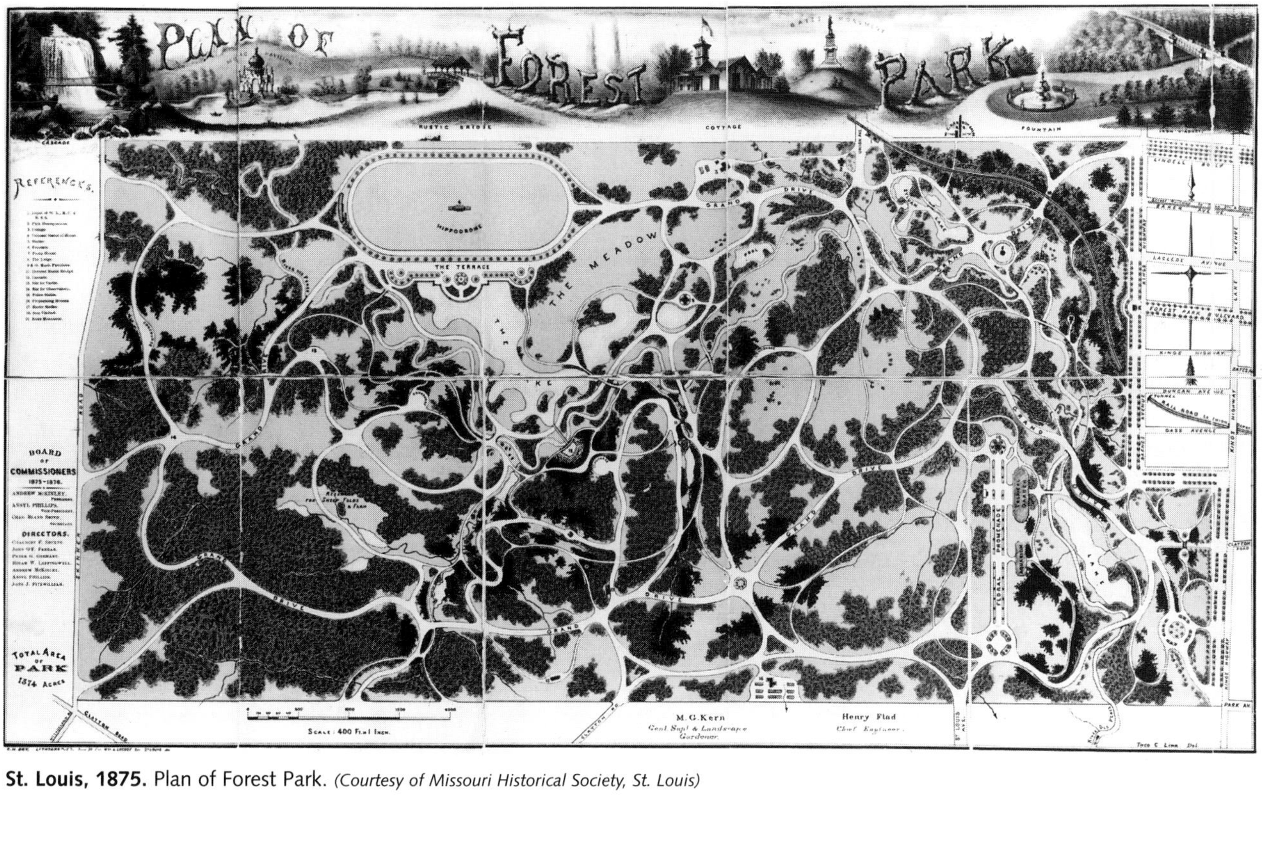

St. Louis, 1875. Plan of Forest Park. *(Courtesy of Missouri Historical Society, St. Louis)*

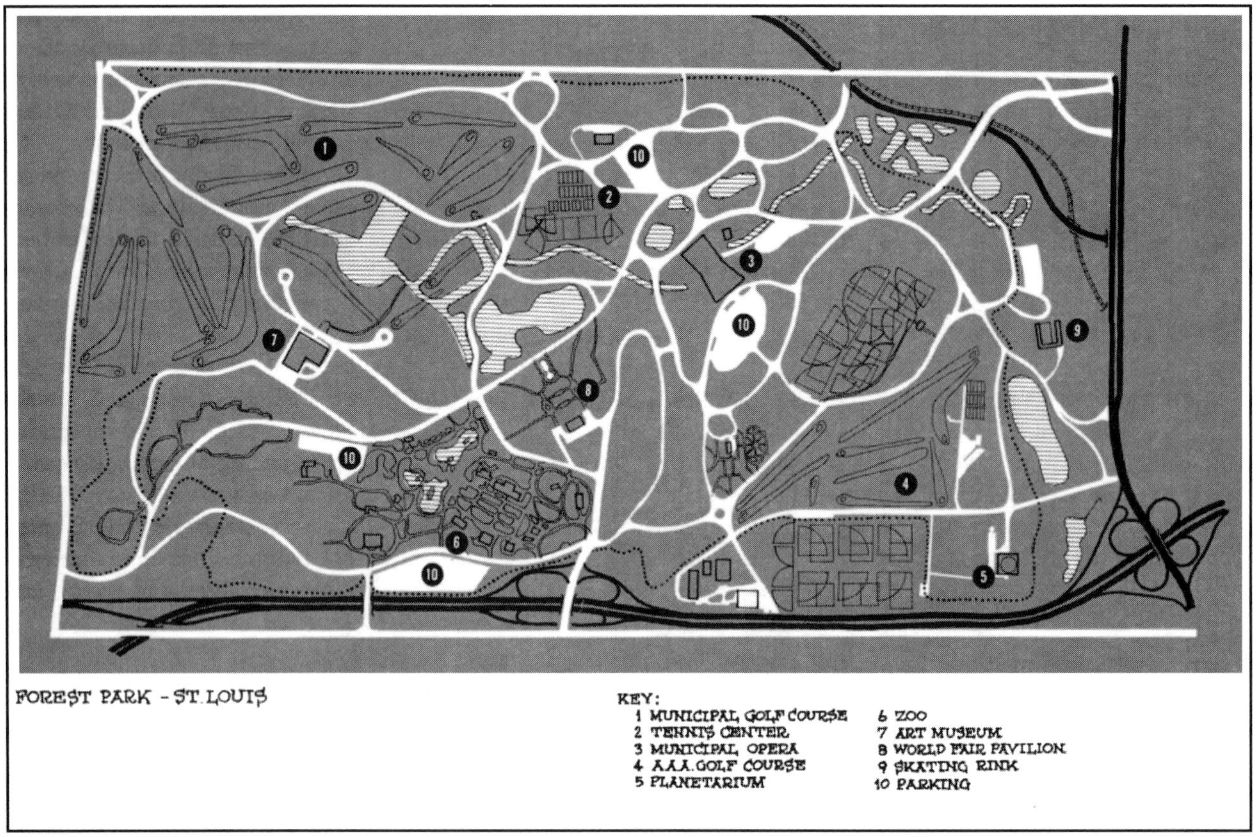

St. Louis, 1976. Map illustrating the changes to Forest Park intended to add the missing element of "social utility" to the original plan. *(From A. Heckscher, Open Spaces, 1977; reprinted with permission from the Twentieth Century Fund, New York)*

When Forest Park officially opened in 1876, developers invested in surrounding properties, which they correctly thought would benefit as much from the presence of the park as from the extension of mass transit running to the central business district. Within 20 years, the Forest Park area included seven streetcar lines, carrying more than 2.5 million passengers annually. Developers reacted to the new park and transit lines by subdividing their properties and selling lots to wealthy citizens (see Chapter 13).

The design of Forest Park, by Maximillian Kern (the park's superintendent and landscape gardener) and Chief Engineers Julius Pitzman and Henry Flad, was inspired by Olmsted. It included similar curvalinear pedestrian paths, winding carriageways, artificial lakes, broad meadows, and wooded rambles. Unfortunately, they copied these features without understanding how carefully Olmsted had tailored their design to fit the specific needs of the people who would use his parks.

From the beginning, Forest Park had to be remodeled to meet consumer demand. Large areas of Forest Park were destroyed for the Louisiana Purchase Exposition of 1904, well-known to movie goers from the film *Meet Me in St. Louis*. Some of the structures the Fair left behind are still in use. The numerous other intrusions that followed reflected the determination of the St. Louis Department of Parks to add "the concept of social utility" to "the element of natural beauty." Had Forest Park, like Central and Prospect Parks, been designed for mass recreation, it would not have needed to be altered to perform its function of "raising of men and women rather than grass and trees."[40]

Unlike Brooklyn, the population of St. Louis began to decline during the 1930s, dropping more than 50 percent over the next 60 years. Despite the resulting decline in market demand, the area surrounding Forest Park has remained the location of the most sumptuous and elegant homes in the city. Without Forest Park, the area would have succumbed to the same forces of decay that affected so many other parts of St. Louis.

Griffith Park, Los Angeles

When Colonel Griffith J. Griffith donated a 3000-acre portion of Rancho Los Feliz to the City of Los Angeles in 1896, it instantly became one of the largest municipal parks in the country. Like Prospect and Forest Parks it was located in undeveloped territory a few miles from the center of a thriving metropolis. (By 1900, the population of Los Angeles had already reached 102,000.) Like these parks, it was the only major facility in the city. But, unlike them, the new Griffith

Park failed to stimulate any significant market reaction. Residential development in Los Angeles did explode after the creation of Griffith Park, but largely westward toward the Pacific Ocean, away from the park.[41]

Griffith Park is in a mountainous area northwest of downtown Los Angeles. The steep topography on three sides limits the amount of construction that is possible. Furthermore, beginning in 1908, the City of Los Angeles enacted a series of land use regulations that restricted construction on the surrounding hillsides to one-family houses. Consequently, developers chose to concentrate their activity on the flat plain below the park.

The greatest difference between Griffith Park and other large city parks is in design. Olmsted's parks and those of his followers are essentially artificially manufactured landscapes. From the beginning, however, most of Griffith Park was left in its natural state. Over the years, the city added riding trails, vehicular roadways, an observatory, an open-air theater, five golf courses, a small picnic and playing area, two freeways, and considerable additional land. Nevertheless, Griffith Park remains a 4063-acre section of wilderness accessible by automobile that is more suitable for hiking than intense utilization by masses of city dwellers.

The Chicago Lakeshore

In 1866, a group of civic reformers and businesspeople, who owned property in the undeveloped Hyde Park Township, 6 miles south of downtown Chicago, began discussing the creation of a park system. Although the Illinois legislature approved their demand for a major park south of the city, it was rejected in a referendum. Finally, in 1869, separate parks commissions for North, West, and South Chicago were approved.[42]

The western facilities, Humboldt, Garfield, and Douglas Parks, were established on open land. Their design, by architect William Le Baron Jenney, combined features of Haussmann's district parks with facilities Olmsted and Vaux had included in Central and Prospect Parks (e.g., boat houses, formal, tree-lined pedestrian malls, and circumferential carriageways).

The three most important parks, Lincoln Park (established by the North Park Commission), and Jackson and Washington Parks in the south, anchored what was to become one of America's most extraordinary waterfront parks: 23 miles of grass, trees, lagoons, beaches, marinas, playgrounds, and landscaped roadway. When these parks were conceived, Lincoln Park was at the end of a horsecar line on the northern boundary of Chicago. The southern parks were not even in Chicago; they were in an undeveloped suburb, with a population of just over 1000, then developing around stations of the Illinois Central Railroad.

The parks with the most natural advantages, those along the shore of Lake Michigan, should have attracted the bulk of the city's expansion. By the middle of the nineteenth century large portions of the lake shore were already occupied by the railroad or were being used as garbage dumps. Consequently development activity was more intense inland. Only in the middle of the twentieth century, when undesirable land uses had been removed, additional parkland had filled in many gaps, and Lake Shore Drive had organized this parkland into a single continuous facility, did an overwhelming amount of real estate activity finally shift toward the lake.

The South Park Commission acquired about 1000 acres, a sandy marsh fronting on Lake Michigan and a desolate stretch of flat prairie further inland. It hired Olmsted and Vaux to transform this land into parks. The design that the firm submitted consisted of four parts: Jackson Park on the lakefront, Washington Park in the interior, a broad, linear Midway Plaisance connecting them, and three landscaped boulevards, similar to what it had recommended in Brooklyn.

As Olmsted and Vaux explained: "the first obvious defect of the site is that of flatness," for which they compensated by creating a series of artificial lakes and lagoons, but without resorting to artificial hills, depressions, or "trivial objects of interest." Much of the land was swampy and the water table frequently was too close to the surface for large trees. This problem was solved by draining the swamps to create the lakes and lagoons, using the scooped-out sand and mud to build up the areas that were to be planted with large trees, and by cutting a drainage channel through to Lake Michigan. Their plan called for a public beach as a barrier to wind and wave damage from Lake Michigan.[43]

The South Park Commission chose not to create the elaborate lagoon that had been proposed for Jackson Park. Nor did it extend a waterway from Washington Park down the Midway to the lake at Jackson Park and out to Lake Michigan. The design, as carried out under the supervision of Horace William Shaler Cleveland, was far less ambitious. It was not till Olmsted worked on the Chicago Fair of 1893 that Jackson Park was dredged, earth moved, and the trees planted to create the elaborate lagoons Olmsted had originally proposed.[44]

As usual, Olmsted's predictions about the activities that would take place in the parks and about the market reaction in the areas surrounding them proved to be correct. He had designed Jackson and Washington Parks as urban facilities meant for active use by large populations, rather than "a distant suburban excursion ground." By 1889, when Hyde Park was annexed by the City of Chicago, its population had grown to 85,000.[45]

The reason the south parks were actively used had as much to do with their character as with the sizable and growing populations that surrounded them. Olmsted and Vaux had, for the first time, specifically designed important sections of a large park (Washington Park) as "an arena for athletic sports, such as baseball, football, cricket, and running games," which they thought would come into fashion.[46]

Olmsted returned to the design of these parks when he worked with Daniel Burnham on the site plan of the Chicago

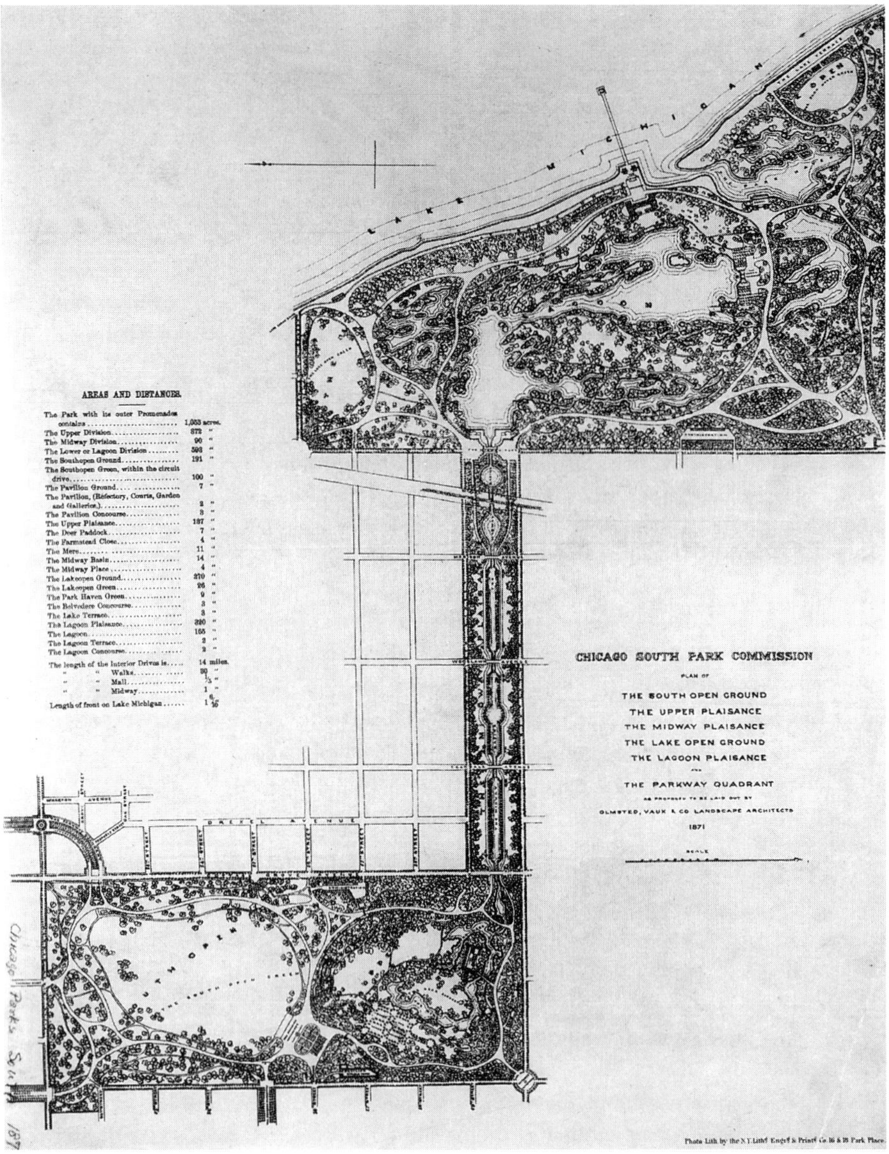

Chicago, 1871. Olmsted and Vaux plan of the South Park System including Jackson Park, Washington Park, and the Midway. *(Courtesy of Chicago Historical Society)*

Fair of 1893 (see Chapters 4 and 18). Once the fair had closed, Jackson Park was relandscaped by the Olmsted firm in a manner that, except for the site of the Museum of Science and Industry and some sections along Stony Island Avenue, was very similar to the 1871 design.

Burnham suggested far more radical action: connecting all of Chicago's waterfront parks to create a single facility. In 1894, he convinced a group of the city's most important businesspeople to advocate a landscaped South Shore Drive connecting Jackson Park with the Loop business district. Burnham's design, completed 2 years later, envisaged the removal of some obsolete rail lines and the creation of a limited access parkway. Between Lake Michigan and the remaining rail lines, he proposed a lagoon, a roadway, and a linear park. At the downtown end, he proposed a boat basin and a major new park. The scheme was not implemented.

Thirteen years later Burnham resurrected the drive, park, and boat basin for *The Plan of Chicago* (see Chapter 18). This time he proposed a broad South Shore Drive, a larger and more elaborate downtown park, and an additional North Shore Drive that included Lincoln Park and extended to the city's current northern boundary.

In 1911, the City Council formally approved adoption of *The Plan of Chicago.* During the next 30 years, it spent hundreds of millions of dollars on landfill, landscaping, roads, beaches, and recreation facilities along the shore of Lake Michigan. The downtown component, Grant Park, became the landfill centerpiece of this extraordinary linear park. The southern portion, especially around Jackson Park, attracted a few developers who built apartment towers that capitalized on the parks and the lovely views of the lake. Along the northern portion, Lake Shore Drive, the impact was spectacular. There,

Chicago, 1982. Lake Shore Drive. *(Alexander Garvin)*

developers created a "gold coast" of expensive apartment buildings, rivaling New York's Fifth Avenue. No park improvement anywhere has had greater impact.

The neighborhoods around Chicago's inland parks prospered until the middle of the twentieth century, when they succumbed to the awesome social and economic forces that swept through much of the city, leaving in their wake a desolate scene of dilapidated buildings, vacant lots, and widespread abandonment. At the same time, market activity shifted back toward Lake Michigan, where, during the half-century following publication of *The Plan of Chicago,* the city had spent so much money moving garbage dumps and railroad uses in order to create the linear park the plan had recommended.

Using Parks to Change Land Use Patterns

Contrary to conventional wisdom, it is as easy to establish new parks in already built-up city districts as in developing areas. The possibilities exist because cities are in constant flux. One section gushes up, while another skids into decline. As economic activity and population shift from one location to another, the properties that are left behind become available for reuse. Transformed into public parks, they can initiate second growth.

These opportunities are often seized by developers who find original ways of adapting property to more profitable uses. City governments usually are blind to such opportunities. But if parks were generally considered to be public investments that could improve surrounding areas rather than (nonessential) recreation facilities, a substantial amount of open land would not now lie fallow. Public agencies would be acquiring underutilized properties at depressed prices and transforming them into new public facilities that would stimulate second growth and reshape the character of surrounding areas.

San Antonio, Texas, is among a small number of cities that have successfully exploited the potential of such underutilized city land. It transformed an abandoned riverfront into the Paseo del Rio, a public park that quickly became a major tourist facility. Developers, attracted by this new market, redeveloped property facing the park and sparked the revival of the surrounding business district.

Other facilities, like Philadelphia's Benjamin Franklin Parkway and Fort Worth's Water Garden that reused sections of the city as parkland, failed to produce the same market reaction. Franklin Parkway offered nothing to attract new customers to the area and—without them—could have no impact on the surrounding city. In Fort Worth, several blocks were cleared to make way for a unique tourist facility that did attract people to a declining section of the business district. Unlike the Paseo del Rio, though, there is nowhere to go after visiting the Water Garden. Consequently, the city is unable to profit from any spillover.

Paseo del Rio, San Antonio

The Paseo del Rio, or Riverwalk, was initiated to terminate a hazard (flooding) and eliminate a nuisance (the garbage-strewn banks of the San Antonio River). When it was first established, few people thought it would also become a tourist attraction. However, by successfully recycling this obsolete waterway its designers provided a powerful illustration of the effectiveness of intelligently planned, public open space as a device for stimulating second growth.[47]

The Spanish colonists, who established the presidio of San Antonio de Bejar in 1718, selected a charming, tree-lined spot along the winding San Antonio River. They chose the site because of its ready supply of water and access to the Gulf of Mexico. The river was so convenient as a transportation route that it attracted commercial activity. Because the riverbed was 15 feet below grade, commercial buildings, fronting the streets above, turned their backs to it. By 1900 the neglected riverbanks had become rubbish-strewn alleys that attracted vagrants rather than economic activity. Its only remaining natural assets were the majestic cypress trees that still shaded the waterway.

The river was subject to periodic flooding. In response to floods in 1913 and 1919, the city commissioned an engineering study, which proposed straightening the river, relegating it to an underground sewer, and paving over its downtown horseshoe-shaped section to create a highway. Residents were unwilling to pay for such radical surgery.

During the flood of 1921, the river rose 35 feet, nearly 10 feet above grade, causing 50 deaths and more than $50 million in damage. City officials immediately resurrected the 1919 study. Once again proposals for consigning the San Antonio River to an underground conduit were defeated. Instead, citizens envisioned a riverfront park that combined the winding streets of "Old Spain" with the canals of Venice. Eventually, they persuaded the city government to establish a River Improvement District and borrow the money to bring their vision to reality. The cost of the improvement, however, was far greater than any bond issue the city administration thought it could afford. Finally, in 1938, San Antonio Congressman Maury Maverick, helped to persuade the Works

San Antonio, 1986. The Paseo del Rio is used by office workers on their way to appointments, tourists going to hotels, restaurants, and shops, and by everybody for casual strolling. *(Alexander Garvin)*

Progress Administration (WPA) to provide a $350,000 grant. The city issued bonds to cover the remaining $75,000.

The Paseo del Rio was created by connecting the ends of the 1.8-mile horseshoe bend in the river with a straight bypass channel. Floodgates were added at each end to control the flow of water. Additional cypress trees as well as 11,000 other trees and shrubs were planted along the river edge. The city also installed 31 stairways, 21 bridges, 17,000 feet of walkways, artwork, fountains, and an amphitheater.

San Antonio, 1986. The Paseo del Rio is so successful that it has become the location of choice for the development of new hotels, office buildings, and restaurants. *(Alexander Garvin)*

When the Paseo del Rio was completed in 1941, the rear sections of the area's underutilized commercial buildings became more attractive than their fronts. Within five years, several stores and two restaurants had broken through to the park. The success of the tourist-oriented facilities that opened along the river was so great that in 1965 voters approved another bond issue to pay for additional entrances and a major extension of the park. By 1968, when a second channel was created to connect the Paseo with the convention center built for the World's Fair/HemisFair, there were 30 retail and tourist-oriented businesses that fronted the Riverwalk. A third channel, connecting the Paseo del Rio with the Alamo, was added in 1981.

Today the Paseo del Rio is lined with outdoor cafes, shops, art galleries, bars, and hotels. City residents and office workers in large numbers walk by the tall cypress trees and dense banks of plants and flowers on their way to downtown appointments. Motor boats give guided tours to fascinated visitors. What had been a costly eyesore has become a profitable tourist attraction and an attractive setting for new real estate development.

Benjamin Franklin Parkway, Philadelphia

In 1892, Philadelphia's director of public works persuaded the city to map a grand diagonal boulevard going from City Hall through Logan Circle (originally conceived as one of the squares in William Penn's plan) to Fairmount Park. The Fairmount Park Art Association commissioned a new plan prepared by a panel of architects that included Paul Cret, Clarence Zantzinger, and Horace Trumbauer in 1907. The final scheme for what became the Benjamin Franklin Parkway, by the French architect Jacques Grébier, was approved in 1917 and completed in time for the opening of the first stage of the Philadelphia Museum of Art in 1928. [48]

The city spent $35 million to pay for acquisition and demolition of some 1300 properties and paving and landscaping of the new roadway. Like Olmsted's parkways, Franklin Parkway was inspired by the Avenue Foch. However, unlike Olmsted and more like Haussmann, Grébier provided ample landscaped park islands on either side of the roadway.

The areas to the south and east of Franklin Parkway included commercial buildings, manufacturing lofts, warehouses, and tenements. The northern and western sections were not yet intensely developed. Nevertheless, both sides of the parkway were largely ignored by the city's expanding residential market, which preferred the suburbs.

Eventually, the sparsely developed area to the north of the parkway attracted a few apartment buildings. Without active market demand, however, there was little reason for developers to assemble and redevelop property in the triangle to the south. After World War II, when urban planners became convinced that private redevelopment was unlikely, the city declared the area's sheds, warehouses, and tenements to be "inefficient and uneconomical," designated it a renewal area, and cleared the worst section for an apartment complex.

Benjamin Franklin Parkway had little effect on surrounding areas because its grass and trees were not enough to attract people who were on their way to other destinations. They had reasons to go to City Hall, the Free Library, the County Courthouse, the Franklin Institute, churches, office and apartment buildings at the eastern end of Franklin Parkway, right in the hub of downtown Philadelphia. However, people going to these places had no reason to walk more than half a mile to the Art Museum. As long as the bulk of city life remained downtown, the grand boulevard could never be a busy pedestrian precinct. As a result, Benjamin Franklin Parkway became a monumental axis: green, filled with motor vehicles, but devoid of people. Its symbolic purpose, connecting a palace of the arts with a palace of politics, may have made geometric sense but had little effect on the daily lives of downtown workers or neighboring apartment dwellers and therefore could not stimulate second growth.

Philadelphia, 1994. Benjamin Franklin Parkway. *(Alexander Garvin)*

Water Garden, Fort Worth

The Fort Worth Water Garden was created as part of an effort to revitalize the neglected southern end of the business district. Its major components included the East-West Freeway, the Tarrant County Convention Center, and a small park. Each was intended to bring customers to this decaying section of downtown Fort Worth. The park, however, seemed the least likely to attract market activity. In fact, because of its brilliant design, it has become a major tourist destination.[49]

The Amon Carter Foundation provided the $7 million to acquire and build the proposed park between the convention center and the freeway. Philip Johnson, the architect who designed the park, understood that 4.3 acres of trees and flowers would not be enough to bring people downtown. Instead, he presented a plan for a "jardin de plaisir" which, like more conventional amusement parks, would entice people seeking to explore their fantasies.

Like the gardens of the Villa d'Este in Tivoli and the palace of Versailles, the Water Garden's main feature is a series of amazing fountains. In comparison with these world-famous gardens, though, the park is tiny and has relatively few waterworks. Its attractions include a cascade, a 650-foot-long wet wall where water drops 22 feet in a single sheet, one pool with a shimmering horizontal slab of water and another with 40 nozzle sprays, tree-shaded walks, and secluded sitting areas.

The most popular spot is the Cascade, where water falls 38 feet in one noisy whoosh. Adventure seekers of all ages, descending on stepping stones, make their way past rushing water down to a trough at the center, where the water disappears. There, at the base of the Cascade, the city is no longer visible and the sound of the water is so overpowering that one is completely engulfed in fantasy.

Since 1974, when the Water Garden opened, this beautiful park has continued to amaze throngs of tourists. But it has not had much effect on the surrounding area because it is so self-contained. Once visitors have completed their tour of the facility, there is no reason to remain in the area. By themselves, these tourists do not provide enough critical mass to attract

Fort Worth, 1990. The Water Garden is located just beyond the Convention Center, too far from the business district to benefit from or contribute to downtown activity. *(Photo by Landiscor Aerial)*

additional businesses interested in their spending power. If, as at the Paseo del Rio, there had been other reasons for people to be in the area, this shabby section of downtown Fort Worth would be profiting from the spillover of tourists attracted by the Water Garden.

Using Park Systems to Change Entire Cities

A park, like any part of a city, is subject to powerful local conditions and major national economic and social trends. Some parks also play an important role in determining how these forces will affect the surrounding city. Conceived and designed as part of a single unified system, they can direct market activity toward certain areas and away from others, shape the character of market activity in those areas, retard or stimulate shifts in population, and even alter the pattern of daily life.

Frederick Law Olmsted was the first American to think about parks in such urban-planning terms. The facilities he designed for Brooklyn, Chicago, and Buffalo were conceived as parts of broader schemes for municipal improvement. Despite creation of a series of remarkable parks, he was unable to persuade civic leaders in these cities to let him implement all his ideas. Finally, in the last quarter of the nineteenth century, the City of Boston hired him to create a city park system that was conceived as a unified whole.

Like the prototypes that Olmsted developed for the large urban park, the playground, and the landscaped boulevard, the park system he devised for Boston became the prototype for similar systems in Kansas City, Cleveland, Cincinnati, Seattle, and many other American cities. These park systems were started by crusading individuals who rarely understood the tremendous scope of what Olmsted actually had in mind nor the importance of hiring designers of similar genius. The most serious difficulty, however, was that their passionate commitment to acquiring parkland usually blinded them to the need for continuing public support, steadily increasing streams of income, and careful nurturing by a dedicated public agency staffed with talented professionals. Only in Minneapolis did all the factors come together to produce a park system that demonstrated, as Olmsted's work in Boston would not, the powerful *continuing* role that a park system could play in shaping the evolution of the surrounding city.[50]

Boston's Emerald Necklace

In 1875, the Massachusetts legislature and the voters of Boston approved the creation of a Board of Park Commissioners, similar to the ones that were responsible for parks in other cities. Luckily for Boston, its desire for new public parks coincided with Olmsted's move from New York to Boston. In 1872, he ended his partnership with Calvert Vaux. Six years later the Commissioners of Central Park dismissed him from his role as superintendent/landscape architect, a position he had occupied in one form or another since the mid-1860s.[51]

In part because of the increasing number of commissions in the Boston area, and in part because of a growing friendship and professional relationship with architect Henry Hobson Richardson, Olmsted spent an increasing amount of time there. The transition to Boston began during 1878, when he spent the first of four summers in the area. In 1881 he established an improvised office in Brookline. Two years later he acquired the farmhouse that would become his home and the headquarters of his firm.[52]

Boston's program of park development began as soon as it had been endorsed by the voters. Mayor Samuel Cobb appointed three prominent businessmen to constitute a Board of Commissioners of the Department of Parks. Its first project was a new park for the Fens, one of Boston's natural salt marshes. The Fens accommodated the outflow of the Muddy River, Stony Brook on its way to the Charles River, and the saltwater backflow from the Charles during high tides. Because it also was used for storm drainage and all manner of waste, the area was rapidly becoming a breeding ground of epidemic diseases.

In 1878, the Board held a design competition for the new park and asked Olmsted to evaluate the 23 submissions. He pointed out that some of the designs failed to consider the flooding, while others only thought of the proposed park as a flood-control problem. The Board was so disenchanted with the submissions that it engaged Olmsted to become its professional adviser and landscape architect.[53]

By the time his work was finished in 1895, Olmsted had created a 2000-acre Emerald Necklace extending from the Common and Public Garden through a variety of neighborhoods to the outer limits of Roxbury and South Boston. Commonwealth Avenue and the Charles River Embankment, the first links in the Emerald Necklace, were not Olmsted projects. Both had long been accepted parts of the park agenda. He included them because he wanted to be sure that they linked the new park for the Fens with the Common and Public Garden. In addition, he proposed linking the inland end of the Fens with five new public parks (Muddy River, Leverett Park, Jamaica Pond, Arnold Arboretum, and Franklin Park), which themselves were linked by new parkways. The resulting scheme was intended to eliminate pestilent swamps and other nuisances that retarded development, provide a convenient means of communication among adjoining districts, stimulate construction in surrounding communities, and integrate each part of the system into a single comprehensive design.

The philosophy behind this design was not different from that of Central Park. But, when Olmsted applied it to the

Boston, 1866. Back Bay from Parker Hill in Roxbury prior to its transformation into a public park. *(Courtesy of the Boston Public Library, Print Department)*

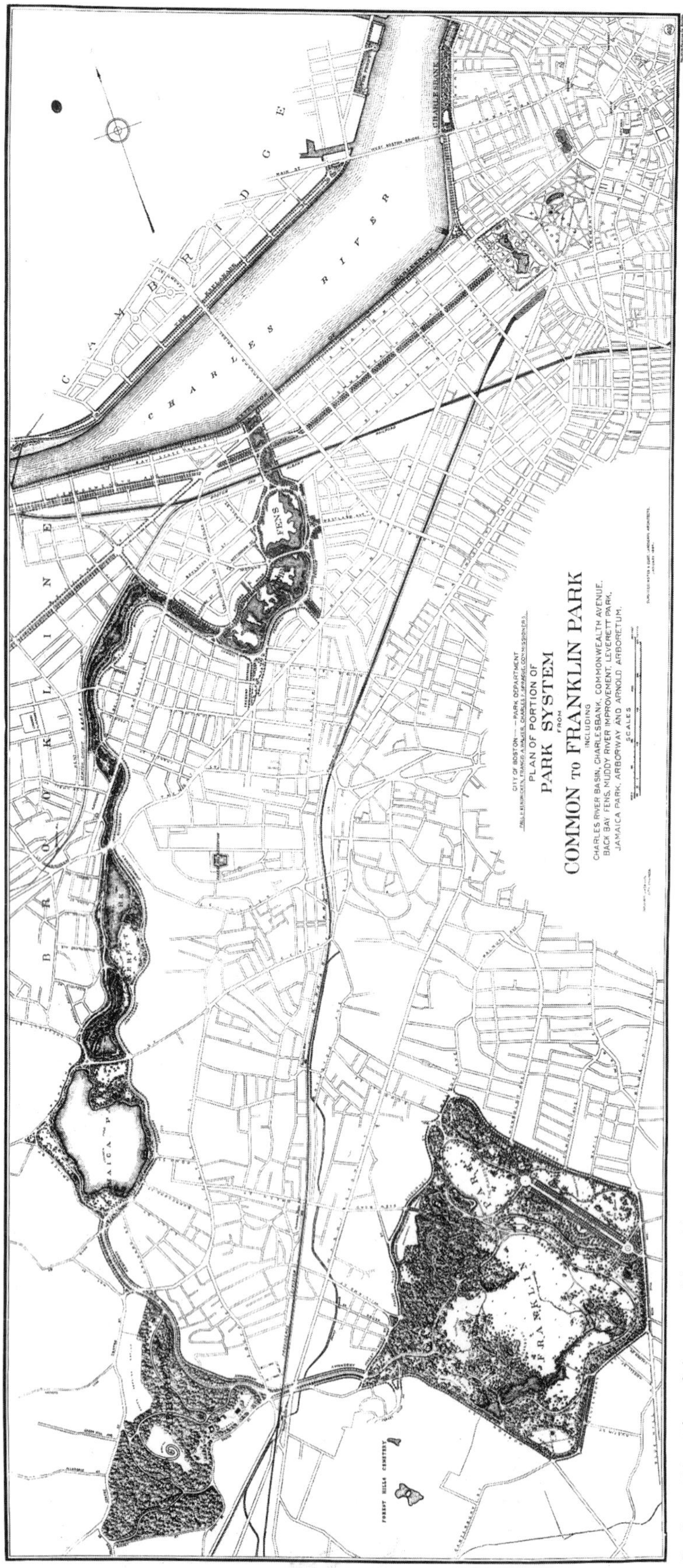

Boston, 1894. Plan of the Emerald Necklace. *(Courtesy of the National Park Service, Frederick Law Olmsted National Historic Site)*

Boston, 1980. Olmsted's design transformed the Back Bay–Fens from a brackish, sewage-filled, breeding ground of pestilent diseases into an ingenious natural drainage scheme that used this winding waterway as a storage basin for storm water and drained its marshy banks as an integral part of a 6-mile-long park system. *(Alexander Garvin)*

design of the Emerald Necklace, he had the benefit of two decades of practical experience with public parks. The first principle was derived from the work of Capability Brown: base the design on the "capabilities" of the site. As always, Olmsted was careful to see that park activities took place where the topography was appropriate. The second principle was market-driven. A park design that met the needs of one neighborhood might not be as effective in serving the needs of another. Since the park that was topographically and functionally most suited to an individual's needs might not be the one nearest to his or her residence, Olmsted contended that it was wrong to think of each park individually, "as if it were to be of little value except to the people of the districts adjoining it."[54] He felt the entire system had to be easily accessible to all classes whether coming by foot, on horseback, or in a vehicle, and be easy to move through to get to any type of facility.

These principles are clearly exhibited in the Fens. Only half the Fens could be used for active recreation. The rest was needed for Olmsted's ingenious natural drainage scheme, which used the winding waterway and marshy banks as a storage basin for storm water and introduced interceptor sewers to handle the flow of the Muddy River and Stony Brook. To accommodate high tides and tolerate sea spray, Olmsted planned for occasional flooding of up to 20 acres. He also restricted tree planting to the borders of the new roads that crossed the marsh or lined its edges.

The original raison d'être for Olmsted's design no longer exists. A dam, completed in 1910, eliminated the flow of salt water. Later construction-fill eliminated some of the marshland. In the 1960s the Charlesgate highway-interchange and network of overpasses into Storrow Drive disfigured the northern end of the park. Nevertheless, enough of Olmsted's original concept remains for anyone to marvel at its ingenuity. Moreover, had the park not been created, it is doubtful that substantial further upland construction could have continued without major expenditures on an extensive sewer system. Even then, developers would have shunned the areas immediately surrounding the increasingly fetid swampland.

The park Olmsted created at Muddy River is an equally extraordinary design. He proposed this joint effort to the Brookline and Boston Park Boards in 1880. At that time Brookline (whose name originates from this narrow winding tidal *brook,* which marked the boundary *line* between the two cities) had a population of about 7000. Muddy River, like the Fens, was fast becoming a brackish, sewage-filled, mosquito breeding-ground. Olmsted's plan, revised several times prior to its completion in 1892, proposed transforming the area into an "attractive suburban residence district, agreeably connect-

Boston, 1992. Muddy River became the centerpiece of an "attractive suburban residence district," which generated an increase in "market and taxable values securing the city a rapid return for its outlay." *(Alexander Garvin)*

ed" to a new park that would induce "advance of market and taxable values securing the city a rapid return for its outlay."[55]

To create this "attractive suburban residence district," Olmsted had to move the earth and plant the shrubs, trees, and flowers, in the process converting a drainage disaster into a useful and attractive public park. The park itself is an artificially constructed landscape with a redesigned river channel, an independent sewer system, and a pedestrian promenade that extends along its entire length. At strategic points, he erected bridges that crossed over the park to connect the adjacent communities; at others, he narrowed the riverbed to accommodate broad meadows that could be used as sports fields. Along the edge of the park, which sometimes rises to a level 20 feet above the waterway, he built a parkway.

The best location from which to see Olmsted's radical transformation of the landscape is near the Longwood station of the contiguous Massachusetts Bay Transportation Authority (MBTA), originally used by Boston & Albany Railroad. Neither the station nor the tracks are visible from within the park because a landscaped berm keeps them out of view. Overhead a bridge connects unseen, adjacent residential neighborhoods. The pedestrian strolling through the park is only aware of the landscaped banks of the meandering Muddy River.

Jamaica Park includes 60 acres of parkland surrounding Boston's largest freshwater lake. This 70-acre lake had been a popular site for ice skating and boating when it was acquired by the Park Board and remained so after Olmsted completed his work. Other than filling in some sections to provide for an attractive circumferential promenade, he did little more than add a few trees to the beautiful pines and beech trees that already grew there. But it was just enough to transform the shore into an attractive setting for strolling and jogging, a place to escape from the noise and confusion of the city.

From Jamaica Park, Olmsted extended a tree-lined "Arborway" with landscaped park islands similar to his park-

Boston, 1992. Selective property acquisition, clever landscaping, and the introduction of a circumferential path for strolling, jogging, and bicycle riding increased the attractiveness of living near Jamaica Park. *(Alexander Garvin)*

Boston, 1994. Franklin Park provides city dwellers with broad meadows for active recreation and rugged forested areas for rambling. *(Alexander Garvin)*

ways in Brooklyn and Chicago. The Arborway leads to the Arnold Arboretum, which already existed when Olmsted began his work on the Boston Park System. The Arboretum was created on the site of a 210-acre farm that was willed to Harvard University by Benjamin Bussey in 1842. However, because the donor's heirs retained a life tenancy, it only became available in 1873. Five years earlier, James Arnold, a respected authority on trees, had died leaving $100,000, which his trustees agreed to donate to Harvard for the purpose of transforming the Bussey farm into Arnold Arboretum. Olmsted became involved with the project in 1874 before he moved to Boston, when the Arboretum's director, Charles Sprague Sargent, wrote to him, suggesting that it be donated to the city of Boston for use as a public park. In response Olmsted wrote: "a park and an arboretum seem to me to be so far unlike in purpose that I do not feel sure that I could combine them satisfactorily."[56]

In 1882 Harvard agreed to sell the property to the city of Boston, which acquired several critical additional acres, and leased it all back to the University for 1000 years, in exchange for managing and maintaining the facility. In spite of his doubts, Olmsted agreed to design a park-arboretum. The plan is based on roadways that wind their way up the hilly terrain. Specimen trees, grouped by family and genus, were planted along these roads so that any visitor can see the many varieties that are native to the northern temperate zone.

From the Arnold Arboretum, Olmsted extended another "Arborway" leading to Franklin Park in West Roxbury. When the Park Board acquired this 500-acre site, the area contained little more than a few farms. Olmsted was delighted with the terrain, which he thought of as a perfect site for a country park that would be "within easy reach of the people of the city" and could counteract "a certain oppression of town life."[57] The money to develop the park came from a $2.5 million bond issue approved by the City Council in 1886 and from a bequest from Benjamin Franklin. Franklin had willed a sum of money to his two favorite cities, Boston and Philadelphia. Upon his death, this money was to be invested for 100 years. The proceeds were to be applied "to some public work" when the investment matured in 1891–1892.[58]

Olmsted's design for Franklin Park is, in many ways, similar to his work for Central and Prospect Parks. Each section of the park, described in writing along the margins of the General Plan of 1885, is intended for a different activity. There are broad meadows for active recreation (baseball, football, tennis, and, later, golf) contrasted with more rugged, forested areas for rambling. The circumferential road is like those in other Olmsted parks. There is a formal tree-lined promenade called the Greeting, similar to the Central Park Mall, that was later converted into a zoo. The only real difference from Olmsted's other large parks is that he did not need to alter substantially the topography or install a major drainage system. Thus, with a minimum of money, he created a large country park with "breadth, distance, depth, intricacy, atmospheric perspective and mystery" at the end of a 6-mile pleasure-route that extended all the way from downtown Boston.[59]

There is no doubt that Boston would have continued growing with or without its park system. The Emerald Necklace created the framework for that growth. By replacing what he called breeding grounds for pestilent epidemics with lovely parks, Olmsted established surrounding territory, rather than more distant suburbs, as prime locations for initial development. Once the areas around the Emerald Necklace had been developed, however, its influence waned.

Boston's population has declined, dropping from 801,000 in 1950 to 574,000 in 1990.[60] During that time there has been little pressure for second growth outside the downtown business district. The Emerald Necklace begins just beyond this area of market activity. Thus, there was little or no second growth for it to influence. Nor could it restrain the region's continuing suburbanization.

The Emerald Necklace demonstrates more persuasively than Olmsted's work in Brooklyn, Buffalo, or Chicago, the appropriateness of developing a single comprehensive park system to meet the needs of an entire city. It has provided an element of stability during a period of significant social and economic change. Despite neglect and deterioration, the power of its design and the effectiveness of the engineering and landscaping have ensured that it will always be a heavily used park system. Its greatest importance, though, lies in its influence on the design of park systems for other cities. Too often, these park systems are parodies of Olmsted—connected swatches of green that appear significant on a map but, because of their location, topography, and design, cannot function as a park system for a large city with a heterogeneous population.

Kansas City

The initial section of the Kansas City park system demonstrates how easy it was to accept Olmsted's rhetoric and imagery without embracing his philosophy or design practices. It was designed by George Kessler, a landscape architect who began his professional career as superintendent of parks for a small railroad outside Kansas City, and in 1890, parks "engineer" for the newly established Kansas City Board of Park Commissioners.[61]

The park system Kessler proposed in a report published in 1893, consisted of landscaped boulevards connecting three new public parks: West Terrace Park, North Terrace Park, and Penn Valley Park. Civic leaders assumed that these proposed parks and parkways, like Boston's Emerald Necklace, were organized into a comprehensive system with a variety of facilities that were easily accessible to all its citizens and took it for granted that the new system would spur real estate development. Instead, they got an opportunistic assemblage of inexpensive land that had only a passing impact on surrounding neighborhoods.

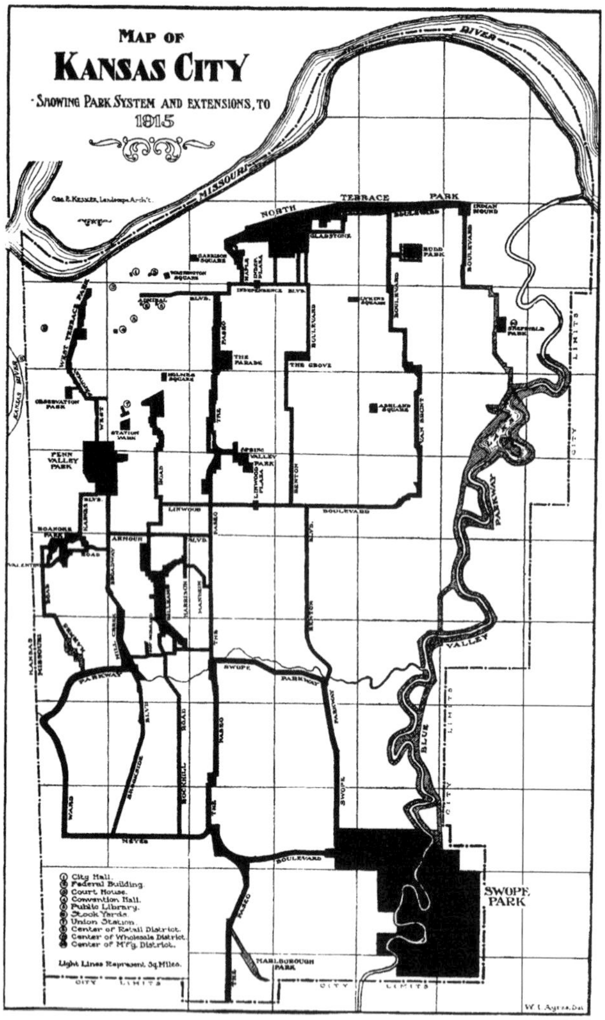

Kansas City, 1915. Plan for a Park System showing newer and larger parkways and parks that were added to Kessler's original 1893 scheme. *(Courtesy of Missouri Valley Special Collections, Kansas City Public Library, Kansas City, Missouri)*

West Terrace Park is a bluff, rising 200 feet above the stockyards, that in 1893 was occupied by unsightly billboards and weatherbeaten shanties. Although the site provided splendid views of the Kansas and Missouri Rivers below, it was unlikely to be developed because it was too steep and too near the odors of the stockyards. Most of the relatively flat land that might have become usable parkland was eliminated from the proposal in 1899 because it was equally usable for tax-paying real estate development. Too many people objected to paying for such costly land.

The views of the Missouri River are even more spectacular from the much larger North Terrace Park. This site was even less likely to be developed because it was both steeper and further from downtown Kansas City. Since most of its 200 acres are wild cliffs cut by high ravines, it is a wonderful place for hiking, but little else. Once again topography prevented Kessler from accommodating the variety of active and passive recreation facilities that Olmsted designed for the Emerald Necklace.

Penn Valley Park was created out of a ravine in the southwestern part of the city. Transforming such ungrateful terrain into a public park required all of Kessler's ingenuity. He formed an artificial lake by erecting a 30-foot-high earthen dam and supplied proper drainage by building a system of cement gutters and underground conduits. The landscape that emerged, like that of the other two parks, provides lovely views. Unlike them, it also provides a setting for some of the activities that are typical of Olmsted's designs.

All three parks may have preserved dramatic topographic features and provided stunning views, but their major attraction to Kansas City's Board of Park Commissioners was that their land acquisition was relatively cheap ($2.3 million) and removed relatively little developable property from the tax rolls. Unfortunately, this resulted in few of the level pedestrian paths, broad meadows, gentle wooded knolls, or ample playing fields that made Olmsted's parks so successful.

In 1896, Kansas City was unexpectedly supplied with land that could support the wide range of activities. Thomas Swope donated 1334 acres of land for a public park, 4 miles southwest of the city limits. Here Kessler and his successors were able to create a landscape with some of the features of Franklin Park in Boston. During the century since Swope Park was added to the system, the city has annexed so much land that the park is now well within its boundaries and has become a major recreation facility for a metropolitan region with more than 1½ million people.

In addition to parks, Kessler's system proposed a "comprehensive, well-planned and thoroughly maintained" system of landscaped boulevards, which he thought would counter "the tendency to…build residences in the suburbs." As he explained,

> *The best and most expensive residences will go up along boulevards, but these avenues will exercise a decided effect upon the character of residences to a considerable distance on each side. They will, in fact, create compactly and well built-up residence sections.*[62]

With the exception of the elaborately landscaped Paseo, which was planned to extend from North Terrace Park south to 18th Street, the boulevards proposed in the 1893 Report were not boulevards at all. Armour, Linwood, and Independence Boulevards were tree-lined, 100-foot-wide rights-of-way that in other cities would be called avenues. Kansas City was unwilling to authorize anything wider because of the high cost of acquisition and the probable opposition to the required condemnation.

Initially these boulevards did attract "the best and most expensive residences." That success was also one reason for their demise. Kessler was able to use them as the arguments for acquisition of much wider rights-of-way and for creation of the broader, better-landscaped parkways that were extended further to the south (e.g., Ward Parkway, Meyer Boulevard,

Kansas City, 1980. Ward Parkway, a 1915 addition to the park system that, unlike Kessler's earlier "parkways," was broad enough to attract and retain some of the city's wealthiest residents. *(Alexander Garvin)*

and South Paseo). He was able to obtain these broader rights-of-way because they were actively supported by neighborhood improvement associations and local subdivider-developers. These realtors and the people who lived in their subdivisions argued that such multilane arteries provided easy access for automobile traffic going downtown. They also understood their importance in increasing property values, an objective that was so important that a few of them actually donated some of the land through which the new parkways were planned.[63]

This second set of parkways was so attractive that it soon supplanted the narrower older "boulevards" as a location for the city's best and most expensive residences. The neighborhoods surrounding these later parks and parkways have retained their allure and remained locations of choice for the city's middle class. On the other hand, Kessler's first "boulevards" are lined with vacant and abandoned buildings and their once handsome trees have succumbed to disease.

The Kansas City park system provides a lesson in the difference between rhetoric and reality. In 1893, Kessler promised that his boulevards would "exercise a decided effect upon the character of the residences to a considerable distance on each side." In reality, they were no different from similar avenues throughout Kansas City, and had no lasting impact. The first three parks appeared to be lovely landscapes enhanced by trellises and pergolas. In fact, they were steep cliffs with relatively little flat land that was usable by large crowds.

The system Kessler proposed in 1893, unlike the Emerald Necklace, included few facilities that were designed to serve the city's future population. Kessler also failed to foresee how quickly the countryside would be engulfed by new residences. The later sections of the park system that were added as a result of private donations, community activism, and lobbying by real estate developers illustrate the importance of Olmsted's vision of a park system as a framework around which the city could grow and develop. They, rather than Kessler's early efforts, demonstrate that a park system can provide a convenient means of communication among adjoining districts, a variety of places for active and passive recreation, and stimulate development in surrounding communities.

Minneapolis, 1979. The ample dimensions, generous facilities, and excellent maintenance of the park system attracts users from nearby neighborhoods and enhances property values. *(Alexander Garvin)*

Minneapolis: America's Outstanding Park System

The best-located, best-financed, best-designed, best-maintained public open space in America is the Minneapolis park system. Its 6380 acres are organized around 22 major stillwater lakes, ranging in size from 2-acre lagoons to 425-acre Lake Calhoun. They are part of an integrated system of 170 park

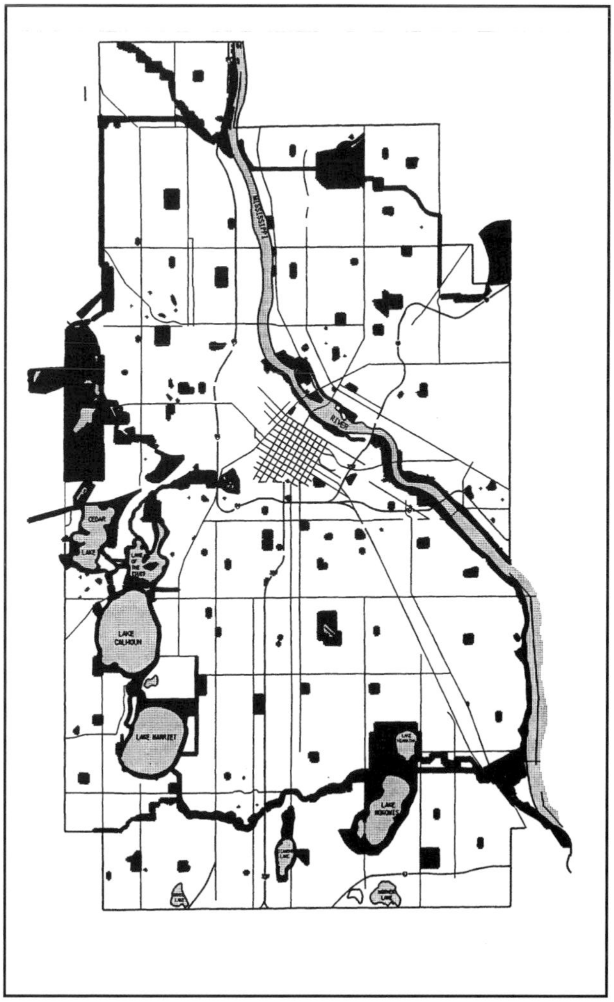

Minneapolis, 1995. Plan of America's finest park. *(Courtesy of the City of Minneapolis Board of Park Commissioners)*

Minneapolis, 1979. Boating on Lake Calhoun. *(Alexander Garvin)*

properties that also includes: 60 miles of generously landscaped parkways, 38 miles of designated walking trails, 36 miles of bicycle paths, 6 public golfcourses, 61 supervised playgrounds, 42 recreation centers, 21 supervised beaches and swimming pools, rose gardens, historic structures, athletic fields, fountains, picnic grounds, bird sanctuaries, waterfalls, even a wildflower garden. This parkland extends throughout the city and the greater portion of it is connected by a continuous system of jogging and walking trails, bicycle paths, and landscaped vehicular parkways. With a Minneapolis 1990 population of 368,000, there are only 58 people for every acre of public open space. More important, this parkland is easily accessible from anywhere in the city, provides the widest variety of facilities, and affords the user an opportunity to go from facility to facility without leaving the park system.[64] The city's comprehensive park system would probably not surprise the members of the Minneapolis Board of Trade, who in 1883 unanimously adopted a resolution calling for the establishment of an independent park commission. As they explained,

> *The rapid growth of our city...warns us that the time has come when, if ever, steps should be taken to secure the necessary land for such a grand system of Parks and Boulevards as the natural situation offer and will give to Minneapolis, not only the finest and most beautiful system of Public Parks and Boulevards of any city in America, but which, when secured and located as they can now be at a comparatively small expense, will, in the near future, add many millions to the real estate value of our city.*[65]

The Board of Trade was fought by the City Council, which opposed any independent entity with the power to issue bonds, levy taxes, condemn property, and develop parks without the approval of property owners, taxpayers, or, of course, the elected members of the City Council. They were overruled by the Minnesota legislature that authorized a referendum in which voters overwhelmingly approved the idea.

Soon after its establishment in 1883, the Board of Park Commissioners engaged H. W. S. Cleveland, a prominent landscape architect who had previously worked with Olmsted on Prospect Park and had been hired by Chicago's South Park Commission, to revise and execute Olmsted's designs. Cleveland urged the Minneapolis Commission to be generous in its appropriations, arguing:

> *Do not be appalled at the thought of appropriating lands which seem now too costly, simply because they are far out of proportion to your present wants....Look forward for a century, to the time when the city has a population of a million, and think what will be their want. They will have wealth enough to purchase all that money can buy, but all their wealth cannot purchase lost opportunity, or restore natural features...which would then possess priceless value, and which you can preserve...from the destruction which certainly awaits them.*[66]

Cleveland may have been wrong in predicting that Minneapolis would have a population of a million. But, he could not have been more correct about the prohibitive cost and difficulty of acquiring land for parks once the city had matured.

Like Olmsted, Cleveland urged the creation of an extended system of parks and boulevards "rather than a series of detached open areas." His arguments, though, were different. Having learned from the Chicago fire of 1871 that "it is hopeless to try to contend with fire when it sweeps from block to block," he explained that when there are broad landscaped boulevards, 200- or 300-feet wide, "the attack is reduced to a skirmish with cinders, and the firemen have an opportunity to hold their ground against it."[67] Like Olmsted, he proposed to exploit the "capabilities" of the site, in this case, by displaying such unique features as the gorge of the Mississippi River, Minnehaha Falls, and the region's many beautiful lakes. Like Olmsted, he proposed to dredge and fill swampy marshes, not merely in order to eradicate the breeding grounds of pestilent epidemics, but also to make the extraordinary lakes of Minneapolis the central feature of the new park system.

H. W. S. Cleveland provided the embryo of the Minneapolis Park System. However, the system is largely the work of Theodore Wirth, superintendent of parks from 1906 to 1935. He is the man who extended the system beyond Minnehaha Falls, the initial lake parks, and the early parkways. He dredged these and other lakes, graded their banks, eliminated flooding, and installed permanent paving. He supervised the addition of thousands of acres of new parkland, miles of connecting parkways, and dozens of smaller neighborhood facilities. He planted thousands of acres with grass, shrubs, trees, and flowers, built the park drives, and installed the recreation facilities which we see today.

The system Wirth built demonstrates the wisdom of Olmsted's view that each component in a park system should be individual in its character, reflecting the potential of the topography and the utility of its individual service function. Thus, decades after they became part of the park system, Lake Harriet is a family facility with picnic grounds, playing fields, a band shell, and other group recreation facilities; Lake Calhoun is a setting for fast-paced iceboating and sailboard-

Minneapolis, 1992. Bicycle riding, roller blading, and volley ball in a section of the park at Lake Calhoun. *(Alexander Garvin)*

Minneapolis, 1908. Hydraulic dredge at work on Lake of the Isles. *(From T. Wirth, Minneapolis Park System, Minneapolis Board of Park Commissioners, 1945)*

ing; Lake of the Isles provides a setting for roller skating, cross-country skiing, and just strolling. The jogging trails, bicycle paths, and parkways connecting these and other facilities make them accessible to anyone coming from any part of the system.

The parks Cleveland and Wirth created were directly in the path of the city's growth. Without them, the character of that expansion might well have been different. The city's lakes included large unattractive swampy sections that frequently flooded surrounding areas and were a favorite dumping ground for refuse. Once they had been dredged and landscaped, they became attractive public parks and, thus, a magnet for development.

The impact of the Minneapolis parks can be seen in the increasing cost of land acquisition. The first 30 acres of Loring Park were acquired in 1883 for $4904 per acre. An addition to this park, made 19 years later, cost $48,096 per acre. Even today, more than a century after the first park acquisitions, the surrounding neighborhoods contain some of the city's most valuable residential property.

The level of maintenance in the Minneapolis park system is perhaps its most impressive achievement. Paths and trails are repaved when they wear down. The grass is cut regularly and replanted when necessary. Signs are repainted or replaced when they are no longer legible. Boathouses, refreshment stands, picnic pavilions, benches, and playground equipment are all in good repair.

The excellent condition of the Minneapolis park system may be attributed to the benign habits of a relatively homogeneous population. I believe it also has a great deal to do with the unique system of administration. From its inception the Minneapolis park system has been separated from the rest of city government. The Park and Recreation Board, as it has been known since 1967, is elected for staggered four-year terms. It consists of nine members, six elected by district and three at large. The board, not the city government, owns the land, enacts the ordinances governing the system, operates the recreation programs, polices the parks, and establishes the budget. It can issue bonds to pay for acquisition and development and has the power to levy taxes within limits set by the City's Board of Estimate and Taxation (on which it holds a seat as it does on the City Planning Commission). There are only two significant governmental checks on its activity: the mayor and the city budget. Since 1975, the mayor has been able to veto its actions, provided the board cannot muster a two-thirds vote to overide him. The more important control over its activities is budgetary. Although the board has the ability to levy taxes, its tax revenues are insufficient to pay all expenses, making it dependent on further city appropriations.

The value Minneapolis places on its park system can be seen from the price its citizens are willing to pay. In 1977, the superintendent of parks was the highest paid official in the city. He received a salary of $48,812 and a house. The superintendent of schools received $188 more, but received no house. The mayor's salary was two-thirds that of the superintendent of parks.

The popularly elected Minneapolis Park and Recreation Board is probably more powerful than any other U.S. entity administering city parks. Because it is accountable to the voters, unlike virtually every other city park agency, it is also more attentive to the wishes of the population it serves. This unique form of governance and financing is what has enabled the residents of Minneapolis to have the best-located, best-financed, best-designed, best-maintained park system in America.

Ingredients of Success

Few people still believe, as did nineteenth-century reformers, that parks can influence the character and development of an entire city. Nevertheless, parks can and should be used in that way. Chicago's lakeshore parks, the Paseo del Rio in San Antonio, and the Minneapolis park system all affected the surrounding city. The explanation for their influence lies in their manipulation of the same ingredients that are responsible for all successful urban planning: market, location, design, financing, entrepreneurship, and time.

Market

During the nineteenth century, there was little need to consider the market for city parks. Once a new park was established, development engulfed it and moved further out toward the suburbs. Satisfying such growing demand for public open space is simple: establish public parks at a pace that keeps up with an ever-increasing population.

As cities matured, however, some cities discovered that parkland could help to retain an existing market and even to attract activity that had not heretofore existed. Olmsted's parks, for example, supplied space for so many types of recreation that they were easily adapted by ever-changing populations, continued to retain their attractiveness, and became stabilizing forces for surrounding neighborhoods. The Paseo del Rio in San Antonio, on the other hand, was specifically designed to attract pedestrians to an area that had up to that time repelled most of the citizens of San Antonio. Once the park was completed, property owners tried to profit from this new market by opening stores and restaurants. That symbiotic relationship between the park and retailing, in turn, attracted tourists and even resulted in hotel construction.

Public investment in city parks fails to generate private market activity in surrounding areas only when the new facility fails to attract people who will spill over into those areas. The motorists who leave downtown Philadelphia, driving out Benjamin Franklin Parkway on their way to the suburbs, for example, have no reason to stop and therefore fail to provide any increase in demand for adjacent property, just as the hikers in Kansas City's North Terrace Park could not possibly constitute a sufficient market for adjacent property owners.

Location

If market was not an issue in planning nineteenth-century parks, neither was location. There was plenty of relatively inexpensive, undeveloped land just outside already settled areas. Furthermore, facilities like Forest Park in St. Louis, or Prospect Park in Brooklyn, could be created at sites that were only a few minutes away on the streetcar. Only when park planners worked with properties, like Griffith Park in Los Angeles, that were outside the path of major population growth or were inherently unattractive for development, like the cliff parks in Kansas City, did they fail to stimulate the desired market reaction.

While proximity, access, and terrain continued to be important ingredients in the success of parks in already developed cities, the inherent characteristics of the location and of neighboring land uses took on greater importance. Chicago's lakeshore parks, for example, provided wonderful views, summer breezes, beaches, marinas, and an opportunity for water sports that increased the attractiveness of living nearby. Property owners responded by building residences for the market that had been attracted by the parks.

Design

In considering the design of Prospect Park, Frederick Law Olmsted thought that the critical considerations were (1) convenience of shape; (2) amplitude of dimensions; (3) topographical conditions, and the surrounding circumstances.[68] These all played a role in the failure of the initial sections of the Kansas City park system to generate any continuing market reaction. Their location, shape, and topography made it difficult for them to affect more than a limited amount of surrounding territory. The parkways were not wide enough to be recreation facilities. West Terrace Park and North Terrace Park did not have sufficient level territory for a great variety of activities.

Familiarity with Olmsted's parks and park systems leads me to add two other elements that were critical to their design: a variety of places that can accommodate a large range of recreational activities and a mutually reinforcing arrangement of those places. Their significance becomes immediately evident in examining Forest Park in St. Louis. Had it been designed for a range of recreational activities, the Department of Parks would not have made intrusions that added the element of "social utility." However, when it did so, it was too late to arrange them in any complementary sequence.

These same factors are among the reasons for the success of the Minneapolis park system. Its designers dredged lakes and filled swamps in order to prevent flooding and provide facilities for all manner of water-based recreation; created parkways that were broad enough to be actively used for jogging, cycling, strolling, and active sports (not just vehicular transportation); and landscaped the edges of parks and parkways in a manner that enhanced the illusion of living in the country.

Financing

A surprising amount of parkland has been acquired through donation. Swope Park in Kansas City, Griffith Park in Los Angeles, and the Water Garden in Fort Worth, are a few notable examples. In most cases, however, governments need money to pay for acquiring land, transforming that land into usable public facilities, and maintaining those facilities once they have been created. They usually get the money for acquisition and development by selling bonds and repay the money in the form of regular debt-service payments to the holders of those bonds.

Nineteenth-century park advocates understood this process very well. Whenever they proposed a new facility they described it as an investment that could then be made at relatively low cost and eventually would produce revenues far in excess of initial cost. They were usually right. Land costs, even in as-yet-undeveloped areas, had continually increased. They argued that it was better to pay less for the land now than considerably more later, when an increasing population insisted on establishing additional facilities. Their second argument was that initial costs would be covered many times over by the increased taxes from surrounding properties whose value had increased as a result of the new park.

Minneapolis and Boulder, Colorado, are among the very few park systems that are adequately financed. For over a century, the Minneapolis Park Board has received a dedicated stream of tax revenues, which it can pledge as payment to bondholders who lend money for capital projects. As a result, it has few problems paying for development or rehabilitation. In the late 1960s Boulder, Colorado, set aside a sales tax of 0.4 of a cent for its parks. Over the next two decades the city invested this money in a park system that now includes more than 40,000 acres.[69]

Other city park systems have to compete for capital funds. This money is usually obtained when a local government issues general revenue bonds to pay for everything from roadways to firehouses. Since parks are rarely priorities, few cities spend large sums on major park acquisition or restoration projects. Whatever park development still takes place is usual-

Boulder, 1993. A city park system acquired, developed, and financed through a dedicated sales tax. *(Alexander Garvin)*

ly financed from external sources, such as the federal government. That was the source of a substantial amount of the money Robert Moses used to pay for the many new facilities and improvements he made to New York City's park system.

Public park systems in Minneapolis and Boulder, which have dedicated sources of income, spend that money to see that their facilities are properly maintained. Park systems in many other cities are starved for funds and continue to deteriorate because they have great difficulty competing for operating funds. New York City provides a particularly stark example. Between 1945 and 1955, while Robert Moses was still parks commissioner, "parks expenditures accounted for approximately 1.5 percent of each annual City operating budget." By fiscal year 1992, the share had dropped to its lowest historical level, less than half a percent.[70]

Entrepreneurship

Park developers with the imagination and drive of Robert Moses are as rare as park designers with the genius of Frederick Law Olmsted. Wherever they surface, cities will have wonderful parks. Good park systems, however, cannot be built on the hope that such individuals will be available. Moreover, they cannot succeed without the determined effort of dedicated public servants who operate within an environment that fosters public entrepreneurship.

During the nineteenth century Brooklyn, Chicago, Boston, and many other cities were able to create wonderful parks because park development was a major part of the public agenda and undeveloped land was so readily available. Those cities also operated with administrative structures that were more open to public entrepreneurship. They had park commissions made up of citizen leaders who actively pursued their mandate and were deeply involved in directing operating agencies. Minneapolis is the only city with a major park system that is still operated by an independent park commission. The results are visible throughout the system.

Today, most city park systems are operated by municipal bureaucracies staffed by tenured civil servants. Bold initiatives are unlikely to emerge from this sort of institutional setting. Agency staff is just not in a position to oppose elected public officials who are eager to reallocate park funds to other pressing demands for municipal assistance. The inevitable result: declining budgets and deteriorating public parks.

Harnessing local initiative is the most effective way to overcome inadequate budget allocations, poor maintenance, and inattentive management. A good example is the Joseph C. Sauer Playground, on Manhattan's Lower East Side. This playground, built by Robert Moses with Public Works Administration (PWA) assistance in 1934, was so badly deteriorated by the 1980s that the 12th Street Block Association had to organize its cleanup, lobby for its redesign, and fight to have its reconstruction added to the city budget.[71] When the enlarged and redesigned Sauer Playground reopened in 1993, the Block Association took responsibility for supervising its management and maintenance. It supplied the entrepreneurial role that had been missing for decades and demonstrated that small public facilities could be successful when there was active public participation in their operation. Similar community-based management of playgrounds will be successful wherever there is a local organization with the necessary drive and dedication.

Manhattan, 1994. By lobbying for the renovation of the Joseph Sauer Playground and then supervising its management and maintenance, the 12th Street Block Association has demonstrated the crucial entrepreneurial role that can be played by dedicated, community-based organizations. *(Alexander Garvin)*

Time

Some of the most wondrous parks are those in which visitors make their way through a structured sequence of experiences. Olmsted choreographed this sort of movement through Prospect Park. Philip Johnson did the same for the Water Garden in Fort Worth. These two very different facilities attract crowds of people because from the moment people enter until they leave, they can spend their time having fun. In other facilities, like Benjamin Franklin Parkway, there is nowhere to go for a good time. Consequently, such parkland does not attract many people.

Parks that function successfully over a 24-hour period, 7 days a week, are rare. Even Olmsted admitted that parks are unlikely to be safe at night. However, whether working with prairie land like Washington Park in Chicago, or a narrow, topographically varied facility like Muddy River in Boston, he was insistent that parks include a wide variety of facilities that could attract people for different forms of recreation at different times.

The most common and serious error in planning parks, however, is thinking of them as development projects that terminate when the facility has been completed. As Olmsted explained not long after Central Park was opened to the public:

> *The people who are to visit the park this year or next are but a small fraction of those who must be expected to visit hereafter. If the park had to be laid out and especially if (it) had to be planted with reference only to the use of the next few years, a very different general plan, a very different way of planting and a very different way of managing trees would be proper.*[72]

The life of every park is just beginning when its development is over. Minneapolis is one of very few cities that understood this simple idea and provided an administrative structure, a guaranteed stream of income, a regularly updated public mandate, and legal powers to ensure that its parks continued to be well-maintained in good times and bad.

Parks as City Planning Strategy

Public investment in public open space is no longer as fashionable as it was 100 years ago when Minneapolis began creating its extraordinary park system. Nevertheless, public investment in parks was then and still is an effective means of stimulating a desirable private market reaction. The trick is to spend public money in ways that will reduce the risk of investing in surrounding property or to spend it in a manner that will attract activity that will spill over into the areas surrounding parkland.

Olmsted's work in the Fens and Muddy River in Boston is a good example of park investment that reduces the risk of investing in surrounding areas. As long as these areas were becoming increasingly pestilent breeding grounds of disease, investment in surrounding areas grew increasingly unattractive. Once these polluted waterways became public parks, surrounding property became attractive sites for development. The same thing happened in Minneapolis after it terminated the danger of flooding by dredging its lakes, landscaping their banks, and transforming them into public parks.

Parks also stimulate private investment by attracting customers to an area. By spending hundreds of millions of dollars over several decades, Chicago created a wonderful string of lakefront recreation facilities that brought tens of thousands of people to the waterfront. Developers were quick to perceive the spending power of this growing market and made fortunes supplying it with new apartments.

Similar opportunities still exist. There are city parks that have now deteriorated so badly that they act as a depressant force for their surroundings. There are inner-city properties that are no longer in demand but can be recycled as new city parks. There still is open land available in rapidly suburbanizing areas. Public investment should be directed to each of these opportunities.

Existing city parks and playgrounds are particularly good candidates for new public investment. In many cases, like the Olmsted parks, they are priceless historical artifacts, whose continuing benefits were paid for long ago. If they were put up for sale, cities could net tremendous amounts of money. Instead of protecting these valuable assets, we allow them to deteriorate. They should be treated with the same respect we accord the artworks in our museums. Once restored they too can attract a substantial and profitable market.

New parks in inner cities can also trigger second growth. Such parks are relatively easy to create from underutilized property that has been left behind by previous users. Among the possibilities are rail yards and rights-of-way; waterfront areas that are no longer needed for shipping, warehousing, or manufacturing; streets, highways, and interchanges whose traffic can be rechanneled to other arteries; even residential areas where local governments already own large blocks of vacant property repossessed for failure to pay taxes. For example, in 1989 Boston opened the 5-mile-long Southwest Corridor Park. This park was part of a $780 million transit project that combined an existing commuter railroad, a new subway line, and vacant and underutilized property that was contiguous to the right-of-way. Seattle created additional public open space in 1976 by building a 5-acre Freeway Park over Interstate Highway 5. The park was so successful in tying together the sections of the city that had been separated by the highway that it was expanded in 1984 and again—with the completion of the Washington State Convention and Trade Center—in 1989. Like San Antonio's Paseo del Rio, these new parks are independent facilities that are substantial enough to attract lots of people and thus to generate a significant market reaction from neighboring property owners who see a chance of profiting from the spillover.

There are also attractive sites for new parks outside center cities. Developers who convert countryside into sites for single-family houses and condominiums usually leave new residents with little more than their own yards for recreation. Larger subdivisions may add a swimming pool, clubhouse, tennis courts, or even golf links. These facilities are usually available exclusively to residents or club members. Only rarely will a subdivision include a genuinely *public* park. If developing areas were to include a continuous and varied public park system, like that of Minneapolis, which could be adapted to the changing needs of future generations, it too would become a stabilizing force for surrounding communities.

Boston, 1994. Southwest Corridor Park built over a transit right-of-way. *(Alexander Garvin)*

Cities continue to miss these opportunities because they do not have park agencies with the necessary political mandate, legal authority, or money. The situation can be reversed by copying Minneapolis. All that is necessary is state enabling legislation that will authorize local governments to map park districts, establish elected park boards, allocate a fixed proportion of sales and property taxes for park purposes, and authorize the park board to use that money for park maintenance and debt service on their bonds.

The revenue base for these elected park boards is central both to their ability to develop new park facilities and to successful urban planning. A set-aside of property- or sales-tax revenues would allow park boards to make long-term plans and use the money to make debt-service payments on bonds issued for property acquisition and development. However, if the only source of revenue is a citywide tax, park boards will conceive and develop facilities that meet the insular requirements of single-function interest groups. Instead, they should be making park investments that will stimulate complementary private-market activity in surrounding neighborhoods.

The great estates of London made such investments because they derived revenues from property surrounding their squares. If park boards derived a part of their income from properties that are in the immediate vicinity of park facilities, they too would have an interest in improving the surrounding city. The means of achieving this is simple: allocate to the park board a fixed portion of the real estate taxes (say, 20 percent) paid by properties within a specific distance (say, 1000 feet) of a public park.

State legislatures and city councils are not likely to enact such enabling legislation. They have had more than a century to copy Minneapolis and have not done so because it means giving up power. Public officials only give up power when the electorate demands it or when they are faced with an offer they cannot refuse.

Congress can make this offer by combining what was successful in Minneapolis, with what was successful in San Antonio, to create a National Urban and Suburban Park Development Program. This new program would lend federal park-development funds on a matching basis of 5 to 1 (as it did for the Paseo del Rio) to local park boards (like the one in Minneapolis) that are prepared to develop and maintain major park systems. In order to qualify for federal park-development loans, a city would have to have an elected park board

Seattle, 1990. Freeway Park built over Interstate Highway 5. *(Alexander Garvin)*

that owned and operated its park system, allocate a fixed portion of its tax revenues to the park board to cover operating costs, and set aside a fixed portion of real estate taxes from property in the immediate vicinity of parkland for park development purposes. The revenues derived from the real estate tax set-aside would have to be allocated first to debt-service payments on any borrowing (e.g., park bonds) made for park acquisition and development and then to debt-service payments on federal matching loans. When this debt was repaid, the park board would have an unencumbered stream of income with which to finance further park development.[73]

Establishing this National Urban and Suburban Park Development Program would completely change the way cities establish, develop, finance, and operate their parks. While it would not guarantee that every American would have access to a decent park system, it would allow those cities that chose to invest public funds to develop and nurture a major park system to benefit from well-maintained and well-managed parks that also significantly improved surrounding neighborhoods.

Notes

1. Ralph Waldo Emerson, *Selected Essays,* Penguin Books, New York, 1982, "Nature" (1836), p. 43.
2. "Capability" Brown received his nickname because he was forever expounding on the "capabilities" of the site.
3. Toward the end of the eighteenth century, Capability Brown's soft, graceful landscapes were supplanted in popularity by more rugged, romantic visions of sublime nature. These newer gardens by Uvdale Price, Richard Payne Knight, and Humphrey Repton still tried to display the natural beauties of the site, but did so while minimizing their apparent interference with nature. They wanted gardens that appeared wild and undisturbed. Both esthetics were eminently picturesque and both continued well into the nineteenth century, when American cities began establishing public parks.
4. Fredrick Law Olmsted, *Walks and Talks of an American Farmer in England,* University of Michigan Press, Ann Arbor, 1967, pp. 52–53.
5. In 1851, Savannah set aside 10 acres for Forsythe Park. The park was later doubled in size, but its final 20 acres are tiny in comparison with the 843 acres of Central Park. In 1812, Philadelphia acquired for a municipal waterworks the first 5 acres of what was to become Fairmount Park. In 1828, in order to protect the purity of the city's water supply, the site was enlarged to 28 acres. However, it wasn't until 1855 that the Pennsylvania legislature authorized acquisition of any substantial amounts of land for purely recreational use.
6. Ambrose Kingsland, "Message to the Common Council," April 5, 1851.
7. John P. Rea, *Minneapolis Tribune,* May 23, 1880.
8. Jane Addams, *The Spirit of Youth and the City Streets,* Macmillan Co., New York, 1909, p. 103.
9. Jacob Riis, *The Peril and the Preservation of the Home,* Jacobs, New York, 1903.
10. Frederick Law Olmsted: "Report on the Charles River Embankment ('Charlesbank')," *Twelfth Annual Report of the Board of Commissioners of the Department of Parks for the Year 1886,* City Document 24-1887.
11. Cynthia Zaitzevsky, *Frederick Law Olmsted and the Boston Park System,* The Belknap Press of Harvard University Press, Cambridge, 1982, pp. 96–100.
12. Ibid.
13. Galen Cranz, *The Politics of Park Design,* MIT Press, 1982, pp. 80–83.
14. Philadelphia City Planning Commission, *Comprehensive Plan for Swimming Pools,* January 1968.
15. Derived from Chicago Recreation Commission, *Suggested Goals in Park and Recreation Planning,* 1959; Denver Inter-County Regional Planning Commission, *Standards for New Urban Development,* 1962; Minneapolis Park Board, Planning Division, *Park and Recreation Facilities and Standards,* 1964.
16. National Parks Service, *Recreational Use of Land in the United States,* National Resources Board, 1938.
17. Robert Moses, *Six Years of Park Progress,* City of New York Department of Parks, New York, 1940, p. 10.
18. Robert Moses, *26 Years of Progress 1934–1960,* City of New York Department of Parks, New York, 1960, p. 52.
19. Clare Beckhardt, "Proposed Redesign of the West 46th Street Playground," The Parks Council, 1972, p. 1.
20. Thomas P. F. Hoving, "Think Big About Small Parks," *The New York Times Magazine,* May 16, 1966, p. 12.
21. *The New York Times,* May 11, 1966, p. 51.
22. Elizabeth Barlow Rogers, *Rebuilding Central Park: A Management and Restoration Plan,* MIT Press, Cambridge, 1987.
23. Robert Brayton Nichols, "A Proposal for Adventure Playgrounds," Council for Parks and Playgrounds and the Park Association of New York City, March 1969.
24. Ibid.
25. Frederick Law Olmsted, letter to Charles Brace, December 8, 1860.
26. Historical and statistical material on the squares of Paris, is derived from Michael Dennis, *Court and Garden,* MIT Press, Cambridge, 1986, pp. 43–51, 79–90, and 128–136; and Pierre Lavedan, *Les Villes Françaises,* Editions Vincent, Freal & Cie, Paris, 1960, pp. 126–142.
27. Historical and statistical material on the great estates of London is derived from John Summerson, *Georgian London,* Barrie & Jenkins Ltd., London, 1988, pp. 73–86, 147–161, and181–187; Donald J. Olsen: *Town Planning in London—The Eighteenth and Nineteenth Centuries,* Yale University Press, New Haven, 1982, pp. 27–96; and Steen Eiler Rasmussen, *London: The Unique City,* MIT Press, Cambridge, 1967, pp. 165–201.
28. Historical and statistical material on the development of Regent Street and Regent's Park is derived from Summerson, op. cit., pp. 162–180; and Rasmussen, op. cit., pp. 271–291.
29. Historical and statistical material on Haussmann and his work on the parks, squares, and boulevards of Paris, is derived from David H. Pinkney, *Napoleon III and the Rebuilding of Paris,* Princeton University Press, New Jersey, 1958, pp. 75–104; George F. Chadwick, *The Park and the Town—Public Landscapes in the 19th and 20th Centuries,* Praeger, New York, 1966, pp. 152–162; and Antoine Grumbach, "The Promenades of Paris," pp. 50–67 in *Oppositions #8,* Spring 1977, MIT Press, Cambridge.
30. Avenue Foch was known as Avenue du Bois, prior to being renamed in honor of Marshal Foch.
31. Carl Feiss, "Early American Public Squares," pp. 237–255 in Paul Zucker, *Town and Square from the Agora to the Village Green,* Columbia University Press, New York, 1959.
32. John W. Reps, *The Making of Urban America,* Princeton University Press, Princeton, 1965, pp. 157–174.
33. Ibid., New Jersey pp. 185–202.
34. H. W. S. Cleveland, "Suggestion for a System of Parks and Parkways

for the City of Minneapolis," read at a meeting of the Park Commissioners, June 2, 1883, reprinted by Theodore Wirth, *Minneapolis Park System 1883–1944,* Minneapolis Board of Park Commissioners, 1945, pp. 28–34.

35. I am indebted to Tupper Thomas, Administrator of Prospect Park, for a multitude of insights on the design of the park and for information on the park's conifers.
36. Frederick Law Olmsted and Calvert Vaux, "Preliminary Report to the Commissioners for Laying Out a Park in Brooklyn, New York," (1866), reprinted by Albert Fein (editor), *Landscape into Cityscape: Frederick Law Olmsted's Plans for Greater New York,* Cornell University Press, Ithaca, 1968, p. 98.
37. Frederick Law Olmsted and Calvert Vaux, "Report to the Landscape Architects and Superintendents to the President of the Board of Commissioners of Prospect Park, Brooklyn" (1868), reprinted by Albert Fein (editor), op. cit., p. 157.
38. Marine Park is larger (1822 acres) than Prospect Park (526 acres). However, it became a park long afterward (1924), involved little landscaping, and is difficult to reach by mass transit. (Source: Office of the Borough President of Brooklyn.)
39. Historical and statistical material on Forest Park is derived from Caroline Loughlin and Catherine Anderson, *Forest Park,* Junior League of St. Louis and University of Missouri Press, Columbia, 1986; and August Heckscher, *Open Spaces, The Life of American Cities,* Harper & Row, New York, 1977, pp. 173–177.
40. *Report of the St. Louis Department of Parks,* (1915), quoted by August Heckscher, op. cit., p. 177.
41. Historical and statistical material on Griffith Park is derived from Robert M. Fogelson: *The Fragmented Metropolis: Los Angeles 1850–1930,* Harvard University Press, 1967, and August Heckscher, op. cit.
42. Historical and statistical material on Chicago's parks is derived from Olmsted, Vaux & Co., "Report Accompanying Plan for Laying Out the South Park" (1871), partially reproduced in *Civilizing American Cities,* S. B. Sutton, MIT Press, Cambridge, 1971, pp. 156–196; Daniel Bluestone, *Constructing Chicago,* Yale University Press, New Haven, 1991, pp. 7–61; Victoria Post Ranney, *Olmsted in Chicago,* R. R. Donnelley & Sons, Chicago, 1972; Harold M. Mayer and Richard C. Wade, *Chicago: Growth of a Metropolis,* University of Chicago Press, Chicago, 1969; and Jean F. Block, *Hyde Park Houses,* University of Chicago Press, Chicago, 1978.
43. Olmsted, Vaux & Co., "Report Accompanying Plan for Laying Out the South Park," in S. B. Sutton, op. cit., p. 161.
44. H. W. S. Cleveland had worked for Olmsted, Vaux & Co., on the design of Prospect Park. He left to establish his own firm and moved to Chicago in 1869.
45. Kenneth Jackson, "Foreword," to Jean F. Block's *Hyde Park Houses,* p. vii.
46. Olmsted, Vaux & Co., "Report Accompanying Plan for Laying Out the South Park," in S. B. Sutton, op. cit., p. 168.
47. Historical and statistical material on the Paseo del Rio is derived from Chris Carson and William McDonald (editors), *A Guide to San Antonio Architecture,* San Antonio Chapter of the AIA, San Antonio, 1986, and Clare Gunn, David Reed, and Robert Gouch: *Cultural Benefits from Metropolitan River Recreation—San Antonio Prototype,* Texas A&M University, College Station, 1972.
48. Historical and statistical material on Benjamin Franklin Parkway and its surroundings is derived from David B. Brownlee, *Building the City Beautiful—Benjamin Franklin Parkway and the Philadelphia Museum of Art,* Philadelphia Museum of Art, Philadelphia, 1989, and John F. Bauman, *Public Housing, Race, and Renewal—Urban Planning in Philadelphia 1920–1974,* Temple University Press, Philadelphia, 1987.
49. I am indebted to Sherwin M. Goldman for his comments on the evolution of the area surrounding the Water Garden. Specific historical and statistical material on Fort Worth and the Water Park is derived from Carla Crane and Theresa Savard (editors), *Dallas/Fort Worth Metroplex Area...Today,* Urban Land Institute, Washington, D.C., 1979.
50. In the late 1960s, Boulder, Colorado, initiated a similar effort. During its first two decades of operation, this program has added more than 12,000 acres to the park system. While it is too early to evaluate its success, it appears as though Boulder will provide a second example of the effectiveness of Olmsted's ideas.
51. Historical and statistical material on the Boston park system is derived from Cynthia Zaitzevsky, op. cit.; Frederick Law Olmsted, *Seventh Annual Report of the Commissioners of the Department of Parks for the City of Boston for the Year 1881,* reproduced in Sutton, op. cit., pp. 221–227; Frederick Law Olmsted, *Suggestions for the Improvement of the Muddy River, Sixth Annual Report of the Board of Commissioners of the Department of Parks for the City of Boston for the Year 1880,* reproduced in Sutton, op. cit., pp. 228–233, and Frederick Law Olmsted, *Notes on the Plan of Franklin Park and Related Matters, (1886),* reproduced in Sutton, op. cit., pp. 233–262.
52. Laura Wood Roper, *Flo, A Biography of Frederick Law Olmsted,* Johns Hopkins University Press, Baltimore, 1973, pp. 324–368 and 383–392.
53. Hermann Grundel won the competition and was awarded $500. (Cynthia Zaitzevsky, op. cit., p. 54.)
54. Frederick Law Olmsted, *Seventh Annual Report of the Commissioners of the Department of Parks for the City of Boston for the Year 1881,* reproduced in Sutton, op. cit., p. 221.
55. Frederick Law Olmsted, *Suggestions for the Improvement of the Muddy River, Sixth Annual Report of the Board of Commissioners of the Department of Parks for the City of Boston for the Year 1880,* reproduced in Sutton, op. cit., p. 231.
56. Frederick Law Olmsted, letter to Charles Sprague Sargent, July 8, 1874, quoted in Zaitzevsky, op. cit., p. 60.
57. Frederick Law Olmsted, *Notes on the Plan of Franklin Park and Related Matters* (1886), reproduced in Sutton, op. cit., p. 248.
58. City of Boston Department of Parks, *Twenty-first Annual Report of the Board of Commissioners for the Year Ending January 31, 1896,* p. 50.
59. Frederick Law Olmsted, *Notes on the Plan of Franklin Park and Related Matters* (1886), reproduced in Sutton, op. cit., p. 249.
60. U.S. Dept. of Commerce, Bureau of the Census, *Statistical Abstract of the United States (1978) and (1991),* Washington, D.C.
61. I would like to thank Marc and Mel Solomon for helping me to understand the difference between the earlier and later sections of the Kansas City parks system. Historical and statistical material on Kansas City and its park system is derived from William H. Wilson, *The City Beautiful Movement,* The Johns Hopkins University Press, Baltimore, 1989, pp. 99–125 and 208–212; William S. Worley, *J. C. Nichols and the Shaping of Kansas City,* University of Missouri Press, Columbia, 1990; and Carla C. Sabala (editor), *Kansas City...Today,* Urban Land Institute, Washington, D.C., 1974.
62. *Report of the Board of Park and Boulevard Commissioners of Kansas City, Mo.,* Board of Park and Boulevard Commissioners, Kansas City, Resolution of October 12, 1893, pp. 14–15.
63. William S. Worley, op. cit., pp. 78–85 and 100–107.
64. Historical and statistical material on the Minneapolis park system is derived from Theodore Wirth, op. cit., Sheila M. Speltz, "The Minneapolis Park & Recreation System," 1987, unpublished; and League of Women Voters of Minneapolis: *Minneapolis—A Guide to Local Government,* Minneapolis, October 1977.
65. Theodore Wirth, op. cit., p. 19.
66. H. W. S. Cleveland, "Suggestions for a System of Parks and Parkways for the City of Minneapolis," June 2, 1883, quoted in Wirth, op. cit., p.29.
67. Ibid.
68. Frederick Law Olmsted and Calvert Vaux, "Preliminary Report to the Commissioners for Laying Out a Park in Brooklyn, New York," (1866), in Albert Fein, op. cit., p. 96.
69. Joseph De Raismes III, Boulder City Attorney, personal communication, July 15, 1992.
70. Hamilton, Rabinovitz & Alschuler, Inc., *New York City's Park Spending in a National Context,* The Urban Center, New York, 1991, p. 6.
71. Patricia Leigh Brown, "Reclaiming a Park for Play," *New York Times,* "The City," section, September 12, 1993, p. 1.
72. David Schuyler and Jane Turner Censer, *The Papers of Frederick Law Olmsted,* vol. 6, The Johns Hopkins University Press, Baltimore, 1992, p. 539.
73. There are several precedents for this sort of federal incentive for states to enact local enabling legislation. The Housing Act of 1937 provided money to local housing authorities that were established pursuant to state enabling statutes. The Housing Act of 1949 did the same for locally established redevelopment agencies. See Chapters 9 and 11.

4

Palaces for the People

Cincinnati, 1970. Riverfront Stadium. *(Alexander Garvin)*

Over a century has passed since the trustees of the Boston Public Library explained that they wanted to build "'a palace for the people' and, as such...a monumental building worthy of the city."[1] Such *palaces for the people,* whether libraries, stadiums, museums, city halls, courts, or other public facilities, are more than fashionable civic embellishments, municipal status symbols, or even promotional edifices. By attracting people who spend millions of dollars, they also become agents of economic development.

Monumental public structures have considerable appeal. Politicians get votes for awarding construction contracts and distributing construction jobs. When the project is completed there are additional operating contracts, permanent jobs, increased retail sales, and new taxes with which to pay for government programs. If the project is a stadium, there is the additional status to be gained by bringing or retaining a major league team.

Any public facility can be claimed to be successful in and of itself as long as revenues exceed expenses. For a public facility to have beneficial impact on the rest of the city, however, it must attract a critical mass of customers and yet be located and designed so that their market requirements *cannot* be fully accommodated within the facility. Only by this seemingly contradictory set of attributes will a public facility generate beneficial interaction with the rest of the city, because only then will its customers have a reason to set foot or spend money anywhere else. In addition, its periods of operation must complement those of surrounding areas, thereby providing customers when these areas would otherwise be empty.

Too often, palaces for the people are conceived of as single-purpose facilities, whose impact on surrounding areas (measured in additional traffic, pollution, noise, garbage, etc.) only generates opposition. Instead, they should be planned and financed in conjunction with improvements to neighboring properties, thereby avoiding a good deal of political conflict. More important, facilities so planned would then spark further market-generated improvements in their immediate vicinity and become engines for continuing prosperity.

World's Columbian Exposition of 1893

One new municipal palace is good; more are better. The World's Columbian Exposition that opened in Chicago in 1893 demonstrated this concept as nothing had before. Visitors saw that the attractions had been combined into a coherent, powerful whole and concluded that this was the key to successful urban planning.[2]

Chicago, 1893. The monumental exhibition structures grouped around the Court of Honor at the World's Columbian Exposition became the model for well-planned civic and cultural centers. *(Courtesy of Chicago Historical Society)*

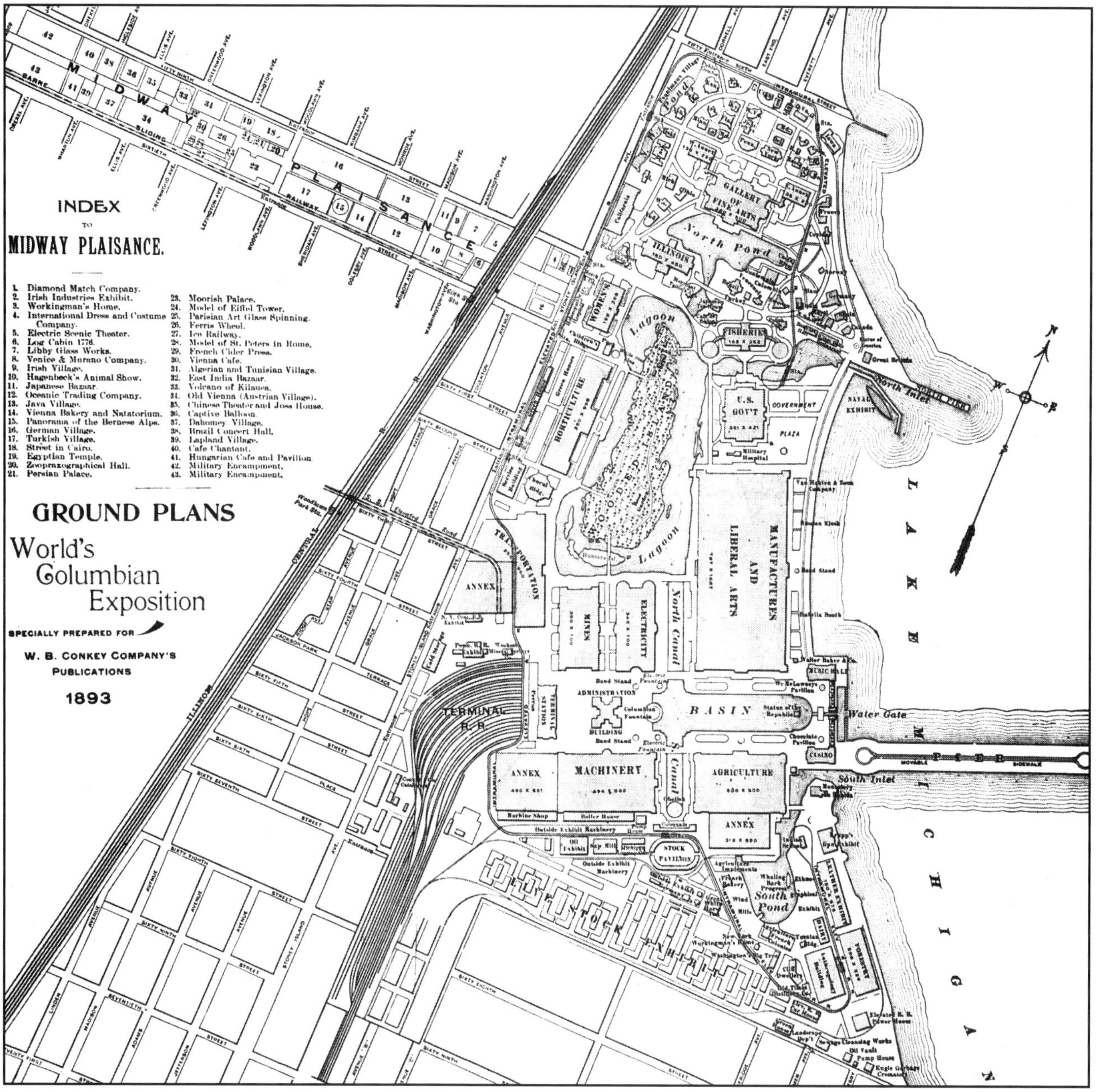

Chicago, 1893. Plan of the World's Columbian Exposition. *(Courtesy of Chicago Historical Society)*

Such planning became conventional wisdom because it was propagated by the people who went to the Chicago Fair. Its 27.5 million admissions (paid and unpaid) equaled 43 percent of the population of the United States.[3] Obviously 43 percent of the United States did not go to the Fair. But any time even 10 percent of the population of the United States sees something, the impact is phenomenal.

Preparation for the Fair began in 1889, when Chicago established a corporation to lobby for, plan, and develop an exposition to celebrate the 400th anniversary of the discovery of America by Christopher Columbus. The corporation promptly issued $5 million in bonds. The following year, after considerable controversy, Congress designated Chicago as the site for a World's Columbian Exposition "of arts, industries, manufactures, and the products of the soil, mine, and sea."

The Exposition Corporation selected the Olmsted firm to be its landscape architect and Burnham and Root as coordinating architects. As a site for the exposition, they recommended Jackson Park, which Olmsted had designed more than two decades earlier. It was a particularly attractive location because the South Side Rapid Transit Company agreed to extend the elevated railroad from its 63d Street terminus to the Park (see Chapter 3).[4]

Olmsted and Burnham proposed gutting the existing landscape, building the exposition, then replacing it with an improved park when the Fair was over. They conceived a three-part exposition: a formal group of major exhibition structures organized around a Court of Honor containing a large water basin (350 feet wide and 1100 feet long) decorated with sculpture and fountains; picturesque pavilions grouped around the park's irregular ponds and lagoons; and an amusement area strung out along the 7/8 mile of Midway Plaisance leading west into Washington Park. The buildings themselves were designed by the nation's most prominent architects, who transformed this exhibition of the world's progress in science, art, industry, and agriculture into a major architecture show.

The artists and architects who designed the Chicago Fair created what Henry Adams called "the first expression of American thought as a unity."[5] Ironically, it did not look like the uniquely American steel and glass skyscrapers then going up in Chicago. The architects of the Fair combined styles then fashionable at the Ecole des Beaux Arts in Paris. The result was an eclectic confection: Roman in civic presence, Baroque in axial organization, and Renaissance in surface decoration. The architects adopted a common design vocabulary and used similar materials. Most structures were built to a common cornice height, included built-in, outdoor incandescent lamps to provide lighting for pedestrians, and were covered with the same white plaster-cement cladding for which the exposition was nicknamed the "White City."[6]

The exposition was both a popular and a financial success. The 21.5 million paid admissions and numerous concessions produced almost $33 million in gross revenues and a $2.25 million return for the exposition's investors. Tens of millions more dollars were spent by visitors to Chicago hotels, restaurants, and stores and by real estate developers who rushed to build on undeveloped sites made attractive by their proximity to the Fair and easily accessible by the elevated railroad. The most important result of the exposition, though, was not its popular renown, or its profitability, or its contribution to tourism and real estate development—it was its extraordinary impact on American architecture and urban planning.

The exposition convinced generations of architects and public officials that careful, coordinated planning resulted in a more convenient and efficient environment (see Chapter 18). It also launched a vision of the "City Beautiful" as the appropriate appearance for municipal improvements, and it demonstrated that public buildings could have even greater impact when collected into a coherent district and designed to function as an ensemble.[7] This idea of grouped public buildings quickly became part of the progressive agenda of municipal reform. Today it lives on in every city as the civic center, the cultural center, the sports center, and the convention center.

Civic Centers

Civic reformers who wanted to implement the City Beautiful strategy in the years immediately following the Chicago Fair faced a major obstacle. There was as yet no way for government to direct the location and design of privately owned real estate. However, government could ensure the thoughtful organization of municipal offices, courthouses, and facilities for legislators. Thus the early manifestations of the City Beautiful were usually proposals for new civic centers.

The idea of clustering government buildings was not new. It went back to the Campidoglio in Rome, and before. Gathering such facilities together into a civic ensemble provided citizens with a physical and symbolic representation of local government. In America the reason for a civic center was more a matter of efficiency and economy than symbolism. Expanding municipal, county, and state governments needed to replace scattered, inadequate, outworn facilities. The people who went to grouped facilities to obtain government services could be counted on to patronize nearby businesses, as would government employees. Tourists might be attracted by the opportunity to see government in action and thus make a small contribution to the local economy. It was beyond imagination, however, that a century after the Chicago Fair, government (federal, state, and local) would employ 17 million people and annually spend $1.7 trillion, in the process occupying a significant portion of every city's land surface and office space and becoming a major component of any city's economy.[8]

The McMillan Plan for Washington, D.C.

The first American city to implement a major plan for the clustering of government buildings was Washington, D.C. The federal government owned more than enough structures to create several civic centers. Unfortunately, they had been built with little regard to their relationship to one another, to the city as a whole, or to generating further private development. In 1902, the Senate adopted a plan, prepared under the leadership of Senator James McMillan of Michigan, that was intended to correct this by applying the principles that had been so successful at the Chicago Fair.

For more than a century, private as well as public development in the national capital had been loosely based on a plan originally conceived in 1791 by French engineer Pierre L'Enfant. His design, based on the chateau gardens of the French landscape architect André Le Nôtre and the emerging modern city of Paris, was an amalgam of diagonal boulevards and a rectilinear grid. The diagonal boulevards allowed carriages and horseback riders to reach their destinations by cutting through whole neighborhoods. The grid permitted the simple survey, sale, and reconveyance of property for the construction of homes and public buildings.[9]

L'Enfant's plan specified the sites of major public buildings. The Capitol was to be placed at the top of Jenkin's Hill where it could dominate the city. It was connected by Pennsylvania Avenue (a broad thoroughfare intended to be

Washington, D.C., 1901–1902. Model showing the Capitol and the irregularly shaped open spaces that at the time included a railroad station and numerous other intrusive structures. *(Courtesy of National Commission of Fine Arts)*

lined with major public structures) to the "Presidential Palace" located on high ground at the north end of a vast public open space leading south to the Potomac. A second "Grand Avenue," lined with sloping gardens that extended from the houses on either side, was to run east-west, connecting Capitol Hill with the Potomac.

During the course of the city's growth, a variety of intrusions significantly altered L'Enfant's initial conception. A canal was extended through the site of the Grand Avenue to connect the eastern and western branches of the Potomac River. When the Treasury Building was erected, it blocked the view between the Capitol and the White House. The Washington Monument, which required foundation conditions that could support an immense obelisk, was built several hundred feet off the crossing of the north-south axis of the White House and the east-west axis of the Capitol. The Smithsonian Institution obstructed the path of the Grand Avenue, which itself had become part of an irregular, asymmetrical public garden. The most serious intrusion was the Baltimore & Ohio Railroad which, in 1872, built its tracks and station right in the middle of this picturesque park.

Proposals for a suitable centennial celebration of the founding of the national capital culminated in 1901 with a Senate resolution directing the Senate Committee on the District of Columbia to report on the development and improvement of the city's park system. The Committee's chairman, Senator McMillan, appointed Daniel Burnham, Frederick Law Olmsted, Jr., Charles Follen McKim, Charles Moore (McMillan's secretary), and Augustus St. Gaudens to prepare the report. With the exception of McMillan and Moore, they had worked together on the Chicago Fair and saw their current project as a logical continuation of these earlier efforts.[10]

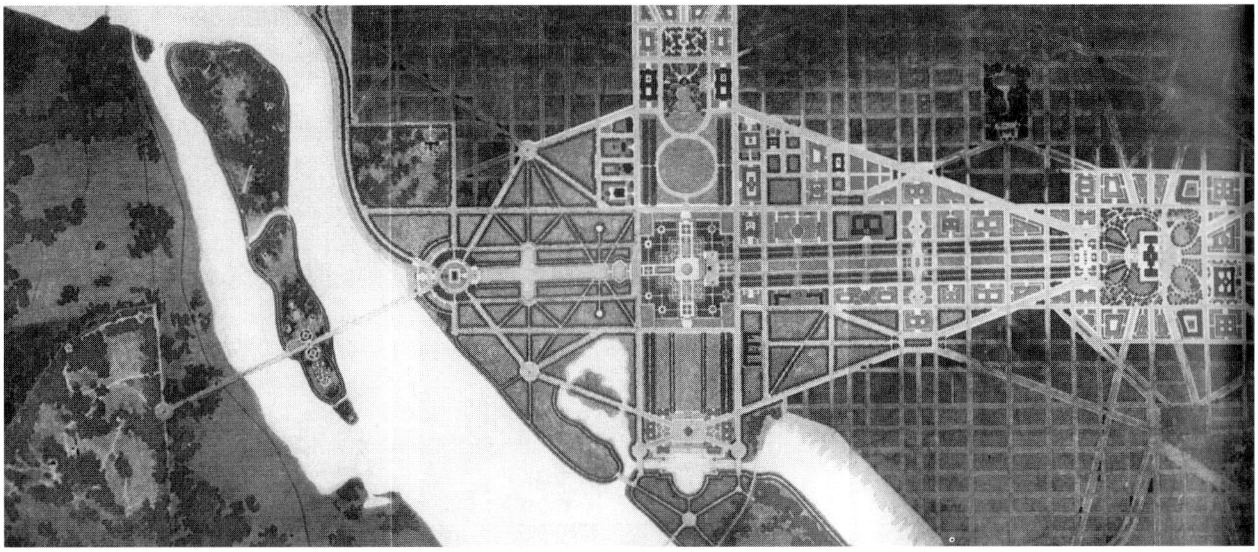

Washington, D.C., 1901–1902. The McMillan Plan for the redevelopment of the Mall created a setting for America's largest concentration of majestic public buildings. *(Courtesy of Senate Park Commission)*

During the summer of 1901, Burnham, McKim, Olmsted, Jr., and Moore traveled together to Europe to examine what they conceived to be the world's finest gardens, palaces, and civic complexes: Versailles, Vaux-le-Vicomte, and the Champs Elysées (which had so influenced L'Enfant); Hadrian's Villa at Tivoli, the Villa Medici, and the grand piazza of St. Peter's (that were so revered at the American Academy in Rome); Vienna, Budapest, and Paris (whose design was so admired at the Ecole des Beaux Arts). Once again, European royal monuments provided the inspiration for the capital of the American Republic.[11]

At every stop they discussed the sites, their design philosophies, and specific proposals for Washington. Their common approach is marvelously captured in an event that occurred in Venice. One night McKim disappeared. When Olmsted wondered how they could find him, Burnham replied: "That's easy.... We will go to the Piazza di San Marco and find him on the axis."[12] Indeed, the plan they devised is essentially a series of imperial axes intended to enhance the symbolic significance of Washington's major monuments.

As was the case at the Chicago Fair, Burnham was responsible for coordinating their work. Together with McMillan and Moore, he handled the promotional aspects of obtaining the support of the administration of Theodore Roosevelt, the Congress, and a variety of civic organizations. Olmsted's firm again prepared the landscape plan; McKim developed and refined the commission's design proposals; St. Gaudens planned the sculptural decoration. In January 1902, the commission presented its report in the form of a written document drafted by Charles Moore and an exhibition of scale models, plans, and perspective drawings prepared under McKim's direction in New York.[13]

Washington could not continue to function at the speed and scale of a leisurely pedestrian. It could not continue to close down for the summer. Nor would it remain what John F. Kennedy later referred to as the perfect combination of southern efficiency and northern charm. Washington had international responsibilities. So Burnham, McKim, Olmsted, Jr., and the others proposed a monumental scheme to transform L'Enfant's design for the capital for a provincial republic into the permanent administrative center of an international empire. It included conversion of L'Enfant's Grand Avenue into a spectacular mall; creation of a second, similarly symbolic axis perpendicular to it; relocation of the railroad tracks and terminal; establishment of three new groups of public structures; and development of an integrated park system.

L'Enfant's Grand Avenue was to be doubled in width to 800 feet and lined on both sides with four rows of trees, a service road, and a procession of majestic public buildings. The axis of the proposed Mall was shifted slightly to accommodate the awkward placement of the Washington Monument. It was extended further westward along a reflecting pool, longer than the one at the Chicago Fair, through a new park (on reclaimed land) to a proposed Lincoln Memorial and from there diagonally across the Potomac on a low Memorial Bridge to the National Cemetery at Arlington.

The imperial character of the new Mall was matched by the enhancement of L'Enfant's north-south vista from the White House to the Potomac. This open space was broadened and extended across reclaimed land to a Memorial Building Group or pantheon on what is today the site of the Jefferson Memorial. Since there was no way to compensate for the placement of the Washington Monument, McKim designed

Washington, D.C., 1901–1902. Bird's-eye view of the McMillan Plan illustrating the monumental design framework for the future development in the national capital. *(Courtesy of Senate Park Commission)*

Washington, D.C., 1901–1902. Park system proposed by the McMillan Plan for Washington, D.C. *(Courtesy of Senate Park Commission)*

an elaborate terraced formal garden with a second reflecting pool marking the crossing of L'Enfant's two axes.

These organizing axes would have been impossible without Burnham and McMillan. Burnham, the architect of a proposed new Union Railroad Station, persuaded Alexander Cassatt, president of the Pennsylvania Railroad, to move its railroad tracks and station north of the Capitol, provided Congress would pay for a tunnel under Capitol Hill. McMillan obtained Congressional approval just prior to his death in August 1902. The following year Congress appropriated the necessary funds. While Burnham's Union Station and the diagonal boulevard connecting it with Capitol Hill were not formally part of the commission proposal, they were an integral part of the plan and were intended to provide a majestic gateway to the proposed monumental government center.

Three new groups of public buildings were to be established. The first was to be created by replacing the old houses on Lafayette Square with large-scale government offices, the second by locating additional public edifices in the triangle between Pennsylvania Avenue and the Mall, and the third by turning Capitol Hill into a vast square defined by huge new structures for the Supreme Court and other government entities.

The most ambitious element of the plan was the park system in which Olmsted, Jr., like his father, proposed to exploit topographic features, provide neighborhood recreation facilities, and tie together Washington's disparate neighborhoods. He achieved this with substantial new park areas, riverside drives, and scenic park-boulevards encircling the city.

Few of the individual projects, when completed, followed exactly the details presented in the drawings. Lafayette Square was not torn down. The Smithsonian Institution was not moved to a Beaux Arts palace.[14] The proposed pantheon of monuments became a single Jefferson Memorial. However, the monumental city that we know today would have been impossible without the conceptual framework provided by the McMillan Plan.

With or without the plan, Washington's massive bureaucratic engine guaranteed a critical mass of expenditures that had to spill over into the surrounding city as well as an avalanche of tourists, who would have even more impact on the local economy. However, the monumental design framework of carefully considered groups of public structures substantially increased its symbolic meaning, attractiveness, and usefulness to millions of visitors who might otherwise have had much less to see, come on shorter visits, and spent far fewer dollars.

Attempting to emulate either the Chicago Fair or the McMillan Plan, virtually every American city prepared plans for a civic center. The authors of these plans seem to me to have failed to understand that no complex of government buildings could attract even a fraction of the 27.5 million who visited the World's Columbian Exposition. They also misunderstood the McMillan Plan. Government is Washington's very raison d'être. In most cities government can only be a small segment of the local economy. A municipality might need a city hall, a courthouse, a police station, a central post office. But, in most instances these facilities can only cover a fraction of the city's land surface, occupy a minor amount of building space, and employ a small portion of its population. Nevertheless, architects and planners sought to use these buildings to provide a monumental framework for urban development and politicians were quick to distribute the resulting patronage.

Ironically, Daniel Burnham was the man responsible for promoting this faulty planning strategy. Upon completion of the McMillan Plan, he became one of three commissioners appointed to advise Cleveland on questions of urban planning and went on to propose similar civic centers for San Francisco and Chicago (see Chapter 18). Unlike Washington and Cleveland, these cities did not implement his civic center designs.

The Group Plan, Cleveland

For nearly a decade after the Chicago Fair, Cleveland's leadership tried to create a group of public structures inspired by the Fair. They believed that this ensemble would attract tourists to "visit the city and enjoy the wonderful picture of municipal enterprise and beauty."[15] In 1902, with the help of Mayor Tom Loftin Johnson, they persuaded the Ohio legislature to allow the governor to appoint an advisory commission that, as expected, proposed a new civic center.

The governor appointed three architects who had been recommended by Mayor Johnson and other Cleveland civic leaders: Daniel Burnham, Arnold Brunner, and John Carrère. They repeated the procedures that had been so successful in preparing the McMillan Plan. Once again Burnham (during

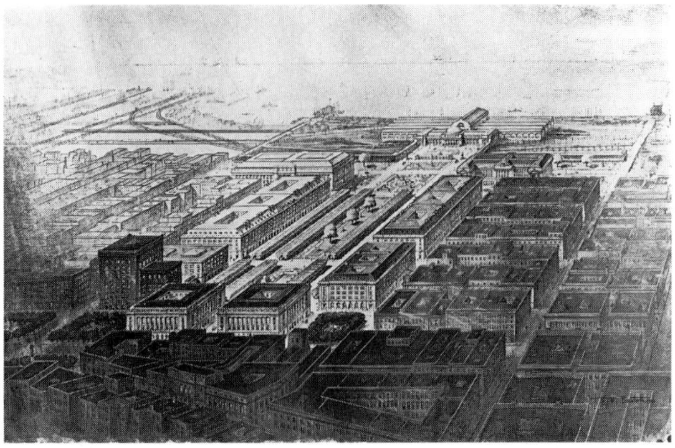

Cleveland, 1903. Group Plan for the redevelopment of downtown Cleveland. *(From Burnham, Carrère, and Brunner, Report on the Group Plan of Public Buildings of Cleveland, Ohio, Board of Supervision for Public Buildings and Grounds, Cleveland, 1903; Courtesy of Avery Library, Columbia University, New York)*

visits from his Chicago office) coordinated the planning taking place at Brunner's and Carrère's New York offices as well as the promotion and lobbying going on in Cleveland. This time he also wrote the text.[16]

The *Group Plan* they released in 1903 was a portfolio-sized brochure filled with handsome, detailed plans and perspective drawings of an entirely new civic center. It showed a monumental group of public buildings organized along a 400-foot-wide mall extending one-third of a mile from the corner of Public Square to a new Union Railway Terminal (for which Burnham had already been designated architect) on Lake Erie. Along the lake shore the plan proposed a new park promenade. The drawings also depicted new buildings that extended for blocks in every direction. Presumably these were to be privately financed and built. Like the structures at the Chicago Fair, they were designed in the appropriate Beaux Arts style, to a common cornice height.

The civic center proposed in the plan was intended to replace the slum that lay between Public Square and Lake Erie. However, the plan's brief text was vague in explaining how all this would happen. It dismissed acquisition and relocation problems saying: "the present population of the district...will have to be moved elsewhere."

In 1903, when the *Group Plan* was released, only three buildings were in the planning stage. Over the ensuing decades other civic structures were erected for occupants who needed space and had the money to pay for it. The plan's most important features were ignored. Burnham's terminal was never built because the railroads serving Cleveland could not agree on its location, design, or funding and the park promenade along Lake Erie remained a dream because the railroads were unwilling to pay the vast sums that would be required to reroute their facilities.[17]

The authors of *Group Plan* had boldly announced that: "the new public buildings" would spur property owners to "develop this territory and extend the business center of the city toward the Lake." They could not have been more wrong. The civic structures that were erected produced little or no market reaction. Only the railroad station would have aimed a steady stream of travelers through the Mall on their way to work, to business appointments, and to hotels and other visitor services.

Some privately financed property redevelopment might have occurred in response to this new market. But even with the additional traffic, the civic center probably would have failed to attract the city's business center because it was located at the wrong end of town. The path of city growth was to the east, out Euclid Avenue toward the wealthier suburbs. Any chance of moving the business district to the blocks surrounding the new civic center disappeared when the city's railroad station was established at Terminal Tower, completed in 1930.

Not only did the Group Plan fail to generate any market reaction in the surrounding area, it also failed to contribute to the vitality of downtown Cleveland. After 5:00 P.M. and on weekends, when all the government buildings are closed, the area is deserted. Even during the day, it appears empty because of the vast distance across the mall. Instead of a "wonderful picture of municipal enterprise and beauty," the *Group Plan* proved to be a hollow core surrounded by monuments for a government bureaucracy.

Municipal leaders in Cleveland had mistakenly thought that civic centers, in and of themselves, provided the critical mass needed to generate both increased commercial activity and further real estate development. This was a convenient delusion that helped civic leaders in Cleveland and elsewhere to obtain political support for the bond issues to pay for proposed civic centers. They argued that the bonds would be paid off with the increased tax revenues from private development in surrounding areas. This strategy failed in Cleveland and other cities when the location and design of these centers precluded any significant spillover spending and, therefore, also precluded sufficient market activity to justify further development.

Memorial Plaza, St. Louis

The clustering of government buildings for St. Louis was initially proposed by the Civic League in 1907 and finally completed in 1960. The first 10 blocks were paid for by a 1923 bond issue; further bond issues in 1933 and 1944 paid for the rest. The resulting procession of public structures extends for more than half a mile along Market Street between City Hall and the railroad station. Commonly referred to as "Central Parkway" or "Memorial Plaza," it includes a Soldier's Memorial, an auditorium, courts, government offices, and the post office. The only special attraction along its entire length is Carl Milles's "Meeting of the Waters," a delightful fountain

St. Louis, 1987. The public buildings of Memorial Plaza are strung out over too great a distance to produce a critical mass of customers. *(Alexander Garvin)*

with 14 bronze figures representing the meeting of the Mississippi and Missouri rivers.[18]

Memorial Plaza was as unsuccessful in stimulating a market reaction in St. Louis as the Group Plan was in Cleveland. This time it was not a matter of location. Central Parkway connected the business district with the expensive residential areas around Forest Park (see Chapter 14). Nor was it the absence of the railroad station, which was already at the site. In the beginning the failure could have been ascribed to an incomplete project with an inadequate number of public buildings and too few government employees. When the plan was completed it became clear that it failed to generate a private-market reaction because of faulty design. The buildings extended over such a long distance that they could not generate the critical mass of activity needed to spark adjacent private development. Even today, when Union Station has been converted into a successful retail-tourist center, there are still not enough people to animate this half-mile-long public open space.

The Los Angeles Civic Center

In Los Angeles, as in Cleveland and St. Louis, the civic center took decades to complete. The first proposal for a civic center appeared in 1909 in a city plan prepared for the Municipal Arts Commission by Charles Mulford Robinson. He proposed to locate a combined civic and cultural center at the northern end of the business district, below Bunker Hill, then a crazy-quilt of frame dwellings, rooming houses, and commercial buildings. A second proposal was made in 1918 by the mayor's Civic Center Committee directed by William Mulholland, chief engineer for the city's Public Service Department. It also suggested building on the northern edge of downtown but eliminated the libraries, museums, and other cultural facilities of the earlier plan and proposed a separate cultural center for the middle of the city. Neither plan was adopted.[19]

In 1923, a voter referendum approved creation of the civic center, ratified a $7.5 million bond issue, and authorized construction of a new city hall. The City Planning Commission hired the firm of Cook and Hall to prepare a plan for the new administrative center. Another proposal was made by the Allied Architects Association. In neither case were there sufficient occupants to fill the proposed structures or money to pay for them. So construction proceeded on a piecemeal basis, starting with the Hall of Justice in 1925 and City Hall in 1926–1928.

Over the next four decades government buildings were erected around a plaza consisting of three landscaped open spaces interrupted by streets and connected by a series of stairs and ramps. The northern end of this axis, a half-mile from City Hall, was completed during the 1960s. It includes the Music Center and the Water and Power Building, which, like the other parcels, are separated from one another by traffic arteries and parking facilities.

The Los Angeles Civic Center has had little influence on the development of the city. Initially there were not enough government buildings to make an impact. Once there were, the sloping site and distances between structures ensured isolation rather than a critical mass of mutually reinforcing activity.

Construction of the Hollywood Freeway, during the 1950s, cut off any potential spillover to the north and east. Government acquisition and clearance of then-seedy Bunker Hill in the 1960s eliminated any possible influence to the west. Perhaps in the twenty-first century, when the redevelopment of Bunker Hill is completed, the Civic Center may provide a monumental focus for the northern end of downtown. So far, like the civic centers of Cleveland and St. Louis, it has proved to be a hollow core attracting only isolated activity during the day and nothing at night.

Los Angeles, 1991. Civic Center at 3:00 P.M. virtually devoid of pedestrians. *(Alexander Garvin)*

Government Center, Boston

Most American civic centers are little more than theatrical settings for the day-to-day activity of government. Boston's is one of the few exceptions. Its government center really did influence city growth and development. Part of its success was a matter of timing. It was created in the 1960s, when government and its customers had become a rapidly growing market. It also exploited a critical location, where the business district converges with the waterfront, Beacon Hill, the West and North Ends, and was designed to encourage anybody who went to the new government center to make use of these surrounding districts.[20]

Boston's City Planning Board first proposed clearing Scollay Square, then a notorious red-light district, for the purpose of building a civic center in 1917. The idea was revived during the Great Depression and again in the 1950s. Finally, in 1961, Mayor John Collins and Edward Logue, his development administrator, obtained federal urban renewal funding for a new government center consolidating federal, state, and municipal facilities at Scollay Square.

The master plan, prepared by architect I. M. Pei, proposed transforming 26 decaying city blocks into a modern townscape composed of 15 large buildings. Its centerpiece was a spacious new plaza and city hall, designed by Kallman, McKinnel, and Knowles, the unanimous choice as winner of a major international design competition.

New Deal and post–World War II legislation had expanded government activity to the point that federal, state, and city offices were scattered in rented space and converted annexes throughout the city. Consolidation meant greater efficiency and reduced cost. More important, with the help of House Speaker McCormick and President Kennedy (both from Boston), Mayor Collins was able to attract federal and state buildings that otherwise might have been located elsewhere.

Government Center brought 25,000 workers where there had formerly been 6000 and located them on 60 acres in the middle of the business district. Downtown Boston is so tightly concentrated that Government Center is an easy walk from almost anywhere. Thus Government Center could benefit from proximity to the financial, general office, and shopping districts, while they could profit from the customers Government Center would provide. The interaction of this critical mass of customers and activity was exactly what was needed to spark developer interest in additional construction on sites adjacent to Government Center.

Pei's design made Government Center an integral part of the cityscape, not an obviously separate district. Unlike earlier City Beautiful civic centers, buildings were not uniform in height, color, material, and scale. Nor did Pei specify a consistent style. Most important, the plan included more than just government buildings. It preserved a few existing private commercial structures, introduced some new ones, and shuffled them together with the new government buildings. Instead of depending on axial symmetry, the design unified this disparate collection of structures through the use of pedestrian walkways, arcades, and open spaces, all leading to City Hall Plaza.

Nevertheless, Government Center suffers from two of the same problems that afflicted earlier civic centers: land use segregation and oversized open space. Because Government Center consists almost entirely of commercial and institutional offices, the plaza remains empty except on those very few occasions when it is the setting for major public events. Like other civic centers, it closes down for the night. During the day, City Hall Plaza may provide a monumental setting for government. But, like the vast central spaces of other civic

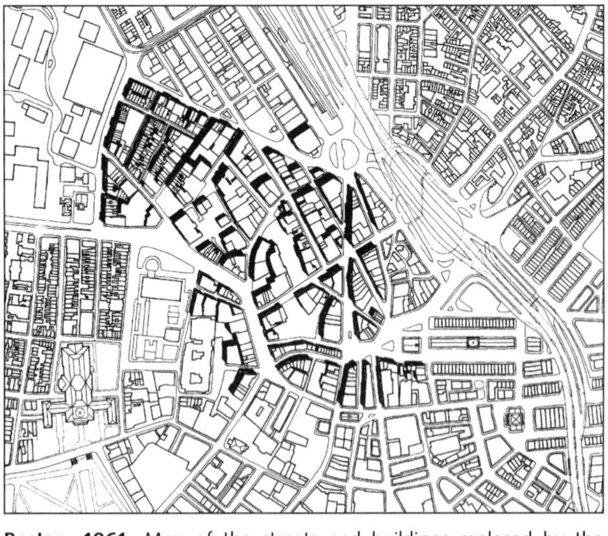

Boston, 1961. Map of the streets and buildings replaced by the Government Center. *(Courtesy of Pei Cobb Freed & Partners)*

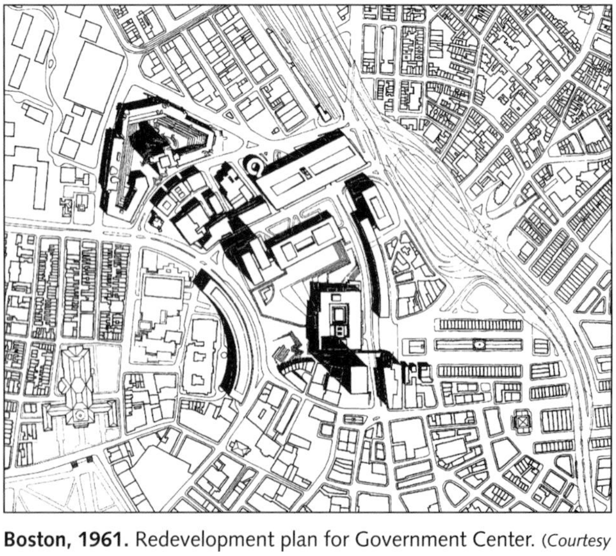

Boston, 1961. Redevelopment plan for Government Center. *(Courtesy of Pei Cobb Freed & Partners)*

Boston, 1989. Government Center buildings accommodate more than 17,000 office workers who patronize the shops and restaurants of the surrounding area. *(Alexander Garvin)*

centers, it is in scale with surrounding public buildings—not with the people who use it.

Cultural Centers

The cultural center is a recent phenomenon. Prior to the mid-twentieth century, theaters were built where profit-motivated owners thought they could maximize box office receipts; so were privately owned concert halls. Operas, museums, and other cultural institutions occupied sites their donors already owned or found convenient to purchase. Occasionally, city governments provided sites for these buildings, often in an existing public park. Cultural facilities simply were not thought of in terms of their impact on the growth and development of the city.

When the Chicago Fair popularized the notion of clustering public buildings, no individual cultural facility had a reason or a mechanism for relocating into a single arts district. With the exception of theaters, which tended to cluster as a method of profiting from the resultant aggregate market, the impetus had to originate elsewhere. Occasional clustering of cultural facilities occurred in civic centers that could not otherwise obtain tenants for the sumptuous facilities that had been envisioned. This happened in San Francisco in 1932 when the Opera and Veteran's Auditorium were added to the scattered government buildings in its Civic Center and in Washington, D.C., during the New Deal when the National Archives and National Gallery began filling the gaps in the McMillan Plan. However, it was not until the advent of Lincoln Center that consolidating disparate arts institutions into a single cultural center became popular.[21]

Lincoln Center, New York City

When Robert Moses, chairman of the Mayor's Committee on Slum Clearance, proposed a renewal plan for Lincoln Square in 1955, New York City was not in decline. More than 9 million square feet of new office space had been built since the end of World War II.[22] The assessed value of taxable real estate had climbed 31 percent, from \$13.8 billion in 1945 to \$18.1 billion in 1955.[23] The 1950 census had reported a population

Manhattan, 1957. Site of Lincoln Square Urban Renewal Project prior to redevelopment. *(Courtesy of the Citizens Housing and Planning Council, New York)*

increase of 436,000. Nobody doubted a continued rosy future. Instead, people worried about specific neighborhoods.

The city's white middle class, especially on Manhattan's West Side, was confronted with a massive influx of African-American and Puerto Rican newcomers.[24] In an effort to accommodate them, once-fashionable, brownstone row houses had been converted into rooming houses or single-room-occupancies (SROs) where no fewer than eight households (and often many more) shared the same kitchen and bathroom. Apartments had been subdivided and rented to tenants whose only way of paying was by packing in more people than these accommodations were designed for. Overcrowding only increased the wear and tear on the buildings. New and old populations, now jammed into the neighborhood, were soon at each other's throats. The most insightful depiction of the scene is the Leonard Bernstein–Stephen Sondheim–Arthur Laurents 1957 Broadway musical, *West Side Story*, which took for its setting the very spot Moses proposed for redevelopment and that later became the location for the film version.[25]

The Lincoln Square Urban Renewal Project was intended to be the centerpiece of Moses' effort to "save" the West Side from destruction by the newcomers. When he proposed it in 1955, he already had 11 renewal projects under way, including 2 that were intended to reverse deterioration of the West Side: West Park at the northern end of the area and Columbus Circle in the south. The West Park Renewal Project (better known as Park West Village) was scheduled to clear 3700 apartments, occupied primarily by poor African Americans

Manhattan, 1955. Rendering of the proposed Lincoln Center for the Performing Arts in a form that recalls St. Peter's Square in Rome. *(Courtesy of the Citizens Housing and Planning Council, New York)*

Manhattan, 1993. The 12,000 ticket holders and 6800 musicians, dancers, actors, costumemakers, stagehands, ushers, porters, and other people who put together the performances at Lincoln Center have transformed the area into one of the city's liveliest neighborhoods. *(Alexander Garvin)*

and Puerto Ricans, and replace them with 2700 apartments for the middle class. Columbus Circle was to remove two blocks of shabby commercial buildings and tenements accommodating 300 households for the purpose of building a convention center, an office tower, and 600 middle-income apartments.[26]

With the extremities of the neighborhood theoretically protected from further intrusion by redevelopment, Moses needed something to spark the revival from within. He knew that the Metropolitan Opera was looking for a new home and that the New York Philharmonic had been told to vacate Carnegie Hall when its lease expired in 1959. They might provide the economic and psychological impetus needed to revitalize the West Side. So he persuaded them to relocate to the West Side and paid for their move with federal renewal funds.[27]

Moses began by announcing a $160 million plan that covered 18 blocks and included new buildings for the Metropolitan Opera, the New York Philharmonic, Fordham University, 3800 apartments, and miscellaneous community facilities. Over the next 2 years he proposed adding a 10-story fashion center, headquarters for a national engineering society, a shopping center, a skyscraper hotel, and a legitimate theater complex with five new halls. None of these proposed additions survived the proposal stage.

When Moses finally submitted a redevelopment plan for public review in 1957, four northern blocks along Broadway had been deleted. Nevertheless, at least 678 businesses and 5268 households (4600 in apartments and the remainder in rooming houses) had to be relocated.[28] In their place he proposed a truly powerful stimulant: the Metropolitan Opera, Philharmonic (now Avery Fisher) Hall, the New York State Theater (to serve as the home of the New York City Opera and New York City Ballet), the Vivian Beaumont Repertory Theater, the Julliard School, the Library and Museum of the Performing Arts, Fordham University Law School, headquarters for the American Red Cross, an 800-car garage, new public schools, a fire station, a public bandshell, and 3800 middle-income apartments to be known as Lincoln Towers. If the activity from these facilities could not revitalize the West Side, nothing could.

Opposition was vociferous. Area residents formed a Lincoln Square Citizens Committee that held protest rallies in front of City Hall. They knew they would have to pay for Lincoln Center, not in dollars or taxes, but in uprooted lives. As one opponent put it: "We are planning to take away what they [the residents] have with the reason being that they are living under bad conditions."[29]

Advocates for the relocatees were not the only critics. There was opposition to the very concept of a cultural supermarket. As Jane Jacobs complained:

> *[Lincoln Center] is planned on the idiotic assumption that the natural neighbor of a hall is another hall. Nonsense. The natural neighbors of halls are restaurants, bars, florist shops, studios, music shops, all sorts of interesting places. Look for instance at what has been generated by Carnegie Hall on West 57th Street, or by some off-Broadway theaters.*[30]

She and other critics felt that the components should be separated and used to revive many declining neighborhoods. Moses knew this to be impractical. He had had difficulty persuading the Philharmonic to move a few blocks north of its previous home at Carnegie Hall. Getting the Metropolitan Opera or the Julliard School to move to one of his renewal projects in Brooklyn or the Bronx was out of the question.

With all this controversy, the City Planning Commission and Board of Estimate hearings on the Lincoln Square Urban Renewal Project were tumultuous. It was time to bend. Moses amended the plan again. This time he added 420 tax-exempt, cooperative apartments. Finally, more than 2 years after it had been proposed, Lincoln Center was approved.

Designing Lincoln Center was as difficult as obtaining project approval. The constituent institutions had selected some of the country's best-known architects: Philip Johnson, Wallace K. Harrison, Max Abramovitz, Pietro Belluschi, Eero Saarinen, and Skidmore, Owings & Merrill. Like their predecessors at the World's Columbian Exposition, the architects of Lincoln Center chose to emulate European models. One version was inspired by St. Peter's Square in Rome, a later one by Piazza San Marco in Venice. What finally emerged was a $175 million group of neo-Beaux Arts containers, built to the same cornice height, out of the same travertine and glass, and differentiated primarily by their structural supports.

The rest of this $280 million project is so disparate in scale, material, height, and color that most New Yorkers have long forgotten that the 45-acre Lincoln Square Urban Renewal Project is more than an internationally known performance emporium. In fact, the only connection between the Fordham University Law School, the American Red Cross Building, Public School No. 199, and the 3800 apartments of Lincoln Towers is that they were built on land acquired and cleared for the same urban renewal project.

Manhattan, 1993. Lincoln Square Urban Renewal Project looking northwest—Lincoln Towers, American Red Cross, and Martin Luther King High School. *(Alexander Garvin)*

Ironically, Lincoln Center demonstrated the validity of Jane Jacobs' observation that "the natural neighbors of halls are restaurants, bars, florist shops, studios, music shops, all sorts of interesting places." It also proved her criticism wrong. The planners of Lincoln Center were after precisely the frictional effect she had described. They understood that concentrating so many cultural institutions in one place would not preclude "all sorts of interesting places" but rather result in greater activity than the individual components could generate separately. But even they underestimated the impact of this critical mass of 12,000 ticketholders and 6800 musicians, dancers, actors, costumemakers, stagehands, ushers, porters, and other people who put together the performances.

Within a few years, Lincoln Center had forever banished the world of *West Side Story* to the musical stage. Today, Broadway and Columbus Avenues, opposite Lincoln Center, are lined with fashionable boutiques, restaurants, and new, privately financed apartment towers. The magnitude of the change is reflected by the $189 million increase in the assessed value (1950 to 1990) of just the four blocks between Lincoln Center and Central Park.[31]

Today Lincoln Center is part of a very different city from the city it helped to change. When the project was conceived, cultural institutions were not considered to be significant components of the city's economy. At that time manufacturing constituted 30 percent of New York City's labor force. By 1979, Lincoln Center already had a payroll of $62 million. In 1990 (when manufacturing employment had fallen to 12 percent of the labor force, when tourism had become its leading industry, and when the arts had become an even more potent force in American society) Lincoln Center had become a major player in a multi-billion-dollar sector of the city's economy.

Lincoln Center, like most Broadway hits, went on the road. Los Angeles, Washington, Louisville, Dallas, and other cities produced their own versions. These might involve a concert hall, a repertory theater, or some other players. Frequently, they were little more than pallid groups of official buildings. The location, the staging, the participants, the design, or something else kept them from being more than just arts facilities. Most cities did not have the critical mass of cultural institutions to produce another West Side story.

The Los Angeles Music Center

Los Angeles opened its Music Center 4 years after Lincoln Center. It was built at the top of the hill, at the far end of the Civic Center. At first glance, the Music Center resembles its New York antecedent. As at Lincoln Center, travertine and glass containers flank a public plaza, this time containing both

Los Angeles, 1987. People come to the Music Center by car, park, attend a performance, and never set foot in downtown Los Angeles. *(Alexander Garvin)*

Los Angeles, 1991. The Music Center seen from undeveloped sites in the Bunker Hill Urban Renewal Area that have remained vacant for nearly a quarter of a century and that can provide nothing but parking for the people who drive there. *(Alexander Garvin)*

a fountain and an impressive sculpture by Jacques Lipchitz. Once again, the buildings are differentiated by the design of their exterior colonnades. On one side is the 3250-seat Dorothy Chandler Pavilion; on the other, the Ahmanson Theater and the smaller Mark Taper Forum, together providing another 2850 seats. However, when the center was conceived, there were not enough players to put on a complete show. So, in the middle, separated from these facilities by Hope Street, stands, not an opera house, but the offices of the Water and Power Company.

The location on a hill at the northern end of downtown keeps the Music Center from having a real impact on its surroundings. Topography, traffic, and distance prevent much interaction with the Civic Center to the southeast. The Harbor and Hollywood freeways cut off interaction to the north and east. The substantial hike up Bunker Hill through the vacant blocks of the Urban Renewal Area prevents interchange with the business district to the southwest. Even if the business district were not so far away, there is nothing to interact with because intervening blocks have remained vacant since they were cleared for redevelopment during the 1960s. This may change when the Disney concert facility is completed and the other vacant blocks of Bunker Hill are finally filled in. However, for the first quarter-century of its existence, the Music Center has been a much appreciated island of culture with no effect on the rest of downtown Los Angeles.

The failure to repeat the remarkable impact of New York's arts emporium is not just a matter of location and topography. It is also a matter of conception and design. Angelenos go everywhere by car. Therefore, the Music Center has to be easily accessible by automobile. By building a 2000-car garage beneath the plaza, the Music Center accommodates automobiles that drive off the adjacent Hollywood and Harbor freeways. Once safely parked, these motorists have no reason for going anywhere else.

Lincoln Center had been planned to throw off sparks that would catch fire along Broadway, Columbus, and Amsterdam Avenues, and throughout Manhattan's West Side. One day the Los Angeles Music Center also may throw off sparks. We will find out only when there is something around it that can catch a bit of the fire.

Kennedy Center, Washington, D.C.

Los Angeles is not the only city to demonstrate that performance halls do not always have "natural neighbors," or induce "all sorts of interesting places." Kennedy Center in Washington, D.C., completed in 1971, proves the same point.

When President Eisenhower appointed the District of Columbia Auditorium Commission in 1955, the general presumption was that the capital's cultural center would become one of the (as yet unbuilt) monuments called for by the McMillan Plan. The site most frequently mentioned was on the Mall, opposite the National Gallery. It was taken for the Air and Space Museum. So, in 1957, the Commission recommended a lovely 28-acre site in Foggy Bottom, overlooking the Potomac. The site had the advantage of requiring the condemnation of only a few structures, the demapping of some streets, and the rerouting of a small section of Rock Creek Parkway. However, it was a location on the edge of the city, where its impact would be minimal.[32]

The design, by architect Edward Durrell Stone, has been described by critics as the largest box of Kleenex in the world. It is essentially a rectangular solid, 630 feet long, 300 feet wide, and 100 feet high that contains the opera house, concert hall, two theaters (one large, the other more intimate), the American Film Institute's projection hall, a performing arts library, restaurants, and reception rooms. The base provides parking for 1400 cars, from which the Center's 6100 ticket holders can proceed by elevator to the single 600-foot-long, air-conditioned lobby. They need never even step outside on their way upstairs. Consequently, this $70 million monument, which makes a major contribution to the cultural life of the

Washington, D.C., 1994. The Kennedy Center is too far from surrounding neighborhoods to have much impact. *(Alexander Garvin)*

national capital, makes no impact on anything except possibly the street level of the neighboring Watergate residential complex.

Dallas Arts District

Cultural centers also can shape areas that lie in the path of development. This did not happen in Los Angeles or Washington because their cultural centers were located and designed to be self-contained. Like them, Dallas is creating a cultural center located along a highway on the edge of the business district. But, rather than build an expensive arts emporium, Dallas is creating a 62-acre, mixed-use district to be developed by different landowners for a variety of purposes.[33]

In 1982, after a decade of discussion, the city hired Sasaki Associates to prepare a master plan for a 17-block area at the northeastern edge of the central business district. They proposed a design scheme, a zoning ordinance, a financing strategy, and a management plan for an arts district that left existing streets in place. New buildings for the Dallas Museum of Art and the Dallas Symphony are intermingled with existing institutions such as the cathedral of Santuario de Guadalupe, the Dallas Bar Association, and the Dallas Arts Magnet High School. Other sites have been set aside for later private development as office buildings and retail centers.

The design scheme establishes Flora Street as a linear axis along which to group new buildings. At one end is the Dallas Museum of Art, in the middle the Morton Meyerson Symphony Center, and at the other end a proposed plaza with a fountain. Flora Street is not intended to be a vast City Beautiful mall. It will remain a sidewalk-lined city street that is intersected by other sidewalk-lined city streets.

The Planned Development District Ordinance, approved in 1983, ensures that the district will remain pedestrian in scale and character by specifying building height, setbacks, ground-floor uses, parking, and loading requirements. Land uses on Flora Street, for example, are restricted to shops, restaurants, plazas, and fountains. Street walls cannot exceed 50 feet. The effect of the ordinance can already be seen in the pavilions, terraces, fountains, and sculpture collection that make up the Flora Street front of the 50-story Trammell Crow Center (formerly the LTV Center).

The financing strategy establishes public/private cost sharing guidelines covering the $2.6 billion in expenditures expected by the year 2000. Pursuant to that strategy, Dallas has already issued more than $100 million in general obligation bonds to pay for land acquisition, infrastructure improvements, a 1600-car garage, and new buildings for the Dallas Museum of Art and the Dallas Symphony.

An Arts District Management Association is responsible for planning, implementation, and operations. Civic groups have set up two nonprofit foundations to raise money from the public and provide support for the arts. In addition, the City

Dallas, 1989. The Morton Meyerson Symphony Center is part of an Arts District that aims to intermingle arts facilities with office buildings and retail stores that are all similarly located within the existing street grid. *(Alexander Garvin)*

Council has appointed an arts district coordinator to be a liaison between City Hall, private developers, and arts interests.

The goal of the Dallas Arts District, like that of Lincoln Center, is to attract customers to a location from which they will spill over into the surrounding city and stimulate a desirable market reaction. But the design, unlike Lincoln Center, rejects a separate precinct for arts-related buildings. Instead, it provides a framework that intermixes sites for conventional commercial activity with sites for arts activities. As the district fills in, it will become an increasingly important model for other municipalities that wish to make the arts a regular part of a cityscape that offers activities and attracts customers at times when city streets might otherwise be deserted.

Sports Centers

At the end of the nineteenth century, athletics were an informal activity engaged in by those with enough leisure time. Organized sports such as baseball, football, and basketball were just being invented. As sports grew in popularity, civic leaders wanted sports palaces in order to enhance municipal self-esteem and project an image of being "in the major leagues."

For many citizens, stadiums and arenas bring an improvement in the quality of life. They contribute customers and jobs that spill over into surrounding areas, stimulating property development by businesses interested in capturing this new market. For others (especially those who live and work around sports centers) the increase in traffic, noise, and pollution is unjustifiable.

The first spectator sports facilities were usually financed, built, owned, and operated by professional teams or franchise owners. Today, however, large stadiums are often too expensive to be privately financed. The Miami Dolphins' open-air Joe Robbie Stadium cost $90 million in 1987; the Hubert H. Humphrey Metrodome in Minneapolis cost $75 million in 1983; Riverfront Stadium in Cincinnati cost $44 million in 1970; the Houston Astrodome cost $45 million in 1964. Moreover, franchise owners are usually able to avoid the entrepreneurial problems of developing these expensive structures. The competition for major league teams is so fierce that most city governments are only too happy to offer them publicly developed and financed facilities.[34]

Atlanta, 1991. Atlanta–Fulton County Stadium is surrounded by empty parking fields that are a long way from the city's business district. *(Alexander Garvin)*

Most sports palaces, like cultural centers, are *not* financially self-sufficient. Typical stadium revenues (rentals, concessions, parking, advertising, etc.) may cover operating costs. Even when they are able to earn substantial revenues from rock concerts, sports centers often fail to cover debt service on the bonds that financed their development. Proponents justify subsidizing stadiums and arenas because they bring money to the local economy—many times the money brought by a concert hall or a theater. America's largest cultural center, Lincoln Center, accommodates 12,000 ticket holders. Major league baseball parks seat 40,000 to 50,000; football stadiums 65,000 to 100,000. Visitors to ordinary games spend about $30. Those attending a super bowl stay for 5 days and spend more than $1100. No wonder every city wants a major league team.[35]

For a city to reap the entire potential of this lucrative market, its sports palaces must be conveniently located, accommodate thousands of vehicles, and encourage spectators to go into town before and after the games. If, like Atlanta–Fulton County Stadium, a facility is placed along a highway in a location far from most commercial activities, the city will be unable to profit from the 60,000 fans who come there for a football game.

Arenas and stadiums cover vast territories, especially when they are surrounded by a sea of automobiles. Atlanta–Fulton County Stadium, for example, requires 19.4 acres. Consequently, it is critical to design each facility and its accessory parking in a manner that avoids smothering its surroundings. Buffalo did so by placing Pilot Field within the downtown street system. The idea is not very radical; Roman arenas were sited that way.[36] The only difference is that Pilot Field has to accommodate the spectators plus their cars. The facility itself only provides parking for 2000 cars. The rest of the fans park in the surrounding business district or use mass transit. Thus, they walk through downtown Buffalo on their way to and from a game.

The Los Angeles Coliseum

Los Angeles was one of the first cities to conceive of a sports arena as a device for municipal improvement. Civic leaders were anxious to do something about Exposition Park, a fairground and racetrack in operation since 1872. They felt it was having an undesirable impact on both area residents and adjacent University of Southern California (USC) students. In 1898, they successfully persuaded the state, county, and city jointly to purchase the 90-acre site.[37]

There was no consensus on the site's reuse. The university wanted a sports arena. However, public officials were doubtful that Los Angeles (whose population in 1900 was just 102,000) could generate enough ticket sales to cover debt service on the necessary bonds. For this reason, development of Exposition Park began in 1910 with the Los Angeles County Museum of History, Science, and Art (today the Museum of Natural History).

Los Angeles, 1992. The Coliseum is set back too far from surrounding neighborhoods to affect more than vehicular traffic before and after big games. *(Alexander Garvin)*

Cincinnati, 1970. Pedestrian bridges provide a welcome connection between Riverfront Stadium and the central business district. *(Alexander Garvin)*

In 1920, when Los Angeles had grown to 577,000 people, the city finally decided that there was a sufficient market for a stadium. Even in 1923, when the Los Angeles Coliseum opened, sports events could not attract anywhere near the 76,000 spectators that it could accommodate. Its primary user was the USC football team, the Trojans, which at that time attracted little more than 13,000 spectators.

The Coliseum was enlarged for the 1932 Olympics and remodeled again for the 1984 Olympics. Only in 1946, when the Rams moved from Cleveland, did the stadium finally begin to attract big-league crowds. At one time or another, the Coliseum has been the home stadium for major league football (the Rams, the Chargers, the Raiders) and baseball (the Dodgers). Today, with 93,000 seats, it can accommodate anything from professional football to a papal mass.

Exposition Park also includes the Los Angeles Sports Arena, the California Museum of Science and Industry, the Los Angeles County Natural History Museum, the California Aerospace Museum, the Mitsubishi Imax Theater, the California Museum of Afro-American History, the Multicultural Center, and the Exposition Park Rose Garden. This extraordinary assemblage, a few blocks from the Harbor Freeway, is easily accessible from anywhere in the Los Angeles metropolitan area. It should be a powerful force generating all sorts of interesting activity. Instead, it is an island of separate public structures, 2 miles south of downtown Los Angeles, too far to permit any interaction with the business district and too self-contained to have much impact on USC or the surrounding, deteriorated, low density neighborhoods.

Cincinnati's Riverfront Sports Facilities

During the 1960s, Cincinnati was in the forefront of downtown redevelopment. Civic leaders planned and built multilane highways to bring the growing suburban market downtown and a second-story skywalk network to distribute customers and encourage pedestrian circulation. Unlike other cities that sought a modern, functional business district, Cincinnati's leadership understood that an office district by itself would not provide enough sparkle to revive its downtown. Offices shut down at night and on weekends. Cincinnati's leaders decided on building sports facilities to fill the gap.[38]

The site selected for Cincinnati's 56,000-seat Riverfront Stadium (completed in 1969) and 17,000-seat Riverfront Coliseum (completed in 1973) was the obsolete warehouse and loft manufacturing district along the **Ohio River**. The district's large properties were easy to assemble into sites that were large enough to accommodate the major leagues. Furthermore, the area's increasingly high vacancy rates and low job density minimized relocation. Most important, I-71, the multilane interstate highway that separates the riverfront from the business district, made these sites easily accessible to tens of thousands of fans from outside the city.[39]

The design exploits the city's topography. Because the sports facilities were in the Ohio River floodplain, they had to provide safely for water levels of up to 80 feet. This was accomplished by setting the new sports facilities on a platform above several levels of parking. Because downtown streets were so much higher than the riverfront, the spectator entry level could be directly connected by pedestrian bridges that easily cleared the highway in between.

Nearby downtown parking facilities reduced the number of spaces that had to be built specifically for the stadium and arena. On weekdays stadium and parking structures could be used by office workers, while on weekends stadium-bound cars were a welcome supplement for downtown garage operators. Thus, on Saturdays and Sundays when there is a Cincinnati Reds or Bengals game, cars start pulling into downtown garages by noon. Fans fill the streets on their way to or from the game, patronizing, on their way, downtown shops, restaurants, and bars.

Buffalo, 1991. During its first year of operation, Pilot Field generated $21.7 million in direct and indirect spending in downtown Buffalo and $1.65 million in additional sales and income taxes. *(Alexander Garvin)*

Pilot Field, Buffalo

Buffalo, like so many Rust Belt cities, had been in decline for decades when Mayor James Griffin announced a major effort to build a new downtown stadium. In 1980 he appointed a private sector committee, established a multiyear development timetable, and initiated the market, environmental impact, parking, and traffic studies that public assistance programs required.[40]

Bringing back baseball to Buffalo was more than an attempt at a psychological shot in the arm. It was an economic development project that was intended to recapture recreational spending that had been lost to cities as far away as Toronto, to provide service employment in a city that was in a 10-year period of double-digit unemployment, and to generate additional retail sales and tourist spending.

The mayor had the support of the chamber of commerce, local labor unions, sports fans, and the media. The missing ingredient was a sports team. A baseball team was supplied in 1985 when the Rich family (owner of the Rich Product Corporation, a frozen-foods conglomerate that produces Coffee Rich creamer) purchased a Wichita baseball franchise for $1 million, renamed it the Bisons, and moved it to Buffalo.

Pilot Field and its two garages opened in 1988. It was designed by the HOK Sports Facilities Group and cost $56 million. The money was patched together from a variety of sources: a New York State Urban Development Corporation (UDC) loan, city bonds, federal Urban Development Action Grant (UDAG)-backed revenue bonds, and contributions from the Bisons, the city, county, and state governments. Because its backers hoped to attract a major league team, the design allows for future expansion.

Thus far, Buffalo has lost out to other competitors for major league franchises. Nevertheless, the city continues to reap real benefits from Pilot Field. The Bisons have a payroll of over 900 (mostly part-time) workers from April through September. They attract an average annual paid attendance of 1.2 million. During the first year that Pilot Field was in operation, these fans generated $21.7 million in direct and indirect spending in downtown Buffalo and $1.65 million in additional sales and income taxes. Whether this level of spending can be sustained without a major league team remains to be seen. In the meantime Pilot Field has been providing nighttime and weekend activity that had long been missing from the business district.

Convention Centers

Cities invest in convention centers because they think they are municipal money-making machines. In fact, convention centers make the other palaces for the people seem like small potatoes. During 1983, every 100,000 convention visitors generated between 1100 and 1900 jobs, *plus* $37 million in direct expenditures, *plus* $110 million in indirect expenditures for hotel rooms, food and beverages, services, retail purchases, and transportation, *plus* $15 million in local taxes.

The impact of all this activity and money is dramatic. In Boston alone, of the 8.6 million tourists who visited the city in 1987, 520,000 were convention delegates who spent $576 million.[41]

Like a stadium, a convention center, to be financially successful, needs to attract enough of this international market to pay operating costs and debt service. Convention centers usually collect sufficient fees to meet operating costs, but often cannot cover the debt service. In those cases, government officials try to justify subsidizing debt service out of public funds by estimating the additional tax revenues that otherwise would not be collected. They also enumerate the jobs that have been created, but usually without any dependable estimate of the proportion of those jobs that will actually go to city residents.

Conventions may be an economic bonanza. But this bonanza can only be tapped when, like the Washington State Convention and Trade Center in Seattle, convention facilities are strategically located, appropriately designed, and integrated into the physical structure and economic life of the surrounding city. Convention facilities, like those along the Detroit waterfront, that are separated from the surrounding city and are designed to satisfy visitors' every desire without those visitors setting foot in the rest of the city will never have much beneficial impact. They occupy such large sites that they also remove customers and activity from their periphery, in the process blighting contiguous businesses.

Renaissance Center, Detroit

Detroit's vast visitor complex is located at the southern end of the city along the Detroit River. It includes Veteran's Memorial Hall (1950), 2900-seat Henry and Edsel Ford Auditorium (1955), and the 2.5-million-square-foot Cobo Exhibition Hall and Convention Arena (1960). The pièce de résistance opened in 1977. It is the Renaissance Center, a $350 million complex designed by architect John Portman, including the world's tallest (73-story) hotel, four 39-story towers containing 2.2 million square feet of office space, and a 14-acre, 4-story podium containing additional retail, convention, and parking facilities. During the 1980s the complex was amplified by two additional 21-story office towers, the Joe Louis Arena and the renovated Cobo Hall.[42]

Millions of tourists make use of these facilities. Businessmen profit from the revenues they generate. Labor unions benefit from thousands of jobs that are located there. The city government raises tremendous amounts of tax revenue. The only loser is downtown Detroit.

When Henry Ford II announced Renaissance Center in 1971, Detroit was in trouble. Its population had declined to 1,511,000, a drop of 339,000 since 1950.[43] He rallied the business community, persuading 50 of the city's major firms to invest $1 million each. In addition to this $50 million in equity, Ford obtained $200 million in mortgage financing ($180 million from a consortium of insurance companies and $20 million from Ford Motor Credit Company).

Detroit, 1989. The city's convention and visitor facilities are located along the Detroit River, just far enough away from the rest of downtown Detroit to preclude serious interaction. *(Alexander Garvin)*

The strategy was to allow Detroit's business district to profit from a lucrative tourist and convention business. Renaissance Center's backers selected a site along the riverfront where it could augment Cobo Hall and the other facilities that were already there. More important, the project would also clear 33 acres of blighted property and hook onto Jefferson Avenue, which was being transformed into a dozen-lane traffic artery that connected directly into the interstate highway system.

When Renaissance Center opened in 1977, it was unable to obtain projected rents or levels of occupancy. Planners had overestimated the convention and tourist market that could be attracted to Detroit. Nor were there enough tenants for office space at high rent levels or enough customers to support the vast network of retail outlets. Consequently, revenues would not cover project debt service. The mortgagees chose not to foreclose. They became equity partners of a financially restructured venture in which they also had an active management role.

Meanwhile, the Detroit business district was dying a slow death. Hudson's, the nation's tallest and second-largest department store, closed its 2.1-million-square-foot store on Woodward Avenue. The 18-story Hilton Hotel on Washington Boulevard was shut down. Vacant office space and retail frontage became the norm. By 1990, the city's population would drop to 1,028,000.[44]

Renaissance Center had exacerbated an already bad situation. The project's office space was designed to attract the city's major firms. Consequently, their move from existing downtown buildings drew customers away from the already declining business district. Still worse, the project was separated from downtown Detroit by the traffic on Jefferson Avenue. Downtown Detroit is just too far away for the 16,000

Detroit, 1989. Traffic on Jefferson Avenue separates Renaissance Center from the rest of the business district. *(Alexander Garvin)*

office occupants of Renaissance Center to use downtown stores and restaurants.

Convention visitors have no reason to leave Renaissance Center. They come from the airport along convenient modern highways. Once safely inside, they are unlikely to risk a visit downtown. Cobo Hall and every other place they might need to go is happily isolated between the Detroit River and Jefferson Avenue.

In an attempt to remedy the situation, the project's administrators hired real estate consultants who recommended eliminating design and marketing flaws. Retail facilities became more appropriate to the project's tenantry and the hotel began to operate more successfully. The city tried to tie Renaissance Center to the rest of town by building an elevated "people-mover" transit line circling the central business district and connecting Cobo Hall and Renaissance Center with the rest of downtown Detroit. But the damage could not be undone. From the time that Renaissance Center opened, the only place that developers have been willing to erect new buildings is directly opposite. Meanwhile, downtown firms have continued to move away, leaving downtown Detroit further in need of activity.

Hynes Convention Center, Boston

A modern convention center requires a single-level exhibition hall of several acres. Creating such a vast space requires removing huge chunks of downtown land and with it huge numbers of people. The result is curiously paradoxical. Conventions bring economic activity to the city while convention centers often remove it from the city streets. Thus, one must be careful to prevent the edges of any convention center from reducing pedestrian activity and thereby having a blighting impact on surrounding areas.

Boston tried to solve the problem by erecting its John Hynes Civic Auditorium, completed in 1965, on top of the Massachusetts Turnpike and the Boston & Albany Railroad. The auditorium, along with Prudential Center, were part of a clever plan that covered 28 acres of railroad yards while providing a right-of-way for the turnpike. The new auditorium was a nondescript, multipurpose facility used for trade shows, concerts, major assemblies, and virtually any other public purpose requiring large amounts of space. It had a chilling effect on Boylston Street because its 500-foot frontage and blank walls set back 90 feet from the sidewalk removed all the customers from one side of the street.[45]

As time passed, it became clear that Boston needed a bigger convention hall. In 1982, the state legislature established the Massachusetts Convention Center Authority, which worked with the Boston Redevelopment Authority to expand and remodel the building on Boylston Street. The renamed Hynes Convention Center, which reopened in 1988, is an 850,000-square-foot structure with 450,000 square feet of rentable space.

The $234 million expansion, designed by Kallman, McKinnel, and Knowles (the architects who won the competi-

Boston 1994. Hynes Convention Center provided a 500-foot arcade without stores or restaurants, thereby reducing pedestrian activity in this section of Boyleston Street. *(Alexander Garvin)*

tion for the Boston City Hall), pasted an L-shaped addition on the Boylston Street and Prudential Center sides of the building and added additional ballroom and exhibition space on top of the existing structure. The handsome granite façade that emerged along Boylston Street was intended to "reconstitute" commercial and institutional activity along the street. It consists of a 500-foot arcade ending with a glass entrance canopy adjacent to Prudential Center. This monumental loggia is mere decoration for, unlike the Rue de Rivoli in Paris, there are no stores or additional building entrances within the arcade. Consequently, pedestrians and retail customers still have no reason to walk along that side of the street.

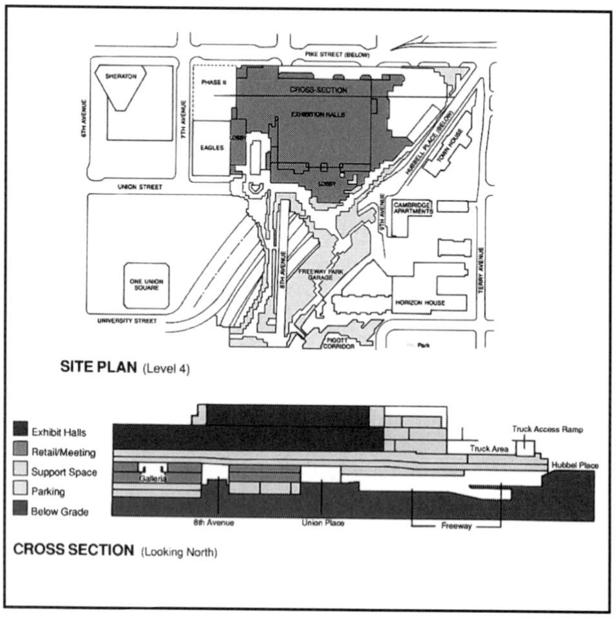

Seattle, 1989. Site plan and cross section showing the vehicular and pedestrian arteries that pass through the Washington State Convention and Trade Center. *(Courtesy of ULI—Urban Land Institute)*

Washington State Convention and Trade Center, Seattle

The enormous size of convention centers, like Detroit's, often condemns them to fringe locations where they become barriers to street traffic, deadening rather than generating activity. The Washington State Convention and Trade Center demonstrates how intelligent planning can transform such behemoths into a force for municipal improvement. Not only is the Convention Center located right in downtown Seattle where it can affect its surroundings, it is designed to bring together once separated sections of the city.[46]

Downtown Seattle is built on a steep, hilly site overlooking Elliott Bay. It is cut off from the eastern sections of the city by an interstate highway that was completed in 1965. Ever since, civic leaders have sought to reconnect both sides of town by bridging the highway. Their first effort, completed in 1976 and expanded in 1984, was the delightful Freeway Park. To that, in 1988, they added nearly 1 million square feet of exhibit halls,

Seattle, 1990. Visitors to the Washington State Convention and Trade Center stay at downtown hotels, patronize nearby restaurants, and use local streets and sidewalks to go to and from its events. *(Alexander Garvin)*

meeting rooms, retailing, parking, and support facilities of the Convention and Trade Center.

The Washington State Convention and Trade Center was developed by a public corporation created by the state legislature in 1982 and designed by a team of architects led by the Seattle architectural firm TRA. The total development cost was $157 million, of which $121 million came from state general obligation bonds, $1 million from the City of Seattle, and most of the rest from private funds. Its operations are paid primarily by a tax on hotel rooms in Seattle and surrounding King County.

The Convention Center bridges the highway and encompasses within itself two city streets, ramps on and off the highway, and a variety of landscaped sitting areas and pedestrian paths. It supplies the hotels, restaurants, and retail stores on surrounding blocks with customers, while they supply conventioneers with everything that is missing from the center itself. As a result, instead of deadening activity along its edges, the Convention Center fills the vacuum created by the highway, attracts pedestrian and vehicular traffic, uses them to tie together different sections of the city, and makes it essential for them to spill over onto nearby commercial streets for parking, restaurants, hotels, and entertainment.

From an economic perspective both the Detroit and the Seattle combination of convention center, hotels, restaurants, and retail stores is desirable. In both cases vast facilities draw a substantial convention and visitor market downtown, bringing with them hundreds of millions of dollars in expenditures that would not otherwise be made in those cities. From an urban planning perspective, however, Seattle's facility has become a major force for municipal vitality while Detroit's has drawn away the city's lifeblood.

Ingredients of Success

Cities continue to invest in ever more monumental palaces for the people because they correctly conceive of them as magnets attracting a lucrative market that can generate the jobs and taxes they desperately need. As these facilities grow larger and more expensive, their increasing appetite for government subsidies makes it important to understand the requirements for their success. After all, why should a city subsidize something that does not produce sufficient benefits?

A successful civic, cultural, sports, or convention center must attract a market that would otherwise not be there and be located and designed in a manner that forces that market to interact with the rest of the city. The financing, development, and management issues are somewhat different from profit-motivated private ventures because so many of these facilities may not be immediately self-supporting. All the more reason to demand that public officials and the development agencies established to build and manage them consider and plan for the private-market reactions these public facilities generate.

Market

In creating palaces for the people, civic leaders must determine the size and character of the market that will be attracted. How much will that market spend and on what? During what periods of time will it be there? What sorts of support services and activities will it require? Most important, how can the rest of the city profit from the people attracted to that particular facility? If these questions are not answered, cities will not be able to plan intelligently for the spillover of that market and, consequently, will not be able to take public actions that will generate desirable private-sector reactions.

For planning purposes, the most important characteristic of any market is its source. Attracting conventioneers from out of town clearly results in a net addition to the local economy. Attracting sports fans who would otherwise be attending games in other parts of the region is also a net plus. Most civic centers, on the other hand, only move an existing market from one part of the city to another.

Only when a market is sufficiently large will it produce any reaction from surrounding property owners. A single auditorium could never have generated the changes that Lincoln Center brought to the West Side of Manhattan; just as a single sports arena could not have brought enough weekend customers to enliven downtown Cincinnati. In every instance there is a critical mass without which little will change.

The most important consideration in accommodating any of these markets is *not* supplying everything within the planned facility. If every concertgoer can obtain a meal, a snack, a drink, or a souvenir right there, there is no reason to go anywhere else. Similarly, if a convention center includes enough hotel rooms to satisfy every conventioneer, there will be no market spillover to surrounding properties. That is why, from the very beginning, the Renaissance Center was guaranteed to flop, while the Seattle Convention Center was bound to generate activity in surrounding areas.

Location

Palaces for the people need to be easily accessible to enormous numbers of users, to the people who work there, and to the vehicles that deliver the goods and services that they provide. That is why cultural centers, stadiums, and convention centers are located along major highways.

Highway access alone is not enough. Vehicles need to be able to enter and exit quickly and easily during peak periods. Nearby city streets and parking lots all contribute to making Cincinnati's riverfront sports facilities and the Seattle Convention Center easily accessible. Peak period traffic at Kennedy Center and Atlanta–Fulton County Stadium, on the other hand, is largely dependent on highway access ramps. As a result, when everybody leaves there is serious congestion.

There also needs to be sufficient parking and loading space, although not entirely supplied on site. Pilot Field achieves this by developing a reciprocal relationship with existing facilities in downtown Buffalo; Lincoln Center by depending on surrounding blocks of the Upper West Side. The sea of parking around Atlanta–Fulton County Stadium and the Los Angeles Coliseum only further isolates them from the surrounding city.

For planning purposes, the most important characteristic of any location is its periphery. Not only are the Los Angeles Civic and Music Centers located at the far end of the central business district, too far away to have much effect on downtown life, they are cut off from their surroundings on two sides by freeways. The Renaissance Center is similarly cut off from downtown Detroit by Jefferson Avenue.

Thus, the key to successfully locating palaces for the people lies in artfully combining convenient highway access with a site in the midst of an existing downtown business district and then encouraging a mutually reinforcing relationship with that district.

Design

Designing successful public facilities is largely a matter of dimensions and arrangement of components. The importance of dimensions cannot be overemphasized. The distances across the plaza in Cleveland's Group Plan made interaction among the buildings difficult. The length of Memorial Plaza in St. Louis precluded the development of a critical mass of customers affecting its surroundings. These civic centers create impressive public open spaces. However, for these spaces to come alive, they require vast crowds that are unlikely to come simply to renew a driver's license or to obtain a building permit.

The size of the facility itself is also critical. Convention centers, stadiums, and their parking facilities cover acres of land, in the process removing the customers who previously patronized the facilities and institutions that remain along their periphery. In many cases the market that is lost cannot be replaced by sports fans or conventioneers. Cincinnati's riverfront sports facilities deal with this problem by placing the parking underneath. This parking serves the business district when the stadiums are not in use. Seattle accommodates the large footprint required by its convention center by placing it over a highway, which itself had removed the customers that previously had been on the site.

The Washington State Convention and Trade Center also illustrates the importance of relationship among traffic arteries, vehicular storage, exhibition halls, meeting rooms, and support services for visitors. The design specifically incorporates an interstate highway and its access ramps, city streets and their access ramps, and pedestrian walkways in a manner that prevents convention center traffic from interfering with other vehicular and pedestrian circulation, even during those times that downtown traffic is at its most intense.

Financing

Neither civic nor cultural centers make any pretense of being self-financing. Federal buildings are paid for by Congressional appropriation. State and municipal buildings are usually financed by general obligation bonds, whose debt service is paid from tax revenues. Museums, concert halls, theaters, opera houses, and other cultural institutions are usually paid for through charitable donations.

Financing, however, is a major issue in the case of sports and convention centers. In most instances they are financed by revenue bonds. Since these facilities are occupied by revenue-generating businesses, these revenues should be adequate to cover operating costs and debt service on the bonds. Too often when the facility is completed, it cannot generate sufficient revenues to cover debt service. As a result, municipal governments use general tax revenues to make up the difference.

No municipality starts out by promising to subsidize these profit-making businesses. They are lured into it by the promise of additional employment and taxes. Indeed, the indirect expenditures by conventioneers on food, hotel rooms, transportation, and retail purchases may generate the taxes needed to subsidize these convention facilities. Only when that proves to be the case are government subsidies justified.

Entrepreneurship

Planning prescriptions are never implemented spontaneously. They require a private or public entrepreneur. Sometimes, entrepreneurship is supplied by business leaders. Buffalo's Pilot Field would not have been built without the backing of the Rich Product Corporation, nor Detroit's Renaissance Center without Henry Ford II and the 50 major corporations that supported him.

The difficulty with depending on corporate entrepreneurship is that it usually confuses financial self-sufficiency with urbanistic success. Pilot Field may generate enough revenues to cover operating costs and debt service. Its contribution to the city, however, comes from attracting a market that would not otherwise be there and accommodating that market in a manner that forces consumers to spill over into downtown Buffalo, where they inevitably spend large amounts of money. The Renaissance Center may have been a financial failure, but its disastrous effect on downtown Detroit has nothing to do with that financial failure. That came about because its very existence skimmed the cream off the downtown office market, while its location and design ensured that its convention business had little or no effect on the rest of the city.

Some of the most successful public facilities are the product of public, rather than private, entrepreneurship. Without the political acumen of Senator McMillan or the persuasiveness of Daniel Burnham, the Mall in Washington, D.C., would be a very different place.

Just as private developers often confuse financial feasibility with desirability, public entrepreneurs often confuse public support with good planning. That is one reason that the creators of the St. Louis and Los Angeles Civic Centers were able to obtain public support and funding for their plans without understanding that the monumental spaces they created produced hollow cores rather than vibrant contributors to the economy and character of the surrounding business district.

Robert Moses never had the luxury of relying on easy public acceptance of Lincoln Center. From the day he first announced this project, he had to fight with citizen organizations, community groups, and skeptical politicians. They forced him to adjust and readjust his proposal until it took into account some of the interests they represented. The same thing happened in Buffalo after Mayor Griffin proposed building Pilot Field. He had to adjust the project to the demands for union workers, minority employment and contracting, cheap replacement parking, and sensitive relocation practices.

The process of public review forced Moses and Griffin to take into consideration conflicting demands and to broaden their view of the public interest. As a result, Lincoln Center and Pilot Field were altered until they each became feasible both financially and politically. More important, they also were altered to accommodate some of the interests of surrounding communities.

Time

Civic, cultural, sports, and convention centers are all dependent on the patronage of large numbers of people. The way they move through these facilities is critical. No city will benefit if people simply park their car, go about their business, and return home. The trick is to get visitors to spend some time in town on their way to and from their destination. The Boston Government Center and the Dallas Arts Center accomplish this by mixing commercial office buildings with sites designated for government or cultural activity. Pilot Field and the Seattle Convention Center force their customers into the city by failing to supply all their needs within the facility itself. Whichever strategy is adopted, the result is to prolong the visit and force visitors to interact with the rest of town during their stay.

The most important benefit that is brought by any of the palaces for the people is activity during those times that the city would otherwise be without it. Lincoln Center brings people to Manhattan's West Side at night and on weekends. Cincinnati's riverfront sports facilities bring additional customers to that city's business district at times when it would otherwise be empty.

Most stadiums and convention centers bring a mass of customers that is large enough to generate a market reaction if those customers spill over into the rest of town. But civic and cultural centers can only achieve this when they include enough individual buildings to aggregate a similar critical mass of customers. In most cases this takes many years. It was three decades before Cleveland's civic center included enough government buildings to develop this critical mass, and half a century in St. Louis. In the interim neither city could benefit from a critical mass of customers. By the time each civic center had been completed it had become obvious that faulty design would preclude the necessary critical mass from ever developing. The Dallas Arts Center, on the other hand, is specifically designed so that there is no need to wait decades before its effects are felt. As buildings fill in the master development plan, they will generate increasing spillover demand.

Palaces for the People as a Planning Strategy

Civic, cultural, sports, and convention centers are magnets that attract customers from the surrounding metropolitan area and beyond. But, as long as they continue to be viewed as projects whose desirability is measured only in terms of financial and political feasibility, cities across the nation will miss the opportunity of profiting from the market they can attract.

Conventional planning procedures will never ensure that public facilities will enrich the cities that surround them. Nor will the parochial efforts of arts organizations, sports enthusiasts, the tourist industry, or local chambers of commerce. The federal government, however, can do so by providing a mechanism that will encourage civic leaders to create municipal facilities—such as the Lincoln Center, Pilot Field, and the Washington State Convention and Trade Center—that have an interdependent relationship with their environs. The simplest mechanism is a monetary incentive. Unfortunately, the federal government currently provides such an incentive for public facilities conceived without any relationship to their surroundings. It subsidizes such projects by exempting from federal income tax the interest on bonds issued to finance them. Tax exemption should not be used to sap the lifeblood from existing cities. It should be available only to those projects that genuinely will improve our cities.

To remedy this situation, I propose a Public Facilities District Act, which would permit tax-exempt financing only for those projects that were a part of a public facilities district that extended 1000 feet beyond the periphery of the buildings themselves. Thus, tax-exempt bonds could only be issued for whole districts, not independent facilities. No more than 75 percent of bond proceeds could be allocated to public facilities. The rest would be set aside for other properties within the district.

The money for the surrounding district would take the form of a mortgage fund available to its property owners. Its use would be restricted to rehabilitation or new construction, not land acquisition. Otherwise the availability of these funds would artificially increase the market price for existing property. Since the interest payments on the bonds would be tax-exempt, this money could be lent at below-market rates of interest, thereby making projects feasible that otherwise might not be self-sustaining.

A board of directors appointed by the mayor would be responsible for administration of the district and the bond proceeds. One quarter of its members would have to be owners of businesses (but not property) located within the district. Another quarter would have to be representatives of those fields affected by the facility itself (e.g., sports, cultural institutions, tourism). The rest would only have to be residents of the surrounding city.

Public financing that is directed to a district rather than a project, and a board of directors that is composed in part of district business owners will make it unlikely that any facility will proceed unless it is of benefit to the surrounding area. In other words, the only public actions (investment in public facilities) that would take place would be those that generate a desirable market reaction (renovation or construction on surrounding properties).

Notes

1. *City Document #13, Thirty-seventh Annual Report of the Trustees of the Public Library,* Boston, 1888, p. 6.
2. Historical and statistical information on the Chicago Fair is derived from James Gilbert, *Perfect Cities, Chicago's Utopias of 1893,* University of Chicago Press, Chicago, 1991; R. Reid Badger, *The Great American Fair,* Nelson Hall, Chicago, 1979; Stanley Appelbaum, *The Chicago World's Fair of 1893,* Dover, New York, 1980; William H. Wilson, *The City Beautiful Movement,* Johns Hopkins University Press, Baltimore, 1989, pp. 53–74; Thomas S. Hines, *Burnham of Chicago,* Oxford University Press, New York, 1974, pp. 73–138; Leland M. Roth, *McKim, Mead & White, Architects,* Harper & Row, New York, 1983, pp. 174–179; and Laura Wood Roper, *FLO—A Biography of Frederick Law Olmsted,* Johns Hopkins University Press, Baltimore, 1973, pp. 425–433 and 444–450.
3. The 1890 Census reported a total population of 62, 947,714. See U.S. Dept. of Commerce, Bureau of the Census: *Statistical Abstract of the United States 1989,* Washington, D.C.
4. Henry Codman, John Wellborn Root, Charles Follen McKim, and Augustus St. Gaudens also played major roles in determining the shape of the Fair. Codman, one of Olmsted's partners, accompanied him on his first trip for the Exposition Corporation and continued to share management responsibilities until his sudden death at the age of 29, several months before the Fair opened. Olmsted, Codman, Burnham, and Root met regularly for over a year, during which Root acted as a sort of graphic stenographer recording their ideas. Root died equally suddenly in early 1891, 2 years before the Fair opened. Burnham never got over the loss. Perhaps this led him, acting as the exposition's Director of Works, to consider McKim his right-hand man during the later stages of the Fair's development. St. Gaudens was responsible for the coordination of the Fair's opulent sculptural decoration and, thus, made a major contribution to its distinctive appearance.
5. Henry Adams, *The Education of Henry Adams,* Boston, 1918, p. 343.
6. The major exception was the Transportation Building designed by Adler and Sullivan.
7. Charles Mulford Robinson first used the phrase "City Beautiful" in 1899 in an article he wrote for the *Atlantic Monthly.* This is one reason that William H. Wilson argues that the City Beautiful movement did not originate with the Chicago Fair (op. cit., pp. 64–65 and 70–71). However, the Chicago Fair surely popularized many of the concepts and esthetic devices that later became known as the "City Beautiful."
8. U.S. Dept. of Commerce, Bureau of the Census, *Statistical Abstract of the United States 1989,* pp. 267 and 294.
9. Historical and statistical information on the L'Enfant Plan is derived from John W. Reps, *Monumental Washington,* Princeton University Press, Princeton, 1967; Frederick Gutheim (consultant), *Worthy of the Nation,* National Capitol Planning Commission, Washington, D.C., 1977; Pamela Scott, "This Vast Empire," pp. 37–60 in *The Mall in Washington 1791–1991,* Richard Longstreth (editor), National Gallery, Washington, D.C., 1991; and Christopher Tunnard, *The Modern American City,* Van Nostrand, Princeton, 1968, pp. 53–54.
10. Frederick Law Olmsted, Jr., was in his early twenties when his father's firm began work on the Chicago Fair. Not only was he familiar with its initial planning and design, he spent one summer working as an aide-de-camp to the superintendent of construction, and was later to say that it was one of the three most stimulating experiences of his professional life (Roper, op. cit., p. 431).
11. Historical and statistical information on the McMillan Plan is derived from Reps, op. cit., pp. 71–157; Gutheim (consultant), op. cit., pp. 111–136; Thomas S. Hines, op. cit., pp. 139–157; Leland M. Roth, op. cit., pp. 251–259; and David C. Streatfield, "The Olmsteds and the Landscape of the Mall," pp. 117–141 in *The Mall in Washington 1791–1991,* Richard Longstreth (editor), National Gallery, Washington, D.C., 1991.
12. Charles Moore, *The Life and Times of Charles McKim,* Houghton Mifflin Co., Boston, 1929, p. 194 (quoted in Reps, op. cit., p. 97).
13. Roth, op. cit., p. 254.
14. This Gothic "obstruction" (never referred to in Moore's text) was carefully eliminated from every drawing and model of the proposed Mall.
15. Herbert B. Briggs, "Municipal Inprovement, Cleveland," *The Inland Architect and News Record,* 34 (August 1899), pp. 4–5 (quoted in Hines, op. cit., note 5, p. 160).
16. Historical and statistical information on the Group Plan is derived from Daniel Burnham, John Carrère, and Arnold Brunner, *Report of the Group Plan of the Public Buildings of the City of Cleveland, Ohio,* Board of Supervision for Public Buildings and Ground, Cleveland, 1903; Holly M. Rarick, *Progressive Vision: The Planning of Downtown Cleveland 1903–1930,* The Cleveland Museum of Art, Cleveland, 1986; and Hines, op. cit., pp. 158–173.
17. The Federal Building and Post Office were completed in 1911, the Cuyahoga County Court House in 1913, City Hall in 1916, the Cleveland Public Library in 1925, the Public Auditorium, Music Hall, and Convention Center in 1927, and the Board of Education Building in 1930.
18. Historical and statistical information on Memorial Plaza is derived from The Civic League of St. Louis, *A City Plan for St. Louis,* St. Louis, 1907; Harland Bartholomew, *Comprehensive City Plan—St. Louis, Missouri,* St. Louis, 1947; and George McCue, *The Building Art in St. Louis,* St Louis Chapter of the American Institute of Architects, Knight, St. Louis, 1981.
19. Historical and statistical information on the Los Angeles Civic Center is derived from Robert M. Fogelson, *The Fragmented Metropolis—Los Angeles 1850–1930,* Harvard University Press, Cambridge, 1967, pp. 262–271 and Paul Gleye, *The Architecture of Los Angeles,* Rosebud Books, Knapp, Los Angeles, 1981, pp. 102–104.
20. Historical and statistical information on the Boston Government Center is derived from Walter Muir Whitehill, *Boston—A Topographical History,* Harvard University Press, Cambridge, 1968, pp. 200–217; Rachelle I. Levitt (editor), *Cities Reborn,* Urban Land Institute, Washington, D.C., 1987, pp. 9–53; and Donlyn Lyndon, *The City Observed: Boston,* Vintage Books, Random House, New York, 1987, pp. 32–42.
21. Although the Brooklyn Academy of Music, erected in 1908, includes four performance halls, it does not include the variety of arts institutions that characterize a true cultural center.
22. Real Estate Board of New York, Inc., *Office Building Construction Manhattan 1947–1967,* New York, 1968, p. 1.
23. *The City of New York Official Directory* (*1946 and 1956*), The City

Record, New York, 1946 and 1956, p. 8.

24. The southern part of the West Side, known as San Juan Hill, was the last of a series of nineteenth-century African-American neighborhoods to be established prior to Harlem. It had been named after the well-known battle in the Spanish American War in parody of the racial conflicts that took place on the slopes leading to 60th Street.
25. Historical and statistical information on Lincoln Center is derived from New York City Department of City Planning, *Transcript of Public Hearing before the Planning Commission,* New York, September 11, 1957; Edgar Young, *Lincoln Center: The Building of an Institution,* New York University Press, New York, 1980; *Community Development Program Progress Report, 1968,* New York City Housing & Development Administration, New York, 1968; and Hart, Krivatsy & Stubee, *Lincoln Square Community Action Planning Program,* Lincoln Square Community Council and New York City Department of City Planning, New York, 1970; and Robert Moses, *Public Works: A Dangerous Trade,* McGraw-Hill, New York, 1970, pp. 519–533.
26. Officially reported statistics on these projects can be found in *Community Development Program Progress Report, 1968.* However, like all official reports, it undercounts the number of relocatees because it included only those tenants on the site at the time of title vesting. A large number of residents vacate during the time between a redevelopment project is announced and the court finally approves condemnation.
27. The owner of Carnegie Hall intended to tear it down and build a more profitable office tower. His plans were upset when violinist Isaac Stern organized a movement to save Carnegie Hall. By then the Philharmonic had made its commitment to Lincoln Center.
28. *New York Times,* July 29, 1958, p. 50.
29. New York City Department of City Planning, *Transcripts of Public Hearing before the Planning Commission,* New York City, September 11, 1957, p. 24, quoting Harris L. Present, Chairman of the New York City Council on Housing Relocation Practices.
30. Jane Jacobs, speech given at the New School, April 20, 1958.
31. The Assessed Value of Tax Blocks 1115-1118 (62d to 66th Streets, Columbus Avenue to Central Park West) was $25.6 million in 1950. By 1990 it was $215 million. Source: Bureau of Real Property Assessment, Department of Finance, New York City.
32. Historical and statistical information on Kennedy Center is derived from Brendan Gill, *John F. Kennedy Center for the Performing Arts,* Harry N. Abrams, New York, 1981, pp. 23–32.
33. Historical and statistical information on the Dallas Arts District is derived from The Arts District Associations, "Dallas Arts District—Fact Sheet," Dallas, May 1985, and "Dallas Arts District—Project Summary," Dallas, April 1986.
34. David C. Peterson, *Convention Centers, Stadiums, and Arenas,* Urban Land Institute, Washington, D.C., 1989, pp. 45–48, 98–100, 111–113, and 117–119.
35. Ibid., p. 5.
36. The Arena of Nimes seated 21,000; the Colosseum in Rome, more than 50,000.
37. Historical and statistical information on the Los Angeles Coliseum is derived from David Gebhard and Robert Winter, *Architecture in Los Angeles,* Gibbs M. Smith, Layton, Utah, 1985, p. 257, and David C. Petersen, op. cit., pp. 101–104.
38. Historical and statistical information on the Cincinnati's riverfront sports facilities is derived from The Architectural Foundation of Cincinnati, *Architecture and Construction in Cincinnati,* C. J. Krehbiel, Cincinnati, 1987, pp. 148–149, and David C. Petersen, op. cit., pp. 111–113.
39. At that time there was little interest in the preservation of the mercantile history of Cincinnati and no experience with the waterfront festival marketplace.
40. Historical and statistical information on Pilot Field is derived from Charles F. Rosenow (President, Buffalo Development Companies), *Presentation to the 1991 ICMA Sports & Events Management Conference,* April 10, 1991.
41. International Association of Convention and Visitors Bureaus.
42. Historical and statistical information on Renaissance Center is derived from Louis G. Redstone, *The New Downtowns,* McGraw-Hill, New York, 1976, pp. 130–137; Carla Crane (editor), *Detroit... Today,* Urban Land Institute, Washington, D.C., 1977, pp. 49–59; Meyer and McElroy (editors), *Detroit Architecture,* Wayne State University Press, Detroit, 1980; and Stephen A. Horn, "Detroit's Renaissance Center—Redevelopment Rescues City Symbol," *Urban Land,* Urban Land Institute, Washington, D.C., July 1987, p. 6–11.
43. U.S. Dept. of Commerce Bureau of the Census, *Statistical Abstract of the United States 1978,* Washington, D.C., 1978, p. 24.
44. U.S. Dept. of Commerce Bureau of the Census, *Statistical Abstract of the United States 1991,* Washington, D.C., 1991, p. 34.
45. Historical and statistical information on Hynes Convention Center is derived from "Civil Center," *Progressive Architecture,* May 1989, pp. 65–77, and David C. Petersen, op. cit., pp. 70–73.
46. Historical and statistical information on the Washington State Convention and Trade Center is derived from the Urban Land Institute, "Washington State Convention and Trade Center," *Project Reference File,* vol. 19, no. 10, the Urban Land Institute, Washington, D.C., April–June 1989; "Only Connect," *Architectural Record,* February 1989, pp. 112–117; and David C. Petersen, op. cit., pp. 77–79.

5

Shopping Centers

Baltimore, 1981. Harborplace. *(Alexander Garvin)*

People often measure the health of a city by the condition of its commercial areas. They believe that vacant and boarded-up stores indicate a withering economy while busy shopping streets reveal a prosperous municipality. Politicians and local officials are particularly sensitive to this indicator because it means changes in the tax base and, therefore, in the ability to pay for government services and jobs. Their most frequent response is to offer land and financing for new shopping facilities because, like sports stadia, cultural facilities, and convention centers, they attract throngs of people who spend large sums of money. Furthermore, these customers come at times when other commercial activity is less significant, bringing 24-hour vitality to streets, sidewalks, and parking facilities that would otherwise be empty and unsafe.

Two types of shopping facilities have been used to revive commercial districts: the shopping mall and the marketplace. Both are as old as retailing itself. The only difference is that in a mall, shopping takes place in a structure protected from the surrounding environment, while the marketplace sprawls in the open air.

In most cases consumers choose among facilities that compete within the same trade area. Consequently, public assistance to one facility produces neither new spending nor new jobs. It simply moves them from one location to another, favoring one group of businesses over another. The justification for such favoritism can only be that it generates other public benefits. Retail activity may be more appropriate in one location because the infrastructure in that part of town may be underutilized. It may generate customers for nearby facilities that otherwise would not be able to survive. The noise and traffic may not be welcome elsewhere. All too frequently, however, these projects divert customers from other commercial districts, causing vacancies and deterioration.

If we are to improve our cities we need to avoid public investment in malls and marketplaces whose success is detrimental to other parts of town. One way is to analyze the impact of government assistance on commercial districts that do not receive subsidies prior to making any major public investment. Another is to earmark the revenues earned from an investment in one retail project for the benefit of other districts that would not otherwise have profited from the investment. Then we can get beyond the identification of that venture's projected retail sales, jobs, and tax proceeds and concentrate instead on strategies for the improvement of the entire city.

London, 1985. Burlington Arcade completed in 1819—one of the earliest retail shopping arcades. *(Alexander Garvin)*

City Shopping Arcades

It is difficult for contemporary readers to imagine, but at the start of the nineteenth century, sizable sections of the world's largest cities were without sewers, sidewalks, or paving. Horses, delivery carts, carriages, and other traffic made streets an inconvenient and sometimes impossible place for shopping. Removing retail activity from city streets was a good way of providing customers with an environment unimpeded by competition from other activity or by the vagaries of climate. There they would be free to examine goods and decide what to purchase.

Like Trajan's Market in Rome and the bazaars of Isfahan, the *galleries, passages,* and *arcades* erected during the first decades of the nineteenth century were an attempt to provide the consumer with precisely this sort of refuge. Seen from above, these early shopping arcades appear to be long, narrow buildings connecting existing streets. On the inside, they are essentially bright, skylit interior walks, flanked with stores.[1]

The contemporary air-conditioned shopping mall is a response to the same phenomenon. Our streets may be paved, sewered, and lined with sidewalks; but they are obstructed by trucks, buses, and automobiles filling the air with noise and pollutants. Often there is nowhere to park and no way to stroll along the street to compare goods and prices. As a result, developers provide structured parking that leads directly to shopping malls where goods can be purchased in an environment free from the noise, foul air, and obstructions of the city street.

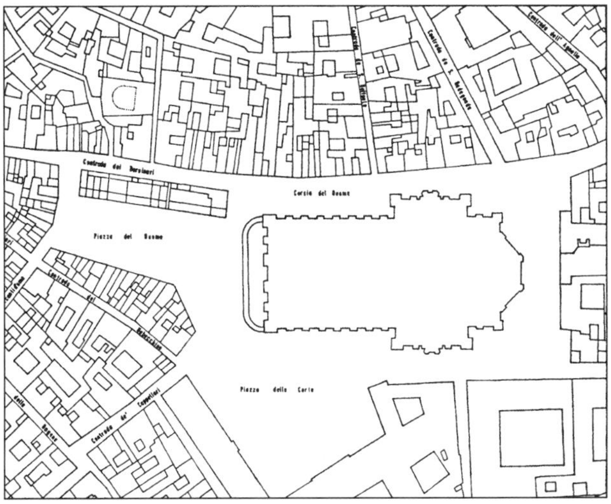

Milan, 1850. Plan of the area around the cathedral prior to redevelopment. *(From Johann Friedrich Geist, Arcades, MIT Press, Cambridge, Mass., 1982)*

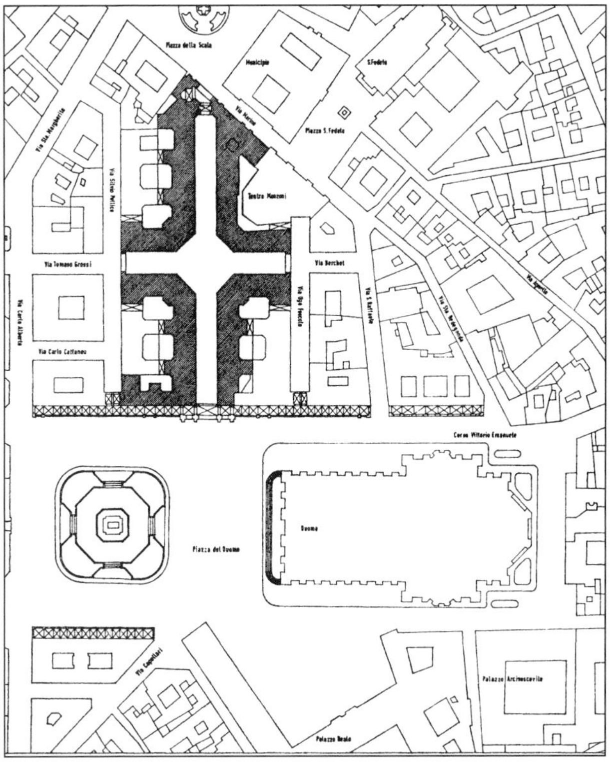

Milan, 1900. Plan of the area around the cathedral after redevelopment. *(From Johann Friedrich Geist, Arcades, MIT Press, Cambridge, Mass., 1982)*

The Galleria, Milan

The world's most famous shopping arcade, Milan's Galleria Vittorio Emanuele II, is an excellent example of how to use a shopping facility as the centerpiece of a municipal improvement scheme. The ostensible reason for this project was to commemorate the struggle for Italian independence, specifically the victory by the French and Sardinians led by King Victor Emmanuel over Austria at the battle of Magenta in 1859.[2] In fact, the project was really intended to create a major, public, open space in the center of the city, a public setting for the Duomo (Cathedral of Milan), a network of new streets wide enough to accommodate heavy traffic, and a connection between the new Cathedral Square and the piazza in front of a similarly important institution, the Scala Opera.

A royal decree in 1860 authorized a lottery, whose profits were supposed to pay for the project. Simultaneously, the city held a design competition that attracted 220 submissions, none of which was accepted. Instead, an 11-member commission was appointed to find a better scheme. The commission held another competition won by Giuseppe Mengoni, an architect from Bologna.[3]

Two problems remained: public opposition and financing. People protested the destruction of six acres in the middle of old Milan. One of the most vocal opponents was the newspaper *Pungolo,* whose offices were in a building scheduled for demolition. In those days preservationists usually failed to stop public improvement projects. Financing was the more serious obstacle because the lottery had only raised 1 million of the 15 million lira required for demolition and construction. So, the government of Milan sought assistance from the private sector.

In 1864, the city entered into an agreement with an English firm, the City of Milan Improvement Company, Ltd., to finance and build what would become the city's central tourist attraction. In exchange the developers were promised a 5 percent return on their 16 million lira investment.

The Galleria Vittorio Emanuele was opened to the public in 1867. It is cruciform in shape and has a four-story interior façade concealing what is really a seven-story building containing 1260 rooms. The two arms, 645 and 345 feet long respectively, are covered with a glass vault that becomes a glass dome at the crossing. The ground level and mezzanine are filled with shops, cafés, and restaurants. The next level

Milan, 1975. Pedestrians protected from the weather walk through the Galleria, sometimes making purchases or stopping for coffee, on their way to and from nearby sections of the city. *(Alexander Purves)*

Cleveland, 1983. Old Arcade completed in 1890 is still functioning as an attractive retail emporium set apart from the noise, fumes, and traffic of local streets. *(Alexander Garvin)*

consists of offices and studios, while the top four floors are residential.

The Galleria is no narrow pedestrian passage accommodating retail trade along a connection between streets. It is an entire district, built to a scale that even Caesar would have found impressive. Nor is the Galleria intended to serve the needs of a particular class of customers or of a specific residential neighborhood. It is intended to serve the complex needs of the vast numbers of people who crowd their way through downtown Milan. More than a century after it was completed, the Galleria still serves hundreds of tourists who mingle with local residents as they stroll, shop, eat, and hustle through one of the world's most successful public spaces.

The Galleria, like the Chicago Fair of 1893, is extremely important because of its extraordinary influence on later development. Newspapers treated its opening as a national event. Architectural journals printed elaborate analyses. Turin, Genoa, and Naples followed suit, building arcades on the pattern and scale set in Milan. The Kaisergalerie in Berlin, GUM in Moscow, and the Old Arcade in Cleveland, are some examples of its influence outside Italy.[4]

Building codes enacted at the beginning of the twentieth century required arcades to prevent smoke accumulation and meet modern safety standards. These code requirements made shopping arcades prohibitively expensive. Nevertheless, architects and planners continued to dream of vast, day-lit interior shopping spaces. However, they just could not get developers to build them or government officials to permit their construction.

Southdale and the Revival of the Galleria

In 1956 the galleria was resurrected in Edina, Minnesota, a suburban community outside Minneapolis. Victor Gruen, then America's premier shopping center architect, understood that "with extremely cold winters and very hot summers...outdoor public pedestrian spaces would be attractive to shoppers during only a few days of the year."[5]

No suburban shopping center developer wanted to lose customers for even one day. Gruen proposed to solve the problem through climate control and his department store client (Dayton's) agreed. The result was Southdale, America's first air-conditioned shopping mall, a 679,000-square-foot complex that initially included two department stores and 139 shops, and parking for 5200 cars all grouped around a two-story skylit, climate-controlled pedestrian walkway.[6]

Southdale opened a new era in marketing. It demonstrated that climate-controlled shopping arcades, adapted to the requirements of modern merchandising, were more profitable than open-air shopping centers. From then on most developers switched to building air-conditioned shopping malls.

At first the new arcades were strictly a suburban phenomenon. New Haven's Chapel Square Mall, completed in the mid-1960s, was an exception (see Chapters 2 and 6). It was not until developers had perfected the design and merchandising techniques of the suburban shopping mall that public officials found ways of successfully applying it to urban settings. Even then, projects could be commercially successful (attractive to the consumer and profitable for the developer), but detrimental to the business district because they pulled customers off the streets and away from existing downtown shopping areas. Crown Center in Kansas City and Santa Monica Place are examples of just such commercially successful but urbanistically questionable projects. Grand Avenue in Milwaukee, on the other hand, succeeded in attracting customers without adversely affecting other retail districts.

Crown Center, Kansas City

Crown Center was conceived in the late 1950s by Hallmark Cards as a way to improve its existing manufacturing, distribution, and office facilities. After 6 years of planning by Victor Gruen and Associates and Larry Smith and Company, the Crown Center Redevelopment Corporation (a wholly-owned subsidiary of Hallmark) settled on a master plan by architect Edward Larabee Barnes. That plan included 450,000 square

Edina, Minnesota, 1993. Southdale—the world's first air-conditioned shopping arcade. *(Alexander Garvin)*

feet of retailing, 1.5–2 million square feet of offices, 1000 hotel rooms, 2200 apartments, and 7000 underground parking spaces.[7]

To obtain possession of the site, Crown Center proposed a Missouri Urban Redevelopment Corporations Law project

Kansas City, 1994. Crown Center—a mixed use redevelopment project that included a major air-conditioned shopping mall. *(Alexander Garvin)*

that was approved by the Kansas City City Council in 1967.[8] It required clearance of Signboard Hill, an 85-acre "urban trash-can" 12 blocks from the central business district. Besides billboards, the site contained parking lots, garages, diners, a few run-down multistory commercial and industrial buildings, and 15 "decrepit" residences.

By 1974, one-third of Crown Center had been completed including five 7-story office buildings, a 20-story 728-room hotel, 305 apartments, three underground garages containing 3450 parking spaces, and Crown Center Shops, an enclosed shopping arcade. While these buildings are visually and operationally independent, they are interconnected by a network of public spaces. Initially these public spaces included the hotel's interior garden, the shopping arcade, and an outdoor plaza in front of the office buildings. Fifteen years after completion, two dramatic, curving pedestrian bridges were added to connect office and hotel structures that had been built in the interim. These bridges allow visitors to get to any part of Crown Center without having to set foot elsewhere in the city.

Crown Center Shops was not designed just to provide for the retail needs of the 5000 Hallmark employees, the hotel, and the 2200 other office workers in the project. It was intended to attract customers from metropolitan Kansas City throughout the entire week.

Most shopping malls follow the simple formula established by Southdale: department stores anchoring each end of a multilevel, sky-lit arcade lined with small stores. Instead, Crown Center Shops was conceived as a cluster of 81 specialty outlets and one department store (Hall's, also a subsidiary of Hallmark) arranged along a three-level, 355,000-square-foot arcade. The marketing strategy was to provide a variety of small shops with a strong identity and a large number of food, music, and entertainment options. It was thought this would attract customers with a wide array of incomes, ages, and lifestyles.[9]

At first, Crown Center Shops was a commercial failure. It provided the wrong mix of stores, many of which were poorly located, producing the wrong flow of customers.

Hallmark had deep pockets and was able to make the necessary changes. To encourage activity at night, a 6-plex movie theater and a 600-seat playhouse were added. Specialty food stores and restaurants were recombined into the Heartland Market. The remaining stores were rearranged in a sequence that allowed them to profit from customer traffic flowing to and from Halls, the Heartland Market, and the theaters.

Crown Center succeeded in creating a pleasant working environment for Hallmark Cards, thereby keeping the company in Kansas City. It has also spurred additional real estate development on adjacent blocks. Since its completion, Mutual Benefit Life Insurance and IBM have built regional headquarters and Hyatt has built a 45-story hotel.

However, this attractive mixed-use project has also damaged downtown Kansas City. Unlike the Galleria in Milan, Crown Center is not in the center of the business district. It is 1.5 miles away. Consequently, it draws away retail, business, hotel tenants, and convention activity that are the life blood of any central business district.

Santa Monica Place

Even when a galleria is built downtown it may, because of its design, draw away customers from existing stores. This is what happened in Santa Monica. Downtown retail activity had been steadily declining. The first effort to reverse this decline came in 1965 when the city transformed three blocks of Third Street into a pedestrian shopping precinct with over 100 retail stores. While the new open-air Santa Monica Mall was itself initially successful, the rest of the business district continued to decline.[10]

The City Council thought new department stores could complete the job that pedestrianization had started. It selected a three-block site at the south end of the Santa Monica Mall, just off the Santa Monica Freeway. The idea was to replace the area's parking lots and scattered buildings (containing more than 35 businesses and 14 residences) with department stores, office buildings, and a hotel. In 1972 the City Council designated it a redevelopment area and sought proposals from developers.

Just as in Milan a century earlier, there was immediate opposition from site tenants, including United Western Newspapers, publisher of the city's newspaper, the *Santa Monica Evening Outlook.* Once again financing, rather than opposition, proved to be the critical problem. The developers were unable to obtain financing for anything except retail shopping facilities. For this reason, in 1974, the hotel and office buildings were deleted and the site was reduced to two city blocks. Thus, what had been a government-sponsored redevelopment project became a government-sponsored shopping mall.[11]

Many of the property owners would not sell at reasonable prices. Consequently, the city condemned the land. Because Third Street cut the projected shopping arcade in half, the city closed the section of Third Street that ran through the project and transferred ownership to the developer. It also rezoned both blocks for department store use.

Planners and developers alike thought that Santa Monica Place would capture the retail business that would otherwise go to the large shopping malls then being built throughout metropolitan Los Angeles. Despite the size of this market, financial institutions were not willing to provide sufficient mortgage financing to cover the cost of development. The necessary additional funds were provided by a \$14.5 million municipal bond issue covering the cost of acquiring the site and building the parking structures.

The project that finally emerged consists of two department stores, a three-story, sky-lit arcade with 163 shops, two six-story garages with 2034 spaces, and a 10,000-square-foot public terrace. Its design is the product of the interplay among the developer (the Rouse Corporation), the architect (Frank Gehry), the City of Santa Monica, and the California Coastal Commission.

Each of the four façades of the building is different. The famous southern façade is made of overlapping layers of chain-link fence spelling out Santa Monica Place in giant letters. It is a superb advertisement aimed at drivers going to or coming off the freeway. The western façade consists of white stucco and tile decks required by the Coastal Commission as a way of allowing people to see and "enjoy the ocean." These decks are empty except when used by paying restaurant patrons. Moreover, neighboring buildings erected after the mall was completed now block the view. It is difficult to imagine a more eloquent demonstration of misguided government regulation. The eastern façade (bland department store and garage walls) brings even less activity to the street. Only the

Santa Monica, 1991. The super graphics on the south façade of Santa Monica Place are aimed at attracting customers who come by car, shop, and can drive away without setting foot anywhere else in the city. *(Alexander Garvin)*

northern façade makes an attempt to tie Santa Monica Place into the retail life of the city. There, at the termination of the pedestrian mall, stands an enticing glass structure, attracting those few customers who come on foot.[12]

The real entrances to Santa Monica Place are through the garages and not through the glass arcade that terminates the Santa Monica Mall (now the Third Street Promenade). These garages are so prominent a design component because most people come to the project by car. Without plenty of visible parking, they would do their shopping in other places where they knew they could get a parking space.

Santa Monica Place rapidly became one of the country's most successful retail malls. By 1989 it was generating $130 million in sales ($227 per square feet). It has been a commercial success because it is conveniently located, provides the necessary parking, and offers both variety and quantity of goods. Local customers drive through the streets of Santa Monica. The rest come by freeway from all over the western part of metropolitan Los Angeles. No wonder that during its first year of operation this shopping arcade attracted as many as 125,000 people per week.

Santa Monica Place may have attracted shoppers who would not otherwise have been in downtown Santa Monica, thereby creating jobs and taxes. They drove to a convenient parking space and went directly from their car to the shopping arcade. Moreover they had little reason to go anywhere else before driving home. Consequently, they had no impact whatsoever on the rest of the business district. Worse yet, Santa Monica Place also pulled away customers from all over the city, especially from the Santa Monica Mall, which went into decline shortly after Santa Monica Place opened in 1980. Many stores were forced to shift their marketing strategy to cater to the lower end of the economic spectrum. Others went out of business. Vacant and boarded-up shop windows became so prevalent that, in 1988, the city embarked on a program to revive its pedestrian mall, redesigning the paving and street furniture, providing zoning bonuses for entertainment-oriented uses, and renaming it the Third Street Promenade.

Santa Monica, 1985. Vacant and underutilized stores on Third Street 5 years after Santa Monica Place opened. *(Alexander Garvin)*

This program has brought additional customers to downtown Santa Monica and made the combination of Santa Monica Place and the Third Street Promenade into one of the most popular attractions in that part of metropolitan Los Angeles (see Chapter 16).

Grand Avenue, Milwaukee

In 1973, 35 Milwaukee firms contributed $500,000 to study the problems of the business district and $2.5 million to form a redevelopment corporation with the power to execute its recommendations. They sought and received an Urban Development Action Grant ($12.6 million) to cover the gap between development cost, city bonds, and private financing. The result, called Grand Avenue in recollection of Milwaukee's once-famous shopping street, opened in 1982. It is a shopping galleria with 150 stores connecting two department stores and three garages with spaces for 3750 cars.[13]

Grand Avenue is different from other urban shopping malls because it is essentially a rehabilitation project. The

Milwaukee, 1986. Shoppers in the climate-controlled Plankinton Arcade at Grand Avenue. *(Alexander Garvin)*

Milwaukee Redevelopment Corporation, working with its architects (the ELS Design Group) and the Rouse Company, created this four-block galleria by connecting existing buildings. It begins with Marshall Field (formerly Gimbel's), bridges over Plankinton Street, continues by reusing the existing arcade in Holabird and Roche's 1916 Plankinton Building, bridges over Second Street to a new three-story shopping arcade that terminates at the Boston Store. The only entirely new elements are the three-story section of arcade, the glass entry on Wisconsin Avenue, and one of the garages.

Inside, the Rouse Company has created a regional variant of the suburban mall. It takes the form of a "Speisegarten," decorated with photomurals of Milwaukee's turn-of-the-century beer gardens and, offering a variety of ethnic and fast foods and a "Bull Market," featuring pushcart vendors who sell regional crafts and novelties.

This $70 million facility supplies a retail environment that cannot be duplicated in metropolitan Milwaukee. As a result, it attracts more than 20,000 shoppers a day on weekdays, 40,000 on weekends, and 100,000 on the heavy shopping days before Christmas. All these customers have helped to revive what had been a declining part of the business district. Property owners have made improvements on nearby blocks (among them a new $25 million Hyatt Hotel) that may lead eventually to reviving further sections of downtown Milwaukee.

The Urban Marketplace

Both the city shopping arcade and the urban marketplace are intended to attract customers who would otherwise spend their money elsewhere. Both try to be "where the action is." But the similarity ends there. Rather than drawing customers into a controlled environment carefully separated from the dangers of the city, the urban marketplace offers colorful outdoor attractions jumbled together with the surrounding city.

The urban marketplace provides more than everyday consumer goods. It is an outlet for surplus leisure time and income, for singles looking for a good time, young parents seeking entertainment for their children, suburbanites seeking a "safe" taste of city excitement, out-of-town visitors eager for fun. Rather than relying on anchor stores, it presents an agglomeration of vendors offering food and drink, and impulse and specialty items. Often capitalizing on nostalgia for a bygone era, the urban marketplace seeks to induce spending by simultaneously emulating and sanitizing the noise, odors, crowds, and vitality of older, city shopping districts.

Public markets existed throughout the world long before there were any automobiles. A few, like the Grand Central Market in downtown Los Angeles and Pike's Place Market in downtown Seattle, are still in operation. However, most city markets went out of business long ago because they offered fresh produce but very little else.

By the 1920s it had become clear that many customers preferred driving to a single location where they could do all their shopping. No public market was able to accommodate this massive onslaught of cars until Jesse Clyde Nichols, a Kansas City real estate developer, found a way to combine retailing with automobiles and so created America's first fully planned, *suburban* shopping center. Ironically, he simultaneously established the image, form, and design principles of what would later become the *urban* marketplace.[14]

Country Club Plaza, Kansas City

In 1906, Nichols began assembling and developing the 5000 acres that were to become Kansas City's Country Club District, one of America's most impressive planned communities. At that time the area consisted of undeveloped land at the southern extremity of the city. By 1920 Nichols was ready to establish a major commercial center intended to serve the residents of his growing new community and the increasingly suburban population of Kansas City. Today, when residential development extends southward for miles, the idea appears obvious. At the time establishing a major retail center in the middle of nowhere was thought to be preposterous.[15]

Nichols engaged Edward Buehler Delk, a young architect from Philadelphia, who submitted his proposals in 1922. The concept and image of the center, however, were Nichols'. He called his shopping center the "Plaza" because he wanted to reproduce the character of the colorful Spanish plaza marketplaces he had so admired on his trips to Europe. For this reason, Delk designed buildings with ornamental ironwork, tile, balconies, fountains, courtyards, and towers, inspired by the architecture of Seville, Spain.

It is not Spanish-style architecture that makes Country Club Plaza America's first shopping center. It is the organization and planning of what eventually became a 978,000-square-foot retail center. Nichols understood that the customers for the Plaza's more than 100 stores would come by car. To accommodate them, he built strategically located (Spanish-style) parking structures, the first to be specifically designed to serve a planned retail center. Today there are 4300 off-street parking spaces plus 700 along the streets.

In order to facilitate automobile circulation and encourage pedestrian exploration and spending, he minimized block size and maximized the number of streets and intersections. Thus, only 54 percent of the Plaza's 40 acres are in commercial use. The rest is used for circulation. This allows complementary groups of stores to attract customers who zigzag from one block to another.

Nichols wanted the Plaza to function as an entity, not as a collection of individual stores. Consequently, he carefully chose the location of his prime tenants and rented adjacent facilities to stores that would profit from and contribute to the business of their neighbors. He pioneered common marketing for all the stores, advertising Country Club Plaza as a whole,

Kansas City, 1981. The Spanish-style architecture of Country Club Plaza presents a single consistent image that provides a common identity to more than 100 different stores. *(Alexander Garvin)*

Kansas City, 1981. Country Club Plaza—America's first planned shopping center. *(Alexander Garvin)*

coordinating shopping hours, and even sponsoring seasonal festivals and Christmas decorations.

Country Club Plaza eliminated the problem of automobile congestion by making street parking, parking lots, and garages an integral part of project design. By preplanning the location of major stores and carefully selecting tenants, it also pioneered sequential merchandising. Most important, it established that an agglomeration of stores unified by a consistent architectural image and managed and merchandised as a single entity would attract more customers than would come separately to each shop.

Nichols' marketing principles have continued to generate a high volume of retail sales at Country Club Plaza. These principles were refined by other developers who found increasingly sophisticated ways of creating suburban substitutes for downtown shopping. They quickly dropped Nichols' thematic decoration and built sparsely landscaped walkways lined with stripped-down retail structures. Had they, like Nichols, created projects with a distinctive architectural image, there might not have been the ever-present nostalgia for urban shopping districts. This latent thirst for more colorful retail environments began to be satisfied when Ghirardelli Square opened in San Francisco in 1968 and Quincy Market opened in Boston in 1976. These projects, which recast old buildings as marketplaces, became the models for center cities that wished to successfully compete with the increasingly efficient, standardized suburban shopping center.

Ghirardelli Square, San Francisco

After World War II, San Francisco's waterfront, like those in most American port cities, was in decline. As shipping, warehousing, and manufacturing moved away, the northern section of San Francisco's waterfront, known as Fisherman's Wharf, began to be turned back to the seamen for whom it had been named. Vacant and underutilized upland warehouses and factories were available at attractive prices. But there were not many users.

William Roth was the first developer to adapt successfully these empty buildings for use as restaurants, shops, and tourist oriented retailing. In 1962 he purchased a 2.5-acre block of early twentieth century buildings from the Ghirardelli Chocolate Company, which had decided to transfer production to modern facilities in San Leandro (see Chapter 2).

Roth wanted to transform the various factory and warehouse structures into an attractive shopping facility for tourists. This required cleaning building exteriors, gutting their interiors, creating a central plaza with a view of the port,

San Francisco, 1992. The factory and warehouse structures of the Ghirardelli Chocolate Company were converted into a 54,000-square-foot urban marketplace that successfully combined nostalgia for old San Francisco with the freshness of a new retail facility. *(Alexander Garvin)*

San Francisco, 1992. Fisherman's Wharf became even more popular after Ghirardelli Square and other retail facilities were opened. *(Alexander Garvin)*

Brooklyn, 1994. Restoration Plaza is an example of unsuccessful adaptive reuse of manufacturing buildings as a shopping facility. It has not attracted one dollar not already being spent by neighborhood residents, and it may have drawn customers away from the marginal, locally owned shops. *(Alexander Garvin)*

adding new structures where appropriate, and slipping a 300-car garage underneath. What emerged was Ghirardelli Square—a 54,000-square-foot urban marketplace that successfully combined nostalgia for old San Francisco with the freshness of a new retail facility.

This combination became an instant favorite with tourists and made Ghirardelli Square the prototype for similar projects in San Francisco and around the country. A few blocks away the old Del Monte Fruit Cannery became a dining, shopping, and entertainment center. Seafood restaurants that had long been located opposite the piers began to multiply. Souvenir shops opened everywhere. Within a decade Fisherman's Wharf had been transformed from a working waterfront into one of San Francisco's major tourist attractions.[16]

Restoration Plaza, Bedford Stuyvesant, Brooklyn

Ghirardelli Square was a model that cities everywhere wanted to emulate. However, as Restoration Plaza in Bedford Stuyvesant illustrates so well, public officials often failed to understand that rehabilitating old buildings, adapting them to the needs of new users, and creating an atmosphere of bygone days is not guaranteed to revitalize decaying city neighborhoods.

During the 1960s, Bedford Stuyvesant, New York City's largest African American neighborhood, became a symbol for the problems and hopes of urban America. Robert Kennedy, while successfully campaigning for the U.S. Senate in 1966, initiated a major effort to revitalize the area. Together with Senator Jacob Javits, he organized the Bedford Stuyvesant Restoration Corporation. They successfully fought for extra federal assistance, attracting tens of millions of dollars to the neighborhood. Money poured in for health, education, job training, daycare, housing, and every other program Washington had to offer.

Once it got going, the Restoration Corporation sought a project that would be the physical embodiment of the effort to revitalize Bedford Stuyvesant. In 1970, it settled on a vacant dairy located on Fulton Street, the neighborhood's primary retail street. The idea was to transform this empty building and the rest of the block into an urban marketplace that would be a catalyst for the revitalization of the surrounding area. Appropriately, the project was named Restoration Plaza.

Restoration Plaza opened in stages between 1975 and 1980, when the entire block had been redeveloped. The final design, by architect Arthur Cotton Moore/Associates, includes 115,000 square feet of retail space, 170,000 square feet of offices, an outdoor skating rink, a community center, and underground parking for 150 cars.[17]

Like Ghirardelli Square, the core of the project is a courtyard that leads to all the commercial tenants. The similarity ends there. Restoration Plaza is not geared to impulse buying or tourists. It is completely oriented to a local market. The prime retail tenant, at one end of the block, is one of Bedford Stuyvesant's few supermarkets. The other end is anchored by chain clothing stores.

Although Restoration Plaza is an attractive shopping center, there is no evidence that it has had any beneficial impact on Fulton Street or any other section of Bedford Stuyvesant. It has not attracted one dollar that was not already being spent by neighborhood residents. In fact it may have drawn customers away from the marginal, locally owned shops that line Fulton Street.

The people who conceived of Restoration Plaza duplicated the courtyard and underground parking of Ghirardelli Square. They reproduced the nostalgic image of the older buildings. However, they failed to understand that for an urban marketplace to generate new economic activity it must attract a new market. Without the attractions that could bring customers from outside Bedford Stuyvesant, Restoration Plaza could never generate additional economic activity. As a result the project only succeeded in moving customers from one part of the neighborhood to another and from one group of businesses to another.

Quincy Market, Boston

Country Club Plaza may have established the effectiveness of a powerful (nostalgic) architectural image, structured parking, and sequential merchandizing. Ghirardelli Square may have demonstrated the attractiveness of reusing ostensibly obsolete buildings in formerly congested mercantile districts. However, it was not until 1976, when the three granite market/warehouse structures behind Boston's historic Faneuil Hall were reopened as an urban marketplace, that this prototypical marketing strategy was perfected and came to be copied in virtually every sizable American city.

The three buildings known as Quincy Market opened for business in 1826.[18] Until then the area had been under water. Like much of Boston, it had been reclaimed in an attempt to satisfy the city's voracious appetite for new land. The buildings, designed by Alexander Parris, continued to house the city's produce and meat markets until the site became too congested and the structures too outmoded to continue as an efficient food distribution center.[19]

Boston, 1968. Quincy Market prior to its transformation into a "festival marketplace." *(Alexander Garvin)*

In 1961, Quincy Market became part of an ambitious scheme by the Boston Redevelopment Authority (BRA) for the redevelopment of the downtown waterfront. Rather than demolish the market, the BRA designated its three structures for

Boston, 1993. Quincy Market attracts office workers, passing tourists, and suburban customers from all over the metropolitan area. *(Alexander Garvin)*

renovation. Nine years later, after a series of feasibility studies and a $2 million HUD grant for historic preservation, the BRA finally issued a request for proposals from interested developers. The winning development team, Benjamin Thompson & Associates (architect) and Van Arkle-Moss (developer), was unable to put together the necessary financing. In 1974 the city designated James Rouse (working with Benjamin Thompson and Associates as architect) as the new developer.

Rouse was a successful, Baltimore-based, suburban shopping center developer, better known nationally as the man behind the "new town" of Columbia, Maryland (see Chapter 15). When Rouse became involved with Benjamin Thompson and his wife and business partner Jane Thompson, Rouse had been looking for a site that could demonstrate that urban shopping centers could be as profitable as their suburban counterparts. He realized that Quincy Market was precisely what he had been looking for. It was located on the edge of the increasingly popular waterfront district, just behind the new City Hall and Government Center (see Chapter 4), next to the financial district, and not far from the city's department stores. There were more than enough daytime workers in the area to support a major new shopping facility. Another 20,000 people lived within walking distance of the site. The most significant factor, however, was the secondary market in the surrounding suburbs. The question he and the Thompsons set about answering was how to attract these affluent consumers to Quincy Market.

They rejected the notion of organizing the project's 6.5 acres of land and 370,000 square feet of interior space around two or three anchor department stores. There was no way to squeeze them into structures that were nearly 550 feet long and 50 feet deep. Moreover, Rouse did not want to compete with Filene's or any of Boston's other existing department stores. He proposed to base the project on small businesses. The scheme contained 160 small stores occupying 219,000 square feet of retail space plus 143,000 square feet of small office suites. Each occupant would lease a small area, do more business per square foot than more conventional tenants, and thus be able to pay more rent per square foot.

At first financial institutions were reluctant to lend money for so innovative a venture. Except for Ghirardelli Square, there had been little experience with adapting older structures for urban retailing. Moreover, banks and insurance companies could not base their projections on the credit rating of the vendors to whom Rouse proposed to rent. Their customary procedure was to require leases from department stores and major retail chains. Nevertheless, Rouse obtained a $21 million mortgage from Teachers Insurance and Annuity Association and raised $9 million in equity capital. The remaining $10 million came from city, state, and federal programs. In addition the City of Boston abated property taxes until the project opened and leased the site to Rouse for 99 years at $1 per year. In exchange the city received 20–25 percent of gross income in lieu of taxes.

The central structure at Quincy Market is reserved for food outlets. Adjoining structures are filled with shops offering fashionable clothing, accessories, jewelry, and gifts. Both outdoor and indoor areas are flooded with pushcarts. As Rouse explains:

> *We hired a bright young woman who went out all over New England identifying artists and craftsmen and small entrepreneurs with narrow specialties. She worked on 900 prospects for those 43 pushcarts, evaluating and recruiting them. We designed the carts and provided boxes and baskets to hang on them.*[20]

The pushcarts and food outlets, like the department stores in a suburban shopping mall, became major attractions, drawing office workers, passing tourists who stop along the way to make additional purchases, and suburban customers from all over the region. Quincy Market has been particularly successful because it also tapped Boston's substantial tourist market. Of the 12 million customers who came to Quincy Market in 1981, 60 percent were tourists.

Quincy Market's success exceeded even the most optimistic sales projections. By 1981 annual sales averaged an astonishing $377 per square foot per year for the food vendors and $345 per square foot per year for the other merchants. Rents ranged from $30 to $45 per square foot per year for the north and south buildings and $50 to over $100 per square foot per year in the central structure. Even three years later, median sales per square foot in most regional shopping centers had only reached one-third that of Quincy Market.[21]

Harborplace, Baltimore

The redevelopment of Baltimore's declining industrial waterfront originated in the late 1950s. The Greater Baltimore Committee, Inc. decided to continue its urban renewal efforts, then successfully under way at Charles Center two blocks to the north (see Chapter 6). Except for the waterfront promenade and the Port Authority Headquarters, each element of its "Inner Harbor Plan" either could not get voter approval or could not obtain financing. Nevertheless, the city proceeded to acquire the necessary 95 acres.[22]

Inner Harbor languished for more than a decade until James Rouse (chairman of the Greater Baltimore Committee, Inc. in 1965 when it published its initial waterfront proposals) proposed to provide Inner Harbor with an urban marketplace like the one he had just created in Boston. At that time the plan for Inner Harbor included a new convention center, 9600 parking spaces, a 500-room Hyatt Regency Hotel, a major aquarium, and a marina. In 1978, Rouse negotiated the long-term rental of a 3.2-acre site for Harborplace, his proposed urban marketplace. This improved version of Quincy Market was just what was needed to transform the Baltimore waterfront into the major downtown tourist center envisioned by the plan.[23]

The Washington-Baltimore suburbs were one of the fastest growing markets in the nation. The boats in Baltimore harbor had always been a regional attraction. The new waterfront promenade, with its decorative paving, benches, and

Baltimore, 1994. Inner Harbor has become a major tourist destination. *(Alexander Garvin)*

streetlights, along with the aquarium, old ships anchored in the harbor, and new parking facilities, made the waterfront attractive, accessible, safe, and convenient for that regional market. Adding an urban marketplace with its many commercial attractions would provide the excitement and gaiety needed to bring that enormous market to Inner Harbor. The adjacent convention center and hotel meant Harborplace would profit from another major market: out-of-town tourists. Moreover, because Inner Harbor had been carefully planned to fit together with Charles Center and the rest of downtown Baltimore, Harborplace would also profit from a third market: daytime office workers.

Unlike Quincy Market, Harborplace was built from scratch. Benjamin Thompson and Associates transformed the opaque masonry of Quincy into two glass pavilions surrounded by covered porches and terraces. By night the brightly lighted glass façades provide a sparkling enticement for outsiders to come in, join the fun, and (naturally) spend money. By day, the prevalent glass also opens up the view to the waterfront for the customers inside doing their shopping. The roll-up exterior doors allow direct contact with outside activities when the weather permits. Porches and terraces provide additional places from which to enjoy the harbor.

Harborplace is almost entirely based on its Boston predecessor. The larger of its two pavilions, like the central structure at Quincy Market, is a food court offering a wide variety of ethnic, prepared, and fresh foods from restaurants, fast-food counters, market stalls, delicacy shops, and pushcarts. The smaller pavilion is for specialty stores and more formal restaurants. Together the two pavilions provide 142,000 square feet of gross leasable area for 142 merchants, including 49 eating places, 20 food stores, 36 specialty shops, 2 florists, and 35 pushcarts and kiosk vendors.

Baltimore, 1994. Harborplace was the key ingredient needed to transform the Baltimore waterfront into the city's major downtown attraction. *(Alexander Garvin)*

During 1980, its first year of operation, Harborplace attracted 18 million visitors. Annual sales per square foot exceeded Quincy Market, which had had four years to build its clientele. The city gained $3 million in new real estate taxes, 2500 new jobs (one-third held by previously unemployed Baltimore residents), and 6 million tourists from outside the greater Baltimore area.

Rouse calls his product a "festival marketplace." Working with Benjamin Thompson and Associates, he has reproduced it at New York's South Street Seaport, Miami's Bayside Marketplace, and elsewhere. But, whether because the size and character of their markets were different or because he knew Baltimore so much better, none of these projects has transformed the city around them in the dramatic way that Harborplace has.

Horton Plaza, San Diego

Horton Plaza violates conventional wisdom about the urban marketplace. It includes department stores as well as small vendors; it offers every sort of merchandise from home furnishings to family apparel, not just specialty items and exotic foods; it is designed as an inward-oriented multistory center, not a pedestrian-oriented extension of other downtown activity. Yet, like Quincy Market and Harborplace, Horton Plaza attracts millions of customers, keeps downtown San Diego alive well into the night, and has revitalized the central business district.[24]

During the 1960s, downtown San Diego experienced the same difficulties experienced by cities around the country: loss of business to the suburbs, decreasing retail sales, and general deterioration. The city's long-established red-light district, which attracted sailors from the busy harbor and carousing vagrants who enjoyed the balmy weather much of the year, extended further and further into the central business district. In an effort to reverse these trends the city embarked on a series of redevelopment projects, one of which turned into Horton Plaza.

The project began in 1969 with a three-block redevelopment plan to improve the area around Horton Plaza Park. Public pressure successfully forced expansion of the project to the 15-block area approved by the city council in 1972. Three years later, as a result of a nationally advertised competition, Ernest W. Hahn Inc., a California-based realtor responsible for dozens of shopping centers, was designated the developer.

It took Hahn and the city 7 years to put the project together. Ultimately the city provided $39 million for property acquisition, relocation, infrastructure improvements, and development of two theater facilities within the project. The rest came from the private sector: $85 million in permanent financing, $15 million in equity from Hahn, and $40 million from the department stores.

In 1985, when Horton Plaza finally emerged, it was a nine-block, 885,000-square-foot shopping complex with 140 tenants including 4 department stores, a 7-plex cinema, a legitimate theater, a nightclub, 19 eating establishments, and a constantly changing number of pushcart and kiosk vendors. Two historic structures, the old Balboa Theater and the Spreckels Building, were incorporated into the design along with two reconstructed façades of Italianate buildings that had been on the site.

The design, by the Jerde Partnership, consists of 10 clusters of shops each characterized by a different color scheme and architectural image, each open to San Diego's benign climate, each on a different level, tied together by a series of stairs, ramps, escalators, and elevators that cross the S-shaped central open space. The combination is a confusing and colorful array of merchandise displayed in pastel-tinted Mediterranean piazzas, neon-clad Victorian arcades, stucco-and-tile Indian pueb-

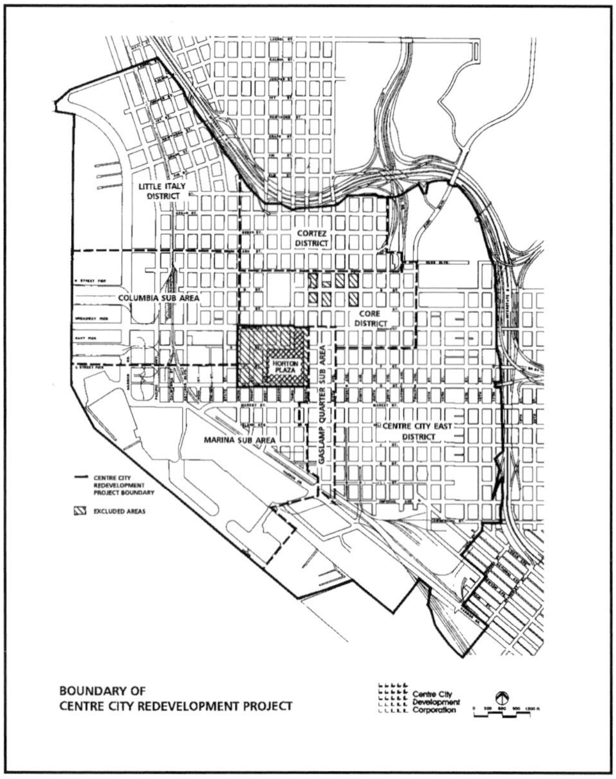

San Diego, 1994. Redevelopment area including Horton Plaza. *(Courtesy of San Diego Center City Development Corp.)*

San Diego, 1991. The Gaslamp Quarter, whose renovation was spurred by the success of nearby Horton Plaza. *(Alexander Garvin)*

San Diego, 1987. Horton Plaza has become a 9-block shopping complex with 140 tenants, a 7-plex cinema, a legitimate theater, a nightclub, 19 eating establishments, and a constantly changing number of pushcart and kiosk vendors. *(Alexander Garvin)*

los, multicolored Gothic palazzos, and ornamented, postmodern emporia—a circus atmosphere that is amplified by mimes, jugglers, bands, aerobics teams, and the like. It is also one of the country's most effective examples of sequential merchandising. Ramps and walkways force customers to pass all sorts of spending opportunities on their way to any destination.

Horton Plaza is commercially successful because it supplies a cleverly designed, unique attraction with plentiful merchandise for a huge market: 60,000 to 100,000 downtown office workers, 310,000 in-town residents, 1,900,000 fashion-oriented metropolitan shoppers, and millions of tourists and conventioneers. It has helped to make downtown San Diego a lively attraction virtually 24 hours a day, 365 days a year. New hotels, office buildings, retail projects, and apartment houses continue to be built on surrounding blocks. Adjacent older buildings are being renovated. In the nearby historic "Gaslamp Quarter," porn shops and cheap hotels are being replaced by upscale restaurants and other more conventional tourist-oriented retailing. There are few more effective examples of downtown redevelopment in the United States.

Ingredients of Success

The health of an urban shopping district is a function of the market it can potentially serve and the strength of the competition. If an area is in trouble it is because one or more of the following are true:

- The market that the district serves has declined in size, income, or both.
- The district no longer serves the tastes of the market.
- Alternative methods of merchandising have rendered the area functionally obsolete.
- Newer, more attractive commercial areas have captured its market.
- Adjacent conditions are having a negative frictional impact, chasing away the district's market.

Improving the health of a retail district by building a new shopping arcade or urban marketplace requires understanding which of these conditions is causing the problem and then manipulating the ingredients of project success to alter those conditions.

Market

Population trends are central to the effectiveness of retail projects. If an area is experiencing population or income growth, building a new shopping facility like Horton Plaza can harness the increasing spending power. It directs the additional spending to a part of town that will profit from that spending without having any serious negative impact on existing retail districts. If population and income are stable or declining, however, a new facility such as Restoration Plaza will simply shift spending from one part of town to another.

Sometimes spending is a matter of consumer taste. During the 1960s and 1970s, Boston and San Francisco had declining populations. Nevertheless Ghirardelli Square and Quincy Market successfully attracted customers without doing damage to other parts of the city because many of these customers were attracted from outside the city.

As long as there are more convenient or attractive alternatives, no new retail facility is likely to capture any significant share of the market. Chapel Square Mall lost customers to suburban shopping centers that were built to attract the growing population of metropolitan New Haven. Instead, new shopping facilities should, like Harborplace or Horton Plaza, offer something unique that cannot be obtained elsewhere. Then they will attract people who would not otherwise be in the city, thereby generating sales, jobs, and tax revenues that would not otherwise be available.

Location

Many urban shopping centers exploit the inherent characteristics of their location. Horton Plaza is able to offer a wide variety of outdoor amusements because San Diego's weather is so benign. Harborplace and Ghirardelli Square benefit from the adjacent waterfront.

Other retail facilities are more dependent on proximity to their customers. The cafés and restaurants of the Galleria Vittorio Emanuele, for example, serve the occupants of the offices and apartments of its upper floors, those of neighboring blocks, and those who have come to visit La Scala or the Duomo. A similarly large number of the people who eat lunch at Milwaukee's Grand Avenue come from nearby office buildings.

Proximity to a new shopping facility does not necessarily bring commercial revitalization. Crown Center, which serves the Kansas City metropolitan area, draws away customers who might otherwise continue driving for another mile and a half to do their shopping downtown. Consequently, it has not had any beneficial impact on the central business district. When Santa Monica Place opened, it drew away so many customers from the Santa Monica Mall that for many years the street was known for its vacant, deteriorating, and transient retail outlets. For those reasons, except in special circumstances, government should only consider assistance to projects that bring new customers, do not pilfer customers from other retail facilities, and generate additional activity in the surrounding neighborhood.

Design

When an area is losing its market to other, better functioning facilities, the best way to fight back is to augment existing retail structures with similar up-to-date alternatives. Santa Monica Place and Grand Avenue are examples of projects subsidized by cities that were not willing to lose customers to suburban malls.

Building a modern, air-conditioned shopping mall, however, is no guarantee of increasing retail sales. As the initial failure of Crown Center Shops demonstrates, the organization of a shopping center's component parts can determine its success. Crown Center's single department store was not enough of a draw. Moreover, insufficient attention had been given to the movement of customers as they made their way to their destination. Adding a multiplex cinema and a 600-seat theater increased the number of customers attracted to the project. Reorganizing the retail outlets so that customers on their way to their destination had to pass merchandise that they might purchase also increased sales.

Character is as important to the design of shopping facilities as the organization of its constituent parts. The theatrical image of Country Club Plaza increases its competitiveness as does the festive atmosphere and historic architecture of Ghirardelli Square and Quincy Market. Harborplace and Horton Plaza may be very different interpretations of the festival marketplace, but they also capitalize on a distinctive atmosphere, in these cases created from scratch by their designers.

Financing

The prototypes of the modern American shopping complex (Country Club Plaza, Southdale, and Ghirardelli Square) were entirely conventionally financed. So are virtually all suburban shopping centers. On the other hand, most downtown malls and marketplaces involve government assistance.

Since banks and insurance companies are understandably wary of investing where there are vacant stores and deteriorating retail facilities, developers find it difficult to finance retail-revitalization schemes. Government should reduce this risk by participating in project planning and assisting in property acquisition. Crown Center, Santa Monica Place, and Horton Plaza and many other commercial revitalization projects would have been impossible without such government assistance in planning, assembling sites, and holding them until financing is in place.

Financial institutions rarely provide enough mortgage financing to cover project costs. In privately financed projects the remainder is equity capital. Most retail-revitalization projects are not able to generate enough revenues to cover both debt service and return on equity. Government should fill the gap. After all, if these projects were able to raise the necessary financing on their own there would be no need for public assistance.

There are many ways for government to provide money without appearing to subsidize the developer. At Santa Monica Place, it was done by financing parking structures; at Quincy Market, by covering the cost of historic preservation and by abating real estate taxes; at Harborplace, by making an equity investment in the project. But, whatever the form of public assistance, it should be restricted to the minimum needed to guarantee financial feasibility.

Entrepreneurship

J. C. Nichols understood, as nobody had before him, that the automobile had made mass marketing possible. For it to take place, however, there had to be a destination (department stores) that attracted huge numbers of customers, a place of arrival (parking), and a path that forced these customers past goods they would wish to purchase on the way to their ultimate destination (sequential merchandising). By sheer force of entrepreneurship he overcame the skepticism of Kansas City's retail merchants, attracting them to an undeveloped part of Kansas City. More important, he persuaded these hesitant retail merchants to locate where they would have the greatest effect on the project as a whole.

When businesses are uncertain about an area or a project, government participation will help overcome their hesitation, coordinate the various players, and take the necessary risks. It can do this by analyzing the market, planning the project, acquiring the property, and sometimes relocating tenants and preparing sites for development. That leaves the ultimate developer with the no-less-difficult job of finding retail tenants, putting the financing together, building the project, and operating the facility.

When government entrepreneurship is inadequate, there is tremendous time lost until a developer is able to put a deal together. In fact, packaging the project may prove impossible. It took the Boston Redevelopment Authority 9 years to put together an ostensibly feasible scheme for Quincy Market. When the developer it selected was unable to bring the project to fruition, it took another 4 years for the BRA to restructure the deal and bring in James Rouse. He had the know-how to hit a home run with the bases loaded. For early success, the trick is to start out with an entrepreneur who has all the abilities needed to bring the project to completion.

Time

Since it may take years to put a retail-revitalization scheme together, government has a crucial role to play. By using its power of condemnation, it can shorten the time needed to assemble a site. By purchasing the site and holding it until a project is ready to go, it can eliminate the cost of carrying the property (i.e., interim interest, real estate taxes, and operating expenses). Both were crucial to the feasibility of Santa Monica Place and Horton Plaza.

However, the single most important time period for the financial success of any shopping facility is the time customers spend there. Country Club Plaza may have been different from the Galleria in Milan in terms of location, appearance, and tenantry, but it manipulated the time its customers spent in the same way. The cafés and restaurants of the Galleria captured visitors on their way to and from specific destinations (the Scala Opera and the Duomo), just as the small shops of Country Club Plaza captured them between parking their car and entering a department store.

If the time that customers spend in a retail facility is central to its financial success, the time they are *not* there is crucial to the health of the surrounding city. Many business districts are dead at night and on weekends because they lack retail, entertainment, and leisure facilities that attract large crowds. As a result, a tremendous investment in infrastructure lies fallow except for one-third of the day, 5 days of the week. Moreover, the city is forced to pay for duplicating that infrastructure in other retail districts that themselves are underutilized during the workday and might be enhanced by addressing both markets. Consequently, retail-revitalization schemes that minimize down time are very cost-effective. They also produce a level of vitality that cannot be duplicated by dividing land uses and activities among separate districts.

Urban Shopping Centers as a City Planning Strategy

Public officials usually discover the impact of proposed malls and marketplaces after they open. In Santa Monica, the city government spent a decade getting an up-to-date air-conditioned shopping arcade. When it opened, people were surprised that the new mall attracted customers from Third

Street. As a result the city spent another decade seeking to replace the customers Third Street had lost.

The unintended consequences of inadequately conceived retail-revitalization projects arise because public officials focus their attention on specific projects, rather than the city as a whole. Not only is this poor urban planning, it is unfair to businesses that do not get public assistance. The best way to avoid unnecessarily assisting one group of businesses at the expense of others is to enact state legislation that requires every local government to commission, pay for, and distribute a *consumer impact study* prior to undertaking any program that would benefit any individual retail establishment. Had such a consumer impact study been available, the Santa Monica City Council might not have voted the site acquisition, street closing, rezoning, or subsidies needed for Santa Monica Place before the merchants of Third Street and their employees knew that they would be put out of business.

There will always be cases when a project's citywide benefits outweigh the damage to local businesses. As long as the project involves a street closing, rezoning, or some other government action that does not involve subsidization, there is no reason for more than public consideration of a consumer impact study. When government also covers the gap between available private financing and project cost it should get a return on its investment. That return should be deposited in a *retail-revitalization fund* operated by the local Chamber of Commerce for the benefit of other retail merchants in need of assistance. In such a way, that income can be invested in the improvement of retail activity throughout the city rather than be used to subsidize only one of the city's businesses.

Notes

1. Johann Friedrich Geist, *Arcades—The History of a Building Type,* MIT Press, Cambridge, 1982.
2. Victor Emmanuel, originally king of Sardinia, assumed the title of the first "King of Italy," in 1861. He is considered, together with Garibaldi, Mazzini, and Cavour, to be responsible for the creation of an independent, unified Italy.
3. Geist, op. cit., pp. 74–75 and 371–401.
4. Carroll L. V. Meeks, *Italian Architecture 1750–1914,* Yale University Press, New Haven, 1966, pp. 290–297.
5. Victor Gruen, *The Heart of Our Cities,* Simon & Schuster, New York, 1964, p. 194.
6. In 1972 and 1988–1991 Southdale was remodeled and expanded to 1,350,000 square feet. It now includes 3 department stores, a food court, 107 specialty shops, and parking for 6100 cars. See Dean Schwanke with Terry Jill Lassar and Michael Beyard, *Remaking the Shopping Center,* The Urban Land Institute, Washington, D.C., 1994, pp. 123–129.
7. Historical and statistical information on Crown Center is derived from Carla Sobala (editor), *Kansas City Today,* Urban Land Institute, Washington, D.C., 1974, pp. 31–49, and George Ehrlich, *Kansas City Missouri—An Architectural History 1826–1976,* Historic Kansas City Foundation, Kansas City, 1979, pp. 155–162.
8. For an explanation of the Missouri Urban Redevelopment Corporations Law, see Chapter 11.
9. When Crown Center opened there were four main groups of stores: Hall's (a 100,000-square-foot department store made up of specialty shops), the Market Place (a complex of 14 specialty food stores), West Village (a cluster of 35 boutiques catering to sophisticated young people), and the International Café (8 ethnic restaurants located at the entrance).
10. Historical and statistical information on Santa Monica Place is derived from Barbara Goldstein, "A Place in Santa Monica," *Progressive Architecture,* July 1981, pp. 84–88; and *Santa Monica Evening Outlook,* March 6, 1972, p. 15, August 31, 1978, pp. 9–10, and October 15, 1980, p. 10.
11. The block between Ocean Avenue and Second Street was eliminated from the redevelopment area.
12. This glass structure was remodeled in 1990.
13. Historical and statistical information on Grand Avenue is derived from J. Thomas Black, Libby Howland, and Stuart J. Rogel, *Downtown Retail Development: Conditions for Success and Project Profile,* Urban Land Institute, Washington, D.C., 1983, pp. 36–38, and Wayne Attoe and Donn Logan, *American Urban Architecture—Catalysts in the Design of Cities,* University of California Press, Berkeley, 1989, pp. 48–73.
14. Commercial blocks at Roland Park, Maryland, (1896), Lake Forest, Illinois (1916–1917), and elsewhere that include a variety of retail shops cannot be considered true suburban shopping centers because they weren't specifically designed to accommodate large numbers of customers who arrived by car. See Kenneth Jackson, *Crabgrass Frontier,* Oxford University Press, New York, 1985, pp. 258–259.
15. Historical and statistical information on Country Club Plaza is derived from William S. Worley, *J. C. Nichols and the Shaping of Kansas City,* University of Missouri Press, Columbia, 1990; and Sobala (editor), op. cit., pp. 10–28.
16. In 1986 Ghirardelli Square was remodeled and expanded to include 91 retail establishments in 155,226 square feet. See W. Anderson Barnes: "Ghirardelli Square Keeping a First," *Urban Land,* Urban Land Institute, Washington, D.C., 1986, pp. 6–10.
17. Carla S. Crane (editor), *New York Metropolitan Area... Today,* Urban Land Institute, Washington, D.C., 1980, p. 76.
18. The buildings were named after Mayor Josiah Quincy, who had been responsible for this landfill and construction project.
19. Historical and statistical information on Quincy Market is derived from Walter Muir Whitehall, *Boston: A Topographical History,* The Belknap Press of Harvard University Press, Cambridge, 1963, pp. 95–98; Mildred F. Schmertz, "Faneuil Hall Marketplace," *Architectural Record,* December 1977, pp. 118–127, and Black, Howland, and Rogel: op. cit., pp. 50–52.
20. Schmertz, op. cit.
21. The Urban Land Institute, *Dollars and Cents of Shopping Centers: 1987,* Urban Land Institute, Washington, D.C., 1987, p. 10.
22. Historical and statistical information on Harborplace is derived from Greater Baltimore Committee, Inc., and the Committee for Downtown, Inc., *The Inner Harbor and City Hall Plaza,* Baltimore, 1965, and Douglas M. Wrenn, *Urban Waterfront Development,* Urban Land Institute, Washington, D.C., 1983, pp. 146–155.
23. The first proposals for the Inner Harbor included an East-West Expressway cutting across the harbor, a civic center organized around an open-air mall connecting the harbor with City Hall, a new head quarters for the Port Authority, an east-west "minirailway," a theater/museum "playground," new apartment towers, and a waterfront promenade.
24. Historical and statistical information on Horton Plaza is derived from *Urban Land Institute Project Reference File,* vol. 16, no. 19, October–December 1986, Urban Land Institute, Washington, D.C.; and Bernard Frieden and Lynne Sagalyn: *Downtown, Inc.: How America Rebuilds Cities,* MIT Press, Cambridge, 1989, pp. 123–131, 145–153, and 191–197.

6

The City of Tomorrow

Pittsburgh, 1983. The Golden Triangle from Point Park. *(Alexander Garvin)*

After World War II the American city experienced cataclysmic change. Broad superhighways thrust into its heart. Spacious pedestrian plazas with shiny glass towers replaced familiar neighborhoods. The impetus for this radical transformation was the idea that cities were terminally ill. The disease seemed obvious wherever there were deteriorated and vacant buildings, a decreasing population, and declining employment, retail sales, and office occupancy. Many experts thought the decline could be reversed by replacing what they observed to be a functionally obsolete physical plant. They prescribed rebuilding decaying cities, section by section, until every corner had been transformed into an efficient, modern metropolis.[1]

This redevelopment prescription was made available to the nation when Congress enacted the Housing Act of 1949, which offered to pay any city that used the remedy two-thirds of its cost. Over the next quarter of a century, the federal government spent $12.7 billion to have the remedy tried in nearly 1000 cities. Some cities had a vision of the modern metropolis that they wished to become. Others just wanted to clear a slum or move its occupants. Many tried redevelopment simply because money was available. In each case the Housing Act of 1949 financed the elimination of large sections of the city, paved the way for new highways and garages, and subsidized the development of massive superblocks.[2]

In most cities, redevelopment was a painful process. From the beginning there was opposition from relocatees, preservationists, and people who opposed public intervention into the private market. With every new project that opposition increased. By 1973, when the Nixon administration abruptly terminated the program, few people still wanted their cities rebuilt. Too many of the program's 2532 urban renewal projects had been shameful failures.

The diagnosis that cities were dying and that the cause was an obsolete physical plant was flawed. In many cities, such as Dallas, Phoenix, and San Diego, the problems that required attention were caused by growth rather than decline. Those cities that had shrinking populations, such as Cleveland, Cincinnati, and St. Louis, were not dying; nor was their population decline caused by outmoded structures. Nevertheless, across the country, city governments established redevelopment agencies to rebuild entire districts.

In Pittsburgh, Baltimore, and other cities where redevelopment projects did not satisfy the demand for new space, they stimulated further private investment and triggered genuine urban renewal. In most instances, however, redevelopment projects caused hardship for the residents, businesses, and workers who were displaced, subsidized the creation of arid districts dominated by mediocre high-rise buildings, and retarded further private-market activity. This history should deter civic leaders from initiating further government-assisted redevelopment except where the decline is truly caused by physical and functional obsolescence, where individual entrepreneurs cannot overcome that obsolescence without government intervention, and where the project is located and designed in a manner that ensures its occupants will generate additional market activity in surrounding areas.

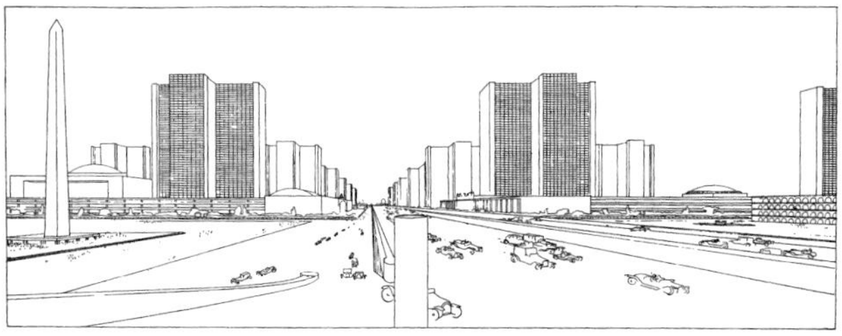

1922. The highways and towers of Le Corbusier's City of Tomorrow inspired the urban renewal program in America. *(Courtesy of Artists Rights Society [ARS] / SPADEM, 1995, Paris)*

Le Corbusier's Vision

The physical paradigm for America's redevelopment program was provided by the Swiss-born French architect, painter, and writer Charles Edouard Jeanneret, better known as Le Corbusier. As early as 1924, Le Corbusier had written that "the city of today is a dying thing," called for "a frontal attack on the most diseased quarters," and demanded their replacement by new districts, "vertical to the sky, open to light and air, clear and radiant and sparkling."[3]

Le Corbusier's summarized his vision in *The City of Tomorrow, and Its Planning* first published in 1924. He proposed to create new cities that consisted of three separate districts: a business center of office towers, a residential area of elevator apartment houses, and a manufacturing-warehousing district. The residential and office areas were essentially a continuous green park divided by elevated highways into superblocks. Citizens were to speed along the highways in their automobiles until they reached the appropriate branch road leading to an "auto-port." There they would garage their cars and enter a green pedestrian precinct containing all the amenities of modern life.

Le Corbusier described the proposed skyscraper business district as:

> *a great open space 2,400 yards by 1,500 yards, giving an area of 3,600,000 square yards, and occupied by garden parks.... In these parks, at the foot of and round the skyscrapers, would be the restaurants and cafes, the luxury shops, housed in buildings with receding terraces; here too would be the theaters, halls and so on; and here the parking places or garage shelters.*[4]

Each 1200-foot-square residential superblock was supposed to include all the necessities of a healthy family life:

> *communal services (catering and household supplies), nursery, kindergarten, open-air playground in the park, primary school... complete stadium, large swimming pool and*

1929. Le Corbusier's towers-in-the-park vision of a new living environment for Buenos Aires. (Courtesy of *Artists Rights Society [ARS] / SPADEM, 1995, Paris*)

sand beach + tennis courts + infants' playground + covered play areas underneath buildings + immense ribbons of sunbathing beaches on roof-gardens.[5]

At ground level these superblocks flowed together to form one immense park, only 15 percent of which was covered with buildings.

Along with its revolutionary combination of public open space, superhighways, and skyscrapers, *The City of Tomorrow* provided a brand-new way of modernizing cities. In sixteenth- and seventeenth-century Rome, the popes had acquired privately owned land to provide necessary public thoroughfares. In nineteenth-century Paris, Napoleon III and Baron Georges Eugene Haussmann did so to provide an infrastructure of public works that would spur private reconstruction of appropriate parts of the city (see Chapter 18). Le Corbusier proposed the next step: condemnation of whole districts to allow the efficient reconstruction of an entire city. In physical terms this evolution to full-scale redevelopment may have been relatively obvious. In economic and political terms it meant rejecting capitalist market economics and assigning to government the functions of the real estate developer.

Creating the City of Tomorrow required condemnation of thousands of privately owned properties. Le Corbusier did not specify whether they would be acquired by negotiation or expropriation. He was equally unclear as to what entity would implement the plan. However, he was clear, if naive, in explaining how to pay for it. Eventually the money would be

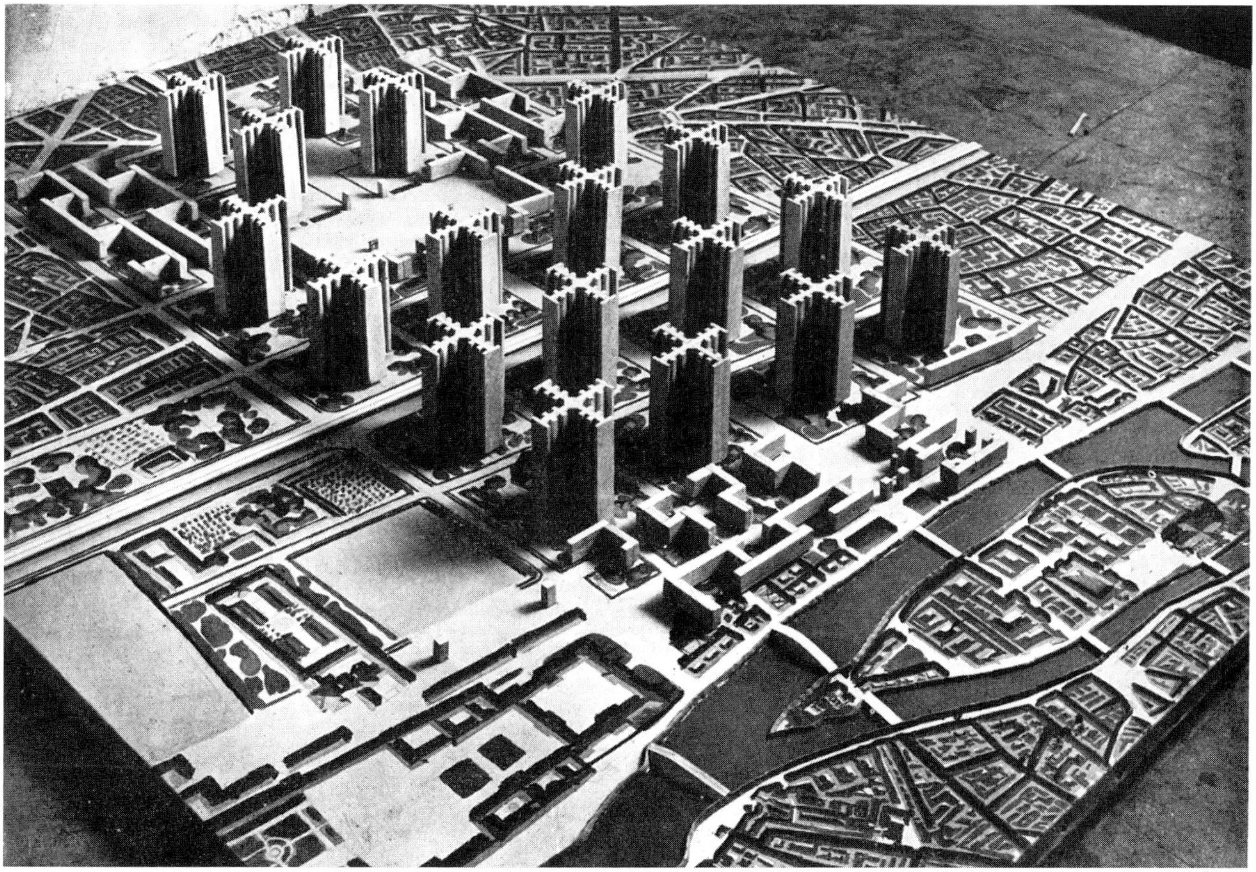

1925. Model of Le Corbusier's Plan Voisin for the redevelopment of Paris. (*Courtesy of Artists Rights Society [ARS] / SPADEM, 1995, Paris*)

earned by "the initiator of this change" (national government?) from the "fourfold or tenfold increase" in land value that would result from more efficient, high-density use of land. How "the initiator" would raise the gargantuan amounts of cash needed to pay for initial land acquisition or the even more massive costs of reconstruction was never explained. Nor did Le Corbusier give any consideration to the problem of relocating millions of residents and thousands of businesses.[6]

Although Le Corbusier's ideas may have been well-known to intellectuals and to the architects who would be hired to design any redevelopment project, most Americans had never heard of him. Nevertheless, millions of Americans were familiar with the brave new world of highways and skyscrapers that he advocated. It was this image of the new utopia, rarely drawn by Le Corbusier himself, that had been hammered into the public consciousness by countless magazine articles, exhibitions, and Hollywood movies. Its most widely known version is the one which was presented to millions of visitors at the New York World's Fair of 1939. There, at the General Motors exhibit, they could see a model of "Futurama," architect Norman Bel Geddes' depiction of America in 1960:

> *traffic mov[ing] at designated speeds of fifty, seventy-five, and a hundred miles an hour along highway surfaces...skyscrapers spaced far apart, the base of each one occupying a full city block. On the roofs of some were landing places for airplanes and autogyros, as helicopters were then called. Parks occupied a third of the total city area. It was a utopia of abundant sunshine, fresh air, and recreational opportunity.*[7]

Adapting the City of Tomorrow to Postwar America

Whether in its pristine version by Le Corbusier, the commercial version presented by General Motors at the 1939 World's Fair, or the more generalized schemes depicted in the mass media, the City of Tomorrow had to be adapted to the needs of America's ever practical population. This meant providing a rationale for a national urban redevelopment program, reducing its size to fit financial and political reality, and then creating financial inducements for local governments and private developers to build it.

Local government was needed for its power of eminent domain. There is no way to redevelop blighted city districts without condemnation of privately owned real estate because some property owners will hold out for prices that make redevelopment financially unfeasible and others will refuse to sell at any price. Moreover, government interim landownership eliminates both the risk and the cost of carrying the site while redevelopment plans are developed, debated, and approved.

Government had little experience in erecting office buildings, retail stores, or apartment houses. The real estate industry did. The obvious solution was to give local government the central role in planning and private developers the responsibility for building. This combination had already been tried in New York and Pittsburgh.

Stuyvesant Town, New York City

In 1943 Mayor Fiorello LaGuardia and Parks Commissioner Robert Moses persuaded the Metropolitan Life Insurance Company (MetLife) to join with the city government in a major slum-clearance project. They chose the notorious "Gas House" District along the East River, north of 14th Street. Together they lobbied the state legislature for passage of the Redevelopment Companies Law, which allowed the city to condemn blighted areas for resale to private developers who agreed to clear and reconstruct them pursuant to a government-approved plan. Once the legislation had been enacted, MetLife prepared a redevelopment plan for the "Gas House" District. It proposed clearing 18 blocks that were home to 16,000 residents and replacing them with Stuyvesant Town, a 75-acre superblock with 8800 apartments.[8]

The traditional street grid was replaced by a district of trees, flowers, grass, playgrounds, curvilinear paths, parking, and residential towers, but not the schools, libraries, and other

Manhattan, c. 1942. Tenements in the Gas-House District that were cleared for the construction of Stuyvesant Town. *(Courtesy of MetLife Archives)*

1943. Model of the Metropolitan Life Insurance Company's proposal for Stuyvesant Town. *(Courtesy of MetLife Archives)*

community facilities, which were part of Le Corbusier's scheme. Stuyvesant Town was followed by Peter Cooper Village, a similar MetLife project directly to the north. But neither project was part of a continuous aggregation of green superblocks through which pedestrians were free to roam. They were separated from the rest of the neighborhood by wide streets. In fact, each had been specifically designed to be "quite independent of any development that might come around it."[9]

Both Stuyvesant Town and Peter Cooper Village seemed to justify the need for a modern residential environment. Life in these projects was so much better than anything around them that applicants clamored to get in. Even a half-century after completion, hundreds of families remain on waiting lists for years in the hope of moving in.

These early redevelopment projects demonstrated that there was public support for redevelopment. They could not, however, demonstrate that replacement of the most diseased quarters would result in city rejuvenation because these projects involved only housing, parking, and stores and did not include the businesses that formed the city's economic base. That demonstration would come from the redevelopment of the Golden Triangle in Pittsburgh.

Manhattan, 1993. Stuyvesant Town provided its residents with apartments in towers in a parklike environment with sidewalks, benches, playgrounds, grass, trees, and flowers. *(Alexander Garvin)*

Pittsburgh, 1945. Fifth Avenue at 11:00 A.M. Air pollution so darkened the skies that street lamps had to be kept lighted 24 hours a day. *(Courtesy of Allegheny Conference on Community Development)*

Pittsburgh, 1983. Gateway Center helped to trigger new office construction elsewhere in the business district. *(Alexander Garvin)*

The Golden Triangle, Pittsburgh

By World War II, Pittsburgh's Triangle, at the point where the Allegheny and Monongahela Rivers join to form the Ohio, had become a jumble of railyards and lofts. Without easy highway access and parking facilities, the entire business district was becoming intolerably congested. Surrounding rivers periodically overflowed their banks. On St. Patrick's Day 1936, they rose 24 feet. Damage was estimated at $200 million. Flooding was one thing; everyday smoke, smog, and grime another. The city, eager to maintain employment in steel mills and coal fields, had refused to implement effective smoke-control regulations. As a result, day often differed little from night, and street lights remained in continuous use.[10]

Richard King Mellon, one of the city's most powerful businessmen, decided that conditions had to change. In 1943, he helped to form the Allegheny Conference on Community Development (ACCD), a group of elite business and civic leaders determined to clean up the environment and transform Pittsburgh into an efficient, modern corporate center. The ACCD developed a comprehensive improvement program that was embodied in a "Pittsburgh Package" of state legislation. Eight of its proposed ten bills were passed, including county smoke control, a public parking authority that was to build 5200 municipal garage spaces, a county traffic and transit commission, county waste-disposal facilities, and new downtown highways. The centerpiece of the package was legislation establishing a redevelopment agency with authority to plan, manage, and implement the transformation of what was to be renamed the Golden Triangle. Mayor David Lawrence appointed himself chairman of the redevelopment authority. In that capacity, Lawrence coordinated every aspect of the transformation of Pittsburgh until 1959, when he became governor.

The redevelopment plan included restoration of Fort Pitt (the 1759 fort from which modern Pittsburgh had grown), a new 36-acre Point Park, new highways and bridges connecting the city with the surrounding suburbs, Gateway Center (a 23-acre office complex financed by the Equitable Life Assurance Society), several independent office buildings, a 750-car underground garage, a hotel, and a 27-story apartment building. This combination spurred other developers to build office towers near the newly redeveloped Golden Triangle and throughout the business district. By the mid-1960s, one-quarter of downtown Pittsburgh had been rebuilt.

A National Program

Redevelopment at Stuyvesant Town and the Golden Triangle was strictly a local enterprise. If it was to be used on a national scale, there had to be a convincing public policy rationale. In postwar America, that proved to be very easy. Cities across the nation were experiencing increasing physical deterioration, loss of population, decreasing employment, declining retail sales, decreasing office occupancy, and a rapidly disappearing tax base. The flight to the suburbs was accelerating.

All sorts of people were clamoring for action: businesspeople who worked downtown, property owners who saw values plummeting, the poor who could not afford to move to the suburbs, and politicians who depended on all these people for votes.[11]

Faced with the demand for action to save America's "decaying" cities, Congress decided on a program that was based on the formula that worked for New York and Pittsburgh. Its purpose was to assist localities to "clear blighted areas" and to develop "well-planned" communities. The mechanism, embodied in Title I of the Housing Act of 1949, was a subsidy of two-thirds of the cost of redevelopment projects that had been approved by the federal government.[12]

The New Working Environment

Pre–World War II office buildings were not designed to meet the rapidly growing needs of their occupants. Tenants wanted up-to-date electrical systems, air-conditioning, and large office floors that could accommodate increasingly sophisticated business machines. Workers expected a pleasant working environment that was easily accessible by automobile. Most older office districts could not provide these conditions. The City of Tomorrow, with its highways, parking garages, broad plazas, and office towers, seemed to be what was needed.

Most city governments had neither the money nor the entrepreneurial skills to provide this brave new world. They hoped to obtain both by participating in the federal urban renewal program. This required a redevelopment agency with the ability to plan, acquire, prepare sites for development, and sell those sites at artificially low prices to developers who agreed to execute their redevelopment schemes; federal approval of their redevelopment plan; and enough money to cover a one-third share of project expenses.[13]

In Philadelphia, Boston, and New Haven, the impetus for redevelopment came from mayors who had been elected promising to redevelop what most people thought of as obsolete business districts. In Baltimore and Cincinnati, the business community led the campaign for redevelopment. It saw urban renewal as the best way of winning a market that would otherwise go to the suburbs. In Hartford, Cleveland, and San Francisco, government officials saw redevelopment as a device for obtaining federal grants. Whether politicians, businesspeople, or bureaucrats took the lead, Title I provided the subsidies to pay for replacing congested downtown districts with local visions of a new working environment. The only exception was New York City, which continued to depend on the private market to provide up-to-date commercial space.[14]

Constitution Plaza, Hartford

Hartford, Connecticut, was one of the earliest cities to seek federal funds for downtown redevelopment. In March 1950 it established a Redevelopment Agency, whose first task was to study possible sites for a Title I project. Within a year business leaders, government officials, and their consultants had agreed on the 11-acre Front–Market Street district, a "slum" that was only a block east of the city's shopping district. In comparison to other proposed sites, the relocation load (108 "marginal" businesses employing 1037 workers, 187 families, and 31 individuals) was relatively low. More important, its location between a proposed highway and the business district seemed ideal for modern office buildings.[15]

In 1952 the City of Hartford was granted Title I assistance with which to plan Constitution Plaza, a complex of glass office buildings, retail stores, and a hotel, all to be built on the Front–Market Street site. The first hurdle came in a challenge to the constitutionality of taking property from one owner for sale to another. This taking issue was overcome in 1954, when the State Supreme Court ruled in favor of the Redevelopment Agency. In 1956, voters approved an $800,000 bond issue to cover the local one-third share of the project's cost. Only in 1958, when relocation was completed, could demolition begin.

Four developers presented plans for the project. F. H. McGraw and Company, the winning bidder, spent 2 years trying to arrange financing for the project. When it failed, the Travelers' Insurance Company came to the rescue, organizing a subsidiary, Constitution Plaza Inc., to finance, build, and operate the project. Travelers', one of Hartford's many insurance companies, needed better office space, understood the local market, and had a commitment to improving the city. Most important, it was in the business of financing real estate development.

Constitution Plaza is an independent enclave built on a platform that covers a 1875-car garage. It was conceived in conjunction with an elevated highway, structured parking, and retail facilities that were intended to serve its occupants. In Hartford, this was a recipe that damaged rather than helped the central business district.

The marginal businesses and deteriorating residences that had occupied the site of Constitution Plaza were not the cause of Hartford's decreasing building occupancy and retail sales. Demand for office space was declining because companies like the Connecticut General Life Insurance Company (2300 jobs) and the Fuller Brush Company (1500 jobs) were moving to the suburbs. Retail sales were declining because office workers also were moving to the suburbs and shopping closer to home. Clearance could not restore this market.

The firms that relocated to Constitution Plaza did not fill the gap. Worse, they moved to an enclave that was designed to be separate from the rest of downtown Hartford. Workers and visitors can park in the project and go directly to their offices without having to set foot in the city. If they need to purchase something they can do so at one of Constitution Plaza's underutilized stores. Those who do visit the business district have to cross Market Street, which was widened as part of the project and only further separates Constitution Plaza from the city.

Hartford, 1953. Front–Market Street prior to clearance for Constitution Plaza. *(From Louis Redstone, The New Downtowns, McGraw-Hill, New York, 1976; courtesy of McGraw-Hill)*

Hartford, 1981. The overpass that became an empty pedestrian-entry level for commercial structures at Constitution Plaza. *(Alexander Garvin)*

Despite its failure to revitalize Hartford's business district, Constitution Plaza proved to be a bonanza for its government sponsors. Prior to redevelopment, the 11 acres that were cleared for the project had been assessed at $2.3 million and paid $103,000 in annual real estate taxes. Upon completion, in 1964, the renewal area was reassessed at $23.4 million and paid $1.05 million in annual real estate taxes. Since the City of Hartford needed only $800,000 to cover the local share of Title I subsidies, it was able to recoup its initial investment in less than 1 year.

New Haven, Connecticut

The redevelopment of downtown New Haven was an outgrowth of the mayoral election of 1953, in which Democrat Richard C. Lee defeated the city's incumbent Republican mayor. A central feature of Lee's winning campaign was the promise to implement redevelopment plans that had been discussed for years, but had never moved beyond the planning stage. The new mayor quickly appointed Edward Logue as Development Administrator. Logue was a recent graduate of the Yale Law School who had been active in his campaign. While Mayor Lee rallied public support for the redevelopment program, Logue packaged the projects. Together they bulldozed Washington into paying for them and were so successful that New Haven received more Title I subsidies per capita than any other city in the country (see Chapter 11).[16]

The Church Street Redevelopment Project was the downtown cornerstone of that program. Its major objective was maintaining New Haven's role as one of Connecticut's premier retail centers. A detailed market survey had concluded that New Haven's population would remain at its 1950 level, 164,000, for the next 40 years. The surrounding suburban market was projected to grow from 156,000 to 746,000. Its authors had reasoned that if the city became more accessible to these suburbanites, it would remain a major retail center.[17]

The idea was to make a three-block section of Church Street the terminus of a highway connector that brought retail customers downtown. Once there, they would park in the garage, do their shopping, and go to a show at the Shubert Theater or at one of the movie palaces that were within a block or two of the site. New Haven's existing streets and blocks were to remain in place. George Street was to be bridged by a six-story garage that connected directly into two department stores. Crown Street was to be bridged by a climate-controlled walkway connecting the garage and department stores with an air-conditioned shopping mall, office building, and hotel.

The well-known Broadway producer Roger Stevens was designated as the project's developer. Stevens had been chairman of the Finance Committee of the Democratic National Committee during the 1952 presidential campaign. More important, he was a successful real estate investor who had recently put together the syndicate that purchased the Empire State Building. His expertise, however, was in financing and operating already revenue-producing real estate, not in developing complex projects.

Stevens was involved in many ventures and could devote only limited time to Church Street. Consequently, Lee and Logue took the lead in developing the project. They worked hard to overcome political opposition, bureaucratic inertia, and lawsuits. They even persuaded one of the city's surviving department stores, Malley's, to give up its prime downtown location and participate in the renewal project. Despite these efforts, in 1961, when Church Street was cleared and ready to go, the only component of their plan that was under way was the 1280-car municipal garage. Lack of progress became a campaign issue and Lee came within 4000 votes of losing the election.

Construction costs and interest rates had increased during the 6 years since the project had been announced. Stevens wanted out. The financial deal that he had envisioned was no longer feasible. Logue had gone on to direct the Boston

New Haven, c. 1954. Church Street prior to redevelopment. *(Courtesy of New Haven Redevelopment Agency)*

New Haven, 1994. Empty department stores on Church Street three decades after redevelopment. *(Alexander Garvin)*

Redevelopment Authority. Mayor Lee had no choice but to take an even more active role in packaging Church Street. In 1962 he persuaded Macy's, which had discussed participating in the project for 5 years, to open a second department store on the site. Two years later the Fusco-Amatruda Construction Company, took over from Stevens.

Finally, more than a decade after the project had been announced, the redevelopment of Church Street was complete. It did not become the commercial center its planners had envisioned. Not long after completion, Malley's Department Store went out of business. The building has remained vacant ever since. The shopping mall was a failure until the late 1980s when a new city administration provided substantial subsidies and brought in the Rouse Company to renovate and remarket the project. That effort was seriously damaged in 1993, when Macy's closed its doors.

From the start, redeveloping downtown New Haven was a mistake. The market survey on which the project was based had incorrectly predicted that the city's population would remain stable for 30 years. By 1980 it had shrunk to 126,000. Although this shrinkage meant fewer customers, the suburban market, which in 1980 had grown to 635,000, should have been more than enough to fill the gap.[18] Instead, this suburban population had chosen to shop elsewhere. Between 1960 and 1973, seven major shopping complexes containing 3,342,000 square feet of floor area opened in surrounding suburbs. They attracted the market New Haven lost.

Charles Center, Baltimore

Like Hartford and New Haven, Baltimore was experiencing declining retail sales (a 10 percent drop in department-store sales between 1952 and 1957) and declining downtown tax assessments (a similar 10 percent drop between 1952 and 1957). Although office occupancy had remained a steady 97 percent since 1942, the business community was sufficiently concerned that in 1954 it formed a Committee for Downtown, Inc. and a year later the Greater Baltimore Committee, Inc. Both organizations were dedicated to fighting what they perceived as alarming deterioration in the central business district, where three-quarters of the office buildings had been erected prior to 1920. In fact, nothing new had been built since 1928.[19]

The two groups came together to form the Planning Council of the Greater Baltimore Committee. This private, nonprofit, planning organization became the technical consultant for the redevelopment of downtown Baltimore and, under contract, for other civic groups and government bodies. Because the Planning Council was not a municipal agency, it was less likely to succumb to political pressure or government inertia. More important, by avoiding out-of-town consultants, it was forced to face local realities and get directly involved with project implementation.

The Planning Council hired David Wallace, an architect-planner who would later head the firm of Wallace-McHarg Associates. He directed a team of experts that included George Kostritsky, later a partner in the architectural firm of Rogers, Taliaferro, Kostritsky, and Lamb, and Dennis Durden, who would later spearhead the redevelopment of downtown Cincinnati. Their goal was to devise a project that would generate further private redevelopment elsewhere in the business district. That meant a project that was big enough to have real impact, but not big enough to fully satisfy the demand. They

Baltimore, 1964. The business district with Charles Center after clearance for redevelopment and after completion of the first new office building. *(Courtesy of ULI—Urban Land Institute)*

wanted to avoid project success at the expense of other downtown development and did so by planning to satisfy only two-thirds of identified demand for additional office space.

The 33-acre site they selected for the project, which became known as Charles Center, was right in the middle of the city, where it could create a focus for and link together Baltimore's retail, government, and financial districts. Because the site dropped 66 feet from one end to the other, there was room to superimpose an entirely new pedestrian level over Baltimore's busy streets and sidewalks without disturbing existing traffic and to simultaneously slip new garages underneath the new pedestrian level.

The Planning Council was determined to avoid cutting out the heart of downtown Baltimore and then waiting, like New Haven and Hartford, for a decade while developers tried to package their projects. So it began by retaining five older buildings whose assessed value represented 47 percent of the entire 33-acre site. These pre–World War II buildings would continue to attract activity both during and after redevelopment.[20]

Instead of a single redevelopment site with one prime developer, Charles Center was subdivided into 16 parcels whose development could be timed to absorb market demand. The size of these sites made them easier to finance and therefore attractive to a broader range of developers. The

Baltimore, 1994. Old and new buildings lining the Charles Street edge of the Charles Center Urban Renewal Project. *(Alexander Garvin)*

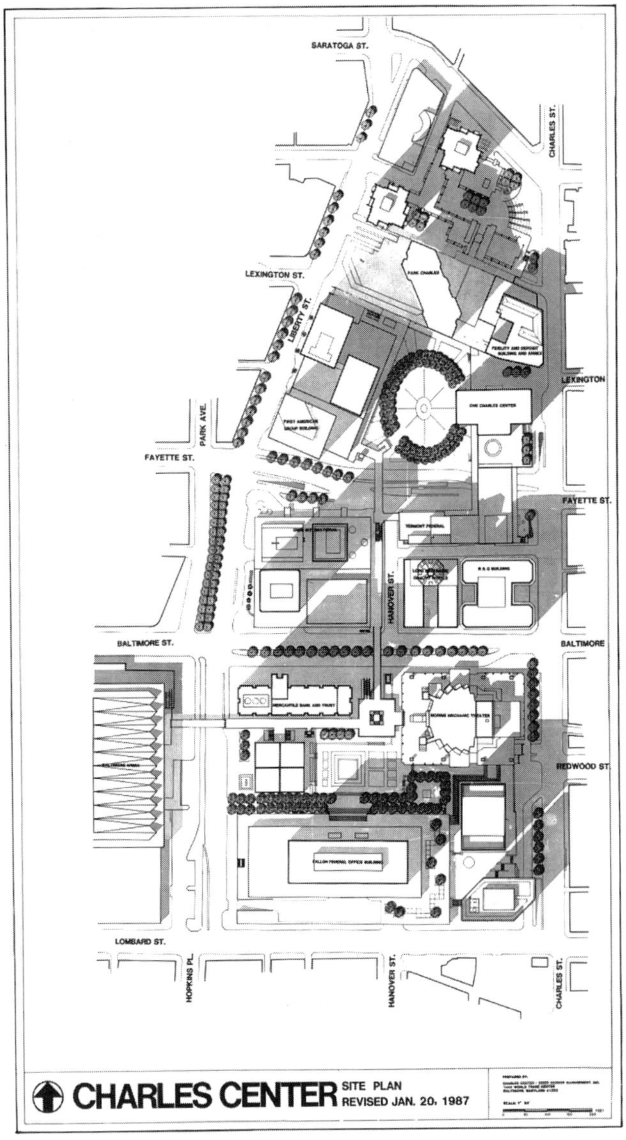

Baltimore, 1987. Redevelopment Plan for Charles Center. *(Courtesy of City of Baltimore Development Corporation)*

decision to subdivide also required careful integration of the project's many components.

Although the Baltimore Urban Renewal and Housing Agency was nominally responsible for Charles Center, and designation as a Title I project involved supervision by federal agencies, the project was implemented by a special management office directed by J. Jefferson Miller, a recently retired businessman. The office was responsible for generating public support, supervising 148 separate acquisitions involving 216 different properties, overseeing the relocation of 350 businesses with 8789 jobs, managing the disposition of the 16 development sites, coordinating public works construction, and making sure everything happened in a timely manner. As Miller explained:

> *The entire project became a Chinese puzzle. For example, the Hamburgers retail store had to be completed so that Hamburgers could move [from its original site within the redevelopment area], before we could start work in the hotel area. The Vermont Federal Savings and Loan Association had to be moved to the Sun Building, which is located in the future theater area, so that they could do business while their former home was being demolished and their new home being erected on the same spot.*[21]

The developer of the first office building was selected by competition. Six organizations submitted proposals. The winner, Metropolitan Structures of Chicago, proposed a scheme by architect Mies van der Rohe. It was selected because the jury felt that the design of this "lead" site should set a standard for the rest of the project. Later projects, whether selected by design competition, by displaced site tenants, by government agencies, or by owner-builders, were carefully adjusted to fit the scheme. Only one them, the Mechanic Theater, designed by John Johansen, can be characterized as architecturally distinctive.

When Charles Center was completed, over a decade later, it included 1.8 million square feet of office space, 430,000 square feet of retailing space, 800 hotel rooms, an 1800-seat legitimate theater, 367 apartments, and parking for 4000 cars. This new working environment was just what local businesses were looking for: convenient parking, easy access to downtown shopping, restaurants, and entertainment, and large office floors equipped to provide all the needs of modern business

Baltimore, 1994. Fayette Street as it passes through the Charles Center Urban Renewal Project. *(Alexander Garvin)*

machines. Where there once had been 12,000 jobs, there were now 17,000. Real estate taxes quadrupled. More important, Charles Center was accomplished without causing undue hardship to the site tenants that were displaced. Although 44 establishments went out of business, "93 percent of the businesses in Charles Center were relocated without liquidating. Of those that moved, 80 percent were relocated within the city of Baltimore and only 3 percent left the metropolitan area."[22]

By demonstrating that there was a market for new office space, but only satisfying a portion of that demand, Charles Center triggered even more investment outside the renewal area. Further government redevelopment projects have shifted development activity to the harbor. As a result, Charles Center itself is no longer the centerpiece of downtown Baltimore. Like the Golden Triangle in Pittsburgh, it reveals that when market demand is frustrated by an obsolete physical plant, intelligently conceived and managed reconstruction can revive a deteriorating business district.[23]

Baltimore, 1994. Truck loading-dock under the pedestrian overpass crossing Baltimore Street in the Charles Center Urban Renewal Project. *(Alexander Garvin)*

The New Residential Environment

Proponents of redevelopment had good reason for thinking that some cities could not retain commercial tenants without major physical changes to their business districts. They were wrong, however, in believing that people were leaving the city only because they found inner city residential districts filthy, congested, and inconvenient or because existing apartments had inadequate plumbing and wiring or obsolete kitchens and bathrooms. Many residents were moving to the suburbs because they wanted to own their own houses, or to give their children access to better public schools, or just to toss a ball around in their own backyards. Nevertheless, proponents of redevelopment tried to retain these people by creating modern residential environments within the city.

Most residential redevelopment projects were not generous superblocks containing all the necessities of a modern urban neighborhood. Nor were they part of a carefully integrated system of highways and autoports that accommodated

Chicago, 1993. Cabrini Green, The City of Tomorrow misunderstood. *(Alexander Garvin)*

high speed automobile traffic, or part of a vast landscaped pedestrian park that provided a verdant setting for the leisure-time activities of the residents. They were grotesque caricatures of Le Corbusier's images of a brave new world.

Portland Center, Oregon

Civic leaders in Portland, Oregon, worried about the same problems that troubled their counterparts in other cities. Taxpaying residents were moving to the suburbs. Downtown retail sales were declining. They also saw the problem in terms of physical and functional obsolescence and decided the solution lay in redeveloping a 54-block "slum" on the edge of the business district. In 1950, the area was filled with junkyards, run-down hotels, dilapidated apartment buildings, and abandoned commercial structures. It also was home for 2300 people, 43 percent of whom were in single-person households.[24]

When redevelopment was first proposed, in 1952, the plan was to clear the entire 83.5 acres for a new civic auditorium and support services for the nearby business district. Four years later, when the area was rejected as the site for the civic auditorium, the project simultaneously lost its raison d'être and its developer. The Portland Urban Renewal Agency then proposed dividing the "South Auditorium" project into three residential superblocks.

The market for downtown apartment towers in Portland had yet to be tested. Consequently, neither real estate developers nor financial institutions were willing to risk their time and money on the project. The necessary entrepreneurial element was supplied in 1958 when Portland voters approved the creation of a new public agency: the Portland Development Commission (PDC) which, together with the newly created Portland Center Development Corporation, accepted responsibility for reviving the ill-fated South Auditorium project.

In 1961, they hired the architecture firm of Skidmore Owings and Merrill (S.O.M.) to redesign the project and Lawrence Halprin and Associates to devise suitable landscap-

Washington, D.C., 1990. A reasonable approximation of Le Corbusier's "new living environment" in the Southwest Urban Renewal Project. *(Alexander Garvin)*

Portland, 1990. Residential apartments at Portland Center. *(Alexander Garvin)*

ing. Their plan for what became known as Portland Center still called for superblocks but retained the city's 200-foot street grid as a series of pedestrian walkways that defined building sites and recreation areas. However, it was redesigned as an integrated complex of apartment towers, low-rise buildings, offices, convenience retail stores, and generous, landscaped public spaces.

Today, residents of Portland Center still stroll past Halprin's landscaped walkways, fountains, and sitting areas on their way to apartments with impressive views of the city. Many continue to do their shopping within the superblock. More important, they live within walking distance of their downtown jobs. Their presence helps to keep the business district alive after the commuters have driven home.

There is no way of knowing whether Portland Center attracted residents who would otherwise have moved to the suburbs. What is clear is that it satisfied the demand for a downtown residential environment.

Portland, 1990. Commercial edge of Portland Center as it merges into the central business district. *(Alexander Garvin)*

The Moses Method

Although New York City rejected Title I as a mechanism for refurbishing its business districts, it enthusiastically adopted it as a way of providing an improved in-town living environment. The program that emerged was based on Stuyvesant Town. Sites had to be at least 12 acres so that, like Stuyvesant Town, they could provide a critical mass that would survive any pressures from surrounding neighborhoods.

Mayor William O'Dwyer, anticipating Congressional approval of the urban renewal program, had appointed a Committee on Slum Clearance chaired by City Construction Coordinator Robert Moses. Moses had built bridges, tunnels, and highways, created vast expanses of public beach, and doubled the city's park acreage. Now he would rebuild whole neighborhoods.

The Moses method was production-oriented and shaped by political reality. He understood that most private develop-

Bronx, 1958. Rendering of the Mott Haven Urban Renewal Project, one of Robert Moses' many unexecuted redevelopment schemes. *(Courtesy of the Citizens Housing and Planning Council)*

ers and financial institutions were not ready to get involved in the untried program Congress had enacted. So he negotiated with builders in private. When both parties arrived at an acceptable plan, Moses printed a brochure that presented the proposal and inevitably resulted in local opposition. The project was then submitted to the City Planning Commission (including Moses as a voting member), which held public hearings prior to approving it and passing it to the Board of Estimate for another public hearing and final approval. The city then condemned the site and immediately transferred it to the developer. From that point on, the developer assumed the burden of relocating the businesses and families on the designated sites.

Skidmore, Owings, and Merrill was the coordinating architect for many of these early projects. The firm produced handsomely illustrated brochures analyzing each neighborhood, proposing a site plan, apartment layouts, and financing, and indicating that a sizable number of site tenants would be eligible for public housing. In practice the results were very different. The projects themselves were not designed by S.O.M. and looked more like dormitory stockades than the sumptuously landscaped superblocks illustrated in the brochures. The waiting list for public housing was so long that relocatees seldom moved to the public housing projects that Moses referred to as relocation resources. Like the relocatees from Portland Center, most could not afford to move back to what had once been their old neighborhood.

Moses had little trouble from Washington because New York City had the most active and successful program in the country. Federal officials could point to New York City where Moses was "getting things done." By 1956, when redevelopment in most cities was only getting started, he had already begun 10 projects involving construction of 15,341 apartments.[25]

Other cities cleared sites before selecting a sponsor and then had trouble interesting developers in their projects. Once new buildings finally began to emerge in other cities, however, federal officials began to pull in the reins on Moses' methods. With so much housing under way, they could afford to pay more attention to the mounting criticism of the urban renewal program.

Opposition

There had been opposition to urban renewal from the very beginning. When Constitution Plaza in Hartford was first proposed, opponents went to court. They claimed that the area was not blighted and the project would eliminate jobs and rob the city of its ethnic heritage. Like the opponents to redevelopment in most cities, they lost. Critics were more successful in New York City, where opposition forced even the redoubtable Robert Moses to drop three of his first five urban renewal projects.[26]

Manhattan, 1958. Morningside-Manhattanville Urban Renewal Project approved after a 2-year battle with area residents and the public housing project (Grant Houses) that was completed too soon to provide housing for relocatees from the Renewal Project. *(Courtesy of the Citizens Housing and Planning Council, New York)*

A substantial number of Moses' projects never proceeded beyond the brochure stage or were altered significantly in response to opposition from site tenants and their political representatives. In 1950, when Moses proposed a project on Morningside Heights, just north of Columbia University, residents objected to characterizing the area as a slum. The residents organized a "Committee to Save Our Homes" that managed to stall approval for 2 years. In 1957, to obtain approval of his twelfth project, Lincoln Center, Moses had to drop 4 of the 18 blocks he had proposed for clearance 2 years earlier (see Chapter 4).

Eventually, the ever-practical Moses began to avoid center city locations, proposing instead sites that were in fringe areas where the relocation load would not be as serious. Nevertheless, criticism continued to mount. In response, Mayor Robert Wagner in 1959 commissioned studies of the city's housing, relocation, and renewal programs. They were part of the Mayor's strategy to force Moses to resign as chairman of the Committee on Slum Clearance and to alter the character of the city's urban renewal program.[27] The strategy worked. When Moses resigned in 1960, 39 urban renewal projects were either still officially under way or in planning. The city eventually dropped 16 of them.[28]

Urban renewal was also under attack from widely read critics such as Herbert Gans, Martin Anderson, and Jane Jacobs (see Chapter 11). Gans argued that many renewal areas were not slums at all, but vibrant neighborhoods whose major problem was the low income of their residents. Anderson insisted that one did not fix city neighborhoods by bulldozing them. Jacobs contended that the mistake lay in accepting Le Corbusier's vision of an ideal city. As she explained, "It was so orderly, so visible, so easy to understand. It said everything in a flash, like a good advertisement....But as to how the city works, it tells....nothing but lies."[29]

Transfiguration and Death

Congress tinkered with urban renewal from the beginning. When it amended the program in 1954 to make housing rehabilitation an allowable activity, it was responding to legitimate complaints from constituents. Members of Congress did not care that investing in old-world leftovers eliminated any chance of creating a completely modern city.

Because of opposition from relocatees and their advocates, Congress amended the Housing Act in 1959 to require relocation plans for every renewal project. It kept increasing relocation benefits until the Uniform Relocation Act of 1970 finally pushed costs to a level that severely restricted anything but the most selective slum clearance.

Civic organizations and community groups often argued for indigenous solutions and questioned the effectiveness of replicating similar project designs for every situation. Congress reinforced this criticism when it amended the Housing Act in 1959 to guarantee the participation of site tenants in the planning process. It now required that each renewal project have a Citizen Project Advisory Committee. As a result, when Logue left New Haven to take over Boston's redevelopment program he established project offices in every community slated for renewal. The staff in these offices worked with the designated Citizen Project Advisory Committee and with local businesses, settlement houses, and every other interest group in the area. The proposals that emerged had little to do with any vision of utopia. Even so, they usually sparked opposition and were often altered to meet neighborhood political reality prior to any formal approval.[30]

Finally, on January 5, 1973, President Richard Nixon unilaterally declared a moratorium on all new housing and renewal projects. He was able to do so because the projects had become too costly and the opponents too powerful. It would be convenient to hold Nixon accountable for the death of urban renewal. However, when he declared his moratorium, urban renewal itself had become a dying thing.

Until the Nixon moratorium, every city had to compete for its share of national urban-renewal funding. As a result, the projects kept coming. Congress ended the competition for urban renewal grants and guaranteed each locality its fair share of federal funds when it passed the Housing and Community Development Act of 1974, a week after Nixon left office (see Chapter 11).

The new act created block grants that could be used for a variety of purposes, not just redevelopment. Everybody assumed that new urban renewal projects, less expensive ones, would be forthcoming. They were not. America had lost faith in government-subsidized redevelopment. Besides, property owners across the country were rebuilding city districts without renewal assistance. Local governments, noticing this unassisted private redevelopment, chose to spend their block grants on all possible other purposes. The effort to rebuild cities section by section was over.

Ingredients of Success

Few people believe urban renewal worked. As evidence, they point to areas still experiencing physical deterioration, declining retail sales, and a decreasing tax base. What they fail to understand is that these are symptoms of continuing urban shrinkage that could well have been worse had there been no redevelopment. Moreover, they are usually referring to those parts of town where redevelopment had either not taken place or was inappropriate from the moment it was conceived.

In some places, urban renewal worked but its critics were so vocal that they drew attention away from its successes. Projects like Pittsburgh's Golden Triangle and Baltimore's Charles Center demonstrated that by removing portions of a city that were impediments to a prosperous economy, an entire city could be revived. They also demonstrated that replacing whole cities section by section was not only politically and financially impossible; it was also unnecessary. Le Corbusier had been mistaken. The city itself was not a "dying thing."

Market

Physical reconstruction is not a solution to urban shrinkage. It may make city districts safer or more convenient. But, as the redevelopment of Church Street in New Haven demonstrates, it cannot provide retail customers, especially when competitors supply rapidly growing suburbs with more convenient alternatives.

Where consumer demand is strong, redevelopment can provide cities with the means of retaining its customers. The Golden Triangle, for example, allowed Pittsburgh to supply the business community with the physical environment it demanded and otherwise would have had to seek elsewhere. Because the project only satisfied the needs of a few large corporations, once reconstruction of the Triangle was under way, developers sought sites for additional new buildings that were needed by other firms and thereby triggered the Pittsburgh Renaissance. It is more difficult to assess the effectiveness of residential redevelopment as a device for retaining population. Stuyvesant Town, Portland Center, and projects like them were meant to provide an alternative to the suburbs. They decreased densities, increased open space, and provided community amenities. Successful as they may have been in attracting largely white, middle-class residents, they could never have reversed the flight to the suburbs that had been under way since the start of the nineteenth century.

In New York City, where the residential vacancy rate was minimal, the urban renewal sites that Robert Moses cleared were virtually certain to be occupied. Although market demand was comparable in surrounding neighborhoods, his housing redevelopment projects were unable to generate further activity because competitors could not match this subsidized competition. They had neither Title I grants to reduce the cost of assembling and holding a site till it was ready for construction, nor FHA mortgage insurance with which to obtain long-term, low-equity mortgages and thereby reduce debt service. Instead, developers built in less deteriorated, more expensive neighborhoods where they could charge enough to recoup their investment and earn a reasonable return.

Location

State laws usually restrict redevelopment to blighted areas. Consequently, projects are automatically saddled with locations where the market is not vigorous. This can be overcome by selecting blighted sites in the midst of otherwise healthy districts. Charles Center, for example, could tap demand from virtually contiguous downtown shopping, government, and financial districts. At the same time its occupants spilled over to increase market demand in those districts. Conversely, Hartford's government and shopping districts, although nearby, were just far enough away to prevent Constitution Plaza from having the same synergistic impact on the rest of downtown.

A blighted location on the edge of a downtown business district may be just what is needed for successful residential redevelopment. Portland Center was close enough to benefit from downtown employment and entertainment opportunities. New York City's transit system provided its early Title I projects with similar proximity to the business district. In most cities the locations chosen for redevelopment were already occupied by thousands of people and hundreds of businesses that had to be relocated. During the 1950s, relocation expenses were low enough that they did not affect project feasibility. Once protest from citizen groups and the politicians they elected forced Congress to adopt the Uniform Relocation Act of 1970 such inner-city redevelopment became feasible only where, as at Charles Center, it did not involve complete clearance and retained economically healthy businesses or, as in downtown Pittsburgh, it removed land uses that had serious negative impact on surrounding properties.

Design

The City of Tomorrow remains a vision that can be experienced only in Le Corbusier's drawings. Since it was never brought to fruition it is a mistake to place the entire blame for the failures of specific redevelopment projects on his image of the future. Too often, the designers of these projects copied his brave new world without fully understanding what he had in mind.

Their most serious error was to assume that a new city could be created one superblock at a time. The cultural and consumer activities needed by any successful city require a critical mass. That critical mass cannot be mathematically divided and apportioned to individual projects. Thus, when redevelopment consists of an independent project, rather than a network of interconnected projects, neither the project nor the surrounding city can benefit from that redevelopment. Constitution Plaza is such a project set apart from the rest of downtown Hartford. It can only support activities needed by the users of its office towers. Charles Center, on the other hand, was conceived as an integral part of downtown Baltimore. Together with the surrounding busy blocks, it attracts a sufficient concentration of people to support the widest array of land uses.

It is also a misunderstanding to equate spacious public open spaces and shiny glass towers with urban renewal. There is nothing inherently wrong with glass skyscrapers. Designed by fine architects they can rival the greatest of architectural monuments. In the hands of the men who designed most of the high-rise boxes of our redevelopment projects, they are as uninspired as the somewhat smaller boxes of their suburban competitors.

New buildings, whether they are well-designed or not, are not the key to economic or social revival. The redevelopment of Church Street replaced hundreds of "obsolete" structures with brand-new buildings. Nevertheless, New Haven continued to decline. On the other hand, Charles Center successfully revived downtown Baltimore precisely because it integrated old buildings with the new.

Large open areas are no more inherently incompatible with an exciting urban environment than new buildings. But, when they take the form of the vast emptiness of many redevelopment projects, they deaden rather than revitalize the city around them. Light, air, and dramatic vistas are not enough. The trees and grass in many redevelopment projects help in providing color, scale, and the pleasure of foliage but they too are not enough. Urban areas need open spaces that attract people and the activities that they bring with them. Where designers provide a program for this parklike environment, they bring these public spaces to life. At Stuyvesant Town, paved playgrounds for younger children, paved ball courts for teenagers, benches for watching parents, and tree-lined walkways for strolling adults provide the setting for social interaction. Portland Center created a verdant atmosphere conducive to leisurely strolling, tranquil meditation, and active recreation. In countless other residential redevelopment projects the vast stretches of dusty grass provide only a setting for conflict between maintenance workers and "trespassing" tenants.

The success of a redevelopment project depends more on the arrangement of its components than on generous open space or new buildings. The parking garage in the Church Street Redevelopment Project, for example, is so located that shoppers can go directly into a department store without setting foot anywhere else in the project or in downtown New Haven. As a result, New Haven does not profit much from the customers attracted to Church Street. At Charles Center, on the other hand, underground parking is scattered throughout the project. This results in mutually reinforcing interaction among the project's retail customers, theater goers, residents, and office workers. Because these garages are also used by people coming and going from other destinations in downtown Baltimore, they increase the synergistic relationship between Charles Center and the rest of the city.

Financing

Lending institutions are not eager to risk their assets prior to project occupancy. If anything goes wrong, they will be left holding the bag. By transferring to government agencies the cost of carrying a project (interest on the money used for site acquisition, real estate tax payments prior to resale to the ultimate developer, professional fees, and site development costs), Title I provided financing when it was least likely to be forthcoming from the private sector.

Ordinarily, development sites are sold at a price that reflects the "highest and best use" of the property. In redevelopment projects, sites are sold at a lower price that reflects the reuse specified in the redevelopment plan. Inevitably, the actual costs of acquiring, carrying, and preparing the property for this reuse will exceed even that lower price. By subsidizing the difference between the gross project cost and a resale price that is justified by this planned reuse, government makes that reuse financially feasible.

Carrying the cost of project development and subsidizing reuse price is no guarantee of success. Early projects like Constitution Plaza and Church Street had difficulty obtaining long-term financing because they had to be financed as a whole and thus required extremely large sums of money. Charles Center overcame this difficulty by subdividing the redevelopment area into smaller parcels that required smaller mortgages and lower equity investments. Once FHA 220 mortgage insurance became available, housing redevelopment projects no longer faced this problem. Institutions were ready to provide mortgage loans for projects in areas that officially had been designated as blighted because lenders were insured against loss by the federal government.

Entrepreneurship

Just as financing has to be provided both for the site and for development, so does entrepreneurship. Most early redevelopment projects had neither the public entrepreneurs to ram through their plans, nor private entrepreneurs with the ability to package financing, design, and construction. Lee and Logue in New Haven were particularly effective public entrepreneurs when it came to obtaining local political support and federal subsidies for their redevelopment schemes. But even they ran into trouble with Church Street because Roger Stevens, the private developer to whom they had entrusted the project, was not effective enough in putting together the development package.

The planners of Charles Center, who had the benefit of seeing this problem in New Haven and other cities, understood that market demand and a suitable site for development, by themselves, did not automatically result in project completion. Without skilled public and private entrepreneurs, "the project itself could fail, and the market growth could express itself elsewhere within the metropolitan area."[31] Their solution to this problem was to offer important parcels for development by public competition. Each developer/architect team had to demonstrate its ability to design, finance, and build its proposal. Other sites were sold directly to users who had the necessary financial strength to develop them.

Robert Moses thought he would avoid the entrepreneurship problem by first negotiating a deal with private developers and then announcing what he hoped would be a fait accompli. This was not always successful. From the beginning, political leaders were able to prevent some of his redevelopment schemes from obtaining the necessary public approvals. As the painful impact of relocation became increasingly evident, community groups also found that they could force delays and changes, and sometimes even defeat him. Eventually, Moses' disdain for his opponents interfered too much with the political feasibility of his projects. His increasingly unsuccessful public entrepreneurship became enough of a liability that Mayor Wagner was able to force him from office.

Time

Early redevelopment projects did little to manipulate the time that people spent as they made their way to their destination. As redevelopment planners became more sophisticated, however, they began to give shape to that time. The planners of early redevelopment projects thought little about what would occur over a 24-hour period, 365 days a year. Consequently, projects such as Constitution Plaza are empty at night and on weekends and thus have a deadening effect on the surrounding city. Later projects considered their impact throughout an entire week. Charles Center, for example, includes apartment buildings, a department store, restaurants, and even a major theater because its planners knew that these facilities would keep downtown Baltimore alive after 6:00 P.M. and on weekends.

Redevelopment as a City Planning Strategy

Today it is clear that America's cities were not terminally ill. Some of them were losing a part of their population, employment base, and retail sales to surrounding suburbs. Downtown redevelopment did not reverse this decline. Nevertheless, where there was steady or increasing demand for downtown locations, as in Baltimore, redevelopment did simplify, accelerate, and reduce the cost of supplying sites that could satisfy the demand for new office buildings, retail facilities, and hotel and convention business.

We will never really know whether widespread residential redevelopment could have attracted the market that fled to the suburbs. The revival of the Dupont Circle and Adams Morgan areas of Washington, D.C., the Haight-Ashbury and Mission districts of San Francisco, and countless other older urban-neighborhoods leads one to doubt that cities needed new residential districts "vertical to the sky, open to light and air, clear and radiant and sparkling" to keep their population from moving to the suburbs.

However, where functional obsolescence is a problem, redevelopment projects can help to reverse downtown decline. New highways can provide access for thousands of trucks that supply the myriad of goods and services needed in any modern city. Multilevel garages can provide parking for tens of thousands of office workers and downtown shoppers, without whom the modern city would have little or no economic base.

Whether such redevelopment requires federal subsidies is not at all clear. In cities with and without downtown renewal projects, private developers continued to assemble sites for large, new office buildings. Highways and garages, not government-created and subsidized redevelopment parcels, were the critical elements in retaining existing businesses and attracting the growing market for new office space.

From the start, the City of Tomorrow has been a tantalizing mirage. There never was any possibility of clearing America's great cities and rebuilding them in Le Corbusier's image, nor of squeezing his utopian vision into the scaled-down projects that met Title I requirements. Instead, the federal urban renewal program became a mechanism for meeting the needs of the politicians, municipal officials, downtown business interest, and developers who wished to alter the character of their cities.

Politicians saw redevelopment, often correctly, as a mechanism for retaining a competitive position within a growing but increasingly suburbanized metropolitan region. Besides, it provided patronage jobs. They supported the program as long as the voters remained in favor of redevelopment.

Municipal officials advocated redevelopment because it generated tremendous amounts of federal money, often at little or no cost to the city government. The City of Hartford, for example, was able to recoup its investment in Constitution Plaza in less than 1 year. New Haven was so adept at manipulating its noncash contributions that redevelopment probably resulted in a cash surplus (see Chapter 11).

Downtown business interests favored redevelopment because it subsidized improvements to their competitive position. The program allowed government to move businesses, land uses, and people that interfered with their market. It also provided these businesses with new locations and modern buildings that might not otherwise have been affordable.

Many developers who participated in the program found it very profitable. They did not have to waste their time assembling property because they could obtain sites that were already approved for development. The price they paid for these sites did not reflect their true cost. Price was artificially set at a level that made development attractive. More important, developers did not have to spend a penny until the necessary government approvals were in place. Their competitors still had to struggle with conventional real estate development.

Eventually, opponents of redevelopment made the program extremely difficult and expensive to execute. Environmental protection and historic preservation statutes precluded indiscriminate use of the power of eminent domain. Relocation requirements greatly increased project costs. Most important, by making redevelopment one among many permitted uses of the Community Development Block Grant, Congress forced its proponents to compete with other demands for federal subsidies.

While redevelopment remains a viable prescription for some situations, further legislation is not needed. When and where cities wish to replace a functionally obsolete physical plant, the necessary enabling legislation is already in place. There are even projects like Baltimore's Charles Center and Portland Center that can serve as models for future development.

Only a handful of cities will have good reasons to choose redevelopment. The experience, both good and bad, with Title I will stand them in good stead. The rest should avoid it, because there are very few situations in which government-subsidized redevelopment is the proper mechanism for fixing the American city.

Notes

1. This chapter is dedicated to Vincent Scully in whose class more than 30 years ago I first was presented with the comparison of Le Corbusier's *City of Tomorrow* and New York City's housing projects.
2. Title I of the Housing Act of 1949 subsidized 2532 projects in 992 cities. In addition, 429 cities (virtually all of which also received Title I money) participated in the NDP program enacted in 1968. These two programs distributed $12,680,880,000 in federal renewal funds. Source: U.S. Department of Housing and Urban Development, Program Completion Division.
3. Le Corbusier, *The City of Tomorrow, and Its Planning* (first published in Paris in 1924), MIT Press, Cambridge, 1971, pp. 171 and 280.
4. Ibid., p. 167.
5. Le Corbusier, *The Radiant City* (first published in 1933), The Orion Press, New York City, 1967, pp. 162–163.
6. Ibid., p. 71.
7. Mel Scott, *American City Planning Since 1890,* University of California Press, Berkeley and Los Angeles, 1969, p. 361.
8. Historical and statistical information on Stuyvesant Town is derived from Arthur Simon, *Stuyvesant Town USA,* New York University Press, New York, 1970.
9. Arthur Simon, op. cit., p. 31.
10. Historical and statistical information on the redevelopment of the Golden Triangle is derived from Roy Lubove, *Twentieth Century Pittsburgh,* John Wiley & Sons, New York, 1969, pp. 106–141, and Robert C. Alberts, *The Shaping of the Point,* University of Pittsburgh Press, Pittsburgh, 1980.
11. Jon C. Teaford, *The Rough Road to Renaissance,* The Johns Hopkins University Press, Baltimore, 1990.

12. In urban renewal projects subsidized by the Housing Act of 1949, *net project cost* (the difference between *gross project cost* [acquisition, relocation, demolition, site preparation, and required infrastructure and community facilities] and the subsidized *resale price* needed to make the planned construction financially attractive to private developers) is divided between the federal and local governments. The federal government pays two-thirds. In many states the local share is split 50-50 between state and city. This local contribution did not have to be made in cash. A city could get a *noncash credit* for the cost of infrastructure and community facilities. Since most urban renewal areas took place in areas where infrastructure and community facilities were obsolete and required replacement, the expenditures eventually would have been made anyway. So the noncash credits effectively reduce local cost still further.
13. Title I restricted eligibility to sites that were "predominantly" residential prior to or after redevelopment. Cities whose proposed downtown projects did not meet either test applied under a 10 percent exception provision. Congress expanded eligibility when it amended the Housing Act in 1954.
14. It is ironic that during the 1980s, when most city governments had abandoned government-subsidized redevelopment, New York adopted it for 42d Street in Manhattan and Hunter's Point in Queens.
15. Historical and statistical information on the redevelopment of Constitution Plaza is derived from Joel R. Fredericks, *The Front-Market Urban Renewal Project: An Evaluation,* unpublished, 1975; and James Armstrong, *Constitution Plaza: A Development Analysis,* unpublished, 1978.
16. Historical and statistical information on the redevelopment of Church Street is derived from Alan Talbot, *The Mayor's Game,* Harper & Row, New York, 1967; Robert A. Dahl, *Who Governs?,* Yale University Press, New Haven, 1961; Raymond Wolfinger, *The Politics of Progress,* Prentice-Hall, Inc., Englewood Cliffs, 1974, pp. 298–356; L. Thomas Appleby, interview November 21, 1988; Jeanne Lowe, *Cities in a Race with Time,* Random House, New York, 1967; *Church Street Redevelopment and Renewal Plan,* New Haven, September 3, 1957, revised through May 27, 1964; and numerous discussions with A. Tappan Wilder.
17. Homer Hoyt Associates, *Market Survey of Stores in the Church Street Project,* Washington, D.C., 1958.
18. U.S. Department of Commerce, Bureau of the Census, *State and Metropolitan Area Data Book 1991,* U.S. Government Printing Office, Washington, D.C., 1991, p. 192.
19. Historical and statistical information on the redevelopment of Charles Center is derived from Martin Millspaugh (editor), *Baltimore's Charles Center: A Case Study in Downtown Development,* Urban Land Institute, Washington, D.C., 1964; Baltimore Department of Housing and Community Development, *Prospectus, Charles Center Development Area 16B,* Baltimore Department of Housing and Community Development, Baltimore, 1968; John Morris Dixon, "Charles Center," *FORUM,* New York, May 1969, pp. 48–57; and Michael Halle, "Charles Center," unpublished, 1977.
20. The buildings that were retained were the Lord Baltimore Hotel, the Fidelity Building, the Baltimore Gas & Electric Building, the Baltimore & Ohio R.R. Building, and the Eglin Parking Garage.
21. J. Jefferson Miller, "Management, Land Acquisition, Relocation," in Millspaugh (editor), op. cit., p. 40.
22. Ibid, p. 43.
23. By 1994 the locus of commercial activity in Baltimore had shifted closer to the harbor. Although Hamburgers was no longer in operation, Charles Center, enhanced by a large apartment building at the northern end of the site, was still an actively used section of the business district.
24. Historical and statistical information about Portland Center is derived from Carl Abbott, *Portland: Planning, Politics, and Growth in a Twentieth Century City,* Lincoln, University of Nebraska Press, 1983; and Gideon Bosker and Lena Lencek, *Frozen Music: A History of Portland Architecture,* Western Imprints Press of the Oregon Historical Society, Portland, 1985.
25. New York City Committee on Slum Clearance, *Title I Slum Clearance Progress,* New York, September 30, 1957.
26. Only Harlem Lenox Terrace (see Chapter 11) and Corlears Hook (see Chapter 9) were built as conceived. The Williamsburg, Delancey Street, and Greenwich Village Projects were eventually dropped.
27. See J. Anthony Panuch, *Relocation in New York City,* New York, 1959, and *Building a Better New York,* New York, 1960.
28. New York City Committee on Slum Clearance, *Title I Progress,* New York, January 29, 1960.
29. Jane Jacobs, *Death and Life of Great American Cities,* p. 23.
30. Langley Carleton Keyes, Jr., *The Rehabilitation Planning Game,* MIT Press, Cambridge, 1969.
31. Dennis Durden, "The Feasibility Study," in Millspaugh (editor), op. cit., p. 32.

7

Planning for Pedestrians

Denver, 1987. 16th Street Mall. *(Alexander Garvin)*

Rotterdam was the first city to spur municipal revival by banishing the automobile. In 1940, the Luftwaffe had bombed central Rotterdam, reducing it to rubble. The Dutch government did not want to recreate the city's crowded, winding streets. Instead, it built a modern business district whose retail centerpiece, the Lijnbaan, opened in 1953. The Lijnbaan is a 3600-foot-long shopping street for pedestrians only, enlivened by trees, flowers, sitting areas, play spaces, and sculpture. It was such a success that planners everywhere were soon proposing similar schemes.[1]

In his 1956 plan, *A Greater Fort Worth Tomorrow,* Victor Gruen took pedestrianization one step further. He proposed that motor vehicles operate one level below a reconstructed central business district in which every street had been converted into a pedestrian mall (see Chapter 18).

> *No traffic laden streets to cross, no impatient waiting for the traffic signal to change, no frantic dodging of cars, no horns blaring, no sharp smell of monoxide fumes. Not even traffic officers.*[2]

Neither Fort Worth nor any other city could afford Gruen's ambitious dream. They could, however, afford to emulate the Lijnbaan by banning vehicular traffic from a few downtown blocks and installing distinctive paving, artwork, fountains, landscaping, and street furniture. No private property had to be taken for public use. Nobody was forced to relocate. Everyone could still drive downtown. Only their downtown destination now included a retail environment from which noise, fumes, and traffic had been banished.

Public officials adopted this prescription as a relatively inexpensive way of helping merchants who were desperately trying to stanch the hemorrhaging of their business. They believed that downtown workers would be more likely to remain in the business district if they could do their shopping on newly pedestrianized streets and that suburbanites would be less likely to patronize outlying shopping centers if they were offered a vehicle-free downtown alternative.[3]

Pedestrian Precincts

The new pedestrian environment took shape as fully pedestrian malls, semi-malls, transitways, and skywalks. Fully pedestrianized shopping streets or *pedestrian malls* eliminated all ordinary vehicular traffic, only permitting emergency access and service vehicles. *Semi-malls* were really avenues with widened sidewalks and narrowed roadways. Their aim was to create promenades which, like the Champs Elysées in Paris, offer an especially attractive setting for the shopper. *Transitways* combined the improved shopping environment with public transportation. In this case, a narrow portion of the old streetbed was dedicated to public transportation.

Rotterdam, 1994. After the Lijnbaan opened in 1953 it became the model for America's pedestrian shopping streets. *(Courtesy Royal Netherlands Embassy)*

Skywalks removed pedestrians from the street and created an entirely new, climate-controlled, vehicle-free system of walkways connecting shops, hotels, restaurants, office buildings, apartment houses, and garages, all one or more levels above the city's vehicular traffic.

In cities like Kalamazoo, Michigan, pedestrianizing a few blocks was enough to reverse the decline in retail sales. In Jackson, Mississippi, and Providence, Rhode Island, as well as many other cities, it failed to restore spending. As these projects reveal, successful pedestrianization is more than just exterior decoration. Brick paving, trees, benches, and new street furniture may demonstrate public concern for a declining area. Such changes are like mercurochrome, which, although it is red-colored and easy to apply, is ineffective for curing serious ailments.

Pedestrianization has worked in cities where these vehicle-free retail precincts were part of more inclusive downtown development programs. Louisville placed an air-conditioned shopping arcade right over a section of its mall and located new convention and performing arts centers within a few blocks of this arcade. Together, these facilities attracted customers who would not otherwise have come downtown. Denver built suburban transit terminals connected by a transitway with free buses running from one end to the other. The combination attracts people who might otherwise avoid the hassle of a trip downtown.

These and other successfully pedestrianized downtown retail streets attract significant additional spending because they are an integral part of a functioning central business district that also includes convenient vehicular access and circulation, parking, regional and local transit systems, and strategically located facilities patronized by large numbers of people.

Kalamazoo, 1989. The Burdick Street Pedestrian Mall, America's first pedestrianized street, opened in 1958. *(Alexander Garvin)*

Kalamazoo, Michigan

America's first pedestrianized shopping mall opened in 1959 in Kalamazoo, Michigan. Like most later pedestrian malls, it was intended to revive what everybody thought was a decaying downtown. Retail sales had been declining. Office occupancy was decreasing. Businesses were moving to more attractive suburban locations.

In 1957, Kalamazoo merchants hired Victor Gruen Associates to devise a plan that would reverse this decline. Like the plans Gruen prepared for so many other cities, the plan for Kalamazoo was a variant of his scheme for Fort Worth. Entitled *Kalamazoo—1980,* it called for a circumferential highway around the 180-acre central business district, parking facilities at regular intervals along the ring road, and downtown streets from which motor vehicles had been banned.[4]

The City Planning Commission approved the plan in 1958. However, it soon realized that there was not enough money to purchase and clear the land for the parking garages, build the circumferential highway, and transform every downtown street into a landscaped mall. As a result, the highway became a one-way ring of existing streets. The garages were turned into parking lots. The automobile-free downtown was cut back to two blocks of Burdick Street. A third block was added a year after the mall opened.

This modest scheme, designed by the city's Department of Parks and Recreation, cost $82,000. Slightly more than half was paid by assessing the abutting property owners; the rest came from the city. The city spent an additional $98,000 on street widening and utility relocation, plus $630,000 for parking facilities.

Where there had once been automobile traffic there were now trees, shrubs, fountains, sculpture, and street furniture. The Kalamazoo Mall may not be as charming or elaborate as the Lijnbaan, but, despite its modest scale and minimal cost, it attracted new customers from a trade area of 250,000 people covering seven counties.

Over its first 10 years of operation, retail sales increased annually by 10 percent. Some stores even reported 150 percent increases in gross sales during the first 5 years. Pedestrian activity throughout downtown Kalamazoo increased 30 percent. This caused sufficient wear and tear to require a $300,000 renovation, completed in 1970. In 1974, a fourth block was added, and a year later, Kalamazoo Center, a multiuse convention facility including a hotel, restaurants, shops, and a theater.

Kalamazoo's pedestrian mall was part of an overall plan for improving vehicular access, providing parking, and making its shopping facilities user-friendly. It continued to attract shoppers because civic leaders continued to make improvements to the convenience of downtown shopping. However, as America's first pedestrian shopping mall, its most important role lay in demonstrating that a vehicle-free shopping street could spark downtown revival.

Louisville, Kentucky

Pedestrianization came to Louisville the same way it came to Kalamazoo, as an attempt to stanch hemorrhaging downtown business. Fourth Street had long been the heart of Louisville's central business district. It was the site of the best hotels, department stores, and specialty shops. In the 1950s, like so many other urban retail districts, it began to face competition from suburban shopping centers. Movie theaters closed, vacant stores appeared, and general deterioration set in.

The Chamber of Commerce responded in 1959 by establishing Louisville Central Area, Inc. (LCA), a nonprofit entity with the mission of analyzing downtown problems and developing proposals to solve them. In 1962, LCA published its proposals in *Design for Downtown.* They were similar to those then being tried across the country: a redevelopment project for the riverfront, a convention center, a cultural center, and pedestrianization for Fourth Street. Since federal Title I funding for riverfront redevelopment was readily available, this part of the plan was approved the following year.[5]

Meanwhile downtown business and civic leaders and public officials tried to find ways of executing the other proposals. By 1967 they had developed a plan for 2440 feet of Fourth Street along three blocks from Broadway to Liberty Street. The plan included removing old streetcar rails, rearranging utility lines, modernizing the service alleys behind the stores, eliminating all vehicular traffic from Fourth Street, and installing decorative paving, landscaping, fountains, and street furniture.

Louisville, 1988. The Fourth Avenue Mall did not attract much additional pedestrian traffic until it was extended northward to connect with a new convention center and Hyatt Hotel. *(Alexander Garvin)*

The city proposed to purchase property along Fourth Street and resell it to developers who agreed to replace any buildings that were incompatible with the redevelopment plan. The city would then install the pedestrian mall and pay for the project by assessing all the property owners of the blocks flanking the mall. This combination was intended to give the city the same control over retail occupancy that shopping-center developers have. In this way, the city would be able to manipulate the sequence of stores passed by customers on their way to their ultimate destination.

In 1968, the state legislature rejected the assessment district because it was too large and refused to grant the power of condemnation because the area was insufficiently blighted to qualify for urban renewal. It finally approved the project 2 years later, after the power of condemnation had been eliminated and the assessment district reduced in size.

In the interim, Victor Gruen and Associates had been hired to develop a planning strategy for the city. The results, which first appeared in 1967 in *Louisville Central City: A Process for Planned Revitalization* and 2 years later in the *Louisville Center City Development Program,* were essentially the same proposals that had been on the table for nearly a decade. There may have been greater emphasis on highway access and parking, plus additional suggestions for the civic center area, two blocks west of Fourth Street. However, little else had changed.

The $1.7 million pedestrian mall, which opened in 1973, failed to stem the decline of downtown Louisville. A few stores reported increased sales; many more went out of business. Sometimes they were replaced with odd-lot discount operations, sometimes by pornography shops, sometimes by empty storefronts. Two of the mall's primary generators of potential pedestrian traffic and tourist spending, the Brown Hotel located at one end and the Seelbach Hotel at the other end, shut down.

When pedestrianization forced cars off Fourth Street, the customers inside the cars also went elsewhere. There just were not enough reasons for most people to continue to shop or spend time downtown. The mere redecoration of Fourth Street could not get the city's increasingly suburban market to avoid increasingly fashionable suburban malls.

Despite the disappointing beginning, as the pieces of the *Design for Downtown* fell into place, customers returned to Fourth Street. When the long-proposed convention center and Hyatt Hotel were completed in 1977 and 1978, the pedestrian mall was also extended north to connect up with them. It was also given a new (and presumably more elegant) name, "The Fourth Avenue Mall."

The $144 million Louisville Galleria, designed by Skidmore, Owings, and Merrill, opened in 1982, just south of the convention center and hotel. It appears to be a 110-foot-high, glazed, climate-controlled section of the pedestrian mall. In fact, it is a 6-acre complex including 890,000 square feet of office space in two 26-story towers, a renovated 1903 building, the lower floors of an atrium, a 750-car parking garage, 65 shops with 250,000 square feet of retail space, and a 90,000-square-foot department store.

Despite these improvements, merchants complained that parking was not readily available near the various destinations that might attract customers. The solution they proposed was a bus that connected the parking with the stores. Accordingly, the city spent $4 million adding a transitway to the previously traffic-free mall and another $1.5 million to purchase nine buses (made to look like old fashioned trolleys) to provide shuttle service.

The convention center, hotel, and shopping arcade provided reasons for pedestrians to return to Fourth Avenue. New and renovated office buildings provided an additional market. The trolley service added an element of fun. More important, it provided transportation from what had previously been inconveniently located parking.

As a result of all these improvements, Fourth Avenue is again a moderately active shopping street. More than half the buildings fronting on the mall when it opened in 1973 have been replaced or totally renovated. The Seelbach and Brown hotels have reopened. Downtown Louisville may not be as busy as Cincinnati or Chicago. Its metropolitan population and economic base are far smaller. However, the combination of elements built in conjunction with the Fourth Avenue Mall generate substantial economic activity. In 1981, 95,000 shoppers came to downtown Louisville during the typical 30-day period. Two years later there were 181,000, and by 1985, 201,000 such shoppers.

Minneapolis, Minnesota

When business and political leaders in Minneapolis formed the Downtown Council in 1955, the city was suffering from the same problems that faced Kalamazoo and Louisville: declining retail sales, declining downtown office occupancy, and a declining tax base. The strategy for dealing with these problems emerged from a collaborative effort between the business community and the city planning department. It began in

1957 with the Downtown Council's Nicollet Avenue Survey Committee and continued in 1959 with the Minneapolis Planning Department's publication of its *Central Area Plan.*[6]

Both survey and plan called for a totally reorganized business district in which the mass-transportation system had been restructured to provide more direct service to retail areas, traffic congestion had been reduced, adequate parking was readily available, and downtown pedestrian circulation was convenient and comfortable. To achieve a separation between pedestrian and vehicular traffic they called for Nicollet Avenue to become a transitway and for a system of *skyways* that bridged over downtown streets in order to connect buildings at the second-floor level.

Southdale, America's first air-conditioned shopping mall, which had just opened in nearby Edina, revolutionized American retailing (see Chapter 5). For the first time consumers could shop in a totally climate-controlled, naturally-lit shopping mall that included every sort of retail store. Minneapolis is the coldest of the country's 45 largest cities. Its merchants knew that retail sales declined during bad weather, a problem that Southdale had solved. If the merchants were to withstand this competition they had to offer their customers a similar climate-controlled shopping environment. The skyway system appeared to be just what they needed.[7]

The first two skyways opened in 1962, as part of Northstar Center, an office-hotel-parking complex developed by Baker Properties. Other skyways followed in 1964 and 1969. However, it was not until 1973, when the IDS(Investigators' Diversified Services) Center opened, that a real pedestrian system was created.[8]

The IDS Center, designed by architects Philip Johnson and John Burgee, includes a 51-story office tower, a 19-story hotel, a 525-car parking garage, all enclosing an eight-story, skylit atrium with cafés, restaurants, and shops, called the Crystal Court. IDS provided what had been missing from the skyway system: a central attraction and connections to anchor stores. Every part of the skyway system now led to the multilevel "Crystal Court" and from there directly into Minneapolis's two major department stores. For the first time, the skyways,

Minneapolis, 1992. The skyway connecting the IDC Center with Dayton's Department Store provided a needed focus for this second-level pedestrian system. *(Alexander Garvin)*

Minneapolis, 1979. When the Crystal Court at IDS Center opened it became a central attraction, connecting every part of the skyway system directly into the city's two major department stores. *(Alexander Garvin)*

like any suburban shopping mall, included sufficient consumer attractions to induce heavy pedestrian traffic. During a typical March day in 1980, for example, more than 20,000 pedestrians crossed the skyways that connected the IDS Center with the department stores.

In 1962, when the first three skyways were built, there were no accepted principles for such privately built facilities. It did not take long for common characteristics to emerge. A minimum street clearance of 17 feet has been established to permit all trucks and buses to drive underneath. All side walls are made of clear glass so that pedestrians can identify the streets they cross, determine their destinations, and relate to the city around them. Where possible, bus stops are located adjacent to the parking garages that connect to the skyway system. Consequently, rents in buildings connected to the skyway system are 10 percent higher than in those without skyway connections.

The second ingredient of pedestrianized Minneapolis is the 10-block-long Nicollet Mall, which opened in 1967. In landscape architect Lawrence Halprin's design, private cars and trucks are banished, sidewalks are widened and lined with trees, flowers, benches, litter baskets, kiosks, sculptures, fountains, and bus shelters. A sinuously undulating two-lane roadway is set aside exclusively for buses and taxis.

Pedestrianizing Nicollet Avenue cost $3,874,000. One-fourth was paid for by the federal government with a $513,000 Urban Mass Transportation Grant and a $484,000 Urban Beautification Grant. The rest came from an 18-block special assessment district in which adjacent property owners paid in proportion to the benefits they were to receive. The district continues to be assessed annually for about 90 percent of the cost of maintenance. The city pays the remaining 10 percent.

When Nicollet Mall opened in 1967, there were only 9000 daily shoppers downtown. Ten years later there were over 40,000. Retail sales had increased by 14 percent. Millions of square feet of new office space were added to the business district. By 1982, the skyway system connected 35 city blocks and

Minneapolis, 1979. When Nicollet Mall opened in 1967, there were only 9000 daily shoppers downtown; within 10 years there were over 40,000. *(Alexander Garvin)*

more than 81,000 jobs. Ten years later it connected 44 city blocks that included 94 percent of downtown retail space, 85 percent of its rentable office space, 70 percent of its hotel rooms, and 48 percent of its parking stalls.

Because of this success, the streetscape was no longer adequately handling pedestrian and bus traffic along the mall. In 1987 the city formed the Nicollet Mall Implementation Board that included public officials, property owners, tenants, and downtown business leaders. It decided to spend $22 million to refurbish the Nicollet Avenue Mall. The project was completed in 1991. At that time there were two new shopping arcades and four department stores (three of which were new) within two blocks of the IDS Center. These facilities along with the skyways, highways, garages, and transitway had turned Minneapolis into the prime retail/office center of the Upper Midwest.

Portland, Oregon

Like downtown Minneapolis, downtown Portland was threatened by a shopping mall (Lloyd Center) that opened on the near-northeast side of the city in 1960. As in Minneapolis, the response was developed by a coalition of business leaders and public officials. They spent a decade unsuccessfully trying to achieve downtown revitalization with unpopular urban renewal, civic center, and highway projects (see Chapter 18). In the early 1970s they switched to a strategy centered on pedestrianization and mass transit. It called for a high-density office district, an overlapping retail core, two transitways, and a suburban light-rail system.[9]

Two events proved to be critical to the implementation of the plan: the creation of a public Tri-County Metropolitan Transportation District (Tri-Met) in 1969 and 5 years later the abandonment of the Mount Hood Freeway that had been planned to connect Portland with its eastern suburbs. Tri-Met was established to take over the city's failing, privately owned Rose City Transit Company and later several suburban bus lines. Once Tri-Met had been established, it reconfigured the region's transit system and traded in the Mount Hood Freeway for the money to pay for the improvements.[10]

The $16 million Transit Mall opened in 1977. It extends for 11 blocks, along two streets: Fifth and Sixth Avenues. As at Nicollet Mall, there are new street trees, flowers, sculptures, fountains, decorative brick paving, and bus shelters. Transit service is free anywhere within the 300-block core of downtown Portland. The buses that run along these malls connect directly to the entire metropolitan region. Their timetables and routes are displayed on television monitors within the bus shelters. The principal differences between most transitways and those in Portland is that those in Portland are crossed by

Portland, 1979. Transitway. *(Alexander Garvin)*

a 15-mile light rail transit system with 27 stations between downtown Portland and suburban Gresham.

Integrated planning for pedestrian circulation and mass transit has made Portland's business district more accessible, more convenient, and far more pleasant. The time required for a bus to pass through the downtown has been cut from 30 minutes to 15. More important, the percentage of people using mass transit to come downtown increased from 10 percent in 1971 to 25 percent in 1978.[11]

By 1980, 6 million square feet of new office space had been built. The downtown workforce had grown from 50,000 in 1960, to 80,000 in 1980. Naturally, retail sales boomed. Portland, which had been losing business to the suburbs, was by 1990 once again the vital center of a growing metropolitan area with a population of 1,478,000.[12]

Denver, Colorado

Most cities pedestrianize downtown streets as a way of reversing decline. Denver chose it as a method for channelling growth. During the early 1950s, Denver was beginning a period of more than 30 years of expansion. William Zeckendorf, Sr., opened a new $8 million department store, a modern 884-room convention hotel, and a 457,000-square-foot office tower. The world's biggest Woolworth's was built downtown. Between 1950 and 1964, the amount of office space in Denver doubled. In spite of a rapidly growing and increasingly prosperous population, retail sales were weak and transit ridership was down 35 percent.[13]

In 1955 business leaders who wanted to improve the commercial environment, formed Downtown Denver, Inc. They brought in a study group from the Urban Land Institute that recommended a new freeway network, one-way downtown traffic, parking structures, improved transit, and federally subsidized redevelopment. In 1961, a Master Plan Committee was formed to propose major redevelopment activity. Finally, in 1967, after years of controversy, the voters approved a 27-block downtown urban-renewal program. Nevertheless, downtown Denver had no focus, nothing tying all the development activities together.

The missing ingredient slowly took shape during the 1970s. It began as a proposed pedestrian mall running for nine blocks along 16th Street. By 1979, when the 16th Street Mall received Urban Mass Transportation funding, the mall had been transformed into a 13-block transitway connecting two suburban rapid transit stations.

The new 16th Street Mall, designed by I. M. Pei and Partners, was completed in 1982. Commuters arrive on

Denver, 1989. Civic leaders created a Mall Management District with a five-member board that establishes policies, levies fees on all properties within the District, determines the annual budget, and contracts with Downtown Denver, Inc. (a business organization) to manage and maintain the 16th Street Mall. *(Alexander Garvin)*

regional and express buses. Upon emerging from one of the two transit terminals, they can take a free shuttle bus that leaves every 70 seconds. The buses travel on 12-foot rights-of-way set aside exclusively for their use. They stop at every intersection until they arrive at the other transit terminal and reverse direction.

The rest of 16th Street is set aside exclusively for pedestrians. Pedestrians stroll on decorative paving, among trees, flowers, benches, artwork, and fountains. There are numerous vendors selling merchandise from festive pushcarts, a double-decker bus selling theater tickets, and a mounted horse patrol. Special events are scheduled on an almost daily basis.

Customers using the shuttle bus can stop to patronize Writers Square (a shopping center with three restaurants and 25 upscale shops), Tabor Center (an air-conditioned shopping arcade with 67 stores), May D & F (a 427,000-square-foot department store), and Latimer Square (a district of renovated "old west" Victorian buildings with 35 shops and 12 restaurants). Every major downtown office building, hotel, and store is within three blocks of this pedestrian/transit spine, as are Colorado University, the convention center, the State Capitol, and the Denver Center for the Performing Arts. No wonder 90,000 people per day use this beautiful boulevard.

The mall cost $76 million to develop; $3.8 million is spent annually on maintenance and management, of which $1.3 million comes from assessments on 865 property owners (based on the square footage of a facility and its proximity to the mall), $2 million from private grants and earned income, and $500,000 from Denver Partnership membership fees. These operating funds are used to fill planters with flowers and to water and weed, to remove litter and empty trash containers, to prune and spray trees, and to police the mall.

Ingredients of Success

The initial failure of Louisville's Fourth Avenue Mall demonstrates that just banishing automobiles from a city's major shopping street is unlikely to spur downtown revival. Successful pedestrian precincts must be located and designed in conjunction with parking garages, mass transit, convention centers, hotels, office buildings, department stores, and shopping malls. Such facilities entice consumers to stay downtown and to make purchases on their way to their ultimate destination. Once property owners find that they can rely on this additional spending, they will make additional downtown investments and thus, spark further downtown improvements.

Market

Pedestrianization cannot attract a market when none exists. As Jane Jacobs so eloquently explains, without "tremendous numbers of people...there would be no downtown to amount to anything."[14] To bring such "tremendous numbers" downtown, pedestrianized districts must contain more than stores. They need a dense concentration of office workers, conventioneers, tourists, and residents. Otherwise there will not be enough customers to support the desired level of retail activity.

Pedestrianization should only be considered where there already is a large concentration of potential retail customers or in conjunction with new facilities that will attract a critical mass of consumers. Sometimes concentration is brought about by property owners. In Minneapolis, construction of the IDS Center at the intersection of Nicollet Mall and the city's premier department store triggered an increase in demand. The office workers and tourists brought by IDS created a critical mass that generated additional hotel, department store, and shopping arcade developments.

Government also can create the necessary concentration of activity. In Portland, the intersection of the light-rail system with the transitways became the site of a new public square. The combination of public transit and open space attracted a critical mass of customers and triggered private development of department stores and shopping arcades on nearby blocks.

Every pedestrianized district faces competition. In most instances the competition is suburban. Sometimes matching the competition involves only minor changes to the business district. Kalamazoo was able to attract customers simply by improving circulation, supplying additional parking, and pedestrianizing a few downtown blocks. Sometimes the only way to compete is to make radical physical changes to the business district. Minneapolis had to create a skyway system with a climate-controlled retail environment that rivaled Southdale and later air-conditioned shopping malls.

Location

Pedestrianization by itself is futile if the proposed pedestrian district is not easily accessible to its market. Louisville's Fourth Avenue Mall suffered from this problem until it added "trolleys" to ferry customers from parking facilities to their destination on the mall. Minneapolis increased accessibility by building strategically located parking structures near Nicollet Mall and encouraging private development of additional parking connected to the skyway system.

In Denver, proximity is the product of public transportation. Customers who arrive downtown by bus then switch to a shuttle bus that takes them to their ultimate destination. Those who come by car park at or near their destination, no more than a couple of blocks from the 16th Street Mall. They too can take the shuttle bus and be virtually anywhere in downtown Denver within minutes.

Design

The pedestrian environment itself must be inviting. This is not a matter of charm or glitter. The Kalamazoo Mall is not a great work of architecture. It attracts customers because it is easy to reach, compact enough to walk from one end to the other in a few minutes, and contains sufficient attractions (two small department stores and a variety store).

When a mall is too big to be quickly covered on foot, shuttle buses can remedy the situation. There is, however, no substitute for major attractions scattered from one end of a pedestrian mall to the other. In Louisville they are concentrated at the north end of the Fourth Avenue Mall. The shuttle bus cannot create the necessary attractions at the southern end of the mall and thus cannot increase its low sales volume. Nor is there any remedy for discontinuous shopping opportunities. Minneapolis's skyways were not very successful until the IDS Center made the necessary connections to the city's department stores.

Financing

It is difficult to raise money for pedestrianization from the businesses who will ultimately profit from increased retail sales. Some firms will be in financial difficulty. If they were not in trouble, there would be little reason to invest in improvements. Other firms will doubt that the increase in business will justify the expense. Thus, government must cover that part of the capital cost that local businesses cannot afford or will not pay.

Pedestrianization is rarely paid for from a single source. The federal government often provides categorical or block grants that can cover a part of the cost. Local governments have to pay the rest. As a result, Kalamazoo covered part of the cost of its mall from its capital budget (financed by issuing general obligation bonds). The rest was paid for by assessing abutting property owners who ultimately profited from an increase in retail sales. Louisville assessed property owners for 85 percent of the cost of pedestrianizing Fourth Street. The city also issued $6.5 million in bonds to pay for a parking garage, applied for and received an $8 million federal Urban Development Action Grant for renovating the department store in the Galleria, and obtained another $8 million from the State of Kentucky to pay for public spaces.

If the pedestrianization program is successful, the initial capital expenditure will be recouped from increased sales and real estate taxes or through annual assessments of abutting property owners and businesses. In Louisville, for example, the properties that were converted into the Galleria paid $70,000 a year in property taxes. After being repackaged as the Galleria and becoming a part of the Fourth Avenue Mall, they paid more than $1 million.

Financing problems do not end when construction does. Somebody has to pay for maintenance of the now pedestrianized precincts. In Louisville it is entirely paid for by local government. In Kalamazoo half comes from the city and the other half from property owners in the assessment district. In Minneapolis, 90 percent comes from the assessment district.

As long as pedestrianization results in increased revenues, property owners will gladly pay their assessment. However, if business does not improve after pedestrianization, everybody suffers. Merchants will either go out of business or force the city to remotorize. Worse yet, there will not be enough tax revenue to pay debt service on the city bonds that financed the project. Everybody's taxes will go up to cover the shortfall. All the more reason to plan very carefully for any government sponsored pedestrianization projects.

Entrepreneurship

Most pedestrianization schemes are the product of a close working relationship between downtown business and local government. In some cases it is the business community that initiates the process; in others government takes the lead. Both have to participate because the public spaces are in government ownership, while the money to pay for improvements will ultimately have to come from downtown business.

In Denver, civic leaders created a Mall Management District with a 5-member board (headed by Denver's manager of public works and including four property owners). The board establishes policies, determines the annual budget, and contracts with Downtown Denver, Inc. (a business organization) to manage and maintain the 16th Street Mall. Its formal budget and management procedures resulted in installation of better lighting and signage, replacement of rain-catching trashcans, encouragement of pushcarts selling food, flowers, and other merchandise, establishment of a mounted horse patrol, and all sorts of other small improvements that make the 16th Street Mall one of the most successful ventures of its kind. Other cities make do with more informal measures of cooperation. But they are less likely to make capital expenditures and operating decisions that will increase consumer spending.[15]

Time

For the most part, cities are unable to affect the flow of consumers along pedestrianized arteries because they neither own abutting properties, nor determine who will lease them. It is, therefore, particularly difficult to manipulate the time that consumers spend between arrival and destination. Louisville tried to do this by subsidizing the creation of a shopping arcade in the middle of the Fourth Avenue Mall. Downtown Denver, Inc. sponsors pushcarts, a double-decker bus selling tickets to 30 theaters and arts organizations and pays for a variety of outdoor entertainers. However, most pedestrian malls have little control over anything but the physical appearance of the street itself.

The longer-term character of the pedestrian environment is easier to affect. In the attempt to create 24-hour life on the Fourth Avenue Mall, Louisville placed its hotel and convention facilities right on the mall. Minneapolis did the same with Orchestra Hall, the home of the Minnesota Orchestra. However, the most important contribution to the Minneapolis pedestrian environment is the skyway system, which, despite bitter cold and heat waves, rain, sleet, and snow, allows downtown activity to thrive during every season of the year.

Pedestrianization as a City Planning Strategy

Since the invention of the automobile, cities have been restructured to fit its traffic requirements. America continues to spend billions planning highways, installing traffic systems, and building garages, but devotes little attention to pedestrian movement after the vehicles have arrived. It is time to retrofit our cities for the automobile's occupants, to shape their activities after they leave the car and before they reach their ultimate destinations, not by redecorating a few downtown arteries, but by creating streets, sidewalks, arcades, and skywalks that encourage interaction among shopping facilities, convention centers, hotels, office buildings, and all the other components of a healthy business district.

The money to pay for retrofitting cities for pedestrian circulation should come from the Highway Trust Fund established to pay for the Interstate Highway System. Heretofore, this money has been used primarily for planning and building vehicular arteries. Little has been spent planning for pedestrian circulation at the vehicle's destination. This imbalance can be corrected by requiring that every city in the Interstate Highway System plan for pedestrian circulation and earmark a portion of the Highway Trust Fund for public improvements at the destinations themselves.

The 90 percent federal funding of the interstate highway projects was intended to attract local support for regional transportation improvements that would otherwise be overwhelmed by parochial opposition. Instead of examining the cost-effectiveness of specific project designs, most cities thought of the Highway Trust Fund as "other people's money" that generated jobs and taxes for the local economy. This 90-10 split should be changed. Since pedestrian circulation is essentially a local matter, local governments should pay at least half the cost of the proposed pedestrian improvements.

Up to now transportation planning has been in the hands of traffic engineers and public officials who neither benefited directly from proposed projects nor had to pay for them out of their own pockets. They are not qualified, acting alone, to plan for pedestrian circulation, consumer purchases, convention and hotel spending, and all the other activities that go on in a business district. Furthermore, because the locality's share of project cost is likely to be financed through assessment districts and real estate taxes, the property owners and businesses that will have to pay are likely to demand to participate in the planning. Thus, planning for the pedestrian will have to be a cooperative venture that includes government officials and a very wide range of participants in the downtown economy.

This modification in the use of interstate highway funds could have as fundamental an impact on living patterns as did the 1956 legislation that created the system. But, instead of financing the exodus from our cities, it will pay for improving them.

Notes

1. Martin Meyerson, *Face of the Metropolis,* Random House, New York, 1963, pp. 85–89.
2. Victor Gruen, *A Greater Fort Worth Tomorrow,* Greater Fort Worth Planning Committee, Fort Worth, 1956, p. 6.
3. Over the past 20 years William H. Whyte had developed simple, effective principles for the design and management of pedestrian circulation. See William H. Whyte, *City—Rediscovering the Center,* Doubleday, New York, 1988.
4. Statistical and historical information on Kalamazoo is derived from Louis G. Redstone, *The New Downtowns,* McGraw-Hill Book Company, New York, 1976, pp. 6–11; Roberto Brambilla and Gianni Longo *For Pedestrians Only: Planning Design, and Management of Traffic-Free Zones,* Whitney Library of Design, New York, 1977, pp. 123–126; and Wayne Attoe and Donn Logan, *American Urban Architecture: Catalysts in the Design of Cities,* University of California Press, Berkeley, 1989, pp. 74–84.
5. Statistical and historical information on downtown Louisville is derived from Redstone, op. cit., pp. 188–190; Brambilla and Longo, op. cit., p. 188; and Rachelle Levitt (editor), *Cities Reborn,* Urban Land Institute, Washington, D.C., 1986, pp. 55–104.
6. Statistical and historical information on downtown Minneapolis is derived from Lawrence W. Irwin and Jeffrey B. Groy, *The Minneapolis Skyway System: What It Is and Why It Works,* City Planning Department, Minneapolis, 1982; Brambilla and Longo, op. cit., pp. 132–135; David Gebhard and Tom Martinson, *A Guide to the Architecture of Minnesota,* University of Minneapolis Press, Minneapolis, 1977, pp. 24–38; and Jennifer Waters, "The Minneapolis Story," pp. 34–40, in *Urban Land,* vol. 52, no. 4, Urban Land Institute, Washington, D.C., April 1993.
7. One heating degree day is accumulated for each degree that the mean daily temperature drops below 65 degrees Fahrenheit. Minneapolis records 8007 heating degree days per year; San Francisco 3161. See Lawrence O. Houstoun, Jr., "Weather Report," pp. 19–21, in *Planning,* American Planning Association, Chicago, December, 1990.
8. Baker Properties later became Investors' Diversified Services Properties (IDS) and then Oxford Properties.
9. Statistical and historical information on downtown Portland is derived from Carl Abbott, *Portland: Planning, Politics, and Growth in a Twentieth Century City,* University of Nebraska Press, Lincoln, 1983, pp. 207–226 and 248–266; John R. Post, "The Portland Light Rail Experience," pp. 63–72 in *Transit, Land Use and Urban Form,* edited by Wayne Attoe, Center for the Study of American Architecture, School of Architecture, University of Texas at Austin, 1988.
10. In 1974 Congress gave localities, acting through their state govern ment, permission to eliminate or scale down portions of already approved interstate highways and transfer the remaining funding authorization to other road improvements or transit use. Portland was one of the first cities to exercise this option.
11. Robert Lindsey, "New Transit Chief Praised for Role in Portland," *New York Times,* August 1, 1978.
12. U.S. Dept. of Commerce, Bureau of the Census, *Statistical Abstract of the United States 1991,* p. 31.
13. Statistical and historical information on downtown Denver is derived from Melvin D. Moore (editor), *Downtown Denver—A Guide to Central City Development,* Technical Bulletin #54, Urban Land Institute, Washington, D.C., 1965; Leo Adde, *Nine Cities: The Anatomy of Downtown Renewal,* Urban Land Institute, Washington, D.C., 1969, pp. 165–193; Donna McEncroe, *Off the Mall Step by Step,* The Denver Partership, Inc., Denver, 1987; and the Denver Metro Convention and Visitors Bureau.
14. Jane Jacobs, *The Death and Life of Great American Cities,* Random House, New York, 1961, p.4.
15. Nancy Fletcher, "Showcasing Downtown Management," *Urban Land,* Urban Land Institute, Washington, D.C., April 1987, pp. 12–15

8

Increasing the Housing Supply

Orange County, California, 1991. *(Alexander Garvin)*

Public intervention into the private housing market in America is a patchwork of local, state, and federal programs indentified by a bewildering array of letters and numbers. The ingredients of this alphabet soup change so frequently that they only matter while they are current. What is important is that this public intervention has concentrated on five objectives: increasing housing supply, reducing housing cost, improving housing quality, eliminating slums, and revitalizing neighborhoods.

At the federal level, public intervention dates back to the Great Depression when banks were foreclosing mortgages at an alarming rate. By 1933, one-half the home mortgages in the country were in default, annual housing production had dropped below 93,000 units, and mortgage lending had come to a virtual halt. If housing production was to be restored even to pre-Depression levels, mortgage financing had to be made easily available to both developers and consumers. This required a stable, orderly, easily accessible mortgage market.[1]

Congress began the process of creating a stable supply of mortgage money by enacting legislation that insured bank deposits, thereby giving depositors the confidence they needed to keep their money in the bank. It went on to assure home buyers and builders that they could obtain this money from lending institutions by insuring mortgages that met standard lending practices. It also created a secondary market for federally insured mortgages, that allowed financial institutions that needed cash to sell standard mortgages and those that had surplus cash to buy them.

In addition to making sure that financing would be available, Congress greatly expanded the market for additional housing by reducing the size of the downpayment on a house with a federally insured mortgage. By extending the term of the mortgage, it also reduced the amount of the monthly debt-service payment on that mortgage. As a result, millions of households had enough money to own a house.

Businesspeople who would not otherwise have entered the home-building industry were attracted by the greatly reduced risk. Moreover, because they could borrow against FHA mortgage commitments that covered 90 percent of the purchase price of each house, they did not have to put up much cash. This provided entrepreneurs with a unique opportunity to get into that business with only a small equity investment.

By creating an easily accessible mortgage market Congress transformed millions of people who dreamed of home ownership into customers with the ability to pay for new houses and thousands of struggling businesspeople into developers with an ability to supply them with the houses they desired. By 1941, national housing production had climbed to 619,000 units, more than six times the 1933 level.[2]

The real impact of this legislation, however, became evident after World War II. In response to burgeoning demand, housing production soared. By 1960 there were 53 million dwelling units in the United States, up 66 percent from 1940. Home ownership had increased from 44 to 62 percent.[3]

The reform in lending practices initially applied to one- to four-family houses, not apartment buildings. Consequently, this extraordinary increase in the housing supply occurred largely outside urban areas. By 1960, single-family houses represented 77 percent of the nation's housing stock.[4] Had a similar approach been adopted for the financing of multifamily housing, millions of apartments would have been created and the shortage of housing in center cities would not have become so serious.

Congress can eliminate this bias in lending practices and provide city dwellers with the benefits that it has long provided to suburbanites by enacting legislation that standardizes institutional lending for existing apartment buildings, insures mortgage loans to purchasers of individual apartments, and creates a secondary market for these loans. Home ownership would be made available to millions of city dwellers and the real estate industry would create thousands of jobs supplying this lucrative market.

Providing a Stable Supply of Mortgage Money

The creation of a stable supply of mortgage money market began with laws that were intended to increase depositor confidence in financial institutions. The Federal Home Loan Bank Act of 1932 established the Federal Home Loan Bank Board with regulatory powers over savings and loan institutions similar to the powers of the Federal Reserve System over commercial banks. The Home Owners Loan Act of 1933 established the Home Owners Loan Corporation (HOLC) to refinance home mortgages in default or foreclosure. The Glass-Steagall Banking Act of 1933 created the Federal Deposit Insurance Corporation (FDIC), which eliminated the risk of depositing funds in participating banks. The Banking Act of 1934 did the same for thrift institutions through the creation of the Federal Savings and Loan Insurance Corporation (FSLIC).[5]

Without these actions, depositors would have withdrawn all their money, leaving most financial institutions without sufficient capital. Instead, they maintained savings accounts that provided the money used to refinance home mortgages when they came due. In its first three years of operation, for example, the HOLC provided more than $3 billion, to refinance over one million mortgages, 10 percent of all nonfarm, owner-occupied residences in the United States.[6]

FHA Insured Home Mortgages

The new banking laws may have helped financial institutions to attract deposits. However, these institutions needed to be coaxed into investing a major portion of that capital in housing. Congress provided the necessary inducement by enacting the National Housing Act of 1934, which created the Federal Housing

Administration (FHA). Section 203 of this Act created a mortgage insurance system which, for a small premium charge, provided participating lenders with insurance on 90 percent (prior to 1938, 80 percent) of the appraised value of one- to four-family houses. When a bank foreclosed on a mortgage it could transfer the mortgage to the FHA and in exchange obtain most of the money it had lent. By covering so large a part of the downside risk, Congress made home loans a safe investment.[7]

The most important effect of this legislation was that it converted the desire for home ownership into consumer demand. By reducing the downpayment on a home mortgage to 10 percent, Congress dramatically increased the number of people who had the cash to make a downpayment on a house. By requiring the mortgage to be fully self-amortizing, it eliminated the risk of facing a hostile mortgage market when the loan came due. By extending the amortization over a period of up to 35 years, it lowered monthly debt service payments and increased the number of people who could afford a home mortgage.[8]

Construction lenders could depend on the eventual sale of a house that met FHA specifications because the purchaser could depend on an FHA mortgage. Consequently, banks decreased the amount of developer equity required for construction financing, thereby dramatically increasing the number of entrepreneurs who had the equity capital with which to enter the home-building industry. No housing program has been more successful in increasing housing supply. Between 1934 and 1991, the FHA insured mortgages on more than 19.7 million one-family houses.[9]

VA Guaranteed Home Mortgages

Congress adopted a similar approach for veteran's housing. It was eager to help GIs avoid the economic and social problems of post–World-War-II readjustment. In particular, it wished to supply millions of returning members of the Armed Forces with the credit necessary to obtain a home, business, or farm. This assistance took the form of the Serviceman's Readjustment Act of 1944, which established the Veteran's Administration (VA) guaranteed loan.

The VA virtually assured lenders that they would not lose money. The federal government guaranteed 60 percent of the value of a VA mortgage loan. This guarantee was the equivalent of 60 percent borrower equity. In case of foreclosure, the bank needed to recoup only 40 percent of the amount of the loan from the sale of the foreclosed property. The rest would be covered by the federal government.

Although VA home mortgage loans were virtually risk-free, lenders continued to require a nominal cash payment by the borrower (often less than 5 percent). Millions of veterans jumped at the chance of putting a few dollars down in order to own their home. As of 1991, more than 13 million dwelling units had received VA loans, mostly before 1970.[10]

Standardized Mortgages for a National Market

Prior to the Depression, mortgage instruments were quite different from what we know today. A first mortgage seldom covered more than 50 or 60 percent of any transaction. Since borrowers usually wished to reduce their equity investment, they frequently obtained additional second and third mortgage loans with higher interest rates reflecting their greater risk. These were short-term loans, usually lasting less than three years. Unpaid principal was due in a single "balloon" payment when the loan came due. At that time property owners would have to refinance their mortgage and pay the expenses involved with each new loan. They were at the mercy of new market conditions in which they might not be able to refinance the "balloon mortgage" and thus lose the property through foreclosure.

Mortgage instruments and loan requirements varied. One lender might require up-to-date electrical wiring, another might be satisfied with minimum code compliance. Even the language of the mortgage varied. The FHA provided the standardization that revolutionized the American housing industry.

All buildings with FHA insured and VA guaranteed mortgages had to comply with FHA *minimum property standards* as to location, neighborhood conditions, subdivision design, structure, room size, quality of materials, mechanical equipment, even sewage disposal. Thus, both borrower and lender could depend on the quality of the product and were protected from subsequent, unexpected hazards.

Each FHA insured mortgage was essentially the same no matter which bank extended the loan, no matter in what state it was originated. It was a first mortgage that precluded additional mortgage liens, carried a fixed rate of interest, required the same debt service payments every month, and was fully self-amortizing. Without this uniformity in lending practices there could not have been mass generation of mortgage loans, or mass production of new houses, or mass consumption of those houses.

Fannie Mae

The legislation that created the FHA authorized private individuals to establish mortgage associations that could borrow money from the public for the purpose of purchasing and reselling FHA mortgages. It was thought that standard FHA insured mortgages would be sold by financial institutions in areas with high demand for mortgages to institutions in other areas with surplus capital seeking safe, predictable sources of income. By selling these mortgages and making new ones with the money they received, lenders would be able to earn more than their assets would have ordinarily allowed.

A national mortgage market did not develop. Banks were comfortable underwriting mortgages in their own area and ignorant of market characteristics elsewhere. Furthermore, they were skeptical about tying down their funds for very long periods. Their needs might change. There might not be a buyer for the mortgages when they wanted to sell.

To correct this situation, Congress, in 1938, established the Federal National Mortgage Association (FNMA or Fannie Mae). Fannie Mae's job was to buy FHA mortgages from participating institutions in need of additional mortgage capital and in turn sell them to others with surplus capital. The initial capital with which to purchase home mortgages came from the sale of its stock to the Reconstruction Finance Corporation and the Treasury. The rest was raised by requiring institutions, whose FHA mortgages were bought by Fannie Mae, to purchase a small amount of its stock. The income it paid on its securities came from the interest on the mortgages and commitment fees from participating institutions.[11]

Multifamily Housing

The New Deal program for one- to four-family houses was paralleled by a similar program for unsubsidized multifamily rental housing: FHA 207. Like the 203 Program, it provided insurance on 90 percent of value (80 percent prior to 1938). That is where the similarity ended. Existing multiple dwellings were not eligible, only new construction. Thus, unlike the owner of a house with an FHA insured mortgage, the owner of an apartment building with an FHA insured mortgage could not depend on finding a purchaser who could obtain similar financing. Naturally, developers were far more likely to risk equity capital in a safer market. As of 1940, fewer than 30,000 apartments had been built under the 207 Program.[12]

The 608 Program

In 1948, hoping to stimulate apartment house construction, Congress revived the little-used FHA 608 Program, which had originally been enacted during the war. It was successful in spurring new construction because its liberal underwriting standards attracted entrepreneurs who often did not need cash up front. During the 6 years it was in existence, this program financed 464,000 new dwelling units.[13]

The 608 Program provided 90 percent insurance on the estimated cost of development. Land values were established on the basis of an appraisal of current market value. Developers who had purchased land some years earlier at a substantially lower figure were able to withdraw in cash the difference between the required equity investment and the appraised value of the property at the mortgage closing. Had this not been the case, they would have sold their land at a profit and never contemplated the risks of apartment house construction.

Cash advanced during construction was based on the estimated cost of the work. Consequently, those builders who were able to build at costs below those prevailing in the area (and below the estimates of FHA appraisers) made money during construction. If this had not been possible, competent builders would never have entered the program. They would have resented the penalty for being more skilled than their competition.

Some public officials were scandalized by such practices. More important, they were outraged by the fraud that was made possible by collusion among loan officers, appraisers, contractors, and developers who had fraudulently overestimated project costs. Rather than blame the crooks who had profited from scams, public officials questioned the validity of the whole program and, in 1954, allowed it to fade away.

In its stead, Congress revitalized the 207 Program, this time with cost certification and regulation of initial rents. Far fewer developers were willing to deal with the additional requirements, paperwork, and processing time. The new procedures increased the opportunities for discretionary action by government officials, a few of whom were willing to act only when helped along with an extra "fee" to cover their trouble. Thus, while the new procedures did not eliminate corruption, they did terminate the mass generation of FHA insured market-rate mortgages for multifamily housing.

The Savings and Loan Crisis

For half-a-century Congress regulated both thrift institutions (the savings banks and savings and loan associations that provided homeowners with permanent mortgages) and commercial banks (that made loans to developers who built houses for customers who financed their purchase with FHA insured and VA guaranteed mortgages). The resulting stable supply of mortgage money provided financing for a steadily increasing supply of decent, safe, and standard housing.

Since the federal government insured the deposits made to savings accounts and regulated the manner in which this money could be lent to homeowners, thrift institutions had to comply with federal regulations that determined the terms they had to offer both depositors and borrowers. Thrifts were not permitted to offer checking accounts (which were the purview of commercial banks, who were not permitted to pay interest on these accounts). They were, however, able to offer a rate of interest on savings deposits that was slightly above the rate permitted commercial banks. Because the government so carefully supervised their mortgage lending, they were allowed to maintain lower cash reserves (4 percent of deposits). Commercial banks, whose investments ranged far beyond home mortgages and were rarely government guaranteed, were required to maintain more generous cash reserves (15 to 17 percent of deposits).

The strict guidelines for accepting deposits and making loans allowed thrift institutions little latitude and required virtually no expertise on the part of bank officials or regulators. Home mortgage lending was so routinized that loans were, in effect, mass produced. Cynical observers called it "the 'three-six-three' business: take in deposits at three percent, lend them out at six percent, and tee up at the golf course at 3:00 P.M."[14]

For four decades interest rates remained stable and thrift institutions faced no difficulties. They could accept short-term deposits on which they paid market interest and then lend their depositors' money to homeowners for long periods of time at fixed rates of interest. As with so much else in the United States, this comfortable situation was profoundly affected by the inflation that began during the Vietnam War and was fueled by a succession of energy crises. Short-term interest rates, which had slowly fluctuated between 3 and 6 percent since the Great Depression, began to change, sometimes on a monthly basis, reaching an all-time high of 21.5 percent.

In a world of wildly fluctuating rates of interest, thrift institutions (whose rates of interest were regulated) found themselves facing intense competition for deposits from money-market accounts, interest-paying checking accounts, and all sorts of new instruments that paid much higher rates of interest. The result was a massive outflow of money from savings accounts. A far more serious problem, however, was that thrift institutions were suddenly forced to pay depositors high rates of interest although they were still earning far lower rates of interest on their long-term mortgages. Unless money market conditions changed they would soon be out of business. Indeed, "in 1972 the nation's savings and loans had a combined net worth of $16.7 billion. By 1980 that figure had plummeted to a *negative* net worth of $175 billion."[15]

Thrift institutions demanded the right to compete on a level playing field. Their demands coincided with the passion for deregulation that hit the United States during the late 1970s and early 1980s. Congress responded by enacting the Depository Institutions Deregulation and Monetary Control Act of 1980 and the Garn–St. Germain Depository Institutions Act of 1982.

This legislation was intended to help thrifts attract deposits by increasing federal insurance from $40,000 per depositor to $100,000 per account. Reserve requirements for thrift institutions were lowered to 3 percent. In order to help thrifts increase the return on their investments, they were no longer restricted to mortgage lending (a large proportion of which had been federally insured). They were even permitted to become joint-venture partners with their borrowers. In order to attract more entrepreneurial management, they did not have to be operated as widely held membership organizations. For the first time, federally chartered thrift institutions could be purchased, owned, and operated by individuals.

The results of these banking reforms were catastrophic. Brokerage firms offered small investors participation in federally insured accounts, combined these deposits into $100,000 packages, and then sought the highest possible rates of interest. Thrift institutions that needed additional deposits had no choice but to pay top dollar for these accounts. Meanwhile the Federal Reserve, in an attempt to combat inflation, forced interest rates to rise far above the average rate of interest paid by long-term mortgages.

Thrift institutions responded by making investments (e.g., junk bonds and joint-venture deals) that were supposed to produce higher returns than conventional, government regulated and insured home mortgages. However, their employees were not used to making risky investments. They were familiar with the routinized world of FHA insured loans, as were the federal regulators responsible for overseeing their activities. They only discovered the risks of such investment when promised returns failed to materialize. By then it was too late.

In some cases long-established thrift institutions were acquired by crooks who exploited deregulation. Their scams, like many criminal exploits, make interesting reading but reprehensible stories. Some crooks even banded together to avoid regulatory supervision, trading bad loans among themselves so that when bank inspectors showed up, the books would look clean.[16]

Fortunately, most deposits were federally insured; consequently, relatively few depositors lost their hard-earned savings. However, when insurance premiums failed to cover losses, Congress had to make good on its guarantee and was forced to appropriate hundreds of billions of dollars. The bail out has been under way since the late 1980s and will extend almost to the end of the twentieth century.

In reaction to the S & L crisis, thrift institutions have tightened lending policies and chosen to invest a substantial portion of their deposits in safe federal securities. As a result, during the early 1990s there has been far less money available for home mortgages and thus a major decrease in home building. What money is available, is no longer available on the same easy terms. Until this situation changes the supply of housing will not increase significantly.

Ingredients of Success

There is no mystery to increasing the supply of housing. It requires a stable, orderly, easily accessible money market such as was created by the banking reforms of the 1930s. Accessibility is as important as stability. As long as equity requirements and interest rates remained at the low levels established during the New Deal, millions of consumers maintained a steady level of demand for one-family houses. The same low equity requirements and interest rates allowed thousands of builders to supply that demand.

Regulation created the necessary stability. Consumers were able to depend on a standard product and standard lending procedures. Regulation also allowed financial institutions to use a relatively unskilled staff to establish millions of savings accounts and provide millions of home mortgages.

However, this money market had a distinctly suburban bias. With the exception of the 6 years during which the 608 Program was in operation, apartment-house developers were unable to obtain easy access to FHA financing. Nor was there any workable program for the refinancing or rehabilitation of existing apartment buildings. Only during the 1970s and 1980s, when the money market was destabilized and obtaining financing became more difficult, did this extraordinary suburban success story slow down.

Market

In a market economy like ours, government can ensure a level of demand that allows the real estate industry to supply that demand. The banking reforms of the 1930s generated that stable level of demand by making home ownership affordable to two-thirds of the population, by establishing physical and financial standards that met its requirements, and then by ensuring the availability of credit.

Lowering the required downpayment on a house to 10 percent, made purchase affordable. Requiring all FHA and VA mortgages to be fully self-amortizing over a long period, made debt service affordable. As a result millions of people, who had previously been unable to own a house, purchased one. Equally important, when they were ready to move they had a standard product that could easily be resold to another buyer who could count on financing the purchase on similar terms.

Location

The beauty of the banking legislation of the 1930s was that it allowed market forces to supply housing at suburban locations that were easily accessible and inherently attractive. However, those market forces were precluded from operating in the central sections of our cities with their preponderance of older apartment buildings. The bias against cities was not only a matter of inadequate FHA programs for existing multifamily housing. It was also the product of underwriting practices.

FHA insured mortgages could not exceed 90 percent of "appraised value." If the appraised value was too low, the mortgage would be insufficient to justify a mortgage of the size the applicant needed. As a result, the project could not proceed. While the FHA had standardized the elements of required bank appraisals, the amount of the loan depended on the judgment of those approving it. That judgment involved an estimate of the property, the borrower, and the neighborhood. If the property failed to meet FHA standards, the mortgage insurance was denied.

Borrowers themselves might be deficient. This was not just a matter of net worth, or income, or credit history. The FHA *Underwriting Manual* specifically stated that, "if a neighborhood is to retain stability, it is necessary that properties shall continue to be occupied by the same social and racial classes," and recommended "suitable restrictive covenants." The *Underwriting Manual* also specified neighborhood criteria, which downgraded "older properties," "crowded neighborhoods," and "lower-class occupancy" common in urban areas. Simply put, the FHA (without the specific approval of Congress) used its underwriting practices to discriminate against cities and to finance further suburbanization.[17]

Design

FHA design standards brought certainty and predictability to the housing market. Consumers purchasing houses with FHA insured mortgages could depend on structural soundness, decent construction materials, minimum room sizes, modern plumbing, and adequate electrical wiring. Developers who produced buildings that met these standards could depend on their customers obtaining long-term, low-interest mortgages. Banks could depend on selling mortgages on these standard products to Fannie Mae.

Developers of one-family houses were able to predict the FHA insured mortgage that could be obtained. This allowed them to budget development expenditures. Consumers could predict the mortgage that would be available when they sold it. Similarly, banks could predict the physical characteristics of the product they were financing and minimize the time and effort devoted to underwriting. The result was mass production of standard houses, mass generation of standard mortgages, mass consumption of both, and a rapidly increasing housing stock.

The minimum property standards that were so important to creating a market for one-family houses proved to be equally central to the bias against multiple dwellings. Section 2 of the Housing Act of 1934 authorized the FHA to insure loans up to $2000 for repairs and improvements. Given FHA procedures, existing buildings that were in need of restoration were bound to be given low appraisals, usually too low to cover the cost of acquisition and/or refinancing.

If a low appraisal was not enough to discourage the borrowers, minimum property standards would preclude any further desire for an FHA insured mortage. When a property was deficient in a few respects, the borrower (often at high cost) was required to remedy the inadequacy or forgo the loan. The cost of the work necessary to bring most urban multiple dwellings into conformance with minimum property standards (suitable for new construction) usually raised required rents beyond marketable levels. Moreover, the minimum property standards also eliminated major categories of housing. Many Philadelphia and Baltimore row houses, for example, could not meet FHA requirements. They were too narrow.

No serious FHA market-rate mortgage program for the rehabilitation of older buildings has ever emerged. None will emerge until there is a recognition of the essential difference between building new housing and renovating structures that were built to the standards and tastes of another era. It may be cost-effective to require all new buildings to have smoke-free fire stairs designed for 4 hours' survival during any conflagration. However, it certainly is not cost-effective to relocate existing tenants, eliminate existing apartments, and reorganize the circulation patterns of most older multiple dwellings in order to accommodate 4-hour-rated, smoke-free fire stairs.

Financing

Without deposit insurance, banks would not have had money to lend. Without FHA insurance, thrift institutions would not have invested nearly as much in home mortgages. Without Fannie Mae to buy FHA mortgages, there would have been no way to get additional mortgage money to banks that needed to satisfy additional demand. The mass origination of home mortgages, however, would not have been possible without standard FHA lending practices, underwriting techniques, and mortgage instruments.

These new lending practices did not just apply to federally insured mortgages. The fixed-rate, long-term, self-amortizing mortgage became the most common form of loan. In fact, lending institutions adopted the underwriting techniques standardized by federal programs for all their mortgages. Consequently, until the deregulation of the 1980s, thrift institutions were able to generate a steady stream of business that could be managed without hiring an expensive team of financial wizards.

However, the problems with and cost of complying with minimum property standards and the bias against lending in "older neighborhoods," prevented the revolution in housing finance from extending to existing multiple dwellings. Balloon mortgages; second, third, and even fourth mortgages; short-term lending; and other pre-New Deal characteristics continued to be common to the financing of existing apartment buildings.

Entrepreneurship

In devising a program for one-family houses, public officials sought to create conditions that would attract small businesses into real estate. The simplicity of obtaining FHA 203 home mortgages greatly reduced the risk to home builders. They no longer worried about customers who could not obtain a mortgage. Nor did they need much equity up front because they could borrow against an FHA mortgage commitment that covered 90 percent of the purchase price (and presumably an even higher percentage of development cost). All that government officials had to do was to verify that banks were complying with regulations. As a result thousands of entrepreneurs who had relatively little cash were attracted to the home building industry.

Public officials dealt with multifamily rental housing in a very different fashion from owner-occupied one-family houses. They desired unlimited apartment-house production but were uncomfortable with "windfall profits." As soon as it became clear that the 608 Program allowed clever developers to put up little or no cash and make lots of money, it was terminated. Replacement programs may have minimized developer risk and allowed paper equity contributions, but they also limited profit, specified the labor force, regulated tenantry, required time-consuming bureaucratic review, and thus were unable to generate the massive amounts of new urban multiple dwellings that resulted from the 608 Program.

Time

One of the least appreciated results of the banking reforms of the 1930s was that they helped to insulate real estate from a changing money market. Millions of borrowers were able to avoid the hazards of trying to refinance balloon mortgages. FHA insured mortages were fully self-amortizing and extended over several decades. They also reduced the hazards of trying to sell a house during periods of tight money. If the FHA already had insured a mortgage on the house, it was likely to do so again.

Similarly, thrift institutions no longer had to worry about liquidity. Whenever they needed cash, they could sell FHA insured mortgages to Fannie Mae. Thus lending institutions were insulated from changing demands on their resources.

FHA insured mortgages on apartment houses, however, were initially restricted to new construction. Thus the home buyer, but not the apartment-house owner, was insulated from the difficulties of selling to a buyer who could not obtain an FHA insured mortgage.

Increasing Housing Supply as a Planning Strategy

It is only fair for city residents to profit from the same home ownership benefits their suburban neighbors enjoy. This can be done by radically redesigning the already existing FHA 234 condominium mortgage insurance program so that it can apply as easily to individual condo units in multiple dwellings as the FHA 203 program applies to one-family homes in the suburbs.

The impact of these changes will be to increase the rate of home ownership in cities like Chicago (42.4 percent in 1985), New York (29.6 percent in 1987), Boston (32.2 percent in 1985), and Washington, D.C. (37.8 percent in 1985) until it matches the national level of 64 percent.[18] Most important, by opening a huge market of potential urban condominium owners and providing it with a stable supply of capital, these programs will allow the private sector to generate a massive supply of affordable owner-occupied urban housing.

One form of FHA condominium mortgage insurance would apply to newly constructed apartments, the second to existing apartments. The program for newly built city condominiums will benefit the urban middle class. The program for already depreciated, less expensive existing apartments will extend urban home ownership further down the economic ladder. However, beyond their side effect of inducing an increase in housing supply, these programs will not help the poor. There is only one way to provide decent housing for very low income families: *to subsidize* (see Chapter 11).

FHA Insurance for New Condominium Apartments

An entrepreneurially based, institutionally financed FHA condo program patterned on the 608 Program is the only way to generate substantial increases in the supply of urban housing. Establishing such a program for newly built urban condominiums requires changes in existing minimum property standards, legal documents, bank lending practices, and Fannie Mae secondary market procedures.

The prospect of a huge, new, and stable market financed by conventional lenders, similar to the market for suburban houses opened up by the FHA and VA after World War II, will create an entirely new group of developers. These developers will produce FHA condos much more quickly and cheaply than HUD subsidy-dependent producers. They will also find ways to minimize their cash equity, maximize institutional financing, and generate substantial profits.

The reaction will surely be condemnation of "windfall profits" and a demand for such additional requirements as cost certification, Davis-Bacon labor practices, affirmative action, and extra design requirements for the disabled. Such political pressures must be resisted because, as more than 50 years of experience with housing programs demonstrates, such requirements not only result in higher costs, they repel profit-motivated, private developers.

FHA Insurance for Existing Condominium Apartments

Despite low downpayments and lower debt service, many families will still be unable to afford a new condo. In many cities, the cost of producing new condominium housing is just too high. The only way for many of these city residents to enjoy urban home ownership is an FHA condo loan program that applies to existing housing. Older buildings were originally less expensive and have been depreciated many times over. As a result, existing housing tends to be more affordable than newly built apartments.

The FHA 234 condo loan program must be redesigned so that it works as easily as the FHA 203 home mortgage program. Making it apply to existing apartments in multiple dwellings is more difficult than making it apply to new construction. But it is no less possible. Since buildings vary depending on the regulations currently in force in an area or existing at the time they were built, minimum property standards will never work. However, in the half-century since the FHA was established, local laws have become far more stringent and consumer expectations have increased dramatically. Thus, to be sure that the purchaser will obtain a decent home, it is sufficient to require that any condominium receiving an FHA insured mortgage meet local code standards.

Appraisal procedures must be adjusted to fairly reflect the value of any apartment. Given the increasing popularity of inner city neighborhoods, this is less of a problem than it was 50 years ago. Nevertheless, adjustments will have to be made to FHA appraisal practices and minimum property standards, among them the elimination of the concept of a "useful life" for any older structure.

Once necessary adjustments have been made to FHA lending procedures and both FHA condominium programs are in place, resourceful, profit-motivated developers will find efficient and economical ways of satisfying this vast new market. The condition of the existing stock of multiple dwellings will steadily improve and millions of new condominium apartments will be added to the housing supply.

Notes

1. I am deeply indebted to my friend Michael Piore for the conceptual framework of this chapter. It is derived from the discussion of New Deal legislation in "Stablizing the Economy," pp. 73–104 in *The Second Industrial Divide,* by Michael J. Piore and Charles F. Sabel, Basic Books, N.Y., 1984.
2. Kenneth T. Jackson, *Crabgrass Frontier,* Oxford University Press, 1985, p. 205.
3. U.S. Department of Commerce, Bureau of the Census: *Statistical Abstract of the United States,* Washington, D.C., 1978, pp. 789–792.
4. Ibid.
5. Semer, Zimmerman, Foard, and Frantz, "The Evolution of Federal Legislative Policy in Housing: Housing Credits," pp. 69–106 in *Federal Housing Policy and Programs Past and Present,* J. Paul Mitchell (editor), Center for Urban Policy Research, Rutgers, 1985.
6. Kenneth T. Jackson, op. cit., p. 196.
7. FHA premium charges cover the cost of operations and any losses from the sale of foreclosed mortgages. The FHA has been self-financing since 1938. By 1954 it had repaid with interest all initial advances made by the Treasury.
8. Most lenders issued mortgages with a 20- or 25-year term.
9. According to the U.S. Department of Housing and Urban Development, Information Systems Division, between 1934 and December 1990, 19,687,309 one-family home mortgages had received FHA insurance. Of these 15,587,556 were insured under the FHA 203 program.
10. Find/SVP information services.
11. Roger Starr, *Housing and the Money Market,* Basic Books, New York, 1975, pp. 167–181.
12. Subcommittee on Housing and Urban Affairs, Committee on Banking and Currency of the United States Senate, *Progress Report on Federal Housing Programs,* U.S. Government Printing Office, Washington, D.C., 1967, p. 38.
13. Ibid, p. 39.
14. Paul Zane Pilzer with Robert Deitz, *Other People's Money: The Inside Story of the S&L Mess,* Simon and Schuster, New York, 1989, p. 63.
15. Stephen Pizzo, Mary Fricker, and Paul Muolo, *Inside Job: The Looting of America's Savings and Loans,* McGraw-Hill, New York, 1990, quoted by Michael M. Thomas in "The Greatest American Shambles," *The New York Review of Books,* New York, January 31, 1991, p. 31.
16. Pilzer with Deitz, op. cit., pp. 80–122.
17. These quotations, reproduced in Kenneth Jackson's *Crabgrass Frontier,* are only part of the FHA's remarkable record of prejudice in lending described on pp. 207–218 of this indispensible account of the suburbanization of the United States.
18. Bureau of the Census, U.S. Housing Survey.

9

Reducing Housing Cost

Los Angeles, 1989. Wyvern Wood Public Housing completed in 1939 still provides a decent home and a suitable living environment for families of low income. *(Alexander Garvin)*

There are two ways to close the gap between the cost of supplying decent shelter (economic rent) and a price that people are willing to pay (affordable rent). One is to lower the cost of supplying housing. The other is to lower the cost to the consumer.[1]

Some supply-side programs reduce the cost of providing housing by lowering the price of land or construction. Others reduce economic rent by lowering real estate taxes, debt service, or return on equity. Whether the reduction is passed through to the consumer depends on how the program is structured.

Demand-subsidy programs either provide consumers with additional money with which to purchase better shelter or provide supplemental payments to cover the gap between affordable and market rent. More money need not result in more or better housing. The money must be spent on housing rather than something else. It also must be sufficient to justify action by property owners. Otherwise, the additional demand that will result may produce higher prices rather than better accommodations. Like supply-subsidy programs, demand-subsidy programs only result in improved housing when they are structured to do so.

Millions of families have benefited from these supply- and demand-side programs. Some are more economical; some are more efficient; some are more responsive to consumer desires. The difficulty is that these programs do not necessarily improve our cities and sometimes damage them.

One of the most unfortunate aspects of subsidized housing programs has been their tendency to locate low- and moderate-income people in buildings that are visibly different from housing occupied by everybody else. As a result, subsidy recipients are identifiable as living in a "project" that also stigmatizes the surrounding community.

Most subsidized housing programs are conceived with little consideration of anything but shelter. The subsidies are used to produce affordable rents, not places for residents to eat, shop, gossip, play, or be involved with their neighbors. For that reason, when the subsidies are translated into physical form, the result is a building that has nothing to offer the surrounding neighborhood.

Worse yet, some subsidy programs concentrate people with acute social problems where they may obtain decent shelter but not the services they desperately need. Residents of surrounding areas fear subsidy recipients will spill over into the neighborhood, bringing their problems with them. Consequently, they vigorously oppose subsidized housing in their community.

The housing-subsidy programs that have been of benefit to urban and suburban areas are those that allow subsidy recipients to enter the marketplace on terms that are similar to those of nonsubsidized citizens. They also provide a subsidy that is large enough to stimulate property owners to make further investments. A good example is the sudsidy provided to homeowners. Since the enactment of the federal income tax, homeowners have not had to pay taxes on the income they use to pay mortgage interest and real estate taxes. In response, developers built millions of homes whose subsidy recipients are indistinguishable from the rest of society. The recently terminated Section 8 Moderate Rehabilitation Program is another example. This program subsidized the difference between 25 percent (later 30 percent) of income and economic rent for those recipients who lived in apartments that were upgraded to include decent plumbing fixtures, electrical wiring that could handle modern appliances, and other improvements that would not otherwise have been installed.

The best way of using subsidies to reduce housing cost is to make home ownership possible for millions of people who have been left out of the American dream. This eliminates the chasm between the nearly two-thirds of the population that owns its own home and those who do not have enough money to purchase their residence. For the first time they would be able to enter the marketplace on their own. Moreover, subsidizing home ownership avoids the high cost and time-consuming administration that has characterized most subsidy programs.

Home ownership will not solve the many problems facing people of low and moderate income. But making it possible for them to own their own residence will transform a huge population that is currently without decent, affordable shelter into a huge market that will stimulate the real estate industry to improve and expand the housing supply.

Subsidizing Supply

Most federal housing assistance has been directed at lowering the cost of supplying decent shelter. Theoretically, if the lower cost of production is passed on in the form of lower prices, there will be additional demand. Increased demand will stimulate developers to increase the housing supply. Construction means jobs and therefore support for and from the housing industry.

Some supply-side programs require relatively little subsidy but create substantial controversy, especially when private property is taken through public condemnation. In other instances the need for subsidies will be overcome by political attractiveness. The subsidies that go to housing built by nonprofit organizations, for example, often are politically more acceptable than subsidies that go to housing built by the private sector. Consequently, the appropriateness of supply-side subsidies must always be measured for political as well as financial feasibility.

The changing character of the political environment means that few programs remain in place for long. The ways in which supply-side subsidies can be used, however, do not change. They directly reduce one of the components of economic rent (operating costs, real estate taxes, debt service, and return on equity) or lower them indirectly by reducing development costs.

Reducing Development Costs

Development costs can be grouped into a few categories: property acquisition, tenant relocation, demolition, site preparation, professional services (e.g., architecture, engineering, legal, accounting), actual "brick and mortar" construction, fees and taxes, marketing, and interim financing to cover these costs until the property has occupants and a permanent mortgage. Sometimes one must also add the cost of supplying the required infrastructure (streets, sewers, water mains, transit systems) and community facilities (schools, parks, hospitals, fire and police stations, libraries, etc.).

Reduction in development cost does not produce a proportionate reduction in economic rent. For example, a 10 percent reduction in development cost will produce a 10 percent reduction in debt and equity requirements. However, debt service and return on equity are only two of four components of economic rent. If they represent half the required economic rent, then a 10 percent reduction in development cost will only reduce economic rent by 5 percent. Despite this limitation, many supply-side housing programs concentrate on reducing the land and construction costs.

Land

The initial cost for any development is property acquisition. If plenty of sites are available, developers negotiate with property owners until they are offered land at a price that is low enough to justify a financially feasible project. When developers need to assemble a site by purchasing specific parcels from a variety of owners, the cost of land can become prohibitive. Property owners may get wind of interest in their land. They will naturally refuse to sell, holding out for the very highest possible price—often threatening the feasibility of the project.

One of the earliest attempts at reducing the cost of assembling a housing site involved condemnation of privately owned land by the federal government. Faced with "widespread unemployment and disorganization of industry," Congress in 1933 had enacted the National Industrial Recovery Act. It authorized the Public Works Administration (PWA) to create jobs through a comprehensive program of public works including "low cost housing and slum clearance." In most cases land acquisition for these housing projects involved condemnation by the federal government.

Within 3 years the Housing Division of the PWA had begun 50 projects in 35 cities, totaling 25,000 dwelling units. All 50 projects consisted of walk-ups, mostly one- and two-story buildings that covered less than half their carefully landscaped sites. Although some of these projects eventually succumbed to problems that afflict publicly owned and operated housing (discussed later in this chapter under "Public Housing"), most have provided decent homes for families of low income for over half a century.[2]

College Court, in Louisville, designed by a team of local architects led by E. T. Hutchings, is a good example of the high

Louisville, 1988. Consistent siting, common materials, and landscaped open space are the only indication that College Court Public Housing, completed in 1938, is any different from its neighboring structures. *(Alexander Garvin)*

quality of these PWA housing projects. A 5-acre city block was acquired for 126 one- and two-story buildings, grouped around beautifully landscaped open areas at the center of the block. White-painted wooden front porches and pitched roofs give the red-brick structures a handsome domestic appearance. The buildings themselves stretch out along the bounding streets, set back from the property line by green lawns. The consistent siting, common materials, and landscaped open space are the only indication that College Court is any different from its neighboring structures. Thus, it is difficult to identify "project tenants." In 1987, College Court was converted into a resident-owned, low-income condominium, completing its integration into the residential fabric of the inner neighborhoods of Louisville.

Louisville's second PWA project, on Algonquin Parkway, may not be as handsome, but the approach is similar. It consists of a group of one- and two-story buildings, in scale with the surrounding neighborhood, sited around landscaped open space.

The city's third project became one of the most significant projects never to be built. In 1935, a property owner whose land was condemned by the PWA objected and went to court, claiming that the federal government had no right to take his property. He invoked the Fifth Amendment to the Constitution, which guarantees that no person's property shall be "taken for public use without just compensation." The implication is that taking private property for a *nonpublic* use is forbidden, even with compensation. In the case of *United States v. Certain Lands in the City of Louisville* the property owner contended that taking one individual's property in order to provide housing for another was not a public use authorized by the Constitution.

The District Court and, a few months later, the Sixth Circuit Court of Appeals ruled in his favor. They held that any taking had to be for the purpose of occupancy by a public agency (e.g., the U.S. Postal Service) performing a statutory or Constitutional purpose (e.g., mail delivery). Since the Roosevelt Administration was in the midst of a major battle with the Supreme Court and feared yet another New Deal program might be declared unconstitutional, it chose to withdraw the case rather than carry the appeal further.[3]

The case of *United States v. Certain Lands in the City of Louisville* is important because it terminated condemnation and housing construction by the federal government. At the same time, another court, in the case of *New York City Housing Authority v. Muller* (see Chapter 10), held that local authorities could condemn property for the purpose of eliminating slums and blight and providing decent shelter for people of low income. This helped the Roosevelt Administration to switch to a program that looked to local authorities (with condemnation powers provided by state constitutions) to own, build, and operate housing for persons of low income. The necessary subsidy would come in the form of direct federal grants to the local housing authority. This same approach was adopted after World War II for the federal urban renewal program.

In addition to condemnation of privately owned land for housing construction by government agencies, there have been hundreds of instances of government condemnation for construction by private developers. In 1943, Missouri, Pennsylvania, and New York became the first states to enact legislation allowing eminent domain to be used for the purpose of condemnation of property for private housing development.

Under the terms of the Missouri Urban Redevelopment Law of 1943, a developer submits a detailed redevelopment plan including evidence of the existence of blight, the presence of a market for the proposed housing, and the project's financial feasibility. The City Council then issues a certificate transferring the power of eminent domain to the developer. If the developer fails to negotiate property acquisition on favorable terms, the court approves condemnation and determines the price to be received by the former property owner.

In other states, the local redevelopment authority drafts a renewal plan. When the local legislative body approves the plan, the redevelopment authority goes to court to obtain possession of the required sites. The court decides on a fair level of compensation. Then the redevelopment authority sells the property for the amount of the condemnation award to a private developer, who has agreed to execute the plan.

Kansas City, 1989. Acquisition costs for the Quality Hill Redevelopment Project completed in 1954, were minimized because the city's powers of condemnation were used to prevent property owners from refusing to sell except for astronomical prices. *(Alexander Garvin)*

Manhattan, 1980. Corlear's Hook was one of the nation's earliest urban renewal projects subsidized with funds appropriated under Title I of the Housing Act of 1949. *(Alexander Garvin)*

Quality Hill was the first housing project in Kansas City to be completed under the Missouri Urban Redevelopment Law. The site had originally been developed as a high-income residential district during the second half of the nineteenth century. As the population of Kansas City moved southward, this once-fashionable neighborhood began to deteriorate. By the time that the bluffs overlooking the river were proposed for redevelopment the area had been labeled a "slum." Given the housing shortage after World War II, slum clearance for the purpose of housing construction was easy to justify.

When Quality Hill was completed in 1954, it consisted of five 11-story red-brick apartment houses containing 510 apartments, off-street parking for 250 cars, two swimming pools, and two picnic areas. More than four decades later, Quality Hill is still in good condition. It provides decent, affordable shelter for many more families than had previously lived on the site. Whether Kansas City might have been better off had the area's residents not been forced to relocate or if its Victorian houses had been restored rather than cleared is still debated. What cannot be debated is that condemnation proved to be an effective means of lowering the cost of housing development.

Reduction in the cost of acquisition greater than can be achieved through condemnation is, by definition, impossible. However, reducing the cost to the developer is a matter of subsidy. When Congress enacted the Housing Act of 1949, which created the urban renewal program, it provided just such a subsidy. In urban renewal projects conceived and executed by local redevelopment authorities but subsidized by the act, a site is sold to a developer at a price that makes redevelopment economically feasible. The difference between actual cost and the sales price is subsidized, two-thirds by the federal government and one-third by the locality.[4]

Corlear's Hook, one of the first projects to use federal urban renewal subsidies, illustrates how the program worked. Robert Moses had proposed the project soon after passage of the Housing Act of 1949. The 15-acre site, along the East River on Manhattan's Lower East Side, consisted of dilapidated tenements containing 878 apartments. Moses' development plan called for creation of 1668 cooperative apartments in four towers built by a union-organized nonprofit housing corporation.

Affordable coop apartments on the Lower East Side were feasible only if land costs were minimal: no more than $675 per apartment. Accordingly, the site was sold for $1,126,000 (1668 x $675=$1,125,900). However, project costs (acquisition, clearance, and site-work prior to resale for housing construction) were $6,411,000. Thus, the required subsidy was $5,285,000 ($6,411,000−$1,126,000=$5,285,000). The federal government provided $3,523,000, two-thirds of the required subsidy; New York City and State subsidized the rest.[5]

Construction

Attempts to reduce "brick and mortar" costs are often unsuccessful because they increase operating costs. The initial cost of an electric heating system, for example, may be less than a comparable oil or gas system. However, the lower initial cost may be more than compensated by the higher cost of electricity. Reducing room sizes, using poor materials, or installing cheap equipment will be more than compensated by increased maintenance and replacement costs during the project's life.

Since World War II, there have been two important attempts to lower the cost of construction. Both concentrated on labor practices, standardization of components, and shortening development time (and thus interim financing and taxes). Only the first, an entirely private initiative, proved to be successful.

Levittown, 1947. Standardizing design, prefabricating building components, and mass production allowed the Levitts to sell houses for $7990. *(Courtesy of the Levittown Public Library)*

Between 1947 and 1951, William and Alfred Levitt built and sold 17,442 homes on former potato fields in Long Island. They named the project Levittown. It was the first of several similar Levittowns built across America. By applying factory production techniques to housing construction, the Levitts were able to sell their houses at prices 20 percent below the competition (see Chapter 15).

House production was divided into 26 separate operations and subcontracted to 80 different firms that were supervised by the Levitt staff. Construction was scheduled in a manner similar to the assembly line that Henry Ford had used to reduce the cost of automobile production. But, instead of components coming down the assembly line to the workers, each of the subcontractor firms brought its workers to the site at the point it was ready for such involvement. This reverse production-line approach was possible because there were only five house models and because every component was standard and prefabricated (lumber, windows, doors, roofing, etc.).[6]

The Levitts needed cheap and continuous supplies of materials and equipment. For this reason, they bought timberland and a lumber mill on the West Coast that precut the lumber. They also established a supply company that manufactured cement block, nails, and other needed construction components. They were able to purchase fixtures and appliances at lower prices by ordering in bulk from suppliers who gave handsome discounts to important clients.

The resulting economies in construction allowed the Levitts to sell houses with two bedrooms, a living room, a bathroom, and a fully equipped kitchen (including sinks, a stove with two ovens, a refrigerator-freezer, and a Bendix washing machine) on prelandscaped lots for about $7990. Nothing comparable was available in the area for less than $9000—and then without washing machines or landscaping.

In the late 1960s a similar approach was tried by George Romney, Secretary of Housing and Urban Development. Romney, who had headed the American Motors Corporation, wanted to introduce mass-production techniques to government-assisted housing. He called this approach "Operation Breakthrough." Unfortunately, Operation Breakthrough had no way of overcoming traditional labor practices, failed to guarantee sufficient continuous production to justify capital investment in large new factories, and was used at sites and for designs that required development periods long enough to wipe out most of the savings in interim costs. It remains the only government effort to transfer housing production to the factory.

Reducing Economic Rent

Most government efforts at lower housing cost have been directed to reducing three of the four components of economic rent: real estate taxes, debt service, and return on equity.

Buildings can be designed to reduce the fourth component (operating and maintenance costs). However, little can be squeezed from maintenance without seriously affecting either the longevity of the structure or the quality of life within it.

Real Estate Taxes

Reducing real estate taxes provides a subsidy without direct government expenditures and, therefore, often is the most politically expedient method for local government to reduce economic rent. Legislators neither need to vote for a budget appropriation nor for specific projects. Agency staff is not employed administering the development process. Everything is done by the owner.

Tax programs usually only subsidize improvements. The justification is that, absent the improvement, there would be no additional tax to be paid. When the tax reduction expires, the municipality will collect additional revenues by taxing the improvements induced by initially lowering taxes.[7]

In 1920, New York became the first state to adopt enabling legislation that permitted tax exemption for new housing development. The following year, New York City passed a law providing all housing that was in construction or would be started between 1921 and 1927 with an exemption from any increase in real estate taxes because of the improvement. The exemption expired in 1932. By the time the program was terminated, it had provided $917 million in tax exemption for the construction of 574,000 apartments.[8]

A similar program, called 421A after its section in the New York City's Real Property Tax Law, has provided a 10-year exemption for new multiple dwellings started after 1971. The exemption begins at 100 percent and declines 20 percent every 2 years till the eleventh year when the project pays full taxes. Between 1971 and 1992, 105,616 newly built apartments received 421A tax exemption.[9]

Real estate tax abatement is used much less frequently than tax exemption, and then usually in conjunction with other government programs. For example, real estate taxes in federally assisted public housing projects are abated. The nominal tax that is paid is determined by formula to be 10 percent of shelter rent (gross rent less utility costs).

Debt Service

Debt service can be reduced either by lowering monthly amortization payments or by reducing the rate of interest. From the beginning, FHA programs reduced amortization by extending the term of the loan. Obviously, if a loan is repaid in equal monthly installments over a 25-year period, rather than 5 or 10 years, those payments will be significantly lower. Of all government projects, the 50 housing projects started by the PWA between 1933 and 1935, had the benefit of the greatest reduction in annual amortization payments: a 60-year mortgage term.

Reducing interest rates did not become a common strategy until 1959, when the FHA 221(d)(3) Program was enacted. At first, interest was only lowered to the average cost of federal borrowing. In 1965 the maximum interest rate for 221(d)(3) projects was set at 3 percent.[10]

The federal government was able to offer lower interest rates because it could borrow money a few percentage points below what conventional borrowers had to pay. The lower interest rates reflected the greater security and tax-deductibility of government bonds. Theoretically, this lower interest rate would be passed through to developers of moderate-income housing. However, the institutions that lent money for development had to pay market-rate interest to their depositors. In order to make up the difference, banks were allowed to sell their 221(d)(3) mortgages to Fannie Mae at a discounted price reflecting this below-market-rate interest.[11] The differential between the face amount of the mortgage and the discounted sale price was subsidized by congressional appropriation. Congress increased the subsidy for the FHA 235 and 236 programs enacted in 1968 to subsidize the difference between market interest and 1 percent.

Only 190,000 apartments were financed through the 221(d)(3) Program and 463,000 through the 236 Program. One reason for the relatively low number of apartments produced under these interest-subsidy programs was congressional reluctance to pay for them. This was not just a matter of budget priorities or housing philosophy. It was also the result of unhappiness with their inefficiency when compared with privately financed housing. Processing an FHA subsidized mortgage for an apartment building, for example, took many times longer than it took to obtain an FHA insured mortgage on a one-family house.[12]

Another reason for the relatively low level of production was that the program was available only to nonprofit or limited-profit developers. There are relatively few developers who are willing to accept a return on equity of 6 percent or less, especially during periods when the prevailing rate of interest is much higher. They agree to do so because these programs often provide unusually attractive tax benefits and allow them to contribute "builders profit" and "professional fees" in lieu of cash equity. In exchange they are willing to accept the added costs and frustrations of government loan processing.[13]

In addition to criticizing the time required for FHA processing, Congress found it difficult to justify construction costs that were more than 20 percent above comparable, privately financed projects. Not surprisingly, when Richard Nixon unilaterally terminated these housing programs in 1973, Congress chose not to replace them.[14]

Return on Equity

Many people believe that return on equity is the obvious place to cut economic rent. However, if private, profit-motivated developers are to be attracted in sufficient numbers to gener-

Brooklyn, 1994. Tower Apartments completed in 1876, kept rents low by limiting the owner's return to a nominal 5 percent. *(Alexander Garvin)*

ate major housing production, it is the last place to cut. Developers will simply flock to other businesses that produce a higher return. The trick is to keep the rate of return on equity high while lowering the amount of cash that the developer must put at risk.

At first, housing reformers concentrated on cutting the rate of return without understanding that this would reduce development activity. One of the earliest such "limited profit" projects was the Tower and Home Apartments built between 1876 and 1878 in the Cobble Hill section of Brooklyn. This "model tenement," designed by William Field, provided direct access to apartments from an open gallery. Each apartment extended to the other side of the building, thereby providing through-ventilation.

The philosophy behind the Tower and Home Apartments is captured by the catchy slogan coined by its developer, Alfred Treadway White: "philanthropy plus 5 percent." White wanted to demonstrate that capitalists could provide decent housing for working people and still make a 5 percent return. The slogan may have been appealing, but not enough to generate much developer activity. Nevertheless, housing reformers remained convinced that reducing return on equity could produce substantial amounts of housing at reduced cost to its tenants. Rather than continue to demonstrate this by building individual model tenements, they decided to try legislation.

In 1926, New York State enacted the Limited-Dividend Housing Corporations Law. This statute provided a 25-year exemption from any increase in real estate taxes for any housing project built by limited-dividend corporations. Over the next seven decades only 22 limited-dividend projects containing 10,300 apartments were built, nothing like the production reformers had hoped for.[15]

Another try at creating a major housing program by limiting the return on equity was made during the New Deal. The PWA experimented with this approach even before developing projects on its own. Eventually, the Roosevelt Administration produced eight limited-profit projects in six states, containing 4100 dwelling units. All but one of the projects were provided with PWA mortgages covering about 85 percent of total development cost.[16]

In contrast, many more entrepreneurs can be enticed into producing low-cost housing by reducing the amount of cash equity required rather than by reducing the rate of return on that equity. For example, a project with a development cost of $1 million, a $750,000 mortgage whose annual debt service is 10 percent, and $250,000 in equity with an annual return on that equity of 20 percent, requires $75,000 to cover debt service and $50,000 to cover return on equity, totaling $125,000 (i.e., [$750,000x0.1]+[$250,000x0.2]=$125,000). The same project with only $100,000 in equity requires merely $110,000(i.e., [$900,000x0.1]+[$100,000x0.2]=$110,000). Furthermore, since the rate of interest paid on a mortgage is likely to be lower than the rate of return on equity, there is a reduction in the economic rent. A greater number of people will be able to afford this lower price. Consequently, the developer's risk will be reduced.

Another method of decreasing equity requirements without decreasing the rate of return is direct subsidization of the gap between development cost and the amount of the mortgage. The PWA, for example, provided a direct subsidy of 45 percent of development cost of its own projects. The remaining 55 percent was covered by a 60-year mortgage at a low rate of interest.

Such capital "write downs" have become increasingly popular with local government agencies. The Los Angeles Community Redevelopment Agency (CRA) used this approach in 1982, in redeveloping a dilapidated block on 11th Street, south of the downtown office district. The project, Vista Montoya Condominiums, provides 180 apartments for low- and moderate-income households. Twenty percent of the

Los Angeles, 1989. Monthly housing costs at Vista Montoya Condominiums were reduced because the city extended a noninterest-bearing second mortgage covering a large portion of the purchase price. *(Alexander Garvin)*

condominium purchasers were low-income families displaced by this and other nearby projects. When Vista Montoya was completed in 1984, they could not afford the monthly payments on the new condos. So the CRA provided a capital write-down in the form of a noninterest-bearing second mortgage covering up to $45,000 of the purchase price. These mortgages only come due when the buyer sells the unit. At that time the CRA will receive the full amount of the mortage plus 50 percent of the appreciated value of the unit.[17]

Public Housing

The obvious way to reduce economic rent to the absolute minimum is to virtually eliminate real estate taxes, debt service, and return on equity—leaving little more than maintenance and operating costs. The Housing Act of 1937 did just that, calling it "public housing." The purpose of this legislation was:

> *to provide financial assistance to states and political subdivisions thereof for the elimination of unsafe and insanitary housing conditions, for the eradication of slums, for the provision of decent, safe, and sanitary dwellings for families of low income and for the reduction of unemployment and the stimulation of business.*

It provided the subsidies to local housing authorities (created by state enabling statutes) that built, owned, and operated housing for "families of low income."

As government entities, local housing authorities need no return on equity. Debt service is covered by an "annual contributions contract" that makes the federal government responsible for paying amortization and interest payments on bonds issued by the local housing authority. In exchange, local governments are required to reduce real estate taxes to a nominal amount (10 percent of shelter rent). Thus, the rent paid by the tenants is reduced to slightly more than maintenance and operating costs.

In 1987 there were more than 1.45 million public-housing units in America.[18] For most people, this conjures up an image of millions of people living in high-rise dormitory stockades.

San Francisco, 1976. Woodside Gardens Public Housing Project completed in 1968 won awards for architectural excellence. *(Alexander Garvin)*

New Orleans, 1981. The low-rise Ibreville Public Housing Project completed in 1941, includes wrought-iron decoration and other design features intended to integrate it with similar neighboring structures. *(Alexander Garvin)*

The reason for this image is that in New York, Chicago, Philadelphia, and many other cities, public housing has taken the form of depressing brick boxes surrounded by fenced-in patches of grass. There is nothing in the Housing Act that mandates, or even recommends, this design.

Local housing authorities also build projects that become local architectural assets. Sometimes they are designed to reflect the city's architectural heritage. Iberville, 858 apartments built in New Orleans between 1938 and 1941, includes traditional brick chimneys and wrought iron balcony railings. Wyvern Wood, a large group of garden apartments built in Los Angeles between 1938 and 1939, is designed to look like Monterey-style haciendas. Sometimes, like the Williamsburg Houses built in Brooklyn between 1935 and 1938, they are examples of the latest architectural fashion. Woodside Gardens, built in San Francisco in 1968, and 2440 Boston Post Road, built in the Bronx in 1972, won design awards. Similar outstanding architecture has been produced throughout the 50-year history of public housing. Unfortunately, as with most construction, this is the exception rather than the rule.

Another vivid image of public housing is the dynamiting of Pruitt Igoe, a 2762-unit public-housing project consisting of 33 11-story buildings, completed in 1954 in St. Louis. This project had so many problems that, in frustration, the St. Louis Housing Authority ordered its demolition. Conditions

Brooklyn, 1969. The Williamsburg Public Housing Project, completed in 1938, was designed to the most modern international standards of the period and included generous recreation facilities, a public school, day care, and 50 retail shops. *(Alexander Garvin)*

similar to Pruitt Igoe have arisen in public housing projects in Boston, Newark, Chicago, and elsewhere. It is these notorious situations that remain in the public consciousness, not the hundreds of well-managed projects providing hundreds of thousands of good apartments for families who otherwise could never afford a decent home.

The Bronx, 1973. Public housing at 2440 Boston Post Road, completed in 1972, was intended to set a standard of architectural excellence for the surrounding neighborhood. *(Alexander Garvin)*

One explanation for the notorious failures is the quality of construction and design. Congress established room-cost limits for public housing, but no controls on the cost of land or the quality of construction. In order to satisfy these cost limits, some projects (especially where land costs were high) were built as cheaply as possible. In other cases, local authorities, as a matter of social policy, chose to minimize housing quality. They found it difficult to justify providing poor tenants with "amenities" that working people could not afford.

It is wrong to blame the failure of public housing on inadequate design or quality of construction. Many projects that are now in trouble were built to optimum standards. In fact, when completed in 1950, Pruitt Igoe was hailed by contemporary architecture magazines as an example of excellence in housing design. The real explanation for the failure of specific public-housing projects involves fiscal policies, tenant selection procedures, maintenance practices, and project management.

When local housing authorities run out of money, they often cut back on services and maintenance. They develop cash-flow problems because the federal government forbids the accumulation of reserves. Rental income in excess of gross expenses (plus a transfer to reserves of no more than 50 percent of rent) must be used to reduce federal contract contributions (i.e., debt service). As a result of such reductions, between

1945 and 1953 the federal government paid less than half the nominal amount of its annual contract contributions.[19]

Public housing is usually conceived without consideration of eventual replacement requirements. Not only do stoves and refrigerators require replacement, so do boilers, plumbing risers, windows, and the like. Without the budgeted funds to take care of these items, many local housing authorities choose to defer replacement and repairs. Such deferred maintenance is a recipe for deterioration, and those projects in which maintenance has been deferred inevitably become slums. Had local authorities been able to use rents to build up proper replacement reserves, many projects would not be in such poor physical condition.

Another problem was created in 1969, when Senator Edward Brooke of Massachusetts succeeded in amending the Public Housing Program to require that no tenant pay more than 25 percent of income for rent. Congress agreed to pay the difference between 25 percent of income (currently 30 percent) and rent. But it has never appropriated enough money to cover this commitment. Local housing authorities have to cover the gap.

Faced with increasing fiscal problems, some housing authorities cut back on personnel. Also,when local politicians force them to hire political cronies, they become employers of last resort. Without personnel competent to manage and maintain the buildings, conditions become even worse.

Not all problems are fiscal or administrative. Initially, public housing was a temporary haven for the "deserving" poor, en route to stable jobs and houses of their own. Since the end of World War II, however, public housing increasingly has become the haven of the dependent poor. These poor need more than annual contract contributions from the federal government. When they move into public housing, they bring a myriad of other problems with them.

Housing authorities across the country have overcome the problems that forced the Boston Housing Authority into receivership and the St. Louis and Newark Housing Authorities to demolish once-sound apartments. This success is due to their relatively strict admission and occupancy standards, administration that has been relatively unaffected by politics, and budgets that are supplemented by city governments to cover the costs of repairs, replacement, renovation, and shortfalls in federal funding. Hundreds of thousands of families are happy to get apartments in public housing, and millions more wish they could. It is the housing of choice for tens of thousands of poor New Yorkers. For years, the waiting list for a New York City Housing Authority apartment has remained at 200,000 applicants.

Increasing After-Tax Income

Reducing housing cost is not simply a matter of reducing the dollars spent to produce shelter or the dollars spent to purchase it. In each case the expenditure is significantly affected by federal, state, and local income taxes. Federal income tax policy, in particular, subsidizes housing by providing benefits for investment in home ownership, rental housing, and state and local housing finance-agency bonds. These subsidies are particularly attractive to legislators because they do not require specific budget appropriations or project approvals.

Home Ownership

The rationale for encouraging home ownership is deeply embedded in our culture and political system. Throughout the English-speaking world, home ownership is thought of as a source of liberty and a guarantor of responsible participation in society. Encouraging home ownership is also considered to be a method for increasing the level of personal savings, ensuring that money is invested in housing, and improving the quality of day-to-day care of the housing stock.

Programs to develop a stable and free society of homeowners can be traced to the beginning of the Republic. Revolutionary War veterans received land certificates. The Homestead Act of 1862 provided 160 acres of land to any family head who lived there for 5 years and paid a fee of less than $40. From the Civil War on, Congress has used the tax code to alter housing costs. The Revenue Acts of 1864 and 1865, permitted taxpayers to deduct local tax and interest payments from their taxable income before calculating their federal tax payments. In 1913, Congress explicitly restated this policy in legislation establishing the federal income tax system. This policy simply continued to reflect the deeply embedded belief that direct payment of property taxes would result in a responsible citizenry willing to participate in the political process and able to determine the proper role of government and correct level of expenditure to pay for it.

What was not immediately apparent was that in doing so Congress had enacted a housing subsidy for homeowners. The deductibility of mortgage interest and local real estate taxes reduces the cost of owning one's home. Renters, unlike homeowners, cannot deduct any part of their payment for housing. The value of this tax subsidy has been estimated to be equal to a 13.75 percent reduction in the cost of housing.[20]

Rental Housing

Congress also uses the tax code to encourage investment in rental housing by manipulating a property owner's actual *after-tax* return. When it wishes to induce investment in rental housing without making (frequently unpopular) budget appropriations, it increases the after-tax return by granting tax credits or altering depreciation schedules.

No building lasts forever. It must eventually be replaced or remodeled. Thus, for accounting purposes, a building depreciates yearly until it is considered valueless. Although the owner does not make cash payments, depreciation is considered an expense for tax purposes. Obviously, the greater the amount of yearly depreciation permitted by the tax code, the greater the attractiveness of investing in housing. For example, if the tax code permits depreciation to be taken in equal installments over 40 years, the owners of a building valued for tax purposes at $5 million, may deduct $125,000 from its taxable income ($5,000,000÷40=$125,000). If the depreciation period is reduced to 20 years, the deduction is increased to $250,000 ($5,000,000÷20=$250,000). Thus, if the property's net cash flow after mortgage-interest payments but before mortgage-amortization payments is $250,000, the 40-year depreciation results in a taxable income of $125,000 ($250,000−$125,000=$125,000). A 20-year depreciation period permits the owner to avoid paying any tax on this income ($250,000−$250,000=0). However, whatever the amount of depreciation that is deducted, it must be repaid when the property is sold.[21]

During the early 1980s, when Congress permitted very short depreciation periods, many projects generated "paper" tax losses. Given the high income-tax rates in effect at that time, such tax deductions were very valuable. As a result, many wealthy individuals invested in real estate in order to obtain tax deductions because they could be combined with other taxable income to lower annual tax payments.

The Tax Reform Act of 1986 changed this. Rates were reduced to levels that made cash returns more attractive. Furthermore, the act eliminated, in all but a small number of cases, the use of tax losses to offset other income. Thus, for the present, private investment in housing is primarily based on the real cash returns rather than paper tax benefits.

Tax-Exempt Government Bonds

Another housing subsidy that does not need a budget appropriation is the tax exemption granted to state housing finance-agency bonds. Forty-seven states, the District of Columbia, and Puerto Rico have established housing finance agencies that issue billions of dollars in long-term bonds whose proceeds have been invested in housing. These bonds are backed by project revenues or by the credit of a state or local government. The rate of interest on state housing finance agency bonds is usually several percentage points below the most secure corporate bonds whose interest is not tax-exempt. Thus, housing financed by these bonds gets the benefits of a lower interest rate and longer amortization periods than available from conventional lenders.

For example, the Massachusetts Housing Finance Agency uses its bond proceeds in combination with FHA, Section 8, and other federal programs for construction loans and permanent mortgages, home-improvement mortgages, and projects without other federal or state subsidy programs in which at least 20 percent of the apartments are for low-income tenants. During the first two decades since its creation in 1970, the Massachusetts Housing Finance Agency issued more than $3 billion in housing bonds. As of 1987, it had financed the construction or rehabilitation of 63,000 apartments and the purchase of 16,500 homes.[22]

With one glaring exception, housing finance agencies have been operated very responsibly. The exception is New York State, where the tax-exempt bonds that financed the construction of 168,000 apartments in 425 projects (269 state and 156 city) nearly caused fiscal disaster for both the state and city of New York. In 1956, New York enacted the Mitchell Lama Law, thereby becoming the first state to use tax-exempt state bonds to finance housing development and use their tax-exempt status to lower debt service. At first, rent covered all costs. Tenants balked at paying increased rent to cover increased operating costs. Faced with tenant opposition and pressure from elected public officials, state and city personnel deferred the rent increases. Rather than cut back on services or defer maintenance, the projects reduced debt-service payments.

These practices could only result in mortgage defaults and thus failure to make interest payments on state and city bonds. In 1975 this situation forced the state legislature to bail out projects financed by the recently created New York State Urban Development Corporation. Similar problems brought the Mitchell Lama Program operated by the New York State Division of Housing and Community Renewal to a halt. Simultaneously, New York City's fiscal crisis revealed over $1 billion in short-term notes used to finance the City's Mitchell Lama Program. These notes could not be placed into permanent financing because the rents would not cover the debt service.

No other state housing programs have experienced such acute problems. Nevertheless, Congress objected to other abuses. Many states used their tax-exempt bonds as a device for lowering the cost of purchasing single-family houses. While this was attractive to middle-class residents within the state, Congress failed to see the public purpose of further subsidies for the middle class. Moreover, these housing bonds were eroding the federal tax base at a time the federal government was experiencing a massive budget deficit. As a result of tax reform, the authority to continue the sale of tax-exempt bonds for these purposes terminated at the end of 1988.

Subsidizing Demand

The real reason for reducing housing cost is eloquently stated in the Housing Act of 1949:

> *The general welfare and security of the Nation and the health and living standards of its people require...the realization as soon as feasible of the goal of a decent home and a suitable living environment for every American family.*

Thanks to the federal programs that greatly increased housing supply, most Americans do not need financial assistance to be able to live in a decent home. Poor people do!

There are many ways of helping the poor. The services strategy does so by supplying them with whatever society considers to be essential. Building publicly owned and operated housing for persons of low income is an example of this approach.

Another way is to help by increasing incomes. This allows low-income people to select the services they feel satistfy their needs. Giving poor people more money with which to purchase a decent home, however, does not guarantee that they will use it for that purpose. Poor families, especially those in acute need of improved clothing, food, and other necessities may choose to spend on something other than housing. Even if they do spend this additional money on housing, there is no way of being sure that the added expenditure will result in a move to higher quality housing (if it is available) or in improvement in the quality of the housing they continue to occupy. The billions of dollars appropriated annually by Congress for welfare payments illustrate this point quite well.

Where there is insufficient decent housing, providing poor people with more money with which to purchase it increases the price of available housing for everybody else. Prices should start to decline when the housing industry builds enough additional housing to meet the increased demand. Since it takes a long time for developers to perceive the increased demand, acquire property, hire architects to make the necessary plans, obtain the financing, and complete construction, the inflationary period can last many years.

If the subsidy is insufficient to cover the cost of supplying new housing, additional income will only allow poor people to outbid those next up on the economic ladder, causing unintended hardship and opposition. Once again, the welfare program illustrates this quite well. Not one unit of housing has been built by developers seeking to satisfy the increased purchasing power of welfare recipients. Furthermore, such subsidies create considerable animosity among working families who do not get supplemental income to pay for better housing.

Without limiting occupancy to people who could not otherwise afford decent housing, no government program to lower the cost of supplying housing can guarantee that the subsidy will be passed through to the poor. For this reason many housing programs (public housing, 221(d)(3), 236, section 8, etc.) restrict occupancy to persons within defined income limits. Restricting occupancy also segregates the beneficiaries from the surrounding neighborhood. It is doubtful that Congress ever intended or even understood that income-specific housing programs increase segregation. Nevertheless, that has been the result.

Supplementing Rent

Demand-subsidy programs need not be inflationary or increase segregation. The Section 23 Leased Public Housing Program avoided not only segregation but also the stigma of conventional public housing projects. Section 23, enacted in 1965 and terminated in 1974, provided local housing authorities with annual contribution contracts covering the cost of renting apartments in existing buildings.

Theoretically, Section 23 guaranteed widespread tenant dispersal by limiting the number of apartments that could be leased to 10 percent of any building or project. In fact, there was little dispersal. In many areas rents exceeded program limits. Even when rents were at or below program limits, landlords often refused to accept public-housing tenants. Any housing authority could waive the 10 percent limit, and many did. Congress never appropriated enough money to disperse more than a few families. The program's most serious flaw was that it did nothing to reduce the inflationary impact on the local housing market.

The Rent Supplement Program, enacted at the same time as Section 23, tried to eliminate both segregation and inflation. It provided a 40-year subsidy covering the difference between "fair market rent" and 25 percent of tenant income.[23] Initial occupancy was restricted to families whose incomes were at or below public-housing levels. Inflationary pressures were eliminated by tying the 40-year subsidy exclusively to newly built apartments. Thus, the increase in demand is matched by an equal increase in supply.

The Rent Supplement Program avoided economic segregation within a project by allowing the tenants receiving the subsidy to remain in the apartment even if their incomes rose. The subsidy simply decreased by 25 percent of any increase in income until rent equaled 25 percent of income. However, the Rent Supplement Program failed to prevent geographic and, by extension, racial segregation. Rent Supplement projects had to receive approval of any locality in which they were built. To nobody's surprise, during the 3 years of its operation virtually no projects were proposed or approved in suburban areas.

In 1973, unhappy with the administrative complexity and expense of government-housing programs, the high cost of government-financed development, and the inequitable geographic distribution of subsidy programs, the Nixon Administration decided to experiment with direct payment of housing allowances. The Housing Allowance Experiment spent $160 million to provide 25,000 families in 12 metropolitan areas with housing vouchers for periods of 3 to 10 years.[24]

The families affected failed to generate sufficient demand either to increase rents or induce housing construction in any of the 12 participating areas. Most participants chose to remain where they were already living and not to spend the allowance on improved housing. They simply reduced the proportion of recipient family income going to rent. Recipients who did choose to move relocated to areas with populations that had higher incomes. One has to wonder why it was necessary to spend $160 million on an experiment that came up with such obvious conclusions.

The most recent demand subsidy program to be terminated is Section 8 of the Housing and Community Development Act of 1974. The Section 8 Program applied only to persons of low income and subsidized the difference between "fair market rent" and 25 percent (later 30 percent) of income. It came in four varieties: *existing housing* (which was essentially a 15-year housing allowance tied to the recipient in the form of a 5-year contract, renewable for two additional 5-year periods and payable for any apartment in acceptable condition which was within fair market rent levels); *moderate rehab* (which tied the same 15-year subsidy to properties undergoing moderate renovation); *substantial rehab* (which provided the same subsidy for 20 to 40 years for gut rehabilitation of apartment houses); and *new construction* (which provided the same 20- to 40-year subsidy for construction of new multiple dwellings). To qualify, each locality had to decide on an annual mix of Section 8 projects based on a "Housing Assistance Plan" designed to meet the objectives of the 1974 Act.

There is little difference between the housing allowance experiment and Section 8 Existing Housing Program, except its nationwide character. On the other hand, Section 8 Moderate Rehabilitation eliminated major deficiencies in previous demand subsidy programs. Because it was tied to existing buildings, it guaranteed significant improvement in the quality of housing supplied to all recipients. Because the amount of subsidy depended on tenant income, there was genuine economic integration. Because existing buildings (rather than large projects) received the subsidy there was no stigma attached to residing in a Section 8 assisted property. Most important, there was no inflationary impact on a city's housing stock because no residents could take their subsidy and bid for housing elsewhere. The same benefits applied to Section 8 Substantial Rehab. In addition, since the subsidy was applied to previously vacant structures, it also effectively increased the supply of available apartments by making previously vacant units habitable. However, it required several times as much subsidy per recipient family. The Section 8 New Construction Program was only different from the other three programs in that the subsidy per family was even greater.

Faced with huge budget deficits and very high cost per recipient, the Reagan Administration terminated funding of Section 8 during the 1980s. As of 1992, 1.5 million families had received Section 8 existing housing subsidies, 109,000 apartments had received Section 8 moderate rehab subsidies, and 831,000 apartments had received Section 8 substantial rehab and new construction subsidies.[25] It is doubtful that many people in Congress, HUD, or local government perceived that Section 8 moderate rehab had achieved previously unfulfilled goals, without the usual ill effects, at a substantially lower cost per unit than any of the previous demand-subsidy programs.

Ingredients of Success

For most of the twentieth century we have been initiating housing-assistance programs that promise once and for all to provide a decent home for every American family. As soon as developers and government officials learn how one program works, a new one takes its place. The resulting lag in production is unnecessary. After spending hundreds of billions of dollars on housing-subsidy programs, we have more than enough experience to know what will be successful.

Market

Most housing-assistance programs affect the price paid by the occupant without having much impact on anybody else. Consequently, they are supported by program participants and ignored by the rest of the population until neighborhood opposition or budget appropriations become intolerable. Only those housing-assistance programs (e.g., federal income-tax deductions for mortgage-interest payments) that improve market conditions throughout an area are likely to remain politically and financially feasible for any length of time and thus make much of an inroad in providing a decent home for every American family.

Occasionally, as in New York City's real estate tax-exemption programs, a locality will provide a housing assistance that genuinely alters local market conditions. Budget constraints make widespread adoption of such local programs unlikely. Consequently, most programs that reduce housing cost are likely to originate with the federal government.

Congress has never funded housing-subsidy programs at a level high enough to produce substantial additions to any city's housing stock and, therefore, to lower prices. Thus, benefits were passed through to building occupants without affecting the housing market of the surrounding city and without gaining widespread public support. Instead, federal assistance should take the form of shallow subsidies that can be distributed to a broad range of recipients and alter local market conditions.

Location

Consumers naturally favor residences with inherent advantages such as good views, plenty of light and fresh air, and beautiful landscaping. They prefer to be able to get to shopping, recreation, and employment facilities easily and quickly. Local programs that reduce real estate taxes and federal income-tax deductions for mortgage-interest payments do not distort these locational considerations. Consequently, buildings that receive such benefits tend to profit from continuing consumer interest and remain in good condition.

Subsidized housing projects, on the other hand, do not have to be built in attractive or convenient locations. More often than not, the limited subsidies that are available result in selection of sites whose low cost reflects their unattractiveness or inconvenience. Artificially low rents overcome most locational disadvantages. Consequently, most subsidized housing ends up on cheap land far from "better" neighborhoods.

Despite the availability of suburban land that is cheap enough to satisfy federal housing assistance requirements, very little subsidized housing has been located in the suburbs. It is almost as if the Department of Housing and Urban Development and its predecessor agencies had no idea there were housing problems or poor people outside center cities. Consequently, public-assistance recipients tend to be concentrated in the least desirable center city locations.

Instead, federal housing programs should replace program criteria and technical review with consumer choice based on the same locational criteria that apply to the rest of the marketplace. This would sidestep time-consuming political controversy, increase program efficiency, and eliminate the cost of project review.

Design

It is impossible to distinguish resident-owned houses that receive income-tax benefits from those that are rented and therefore do not receive this federal subsidy. Publicly assisted housing projects, on the other hand, are usually visibly different from the neighborhoods around them. Public-housing projects are even more different. Consequently, they become lightning rods for discrimination and opposition.

These differences extend to the way homes and projects affect the landscape. Normally, urbanization is incremental: A few houses are replaced by an apartment building; several years later a movie theater is replaced by an office building; and so on. The resulting urban fabric is a complex mix of colors and materials, periods of construction, styles of architecture, land uses, and human activities. Publicly assisted projects, on the other hand, are usually large enough to vary significantly from the surrounding neighborhood.

If recipients of housing subsidies are to avoid the stigma of public assistance they must be able to participate in the housing market without being identifiable. The only way for this to happen is for government to stop financing "projects" and operate within the context of incremental development by conventional developers whose buildings are financed by conventional lending institutions.

Financing

Using state and local bonds to create a pool of long-term, below-market-interest-rate mortgage money is an efficient method of lowering debt service and thus the cost of housing. However, when underwriting procedures are based on allowable costs, fixed fees, and limited returns on equity there is no reason for borrowers to reduce the size of their loan and, therefore, to further reduce economic rent. That is why some local agencies transfer their bond proceeds to local banks whose conventional underwriting procedures avoid this problem (see Chapter 12).

The subsidy directed to local bonds that are exempt from income taxes is equal to the value of the uncollected taxes. That subsidy could be more efficiently applied if it took the form of equity participation in individually subsidized residences. Not only could the same money be recirculated each time the subsidy was repaid, it could also grow in proportion to any appreciation of value.

Entrepreneurship

The home-building industry is largely made up of small businesses that erect fewer than five houses a year. The small size of their operations allows them to respond quickly to changes in demand, to maintain tight supervision over every aspect of their business, and to exploit unusual opportunities for minor economies. Most government-subsidy programs clash with this low overhead approach to development. Small builders are not willing to comply with time-consuming requirements, prior reviews of proposed activity, and post-factum audits. Consequently, they avoid most government-subsidy programs. The tax deduction for home ownership is an obvious exception. Home builders benefit from this deduction but do not have to apply for it. This cost-effective approach completely eliminates the need for a government agency or for time-consuming operations that true entrepreneurs make every effort to avoid.

The developers of subsidized-housing projects have to be able to withstand government scrutiny. Such developers need well-organized staffs and routinized business procedures. They employ a different labor force and very different construction practices from the more informal home builders. It is, therefore, relatively easy for them to comply with the provisions of the Davis-Bacon Law, HUD cost certification, Equal Opportunity regulations, and whatever else Congress decides to require. Compliance with these requirements is time consuming and increases the cost of development. In a competitive market, this situation would reduce profitability and deflect entrepreneurs to other businesses. It has no effect on the subsidized-housing business because the government fixes both allowable costs and the percentage of return on equity. Thus, there is no incentive to bring costs below government-approved, cost-certified limits. Moreover, because the allowable return is limited to a fixed percentage of project cost, there is every reason to reach those cost limits. Instead, housing-assistance programs should be conceived in a manner that limits cash-equity requirements, but does not limit costs or the return on equity. The control on windfall profits would shift from government regulation to the consumer's willingness to pay the resulting rent and the legislature's subsidy appropriations.

Time

Subsidies neutralize the effect of time on public and publicly assisted housing projects. The cost of carrying a property until it is occupied (and therefore total development cost) may be increased by the time it takes to obtain government subsidies and to comply with government requirements. But that increase is neutralized by project subsidies. Real estate taxes on government-subsidized projects are usually reduced by local statutes. Cash equity has been minimized and therefore also the payment for the use of that money. Increases in interim interest are offset by subsidized interest rates. Even if these costs did amount to substantial sums, none of them are significant because, upon completion, the increased cost of development is rolled into the permanent mortgage and its effect is thereby mitigated by other government subsidies.

None of these additional costs apply to income tax or real estate tax programs that lower housing prices because of the financial incentive to reduce development time. Thus, the best way of applying the same financial incentive to other housing subsidy programs is to shift all financing to conventional lending institutions.

Reducing Housing Cost as a City Planning Strategy

Even if there was a suitable residence for every American, some people would not be able to afford it. There is a rich history of ways to provide them with the necessary subsidies. But if housing subsidies are to have a beneficial effect on our cities and suburbs, they must be embodied in programs that are economical, efficient, equitable, responsive to the desires of the recipients, and generate desirable market activity. They must be economical because minimizing the subsidy per unit maximizes the number of people who can benefit. They must be efficient, otherwise relatively few entrepreneurs will be interested in supplying subsidized shelter. Thus, it will take longer to produce the same number of dwelling units and fewer people will have access to affordable shelter. They must be equitable, otherwise there will be legitimate opposition from those who do not receive subsidies and from those who believe their subsidy is inadequate. They must be responsive to the desires of the recipients, otherwise recipient dissatisfaction will be directed at the housing they are forced to accept. They must generate desirable market activity, otherwise those who do not receive subsidized housing will not benefit from the program and therefore oppose it. The best way to achieve all these goals is to provide everyone who does not own his or her home with the opportunity to do so.

Nearly Universal Home Ownership

The nearly two-thirds of the population that owns its residence is able to do so because at some point it had the cash to make the necessary equity investment (downpayment) and because it currently earns enough money to cover operating costs, real estate taxes, and debt service on a mortgage. Tens of millions of others have the income to cover the monthly costs of owning their home, but do not have the downpayment or have savings that could cover the downpayment but not enough income to pay debt service on a sufficiently large mortgage. Thus, for a relatively small subsidy per recipient we could provide most working people with the opportunity to own their residence. A national program that provided such shallow subsidies would produce a demand-generated increase in the housing supply of the sort that swept the country after World War II.

Subsidizing this group without providing for the dependent poor consigns those suffering from the most serious social and economic privations to live apart from the rest of the nation, probably in the least desirable housing. Segregation of this sort is intolerable. Futhermore, it guarantees the persistence of slums that damage surrounding cities and suburbs. Thus, despite the substantial additional cost, any national program of home ownership must be applicable to virtually everyone.

A program to open home ownership to all Americans is dependent on Congress terminating its discrimination against cities and multiple dwellings by enacting the changes in FHA condominium-mortgage programs described in the previous chapter. Without those changes we would be forced to build and subsidize houses for everybody on public assistance. Doing this on open land in distant suburbs would require so much money that it is beyond imagination. Furthermore, it is unnecessary because the nation's large stock of relatively inexpensive rental apartments could be converted to resident ownership at a fraction of that cost.

The national program of home ownership that I recommend would take three forms. One category of resident-owned dwelling would consist of existing houses and condominium apartments that met program requirements. A second would be created by requiring developers of new subdivisions and condominiums that qualified for FHA mortgages to reserve a preestablished number of dwellings for the program. A similar set-aside would apply to all rental apartment buildings whose conversion to condominium ownership involved FHA mortgages. In all three cases, the number of subsidized units in any complex and geographic area would be limited to 10 percent. This limitation would guarantee a meaningful level of integration and avoid serious political opposition.

Ninety percent of the money to pay for the purchase of subsidized one-family houses and condominiums would come from the financial institutions that provided purchasers with FHA insured mortgage loans. Some portion of the remaining 10 percent would come from occupant-equity contributions. The rest would come from the federal government.

Resident owners would contribute a legislated percentage (20 to 30 percent) of their income to cover operating costs, real estate taxes, and debt service. This monthly payment would go first to cover operating costs (including homeowner-association and condominium charges), then to real estate taxes, then to interest on the mortgage, and finally to amortization. Any deficiency would be paid pursuant to an annual contributions contract similar to that used for public housing. Residents who had more than enough income to cover all monthly costs, would be permitted to make additional payments to the housing authority to amortize up to half the equity investment in the property.

The process of acquiring subsidized residences would begin with Congress deciding on an annual level of housing subsidy. The money would be distributed by HUD to each locality, based on a formula reflecting the local conditions (e.g., population, degree of poverty, condition of the housing stock). The program would then be implemented by local public-housing authorities, which would decide on the mix of existing and new units based on local-market conditions, determine the number of recipients that could be funded in that year, and establish criteria for their selection.

Eligible recipients would purchase their residence on a shared-equity basis with the housing authority. In order to underscore the reality of ownership, each subsidy recipient would have to put up at least one-quarter of the initial equity requirement (a downpayment of 2.5 percent). The local subsidy-allocation would cover the rest.

The housing authority would guarantee annual debt-service payments for the life of the FHA insured mortgage. In exchange for the federal-subsidy allocation and the certainty that the resident was paying a fixed percentage of income on housing, the local government would grant any residence in the program an exemption of up to 100 percent of local real estate taxes.

Owner-occupants could either sell their residence to a purchaser at the market price or sell their share of the equity to the housing authority for occupancy by another eligible applicant. In order to avoid collusion between buyer and seller and to ensure a fair geographic distribution of subsidized units, the housing authority would have the right of first refusal on the sale of any residence receiving an FHA insured mortgage.

In the case of an ordinary sale, the bank would be paid the oustanding balance of the mortgage. The remaining proceeds would be divided so that the owner and the housing authority would first receive their equity contributions. Any balance would be divided in proportion to the cash equity (including mortgage amortization) invested by the occupant and the housing authority. Thus, subsidy recipients, like middle-class suburban homeowners, would be able to build equity and share in any appreciation of value. The housing authority would be able to recirculate its initial capital and use its share of any appreciation of value to acquire additional units.

A national program of home ownership of this sort is economical because it minimizes the cost of acquiring decent shelter for people who could not otherwise afford it. In fact, many residents will be paying half the capital cost and all monthly payments once their income becomes large enough. The program also minimizes operating costs by eliminating service personnel and depending on the resident maintenance.

The program is efficient because it avoids establishing an elaborate bureaucracy and uses existing institutions and market mechanisms. Unlike current subsidy programs, it would be very sensitive to changing market conditions. During periods when existing housing is cheaper than new construction the local housing authority would alter the mix of expenditures to favor existing housing, and vice versa.[26]

Since subsidized residences will be indistinguishable from those that are not subsidized, there will be no segregation by location, appearance, or occupancy. The 10 percent limitation prevents any concentration of subsidy recipients from developing. More important, the program will be as easy to operate in suburban areas as it will be in the inner city.

Once a national home-ownership program is in place, the entire real estate industry (not just a small group of specialized entrepreneurs) will get involved in supplying this huge, newly created market. For the first time, the beneficiaries of subsidized housing will include both its occupants and surrounding urban and suburban communities where existing residences will be improved and new residences will be built. Thus, also for the first time, the consistuency for subsidized housing will include the entire nation.

Notes

1. The "rent" people refer to may mean different things and represent different sums of money. *Affordable rent* is the amount a tenant can pay and still retain enough money to pay for food, clothing, medical care, transportation, and other necessities. *Market rent* is the amount that people will pay for similar facilities, similarly situated. *Contract rent* is the payment required by written aggreement between the owner and tenant. *Regulated rent* is the amount established by those local governments that control everything from the price the owner can charge to the level of service that must be provided. *Economic rent* is the amount required to justify any real estate venture; that amount that will cover all the expenses of running the property. Those expenses include: (1) maintenance and operating costs, (2) real estate taxes, (3) debt service on mortgage loans, and (4) payments to equity investors.
2. James Ford, *Slums and Housing,* Harvard University Press, Cambridge, 1936, pp. 716–736.
3. *United States v. Certain Lands in the City of Louisville,* 9 F. Supp. 137, 141 (D.C.W.D. Ky. 1935) and 78 Fed. 2nd. 684 (C.C.A. 6, 1935). See Lawrence M. Friedman, *Government and Slum Housing,* Rand McNally, Chicago, 1968, pp. 102–103.
4. See Chapter 6, note 12.
5. New York City Housing and Development Administration, *Community Development Program Progress Report 1968,* New York City, p. 215.
6. Historical and statistical material on Levitt and Sons and their new towns in Long Island, Pennsylvania, and New Jersey is derived from: Rachlis and Marqusee, *The Landlords,* Random House, New York, 1963, pp. 228–256; Herbert Gans, *The Levittowners,* Pantheon Books, Random House, New York, 1967; and John T. McQuiston, "If you're thinking of living in Levittown," *New York Times,* November 27, 1983.
7. Government reduction of real estate taxes can take two forms: (a) exemption for a specified period of time from any tax increase in the value of the property due to an improvement, and (b) abatement for a specified period of time of some or all of the taxes to be paid. Sometimes, to ensure that the property owner passes this reduction on to the tenants, the tax reduction will be restricted to buildings

with regulated rents or whose occupancy is exclusively for persons of low, moderate, or middle income.

8. Initially, the benefits were restricted to multiple dwellings of four or more stories and to increases in tax assessment up to $1000 per room and $5000 per apartment. Later benefits were restricted to $15,000 per building. See Citizens Housing and Planning Council, *How Tax Exemption Broke the Housing Deadlock in New York City,* New York, 1960.
9. New York City Department of Housing and Development, Division of Financial Services. The figures are for fiscal years ending June 30. In 1986, the 421 Program was amended to exclude certain sections of the city (thought to be high-rent areas) unless the developer also provided "low-rent" apartments. In other geographic areas the exemption period was extended to 10 years.
10. Initially the 221 (d)(3) Program was restricted to families "displaced from urban renewal areas or as a result of government action." In 1962 it was broadened to also cover all "low- and moderate-income families."
11. Later the Congress removed Fannie Mae from this role and established a new institution, Ginny Mae (the Government National Mortgage Association), specifically for the purpose of acting as a secondary market for such federally subsidized mortgages.
12. U.S. Department of Housing and Urban Development, *H.U.D. Statistical Yearbook,* Washington, D.C., 1978.
13. U.S. Commission on Urban Problems, "Public Assisted and Subsidized Housing," pp. 319–336 in *Federal Housing Policy and Programs Past and Present,* J. Paul Mitchell (editor).
14. U.S. Department of Housing and Urban Development, "Interest Rate Subsidies: National Housing Policy Review," pp. 337–364 in *Federal Housing Policy and Programs Past and Present,* J. Paul Mitchell (editor).
15. New York City Department of City Planning, *Public and Publicly Aided Housing 1927–1973,* New York, 1974.
16. With the exception of Knickerbocker Village, which was financed by the Reconstruction Finance Corporation, they were low-rise complexes, designed and developed by individuals interested in housing reform. The best of these projects, Hillside Homes in the Bronx, was designed by Clarence Stein. It replaced 26 undeveloped acres with 1416 apartments primarily in four-story, walk-up structures organized around a series of landscaped recreation areas connected by a pedestrian spine. Community rooms, workshops, and a nursey were provided in the basements.
17. Urban Land Institute, *Project Reference File,* vol. 15, no. 4, January–March 1985.
18. U.S. Department of Commerce, Bureau of the Census, *Statistical Abstract of the United States,* Washington, D.C., 1991, p. 732.
19. Eugene J. Meehan, "The Evolution of Public Housing Policy," pp. 287–318 in *Federal Housing Policy and Programs Past and Present,* J. Paul Mitchell (editor).
20. Richard E. Slitor, "Rationale of the Present Tax Benefits for Homeowners," p. 173 in *Federal Housing Policy and Programs Past and Present,* J. Paul Mitchell (editor).
21. I have used 20-year and 40-year straight-line depreciation for simplicity and because any attempt to use current depreciation schedules would be obsolete as soon as Congress altered the tax laws.
22. Massachusetts Housing Finance Agency, *Annual Report for the Year Ended June 30, 1987.*
23. Fair-market rent is a term of art. It is a number determined by HUD to meet the objectives of whatever program is financing the project in question. In the case of the Rent Supplement Program, fair-market rent was computed to include up to 6 percent interest plus the 0.5 percent FHA fee.
24. See "Housing Allowances: An Experiment That Worked," by Bernard J. Frieden, and "Housing Allowances: A Bad Idea Whose Time Has Come," by Chester Hartman, pp. 365–389 in *Federal Housing Policy and Programs Past and Present,* J. Paul Mitchell (editor).
25. Section 8 program statistics are derived by Find/SVP information services from HUD printouts for December 13, 1991. The 1.5 million recipients of Section 8 existing housing include Section 23 and Rent Supplement conversions, public-housing demolition, and reallocations from other programs.
26. There will be times when purchasing an existing condominium will be very cost-effective. In 1992, for example, condominium apartments in Queens County, New York, could be purchased at less than half the cost of building public housing.

10

Housing Rehabilitation

Charleston, S.C., 1975. *(Alexander Garvin)*

In Boston's South End, San Francisco's Haight-Ashbury, and Washington's Dupont Circle, rehabilitation is an ongoing activity. In too many other neighborhoods, buildings deteriorate because lending institutions are not prepared to finance improvements, occupants are not willing or able to pay for those improvements, property owners cannot justify capital investment, and local governments discourage rehabilitation of the existing housing stock.

There is no reason for dilapidated housing. We know how to stimulate the private sector to improve housing quality through rehabilitation. The programs that are needed will vary from city to city because the housing stock and the laws that affect it vary. The techniques, however, will be the same: real estate tax policies that do not discourage property improvement, rent regulations that allow property owners to recoup capital investments, and an investment climate that allows lending institutions to provide the financing.

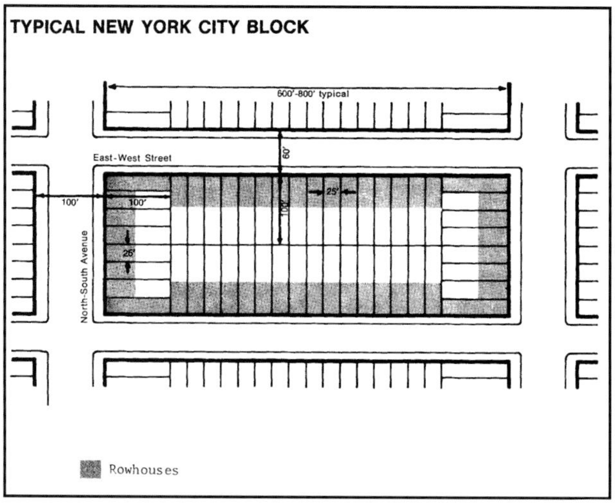

New York City, 1811. Lot and block dimensions of the Commissioners' Plan. *(Courtesy of New York City Department of City Planning)*

The Housing Stock

Housing rehabilitation programs must be local in nature. They depend on the design and condition of specific buildings, the characteristics of their owners and occupants, the laws that govern what can be done with them, and lending practices in the area. I have chosen to examine housing rehabilitation in New York City because any account of its rehabilitation programs will cover most situations facing other cities.

There is a more personal reason. As an architect, city planner, real estate developer, and native New Yorker, I have very specialized knowledge of the city's building stock and laws. I also have the unique perspective of a former government official charged with the responsibility of improving New York's housing stock. Between 1974 and 1978, I was Deputy Commissioner of Housing, in charge of all New York City's housing rehabilitation and neighborhood preservation efforts.

Block and Lot Patterns

America's first cities were founded on virgin territory. Colonists established plats that identified public thoroughfares, public open space, and the boundaries of individual lots for development. Thereafter, everything was at the option of the property owner.[1]

Since each colony was established by a different entity, plats differed as to street width, block and lot size, and organization. By far the most popular design was the rectangular grid, either oriented to the points of the compass or parallel and perpendicular to rivers, cliffs, and other major geographic features. Such plats were easy to survey, easy to divide into rectangular lots that could be subdivided or recombined, easy to describe when conveying title, and easy to add onto if the town outgrew its borders.

The rectangular grid was so popular that it was adopted by Congress in the Northwest Ordinances of 1785 and 1787

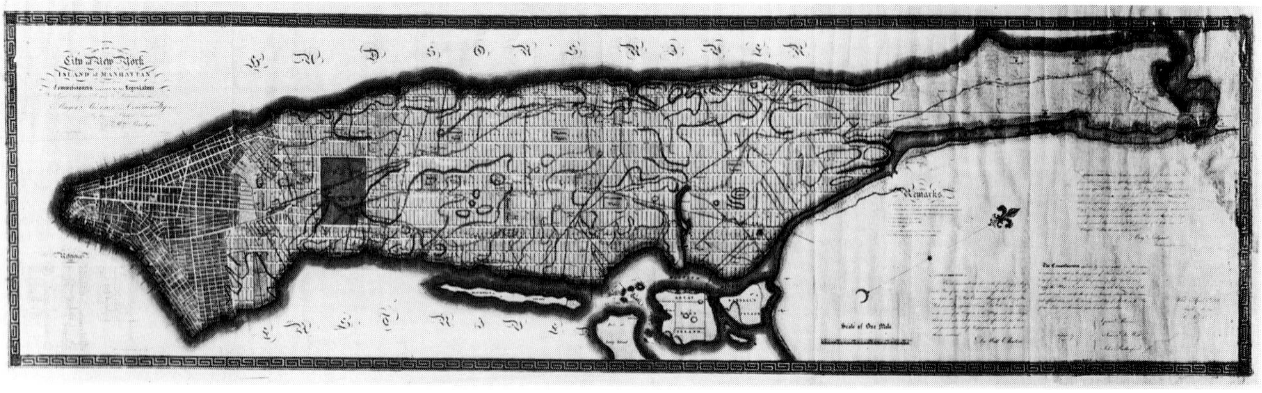

New York City, 1811. Commissioners' Plan showing how the grid was fitted to the topography of Manhattan island. *(Courtesy of Museum of the City of New York, The J. Clarence Davies Collection)*

Manhattan, 1882. Row houses in construction at Lenox Avenue and 133d Street, illustrating what the Commissioners had envisioned for Manhattan. *(Courtesy of Collection of the New York Historical Society)*

as the basis for surveying and conveying virtually all land outside the original 13 colonies. This north-south, east-west grid, 6 miles square, was extended across the landscape, without reference to hills, mountains, cliffs, lakes, rivers, or any topographical features. The 6-mile squares that were created were called townships, sometimes—but frequently not—synonymous with political designations. Each geometrical township was in turn divided into 36 sections, each 1 mile square and each totaling 640 acres. These squares were then further divided into quarters, and again into smaller segments, resulting in a mostly rectangular landscape. Anybody who has flown across the country will instantly recognize the image.

There is no direct connection between a predominantly rectilinear system of property subdivision and slums. However, because property owners have to fit their buildings into specific sites, block and lot dimensions play a major role in determining what is built. Sometimes they produce build-

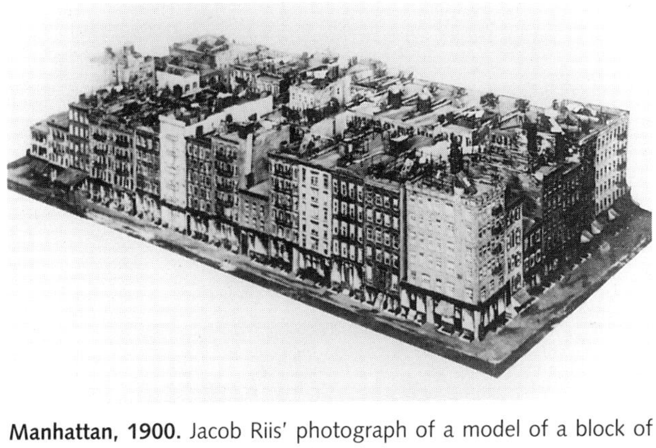

Manhattan, 1900. Jacob Riis' photograph of a model of a block of tenements on the Lower East Side. *(Courtesy of Museum of the City of New York, Jacob A. Riis Collection)*

Manhattan, before 1895. Jacob Riis' photograph of the rear yard of an unidentified Lower East Side tenement. *(Courtesy of Museum of the City of New York, Jacob A. Riis Collection)*

ing configurations that are undesirable. In New York City, for example, because buildings are squeezed into long, narrow lots, it is difficult to provide a desirable level of natural light and ventilation to the rooms in the middle of these lots.

Manhattan's plat was designed by John Randall, Jr., a professional surveyor, who chose to ignore the island's existing roads, streams, and sharp changes in elevation. His plat, approved by the New York State legislature in 1811, envisioned handsome airy neighborhoods with blocks separated every 200 feet by 60-foot-wide east-west streets and divided at intervals of 350 to 800 feet by 100-foot-wide north-south avenues. The blocks were divided into 25- by 100-foot lots, on which it was believed developers would build row houses with spacious rear yards. Since the row houses were expected to be two rooms deep, the buildings would extend 40 to 60 feet from the street. Thus, the rooms inside would receive light and air from the wide streets in front or the ample yards behind.

While much of New York was built on this pattern, property owners soon found it more profitable to do otherwise. They tried to fit in as many apartments as possible, covering as much of each lot as possible, and building as high as their customers were **willing to climb.** Four 25-foot lots were combined to fit five 20-foot buildings, three 25-foot lots to fit four build-

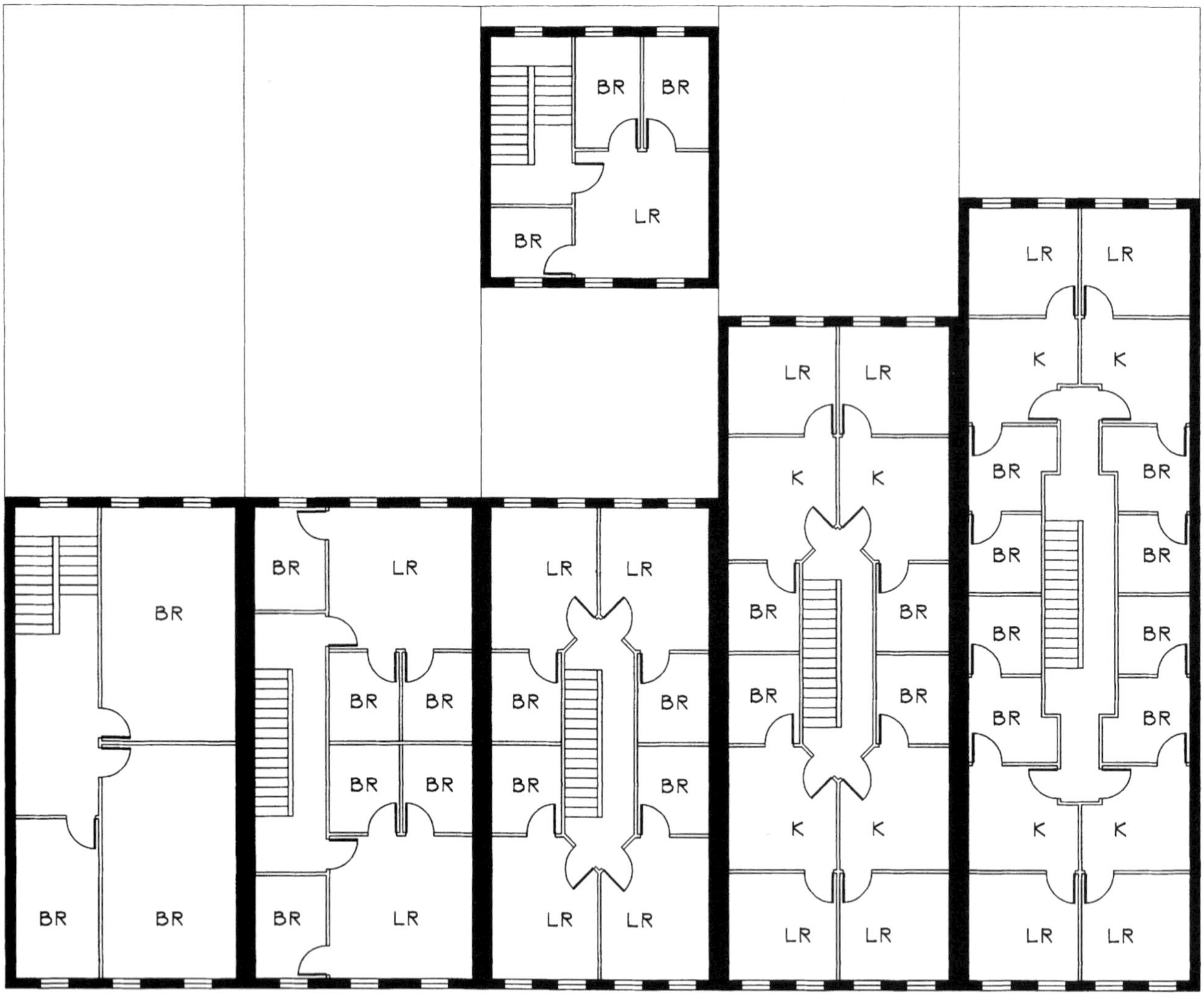

New York City, before 1867. Prior to regulation, property owners tried to maximize their rental revenue by jamming as many rooms as possible into tenement buildings (many without natural light and ventilation) and placing additional buildings at the rear of their lots. *(Alexander Garvin and C. Christopher Koon)*

ings 18 feet 9 inches across, or worse. There was even a building that was only 8 feet wide. Instead of row houses facing other row houses at least 60 feet away, developers built tenements that routinely extended almost to the full 100-foot depth of the lot, leaving only a narrow alley between buildings five or six stories high and sometimes higher.[2]

The resulting apartments were similarly long and narrow. Some tenements had as many as sixteen rooms to the floor, only four of which (two in front and two at the rear) had windows. Living in such conditions was not just unpleasant; it was dangerous. Thousands died from tuberculosis, cholera, smallpox, and a variety of infectious diseases that spread easily in poorly lit and ill-ventilated apartments. Others perished in fires. Small children, the elderly, and others who were not able to move quickly, suffocated when flames sucked the oxygen from their rooms. The rest were unable to escape because there was no emergency means of egress.

Reformers horrified by these conditions built "model tenements" that were not much better. At Gotham Court, a model tenement built in 1850 for the express purpose of rescuing the poor from such noxious conditions, Jacob Riis reported:

> *[T]en years after it was finished, a sanitary official counted 146 cases of sickness...and reported that of the 138 children born in it in less than three years 61 had died, mostly before they were one year old....Seven years later the inspector of the district reported to the Board of Health that "nearly ten percent of the population is sent to the public hospitals each year."*[3]

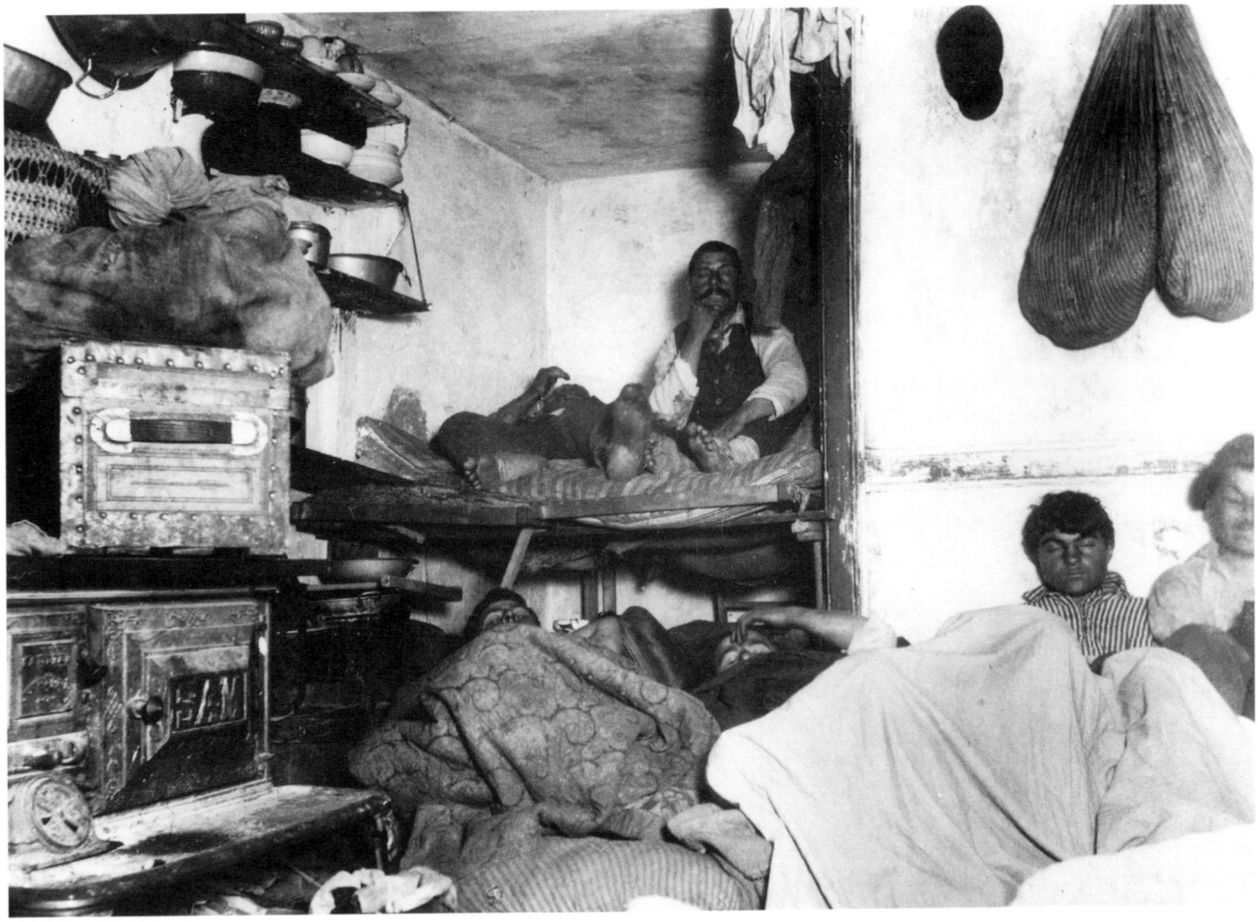

Manhattan, c. 1889. Jacob Riis' photograph of living conditions in a "Bayard Street tenement," on the Lower East Side. *(Courtesy of Museum of the City of New York, Jacob A. Riis Collection)*

While some developers adopted ideas from these "demonstration" projects, they continued to build dark and deadly dens because demand for housing was so intense that virtually anything could be rented.

Construction Regulations

Conditions grew so bad that, in 1867, the New York State Legislature passed a Tenement House Act regulating multifamily housing construction. It required at least 3 square feet of transom window for each room, provided that the window opened onto another room which had a window with "a connection with the external air." There had to be at least one source of water in the house or yard for every 20 apartments. Most important, the law required installation of fire escapes in all nonfireproof buildings that did not already have a secondary means of egress. While it took years to enforce this provision, block after city block eventually took on the pervasive character of its fire escapes.[4]

This statute, also known as the Old Tenement Law, was amended in 1879 to require every room to have a window that opened directly onto a street, yard, or air shaft. These shafts, often barely 2 feet across and more than 60 feet high, were more effective as garbage chutes and sound amplifiers than as conduits for light and air.

In 1901, the state legislature decided that even Old Law tenements were unfit for human habitation. It enacted a New Tenement Law requiring new multifamily buildings to include one toilet per apartment. The air shaft was replaced with a courtyard of not less than 25 square feet (with a minimum dimension of 4 feet). The New Law also limited lot coverage to 70 percent and building height to one and one-third the width of the street it faced.[5]

Finally, in 1929, a new state Multiple Dwelling Law prohibited further construction of tenements. It required that every building with three or more apartments have a toilet and a bath in each dwelling unit and a sink with running water in every kitchen. It also mandated that every room have at least one window that opened on a street or courtyard. Inner courts

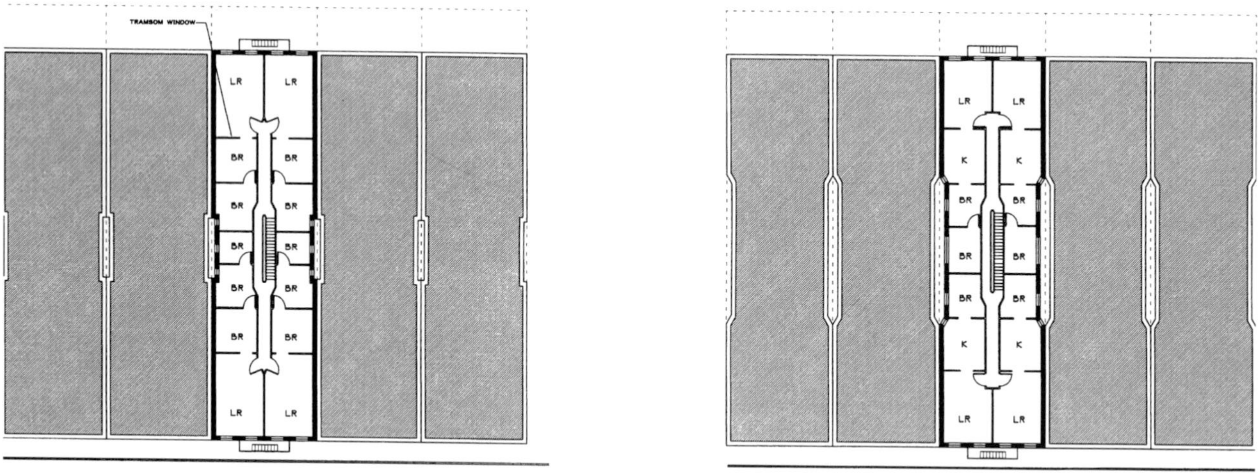

Manhattan. Floor plan of a typical tenement built under the provisions of the Tenement House Act of 1867, and after the 1879 amendments to the Tenement House Act. *(Alexander Garvin and C. Christopher Koon)*

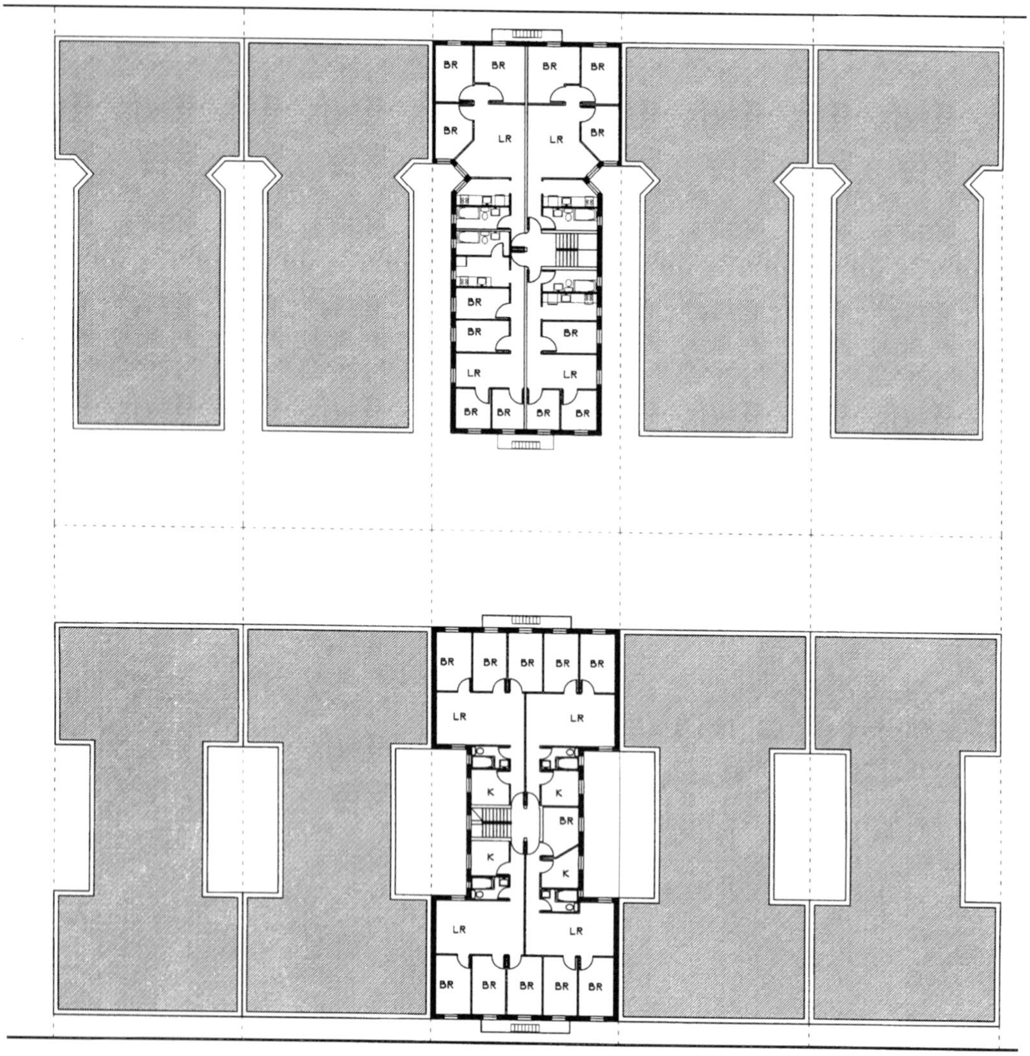

New York City, after 1901. Floor plans of typical tenements built under the provisions of the new Tenement Law of 1901. *(Alexander Garvin and C. Christopher Koon)*

Manhattan, 1915. Interior room in a pre-1879 tenement. Natural light and ventilation is provided by a window opening onto another room. *(Courtesy of Museum of the City of New York)*

Manhattan, 1995. Fire escapes mandated by the Tenement House Act. *(Alexander Garvin)*

had to be at least 30 by 36 feet if completely enclosed or 20 by 30 feet if on a lot line.

As a result of these laws, New Yorkers speak in terms of Old Law tenements, New Law tenements, and post-1929 multiple dwellings. Anybody familiar with these terms can identify probable apartment layouts within. In other cities building design may be different, but the relationship to local construction regulations is the same. Thus the Boston "triple decker," the Chicago "six-flat," the Los Angeles "courtyard house," and the San Francisco "painted lady" refer to housing types shaped by the interaction between local block and lot dimensions and building regulations.

Determining the Level of Rehabilitation

Buildings in Boston's South End, San Francisco's Haight-Ashbury, and Washington's Dupont Circle are renovated because equal or better housing cannot be produced at the same cost, people are ready to pay enough to justify the improvements, and institutional lenders are willing to provide the necessary financing. In districts where one-family homes predominate, it is relatively easy to determine whether these conditions exist. When multiple dwellings are involved, however, the parties concerned may not interpret conditions in the same way. Some tenants may desire improvements; others may not. Some may be willing and able to pay more rent; others may not. Whether tenants desire improvements or not, property owners will only rehabilitate if they receive a return that justifies any additional investment in time and money. Lending institutions will provide mortgage financing only if they are sure the scope of work is sufficient for the property to remain in good condition for the duration of the loan, if building revenues will more than cover expenses, and if the property will not be adversely affected by conditions in the surrounding neighborhood. Thus, any housing rehabilitation program will have to balance often conflicting physical, social, and economic constraints.

Physical Constraints

Rehabilitation includes a continuum of possible work—starting with minor repairs and extending all the way to complete reconstruction. That continuum can be divided into three levels of rehabilitation: moderate, gut, and extensive. *Moderate rehabilitation* includes new wiring, plumbing, boilers, bathroom fixtures, kitchen appliances, windows, bell-and-buzzer

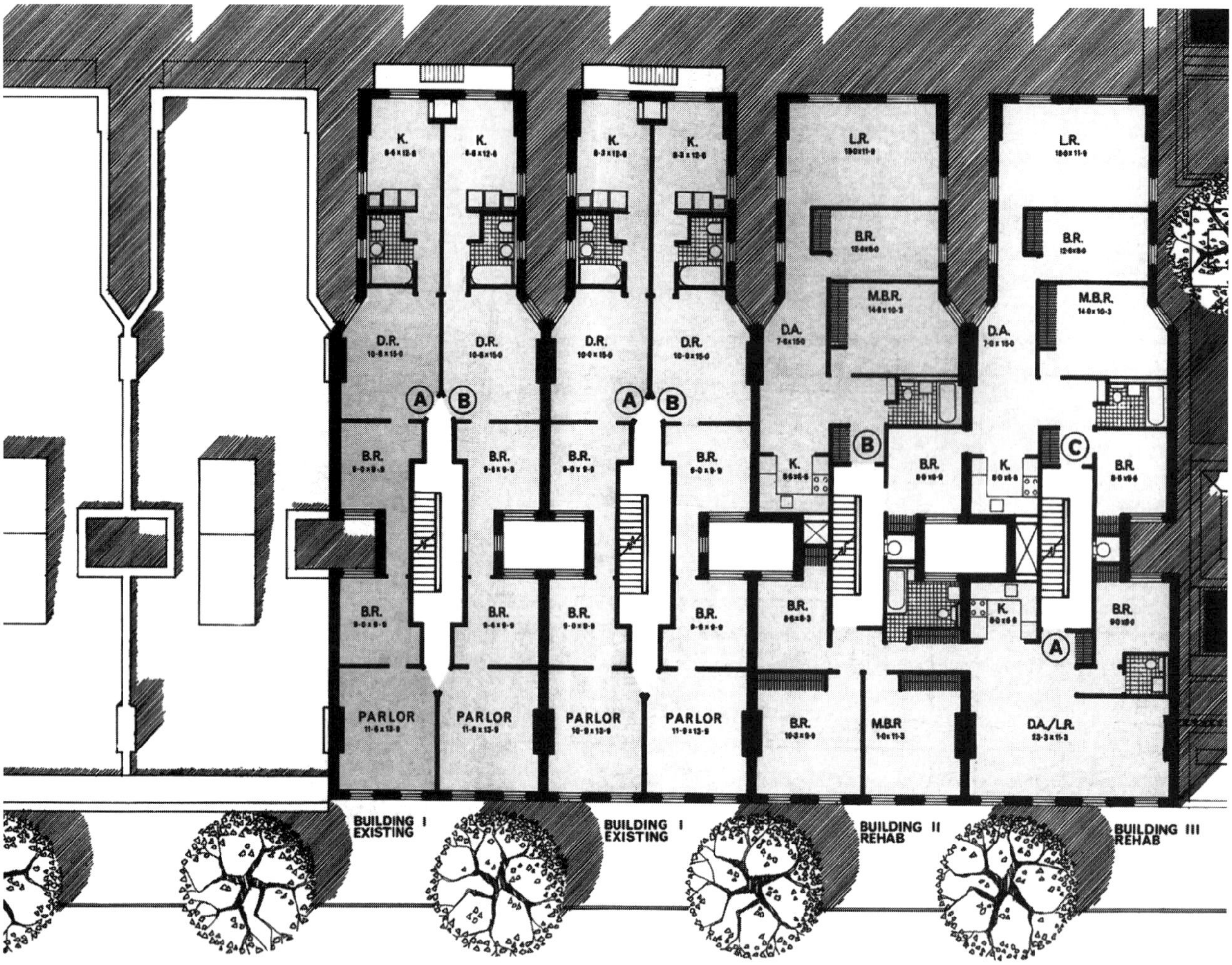

The Bronx, 1967. Old Law tenements before and after *gut rehabilitation,* which improved apartment lay-outs but did nothing to increase the inadequate natural light and ventilation supplied from narrow air shafts. *(Courtesy of New York City Model Cities Program)*

intercom systems, entry doors, repointing, and roof resurfacing. Inconvenient though it may be, tenants can remain in place while work is in progress because apartment layouts remain the same. If the existing apartments have inadequate natural light and ventilation, poor layouts, and minuscule rooms, however, moderate rehabilitation will not provide them.

Gut rehabilitation involves the same items as moderate rehabilitation plus new apartment layouts, and therefore new walls, floors, ceilings, and partitions. *Extensive rehabilitation* reconfigures whole structures, often removing large sections of buildings to permit improved light, ventilation, and apartment layouts. Neither gut nor extensive rehabilitation can take place with tenants in occupancy.

Because apartment layouts and room sizes in masonry row houses are acceptable, moderate rehabilitation usually is all that is needed. Other building types may have to be gutted if they are to provide decent apartments. Old Law tenements, for example, tend to contain apartments with terrible lay-outs. Small, narrow rooms with minimal light and ventilation are strung out one after another like railroad cars. Reconditioning these so-called "railroad flats" perpetuates designs already deemed unfit for human habitation in the era of Grover Cleveland. Moreover, retaining still awkward apartment lay-outs may not be worth the cost of gut rehabilitation.

The best way to obtain good apartment layouts in Old Law tenements is to cut away a substantial portion of the structure, removing the rear portion of the building or cutting out a broad courtyard in the middle. Sometimes such extensive rehabilitation can only be accomplished by combining buildings. This requires nearly as much work as building from scratch. Extreme reconstruction of this sort is justifiable only if it produces better or cheaper apartments than new construction.

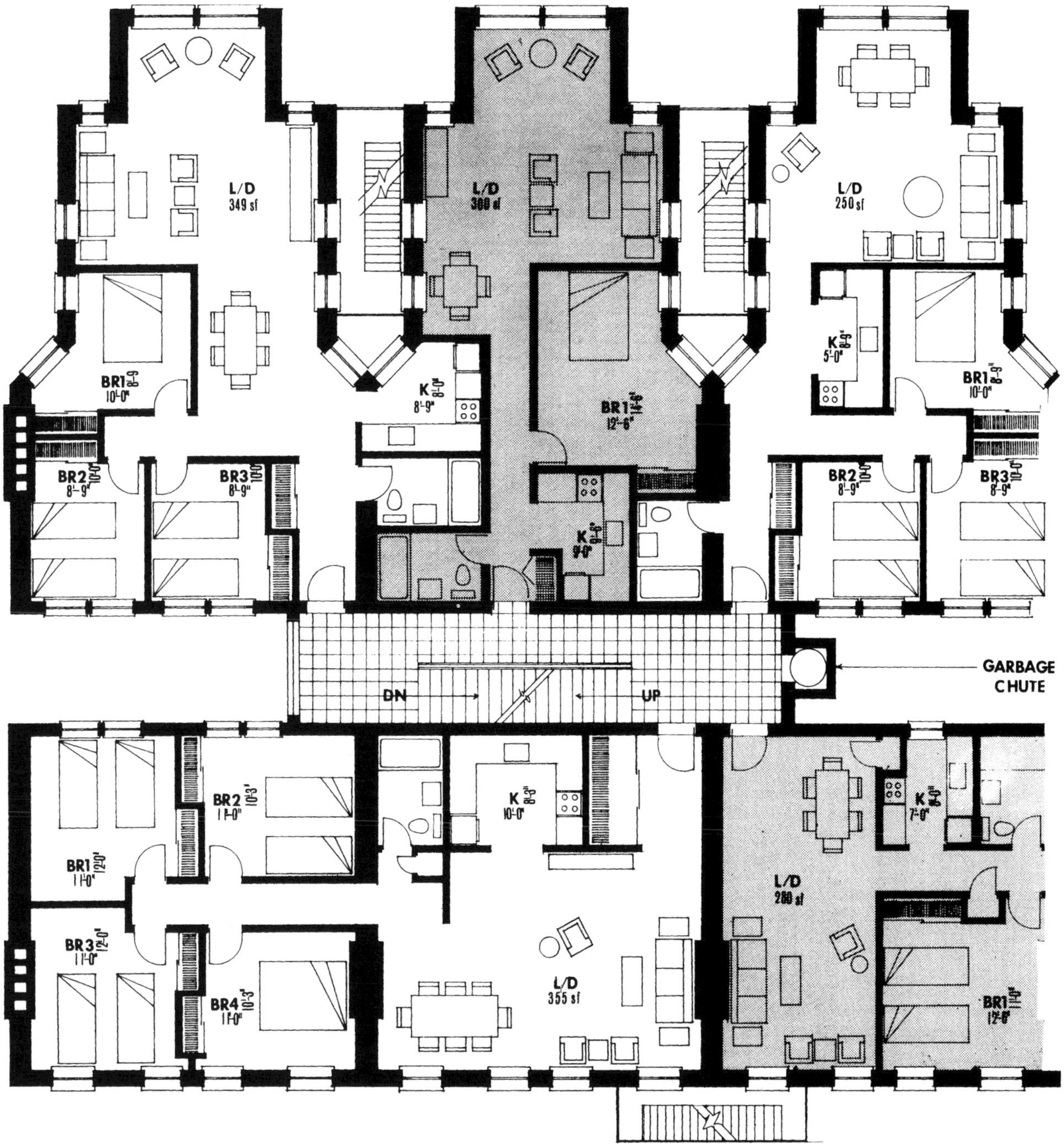

Manhattan, 1967. Old Law tenements after *extensive rehabilitation,* which improved circulation, apartment layouts, and ventilation. *(From Architect's Renewal Committee in Harlem: Housing in Central Harlem, New York, 1967)*

Social Constraints

Because familiar buildings remain in place, people erroneously ignore the social problems that come with housing rehabilitation. Everybody has to move from a building undergoing gut or extensive rehabilitation. Moreover, property improvement inevitably leads to higher rents. Thus, improvement of the housing stock inevitably results in changes to the social composition of the neighborhood.

Although while moderate rehabilitation is in progress living conditions will not be ideal, most tenants will accept the inconvenience. They usually desire building improvements enough to pay moderate rent increases. Inevitably, some tenants will not want the inconvenience or may not be willing to pay increased rent. The more serious problem is that some tenants may not be able to pay higher rents. In such cases the scope of work can be reduced sufficiently to lower rents to an acceptable level or subsidies found to make the new rent affordable or to permit tenants to relocate. Otherwise, physical improvement will be accompanied by tenant hardship.

Gut rehabilitation requires empty buildings. Thus, like clearance and redevelopment, it requires tenant relocation. Unless displaced tenants are paid enough for them to afford improved accommodations, they will be forced out, often to even more dilapidated housing. Even if relocation payments are sufficient to compensate for these and other hardships, most displaced tenants will make long-term moves and rarely return to their former residence.

Intelligently conceived rehabilitation projects often stimulate neighboring property owners to follow suit, thereby attracting new residents. Such gentrification is at once the cost and benefit of policies that improve the quality of the existing housing stock. The best way for government to cushion the impact of gentrification is by pursuing policies that increase the supply of decent housing. That gives everybody a better chance to find affordable accommodations.

Financial Constraints

Moderate rehabilitation is much less expensive than complete restoration. This is not just a matter of construction cost. Labor practices and wage rates for moderate rehabilitation are usually quite different from gut rehabilitation (especially for larger projects that mirror new construction practices). The labor force is predominantly nonunion and includes a high proportion of minority workers. Moderate rehab also requires significantly less time, and, therefore, less in interest and tax payments during construction. Most important, tenants continue paying rent during renovation, helping to defray carrying costs during the development period.

Most structures requiring gut rehabilitation are in neighborhoods suffering from a multiplicity of problems. Banks are reluctant to risk their depositors' money in such areas. Consequently, gut rehabilitation projects usually involve additional expenditures for lighting, security, and other community improvements that reassure the permanent lender.

Given the significantly lower cost of moderate rehabilitation, one would expect this to be the predominant form of renovation. Instead, financial institutions concentrate on gut and extensive rehabilitation. They lack the expertise to balance the messy physical, social, and financial constraints involved in renovating tenanted buildings. The resulting difficulty in getting mortgage financing for renovation is one reason for the continuing deterioration of the existing housing stock.

Three Government Rehabilitation Experiments

Whether because of unhappiness with the high cost of new construction, its insensitive design, or the destruction of our architectural heritage, concerned citizens keep demanding the rehabilitation of deteriorating buildings. New York City has a rich history of such projects. Their strengths and weaknesses can best be explained by retelling the stories of three experiments, all of which involved the Lower East Side tenements that reformers already considered unsatisfactory when they were originally built. They are First Houses at 112–138 East Third Street and 27–41 Avenue A (1933-1935), Instant Rehab at 633–637 East 5th Street (1967), and Sweat Equity at 507–509, 517–519, and 533 East 11th Street (1976–1978).

First Houses

During the mayoral campaign of 1933, Fiorello LaGuardia promised to eliminate slums and provide decent housing. Within weeks of his inauguration he established the country's first municipal housing authority.[6] Two years later the New York City Authority completed "Experiment No. #1," America's first housing project created, owned and operated by a municipal housing authority. It was appropriately named First Houses.[7]

The Housing Authority wished to provide housing that low-income people could afford—apartments that rented for about $6 per room per month. It thought this could be done by replacing slums with new apartment buildings, but soon discovered that sites could not be acquired at prices that allowed it to rent at low enough prices. It decided to try rehabilitation. In December 1934, the authority persuaded Vincent Astor to sell some four- and five-story Old Law tenements. These were the sort of buildings with windowless rooms and

Manhattan, 1934. Avenue A frontage of First Houses before rehabilitation. *(From The Livable City, courtesy of the Municipal Art Society)*

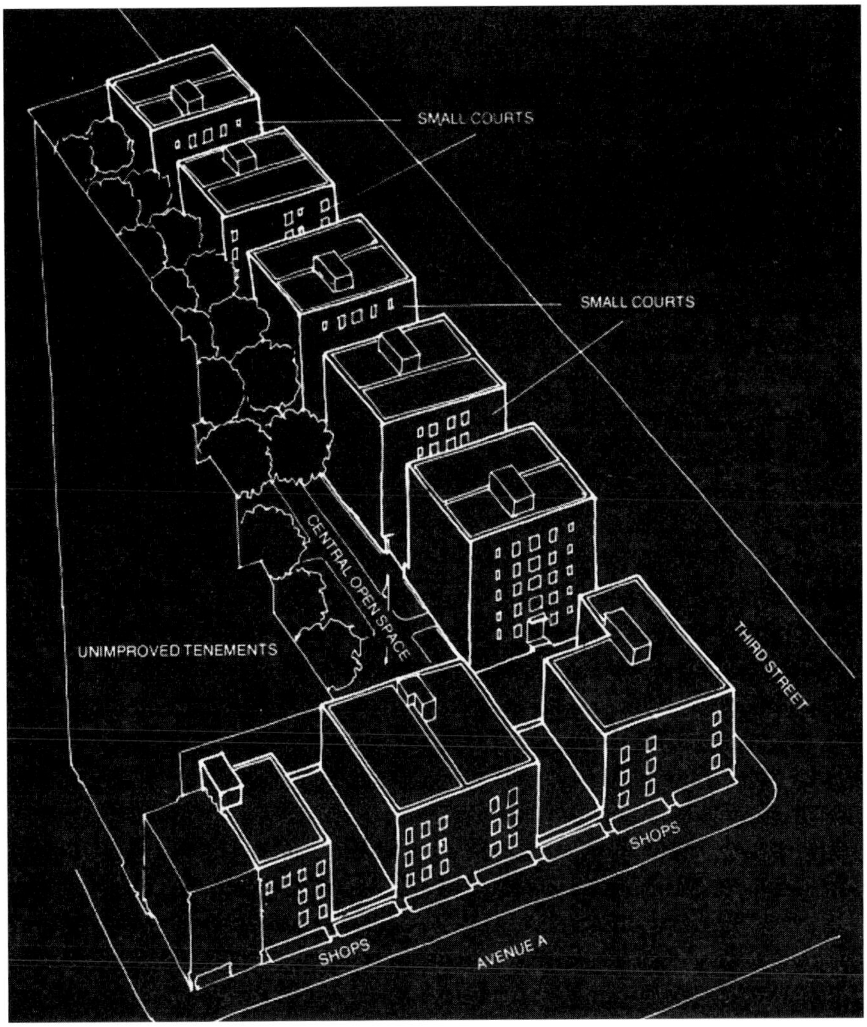

Manhattan, 1935. Isometric drawing of First Houses showing the elimination of every third building. *(From The Livable City, courtesy of the Municipal Art Society)*

long dark corridors that Riis had so bitterly denounced. When the owner of two tenements separating the Astor properties refused to sell, the authority proceeded to condemnation. In March 1935, the New York State Supreme Court in the case of *New York City Housing Authority v. Muller,* held that condemnation by a duly constituted local authority for the purpose of providing housing for persons of low income was permitted by the New York State Constitution.[8]

Experiment #1 demonstrated the utility of rehabilitating Old Law tenements, provided that they were part of an overall redevelopment scheme that created functional apartment lay-outs. To provide adequate light and ventilation, the Housing Authority demolished every third building and cut away the rear third of all those remaining. It installed windows along the side of each building, 25 feet away from the neighboring structure. On Avenue A, the demolished buildings were filled in with one-story shops, thus maintaining the commercial character of the street. On Third Street, the vacant lots provided access to the rehabilitated buildings and the rear yard. The new enlarged rear yards were combined

Manhattan, 1994. Avenue A frontage of First Houses six decades after rehabilitation. *(Alexander Garvin)*

into a single play-area with trees, benches, and WPA-style artwork.

The original structures were reinforced by installing steel beams. All the roofs were replaced. The façades were rebuilt using some of the original bricks. The interiors were redesigned to accommodate only two apartments per stair landing, thereby minimizing building circulation and maximizing cross ventilation. Modern wiring, plumbing, and heating systems were installed. Even the kitchens and bathrooms were completely rebuilt.

A monthly rent of $6.05 per room covered all the expenses of this 123-unit project. It was a bargain for the working-class tenants who moved in. Their average income was $23.20 per week.

Given the pervasive image of public housing as high-rise dormitory stockades segregated from surrounding communities, it is indeed ironic that the nation's first public housing was a rehabilitation project—a walk-up, in scale with the surrounding neighborhood, with stores on the ground floor.

More than 60 years after completion, First Houses remains in excellent condition. If there were not a plaque on the buildings, passersby would never guess that it is public housing, much less a landmark in the history of government housing.

Instant Rehab

It was 30 years before New York City resumed serious efforts at housing rehabilitation. The most publicized project of that period (the late 1960s) entitled "instant rehab," was another experiment with rehabilitation of Old Law tenements. It was intended to show that standardized prefabricated materials could reduce the cost of construction and reduce the time and relocation required in gut rehabilitation.[9]

Its sponsor, the Carolyndale Foundation, selected three Old Law tenements for the demonstration. Two were vacant. The third was occupied by 20 tenant households. Nine households moved while the project was being planned. Consequently, only 11 households needed to be relocated during the projected 72-hour construction period.

The buildings were gutted, leaving only outside walls, floor joists, usable subflooring, and a few interior partitions. Holes were then cut through from the roof to the basement to accommodate two different mechanical cores that were lowered into place by cranes. These cores contained a three-fixture bathroom, a three-fixture kitchen, and wiring and plumbing chases. While the cores were being installed, conventional rehabilitation proceeded on an around-the-clock basis. The heating plant was renovated; new flooring, ceilings, and partitions were installed; and windows and doors were replaced.

Construction took 48 hours. At the opening ceremony, Housing and Urban Development Secretary Robert Weaver called the project an "answer to the problems of housing renewal without tenant dislocation" and Mayor John Lindsay urged "wide application" of the approach throughout the city. Proponents of rehabilitation disagreed. To them the project was an obvious failure. Not only were construction costs more than three times that of FHA rehabilitation projects (which themselves cost several times more than conventionally financed rehabilitation); they also were more than three times the cost of new construction. Even the prefabricated kitchen and bathroom cores were more expensive than equivalent conventional construction.

Manhattan, 1967. Instant rehabilitation at East 5th Street. *(Courtesy of New York City Department of City Planning)*

Because the work had to take place in 2 days, the quality of construction was below standard. It cost substantially more because work took place continuously over 48 hours. The majority of the labor force was paid overtime. Furthermore, given the complexity of the project, new-construction labor practices and wage scales were applied, rather than cheaper rehabilitation rates.

Even if the costs had not been excessive, the quality of the product was grossly inferior. Unlike First Houses, no buildings had been demolished, thereby preventing either improved apartment layouts or adequate natural light and air. Tenement air shafts were left in place. In fact, with the exception of the new fixtures, apartment layouts remained the same.

Worst of all, "instant rehab" was a demonstration project not worth replicating. Since New York, like all cities, was built piecemeal by different developers using different designs, the most appropriate prefabricated standard components were wallboards, doors, windows, sinks, bathtubs, stoves, ceramic tile, and *not* complete kitchen-bathroom cores whose installation required expensive cranes and careful calibration by an expensive, specially trained work force. Ordinary (prefabricated) sinks, stoves, tile, and wallboard were already commonly used in conventional, privately financed rehabilitation. No demonstration was needed to prove their appropriateness.

Unlike First Houses, the instant rehab project rapidly ceased providing decent homes for the poor. Nearby tenements charged very low rents. Customers were not willing to spend more for similar apartments. Thus, the rents that could be charged did not cover the debt service on the mortgage incurred to pay for the renovation. The project stopped making payments on its below-market interest rate FHA mortgage, which was foreclosed 6 years after completion. Two years later the property was sold to a buyer who abandoned it. Finally, in 1977, 10 years after the project had been hailed as an "answer to the problems of housing renewal," the *New York Times* reported:

> *the prefabricated kitchens and bathrooms, some pulled out by their roots, have been stripped of fixtures and hardware by vandals. In one apartment a single switchplate seemed to be the only piece of hardware overlooked.... Snow and ice, resulting from broken windows, lay amid the garbage on floors and steps.*[10]

Today the instant rehab project is no more. It was torn down to make way for the construction of new three-story public housing.

Sweat Equity on East 11th Street

In 1974, when I was Deputy Housing Commissioner, Interfaith-Adopt-A-Building, a neighborhood group from the Lower East Side, approached the city demanding to rehabilitate some vacant, city-owned Old Law tenements on East 11th Street, eight blocks north of First Houses. The buildings had been taken for failure to pay real estate taxes. Not only were they a physical hazard, they attracted drug addicts and were subject to frequent and dangerous fires. It was easy to agree with neighborhood residents that everybody would be better off with the buildings repaired and occupied.

Interfaith-Adopt-A-Building asked the city to donate the buildings. Since it had neither money nor construction skills, Adopt-A-Building was in no position to rehabilitate these buildings. But the group did have enthusiasm, charismatic leadership, and superior technical assistance. It organized block clean-up days, cleared the buildings of garbage and debris, protected them from squatters and addicts, and obtained assistance from the Urban Homesteading Assistance

Manhattan, 1976. East 11th Street just before the Sweat Equity Program began. *(Alexander Garvin)*

Board (U-HAB), the Consumer Farmer Foundation, and the federal Comprehensive Employment and Training Act (CETA).

U-HAB had been organized in 1974 by a group of former city employees who were unhappy with the government's lack of commitment to restoring older buildings and providing housing for the poor. It proposed to use government funds to finance housing rehabilitation and to train prospective low-income homeowners to restore their own homes. It also argued that required equity should be calculated in sweat rather than currency. As U-HAB explained it:

> *Over half of the ghetto youth have no employment prospects. Few incentives exist for positive, socially productive behaviour. A decent home of one's own is an almost unreachable dream.... For many homesteaders the opportunity to own a decent home and to learn marketable job skills represents a turning point in their lives. The realization comes that there is now a new source upon which to depend and it is they, themselves.*[11]

In other words, U-HAB expected far more than renovated apartments from sweat equity. The program was expected to

Manhattan, 1988. East 11th Street a decade after the sweat equity rehabilitation of 517–519 East 11th Street. *(Alexander Garvin)*

provide training, employment, income, and a sense of community for young people who had no other chance of acquiring skills, jobs, or money.

Once established, U-HAB developed the know-how to prepare cost estimates, to hire architects, lawyers, appraisers, accountants, and construction supervisors, to draft grant applications, to process loan documents, and to negotiate with the municipal bureaucracy. However, it could not provide Adopt-A-Building or any other group with the initial cash required to package a rehabilitation project. The necessary seed money came from the Consumer Farmer Foundation.

Construction training stipends for the self-helpers working on the buildings were underwritten by CETA. Thus, substantially less money was required to cover the labor costs of any rehabilitation. A municipal rehabilitation loan covered 100 percent of the remaining cost. The extent of rehabilitation was reduced to ensure that development and operating costs were affordable for future occupants. In addition, the federal government provided a grant to install a solar-powered hot-water heating system and a rooftop electricity-producing windmill. This energy conservation and production equipment was intended to lower dramatically the monthly fuel expenditures and, thus, further lower operating costs.[12]

Adopt-A-Building began with the rehabilitation of one Old Law tenement. Within 2 years the group had obtained the money to rehabilitate another three buildings and transform an adjacent vacant lot into a garden. The projected cost of rehabilitation ranged from $8000 to $13,700 per apartment, one-third the cost of the instant rehab project that had been completed a decade earlier, six blocks to the south.

Despite lower costs, free labor, tenant ownership, and neighborhood support, only one of the buildings, the one with the solar hot-water system and the electricity-producing windmill, was completed. It was also the only building without a CETA training component.

CETA labor stipends were for a fixed period. Once the training period was over, stipends were terminated. Recipients were then expected to move on to construction jobs. Unfortunately, when the stipends ended, construction was far from finished. Recipients had trouble finding jobs in the construction industry. They had no way of paying for basic necessities without abandoning the project. Since the loans only covered interest payments during an underestimated construction period, the project was in default even before the tenants moved in. Without a steady source of income, they had no choice but to stop paying the co-op's debt service.

Sweat equity on East 11th Street had been far too ambitious. Housing rehabilitation is difficult enough. It is impossible when the project is also expected to provide what society as a whole has failed to provide: training for the unskilled, jobs for the unemployed, income for the poor, and a sense of belonging for the rootless.

Three Citywide Rehabilitation Programs

Most people think of rehabilitation in terms of individual projects. Rehabilitation, however, has a much broader role to play as part of a comprehensive, citywide housing strategy. The complexities of site acquisition, design, bureaucratic processing, construction, and marketing are such that few apartments will be added to a city's housing stock in any one year. Whatever is built will inevitably rent or sell at much higher prices than already existing apartments. More important, new construction does not deal with housing conditions where most city residents live. Thus, any housing policy that fails to ensure that the existing housing stock is maintained and concentrates instead on new construction will fail to ensure a supply of decent housing for most of the city's current residents.

New York City has operated three programs that encourage housing rehabilitation by the private sector. The earliest of them, the J-51 Program, reduced real estate tax payments to compensate for the increased debt service incurred to pay for rehabilitation. This was followed by the Municipal Loan Program, which also lowered debt service payments by providing long-term mortgages at the city's cost of borrowing (usually two percentage points below conventional bank mortgage rates). Then in the mid-1970s the city began using its money as leverage to get banks to invest in rehabilitation. Only the J-51 Program generated sufficient production to have a major impact on the city's housing stock.

New York City's J-51 Program

New York City is the first municipality to establish a real estate tax-incentive program that operated on a volume basis to encourage maintenance and rehabilitation of existing residential housing. This program, called J-51 after its section number in the city's administrative code, was enacted in 1955. Initially it provided incentives for the elimination of unhealthy or unsafe housing conditions in tenements. Over the years, its scope was expanded to include upgrading of all existing multiple dwellings as well as the conversion of hotels, rooming houses, and nonresidential space into multiple dwellings. Between 1961 and 1988, J-51 provided benefits to more than 1,400,000 apartments.[13]

J-51 provides two sorts of benefits for eligible buildings: tax exemption and tax abatement. The exemption is from any increase in real estate taxes resulting from improvements to the property. It lasts 12 years. Thus, property owners are not punished for improving their buildings with increased real estate tax assessment. The abatement equals 90 percent of the reasonable cost of the improvements. In effect, it is a refund of 90 cents of every dollar spent on restoration (see Table 10.1). The abatement cannot be taken at once. A limit of 8.33 percent of the certified reasonable cost of rehabilitation may be deducted from the property's real estate tax bill in any one

TABLE 10.1
MODERATE REHABILITATION WITH J-51 BENEFITS

Year	Tax without Exemption or Abatement, $	Tax after Exemption before Abatement, $	Abatement, $	Final Tax Bill, $
1	9,180	4,140	4,140	0
2	9,180	4,140	4,140	0
3	9,180	4,140	4,140	0
4	9,180	4,140	4,140	0
5	9,180	4,140	4,140	0
6	9,180	4,140	4,140	0
7	9,180	4,140	4,140	0
8	9,180	4,140	4,140	0
9	9,180	4,140	4,140	0
10	9,180	4,140	4,140	0
11	9,180	4,140	4,140	0
12	9,180	4,140	4,140	0
13	9,180	9,180	7,081	2,099
14	9,180	9,180	7,081	2,099
15	9,180	9,180	7,081	2,099
16	9,180	9,180	5,577	3,603
17	9,180	9,180	0	9,180
18	9,180	9,180	0	9,180
19	9,180	9,180	0	9,180
20	9,180	9,180	0	9,180
Total	183,600	123,120	76,500	46,620

Property: 19 unit, four-story walk-up apartment house
Preimprovement real estate tax assessment: $46,000
Preimprovement taxes: $4140 (.09 x $46,000)
City-issued certificate of reasonable cost of rehabilitation: $85,000
Maximum annual tax abatement: $7081 (.0833 x $85,000)
Maximum total tax abatement: $76,500 (0.9 x $85,000)
Postimprovement real estate tax assessment: $102,000
Postimprovement taxes without J-51 benefits: $9180 (.09 x $102,000)
Assumed tax rate for the duration of J-51 benefits: $9 for each $100 of assessed value

year until the abatement is exhausted or 20 years pass, whichever is shorter.

Two elements have made J-51 effective: its certainty and its predictability. The law provides the certainty that specific repairs which meet the requirements of the law will receive benefits and predictability as to the amount of those benefits. No public official may withhold approval. It is this nondiscretionary nature of the program that protects it from political pressure and graft. More important, banks can rely on J-51 benefits and will issue mortgage commitments based on these benefits.

J-51 is no panacea. If benefits are insufficient to reduce a building's economic rent to market level, owners will not renovate. Nor does J-51 necessarily provide housing for the lowest income group. That aspect requires further subsidy.

In cities where market forces determine rents, exemption by itself will be cost-effective. Without the inducement of tax exemption, a substantial amount of rehabilitation would not be likely to occur and, thus, the city never would receive the additional taxes. It does not cost anything to forgo taxes you would not otherwise receive. Besides, when the exemption expires, the city collects additional taxes from any increased assessment.

In cities where rent regulations virtually preclude rent increases to recoup the costs of rehabilitation, tax abatement is the only way government can assist an owner to pay for restoration. Even then, the resulting increase in net operating income after taxes may not be enough. Owners also must be able to obtain financing to pay for rehabilitation. They will only be able to do so if banks and other lenders can count on fixed, nondiscretionary tax benefits large enough to justify a rehabilitation loan.

Municipal Rehabilitation Loans

New York City has also provided direct financing for housing rehabilitation through its Municipal Loan program. The program was established in 1962, when the State legislature enacted Article VIII of the Private Housing Finance Law. Initially Article VIII permitted municipalities to make mortgage loans to owners of multiple dwellings constructed prior to 1929. Thus, it restricted lending to the city's oldest buildings with the worst apartment layouts.

Funds for the program came from serial revenue bonds authorized by the mayor. Bond proceeds were supposed to establish a self-sustaining pool of mortgage money to be recirculated as loans were amortized. The costs of operating the program and paying debt service on the bonds were to come from mortgage-interest payments. Before the program was terminated in the mid-1970s, more than $125 million had been loaned for the rehabilitation of 7000 apartments. As of 1988, virtually all of these loans had been foreclosed or were in default.

The law required 10 percent borrower equity, but it was often phantom equity. In some cases owners of dilapidated properties had them appraised at unrealistically high values in order to show more than the required equity. That way they could cover all possible expenditures with the municipal loan and walk away with cash.

Loan proceeds were advanced in stages as construction was completed. The officials who decided how much rehabilitation had been completed and how much money to release were underpaid. They were happy to augment their earnings with payments from borrowers who collected money for work that had not been done. Eventually, these crooks went to jail.

Ten years after it had begun, the City Council determined that the Municipal Loan program was

> *ill-conceived, badly executed and fraught with corruption...[that] many persons associated with the program were either charlatans, thieves or incompetents...[and that it] was poorly thought out and foredoomed to failure.*[14]

New York City's experience with the Municipal Loan program did not invalidate rehabilitation mortgage lending. Banks had a long history of successfully lending to existing property owners for rehabilitation. The Municipal Loan scandal simply highlighted the need for intelligent lending practices.

Joint Bank–City Rehabilitation Loans

The fiscal crisis of the mid-1970s temporarily precluded further municipal lending for any purposes. The inability to continue lending was an opportunity to make additional reforms. The results were embodied in Article XV of the New York State Private Housing Finance Law, enacted in 1976.

Article XV established the Participation Loan Program (PLP), which was supposed to terminate the practice of making municipal loans directly. It authorized the city to join with financial institutions as a co-lender in mortgages for the rehabilitation of multiple dwellings and pay for its share from the city's annual federal Community Development Block Grant (CDBG), thereby avoiding a drain on the city's bonding capacity.

In a PLP project, the city lends CDBG money at 1 percent interest, as part of a joint mortgage with a permanent lender who charges market interest rates. The city determines the amount of the loan based on an adequate level of rehabilitation and an interest rate that will enable the borrower to charge marketable rents that will cover operating expenses, real estate taxes, debt service, and a minimum return on equity. The proportion of 1 percent money and market-rate bank money is established so that the composite interest rate will produce the required economic rent (see Chapter 9, note 1).

Banks had not been willing to make rehabilitation loans because government rent regulation prevented adequate rent increases. Article XV allowed the city to restructure existing rents. Thereafter, the property, like most older buildings, is subject to rent regulation. Thus, from the start there was a presumption that Participation Loans would be made to occupied, not to vacant, buildings and that rents would have to be acceptable to existing tenants.

Even if rent increases were small, some tenants would not have been able to afford the new rents. Section 8 rent subsidies were set aside for those tenants who could not afford higher rents and who otherwise would have had to move (see Chapter 9). Only 15 percent of the tenants proved to need such subsidies.[15]

When the city and the participating financial institution issue a commitment letter for a permanent mortgage loan, the applicant is required to secure construction financing, either from the participating lender or from a government supervised construction lender, usually a commercial bank. The institution responsible for construction financing, using a licensed architect or engineer (on a consultant basis), supervises construction and makes progress payments to the borrower. It certifies satisfactory completion of the work before the participation loan will take effect and the construction lender will recoup its money. The construction lender does not give out one penny unless the work is independently certified as satisfactorily completed. Upon completion of the renovation, the participation loan is serviced by the participating financial institution, thereby eliminating the need for a city debt-service collection bureaucracy and the possibility of political pressure against foreclosure for failure to repay the loan.

With both the permanent and construction lenders checking the borrower's credit history, the validity of any refinancing, the scope of the work, the reasonableness of construction costs, and the marketability of projected rents, there is little chance of the abuses which plagued the Municipal Loan program. This allows the city to concentrate on selecting projects and deciding how large its participation in the loan should be.

As of September 1988, $415 million had been lent for the rehabilitation of 635 buildings, containing 23,600 apartments. Of that, 55 percent had come from private institutions and 45 percent from CDBG funds. Only a few loans are behind in debt-service payments or have been foreclosed.[16]

Ingredients of Success

The rationale behind government housing rehabilitation programs should change with changes in each area's population, housing stock, and mortgage market. What may make sense during a period of rapid population growth will no longer make sense when it is declining. Similarly, a rehabilitation program, ill-conceived for an area whose predominant building type is costly to convert to modern standards, may be appropriate in another neighborhood with charming older structures. But whatever the rationale behind government rehabilitation programs, success will depend on the same ingredients that determine the success of any program for fixing the American city.

Market

Demand for secondhand housing continually changes. When the elaborate ornament of the Victorian period is out of fashion, "tarting up" nineteenth-century structures is not likely to attract home buyers. During periods in which Victoriana is again in fashion, renovation of these same buildings is likely to be prevalent. Private-sector rehabilitation continuously adapts to these changes in consumer taste. Government programs, on the other hand, have to remain in place after the current fad is long forgotten.

The best insulation from changes in fashion is for rehabilitation projects to offer lower-than-market rents. The New York City Housing Authority was particularly sensitive to this consideration at First Houses. If there were to be further public housing projects, it had to demonstrate that government-built, -owned, and -managed housing could successfully provide decent shelter on an ongoing basis. Consequently, it offered *at lower prices* a better product than was generally available in the surrounding area. Had the Instant Rehab Project offered rehabilitated walk-ups at competitive prices, its occupants would not have moved to nearby unrenovated apartment houses.

Affordability alone is not enough. The Sweat Equity Project on East 11th Street avoided major capital investment, and so kept housing costs consistent with neighboring buildings. However, the project could not guarantee steady income or employment for its construction trainee–cooperative owners, who needed additional assistance to cover otherwise marketable project costs.

Location

The character of the buildings in any particular neighborhood is essential to any rehabilitation program's success. All three projects discussed in this chapter involved the rehabilitation of Lower East Side tenements. Even before these tenements had been occupied they were already being described by Jacob Riis and other nineteenth-century reformers as slums.

As First Houses demonstrates, tenements can be altered to meet contemporary living standards. The cost of such extensive renovation, however, is substantial. Private-sector tenement rehabilitation will proceed as long as the resulting rents are marketable. In many tenement neighborhoods such renovation is too expensive for most residents. Rehabilitation in these neighborhoods will require substantial government subsidies and widespread owner participation. Neither is likely.

A more economical and easily implementable approach to government-assisted rehabilitation is to offer shallow subsidies to properties that need only moderate renovation. This will bypass neighborhoods like the Lower East Side that require extensive rehabilitation. If local governments wish to direct their efforts to these locations they must be prepared to appropriate large sums of money.

Design

The dimensions and arrangement of rooms within an apartment determine the degree of privacy provided to each occupant, the ease with which it can be furnished, and thus its marketability. Any program involving extensive rehabilitation must balance the cost of altering the dimensions and arrangement of rooms with the rents that can be obtained for the altered apartments. Developers who have to compete for tenants are sensitive to these trade-offs. Public officials seldom pay much attention to this balance because subsidies allow them to avoid such choices. Unlike extensive rehabilitation, moderate renovation does not suffer from this problem because the tenants who remain in occupancy during the renovation will allow construction workers into their apartments only if they consider postrehabilitation rents to be affordable.

Tax-abatement and -exemption programs spur privately financed rehabilitation projects that would not otherwise be cost-effective. Loan programs, on the other hand, tend to impose design requirements that inevitably result in extensive rehabilitation. Too often, new construction is more cost-effective. Consequently, rather than depend on publicly administered lending programs, we should provide banks with pools of below-market-rate-interest mortgage money and let them do the underwriting. This will direct subsidies largely to those items that would not otherwise be financially justified. More important, it will significantly expand lending for housing rehabilitation.

Financing

Publicly financed housing rehabilitation will never be a major government activity. There are too many competing demands for public expenditures. Even if there were enough money, too few public employees have the expertise to generate billions in secure mortgages. Nor should they. There is no need for government financing if safe loans can be made by private financial institutions.

Government assistance is required only where local banks are afraid to risk their depositors' money on housing rehabilitation or where developers cannot achieve marketable rents given prevailing rates of interest. The Participation Loan program dealt with both situations. It provided the portion of the loan that covered the extra financial risk lending institutions were unwilling to take and the 1 percent interest rate that reduced rents to a level that most tenants could afford. Those few residents for whom this was a hardship were provided with additional government subsidies.

Government housing rehabilitation programs work best when borrowers and banks make market decisions and the public sector subsidizes desired results on a citywide basis. This approach is more equitable than tailoring the program to specific buildings. It also directs the subsidy to those rehabilitation projects that are marketable as a result of public assistance. Therefore, if any city wishes to encourage housing rehabilitation it should establish a program, like New York's J-51, that lets the lenders and borrowers decide what changes are most likely to attract the tenants they need.

The best way to induce banks to increase lending for housing rehabilitation is to develop local joint-mortgage programs, like New York's Participation Loan Program, in which government provides a large enough portion of the gap between the cost of a rehabilitation project and what the bank would otherwise lend to justify a bank mortgage and an owner's equity investment.

Just as the housing stock of each city is different, so are lending practices. There is no way to develop a program that will be equally appropriate to every neighborhood. Thus, local government agencies will have to negotiate with local institutions the specific form of joint mortgage that best meets local conditions.

Entrepreneurship

Property owners will only invest in housing rehabilitation when they believe it is relatively safe and lucrative. J-51 created an investment climate of this sort. Once a property owner had complied with program requirements, the amount that real estate taxes would be reduced could be predicted from a published schedule of allowable costs for every expenditure on rehabilitation.

Even if the risk is low, developers will only invest in rehabilitation when most of the money comes from somebody else. J-51 provided banks with the certainty and predictability they needed to extend credit for housing rehabilitation. Initial loans were calculated as if there were no tax benefits. Once rehabilitation was completed and tax abatement was in place, loans were increased in proportion to increased project revenue. Thus, developers made large equity investments only for the short period needed to complete rehabilitation, obtain J-51 benefits, and draw down the remaining portion of their mortgage commitment.

The Municipal Loan program provided none of these conditions. The amount of the loan was left to the discretion of program officials. Once the loan was granted, progress payments were based on inspections by other government employees. Allowable rents were the responsibility of still others. Long-term property owners who avoid entanglement with government agencies kept out of the program. Instead, it attracted developers who were good at government processing or who found (often illegal) ways of obtaining government action.

If we are to maximize the number of property owners and developers who rehabilitate older buildings we must create conditions that minimize their equity investment, maximize mortgage lending, reduce development costs, and reduce the time required to obtain financing and complete the renovation. This can best be done by relying on local banks to provide financing and on government to provide the marginal funding needed to close the gap between the amount banks will lend without government assistance and the amount needed to make rehabilitation attractive to property owners and developers.

Time

All government rehabilitation programs must consider the time required for work to be completed. Some programs have reduced that time substantially. The Instant Rehabilitation project took only 48 hours to complete building renovation. This eliminated the cost of real estate taxes and debt service during construction. Unfortunately, these savings were more than exceeded by costly labor and construction practices.

Maintenance and renovation of existing housing can only take place when lenders and borrowers are assured that they will not be adversely affected by business cycles. Five- or even ten-year exemption from any increase in real estate taxes due to rehabilitation is not enough. By extending the tax abatement period over 20 years, the J-51 Program increased cash flow and assured a steady tax payment for the probable life of any mortgage used to finance the rehabilitation. Consequently, property owners were in some measure insulated from changing market conditions.

Public officials must stop considering housing maintenance as a short-term effort. Ongoing private housing rehabilitation requires a continuing role for government in creating stable financial conditions for the institutional lenders that provide rehabilitation mortgages. Anything less will guarantee continuing deterioration of the housing stock. Local governments have no way of ensuring a stable money market and stable interest rates. However, they can and should provide stable, predictable real estate taxes.

Rehabilitation as a City Planning Strategy

Too many local governments pursue policies that discourage housing rehabilitation. They punish property owners who improve existing buildings by increasing real estate tax assessments. Eliminating this obstacle to improving the housing stock is easy: exempt all residential properties from any increase in taxes due to rehabilitation. This requires neither a new government program nor additional government employees. It may even reduce the number of people on the public payroll because there will be no need for tax assessors to calculate the value of private investment on housing improvements.

A small number of cities discourage housing rehabilitation by making it difficult to recapture these expenditures in increased rent. Eliminating this obstacle to housing rehabilitation is also easy. In cities with rent regulatory systems that allow property owners to pass through the cost of renovation in the form of a rent increase, that increase should be automatic and allow a suitable period for the amortization of any expenditure (e.g., 5 years for building-wide improvements and 3 years for work done within an apartment). In situations where the municipal government wishes to avoid rent increases it can, as New York City does with J-51 benefits, subsidize those improvements by abating real estate taxes.

Such policies will allow financial institutions to make loans for the rehabilitation of those buildings in which higher rents are marketable. In some cases market rents will not be high enough to cover all the improvements that are needed. In such situations government rehabilitation programs can close the gap. Below-market-interest loan programs, like the Participation Loan program, can be established to cover the nonbankable portion of a rehabilitation loan while proportionately reducing debt service to a marketable level. If there is also a desire to avoid displacing the small percentage of tenants who cannot afford rent increases, a municipality can set aside special subsidies, as New York City did with Section 8, for those few residents who otherwise would have to move.

Notes

1. A *plat* can be defined as a plan for the actual or proposed territorial organization of a city or any of its parts, including the arrangement and dimensions of public spaces, streets, blocks, and building lots.
2. Historical and statistical material on New York City's building laws is derived from James Ford, *Slums and Housing,* Harvard University Press, Cambridge, 1936, and Richard Plunz, *A History of Housing in New York City: Dwelling Type and Social Change in the American Metropolis,* Columbia University Press, New York, 1990.
3. Jacob Riis, *How the Other Half Lives,* originally published in 1890 and reproduced in *Jacob Riis Revisited,* Francesco Cordasco, editor, Anchor Books, Doubleday, Garden City, NY, 1968, pp. 30–31.
4. New York State Legislature, *Laws* (1867), ch. 980, sec. 17, pp. 2265–2273.
5. New York State Legislature, *Laws* (1901), ch. 334, sec. 17, pp. 889–923.
6. In September 1933, Ohio enacted the first state enabling legislation permitting the creation of municipal housing authorities. In February 1934, New York followed suit.
7. Historical and statistical information on First Houses is derived from James Ford, op. cit., pp. 727–731, and Ira Robbins with Gus Tyler, *Reminiscences of a Housing Advocate,* Citizens Housing and Planning Council of New York, New York, 1984, pp. 27–30.
8. *Matter of New York City Housing Authority v. Muller,* 78 F 2d 684, 1935.
9. Historical and statistical information on Instant Rehab is derived from Institute of Public Administration, *Rapid Rehabilitation of Old-Law Tenements: An Evaluation,* New York City, 1968, pp. 35–49, and Laurie Johnston, "'Instant' Rebuilding Ends In Instant Ruin," *New York Times,* January 20, 1977, p. 41.
10. Johnston, op. cit.
11. The Urban Homesteading Assistance Board, *Third Annual Progress Report,* U-HAB, New York, 1977, p. 3.
12. The grant was from the Community Services Administration to the 519 East 11th Street Cooperative Apartment Corporation.
13. New York City Department of Housing Preservation and Development, Office of Development, Division of Financial Services.
14. New York City Council, Committee on Charter and Governmental Operations, *Report on the Municipal Loan Program—Blueprint for Failure,* February 29, 1972, p. 1.
15. Barbara Leeds, Assistant Commissioner, Division of Financial Services, New York City Department of Housing Preservation and Development.
16. Ibid.

11

Clearing the Slums

Detroit, pre-1951. Site of Lafayette Park prior to clearance. *(Courtesy of City of Detroit Housing Commission)*

The rationale behind housing redevelopment is best captured in a single sentence by Jacob Riis:

The bad environment becomes the heredity of the next generation.[1]

In common with many nineteenth-century reformers, Riis believed that rooting out tenements would eliminate a major impediment to safe, healthy family life. But replacing hovels with sanitary dwellings does not produce a good environment if the problems of surrounding slums soon engulf the new buildings.

Some reformers believe surrounding slums can be prevented from overwhelming the new environment by creating separate enclaves whose critical mass precludes such intrusions. Others propose creating superblocks that supply all the elements needed for a healthy family life (schools, stores, recreation facilities, etc.) so that residents can spend almost all their time, should they want to, without having to leave their chosen living environment.

Critics of both approaches argue that there is no way to isolate redevelopment projects from the surrounding city. One group of critics demands steady elimination of substandard housing. They believe that a growing supply of decent dwellings will inevitably draw away customers from unsound housing and eventually force its complete elimination from the market. Another group advocates government action to root out the pockets of blight that presently act to preclude private investment in an area. It believes that private-market forces will create a decent living environment once government has cleared away any blighted areas. A third group relies primarily on multifaceted public action that goes beyond "salvation by bricks" alone and proposes that government implement a coordinated strategy that also includes social and economic programs for area residents.

Obviously, there is wisdom in each of these strategies; obviously, none of them is applicable to every situation. Applied to the wrong place, each has the potential of making things worse. Even when redevelopment is appropriate, there is unlikely to be enough government money with which to implement every desirable project. Consequently, public assistance should be directed only to those redevelopment projects whose benefits will spill over to improve housing conditions throughout the city. Then, instead of thinking in terms of housing units demolished or built, public officials will make redevelopment a part of a citywide strategy for establishing the good environment.

The Bad Environment

Riis and other reformers went to war with one particular slum, Mulberry Bend, a notorious tenement district, on the western edge of what is today Manhattan's Chinatown. He knew the area well, having covered its shootings and stabbings as a reporter for the *New York Tribune.* Riis argued that the only way to eliminate this infamous slum was for the city government to acquire the area's dilapidated tenements, then level them. This strategy already had been tried in London, where The Common Lodging House Act of 1851 authorized the Metropolitan Board of Works to condemn and clear slum property for the purpose of providing replacement housing.[2]

In spite of Mulberry Bend's notoriety, the New York State legislature had difficulty justifying a public taking of private property. There had to be a public use for the land. Proponents of clearing Mulberry Bend had one in mind: a public park. They believed that playgrounds were essential to the battle with the slums (see Chapter 3). The legislature accepted this argument and, in 1887, approved of the Small Parks Act which authorized condemnation of privately owned land for the purpose of creating public playgrounds. Mulberry Bend thus became one of the nation's earliest public playgrounds and its first slum-clearance project.

Riis used the example of Mulberry Bend to advocate further slum clearance, arguing eloquently that during the 5 years since its clearance, "not once has a shot been fired or a knife been drawn."[3] For decades afterward, reformers continued to make this argument by showing a correlation between slum clearance and a decline in criminal arrests, juvenile delinquency, tuberculosis, venereal disease, and other social or physical pathologies.

Techwood Homes in Atlanta provides a vivid example of this thinking. Charles Palmer, a past president of the National Association of Building Owners and Managers, used to drive to work past the Georgia Institute of Technology. He was horrified by what he saw on his trip downtown: "crowded, dilapidated dwellings, ragged, dirty children, reeking outhouses—a human garbage dump."[4]

At the library, Palmer came across Jacob Riis' *How The Other Half Lives.* Riis' theories made such an impression that he went on to organize local support and obtain federal assistance to replace this slum with decent housing. Techwood Homes, the project that Palmer persuaded Washington to subsidize, opened in 1936. Where there had once been crowded, dilapidated dwellings, stood an island of grass and trees containing two- and three-story red-brick buildings with 603 apartments and 109 dormitory units for Georgia Tech.

What Riis, Palmer, and other advocates of slum clearance ignored is that clearing slums also destroyed cheap housing and forced out residents who probably lived there because they could not afford anything better. They thought that replacing a slum and creating a desirable environment for future generations was sufficient justification for the slum dwellers to lose their homes.

The national slum-clearance effort began with enactment of the National Industrial Recovery Act of 1933. This legislation authorized the Public Works Administration (PWA) to

Manhattan, before 1887. Jacob Riis' photograph of living conditions in the "Bottle Alley" section of Mulberry Bend. *(Museum of the City of New York, Jacob A. Riis Collection)*

build low-cost housing as part of its emergency action to create jobs. Techwood Homes was one of the first of 26 slum-clearance projects that the PWA started before litigation terminated its program. The effort was resumed under the Housing Act of 1937, which subsidized local public housing authorities that sought "the eradication of slums" through clearance and construction of replacement housing for persons of low income (see Chapter 9).[5]

It soon became clear that there never would be enough money, entrepreneurial talent, or public support for municipal agencies to replace every slum with government-built, government-owned housing. Since the necessary resources could only be found in the private sector, state legislatures, starting in 1943, began to enact legislation that would permit local governments to use the power of eminent domain for the combined purpose of slum clearance and housing construction by private developers (see Chapter 9).

The Taking Issue

Opposition was immediate and serious. While courts had decided that state governments and local governments could take private property for the purpose of providing government-owned housing to persons of low income, opponents insisted that the Constitution did not permit the federal government to take one person's property for the purpose of selling it to another. The issue was settled in 1954 by the Supreme Court in a landmark case known as *Berman v. Parker,* which involved the Southwest Urban Renewal Area (SWURA) in Washington, D.C.[6]

In 1946, Congress had enacted the District of Columbia Redevelopment Act, which determined that "substandard housing and blighted areas," such as SWURA, were "injurious to the public health, safety, morals, and welfare" and should be eliminated "by all means necessary and appropriate." It further

Washington, D.C., pre-1950. Southwest Urban Renewal Project prior to redevelopment. *(Courtesy of The Washington Post)*

determined that this could not be done "by the ordinary operations of private enterprise alone" and, therefore, required "comprehensive and coordinated planning...[and] the acquisition and assembly of real property and the leasing and sale thereof for redevelopment pursuant to a project area redevelopment plan." The Act clearly stated that "redevelopment pursuant to a project area redevelopment plan...is hereby declared to be a public use."

The National Capital Planning Commission designated three areas as possessing potential threats to public health. One of these areas, SWURA, was located in eyeshot of the Capitol. Redevelopment of this strategic location, it asserted, would determine the future character of the city itself.[7]

The 560 acres known as the Southwest Urban Renewal Area had once been a prestigious residential neighborhood. But when the area was designated for redevelopment, 76 percent of its 5600 dwelling units were judged substandard, 43 percent had outside toilets, 44 percent had no baths, 70 percent had no central heat, and 21 percent were without electricity. However poor the housing, its residents (more than 80 percent African American) were firmly rooted in the neighborhood, 65 percent having lived there for more than 10 years. What they lacked was decent shelter.

The Planning Commission hired Elbert Peets, a landscape architect, to prepare a redevelopment proposal for the Southwest. Peets proposed retention of the area's predominantly low-income population, rehabilitation of many of its traditional row houses, and selective replacement of the worst buildings with new low-rise structures.

The Washington, D.C. Redevelopment and Land Agency, established to execute urban renewal plans, felt the plan was impractical on physical and financial grounds. It did not believe that the Southwest contained sufficient structures "susceptible to the Georgetown kind of rehabilitation." Moreover, it believed the area was so blighted that banks would be unwilling to finance anything unless the area was radically altered.

The Redevelopment Agency commissioned a second plan from Louis Justement and Chloethial Woodard Smith, two architects well-known for their support of clearance and redevelopment. The new plan envisioned a modern residential district with few streets, ample open space, plenty of parking, apartment towers with handsome views of the Potomac, an area for low-rent public housing, and commercial buildings along the main thoroughfare. Eventually the Redevelopment Agency adopted a compromise that reduced the number of multistory apartment houses, included a substantial number of two- and three-story buildings, and paid lip service to the "historic and sentimental interest" of the area's street plan and architecture.

In 1953 the Redevelopment Agency began assembling land, demolishing buildings, preparing sites, and issuing invitations to developers to submit plans for redevelopment of the Southwest. At this point a major legal struggle began. A department-store owner whose property was to be taken went to court claiming that his store was not a slum "injurious to the public health, safety, morals, and welfare." He argued that his property was being taken in violation of the prohibition against taking private property without due process of law established by the Fifth Amendment to the Constitution. Perhaps slum clearance would improve the health, safety, and welfare of the community, but how could there be a justification for taking a person's property merely to create a more attractive community?

The counter-argument was that redevelopment would be impossible without a carefully considered plan for the entire renewal area. That plan assured developers and financial institutions that all slum properties would be eliminated and replaced by a suitable living environment. Without such assurances, developers would not be interested in building nor financial institutions ready to provide the money.

In *Berman v. Parker,* the Supreme Court decided that any property (blighted or not), which was required for a project, could be taken. The decision was explicit:

Washington, D.C., 1994. "Wheat Row" completed in 1794–1795 and retained as part of the Southwest Urban Renewal Project. *(Alexander Garvin)*

Washington, D.C., pre-1950. Row houses scheduled for demolition in the Southwest Urban Renewal Project. *(Courtesy of The Washington Post)*

> *When the legislature has spoken, the public interest has been declared in terms well-nigh conclusive.... This principle admits of no exception merely because the power of eminent domain is involved.*[8]

After this case was decided in 1954, there was no longer any question that legislatures established what constituted "public use" of land. What remained in doubt was whether redevelopment would provide new life to the country's aging cities and whether redevelopment would result in an improvement in the housing occupied by area residents. Neither could be assured without financing for the replacement housing.

Rebuilding Southwest Washington, D.C.

Until 1949 there had been no way to reduce a developer's site costs sufficiently to result in the production of marketable new housing. Congress provided the mechanism in the urban renewal program established by Title I of the Housing Act of 1949. This legislation subsidized the difference between project cost and the resale price needed to make planned new construction financially attractive to private developers. Two-thirds of the subsidy came from the federal government, one-third from the locality (see Chapter 6, note 12).[9]

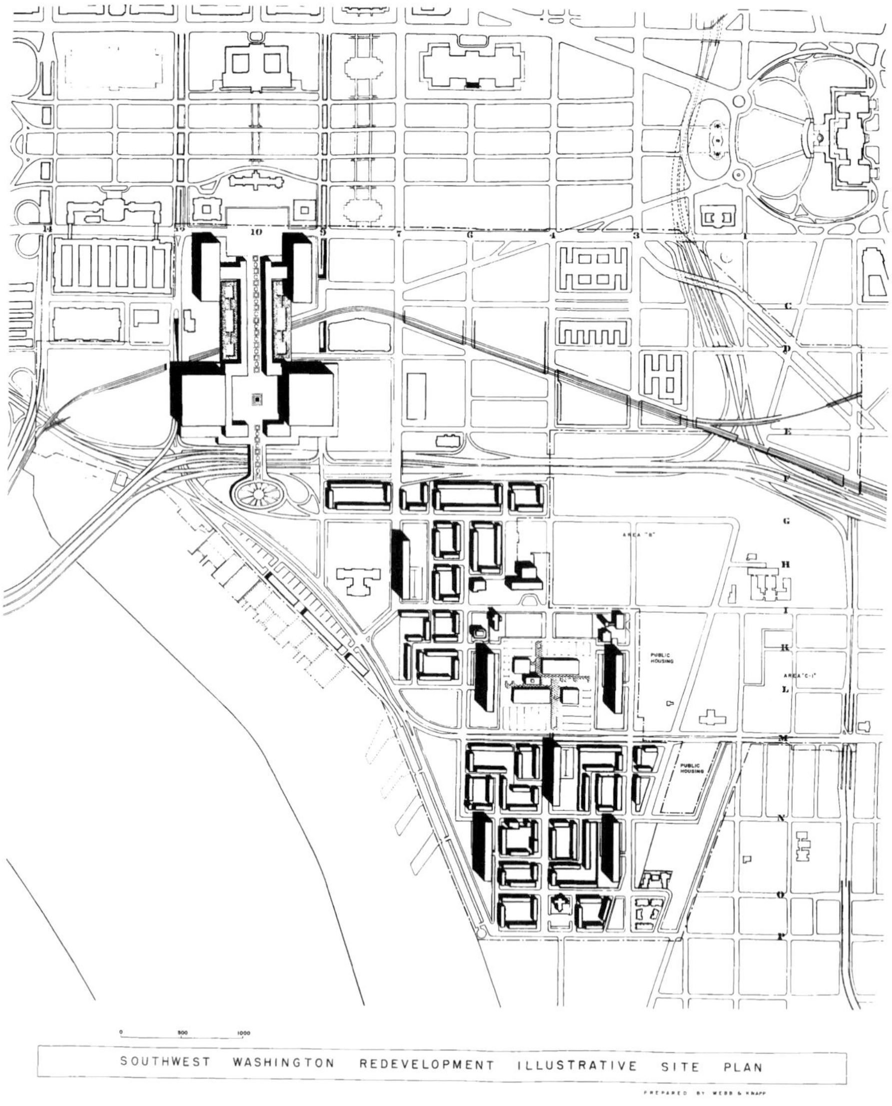

Washington, D.C., 1955. Redevelopment proposals made by I. M. Pei and William Zeckendorf for the Southwest Urban Renewal Area. *(Courtesy of Pei Cobb Freed & Partners)*

Very soon after enactment of the Housing Act of 1949, Congress realized that lenders were not providing mortgages in the federally approved urban-renewal areas; nor were developers ready to risk the equity capital required by mortgage lenders skeptical about the wisdom of lending in these areas. To solve the problem Congress adopted an approach that had worked during the Depression: mortgage insurance. It amended the Housing Act in 1954 to establish the FHA 220 Program, which insured bank mortgages in federally assisted urban-renewal areas. These mortgages were insured for up to 95 percent of the "replacement cost" of newly built or rehabilitated housing.

Before Congress had established the FHA 220 Program or the Supreme Court had decided *Berman v. Parker,* the Redevelopment Agency had already divided the Southwest into three sections and invited developers to submit proposals for redevelopment. One small area was set aside for light industry. James Scheuer, later a congressman from New York City, and Roger Stevens, a successful Broadway producer who later became the power behind the Kennedy Center, submitted the successful proposal for the second area, known as Capital Park. It became a 30-acre complex of moderate-size apartment buildings and row houses accommodating 1750 households. The third parcel, more than three-quarters of the renewal area, was assigned to William Zeckendorf, Sr., one of the country's best-known and most adventurous developers.

Zeckendorf and his architect, I. M. Pei, conceived the strategy that literally reconnected the Southwest with the rest of the city. As they saw it:

> *the elevated tracks of the Pennsylvania Railroad, which rose just below [Independence Avenue] and cross the river to Virginia...form the visual and psychological boundaries of the area...separat[ing] and segregat[ing] Southwest Washington from the rest of the city.*[10]

Washington, D.C., 1994. Federal office buildings along I-395, the interstate highway that cuts the Southwest Urban Renewal Project into two pieces. *(Alexander Garvin)*

Moreover, they felt the proposed eight-lane Southwest Freeway would add a second barrier permanently disfiguring the neighborhood and eliminating any chance of attracting profit-motivated developers to rebuild the area.

Zeckendorf and Pei proposed to eliminate this barrier by building a 300-foot-wide mall that would stretch south from the Smithsonian Institution along 10th Street, bridge both the railroad and the freeway, and extend almost to the river. Along the mall they envisioned an office, cultural, and entertainment center named L`Enfant Plaza in honor of the author of the original plan for the national capital. At the riverfront they proposed a promenade, marina, and recreation area. For the rest of the area they planned row houses and elevator buildings containing 4000 apartments plus a "town center" with the retail stores necessary to serve all the residents of the Southwest.

Although the project was constantly revised, took years to complete, and was largely built by others, Zeckendorf and Pei's vision is what determined the future of the Southwest. New office buildings provided much-needed relocation space for federal agencies housed in temporary buildings erected on the Mall during World War I as well as headquarters for the growing bureaucracies at HUD, HEW, Comsat, and the Department of Transportation. Developers built apartments for the growing market of government employees working in the area's new office buildings and throughout the city.

When it was finally completed in the 1970s, the Southwest Urban Renewal project had eliminated 5600 "slum" dwellings, provided 5838 new apartments and improved a critical section of Washington. It also improved the housing and living environment of the residents who had been displaced. Virtually everybody moved to significantly better accommodations. More than a quarter moved to public housing built at the time they were forced to move. The rest moved to better apartments in older buildings elsewhere in the city. This was possi-

Washington, D.C., 1974. Arena Theater, Town Center Plaza and Waterside Towers flanking 6th Street in the Southwest Urban Renewal Project. *(Alexander Garvin)*

Washington, D.C., 1994. Tiber Island apartment complex (designed by Keyes, Lethbridge, and Condon) in the Southwest Urban Renewal Project. *(Alexander Garvin)*

HOUSING OCCUPIED BY SOUTHWEST RENEWAL AREA RELOCATEES[12]		
Condition	**Prior to relocation, %**	**After 5 years, %**
Good	22.2	85.7
Needs minor repair	26.4	14.3
Needs major repairs	19.9	0
Dilapidated or unfit	16.0	0
No answer	5.6	0

ble because the flight of the middle class to the suburbs had increased the availability of such housing.[11]

SWURA helped to spur a revival of middle-class interest in other sections of the city. Rehabilitation of Washington's many row houses probably would have proceeded anyway, as would construction of new apartment buildings. However, without the successful redevelopment of this very visible part of the city, it would have taken longer for the process to get started. Thus, the Southwest Urban Renewal Project provided both the Constitutional basis for urban renewal and a model that could be copied on a building-by-building basis by developers throughout Washington. However, it did not provide a strategy that could reverse urban decay or be copied successfully by other cities.

Washington, D.C., 1994. Public housing flanking M Street on the eastern edge of the Southwest Urban Renewal Project. *(Alexander Garvin)*

Washington, D.C., was not alone in considering subsidized redevelopment as the path to a slum-free environment. As soon as Congress had enacted the program, Boston's Planning Board proposed housing redevelopment for the West End, a run-down Italian-American neighborhood on the edge of the downtown area. In the same year, the Newark Housing Authority identified the city's 16 most blighted areas and embarked on a renewal program that by 1957 included 395 blocks covering 25 percent of the city's residential areas.[13] In New York, Robert Moses, Chairman of the newly created Committee on Slum Clearance identified 9000 acres of slums requiring clearance and proposed five renewal areas. By 1959, he had proposed more than 39 projects covering more than 900 acres, 16 of which were in execution.[14]

Most cities, however, chose to concentrate on commercial redevelopment rather than residential reconstruction (see Chapter 6). They did not start serious housing redevelopment efforts until Congress amended the Housing Act in 1954 to include a mortgage-insurance program for lenders who agreed to finance housing construction and rehabilitation in urban-renewal areas.

Five redevelopment strategies emerged. Their success depended on the locations to which they were applied, the market in those areas, the appropriateness of redevelopment plans, the willingness of developers to risk their money on local development objectives, and the time they took to implement. However, they all required relocation of families and businesses from the sites selected for redevelopment and they generated political opposition.

Strategy 1: The Self-Contained Enclave

Until the 1920s, private developers engaged in clearance on a scattered, lot-by-lot basis. The validity of redeveloping entire areas was demonstrated in 1928 when Fred F. French, a pioneering New York City real estate developer, completed Tudor

City. He believed that only a giant, economy-size, self-contained enclave could survive negative pressures from surrounding areas and provide the necessary critical mass of new residents for community rebirth.

Tudor City

French demonstrated his theory by assembling a large number of slum properties along East 42nd Street on the edge of the Manhattan business district. The site was sandwiched between the noisy Second Avenue Elevated Railway (the El) and the smelly slaughterhouses beside the East River. Few believed that housing at this location, although in walking distance of Grand Central Station, could attract the large potential market of people working in midtown Manhattan. Others were scared off by the cost and complexity of assembling sufficient land to overcome surrounding negative influences.

French attracted customers by creating a residential enclave 30 feet above First Avenue and 42nd Street. There he built 3300 apartments in Tudor-style buildings that enclosed two 15,000-square-foot private parks and a private roadway bridging 42nd Street. The buildings turned their backs on the slaughterhouses along First Avenue, opening instead onto Tudor City's parks and streets.

From the beginning Tudor City was popular with midtown office workers who eagerly rented apartments in the project. In the decades that followed, other builders erected apartment and office buildings in the area. Today, when the slaughterhouses have been replaced by the United Nations, the El has long been demolished, and east midtown is a busy and expensive area it is difficult to realize the enormous risk French had accepted in redeveloping the area.

The first Title I projects in Washington, Boston, and New York accepted French's notion that since redevelopment took place in slum areas, it had to proceed on a sufficiently large scale to withstand the spillover of these slums. This, plus the desire for economies of scale, undoubtedly contributed to the large size of the nation's first urban-renewal projects.

Manhattan, 1994. One of Tudor City's private parks. *(Alexander Garvin)*

Harlem-Lenox Terrace

Despite the careful planning, self-contained apartment enclaves rarely revive the surrounding neighborhoods. Harlem-Lenox Terrace, one of New York City's first two redevelopment projects, illustrates this very well. The 15-acre site consisted of three full blocks between 132nd and 135th Streets, and Fifth and Lenox Avenues. It was described by The Committee on Slum Clearance, chaired by Robert Moses, as:

> *a group of buildings which are almost all ancient, poorly lighted, badly laid out, inadequately ventilated, and generally occupied by more families than they were originally designed to accommodate...146 out of 164, or 89 percent, were classified as "run down..." 71 percent of the residential structures were...tenements built before 1901, with their excessive coverage of the lot, and inadequate courts and air shafts.*[15]

Clearing these three blocks required demolition of 2068 apartments.[16] Most relocatees paid an average monthly rent of $29 for their "run down" apartments and probably could not afford the projected monthly rent of $29 *per room* in the new buildings. The committee estimated that 1010 families were eligible for public housing, many of whom might go to the recently completed 1286-unit Abraham Lincoln Public Housing Project just across Fifth Avenue. Few people seemed to care that this project would probably not have enough vacancies to accommodate the relocatees. Nor did they wonder how public housing in other locations, given the low vacancy rate and high demand, could provide replacement housing for all the renewal projects Moses had recommended. As for the rest of the relocatees, they were on their own to find private housing.

When Lenox Terrace was completed, in 1961, two streets had been closed to create a separate enclave that included a few retail stores, the already existing Harlem Boys Club and Playground, parking lots, and six 16-story red-brick apartment slabs financed with FHA 220 mortgages. The apartment buildings accommodated 1716 families who paid monthly rents in excess of $50 per room, far more than the relocatees could have afforded.

Lenox Terrace immediately became a desirable residence for middle-class African Americans and remains so more than 40 years after Moses conceived it. It has become a "high rise luxury oasis in the heart of Harlem," where:

> *doormen dress in spiffy blue uniforms and work around the clock. The private parking lot has trees and benches and glistening cars. And the long tenant list includes a roster of leading New York politicians, executives, lawyers and doctors.*[17]

It is part of a complex of six slum-clearance projects extending along the Harlem River, only one of which,

Manhattan, before 1951. Harlem-Lenox Terrace. *(Courtesy of the Citizens Housing and Planning Council, New York City)*

Manhattan, 1994. The Harlem-Lenox Terrace Urban Renewal Project became a "high-rise luxury oasis in the heart of Harlem." *(Alexander Garvin)*

Abraham Lincoln Houses, is for families of low income. Each of these projects is designed as an enclave set apart from the rest of Harlem. The 6800 new apartments that these projects provide are certainly an improvement over the slums they replaced. But neither Lenox Terrace nor any of its neighboring enclaves have had much impact on the rest of the neighborhood. The adjoining blocks are still run down—only more so. Lenox Terrace tenants now worry that the problems of neighboring "ghostly abandoned buildings and street-corner drug markets" may spill over into what one famous resident called "a substitute for moving to the suburbs."[18]

Harlem-Lenox Terrace did not generate further neighborhood improvements because poor residents who lived outside redevelopment projects could not muster sufficient rent to cover the cost of needed housing repairs, much less afford even more expensive redevelopment. Since they could not pay, private developers had no way of financing additional improvements.

Manhattan, 1970. Deteriorating tenements across Lenox Avenue from Harlem-Lenox Terrace remained unaffected for decades after the project was completed. *(Alexander Garvin)*

Strategy 2: The Superblock

At the start of the twentieth century, reformers argued that existing cities had become obsolete. They saw traffic hazards, noise, air pollution, disease, and crime as evidence that streets and blocks "built for an ancient pedestrian age" did not meet "the requirements of our motor age." As an alternative, city planner Ludwig Hilberseimer suggested building superblocks that included all the essentials of community life within walking distances that did not "exceed 15 to 20 minutes." These superblocks would be large enough "to support necessary communal, cultural, and hygienic institutions" and small enough "to preserve an organic community life."[19]

The superblocks, presented by their proponents in drawings, models, and photomontages, were diagrammatic at best. At worst they were anonymous rows of high-rise apartment buildings arranged in geometric patterns that ignored the complexity of daily life. Vehicular traffic was dispatched to regional highways so that the area devoted to local streets could be reduced to an absolute minimum and through traffic eliminated from every superblock. Densities were kept to a minimum in order to prevent the overpopulation that was thought to be responsible for social, moral, and physical diseases prevalent in congested, obsolete cities. Space for day care, education, recreation, shopping, and institutional use was allocated by formulas that were intended to prevent wastage and optimize accessibility.

These superblocks remained theoretical abstractions until the Housing Act of 1949 made their realization possible. Public officials eagerly proposed them as the best way of eliminating the bad environment. Too often the result of their efforts was another depressing dormitory stockade that could be ridiculed by anybody who opposed urban renewal. Only

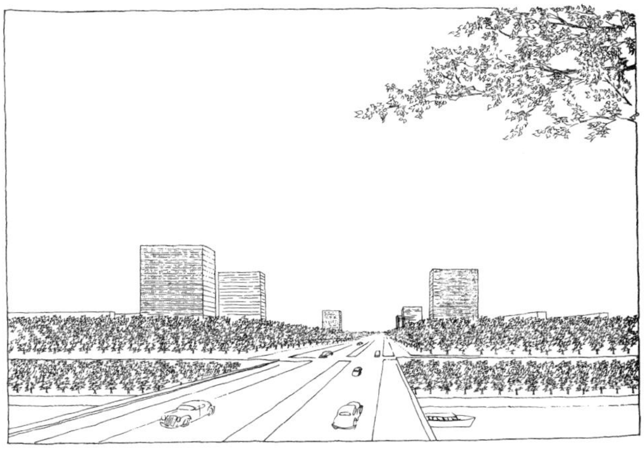

Berlin, 1937. Ludwig Hilberseimer's idealized conception of a housing development for the Heerstrasse and the University of Berlin. *(Photograph copyright 1994, Courtesy of The Art Institute of Chicago)*

occasionally did such efforts result in projects like Portland Center (see Chapter 6) and Lafayette Park that approximated what proponents of the superblock had envisioned.

Lafayette Park, Detroit

Lafayette Park was conceived in 1946, before Congress had embarked on the national effort at urban renewal. As initially proposed, it was a city-sponsored redevelopment project on the edge of downtown Detroit. The 129 acres selected for redevelopment were to be cleared of 1953 families and 989 individuals, 98 percent of whom were African American, more than three-quarters of whom had annual incomes of less than $3500, and nearly a fifth of whom were receiving public assistance. Civic leaders believed that clearing this "slum" would remove a blighting influence on the central business district and that replacing it with a residential superblock would attract families who would otherwise leave Detroit for the suburbs.[20]

The project successfully overcame both community opposition and a taxpayers' suit challenging the validity of public condemnation.[21] But it was unable to overcome the need for a talented and experienced developer, a financial institution that would provide mortgage money, or substantial government subsidies to close the gap between project cost and any sales price that developers were willing to pay or banks to finance.

The necessary subsidies became available when Congress enacted the Housing Act of 1949. Within a year Lafayette Park, then known as the Gratiot Urban Renewal Project, was converted to an urban-renewal project with $4.3 million in federal subsidies reserved for its execution. Finding a suitable developer was much more difficult. Local builders had never tackled anything as large or complex. When the site was put up for auction in 1952, nobody came forward. The following year a developer finally offered $1.27 million for the site, but had to drop out because he was unable to obtain financing (see Chapter 2).

When Congress amended the Housing Act in 1954 to include FHA mortgage insurance for urban-renewal areas, banks and insurance companies were finally willing to finance housing development in Lafayette Park and dozens of renewal projects like it. The following year the city accepted a $1.17 million offer from Cities Redevelopment, Inc., a Chicago firm owned by Herbert S. Greenwald and Samuel N. Katzin.[22]

Greenwald and his design team proposed a 78-acre superblock that included 2000 apartments in six towers surrounded by clusters of one- and two-story row houses. Within a year the first phase was in construction. When residents arrived in 1958, Lafayette Park seemed the beginning of Detroit's transition into a new world "vertical to the sky, open to light and air, clear and radiant and sparkling." There never were any other phases. This brave new world died along with Herbert Greenwald in a plane crash a year later. Unfortunately, the project was completed by a different group of designers, whose work detracts from the ideal physical environment that Greenwald was trying to create.[23]

Arriving at Lafayette Park by car, you first see the encircling trees and an occasional glimpse of the residences behind them, then turn down a cul-de-sac past one- and two-story row houses, and park either in a driveway or a parking lot. There, safe from the intrusions of the surrounding city, you walk directly into an ideal living environment.

Lafayette Park is no isolated enclave. At its heart is a 19-acre park with broad expanses of grass, a clubhouse, and swimming pool.[24] Greenwald understood that its 2000 apartments could not provide enough customers to justify a full range of shops, schools, and other services to the project's perimeter, where they did not exist at the time. As a result, Lafayette Park also includes a small shopping complex and an elementary school that also serve those who live outside Lafayette Park.

Greenwald's design team created one of the nation's most urbane combinations of the natural and manmade. Despite Hilberseimer's insistence on spacing buildings to ensure four hours of direct sunlight in every room, neither the spaces between buildings nor apartment layouts are determined by formula. Furthermore, the landscaping makes Lafayette Park a

Detroit, before 1956. Model of Lafayette Park. *(Courtesy of the City of Detroit Housing Commission)*

Detroit, 1989. Cul-de-sac entry into Lafayette Park with parked cars hidden from view in driveways 2½ feet below garden level. (*Alexander Garvin*)

very special place. Even circulation is not simply a matter of connecting destinations. Residents stroll past the front lawns and secluded yards of the low-rise residences and pass through intimate tree-covered, common sitting areas on their way to broad expanses of grass with plenty of room to toss a ball or play touch football.

Although Detroit has continued to deteriorate and lose population, Lafayette Park has remained occupied and well maintained, perhaps because it is conveniently located only a few minutes' walk from the heart of the business district. Some of the buildings are owner-occupied. Others are inhabited by middle-income renters, who include a broad spectrum of racial and ethnic backrounds. Lafayette Park is a unique island of stability surrounded either by later, similarly located and financed but poorly designed housing projects, or by the abandoned wasteland of blocks untouched by redevelopment.

Strategy 3: A Net Increase in Apartments

A different strategy for eliminating the bad environment is implicit in Fred French's other housing-redevelopment project, Knickerbocker Village on Manhattan's Lower East Side. It calls for a two-pronged attack on a city's worst housing: first by clearing the worst slum housing and then by building more apartments than are eliminated. In this variant of the *filter-down theory,* the families who move into the new buildings vacate slightly less desirable apartments that are then occupied by other families, who in turn, move from other less desirable apartments until the city's least desirable apartments are left without occupants and eventually are removed from the housing stock.

New York City

In 1928, flush from the success of Tudor City, French embarked on an attempt to assemble 50 acres of the Lower East Side, and to create an even bigger self-contained enclave of 40,000 apartments. He acquired one-third of the site before the Depression forced him to sell all but 5 acres of the infamous "Lung Block." Robert W. DeForest, Commissioner of the City's Tenement House Department, had recommended that block for clearance in 1903, saying:

> *I know of no tenement-house block in this city which is so bad from a sanitary point of view, or from a criminal point*

Manhattan, 1995. Knickerbocker Village on the Lower East Side, completed in 1934. *(Alexander Garvin)*

of view...I understand that...these houses are permanently infected with the germs of tubercular disease, and that the only remedy and method of preventing the further spread of this disease from these houses is the destruction of the buildings.[25]

There, with the help of a Reconstruction Finance Corporation mortgage and 25-year real-estate tax exemption, French erected a 13-story enclave that, like Tudor City, was organized around private open space, in this case two huge courtyards.

Knickerbocker Village replaced 1085 slum dwellings with 1593 well-designed new apartments. The net gain of 508 apartments, it was thought, might generate further neighborhood revival because even if the original-site tenants moved to tenement apartments without hot water or bathrooms, the families that moved to Knickerbocker Village would free up better apartments for other city residents living in worse conditions. They, in turn, would free up other somewhat worse apartments, and so on, until 508 of the worst apartments would be filtered out of the city's housing stock.[26]

The economic dislocations caused by the Depression made it difficult to determine whether slum clearance combined with sizable net increases to the housing stock would, in fact, result in improved housing for families outside redevelopment areas. Far too little was built. After World War II, using Title I funding, Robert Moses conceived a massive slum-clearance effort that he believed would work in just this fashion. By 1959, when he was forced to give up chairmanship of the Committee on Slum Clearance, Moses already had an approved redevelopment program that called for a net gain of 22,000 apartments.[27]

Despite Moses' massive redevelopment program, anybody living in New York City in 1940, or 1960, or 1980, could tell you that it was still suffering a major housing crisis. In those 40 years, although 1,050,351 housing units had been built and the population had *declined* by 383,356, there still was a terrible shortage of apartments. The shortage was caused by a decrease in the average household size from 3.64 to 2.54 persons, producing an increase of 738,213 in the number of households that required shelter.[28]

New Haven, Connecticut

In New Haven, which also tried to achieve a net increase in apartments, the filtering process produced much more apparent results. Not only had the city pledged to "free itself of slums," it was more successful than any other American city in obtaining federal redevelopment subsidies. As of 1966, New Haven had received $745 in per-capita federal urban-renewal allocations, 20 times New York City's, 16 times Chicago's, and 7 times Philadelphia's. The nearest competitor was Newark, which had received $277.[29]

New Haven had considered housing redevelopment long before passage of the Housing Act of 1949. The city's first comprehensive plan, jointly prepared in 1910 by architect Cass Gilbert and landscape architect/urban planner Frederick Law Olmsted, Jr., proposed the redevelopment of the area between the railroad station and the downtown business district. Their proposal was not implemented. During the late 1930s the city had surveyed its blighted areas and proposed clearance for the purpose of building new public housing. In 1941–1942 it hired Maurice Rotival, a French city planner on the Yale faculty, to prepare another master plan. Like Olmsted and Gilbert's redevelopment scheme, it was not executed. However, both plans contributed the framework for the redevelopment projects initiated after World War II.

While there were areas of unsafe, inadequately heated, overcrowded housing, New Haven had nothing like the tenement districts of New York or Chicago. Most of the city's housing consisted of low-rise, low-density buildings whose renovation was neither complicated nor expensive. Furthermore, the relatively small quantity of housing that had to be replaced was within the financial capacity of Connecticut lending institutions. Thus, the promise of a slumless city was believable and realizable.

New Haven's redevelopment effort was conceived and directed by one of the best and brightest teams of municipal officials anywhere in the country. The man responsible for bringing it together and providing vision, leadership, and political moxie was Richard C. Lee, mayor from 1953 through 1969. He made the redevelopment proposals that had been discussed for years the cornerstone of his election campaign and 16-year mayoralty. As Mayor Lee explained:

> *I went into the homes on Oak Street...I went to block meetings...three and four in one night. And I came out of one of those homes on Oak Street, and I sat on the curb and I was just sick as a puppy. Why the smell of this building; it had no electricity, it had no gas, it had kerosene lamps, light had never seen those corridors in generations. The smells...It was just awful and I got sick. And there, there I really began...right there was when I began to tie in all these ideas we'd been practicing in city planning for years in terms of the human benefits that a program like this could reap for a city.*[30]

Lee needed talented administrators to develop imaginative but practical redevelopment proposals and then to shepherd them through the maze of bureaucratic stumbling blocks that could prevent their realization. As his first development administrator, he picked Edward Logue (see Chapter 6). Logue and the other members of this team produced plans for every dilapidated section of the city. Meanwhile, Lee worked with the city's political leaders to obtain the active local constituencies needed for acceptance by the Board of Aldermen. The mayor believed that when all these elements were in hand Washington would have to provide the necessary financing—and Washington did.

The team's first undertaking, the Oak Street Area Redevelopment Project, obtained federal funding in 1956. The previous administration had already obtained conceptual approval for razing 15 acres. Lee and Logue tripled the area to be cleared and completely altered the redevelopment strategy. The centerpiece was a highway connector to the Connecticut Turnpike, which was intended to provide fast, easy access for suburbanites on their way to and from working or shopping in downtown New Haven. The plan also included 600,000 square feet of new office and retail space to be built on renewal land, minor expansion by Yale University, and four new apartment buildings.

Public officials accepted demolition of 811 apartments because there was sufficient turnover of existing low-rent public and private housing to accommodate the relocatees. In 1955 there was as yet no way for the private sector to finance replacement housing for persons of low and moderate income. Construction of 812 new apartments guaranteed that there would be no net loss of housing. The officials also accepted displacement of the businesses occupying 62 commercial and 25 industrial structures. They believed that the benefits of slum clearance would surely outweigh the hardship of a move and thought that businesses would be able to carry the financial burden. Besides, redevelopment officials reported that 41 percent of the area's structures were substandard and required replacement.

Mayor Lee described the new apartment buildings in the Oak Street Project as "the most God-awful-looking things I ever laid eyes on."[31] He vowed there would be no more dull buildings and proposed to rebuild other areas with the help of some of the nation's best-known architects. He also shifted the redevelopment program away from large-scale clearance and

New Haven, 1989. The Crown, University, and Madison Towers in the Oak Street Urban Renewal Project that Mayor Lee thought were an ugly mistake. *(Alexander Garvin)*

toward selective redevelopment, housing rehabilitation, and affordable housing financed through federal programs.

Lee and Logue altered the original plan for the Wooster Square Urban Renewal Area to include a major housing rehabilitation effort, scattered clusters of new low-rise housing, small parks, and new community facilities (see Chapter 12). Tom Appleby, who succeeded Logue as development administrator in 1961, continued this approach. The next projects, Dixwell (247 acres) and Dwight Street (215 acres), covered whole neighborhoods still "basically in sound condition." Most of these areas were to remain untouched by redevelopment. Instead, small pockets of blight were replaced with small-scale buildings that blended into their surroundings.

New Haven, 1965. Florence Virtue Homes—a moderate-income cooperative designed by John Johansen for the Dixwell Urban Renewal Project. *(Alexander Garvin)*

Title I permitted a locality's payment of one-third project cost to be made in noncash credits rather than cash. Many cities used necessary expenditures for infrastructure improvements and community facilities as noncash credits. New Haven turned this into a fine art. Not only did the city build 12 new schools in renewal areas—as a way of covering its one-third project cost, it counted every allowable noncity expenditure. For example, when Yale University purchased city land for the construction of two new residential colleges, the sales price became a noncash contribution to the nearby Dixwell Urban Renewal Project. The acquisition cost for the site of the Yale School of Art and Architecture became a noncash credit for the Dwight Renewal Project.

Prior city improvements that served the project area could also be counted. For this reason, New Haven regularly scoured old budgets for "catch basins, tree stump removals, even an abandoned public bathhouse," and other eligible items. Since the noncash credits in excess of the required one-third local contribution could be pooled and credited to other redevelopment projects, the city planned its renewal projects around much-needed local improvements and then used the surplus federal contributions to finance similarly needed improvements in other redevelopment projects. Thus, for New Haven, the Housing Act of 1949 could have appropriately been renamed the capital-budget substitution act.

No federal subsidy was left untapped. When Congress enacted the 221(d)(3) Program (see Chapter 9), New Haven rushed to use it for a series of moderate-income cooperative or nonprofit rental projects within already approved renewal areas. Columbus Mall Houses, 72 apartments in the Wooster Square Renewal Area; Florence Virtue Houses, 129 apartments in the Dixwell Renewal Project; and Trade Union Plaza, 77 apartments in the Dwight Renewal Area, are typical in terms of scale and quality of architectural design.

New Haven, 1989. Trade Union Plaza—a 77-apartment cooperative completed in 1968, designed by Victor Christ-Janer for the Dwight Urban Renewal Project. *(Alexander Garvin)*

When Richard C. Lee left office, almost every area of the city was involved in some effort at redevelopment. There was also major opposition to further government slum clearance, especially in the "Hill," a poor neighborhood with a substantial African-American and Puerto Rican population. Despite growing criticism of the redevelopment program, New Haven's housing market had improved markedly. The city's worst slums had been demolished. Most of the housing that remained was structurally sound and with minor expenditures on rehabilitation could have been expected to provide decent homes for many years to come. Since New Haven's population declined by 25 percent between 1950 and 1980, relocatees had been able to move to steadily improving accommodations. Clearly, the city's ambitious redevelopment program had made great strides in providing a better environment for the next generation. If the process had continued, the revitalization of New Haven's residential neighborhoods might have become a model for the nation.

Strategy 4: Removing Frictional Blight

Another approach for eliminating slums calls for removing impediments to private investment. The argument is that if unsightly structures, incompatible land uses, and noxious activities blighting an area are removed, neighboring property owners will make improvements, developers will purchase and rehabilitate or build, and banks will lend the money to pay for this. Therefore, government should acquire these blighted properties and resell them to developers who will execute the city's renewal plan.

Society Hill, Philadelphia

The strategy of eliminating blight that is having a negative frictional effect on neighboring property is well illustrated by Philadelphia's Washington Square East Renewal Project, better known as Society Hill. This 120-acre area is located in the southeastern section of downtown Philadelphia, just west of the Delaware River (see Chapters 2 and 18).

Society Hill received its name from the "Free Society of Traders" established in 1682, whose members originally purchased most of this land. The houses they built were called "Society houses." Although the society has been gone from the area for three centuries, the name persists.[32]

During the nineteenth century, the area was dominated by the expanding operations of the Dock Street Market, its wharves, warehouses, and traffic. Only poor families and transients moved into the midst of the noise, filth, and odors generated by the rat-infested market. By the midtwentieth century many of the area's formerly gracious Georgian, Federal, and Greek Revival townhouses had been converted into storage facilities, manufacturing lofts, bars, rooming houses, and cheap tenements. Even Washington Square, one of Philadelphia's four original 8-acre park squares located in Society Hill, had become a favorite hang-out for "bums, perverts and other undesirables."

The Dock Street Market had become outmoded. Not only was its downtown location inconvenient to truck, rail, and air freight, it had become a traffic bottleneck. "Even the loading docks were not of a height adapted to trucks which brought the produce in." Philadelphia needed a functional produce market in a convenient location easily accessible to trucking.[33]

In 1954, the Greater Philadelphia Movement, an organization of public-spirited business leaders, proposed moving the market. The site selected was a 388-acre garbage dump in South Philadelphia, easily accessible by highway and railroad to the rest of the country. It was acquired by the Philadelphia Redevelopment Authority for $7 million. After spending $10 million on streets and utilities, it transferred the site to a newly formed Food Distribution Corporation, which spent another $100 million to create the country's first municipally sponsored industrial park for processing, packaging, distribution, and wholesaling of food products.

While the new Food Distribution Center was being planned, Edmund Bacon, executive director of the City Planning Commission, conceived a strategy that used the relocation of the market as the basis for the revival of all of Society Hill. He also proposed the acquisition and removal of every incompatible land use, dilapidated building, and unsightly structure in the neighborhood, whether or not it was connected to the market. His plan, approved for Title I funding in 1957, called for preservation of the area's historic character and sizable stock of eighteenth- and nineteenth-century row houses; construction of new housing, compatible in color, scale, and design with the buildings that were retained; and creation of the commercial, institutional, and recreational amenities needed in any healthy neighborhood.

Philadelphia, 1940. Dock St. Market, cleared to make way for Society Hill Towers. *(Courtesy of The Free Library of Philadelphia)*

Philadelphia, 1993. Rehabilitated late eighteenth and early nineteenth century row houses along Pine Street in Society Hill. *(Alexander Garvin)*

Philadelphia, 1993. Old and new row houses on Delancey Street in Society Hill. *(Alexander Garvin)*

FHA 220 mortgage insurance was the key to restoration of Society Hill's lovely houses. But by themselves, ensured bank loans were insufficient. There had to be property owners who were interested in and financially capable of rehabilitating their buildings, people willing and financially able to live there, and a method of being sure that the rehabilitation would be consistent with the rest of the neighborhood.

The Redevelopment Authority surveyed every structure in Society Hill. It found almost 700 buildings (more than 500 built before 1850) that could be economically rehabilitated. Then it established both general rehabilitation standards for the area and specific requirements for many of the buildings.

Philadelphia, 1974. Penn's Landing Square Apartments, on Society Hill, designed by Louis Sauer. *(Alexander Garvin)*

Property owners were given 30 days to commit to restoration and an extended period to plan and start rehabilitation. If they failed to agree to renovate or to complete the rehabilitation, the Authority threatened to acquire their property through eminent domain.

In 1956, a group of civic-spirited business leaders established the Old Philadelphia Development Corporation to be the nonprofit implementation arm of the renewal effort. It acted as a general promoter of Society Hill, a consultant to the Redevelopment Authority, and, where necessary, as interim developer for buildings and vacant properties that had to be acquired. It found purchasers for these sites, helped them to obtain necessary mortgage financing, and then led them through the maze of renewal requirements. The new owners were given at least 1 year to begin construction. If they failed, the Redevelopment Authority could take the property back and find another more effective owner.[34]

During the 1950s, when millions of city dwellers were departing for what they thought to be more attractive suburban homes, some experts doubted that there would ever again be substantial demand for city residences. If Society Hill was to attract a market interested in living adjacent to the business district, potential residents had to be convinced that the area was going to improve and would soon have all the amenities needed to keep them from choosing a suburban alternative.

Once the Dock Street Market had moved, the Redevelopment Authority sought proposals for the site. The winning scheme was submitted by New York developer William Zeckendorf, Sr., on behalf of his firm, Webb & Knapp. His team, which always included I. M. Pei as architect, had already been selected as a developer for Washington's Southwest Urban Renewal Area and for several of Robert Moses' redevelopment projects in New York City.

The Zeckendorf-Pei plan called for construction of 720 apartments in three towers sited in a vast grassy area farthest away from the historic structures. It also included a supermarket, underground parking for 400 cars, and 14 three-story, brick, one-family town houses. The new town houses were intended to provide a transition between the modern apartment buildings and the historic brick rows.

The Society Hill Towers were concrete and glass. All the rooms had floor-to-ceiling windows with views of the Delaware River on one side or downtown Philadelphia on the other. These conveniently located apartments with splendid views and attractive rents made possible by the subsidized land sale and FHA 220 mortgages, were just what was needed to attract new residents to the area.

The towers, completed in 1964, soon became a beacon announcing the revival of downtown living and attracting other developers eager to profit from the new market. Sometimes these developers built one-family town houses, filling the gaps between older row houses; sometimes, new groups of row houses; sometimes, apartment buildings. The townhouses were often sited in combination with new open spaces and off-street parking. One of the most attractive additions is Penn's Landing, a low-rise, 85-unit complex designed by Louis Sauer. The infill structures, occasionally of radical modern design, were sympathetic in scale and materials to the rest of the neighborhood. Contextual design was required by the design regulations written into the renewal plan. Moreover, each proposal had to be approved by an Advisory Board of Design.

Philadelphia, 1982. Delancey Park, part of the greenway system Edmund Bacon created for Society Hill. *(Alexander Garvin)*

Society Hill is unique among redevelopment projects because of the carefully designed system of handsome public open spaces conceived by Edmund Bacon. There are tree-lined, brick and cobblestone streets and sidewalks lit by Franklin streetlamps, small parks designed to provide play areas for children and sitting areas for the elderly, and pedestrian greenways that connect the streets with the parks. These greenways were created by replacing vacant lots, dilapidated structures, and incompatible land uses with pedestrian ribbons that provide vistas to local landmarks.

Critics point to the decrease in the African-American population as evidence for the contemporary charge that urban renewal amounted to "Negro removal." African Americans (77 families and 63 individuals), however, amounted to fewer than 15 percent of the relocatees. Critics also denounce gentrification and point to the absence of low- and moderate-income housing. Redevelopment certainly increased the number of middle- and upper-income white residents in Society Hill. They had the money to pay for the area's new and rehabilitated housing.

Despite the relocation of 483 families and 551 individuals, the area's population increased from 3378 in 1960 to 4841 in 1970, and is even larger today. More than 1000 new dwelling units have been built and another 600 residential structures rehabilitated. Prior to redevelopment, Society Hill generated $454,000 in annual property tax payments. By 1974, this sum had climbed to $2.47 million, an increase of 444 percent.

The Washington Square East Renewal Project restored Society Hill to its former stature as a respectable and fashionable residential neighborhood. It sparked a revival of interest in simultaneously living and working in the center city. It also ended redlining by banks, of Philadelphia's downtown residential areas. In less than 10 years, $180 million in private funds were invested in Society Hill. Tens of millions more were invested over the next two decades. Most important, it demonstrated to the country the effectiveness of removing frictional blight as a strategy for urban renewal.

New York City's Vest-Pocket Redevelopment

New York City also tried renewing neighborhoods by selectively removing unsafe, unsanitary, and incompatible structures in the West Side (1956–1994) and Bellevue South (1956–1976) Urban Renewal Projects in Manhattan. But, the planning process and the results were quite different from those in Philadelphia. In New York, community groups were

Manhattan, 1994. By planning street-level retailing and retaining the street wall along 23d Street in the Bellevue South Urban Renewal Project, the designers (Davis, Brody & Associates) were able to re-create New York City's active street life. *(Alexander Garvin)*

Manhattan, 1981. Apartment towers erected on Columbus Avenue in the West Side Urban Renewal Area. *(Alexander Garvin)*

Bronx, 1974. Apartment buildings designed by Richard Meier for the Twin Parks Urban Renewal Project. *(Alexander Garvin)*

actively involved in selecting sites for clearance and determining their reuse. The beneficiaries were not just middle- and upper-income home owners or profit-motivated private developers. Each renewal area included sites for middle-, moderate-, and low-income housing that were transferred for development to nonprofit organizations and to the New York City Housing Authority. Of the 7800 new apartments in the West Side Urban Renewal Project, 800 were low-rent public housing, 4200 subsidized moderate- and middle-income dwelling units (15 percent of which had rents comparable to public housing) and only 2800 were fully tax-paying, privately financed apartments. Another difference was staging. Certain cleared sites were given construction priority so that relocatees from other redevelopment sites would not have to move from the neighborhood.

While both the Bellevue South and West Side Urban Renewal Projects are less visually charming and took far longer to complete than Society Hill, they were equally successful in attracting new middle-income residents. In each case there was virtually unlimited demand for market-rate housing at these desirable locations a few minutes away from the midtown business district. By removing blighted and incompatible structures from the neighborhood and providing financial incentives (below-market-interest-rate mortgages and real estate tax abatement) government eliminated impediments to private development. As in Society Hill, the market that these projects attracted spilled over to property not taken for redevelopment.

Bronx, 1974. Lambert Houses, a subsidized apartment complex in the Bronx Park South Urban Renewal Project, designed by Davis, Brody & Associates for the nonprofit Phipps Houses. *(Alexander Garvin)*

Mayor John Lindsay came to office in 1966 with a commitment to apply this same approach to other sections of the city. He believed that "vest pocket" redevelopment was the appropriate alternative to Moses-style Title I renewal because it encouraged contextual architecture rather than immense housing projects. There was little support from Washington, however, until Congress adopted the same strategy of staged redevelopment for the Housing Act of 1968. This legislation established a Neighborhood Development Program (NDP) alternative to conventional Title I renewal. This program permitted housing redevelopment in designated areas to proceed on a year-to-year basis, based on the availability of financing, subsidies, and relocation resources.[35]

New York, like other cities, rushed to make use of these new funds. However, the Lindsay Administration made sure that new redevelopment sites would include more new apartments than the number of units demolished and that these new developments could serve as relocation resources for the next stages of a comprehensive NDP.

Sections of Harlem, Mott Haven and Twin Parks in the Bronx, and Coney Island and parts of Bedford Stuyvesant in Brooklyn were earmarked for NDP funding. In many cases the designated builder-developer was the New York State Urban Development Corporation, whose first president and chief executive officer was Edward Logue, who had cut his redevelopment teeth in the renewal areas of New Haven. That experience had convinced him that mediocre design could ruin an otherwise successful redevelopment effort. The Lindsay

Administration was similarly committed to "good urban design." Together they made the program a showcase for design by more fashionable architects (e.g., Richard Meier, James Polshek, Giovanni Passanella, Prentice & Chan, and Davis, Brody & Associates).

The first NDP sites were the only ones completed. In January 1973, President Nixon unilaterally terminated the country's entire renewal program and declared a moratorium on additional subsidized housing. Further action in Twin Parks, Mott Haven, and other vest-pocket renewal areas was dependent on further subsidies. Without federal assistance the city had no choice but to terminate further development.

The aborted vest-pocket renewal projects demonstrated that by itself, selective replacement of dilapidated buildings is insufficient. For there to be further neighborhood improvement, the remaining property owners have to be able to obtain necessary financing. Residents of the areas selected by the Lindsay Administration for vest-pocket renewal, unlike those of more prosperous areas of Manhattan or of Society Hill, could not afford the necessary rent increases. In the absence of this middle-income market, neither developers nor lending institutions would initiate additional action. Thus, when Nixon terminated redevelopment subsidies, he also terminated further neighborhood improvement in the vest-pocket renewal areas.

Strategy 5: Concentrated, Coordinated Government Action

Many urbanists believe physical redevelopment, by itself, is not enough. They argue that success requires also treating residents' social, economic, and political ailments. This approach calls for active program coordination among quite different government agencies, intense involvement by area residents, and enormous amounts of money. Moreover, the taxpayers are rarely willing to foot the bill. Despite these difficulties, every so often Congress does try this strategy.

Model Cities

The nation's most ambitious attempt to integrate physical redevelopment with social, economic, and political action was embodied in the Demonstration Cities and Metropolitan Development Act of 1966. This legislation, popularly known as Model Cities, called for concentrated and coordinated government action (federal, state, and local) in specially designated *model neighborhoods*. In these model neighborhoods, the federal government paid 80 percent of the cost of planning, administration, and the nonfederal share of federal categorical grant programs, plus 100 percent of any new nonfederal programs.[36]

Cities everywhere wanted their share of Model Cities money. Community leaders, working with a wide range of professionals, prepared analyses of proposed model neighborhoods, established goals and objectives, and devised programs to achieve them. These were embodied in 5-year strategies and 1-year action plans that were submitted to Washington as the basis for inclusion in the program. By 1973, when the Nixon moratorium terminated Model Cities, $2.34 billion had been spent in 150 cities with designated model neighborhoods.[37]

Three huge sections of New York City were selected for the program and approved by HUD: Harlem-East Harlem in Manhattan, the South Bronx, and Central Brooklyn. By itself, the Central Brooklyn Model Neighborhood, included 425,000 residents in three blighted neighborhoods: Bedford-Stuyvesant, Brownsville, and East New York.[38]

The Lindsay Administration was ready to tap Model Cities money even before the legislation had passed. It appropriated "early action" money for acquiring sites and hiring "advocate planners" to work with community residents. The program they developed for East New York was probably the most carefully thought-out by its planners and the most strongly supported by community residents.

Planning for a Target Area: East New York, Brooklyn

East New York, a community of 100,000 located in the southern section of the Central Brooklyn Model Neighborhood, was experiencing rapid population transition. Its Jewish, Italian, Polish, and Lithuanian middle class began moving away in the 1950s. This exodus was accelerated when African Americans and Puerto Ricans, who had been displaced from their homes to make way for public housing projects in neighboring Brownsville, spilled over into East New York.

Residents of East New York moved on average every 18 months. Rapid turnover in apartment occupancy led to strained landlord-tenant relations. Inadequate management and increasingly deferred maintenance exacerbated the deterioration of the area's already dilapidated buildings. By the time East New York was designated as part of the Central Brooklyn Model Neighborhood, it was filled with vacated, burned-out, and destroyed houses.

In November 1966, Walter Thabit, the advocate planner hired by the city, began a series of 17 Wednesday-night planning sessions with community leaders. Over 250 people came to at least one meeting of what was called the East New York Housing and Urban Planning Committee. Eighteen "faithful" members attended five or more sessions. In the end, more than 30 community organizations and churches had been represented. Thabit presented these meetings with detailed analyses of industry, retailing, housing, transportation, population, community facilities, public services, and neighborhood organizations. By April, residents, municipal officials, and Thabit had completed a thorough analysis of the neighborhood.

The Model Cities Program in Central Brooklyn included proposals for everything: early childhood centers, after-school tutoring, bookmobiles, community service officers, fire prevention, sanitation, work release, ambulance services, addic-

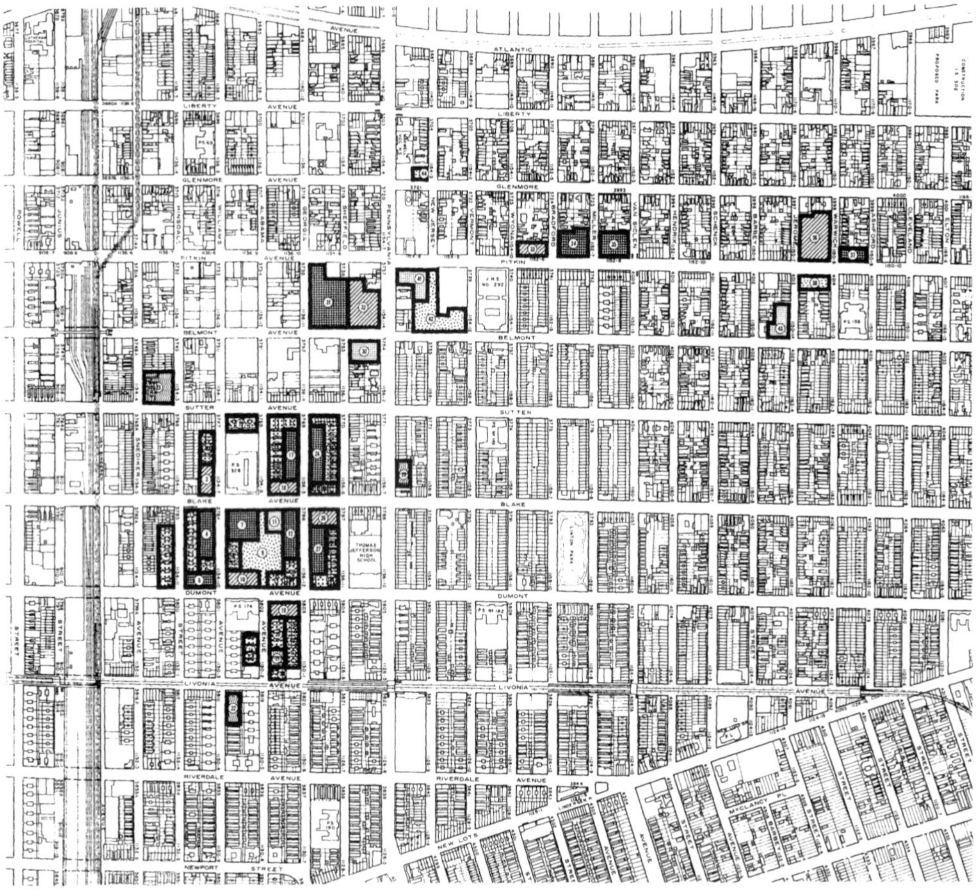

Brooklyn, 1967. Vest-pocket housing strategy prepared by Walter Thabit for the East New York Model Cities Program. *(New York City Housing and Development Administration)*

tion treatment, college scholarships, industrial development, job training.…Its first-year budget totaled $25 million.

East New York chose to concentrate these programs in a "target area" that had the most vacant buildings, fires, and crime. As Thabit explained, those who lived in the area wanted it made livable, safe, and clean for present tenants. Those who lived outside wanted…the "welfare pesthole" removed.[39]

Brooklyn, 1981. Two blocks at the heart of the East New York Section of Central Brooklyn Model Cities Area were combined to create Unity Plaza, a superblock that combined housing with a paved, open space designed and equipped for active recreation. *(Alexander Garvin)*

There were disagreements as to tactics, but the strategy was clear: target 800 to 1000 new public housing units and an equal number of substantially rehabilitated apartments to the "pesthole" and proceed from there. Two blocks at the heart of the area were combined into a single superblock. Six-story buildings were sited along its perimeter to create "Unity Plaza." Open space within Unity Plaza was increased by closing the street that ran through it. Instead of open grass, common areas were paved and equipped for active recreation.

Unity Plaza opened in 1973, a few months after Nixon had terminated Model Cities and decreed a moratorium on further federal housing assistance. It stood alone, surrounded by even more vacated, burned-out, and destroyed buildings. The city government was not able to replace federal Model Cities money. It was facing fiscal disaster. Without money, there was no way to proceed with the ambitious program for East New York.

Brooklyn, 1974. Unity Plaza has stood alone surrounded by an increasing number of empty lots and abandoned buildings since its completion. *(Alexander Garvin)*

Neighborhood Strategy Areas

When federal funding was resumed in the Housing and Community Development Act of 1974, the burden of deciding the mix and level of funding for clearance, rehabilitation, economic development, public improvements, and other renewal activities was shifted from Washington to each recipient local government. The act created *block* grants for every locality, not just for those who successfully applied for *categorical* grants. The amount of the Community Development Block Grant (CDBG) was determined by a formula including population, extent of poverty, and degree of overcrowding. Never again could talented administrators in New Haven or any other city get their citizens 19 times the money allocated to New Yorkers.

Previously, each city had proposed specific projects that were approved by the Department of Housing and Urban Development (HUD) because they met the categorical requirements of specific federal programs. Now federal grants were equitably distributed, funding levels were predictable, and local actions could satisfy local priorities. CDBG paid for 100 percent of the costs of housing rehabilitation, public improvements, open space, historic preservation, and economic development, not just redevelopment.

Most local governments faced with local political pressures and a multiplicity of local needs, chose to avoid new slum-clearance projects. They preferred using the grants to pay for such diverse items as playground renovation, sewer replacement, sidewalk repaving, street trees, and housing rehabilitation. Often the Community Development Block Grant simply paid for local budget items that might otherwise have been dropped.

The Carter Administration decided CDBG would have greater impact if cities targeted funds based on a comprehensive community development program. In doing so it revived the Model Cities approach but without the previous exceptionally high level of funding. Localities were asked to designate Neighborhood Strategy Areas (NSA) and concentrate and coordinate both CDBG funds and municipal-budget expenditures in those areas.

Many cities made a mockery of the process. In New York City, virtually every eligible section of the city was designated to become an NSA. For the first 10 NSAs, concentration and coordination consisted of listing all current and future government budget expenditures and transferring from the municipal budget those that were eligible for CDBG funding.

Just as NSA "targeting" was getting under way, the Reagan Administration brought it to an end by reverting to the more pristine revenue-sharing philosophy that Congress had originally enacted in 1974. Localities could again obtain CDBG funds without complying with complex regulations. Lacking federal interference, most governments chose to ignore former federal stipulations requiring them to concentrate and coordinate their expenditures.

The Clinton Administration revived the notion of coordination and concentration of the full range of social and economic programs for a few selected areas when it announced an Empowerment Zone Program. This program had even less chance of success because it proposed spending a fraction of the funds available for the Neighborhood Strategy Program or for the Model Cities Program.

The Critics

Anger and opposition sprang up wherever clearance and redevelopment were proposed. In Boston, a "Committee to Save the West End" argued that while buildings might have needed repairs and apartments might have been overcrowded, the neighborhood was a good place to live. It managed to forestall final approval of the project until 1958. In New York, political opposition defeated nearly half of the projects Robert Moses proposed before retiring from the field in 1959. Opponents argued against both clearance and redevelopment.

Opposition to Clearance

Critics of clearance observed that you do not eliminate a slum by tearing it down and removing the people; you move the problem elsewhere. In 1949, when the federal urban-renewal program was enacted, there had been few "scientific" studies of the relocatees and where they went. Consequently, there was little evidence of the assertion that slum clearance simply moved the problem elsewhere.

One of the earliest studies, a 1933 analysis of relocation from the site for the Knickerbocker Village, seemed to support the opposition. It found that of 386 families that had occupied the tenements that were cleared, 83 percent moved back to Old Law tenements, 53 percent to apartments without toilets, 34 percent to apartments without hot water, and 38 percent to apartments without bathtubs.[40]

Studies of relocatees from federally subsidized urban-renewal projects seem to prove the opposite. Analysis of relocatees from Washington's Southwest Urban Renewal Project found:

> *nearly five years after the relocation, not a single family was in a home that was judged by a team of investigators as in need of major repair.... [There is] a significant increase in both the cleanliness and the orderliness of the dwellings.... [Today] only 1 percent of the families interviewed live in apartments that do not have bathtubs or showers with running water.*[41]

As for relocatees creating new slums, wall charts and pin maps showing where each family moved from the renewal areas of New Haven between 1956 and 1966 "demonstrated visually that no new ghettos were being created."[42] The only clustering was in public-housing projects. A map of relocatees from Boston's West End produced similar results. Certainly, the relocatees brought their problems with them to new apartments. Whether these problems also spilled over with sufficient force to transform their new neighborhoods into slums is still debated.

By demolishing major amounts of unsanitary and unsafe housing, renewal projects reduced the opportunities for relocatees to move back into slum housing. In many cities this was less of a hardship than critics maintained. Relocatees were able to improve their housing because during the 1950s and 1960s, these cities had declining populations. As a result, it was relatively easy to find housing that had been left behind by people moving to the suburbs.

In New York, where the drop in population came later, the experience was quite different. In 1954, the New York City Planning Commission found that many relocatees "doubled up or moved into furnished rooms or rooming houses."[43] The same thing happened in the West Side Urban Renewal Areas and later in redevelopment programs funded by the Model Cities Program.

Proponents of slum clearance argue that demolition removes the dangers of rats and other vermin, fire, trash, and other threats to a person's health and safety. They also argue that it removes a haven for criminals and thus reduces the risk of theft, assault, rape, and murder. Opponents respond saying that the cost, in terms of disrupted lives, severed personal relationships, and destroyed identity, is not justified, especially given the vulnerability of slum residents. They point out that a person's home, on the most primal level, provides shelter from threats in the environment and that being forced to move from one's home, however inadequate, is a profoundly disturbing experience.[44]

It is difficult, perhaps impossible, to translate into dollars the psychological cost of being forced from one's home. However, it is possible to estimate the economic impact of the move. Originally, the Housing Act of 1949 neither provided compensation for moving expenses nor recognized the need to compensate relocatees for any increased housing cost. As a result of Boston's West End Urban Renewal Project, for example, 86 percent of those moved were paying higher rents after relocation and the median monthly rent had risen from $41 to $71. By 1964, Congress permitted reimbursement of up to $200 in moving expenses and up to $1000 over a 2-year period to cover the cost of securing "a decent, safe and sanitary dwelling."[45]

In response to mounting criticism Congress enacted the Uniform Relocation Assistance and Real Property Acquisition Policies Act of 1970. This legislation, which is still in effect, finally recognized the need for more generous compensation to the victims of slum clearance. It also established sufficiently high levels of payment to force municipal officials to consider the cost of relocation before deciding on further slum clearance.

Opponents also claim that areas chosen for renewal may have been characterized by badly maintained structures and poor residents, but frequently were vibrant neighborhoods that provided a cohesive sense of community for the residents. The most persuasive advocate of this view is Herbert Gans, a sociologist whose book, *The Urban Villagers,* a study of Boston's West End, revolutionized public perception of areas chosen for renewal.[46]

The West End had been labeled "detrimental to the safety, health, morals, and welfare of the inhabitants" by Boston's renewal officials. Instead, Gans saw the West End as a "run-down area of people struggling with the problems of low income, poor education, and related difficulties." He observed that apartments "were usually in much better condition than the outside hallways," that the residents "could live together side by side without much difficulty," and "when emergencies occurred, neighbors helped each other readily."[47]

Gans' study came too late. A 48-acre section of the neighborhood was cleared and 7500 people forced to move. Today the West End is a pallid complex of modernistic boxes containing 2300 apartments, 2 office buildings, 3 shopping areas, 2 pools, a tennis club, and garages for 1200 cars. Except for one building containing subsidized apartments for the elderly, it is an enclave of the upper middle class.

Boston, 1989. Some 7500 people who lived in 48-acre "urban village" described by Herbert Gans were forced to move so that their tenements could be replaced by the pallid complex of modernistic boxes known as the West End Urban Renewal Project. *(Alexander Garvin)*

Opposition to Redevelopment

Unlike opponents of clearance who consider the cost excessive, opponents of redevelopment believe the product unsatisfactory. Since new buildings in redevelopment projects had little ornament and few historical references, the initial criticism was from those who admired traditional architecture. Later it came from those who were unhappy with the new buildings. The problem they identified is best explained by architectural historian Vincent Scully, who observed that in a proposed redevelopment plan for the "Hill" neighborhood in New Haven, "purism and a distaste for life's messy multiplicity could go no further."[48]

There also was opposition from property owners and developers who argued that government-subsidized redevelopment constituted unfair competition with the private market. Owners of existing apartment houses and developers of conventionally financed new housing had reason to object. Their competitors were not only provided with land at subsidized prices, they also received better financing and paid lower real estate taxes.

These property owners had neither the know-how nor the ability to finance large projects, nor were they plugged into the political power structure. Consequently, public officials could dismiss their criticism as sour grapes while explaining that each proposed redevelopment project was a much-needed public action justifying temporary hardship on the part of a very small number of greedy landlords incapable of participating in the urban-renewal program.

Ingredients of Success

Until 1961, when Jane Jacobs published her eloquent book *The Death and Life of Great American Cities,* few critics challenged the effectiveness of redevelopment as a method of curing urban blight. Her indictment was loud and clear. Urban renewal was "a mirage, a pitiful gesture…to combat disintegration and instability that flow from the cruelly shaken-up city" that only created new slums.[49]

Instead of favoring large-scale clearance of aged and inefficient cities, she rejoiced in day-to-day neighborhood living and proposed that we emulate not some Utopian image, but the organic patterns of change common to our currently disorganized but vital cities. While she tried to diagnose the reason for failure and propose alternative action that would be more successful, she never differentiated among the various strategies for eliminating slums and blight, nor understood that there were circumstances in which one or more of these strategies might succeed.

Market

Redevelopment makes sense when the population of an area is declining. In such instances, there will be an increasing stock of available housing to which relocatees can move. Consequently, removing apartments from the market will not cause undue hardship. New Haven's massive redevelopment program, for example, eliminated the very worst housing during a period in which its population was declining. The result was an improved living environment along with an increasing vacancy rate. In New York City, on the other hand, even the net gain in available housing brought about by Robert Moses' redevelopment program could not satisfy the increasing demand for apartments.

Change in demand is not the only market factor that will determine the effectiveness of a redevelopment project. Income and taste play important roles. Removing blighted properties from an area like Society Hill attracts customers who can afford to pay for new and renovated housing. But it cannot revive neighborhoods like East New York, where residents cannot pay for repairs, much less full-scale rehabilitation or new construction, and where small changes in appearance are not enough to interest a large number of outsiders.

Location

Whether a renewal strategy is based on complete clearance and redevelopment or selective clearance and rehabilitation, the same approaches to location come into play: (1) exploitation of proximity to neighboring sections of the city that enhance marketability or screening out of those sections that have a negative frictional impact and (2) exploitation of area characteristics that are in high demand or introduction of new elements that will enhance its marketability.

Fred French demonstrated the importance of proximity to employment, shopping, and entertainment when he built Tudor City on the edge of the midtown Manhattan business district. He also demonstrated the importance of screening out the negative effects of traffic and uncongenial land uses. Such widely different renewal schemes as the Southwest Urban Renewal Project, Lafayette Park, and Society Hill had the benefit of locations that were similarly close to downtown Washington, D.C., Detroit, and Philadelphia. In addition SWURA screened out the blighting influences of the highway and railroad by covering them with a platform, Lafayette Park entirely eliminated through traffic, and Society Hill replaced the Dock Street Market, thereby removing the source of the traffic.

Each of these projects dealt with the character of its location in a different way. Lafayette Park originally was flat terrain covered with substandard wooden dwellings in various states of dilapidation, often without running water, toilets, and central heating. Greenwald and van der Rohe cleared this slum and started over again with a radically different living environment. Society Hill had the benefit of some of the nation's finest eighteenth- and early nineteenth-century brick buildings. Bacon's solution exploited these lovely buildings. The Southwest Urban Renewal Area combined both approaches.

Philadelphia, 1993. The carefully placed combination of new low-rise and high-rise buildings that augmented Society Hill's historic row houses attacted new residents to what had been thought of as one of the city's worst slums. *(Alexander Garvin)*

Design

All the components of a redevelopment project must be arranged in a manner that reinforces the particular renewal strategy. At Tudor City, Fred French exploited the drop in elevation between Second and First Avenues to create two private parks and a private street that bridges over 42nd Street. These amenities contribute to the project's market appeal. This arrangement of buildings and open space created a place that has been distinctive enough to attract customers for 70 years.

Like Tudor City, Moses' urban-renewal projects were giant-size. Their distinctiveness, however, is not the result of a thoughtful arrangement of open space, streets, and buildings. Moses and his architects were more concerned with design standards than with the character of the living environment. New buildings are evenly spaced to provide each apartment with an equitable amount of light and air. Thus, residents have the worst of all possible worlds. They neither live in a protected living environment nor are they integrated into the surrounding city.

Society Hill takes a different approach to the arrangement of pedestrian circulation, public spaces, and buildings. Its new apartment towers were intended to announce the neighborhood's renewal. Customers interested in moving downtown drove toward the towers. Once they parked, pedestrian greenways and brick-paved sidewalks led them past the sitting and playing areas that their families would be able to enjoy if they chose to move either to a tower with windows overlooking Philadelphia or to one of the nearby row houses.

Detroit, 1989. Nineteen acres of exquisitely landscaped open space provide a setting for a wide range of recreation activities at Lafayette Park. *(Alexander Garvin)*

Lafayette Park uses architecture and landscaping to market a very different product. The generous, landscaped, open spaces underscore the special character of the architecture, enhance the privacy of the residences, camouflage parked automobiles, and provide a sylvan setting for sitting, strolling, and playing ball. Consequently, customers have the benefit of a living environment quite different from the surrounding city.

Queens, 1958. Rendering of the Seaside Urban Renewal Project proposed by Robert Moses for Rockaway Beach, a site that only required the demolition of summer bungalows and was therefore presumed to be without serious relocation problems. *(Courtesy of the Citizens Housing and Planning Council, New York City)*

Financing

The Housing Act of 1949 provided financial assistance that made redevelopment easy. Without the power of eminent domain, developers would have had to pay far more to buy properties from owners who were unwilling to sell. They also would have had to pay more to compensate tenants whose leases had not yet expired. More important, government paid the costs of planning, acquisition, holding property, and—frequently—relocation and demolition as well, until development could begin. At Lafayette Park and Harlem-Lenox Terrace, those activities extended for nearly a decade. The Southwest Urban Renewal Project took even longer. Few developers could have financed this activity without earning a penny during so long a period.

Equally important, when sites were ready for development they were sold at a discounted price determined by their planned reuse, rather than the cash invested or their true market value. Nevertheless, until 1954 most developers avoided redevelopment areas because they could not get financing. Banks were unwilling to make loans in areas the government had designated as blighted. Once financial institutions were protected from losses by FHA 220 mortgage insurance, they rushed to provide designated developers and property owners with permanent mortgages for new construction and rehabilitation.

Entrepreneurship

When the federal government initiated the urban renewal program, there were no developers with experience in redevelopment. The program made it relatively easy to get into the business. Nor were developers at risk for long. In many cases they did not take title to property until financing had been guaranteed. As a result, the risk extended only from the start of construction until apartments were rented. The tough period from project inception through to the entitlement to build was the responsibility of the local redevelopment agency.

The amount of cash at risk also was minimized. Conventional mortgages, if they had been available, would have required at least 25 percent cash equity. An FHA 220 mortgage could be obtained with a nominal equity investment, a large portion of which came from mortgagable builder-sponsor fees rather than cash.

Thus, unlike many government programs, Title I had built-in incentives to encourage entrepreneurs to enter the redevelopment business. Any future program that seeks active entrepreneurial participation in redevelopment need only replicate the procedures of the federal urban-renewal program.

Time

Title I eliminated financial risk during the development period; FHA 220 mortgage insurance assured project financing for decades afterward. However, the program did not give adequate attention to the period of time people spent within a redevelopment area. Thus, success depended entirely on what developers and architects created.

Herbert Greenwald's planning team made circulation through Lafayette Park an esthetic experience. Their approach to daily life in the superblock assured a suitable living environment 24 hours a day, 7 days a week. Although completely different in conception and design, Edmund Bacon's scheme for Society Hill achieved the very same result. Pedestrian and vehicular circulation as well as shopping and recreation facilities were carefully arranged to accommodate everyday life. In most redevelopment projects in New Haven, New York, and elsewhere, such concerns were peripheral at best. No wonder Lewis Mumford could call such urban renewal: "prefabricated blight."[50]

Housing Redevelopment as a City Planning Strategy

As Jacob Riis has so graphically explained, redevelopment is intended to replace the bad environment that otherwise "becomes the heredity of the next generation." But redevelopment is not necessarily a way of increasing the housing supply, nor of improving the housing of slum dwellers. It eliminates housing (however dilapidated) and causes hardship for relocatees.

By itself, redevelopment will not eliminate slums. It must be accompanied by strategies for the survival of the new housing *still* surrounded by uncleared slums and for the improvement of untouched older housing *still* occupied by slum dwellers.

It has been years since anybody seriously proposed a major housing redevelopment project. It is time we recognized that redevelopment can revitalize appropriate sections of our cities. The errors of the past need not be repeated. In the right area, clearance and redevelopment can be a catalyst that triggers genuine urban renewal. But redevelopment is only desirable if the costs (in terms of disrupted lives and business) are low and if it truly results in a good environment. Then redevelopment can become a force for the improvement of living conditions throughout the city.

If, as in so many of Robert Moses' projects, new land uses, activities, buildings, and residents are set apart from their neighbors, the result is not just segregation. This separation prevents project benefits from spilling over into surrounding neighborhoods and thus from stimulating further private activity. Instead, redevelopment must be integrated into the life of the surrounding city.

Once we accept the fact that clearance does not necessarily eliminate slum problems, nor redevelopment necessarily increase the supply of affordable housing; once we understand that its primary utility is as a method for stimulating additional private development that would not otherwise occur, we can make housing redevelopment an effective device for fixing cities. Nothing more is needed because governments already possess all the powers they need for eliminating the bad environment.

Notes

1. Jacob Riis, *A Ten Years' War: An Account of the Battle with the Slum in New York,* originally published in 1910 and reproduced in *Jacob Riis Revisited,* Francesco Cordasco, editor, Anchor Books, Doubleday, Garden City, N.Y., 1968, p. 301.
2. Susan Beattie, *A Revolution in London Housing,* Greater London Council, The Architectural Press, London, 1980.
3. Jacob Riis, *The Peril and the Preservation of the Home,* 1903.
4. Charles F. Palmer, *Adventures of a Slum Fighter,* Tupper and Love, Inc., Atlanta, 1955, especially pp. 7–30.
5. James Ford, *Slums & Housing,* Harvard University Press,

Cambridge, 1936, pp. 714–736.
6. *Berman v. Parker,* 348 U.S. 26 (1954).
7. Historical and statistical information on the redevelopment of Washington's Southwest Urban Renewal Project is derived from Frederick Gutheim, consultant, *Worthy of a Nation: The History of Planning for the National Capital,* National Capital Planning Commission, 1977; *Berman v. Parker,* 348 U.S. 26 (1954); William Zeckendorf and Edward McCreary, *Zeckendorf,* Holt Rinehart, and Winston, New York, 1970; Daniel Thursz, *Where Are They Now?,* Health and Welfare Council of the National Capital Area, 1966; and the District of Columbia Department of Housing and Community Development.
8. *Berman v. Parker,* 348 U.S. 26 (1954).
9. Project cost was defined as including property acquisition, relocation, demolition and site preparation, and planning.
10. Zeckendorf and McCreary, op. cit., p. 207.
11. Critics of government housing redevelopment could well ask whether public action was necessary if sufficient improved housing accommodations were already available.
12. Thursz, op. cit., p. 28.
13. Harold Kaplan, "Urban Renewal in Newark" pp. 233–258 in *Urban Renewal: The Record and The Controversy,* James Q. Wilson (editor), MIT Press, Cambridge, 1967, and Central Planning Board of Newark, *Re: New Newark,* 1961, p. 14.
14. New York City Committee on Slum Clearance, *New York City Title I Progress,* July 20, 1959.
15. Committee on Slum Clearance, *Report to Mayor Impellitteri and the Board of Estimate,* New York City, January 1951, pp. 36–38.
16. Committee on Slum Clearance, *New York City Title I Progress,* New York City, July 20, 1959, pp. 24–25. I use the number of apartments demolished (2068) because Moses, in all the publications of the Committee on Slum Clearance, probably underestimated the number of relocatees as 1683 families.
17. Donatella Lorch, "Stray Bullet Makes Oasis in Harlem Fighting Mad," *New York Times,* June 13, 1990, p. B1.
18. Former State Senator Basil Patterson, quoted in Lorch, op. cit., p. B1.
19. Ludwig Hilberseimer, *The Nature of Cities,* Paul Theobald & Co., Chicago, 1955, pp. 192–193.
20. Historical and statistical information about Lafayette Park is derived from Robert Mowitz and Deil Wright, *Profile of a Metropolis,* Wayne State University Press, Detroit, 1962, pp. 11–79; Roger Montgomery, "Improving the Design Process in Urban Renewal," in Wilson, op. cit., pp. 454–487; and City of Detroit Housing Commission, *Gratiot Redevelopment Project, Final Project Report,* Detroit, June 30, 1964.
21. *General Development Corporation v. City of Detroit,* 322 Mich. 459, 33 N.W. 2nd 919.
22. Herbert Greenwald was an unusual developer who sought to combine the economic realities of real estate with a desire to create excellent architecture. Together with architect Mies van der Rohe, he was responsible for some of the finest apartment buildings in Chicago: Promontory (1946–1949), 860–880 and 900–910 Lake Shore Drive (1948–1951 and 1953–1956), and Commonwealth Promenade Apartments (1953–1956). In addition to Mies van der Rohe, the team he assembled to work on Lafayette Park included planner Ludwig Hilberseimer and landscape architect Alfred Caldwell.
23. Most of the low-rise buildings and three towers were completed as designed. The rest of the project was completed by other architects.
24. Peter Carter, "Mies' Urban Spaces," in *The Pedestrian and the City,* David Lewis (editor), Van Nostrand, Princeton, 1965, pp. 11–26; and Richard Pommer, David Spaeth, and Kevin Harrington, *In the Shadow of Mies: Ludwig Hilberseimer Architect, Educator, and Urban Planner,* Art Institute of Chicago, 1988, pp. 62–67.
25. James Ford, *Slums and Housing,* Harvard University Press, Cambridge, 1936, p. 897.
26. Ibid, pp. 591–593 and 706.
27. Committee on Slum Clearance, *New York City Title I Progress,* New York, July 20, 1959, pp. 24–25.
28. New York City Deptartment of City Planning, *New Dwelling Units Completed 1921–1972,* New York, 1973, and *Socioeconomic Profile,* New York, 1986.
29. Historical and statistical information on the redevelopment of New Havenis derived from Alan Talbot, *The Mayor's Game,* Harper & Row, New York, 1967; Robert A. Dahl, *Who Governs,* Yale University Press, New Haven, 1961; L. Thomas Appleby, interview November 21, 1988; City of New Haven Development Departments, *Oak Street Area Redevelopment Plan,* New Haven, November 4, 1955, revised March 1959; City of New Haven Development Departments, *Church Street Redevelopment and Renewal Plan,* New Haven, September 3, 1957, revised through May 27, 1964; City of New Haven Redevelopment Agency, *Dwight Renewal and Redevelopment Project Application for Loan and Grant,* May 1, 1962; City of New Haven Redevelopment Agency, *Dwight Renewal and Redevelopment Plan,* 1963; and Howard W. Hallman, *The Middle Ground: A Program for New Haven's Middle-Aged Neighborhoods,* New Haven Redevelopment Agency, September 1959.
30. Dahl, op. cit., p. 126.
31 Talbot, op. cit., p. 80.
32. Historical and statistical information on the redevelopment of Society Hill is derived from Philadelphia Redevelopment Authority, *Washington Square East Urban Renewal Area: Technical Report,* May 1959; Edmund Bacon, *The Design of Cities,* Viking Press, New York, 1967, pp. 242–271; Leo Adde, *Nine Cities: The Anatomy of Downtown Renewal,* Urban Land Institute, Washington, D.C., 1969; Jeanne R. Lowe, *Cities in a Race for Time,* Random House, New York, 1967; and the Philadelphia Redevelopment Authority Public Information Office, 1979.
33. Adde, op. cit., p. 31.
34. During its 12-year involvement with Society Hill, the Old Philadelphia Development Corporation participated in the rehabilitation or reconstruction of more than 325 properties. See Lowe, op. cit., pp. 345–347.
35. Unlike conventional Title I urban renewal which required a comprehensive redevelopment plan including clearance of every blighted property, NDP permitted a city to time acquisition, relocation, and demolition to match available relocation resources and housing subsidies. Federal funds were allocated on an annual basis based on cash flow requirements. In most other ways, redevelopment under NDP was similar to redevelopment under conventional Title I.
36. For example, in urban renewal areas located in model neighborhoods, the federal government would cover 80 percent of the nonfederal portion of project cost, thereby increasing its share from 67 percent to 93 percent of project cost [i.e., 67 percent+(.8)33 percent=93 percent].
37. Historical and statistical information on the Model Cities Program is derived from Bernard J. Frieden and Marshall Kaplan, *The Politics of Neglect: Urban Aid from Model Cities to Revenue Sharing,* MIT Press, Cambridge, 1975, and U.S. Department of Housing and Urban Development, *The Model Cities Program—A Comparative Analysis of the Planning Process in 11 Cities,* U.S. Government Printing Office, Washington, D.C., 1970.
38. Historical and statistical information on the Central Brooklyn Model Cities and its program for East New York is derived from City of New York, Office of the Mayor, Model Cities Administration, *Partnership for Change,* New York, 1970; New York City Model Cities Committee (Donald Elliott, Chairman; Eugenia Flatow, Executive Secretary), *Central Brooklyn Model Cities Comprehensive City Demonstration Program,* vol. 1, New York, May 22, 1969; and Walter Thabit, *Planning for a Target Area—East New York,* New York City Housing and Development Administration, New York, October 1967.
39. Thabit, op. cit., p. 7.
40. Fred L. Lavenburg Foundation and Hamilton House, *What Happened to 386 Families Who Were Compelled to Vacate a Slum to Make Way for a Housing Project,* New York, 1933.
41. Thursz, op. cit., pp. 28–33.
42. Alvin A. Mermin, *Relocating Families: The New Haven Experience 1956 to 1966,* National Association of Housing and Redevelopment Officials, Washington, D.C., 1970, p. 127.
43. New York City Planning Commission, *Tenant Relocation Report,* January 20, 1954.
44. Marc Fried, "Grieving for a Lost Home: Psychological Costs of

Relocation," pp. 151–171 in *The Urban Condition,* Leonard J. Duhl (editor), Basic Books, New York, 1963.
45. Chester Hartman, "The Housing of Relocated Families," *Journal of the American Institute of Planners,* vol. 30, no. 4 (November 1964), pp. 266–286.
46. Herbert J. Gans, *The Urban Villagers,* The Free Press, Glencoe, Illinois, 1962.
47. Ibid., pp. 13–16.
48. Vincent Scully, *American Architecture and Urbanism,* Henry Holt, New York, 1988, pp. 250–251.
49. Jane Jacobs, *The Death and Life of Great American Cities,* Random House, New York, 1961, p. 5.
50. Lewis Mumford, *From the Ground Up,* Harvest Books, New York, 1956, p. 108.

12

Revitalizing Neighborhoods

Boston, 1994. Newberry Street. *(Alexander Garvin)*

America has spent hundreds of billions on slum clearance but very little combating deterioration. While there is every reason to concentrate resources where the need and situation are desperate, there is no reason to wait until then, just as there is no reason to withhold minor medication until a patient requires major surgery.

Despite the pittance that has been spent on neighborhood revitalization, there is enough experience to demonstrate that deterioration can be reversed, abandonment can be prevented, and older neighborhoods can regain their health. Unfortunately, few neighborhood residents or public officials know much about these neighborhood revitalization programs or how little money they require. As a result, cities continue to avoid them.

Neighborhood revitalization programs succeed in areas with a basically sound building stock that can be restored with relatively little effort and money. The residents and property owners in these areas are usually able to put time and money into improvements, but have difficulty obtaining the necessary financing. Banks ought to rely on these additional expenditures to justify improvement loans. Too often they lack the confidence to make a major commitment. Such areas need an extra little something to trigger private sector spending. Government can provide the extra push by directing capital improvements, tax incentives, and lending programs to these neighborhoods.

Cities as diverse as New Haven, Charlotte, and New York have established programs that stimulated private sector action to revitalize deteriorating neighborhoods. These programs involved mortgage insurance, local lending offices, below-market-rate-interest loans, and capital improvement programs. In none of these cases, however, did government establish programs and wait for people to apply for them. Instead, officials worked with lending institutions that were persuaded to take special interest in the neighborhood and supported or created neighborhood institutions that helped property owners to apply for and obtain rehabilitation financing.

Cities across the country need neighborhood revitalization programs like those that worked in New Haven, Charlotte, and New York. The best way to obtain them is for Congress to enact legislation that provides assistance to localities in which local lending institutions and governments make a commitment to neighborhood reinvestment and enter into a partnership to devise and administer revitalization strategies that are tailored to specific transitional neighborhoods.

Neighborhood Dynamics

Although their boundaries are frequently imprecise and continually changing, every city has well-known, identifiable neighborhoods. They may reflect physical appearance, social composition, cultural values, political interests, history, or any combination of these factors. Their physical manifestation may be topographical features such as San Francisco's Russian Hill, Nob Hill, and Pacific Heights, or a particular building stock, such as Boston's Beacon Hill, South End, and Back Bay.

Neighborhood identity also may reflect its residents' country of origin, as is the case in Los Angeles' Mexican-American, Vietnamese-American, Korean-American, Japanese-American, and other ethnic enclaves. Sometimes it arises from a neighborhood's social function. In New York City, Greenwich Village has long been a center for artists, writers, and a wide variety of nonconformist populations; the Lower East Side has sheltered successive waves of poor immigrants seeking the promise of a new world; the one-family-house sections of Queens have accommodated those seeking greater neighborhood stability. These neighborhoods take on their character by becoming congenial places for sharing activities, life styles, and institutions.[1]

A neighborhood's cultural dimension is only in part a reflection of its social composition. New York City has many African-American neighborhoods. Only Harlem, which is not its oldest, nor its most populous, nor its most depressed African-American neighborhood, is internationally known. And only because Harlem has a unique cultural significance to African Americans could Langston Hughes write:

> *I was in love with Harlem long before I got there and still am in love with it. Everybody seemed to make me welcome. The sheer dark size of it intrigued me. And the fact that at that time poets and writers like James Weldon Johnson and Jessie Faucet lived there, and Bert Williams, Duke Ellington, Ethel Waters, and Walter White, too, fascinated me. Had I been a rich young man I would have built musical steps up to the front door and installed chimes that at the press of a button played Ellington tunes.*[2]

or Malcolm X:

> *Harlem was seventh Heaven! I hung around Small's and the Braddock bar so much that the bartenders began to pour a shot of bourbon, my favorite brand of it, when they saw me walk in the door.*[3]

The least discussed and perhaps most uncomfortable dimension of any neighborhood is political. Neighborhood residents share interests that may be at variance with public policies, surrounding communities, or accepted citywide standards. Chicago's Hyde Park–Kenwood neighborhood gained cohesion by opposing urban-renewal projects; its Gold Coast reinforced its identity by restricting occupancy to certain "desirable" population groups; its Stockyard District became prominent by protesting environmental conditions and organizing labor representation.

The most admired and increasingly prominent dimension is historical. A good way to understand New Orleans is to get to know the history of its successively settled neighborhoods: the French Quarter, Marigny, Treme, the Garden District, etc. Sometimes identity is derived from a past that has little to do with the present. Laclede's Landing in St. Louis, is no longer a riverside commercial district; New York's Ladies Mile is no longer the home of major department stores; Kansas City's Westport District is no longer a pioneer settlement supplying the Santa Fe and Oregon Trails. Yet they are identifiable because of activities that took place in another era.

Patterns of Change

Neighborhoods continually change. These changes may reflect physical condition, social composition, patterns of consumption, and other internal neighborhood characteristics. They also may be caused by changing tastes, migration, price and availability of credit, and other external factors. Sometimes the factors operate independently. San Francisco's Chinatown, for example, began to spill over into other areas during the 1970s because of a purely external factor—the Immigration Act of 1965 opened America, and San Francisco in particular, to increasing immigration from Hong Kong, Formosa, and China.

In Washington's Dupont Circle, external forces and internal characteristics interact. The combination of changing consumer demand (an external market factor) with a highly ornamented nineteenth-century building stock (an internal locational characteristic) was responsible for its decline after World War II and conversely responsible for its gentrification during the 1970s and 1980s.

Washington, D.C., 1993. Row houses on "S" Street in the Dupont Circle area that were renovated during the 1970s and 1980s. *(Alexander Garvin)*

Dupont Circle's large, elegant mansions and more intimately scaled row houses were originally built for large upper-

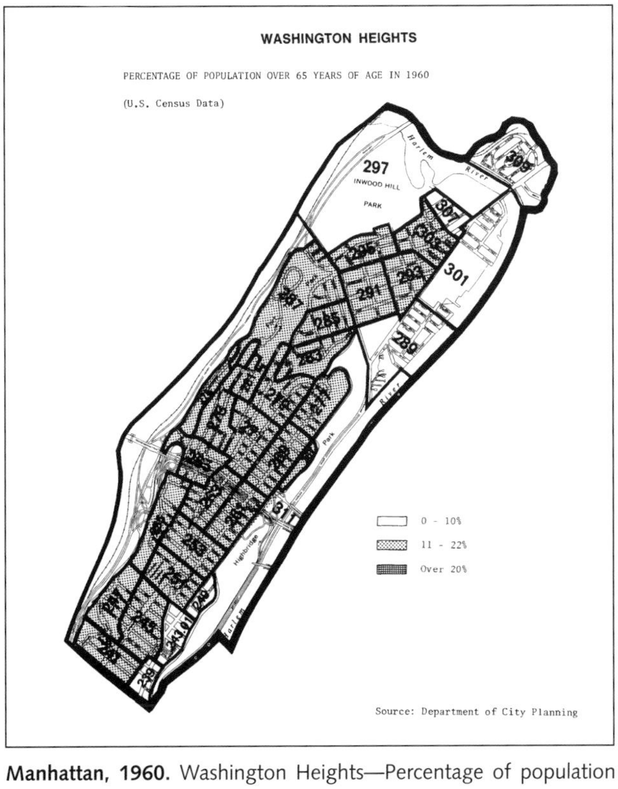

Manhattan, 1960. Washington Heights—Percentage of population over 65 years of age. *(Courtesy of New York City Department of City Planning)*

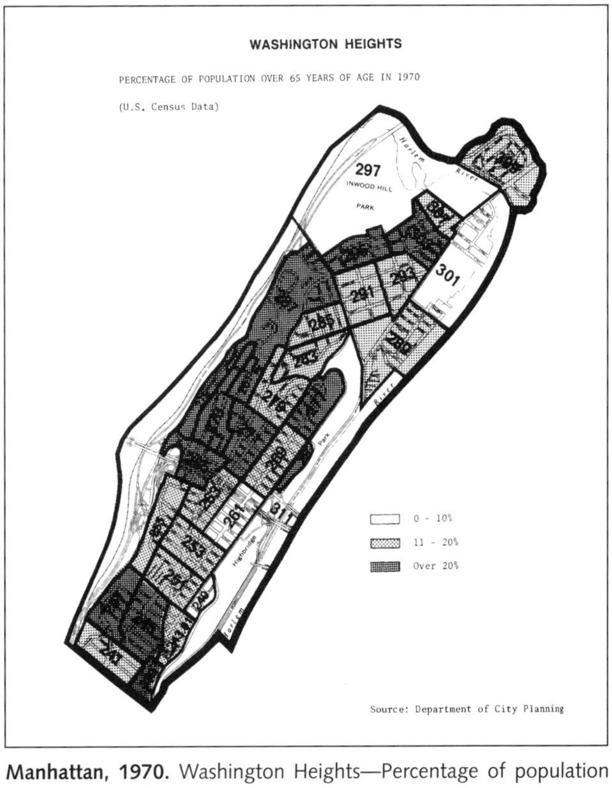

Manhattan, 1970. Washington Heights—Percentage of population over 65 years of age. *(Courtesy of New York City Department of City Planning)*

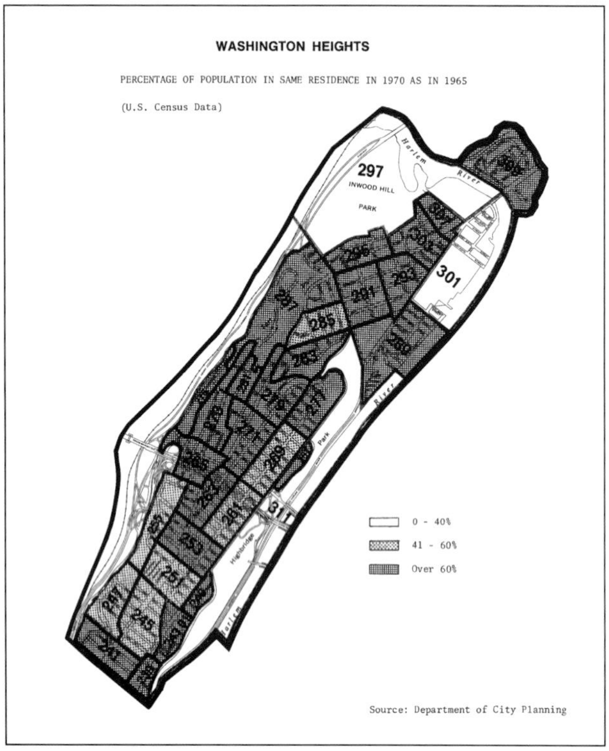

Manhattan, 1970. Washington Heights—Percentage of population in the same residence in 1970 as in 1965. *(Courtesy of New York City Department of City Planning)*

middle-class families with plenty of servants. That lifestyle began to wane even before the stock-market crash of 1929. With fewer families ready to live as their parents had, there was less demand for these ornate mansions. Inevitably, many once-elegant Beaux Arts buildings were converted into boarding houses or multiple dwellings. Since Dupont Circle offered none of the suburban amenities so favored by young families of the day, its accommodations were not in great demand and building owners spent as little as possible on maintenance. By the early 1960s Dupont Circle was a sadly deteriorated neighborhood.

If changing tastes were responsible for the neighborhood's initial decline, they were as responsible for its revival. During the 1960s, when neighborhood conditions had hit a nadir, many young adults chose to settle in the inner city rather than the suburbs. Dupont Circle was an easy walk for a large number of Washington's office workers. These relatively young city dwellers thought the area's older buildings had a charm and character that could not be duplicated. Besides, they could be purchased at low prices.

The "pioneers" who bought, rehabilitated, and usually reconverted the buildings to single-family occupancy often had difficulty getting bank financing for the necessary work. Paying for restoration was easier for two-income households (often gay or lesbian couples) who had knowledge of and interest in design and were willing to put their sweat into renovation. Some pioneers chose to create one or two rent-paying apartments to help cover their costs. They set an example for more conventional developers who followed them into the neighborhood, converting the larger buildings into condominium and rental apartment houses. By the late 1980s Dupont Circle was once again a fashionable middle-class residential enclave, one that has become too expensive for another generation similar to the one that pioneered its revitalization.

The natural life cycle of an area's population (a purely internal factor) also may cause the neighborhood to change. In New York's Washington Heights, for example, the elderly population increased between 1960 and 1970. Since most people remained in the same residence during that period, the increase in the elderly was not due to in-migration. As older residents retired, moved away, and died, apartment turnover was inevitable. This probable population transition was identified by the New York City Planning Department in the early 1970s and resulted in Washington Heights being designated for the city's just-announced Neighborhood Preservation Program.

Fighting Neighborhood Deterioration

No municipal government has the ability to prevent a population from aging, or an ethnic group from settling in an area, or young people from taking a fancy to a neighborhood; nor should it. If government gets involved at all, it should be to prevent living conditions from deteriorating for both existing residents and newcomers.

One of the more important forces responsible for undesirable changes in a neighborhood is a deteriorating physical plant. Every building starts to deteriorate as soon as it is built. As long as property owners make necessary repairs and pay for ongoing maintenance, their buildings can provide decent housing for generations. Government has a responsibility to foster an investment climate that makes it easy for residents to maintain their buildings, no matter who moves in or out of the neighborhood.

An obvious way for government to foster private investment in an area is by making visible, public improvements. Once residents see that government is spending money on the public areas in the neighborhood, they will more readily invest their own time and money on improvements to their own property. Most federal urban-renewal projects relied on this principle. Government invested in new streets, sidewalks, street trees, lighting, schools, and other community facilities that would make an area more attractive, thereby increasing its marketability and thus justifying further investment by the private sector.

No owner of property willingly lets it deteriorate. Maintenance may be deferred out of ignorance or neglect. More often, it is caused by rents that do not cover operating costs, real estate taxes, debt service, and a reasonable return on equity. This revenue gap may be caused by spiraling operating costs, increasing municipal real estate taxes, decreasing availability of mortgage credit, or increasing interest rates. It can also be caused by the limited rent-paying ability of tenants or rent regulations that prevent rent increases. Successful neighborhood revitalization programs deal with all these problems.

Deteriorating buildings need more, not less, money spent on ordinary repairs and maintenance. Moreover, government has little or no ability to affect these expenses. However, it has complete control over real estate taxes. Wherever governments punish owners who repair and restore buildings by increasing their tax assessments, property owners avoid capital improvements and neighborhoods deteriorate. Some municipalities know better. In designated areas, Louisville provides a 5-year moratorium on increased tax assessment resulting from housing rehabilitation. San Antonio offers a 10-year freeze on assessed value after rehabilitation. New York City's J-51 Program provides a 12-year exemption from increased taxes due to renovation plus an abatement of taxes equal to 90 percent of the fair value of the rehabilitation (see Chapters 1, 10, and 17).

Banks are rarely eager to lend in neighborhoods with deteriorating buildings. Government can change their attitude by insuring their mortgages. Once Wooster Square in New Haven was designated an urban-renewal area, banks that lent in the area became eligible for FHA 220 mortgage insurance. Consequently, they became far more willing to make rehabilitation loans.

Where the price of housing cannot be significantly increased because residents are unable to pay more, government can provide subsidies. One of the most effective methods is by reducing mortgage interest payments. The increased cash flow becomes the basis for financing building improvements. Charlotte decided on this strategy for the Fourth Ward. It raised the money by issuing tax-exempt municipal bonds that carried below-market-rate interest. The money was turned over to a consortium of local banks to be lent in the Fourth Ward. People responded by applying for mortgages that they otherwise might not have been able to afford.

Government also can discourage owners from maintaining their property. The most effective method is by imposing rent regulation. As Anthony Downs explains:

> *Owners of housing units under stringent rent controls will discover themselves earning less-than-competitive current yields on their equity investments. To make up for this deficiency, many will cut back on current spending for repairs, maintenance, modernization, and certain services. They will reduce spending on...minor repairs first....They will then cut back spending on long-run maintenance and modernization. [Housing] units will then suffer from greater deterioration and obsolescence than would identical non-controlled units.*[4]

Ironically, New York City, which has just this sort of stringent rent regulation, recognized it was a disincentive to housing renovation and made rent restructuring a significant element in its rehabilitation loan programs. The Participation Loan Program, for example, invalidates previously regulated rents upon rehabilitation and establishes new rents that cover operating and maintenance costs, real estate taxes, debt service (subsidized by the program), and a minimal return on equity (see Chapter 10).

Neighborhood Revitalization Programs

Successful neighborhood revitalization programs are usually community initiated. New Haven's program for Wooster Square grew out of the neighborhood's opposition to federal highway and redevelopment projects. The revival of Ansonborough was the product of Charleston's commitment to historic preservation. The transformation of Charlotte's Fourth Ward was the product of a few dedicated residents who were determined to live in a safe neighborhood within walking distance of their downtown jobs.[5]

The amazing thing is that so many revitalization efforts are successful. Unfamiliar with revitalization efforts in other cities, each preservation group usually begins by reinventing the wheel. For example, when people began efforts to revitalize the Fourth Ward in Charlotte, there was little awareness that they were adopting a strategy similar to the one used successfully in Wooster Square, nearly two decades earlier.

One reason for this ignorance is that, unlike downtown redevelopment or planned new towns, neighborhood revitalization is not glamorous enough to capture national attention. It is too narrow in scope, affects too little territory, and is too local in impact. Thus, success stories never get far beyond the local press.

Once a revitalization effort has been successful, its leaders go back to their homes, enjoy their neighborhoods, and seldom move on to work in other deteriorating areas. Thus, with the exception of New York City's Neighborhood Preservation Program, no city has developed the necessary cadre of trained technicians, proven programs, and political support to carry the work on to other deteriorating areas.

The only national institution that has for many years given assistance to groups interested in a coordinated neighborhood reinvestment strategy is Neighborhood Housing Services, Inc. (NHS), established and funded by the Federal Home Loan Bank Board and HUD. It has provided grants to dozens of neighborhood revitalization efforts. These NHS-assisted local programs have varied greatly in scope and success. They also have had little impact nationally.

Most neighborhood revitalization programs, like those of Charleston, New York City, and Charlotte, were generated independently of NHS. But, whether or not a neighborhood revitalization program received NHS assistance, when it has been successful it is because of certain common features:

- A neighborhood with an attractive, basically sound housing stock that can be restored with relatively little effort and money
- Financial institutions that are prepared to make market-rate loans to property owners who can meet common underwriting requirements
- Residents and property owners who are willing and able to put time and money into improving the neighborhood
- A local government that invests in neighborhood infrastructure, community facilities, and public areas
- A local staff that provides property owners with assistance in dealing with city agencies and financial institutions

Wooster Square, New Haven

Wooster Square is a 235-acre neighborhood centered around a charming landscaped green created in 1825. Originally, it had been a resort fashionable enough to attract families from the South who traveled by boat from New Orleans and Charleston to spend their summers in New Haven. As the city grew, factories sprang up, and the resort changed into a working-class community—first primarily Irish- and later Italian-American. Single-family homes were converted into multifamily dwellings and rooming houses. Conditions deteriorated sufficiently that, in 1951, Wooster Square was one of nine areas identified by city planners as suitable for redevelopment.[6]

Maurice Rotival, consultant to the New Haven City Plan Commission since 1941, advocated virtually complete clearance and construction of a heliport and an elevated vehicular connector for regional traffic going from downtown New Haven to New York, Hartford, and Boston. In 1952, the Connecticut Highway Department released a plan for construction of a turnpike that would run through the western edge of the neighborhood and forever separate it from downtown New Haven. The following year the New Haven City Plan Commission published a different scheme that moved the highway (now Interstate Highway 91) several blocks east so that the area could still provide residences that were a short stroll from downtown. It also advocated complete clearance and redevelopment with modern residential superblocks west of the highway and industrial parks on the other side.

Wooster Square's residents wanted neither superblocks with apartment towers nor superhighways. They liked their neighborhood and felt that all it needed was to be upgraded. Once it was fixed up, they believed that those whom they considered "undesirable" would move elsewhere and Wooster Square would again be a safe, comfortable place to live.

Few officials paid attention until 1955, when newly elected Mayor Richard C. Lee and his development director, Edward Logue, applied for Title I "survey and planning" funds for Wooster Square. After 2 years of active community participation in renewal planning, they proposed a strategy that included rehabilitation of 558 buildings, a new school, a new firehouse, numerous small parks and landscaped residential parking lots, 350 new street trees, and clusters of new low-rise housing. The approach was similar to Society Hill in Philadelphia: spot clearance, scattered small-scale new construction, vest-pocket parks, and housing rehabilitation.

Many Wooster Square property owners were paying a small proportion of their income for housing and were ready to pay

New Haven, before 1965. 10 Academy Street before renovation. *(Courtesy of City of New Haven Redevelopment Agency)*

New Haven, c. 1965. 10 Academy Street after renovation. *(Courtesy of City of New Haven Redevelopment Agency)*

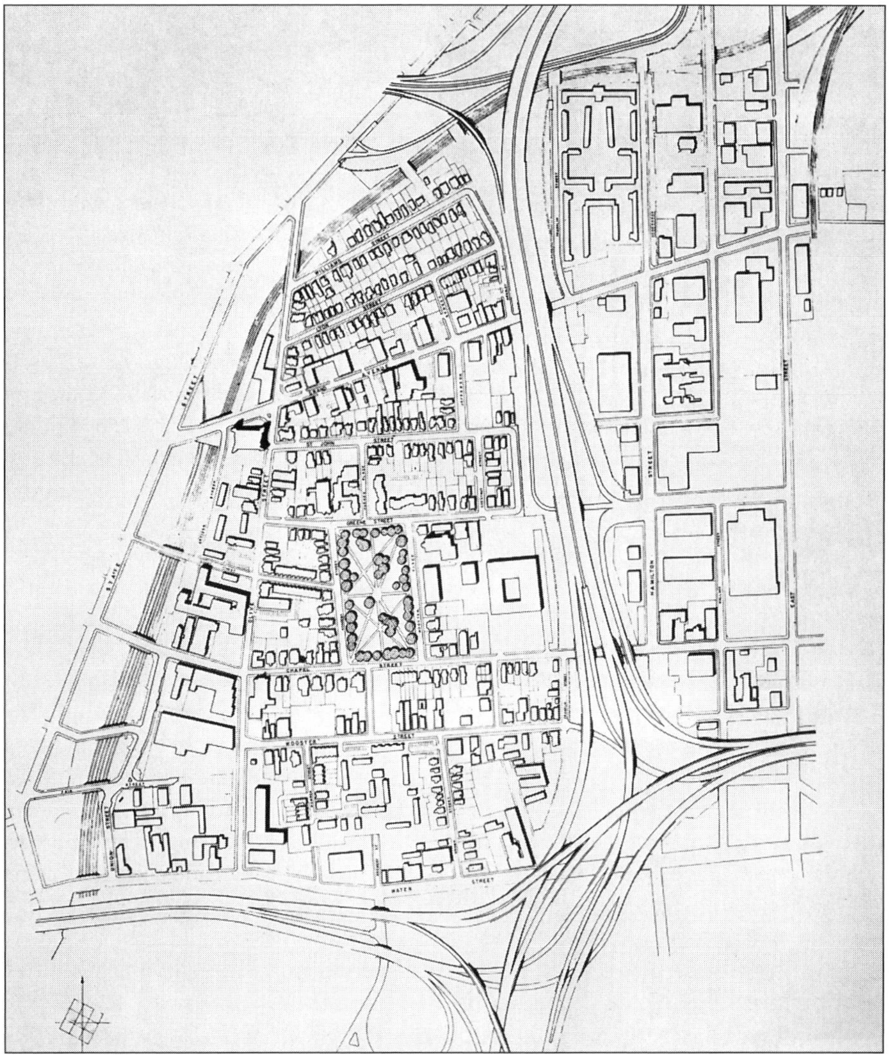

New Haven, 1965. Site plan for the Wooster Square Urban Renewal Area. *(Courtesy of City of New Haven Redevelopment Agency)*

more for better accommodations. Their problem had been getting money to pay for the improvements. Once Wooster Square was approved as a Title I project, mortgages became eligible for FHA 220 insurance. Consequently, banks began lending money for rehabilitation. By 1967, 353 residential structures had been or were in the process of being rehabilitated.

Public improvements qualified as noncash credits toward the city's one-third share of Title I project cost (see Chapter 6,

New Haven, before 1965. Court Street before renovation. *(Courtesy of City of New Haven Redevelopment Agency)*

New Haven, 1974. Court Street after renovation. *(Alexander Garvin)*

New Haven, 1974. Columbus Mall, one of the small-scale new construction projects in the Wooster Square Urban Renewal Project. *(Alexander Garvin)*

note 12). Mayor Lee and Administrator Logue wanted to maximize these noncash credits. Consequently, they made sure that the Wooster Square Urban Renewal Project included every possible municipal improvement. Its new school and firehouse, which would have been built anyway, were counted as part of the local contribution. The small parks, street trees, and landscaped parking lots were simply the bonus that the neighborhood accrued as a result of clever financial planning.

Title I grants paid for a local office with a project director, a housing code inspector who could identify all essential repairs, an architect expert in property restoration, a rehabilitation specialist experienced in all areas of building practice, a mortgage advisor familiar with the intricacies of FHA processing and conventional bank financing, and a neighborhood representative skillful in working with property owners and neighborhood leaders. These specialists surveyed area buildings, prepared illustrative plans, made recommendations for property improvements, worked on mortgage applications, prepared lists of competent contractors, coaxed neighborhood residents into making minor improvements, cajoled property owners into major renovation, and smoothed the way with banks.

Within a decade of the project's approval, Wooster Square was again one of New Haven's most attractive neighborhoods. The Italian-American community remained. Its homes had been rehabilitated. Rooming houses had been reconverted to row-house apartments or single-family homes, and virtually all existing housing had been brought to modern standards.

Crown Heights, Brooklyn

Congress enacted the Housing Act of 1964 as a way of expanding on initial neighborhood improvement experiences in Wooster Square and other renewal areas. Under Section 117 of the act, localities applied to HUD to qualify designated neighborhoods for Federal Area Code Enforcement (FACE). The act paid one-third the cost of government offices, personnel, and providing municipal improvements, such as paving, traffic signals, street lighting, and tree planting. Eventually 171 cities were approved for FACE.[7]

Under Section 312, owners of one- to four-family houses in FACE areas could apply for mortgages that carried the below-market-interest rate of 3 percent. These Section 312 mortgages, however, were only available to owners with incomes at or below the level permitted for public housing. Under Section 115, owner-occupants with incomes of less than $3000 per year also could apply for rehabilitation grants of up to $3500 for their one- to four-family houses. Few property owners were likely to meet these very low-income requirements. Consequently, FACE failed to generate major housing rehabilitation.

New York City's application for Federal Area Code Enforcement was approved by HUD in 1967. It included a section of the South Bronx, just east of the Grand Concourse, and central Crown Heights in Brooklyn. The program had little applicability to the multiple dwellings of the East Concourse, but seemed better suited to Crown Heights, which had a substantial stock of owner-occupied row houses.[8]

The 510-acre, 109-block section of Crown Heights designated for FACE contained 3734 buildings, almost half of which were one- and two-family dwellings. From 1820 to 1870 the neighborhood had been the home of a relatively prosperous African-American settlement known as Weeksville. This

Brooklyn, 1974. Row houses in the Lefferts Gardens section of Crown Heights. *(Alexander Garvin)*

Brooklyn, 1972. Deteriorating apartment buildings in Crown Heights that did not qualify for federal assistance even though they provided housing for 83 percent of the residents of the Federal Area Code Enforcement Program. *(Alexander Garvin)*

community persisted until white, middle-class families began moving into the handsome brownstone and limestone row houses that speculative builders erected during the closing decades of the nineteenth century. The neighborhood experienced a second building boom after 1920, when the IRT subway began transit service under Eastern Parkway. This time developers erected four- and six-story apartment buildings in then-popular Tudor, Hispanic, and Colonial styles.[9]

Shortly after World War II the neighborhood started to change. Rents had been frozen since the imposition of wartime price controls in 1942. Consequently, landlords deferred nonessential maintenance. The state imposed rent control when the federal government lifted price controls in 1947. The continuing combination of frozen rents and escalating operating costs led to further deferred maintenance.[10]

Meanwhile, the population began to change. Jewish families moved to the suburbs and were replaced by nonwhites, frequently middle-income immigrants from Jamaica, Haiti, and other Caribbean islands. By 1960, over half the population was nonwhite. The remaining Jewish population, especially its large Hasidic component, had trouble adjusting to ethnic change. Many nonwhite homeowners distrusted the apartment house tenants, especially the increasingly prevalent households receiving welfare. While this change in ethnicity was not accompanied by a drop in income, it was accompanied by building deterioration and social tensions and, by the late 1960s, led the City Planning Commission to designate Crown Heights as an area that needed "preventive renewal."

During the mid-1960s the Planning Commission had divided the city into areas that were considered sound, areas that required major action, and areas that required "preventive renewal" (see Chapter 18). In its *Plan for New York City,* it had advocated an allocation of about 30 percent of the city's housing resources to preventive renewal. Nothing approaching this amount was actually spent on transitional areas such as Crown Heights. However, the insistence on targeting some resources to transitional areas helped to persuade the New York City Housing and Development Administration (HDA) to apply to HUD for the FACE program.[11]

With the generous federal funding it received for FACE, HDA established a central office with eight professionals under the direction of an assistant commissioner and an office in Crown Heights that employed more than 20 professionals, including mortgage analysts, rehabilitation specialists, housing inspectors, plumbing inspectors, construction inspectors, community organizers, and even a sanitation patrol. They logged 7568 landlord interviews, 10,235 tenant interviews, 688 meetings, 1627 field visits, and 18,298 phone contacts.

Unlike New Haven, which had a clear strategy for Wooster Square, there was no plan for Crown Heights. The staff simply proceeded with the activities that HUD funded and the municipal government authorized. Statistically their work resulted in 2757 residential buildings inspected, 1476 court summonses requested, 69 Section 312 loans and 14 Section 115 grants approved, 9 municipal rehabilitation loans issued, plus $1.2 million spent for sidewalk repair, new street name signs, new sanitation signs, new traffic signals, new street lights, and new street trees. With the exception of the rehabilitation loans, the list is really a catalogue of city expenditures selected because they were eligible for FACE reimbursement.

Half the buildings and 83 percent of the area's housing units were multiple dwellings that were *not* eligible for Section 312 loans or Section 115 grants. Nor were these programs likely to help the resident owners of the area's large stock of row houses. Crown Heights was not a poor neighborhood (see Table 12.1). Most of the owners of its 1839 one- and two-family dwellings had incomes that were too high to be eligible for these programs. Consequently, over the 5 years that FACE was in operation, only 69 buildings qualified for Section 312 loans and 14 for Section 115 assistance.

The neighborhood's multiple dwellings (that were not eligible for FACE assistance) faced the greatest problems. In the absence of FHA insured bank mortgages, the city offered municipal loans. However, the Municipal Loan Program did not have the necessary staff or funds to meet citywide demand for rehabilitation financing. Nor was there any mechanism for eliminating rent control. Besides, most property owners in Crown Heights wanted nothing to do with this scandal-ridden program (see Chapter 10).

TABLE 12.1

CROWN HEIGHTS MEDIAN FAMILY INCOME IN 1959 DOLLARS[12]

Year	Crown Heights	Brooklyn	New York City
1959	$6078	$6245	$6554
1969	6356 (+5%)	7092 (+14%)	7671 (+17%)

CROWN HEIGHTS—AREAS WITH SOCIAL AND PHYSICAL PROBLEMS

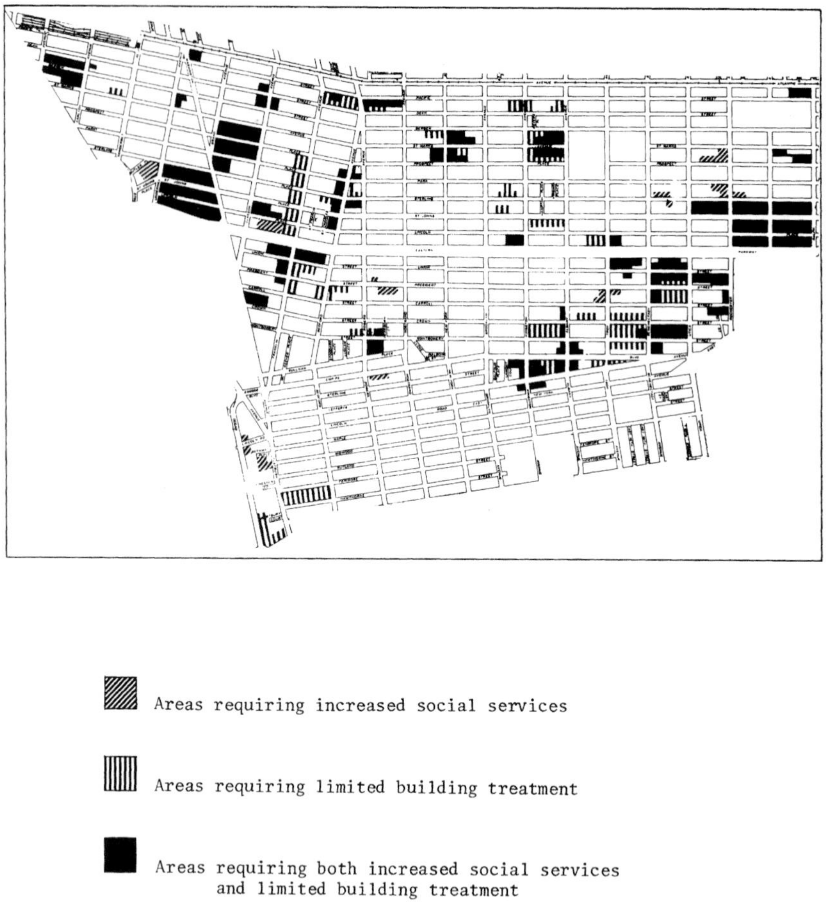

Brooklyn, 1972. Crown Heights. *(Courtesy of New York City Department of City Planning)*

Code enforcement was the least appropriate HUD-funded activity directed to Crown Heights. The only certain result of code inspection is an increase in the number of violations reported. Property owners may or may not make the repairs that will cure violations. Furthermore, the city is usually behind in removing violations from the record, or just fails to remove them. Thus, despite the record, the violations may have already been cured.[13]

Although code inspection in New York City is restricted to multiple dwellings and, therefore, did not apply to half the structures in Crown Heights, city inspectors somehow managed to gain access to 55 percent of the one- and two-unit structures. However, they were not authorized to issue violations. As if to make up for this, the Crown Heights FACE program completed cellar-to-roof inspections of all of its 1747 apartment buildings. Program records indicate that most of these buildings were brought into compliance with housing code requirements.[14]

Despite this high level of code compliance, Crown Heights was still filled with deteriorating buildings. In 1972, the year that the FACE program was concluded, a HUD-funded study of the neighborhood found that conditions in Crown Heights had worsened.[15]

It is not fair to dismiss Federal Area Code Enforcement because it was neither appropriate to Crown Heights nor successfully used there. In some cities with an appropriate housing stock and ownership, and combined with significant additional activity, FACE was very helpful. By itself, however, FACE did not provide all the tools necessary to generate private-sector reinvestment and New York supplied neither the necessary additional ingredients nor the strategy to make them work.

Ansonborough, Charleston

By the 1950s, Ansonborough, the area just north of Charleston's "old and historic district," was a victim of deteri-

Charleston, 1974. Abandoned and deteriorating buildings acquired with money from its revolving fund by the Historic Charleston Foundation in Ansonborough. *(Alexander Garvin)*

oration. Most of its 135 antebellum structures were vacant or dilapidated. The Historic Charleston Foundation, a local preservationist group, began a drive to preserve this decaying seven-block neighborhood. A first step came in 1966, when the foundation persuaded the city to enlarge its historic district to include Ansonborough. Next, it persuaded the city to install distinctive street signs identifying the area's special character.[16]

Charleston, 1991. The same buildings in Ansonborough (now restored) more than 15 years after they were sold by the Historic Charleston Foundation. *(Alexander Garvin)*

Charleston, 1991. St. Andrews Lutheran Church, whose parishioners were among the pioneers in the revitalization of Ansonborough. *(Alexander Garvin)*

Decades of experience had demonstrated that landmark status, by itself, did not result in preservation. There also had to be a way of getting Ansonborough's fine old buildings into the hands of owners who would restore them. The foundation did this through a revolving fund, which it used to acquire buildings, occasionally demolishing them, sometimes restoring their façades, rarely restoring interiors, and always reselling them with protective covenants that ensured appropriate restoration and continuous exterior preservation (see Chapter 17).

By December 1972, The Historic Charleston Foundation had acquired and demolished seven buildings that were incompatible with the rest of Ansonborough. It also bought and moved four historic structures into the area and purchased another 54 buildings. Eight of these buildings were rehabilitated inside and out, five as rental properties and three for resale. Most important, the foundation persuaded banks to provide their ultimate owners with the mortgages they needed to finance acquisition and renovation.

In less than a decade, the revolving fund had been involved with one-third of Ansonborough's buildings. Another third were improved by their owners. As a result, between 1959 and 1972, property values tripled, and by 1980, nearly every building in Ansonborough had been rehabilitated.

Many Charleston-area residents, both natives and new arrivals, perceived Ansonborough's potential. They were attracted by the comparatively low prices of its historic buildings and eager to settle in this extremely convenient inner-city neighborhood. But they were not willing to become pioneers unless a substantial number of its vacant and dilapidated buildings were renovated.

The Historic Charleston Foundation acted as the catalytic agent needed to generate market interest in Ansonborough and to persuade banks to lend money in the area. Once a ready market of potential residents had been attracted and banks had been persuaded to provide financing, Historic Charleston used its revolving fund to keep the rehabilitation ball rolling. Restrictive covenants provided the necessary guarantees of continued maintenance and, thus, confidence in the area's future. Ansonborough's new residents did the rest.

Victorian District, Savannah

Like Charleston, Savannah had had substantial experience with historic preservation when civic leaders decided to address the problems of its Victorian District (see Chapters 2 and 17). Preservationists hoped that a revolving fund, similar to the one that had been so successful in Ansonborough, could be used to revive the Victorian District. Moreover, they were particularly eager to demonstrate that revitalization could be accomplished without significant gentrification.[17]

The dozen wards that make up Savannah's 150-block Victorian District were built up after the Civil War with opulent one-family houses and more modest row houses. Like countless other inner-city neighborhoods, its larger residences went out of fashion after World War II. The district's lovely housing, however, appealed to the city's African-American population, a portion of which had lived in the modest Beach Institute section of the neighborhood since the Civil War. Because many African-American households could not afford the Victorian District's larger residences, some owners con-

Savannah, 1990. Restored buildings in the Victorian District. *(Alexander Garvin)*

verted their buildings into multiple dwellings. Others just cut back on maintenance.

Leopold Adler II, the man who spearheaded the effort to save the district, was an investment banker who had been deeply involved with the Historic Savannah Foundation (HSF) in its successful efforts to preserve the city's 26 antebellum wards. Now he wanted to prove that classic structures could be restored while at the same time "preserving the neighborhood's racial and economic mix, its social fabric." Rather than depend on Historic Savannah with its citywide constituency and downtown focus, he organized a nonprofit corporation, the Savannah Landmark Rehabilitation Project (SLRP), to concentrate on the Victorian District. SLRP scrounged for money everywhere: grants from the National Endowment for the Arts, the Ford Foundation, the federal Comprehensive Employment Training Act (CETA), and a variety of public institutions; charitable contributions from interested individuals; loans from HUD, the National Trust for Historic Preservation, and virtually every bank in Savannah.

In 1979, 5 years after Adler began the fight to revitalize the neighborhood, the Historic Savannah Foundation joined the fray, establishing its own Victorian District Rehabilitation Project. It was a classic revolving fund with $100,000 from the foundation combined with $130,000 of Savannah's CDBG funds. The city added another $100,000 in 1983. HSF continued its proven policy of acquiring clusters of properties depending on their availability, price, and architectural significance, then reselling them with restrictive covenants requiring prompt authentic restoration and ongoing maintenance.

Unlike New York City, where CETA-assisted sweat-equity rehabilitation resulted in mortgage defaults and virtually no job placement in private industry, SLRP's mortgages are current in debt-service payments and two-thirds of its 200 CETA workers were able to obtain jobs in private industry (see Chapter 10). However, as in New York, when Congress terminated the CETA Program, subsidized sweat-equity rehabilitation came to an end. Similarly, HUD cutbacks in its low-interest mortgage programs resulted in termination of subsidized construction.

When Historic Savannah terminated its project in 1988, it had rehabilitated 24 structures containing 51 dwelling units and returned $102,500 to the city of Savannah. By that time SLRP had rehabilitated another 260 housing units and built 44 infill units.[18]

After nearly 15 years of hard work by both SLRP and HSF, the Victorian District was still riddled with vacant and dilapidated structures that were a major fire hazard. The situation became sufficiently serious that in 1989 the Savannah City Council passed an ordinance empowering the city to demolish any privately owned structure considered to be a public nuisance.[19]

SLRP and HSF had been unable to generate enough private investment to preserve the bulk of the neighborhood's many beautiful buildings because existing neighborhood residents were too poor to pay more for their housing and thus to cover either additional maintenance expenditures or the additional debt service on loans that paid for rehabilitation. With little hope of additional revenue, property owners continued their inadequate spending on maintenance. Thus, the pioneers who renovated buildings in the Victorian District were not followed by their neighbors.

Savannah, 1990. Two decades after the establishment of two revolving funds, dozens of buildings remained unaffected by this effort to reverse further deterioration in the Victorian District. *(Alexander Garvin)*

The admirable efforts to preserve Savannah's Victorian District demonstrate that a charming housing stock, a beneficent government, determined nonprofit preservation agencies, and willing lending institutions are not enough. There also must be existing residents, as there were in Wooster Square, or migrants, as there were in Ansonborough, who have the money to pay for renovation.

New York City's Neighborhood Preservation Program

New York City's Neighborhood Preservation Program (NPP) is one of the few neighborhood revitalization programs created by city planners. Beginning in the 1960s, the City Planning Commission had recognized the need for a balance between preservation and new construction. It insisted on including housing rehabilitation in most urban renewal projects, allocated money for housing rehabilitation when it issued the city's draft capital budget, called for a major commitment to preventive renewal in the city's master plan, and prepared a number of program proposals for Mayors Robert F. Wagner and John Lindsay, both of whom were eager to develop successful strategies for neighborhood conservation.

When I entered city government in 1970, Donald Elliott, then chairman of the City Planning Commission, asked me to develop a neighborhood revitalization strategy that the Lindsay Administration could implement. We spent the next three years fighting to have the Housing and Development Administration (HDA) try it. The city's housing establishment opposed any major allocation of funds to neighborhood revitalization because it did not produce *additional* housing. Besides, it believed that the city's housing programs should be determined by federal assistance, which was largely devoted to new construction. Skepticism about neighborhood revitalization was further fueled by unhappy experiences with federally assisted code enforcement and city-assisted municipal rehabilitation loans. As long as Washington provided billions for redevelopment and new construction, there was little hope of changing this attitude.

In 1973, in the wake of Nixon's moratorium on all federal housing assistance, John Zuccotti, Elliott's successor as chairman of the City Planning Commission, persuaded Mayor Lindsay to issue Executive Order Number 80. It instructed the City Planning Commission to designate neighborhood preservation areas and the HDA to establish local offices "to coordinate governmental and community activities for neighborhood preservation...and to provide adequate public investment to support coordinated improvement programs."[20]

The City Planning Commission held public hearings and designated five neighborhood preservation areas: Washington Heights and Clinton in Manhattan, Crown Heights and Bushwick in Brooklyn, and West Tremont in the Bronx. HDA hired a staff of 100 and opened five neighborhood offices. However, it had neither a clear notion of what "neighborhood preservation" meant, nor specific strategies for any of the very different areas that had been designated.[21]

As devised by the City Planning Department, NPP was directed to neighborhoods where the existing housing stock was still essentially sound and attractive but deteriorating and only in need of moderate rehabilitation. The idea was to target minimal amounts of city money and personnel in a manner that would induce the private sector to eventually resume full operation in these neighborhoods.

City money and personnel were used to create two new entities that together were intended to stimulate the necessary private sector activity: decentralized housing offices and the New York City Rehabilitation Mortgage Insurance Corporation (REMIC). In response, 11 commercial banks and 23 savings banks established an independent, not-for-profit corporation, the Commmunity Preservation Corporation (CPC), to provide rehabilitation mortgage financing.

Local offices were essential to program effectiveness. They were catalytic agents, on one hand, stimulating property owners to spend small sums on building repair and maintenance while, on the other, persuading fellow bureaucrats in city agencies to be more responsive to community needs. Like the Wooster Square urban-renewal office, they provided a place in the neighborhood where both residents and property owners could come with their problems. The local offices were soon familiar with every community complaint. They had to be responsive because they would be judged by improvements in the neighborhood, rather than by the amount of paper they processed. As a result, the staff did not wait passively for neighborhood business; it went out to generate it.

The city appropriated $7.9 million from its capital budget to start REMIC. Most of the money went into a mortgage insurance fund, initially limited to covering 20 times the amount in potential coverage. Borrowers paid an annual premium of approximately one-half of 1 percent of the outstanding principal balance of each insured loan. The income from premium fees and investments was intended to cover REMIC's operating expenses and any mortgage insurance contract obligations.[22]

REMIC insurance successfully overcame the reluctance of lending institutions to provide mortgages. It also established standards that would be used for mortgages outside the preservation areas. By 1990, REMIC had insured more than $102 million in mortgages for the rehabilitation of 291 buildings containing 14,284 apartments. Only $122,000 in insurance had to be paid—to cover a mortgage default on 1 building containing 36 apartments.[23]

During the 1980s, REMIC declined in importance because the state of New York established its own mortgage insurance program, SONY MAE. Its requirements were less rigid. More important, banks were more comfortable relying on the financial stability of the state.

In the beginning, most bank lending officers knew little about the city's Neighborhood Preservation Program or about REMIC. They were so worried about their existing loan portfolios that they avoided all but the very safest mortgages. Thus, a new lending institution for the five neighborhood preservation areas was essential. However, when the Community Preservation Corporation was established, its directors and officers were just as skeptical about lending in these areas. They began by restricting their lending to two neighborhoods: Crown Heights and Washington Heights.

Over the next few years, CPC developed underwriting techniques and skilled personnel that allowed it to expand into other neighborhoods and even provide mortgage money for new construction. By 1994, CPC had extended more than $1 billion in mortgages for 34,500 apartments.[24]

In 1974, when I became HDA deputy commissioner, REMIC only had printed application forms; CPC had just opened its offices; and, in an indication of the city's fiscal crisis to come, I was instructed to terminate 15 percent of the staff. The next 6 months were spent reorganizing, training personnel, and devising preservation strategies for each area.

Just as the neighborhood offices were beginning to generate owner-sponsored repairs and to issue city-financed rehabilitation mortgages, New York City's fiscal crisis nearly terminated the program. With the city unable to issue additional bonds, there was no way to continue raising money to lend to property owners for rehabilitation. The budget crisis made it difficult to maintain enough staff to run five offices. Consequently, the program had to concentrate on Crown Heights and Washington Heights, the neighborhoods to which CPC had decided to restrict its operations. The other three offices became token operations.[25]

With virtually no city money and minimal personnel, HDA revised the program to become more dependent on private sector activity. It obtained state legislation altering the J-51 Tax Exemption/Abatement Program and establishing the Participation Loan Program (see Chapter 10). It shifted all construction lending to commercial banks. It began making joint bank-city rehabilitation loans at below-market interest rates. It replaced city bond proceeds with federal Community Development Block Grant assistance as the source of funds for city mortgages. For the first time, the city was generating several dollars of private money for every public dollar lent for housing rehabilitation and doing so without charging a cent to the city budget.[26]

In order to avoid displacing neighborhood residents who could not afford higher rents, the administration asked Washington to set aside federal Section 8 subsidies for qualified tenants in buildings whose rehabilitation was financed with Participation Loans. These subsidies, which had not been available prior to 1974, permitted the program to subsidize neighborhood residents who could not afford increased rent and would otherwise have had to move.

Instead of more government spending or more government services, each preservation office directed existing government activity to critical sections of the neighborhood. The notion was that if a small number of problem buildings in each neighborhood were improved, local conditions would improve overall. In Crown Heights, for example, activity was targeted to large corner apartment houses. In Washington Heights, it was directed to small clusters of blocks.

Once critical buildings were identified, the preservation office sent rehabilitation specialists to ascertain what required immediate attention. With this list in hand, the office estimated the cost of repairs and negotiated with the owner to voluntarily make repairs. In exchange, local office reached into the bureaucracy downtown to help owners obtain services that owners were entitled to receive but were either inadequately represented or insufficiently skilled to obtain.

This selective effort to obtain "voluntary repair agreements" was far more effective in producing repairs than official inspections, which catalogued code violations for the city's computer without obtaining improved living conditions. It was particularly effective when combined with mortgage financing for moderate rehabilitation. In Washington Heights, over the next 15 years, nearly *one-fifth* of the housing stock was renovated.

Washington Heights, Manhattan

Washington Heights is the northern portion of Manhattan Island, extending from 155th Street to the Harlem River. In 1970 approximately 187,000 people lived in the neighborhood's 75,500 apartments: 15 percent were African American and 9 percent, Hispanic; 11 percent were on welfare, a figure

Manhattan, 1994. Aerial view of Washington Heights where two decades of effort by the staff of New York City's Neighborhood Preservation Program resulted in the renovation of 14,000 apartments. *(Alexander Garvin)*

Manhattan, 1992. Apartment buildings on West 181st Street in Washington Heights that continued to remain in good condition or were renovated with assistance from the Neighborhood Preservation Program. *(Alexander Garvin)*

lower than the city average. When Washington Heights was designated a Neighborhood Preservation Area, there was almost no abandoned housing. Its 3000, largely post-1929 structures were built to modern standards and contained better apartment layouts with larger rooms.[27]

Many of the neighborhood's predominantly five- and six-story apartment buildings were deteriorating. They required replacement or upgrading of basic mechanical systems, weatherproofing, and security systems. This work had been deferred because banks were unwilling to make new mortgage loans.

The social stress of adjusting to population changes only complicated matters. Although large areas of Washington Heights continued to be German, Jewish, and Irish enclaves, there had been a significant increase in the Hispanic population. If population change was perceived as a downgrading of the neighborhood, property owners might be less attentive to building management and maintenance. Consequently, the Preservation Office targeted its activity in a manner that was intended to reassure older neighborhood residents that landlords were investing in property improvements. It also directed attention to those sections that were receiving increasing numbers of newcomers.

Responsibility for the program's success in Washington Heights lies with the directors of the neighborhood office, in particular Michael Lappin and Barbara Leeds. Lappin became director in June 1974. For the next year and a half he trained the staff, established an ongoing relationship with community leaders, and reached out to property owners to bring them into the program. Lappin became the Washington Heights loan officer for Community Preservation Corporation, and in 1980 its president. He was succeeded by Barbara Leeds who remained director until 1984. In 1990, she became Assistant Housing Commissioner for Rehabilitation Finance in charge of all the city's real estate tax- and mortgage-assistance programs for housing rehabilitation.

Leeds devised the strategy that targeted the post-fiscal-crisis programs to the critical sections of Washington Heights. It ignored the very strongest market areas, where little help was required. Instead, the office directed its initial attention to the rest of the neighborhood's fundamentally sound housing and later expanded into nearby weaker areas. Activity in the most deteriorated areas, which required massive subsidies, was deferred until suitable programs became available (as they did in the early 1980s when the New York City Housing Authority and private developers were able to undertake gut rehabilitation with the heavy subsidies provided by the Section 8 Program).

When Edward I. Koch became mayor in 1978, 1500 apartments had been rehabilitated under a variety of mortgage-assistance programs; 9300 apartments had been upgraded through landlord repair agreements; and 4000 apartments had benefited from buildingwide improvements assisted by J-51 Tax Exemption/Abatement. The new administration added the one element of a true neighborhood revitalization effort that the city's fiscal crisis had precluded: additional funds for public services and community facilities. The public services were distributed by a task force that coordinated city activities in Washington Heights. In addition, the City Planning Commission designated Washington Heights a Neighborhood Strategy Area, in which it concentrated CDBG and Capital Budget projects. This resulted in a major program of park rehabilitation, sanitation services, infrastructure replacement, and assistance for the elderly.[28]

No neighborhood revitalization program anywhere in the country has resulted in as much private investment as was generated in Washington Heights. As of 1990, the Neighborhood Preservation Program had obtained more than 1336 voluntary repair agreements involving 49,370 apartments. By 1993, the Community Preservation Corporation and the City of New York had extended $92.2 million in joint mortgages for the rehabilitation of 193 buildings containing 7064 apartments; and more than 405 buildings with 13,898 apartments had been rehabilitated under various public programs.[29]

In those sections of Washington Heights, north of the George Washington Bridge, for which the program had been devised and to which it was intensively directed, housing deterioration has been reversed and abandonment is minimal. In fact, dozens of buildings have been successfully converted to resident-owned cooperatives. In some spots developers have even resumed building small apartment buildings. Only south of the bridge, where moderate rehabilitation was insufficient and where residents were unable to afford higher rents, has the neighborhood continued to deteriorate.

The Fourth Ward, Charlotte

During the 1970s, when neighborhood revitalization efforts began in the Fourth Ward of Charlotte, North Carolina, the area had been disfigured by fire, unsafe building demolition, and increasing structural dilapidation. Three dozen structures

Charlotte, 1990. The John Newcomb House, whose renovation by the Junior League helped to spark the revitalization of the Fourth Ward. *(Alexander Garvin)*

Charlotte, 1990. New housing built by private developers attracted by the relandscaping of Fourth Ward Park and the housing rehabilitation projects throughout the neighborhood. *(Alexander Garvin)*

remained standing in the 20-block residential neighborhood, less than a 5-minute walk from Charlotte's business district.[30]

The Fourth Ward's increasing deterioration was especially startling because it had continued during a period when Charlotte's burgeoning economy had become a showpiece of the "new South." Furthermore, the city's residential market was expanding rapidly. Its population had grown from 134,000 in 1950 to 241,000 in 1960, and would be 315,000 in 1980.[31]

In 1975, a group of Charlotte residents came together to form an organization called Friends of Fourth Ward. They were united by their belief in the positive aspects of Charlotte's future, a commitment to living right in town, and a love of the dilapidated but charming Victorian buildings that remained in the Fourth Ward. James Dennis Rash, dean of students at the University of North Carolina at Charlotte (UNCC) became their informal leader.

Working with representatives of the city government and the business community, they developed a program that required action from both. The city agreed to close streets to through traffic, install new decorative brick paving, street lamps, street signs, and street trees, and acquire land for new neighborhood parks. It was also persuaded to rezone the area and to create a Historic District Commission for The Fourth Ward that would review all development for compatibility with the area's historic character.

The Junior League took the lead by acquiring and renovating one of the Fourth Ward's most significant structures, the John Newcomb House. Duke Power Company paid for burying the Fourth Ward's utility lines. A consortium of seven local banks joined with the city government to create a below-market-rate-interest mortgage fund that lent money to residents ready to purchase, build, and renovate houses or apartments in the neighborhood. North Carolina National Bank (NCNB) established a wholly owned, nonprofit subsidiary to act as a development catalyst.

The mortgage fund was established by selling tax-exempt city revenue bonds to local banks. The lower rate of interest paid on tax-exempt bonds allowed the fund to lend money at lower than market interest rates. During its 6 years in existence, the fund issued $25 million in mortgages to purchasers of new and old one-family structures, row houses, and condominium apartments. These loans were especially attractive because the fund had been established before the escalation in interest rates during the late 1970s and early 1980s. Thus, they carried interest rates that were often less than half those available anywhere else in the region.

These mortgages could be assumed by any purchaser. Consequently, reselling a house or condo in the Fourth Ward was easier than in many suburban areas. By the time the fund ran out of money in 1981, it had financed the restoration of 32 old houses, the construction of 10 new one-family homes, and the purchase of several hundred new and converted condominium apartments.

The role of NCNB Community Development Corporation (CDC) was no less critical than its mortgage fund. NCNB-CDC acquired and renovated a 1929 apartment building and built new townhouses. Altogether, it initiated four projects involving 112 apartments. These efforts triggered the interest of other developers who went on to erect additional buildings.

By 1990, the Fourth Ward's image had changed. Its 1164 housing units had become a popular alternative for Charlotte residents seeking attractive in-town living opportunities. Real estate tax assessment increased more than nine times for just the period from 1975 to 1982, and tax revenues during that period jumped from $23,000 to $300,000.

Ingredients of Success

Any successful neighborhood revitalization effort must attract or retain a residential market large enough to occupy all existing buildings, provide these consumers with the amenities they demand, and make available the credit needed by property owners, developers, and purchasers who want to renovate and build residences that they can afford. This requires a strategy and some entity to implement it.

Market

Many cities have attractive but deteriorating neighborhoods. Like Wooster Square, they may be losing population and need to keep residents from moving away. Or, like Ansonborough and the Fourth Ward, they may have already lost much of their market and need to attract new residents. In either case, successful revitalization programs will have to alter consumer perceptions and make the neighborhood competitive in price with its rivals.

The techniques for successfully altering market perception are the same for neighborhoods that need to retain residents as they are for neighborhoods that are seeking newcomers. Blighted structures must be renovated or, where necessary, replaced with attractive new residences that are compatible in size, scale, and character with the rest of the neighborhood. In both New Haven and Charlotte, pockets of blight were removed, and with them, their negative impact on perceptions of the neighborhood.

There also must be visible evidence of investment. A neighborhood need not have special signs that designate it as being in a preservation area, as does Ansonborough. But streets and sidewalks must be kept in good repair and be well lighted. Street trees help, as do new park facilities. Without $8 million in municipal expenditures for street and sidewalk repaving and relighting, new vest-pocket parks, and new street trees, New Haven residents would have had little confidence in the continuing improvement of Wooster Square. Similarly, without the $4 million that Charlotte spent on repaving streets and sidewalks, creating and landscaping parkland, and installing new street signs and street lamps in the Fourth Ward, few city residents would have considered moving into the neighborhood.

Reassurance can also come from visible investment in privately owned residential buildings. New York's Community Preservation Corporation requires every rehabilitation mortgage to include money for steam-cleaning building façades. In Ansonborough, Historic Charleston often restored building façades before putting houses up for sale and always put up prominent signs indicating that preservation was under way.

Visible community investment, however, will not spur further rehabilitation if people are not willing or able to pay for it. A variety of subsidies can lower prices and thereby reach a larger market. Charlotte issued revenue bonds, which because of their tax-exempt status, had a below-market-rate interest. New York City allocated CDBG funds to be lent at one percent interest.

Location

Neighborhood revitalization can exploit locational advantages. Wooster Square and the Fourth Ward had the benefit of proximity to downtown business districts. Proximity, however, is less important than an attractive housing stock. Wooster Square and Ansonborough had lovely wood frame houses. Washington Heights was filled with handsome masonry apartment buildings. There are areas, however, like the Lower East Side tenements described by Jacob Riis or the dilapidated shacks cleared for Techwood Homes in Atlanta, that cannot be made attractive enough to be part of a successful neighborhood revitalization program. Thus, successful revitalization strategies must be tailored to the specific area characteristics. There is no point to targeting a program like FACE, which provides no assistance for multiple dwellings, to a neighborhood like Crown Heights, where most people live in multiple dwellings. In the same way, there was no reason to restrict activity in the Fourth Ward to preservation of the area's historic structures, when the area's many empty lots called for a program that included scattered new construction.

Design

Revitalization programs cannot alter a neighborhood's basic physical characteristics. A neighborhood with historic antebellum structures like those of Ansonborough may need a promotional effort to highlight its attractions. In such areas, installing street signs that dramatize its historic character, planting street trees, and repairing and resurfacing streets and sidewalks may be enough to trigger private investment. Washington Heights, on the other hand, was already a popular area when New York City decided to make it the centerpiece of its Neighborhood Preservation Program. Its buildings required rewiring, replumbing, new windows, and general reconditioning—not promotion.

Financing

Neighborhood revitalization is not possible unless lending institutions provide mortgage financing. Often banks avoid involvement in deteriorating neighborhoods because lending money for rehabilitation is not as simple as underwriting new construction or issuing mortgages for the purchase of a one-family house. The process cannot be standardized. Buildings vary too much in design, condition, neighborhood setting, and marketability. In Charleston and Savannah preservation enthusiasts, community leaders, and public officials persuaded banks to provide mortgages for their cities' historically significant, older housing stock. In Charlotte they persuaded the NCNB to sponsor the revitalization effort in one neighborhood, the Fourth Ward.

Some banks are willing to pioneer preservation areas. NCNB did so because it understood that the bank's success was "tied directly to the vitality of the economy where it does business [and that] if NCNB was to continue to thrive in Charlotte, the local economy must also continue to thrive."[32] Taking a risk on the Fourth Ward was quite profitable. NCNB became the prime construction lender in the neighborhood and obtained market-interest rates on all these loans. The new residential market that was created also allowed it to become the neighborhood's leading permanent lender of conventional market-rate mortgages.

In New York the city government established a corporation that insured institutional mortgages in neighborhoods designated by the City Planning Commission for preservation. New York's Community Preservation Corporation then concentrated on the designated neighborhoods, developed underwriting techniques that were appropriate to building conditions in those neighborhoods, and trained its staff to make the necessary loans.

Entrepreneurship

Neighborhood revitalization does not occur spontaneously. Somebody must own, renovate, and maintain the housing. In Charleston and Savannah, local preservationists established nonprofit entities to purchase vacant and dilapidated buildings. Then they either sold the property to an owner who agreed to do the necessary work or the preservationists did the work themselves and then sold the property to a responsible new owner. The NCNB Community Development Corporation entered into joint ventures with local developers to purchase, build, and renovate houses and apartment buildings in the Fourth Ward.

One thing is certain: Without a catalytic agent to start the ball rolling and generate the necessary level of activity the only neighborhoods that will improve are those like Washington's Dupont Circle that will get better on their own and need no government assistance. The type of catalyst should reflect local conditions. In Ansonborough and the Fourth Ward, it was a nonprofit foundation. In Wooster Square, this role was performed by the urban-renewal office. New York established and staffed neighborhood offices that reached out to building owners to offer them help in obtaining mortgage financing and then reached into the bureaucracy to speed processing by the city's own agencies.

Time

Changing a neighborhood requires time. That means a long-term commitment. The FACE Program was intended to last 3 years. In Crown Heights and many other neighborhoods it was extended to 5 years—not enough to reverse the results of decades of deterioration. It took a dozen or more years to revitalize Wooster Square, Ansonborough, and the Fourth Ward. We must, therefore, stop thinking of neighborhood revitalization as a temporary government function and make it an ongoing operation.

Neighborhood Revitalization as a Planning Strategy

Continuing neighborhood deterioration only leads to expensive remedial action. The year before New York established its Neighborhood Preservation Program, it spent more than $28 million just for emergency-vacate relocation, unsafe-building demolition, and emergency repairs. Even if such remedial expenses are ignored, the replacement cost of the lost housing represents a capital investment larger than most cities will make over several generations. Adding the cost of rebuilding the wide variety of lost community facilities, boarded-up stores, and abandoned institutions makes the price staggering. Duplicating the "community glue" that they provided takes far longer than just rebuilding them. Surely it is far cheaper and less time-consuming to spend a little now than vast sums over many years replacing whole neighborhoods.

The amazing thing about the failure to invest in neighborhood revitalization is that there is hardly any opposition to such expenditures. Suburban communities support it because it reduces pressure on the suburban market. Stable urban communities support it because it eliminates the threat of spreading blight. The only opponents are self-appointed advocates of the poor, who decry possible displacement sometime in the future when neighborhood deterioration has been reversed.

Displacement need not occur. As has been demonstrated in Washington Heights, existing low-income neighborhood residents who cannot otherwise afford renovated housing can be retained by targeting subsidies. Such directed expenditures are cheaper and less disruptive than allowing the neighborhood to deteriorate around residents who have to remain until unsafe conditions finally force them out.

Sporadic efforts to fight neighborhood deterioration are not good enough. The effort must be determined, ongoing, and national. I propose that Congress enact a National Neighborhood Revitalization Act that provides assistance to locally designated and federally approved neighborhood revitalization areas. The program would be administered at the local level and paid for jointly by local lending institutions, the city, and federal governments. Like Title I urban renewal, each locality would establish an agency that would prepare and administer its revitalization strategy. But, unlike Title I, it would not require billions in federal appropriations, nor would the revitalization agency be an entirely government entity. It would be jointly operated and funded by local lending institutions and the city government.

The program would include mortgage insurance, local lending offices, a below-market-interest loan pool created from the proceeds of tax-exempt municipal bonds, subsidies for residents who cannot afford a moderate increase in the cost of their housing, and a capital improvement program for city-owned infrastructure and community facilities. Of these, mortgage insurance and antidisplacement subsidies would come from the national government. The rest would be tailored to local conditions and be operated as local institutions.

The mortgage insurance would be similar to the FHA-220 program that operated so successfully in urban-renewal areas. It would require an initial Congressional appropriation to begin operations. The program itself would be financed from standard FHA mortgage insurance premiums.[33]

The antidisplacement program would be patterned after the Section 8 Existing Housing Program, which was so effectively used in Washington Heights. It would apply to persons of low income living in buildings that were renovated with FHA insured mortgages. If these low-income residents could not afford postrehabilitation rents they would receive a housing voucher subsidizing the difference between 30 percent of income and the new rent.

Each locality's revitalization strategy would be jointly developed by the local government and the lending institutions with responsibility for its implementation. While program components, like FHA mortgage insurance and antidisplacement subsidies would be the same everywhere, they would be targeted based on local information and local objectives. Much of the data upon which these strategies would be based on is already collected. It is just not gathered in a manner that is useful to communities trying to fight neighborhood deterioration or to banks trying to decide whether to make mortgage loans. We now have the computer technology to match the necessary data and to display and map this information by block, lot, and building. Under the National Neighborhood Revitalization Act, HUD would specify the format for the data, prepare the software, and provide it free to all cities that participated in the program. Each local revitalization office would operate the system, publish reports, and pay for maintaining the resulting information system.

The prime lending agency for each revitalization area would differ depending on the strategy that has been selected. Like Charlotte, some cities may prefer existing institutions operating an office within the revitalization area. Others may choose to establish an entirely new entity, like New York's Community Preservation Corporation. But whatever the format, specific lending institutions would be committed to investing in the area.

Similarly, some cities would establish below-market-interest-rate mortgage pools from the proceeds of tax-exempt local borrowing. Others would allocate a portion of their Community Development block grant. These mortgage pools might be operated by the local revitalization agency, as is the case in New York, or by a local bank, as happened in Charlotte. Whatever the source of the money or the mechanism for distributing it, property owners would be able to get conventional mortgages at low enough rates of interest to allow them to make repairs and improvements that would not otherwise be financially feasible.

No bank is likely to agree to invest in a neighborhood if its government partner defers expenditures on needed public improvements. Thus, the extent and pace of public improvements would be determined by a revitalization strategy that lending institutions and local governments jointly prepared and administered.

Once Congress enacts the National Neighborhood Revitalization Act, local governments will have to cease ignoring transitional neighborhoods. They will be forced into a dialogue with residents and property owners who will wish to participate in the program. They also will be forced to stop deferring needed public improvements in these areas. Lending institutions will have to develop practices and train staff to make rehabilitation loans. Thus, for the first time, residents, property owners, lending institutions, and local governments will be devoting the time and money needed to prevent decent city neighborhoods from deteriorating.

Notes

1. Walter Firey, *Land Use in Central Boston,* Harvard University Press, Cambridge, 1947, and Brian J. Godfrey, *Neighborhoods in Transition: The Making of San Francisco's Ethnic and Nonconformist Communities,* University of California Press, Berkeley, 1988.
2. Langston Hughes, "My Early Days in Harlem," *Harlem: A Community in Transition,* J. H. Clarke (editor), The Citadel Press, New York, 1964, p. 62.
3. Malcolm X, *The Autobiography of Malcolm X,* Grove Press, Inc., New York, 1964, p. 76.
4. Anthony Downs, *Residential Rent Controls, an Evaluation,* The Urban Land Institute, Washington, D.C., 1988, p. 19.
5. Karen Kollias with Arthur Naparstek and Chester Haskell, *Neighborhood Reinvestment—A Citizen's Compendium for Programs and Strategies,* The National Center for Urban Ethnic Affairs, Washington, D.C., 1977; Stephen A. Kliment (editor), *Neighborhood Conservation—A Source Book.* The Whitney Library of Design, New York, 1975; Real Estate Research Corporation, *Neighborhood Preservation—A Catalogue of Local Programs,* The Office of Policy Research, Department of Housing and Urban Development, Washington, D.C., 1975.
6. Historical and statistical information on Wooster Square is derived from Mary Hommann, *Wooster Square Design,* New Haven Redevelopment Agency, New Haven, 1965; New Haven Redevelopment Agency, *1967 Annual Report,* New Haven Redevelopment Agency, New Haven, 1967; and Alan Talbot, *The Mayor's Game,* Harper & Row, New York, 1967, pp. 107–109 and 136–147.
7. Find/SVP information services.
8. A third FACE area, Highbridge in the Bronx, received HUD funding

between 1971 and 1973. Its housing stock was as inappropriate for code enforcement and Section 312 mortgages as was the East Concourse.

9. Historical and statistical material on Crown Heights is derived from Edward A. Gibbs (Assistant Commissioner FACE), *Crown Heights Federal Code Enforcement Program, March 7, 1967–March 6, 1972,* City of New York Housing and Development Administration, New York, 1972 and Alexander Garvin (Project Director), *Crown Heights Area Maintenance Program (CHAMP),* vols. 1, 2, and 3. New York City Planning Department, New York, 1972.
10. Between 1943 and 1971, when the N.Y. State Legislature instituted a "Maximum Base Rent" formula permitting annual 7.5 percent rent increases, owners of continuously occupied rent-controlled apartments in New York City were only permitted two across-the-board rent increases—15 percent in 1953 and 8 percent in 1970.
11. Alexander Garvin (Project Director), op. cit., vol. 3, p. 21.
12. For the evolution of the city's commitment to "preventive renewal" see, New York City Planning Commission, *New York City's Renewal Strategy/1965,* Community Renewal Program, New York City, 1965; *Between Promise and Performance…,* Community Renewal Program, New York City, 1968; and *Plan for New York City vol. 1: Critical Issues,* New York City, 1969, pp. 138–143.
13. Violations per se are meaningless. A building with recorded violations, even a myriad of violations, may be in very good condition. For example, failure to have the proper frame around a required document is a violation; so is a nonfunctioning boiler. One has no impact on living conditions; the other is fundamental.
14. Housing inspectors could only enter one- or two-unit buildings in which their visit had been authorized by the owner-occupant, a complaint had been filed, or a warrant had been issued.
15. Alexander Garvin (Project Director), op. cit., vol. 1, pp. 41–43.
16. Historical and statistical material on Ansonborough is derived from Arthur P. Ziegler, Jr., Leopold Adler, II, and Walter C. Kidney, *Revolving Funds for Historic Preservation: A Manual of Practice,* Ober Park Associates, Inc., Pittsburgh, 1975, pp. 56–61, and the Historic Charleston Foundation.
17. Historical and statistical material on the Victorian District is derived from Mary L. Morrison (editor), *Historic Savannah,* Historic Savannah Foundation, Savannah, 1979; Historic Savannah Foundation, "Victorian District Revolving Fund Report 1979–June 1988," unpublished, 1988; Chris Warner, "Attractive Housing For Savannah's Poor," *Urban Land,* Urban Land Institute, Washington, D.C., February 1989, pp. 21–23; and Stephanie Churchill (Executive Director Historic Savannah Foundation), interview, June 15, 1990.
18. HSF ended its efforts in the Victorian District because it decided that, without massive subsidies, there was no way to preserve the Victorian District's deteriorating housing.
19. Michael Homans, "Nuisance Code Ready for Council," *Savannah Evening News,* October 4, 1989 and "City Council OK's Ordinance On Crack House Destruction, *Savannah Morning News,* October 20, 1989.
20. Alexander Garvin (Project Director), *Neighborhood Preservation in New York City,* New York City Planning Commission, New York, 1973, pp. 49–82 and 106–145.
21. The Neighborhood Preservation Program was made operational while Roger Starr was Housing Commissioner during the mayoralty of Abraham Beame and became a major production program under Housing Commissioner Nathan Leventhal when Edward I. Koch was mayor.
22. REMIC insures qualified portions of first mortgage loans by publicly regulated financial entities (i.e., savings banks, commercial banks, savings and loan associations, insurance companies, and pension funds). To be eligible for REMIC mortgage insurance, loans must be made to apartment buildings erected after 1901 within designated neighborhood preservation areas. They also must be at an interest rate not in excess of the ceiling imposed by the State Banking Board and be self-amortizing over terms ranging from 10 to 30 years. The insurance covers losses up to 90 percent of loans on the outstanding principal indebtedness incurred by rehabilitation and 20 percent of the outstanding principal indebtedness on funds used to refinance existing debt or to finance acquisition. However, in no case can the insurance exceed 50 percent of the total of both.
23. New York City Rehabilitation Mortgage Insurance Corporation (statistics cover the period from inception through October 31, 1990).
24. The Community Preservation Corporation, *1993 Annual Report,* New York, 1994 (statistics cover the period from inception through 1993).
25. In 1979 the program was expanded to cover 13 neighborhoods.
26. When the city's fiscal crisis was over, during the 1980s, the Koch Administration resumed using city capital funds for housing rehabilitation.
27. New York City Planning Commission, *Community Planning District Profiles,* New York City Planning Commission, New York, 1973.
28. Barbara Leeds, *New York City's Neighborhood Preservation Program in Washington Heights,* unpublished master's thesis, New York, 1981.
29. The Community Preservation Corporation (statistics cover the period from inception through April, 1993), New York City Department of Housing Preservation and Development. (Statistics for voluntary repair agreements cover the period January 1975 through June 1989. These figures include repeat agreements over this 15-year period and, thus, the actual number of buildings and apartments affected is lower than these totals.)
30. Historical and statistical material on Fourth Ward is derived from Christine Madigan, "The Revitalization of Fourth Ward, Charlotte North Carolina," unpublished, 1990; James Dennis Rash, "Privately Funded Redevelopment in North Carolina," *Urban Land,* Urban Land Institute, Washington, D.C., October 1983, pp. 2–7; Friends of Fourth Ward, *A Walk Through Historic Fourth Ward,* Loftin & Company, Charlotte, undated; M. S. Van Hecke, "Cheap Loans Ending, But Fourth Ward Survives," *The Charlotte Observer,* April 12, 1981; and correspondence and conversations with James Dennis Rash, during October and November, 1990.
31. U.S. Department of Commerce, Bureau of the Census, *Statistical Abstract of the United States, 1978,* p. 24, and *Statistical Abstract of the United States, 1989,* p. 33.
32. James Dennis Rash, op. cit., p. 3.
33. There would be no need for a special neighborhood revitalization mortgage insurance program if the mortgage insurance program I proposed had been enacted.

13

Residential Suburbs

East San Francisco Bay, 1993. *(Alexander Garvin)*

Many Americans think of suburbanization as a chaotic process that squanders both land and money. James Rouse, the developer of Columbia, Maryland, is eloquent in his denunciation:

> *Relentlessly, the bits and pieces of a city are splattered across the landscape. By this irrational process, non-communities are born—formless places without order, beauty, or reason; with no visible respect for people or the land.*[1]

The alternative that he and many others have proposed is the planned new community. This is not an alternative; it is the prevailing situation.

As urban historian Kenneth Jackson explains in *Crabgrass Frontier:*

> *The theory that early suburbs just grew, with owners "turning cowpaths and natural avenues of traffic into streets," is erroneous.... Each city and most suburbs were created from many small real estate developments that reflected changing market conditions and local peculiarities.*[2]

These small suburban real estate developments grow out of a very rational human impulse: the attempt to escape the worst aspects of city life while simultaneously settling into an improved living environment. The combination of the PUSH away from the city with the PULL of something better is as old as city life itself. Pliny the Younger, writing nearly 2000 years ago about the commute from downtown Rome to his suburban home, tells a story that is repeated daily by tens of millions of Americans:

> *The place... is situated seventeen miles from [the city], so that after... having passed a constructive day, you come here to stay. It may be approached by more than one road.... [The roads] are difficult and long... In one area the road is hedged in by woods and in another it opens up and spreads out in broad meadows.*[3]

In latter twentieth-century America the commute is through a landscape that is filled with houses. There are more houses now because there are many more people in the United States who want and can afford the privacy, security, and independence of home ownership. As Herbert Hoover explained:

> *To possess one's own home is the hope and ambition of almost every individual in our country, whether he lives in*

Pelham, New York, 1988. Suburban residences "approached by more than one road...hedged in by woods...[and] broad meadows" [Pliny the Younger]. (*Alexander Garvin*)

hotel, apartment house, or tenement.... Those immortal ballads, Home Sweet Home, My Old Kentucky Home... were not written about tenements or apartments... they never sing songs about a pile of rent receipts.[4]

The woods and meadows are gone because every American wants his or her own little bit of nature: a green lawn sweeping up to a house, nestled among the trees and flowers, with blue sky and drifting clouds above—a vision that is not easily available in noisy, dirty, congested cities.

Developers have been supplying this market for two centuries. They acquire relatively inexpensive land and hold it until they can sell lots to home builders at a price that covers the costs of carrying the property (e.g., maintenance, taxes, and debt service), subdividing it into building lots, installing the necessary infrastructure (streets, water mains, drainage pipes, sewers, and utility lines), and a return on equity that justifies their time, effort, and risk.

Shrewd developers often profit from cheap land in outlying areas by exploiting changes in transportation technology. In the nineteenth century many developers invested simultaneously in land and the ferry, railroad, and mass transit systems that connected it with center cities. In the twentieth century outlying territory has been made accessible by government financed highways. Whatever the transportation technology, once their property is sufficiently accessible to the growing market for new homes, developers profit from their investment by selling to home builders.

Another method of profiting from suburbanization is by supplying building lots that include amenities not available at other locations. Some developers market gated communities that underscore an area's privacy and special character. Others offer swimming pools, golf courses, or tennis courts.

Local governments used to determine the location and character of suburbanization by installing the infrastructure prior to development. This altered the sequence of suburbanization because, all other factors being even, developers favored sites with infrastructure already installed rather than land that still needed major investment.

Despite the widespread abandonment of this planning technique, small, suburban, real estate developments are not now and never have been "splattered across the landscape." They have to meet community standards and be approved by government agencies. Nor are they "formless." They come in three identifiable varieties: rectilinear *plats,* curvilinear *subdivisions,* and (more recently) *cluster communities.* All three can provide attractive living environments. Unfortunately, when these individually satisfactory forms are combined, the resulting landscape can be quite disappointing for there is rarely any overall pattern to provide a means of orientation.

Not only have many local governments abandoned their responsibility for infrastructure, they also have abdicated their responsibility for providing public facilities, access to nature, and places for community interaction. The only truly public component of the suburban landscape, its traffic arteries, is usually a confusing hodgepodge.

We can change this pattern of suburbanization by giving it a public-space backbone that will provide pedestrians with a powerful means of orientation, establish a series of places for community interaction, and lessen the fragmentation of suburban life. This can be accomplished in newly developing areas by requiring individual developers to set aside for *public* use not just roadways but also open space. Private yards and commonly used facilities would not qualify. It would have to be new, open space available for general public use. A different open-space backbone is needed for existing suburbs. It can be established by acquiring leftover and underutilized property and combining it into a continuous system of public places. Both prescriptions require local legislation that is based on an informed understanding of the three principal varieties of suburban development: the plat, the subdivision, and the cluster community.

Suburban Plats

Some cities, such as Philadelphia, Chicago, and Detroit, expanded by filling in a preestablished plan. In states where settlement conformed to the rectilinear land surveys of the Northwest Ordinance or the Homestead Act, cities simply continued the legislated street grid. In other cases, they grew either by extending the existing street pattern to new territory, or, like St. Louis, New Orleans, and Atlanta, by starting a new one, parallel and perpendicular to such topographic features as a bend in the river, a cliff, or a railroad line. Still others grafted plats onto existing regional roads. In every instance, expansion had to satisfy two needs: circulation and lot sales. The only requirements were binding rights-of-way and legal documents that could be used to establish property boundaries, record ownership, easements, and liens, and title to the land.

Savannah

Savannah is a unique example of a more civilized approach to suburbanization. Until the Civil War, each time population pressures required the opening up of new territory, the city fathers simply extended James Oglethorpe's initial grid by adding another ward. Every ward was centered around a landscaped public square bounded by eight rectangular blocks (see Chapter 3). Four of these blocks were set aside for churches, schools, or other public buildings. The other four were each bisected by a service alley and divided into ten 60- by 90-foot house lots.[5]

In 1856, when Savannah abandoned this approach to expansion, there were 26 such wards. Thereafter developers accommodated new buildings by subdividing and recombining lots within existing wards (often replacing one-family homes

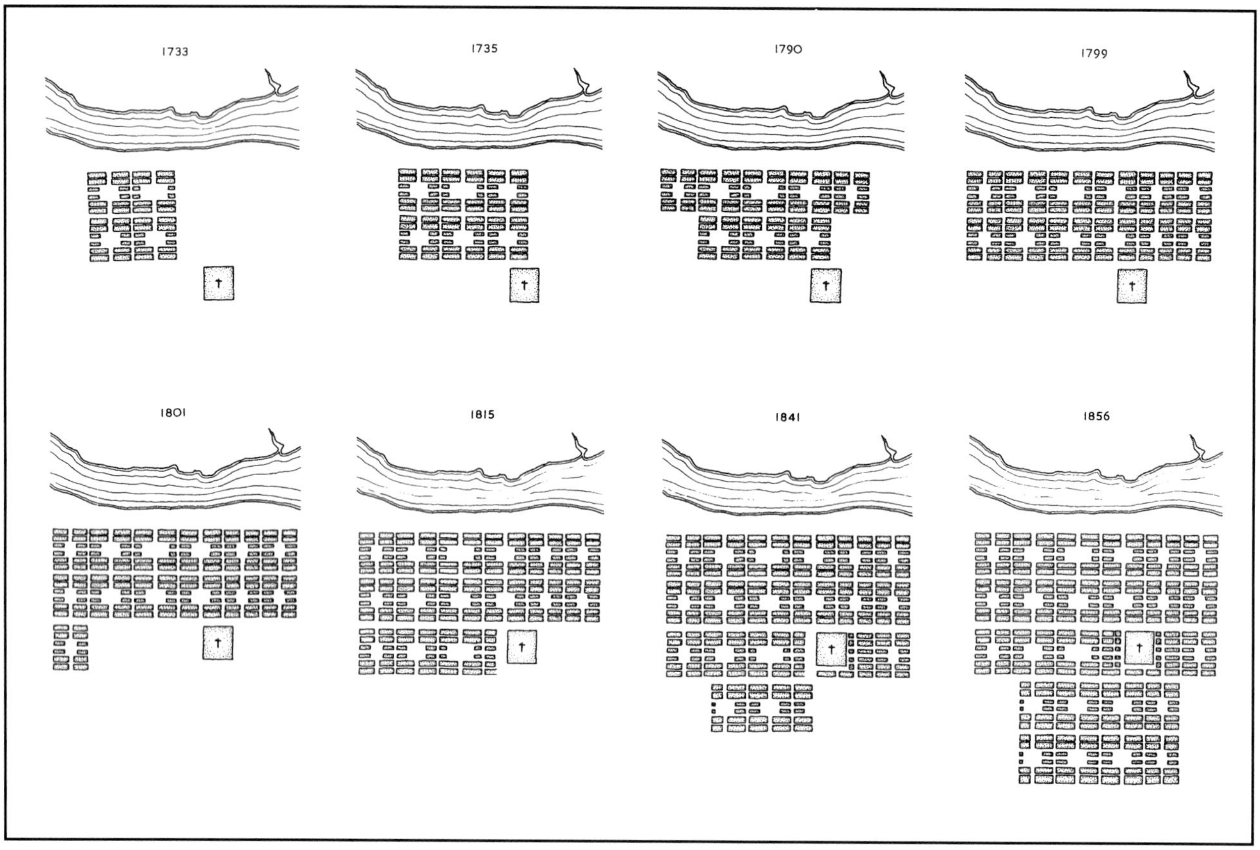

Savannah, 1733–1856. Suburban extension proceeded ward by ward in response to market demand. *(From John W. Reps, The Making of Urban America. Copyright by Princeton University Press 1965, reproduced by permission of Princeton University Press)*

with attached row houses) or by further extending a rectilinear pattern of streets and blocks, but without landscaped squares.

There is another type of suburban plat that goes beyond the creation of streets, blocks, and building lots. Like Savannah's wards, such plats often include open space, but augment it by also considering the commute into town and establishing property regulations that determine the future character of the community itself.

Brooklyn Heights and Prospect Park South

America's first suburban plat was Brooklyn Heights. In 1819, when developer Hezekiah Pierrepont first advertised lots for sale, Brooklyn was an agricultural hinterland inhabited by no more than a few thousand people. They were clustered around a village that had only been chartered three years earlier. The new suburb was a short walk from the village. More important, it was directly across the East River from New York City, which already had a population of nearly 123,000.[6]

Hezekiah Pierrepont was a financial backer of Robert Fulton, the man who built and operated America's first commercially successful steamboat and who, in 1814, established the world's first steamboat ferry service. The steam ferry took a mere 8 minutes to ply the waters between what is today Fulton Street in lower Manhattan, and Fulton Street in Brooklyn. Pierrepont owned 60 acres of relatively cheap agricultural land, with a spectacular view of New York harbor. By investing in the ferry, he transformed this Brooklyn acreage into valuable residential real estate.

Pierrepont's plat for Brooklyn Heights consisted of 50-foot-wide streets and 200- by 200-foot blocks subdivided into 25-foot-wide house lots. His advertisements described "a place of residence combining all the advantages of the country with most of the conveniences of the city...*for a summer residence, or the whole year*."[7] The first houses were built on sites made up of several lots. Within decades many of these sites had been subdivided and filled in with masonry row houses. Today, when many row houses in turn have been converted to multiple occupancy and others have been replaced by apartment buildings, it is hard to remember that Brooklyn Heights was once a low density commuter suburb.

Prospect Park South is another Brooklyn plat developed for the express purpose of exploiting mass transit. The opportunity was provided by the Flatbush Avenue trolley and the

New York City from Brooklyn Heights, 1823. Hezekiah Pierrepont subdivided the undeveloped land in the foreground to create America's first suburb. *(Courtesy of I. N. Phelps Stokes Collection, Miriam and Ira D. Wallach Division of Arts, Prints and Photographs, The New York Public Library Astor, Lenox and Tilden Foundation)*

New York City from Brooklyn Heights, c. 1836. In less than two decades, the 8-minute steamboat ferry ride between Brooklyn Heights and Manhattan had transformed Brooklyn Heights into a popular commuter suburb with houses lining the shore in order to benefit from the view. *(Courtesy of I. N. Phelps Stokes Collection, Miriam and Ira D. Wallach Division of Arts, Prints and Photographs, The New York Public Library Astor, Lenox and Tilden Foundation)*

Brooklyn, 1994. Trees planted on the property line of Argyle and Albemarle Streets in Prospect Park South made the street appear broader and provided houses with additional shade and privacy. *(Alexander Garvin)*

BMT subway, which had only recently extended across the Brooklyn Bridge into Manhattan.[8]

In 1899 real estate developer Dean Alvord purchased 50 acres just south of Prospect Park (see Chapter 3) where he, architect John Petit, and landscape gardener John Aitkin created a charming community in which "wife and children in going to and fro are not subjected to the annoyance of contact with the undesirable elements of society."[9] Privacy was emphasized at the entry points by brick piers decorated with a monogram formed from the letters PPS. Exclusivity was underscored by giving streets British names such as Albemarle, Argyle, and Buckingham. Protection from "undesirable social and moral influences" was provided by restricting construction to one-family houses costing more than $5000. Consistent design was guaranteed by deed restrictions requiring every lot to have a minimum street frontage of 50 feet, every house to be sited not less than 5 feet from its north lot line, and every yard to be open and unfenced.

Prospect Park South provides a parklike environment within the constraints of a rectangular street grid. Aitkin created beautifully landscaped islands in the middle of Buckingham and Albemarle Roads. He planted shrubs to conceal the subway line. Because trees stand at the front of each house lot, rather than at the street curb, residents are less aware of the proximity of their neighbors. Visitors passing through think the tree-lined roadways of the district are wider than conventional streets—an illusion created by the landscaping.

When Pierrepont pioneered Brooklyn Heights, his customers could not have imagined that the houses they built on the edge of rural Long Island would soon be engulfed by an international metropolis. Eighty years after Pierrepont had established his suburban plat, Alvord's customers understood this only too well. To guarantee home ownership in an environment with privacy and a bit of nature, he had to do more than just provide a street grid within a short distance of a transit line. For this reason, he provided dedicated open-space islands and deed restrictions specifying the location and type of building for every lot. In the process Alvord ensured that Prospect Park South would remain an enclave of one-family houses that would not be torn down for the construction of more profitable multiple dwellings.

The Private Places of St. Louis

St. Louis and Savannah are among the few American cities in which landscaped open space was central to the extension of suburban plats. In St. Louis these plats are called "private places" because, unlike Savannah's wards, they are private real estate ventures. The streets and park islands are owned and maintained by surrounding lot owners, not by the city. To emphasize this, most of the private places are defined by ornamental gates that also limit through traffic.[10]

Starting with Lucas Place in 1851, developers created more than 50 private places, mostly designed by city surveyor Julius

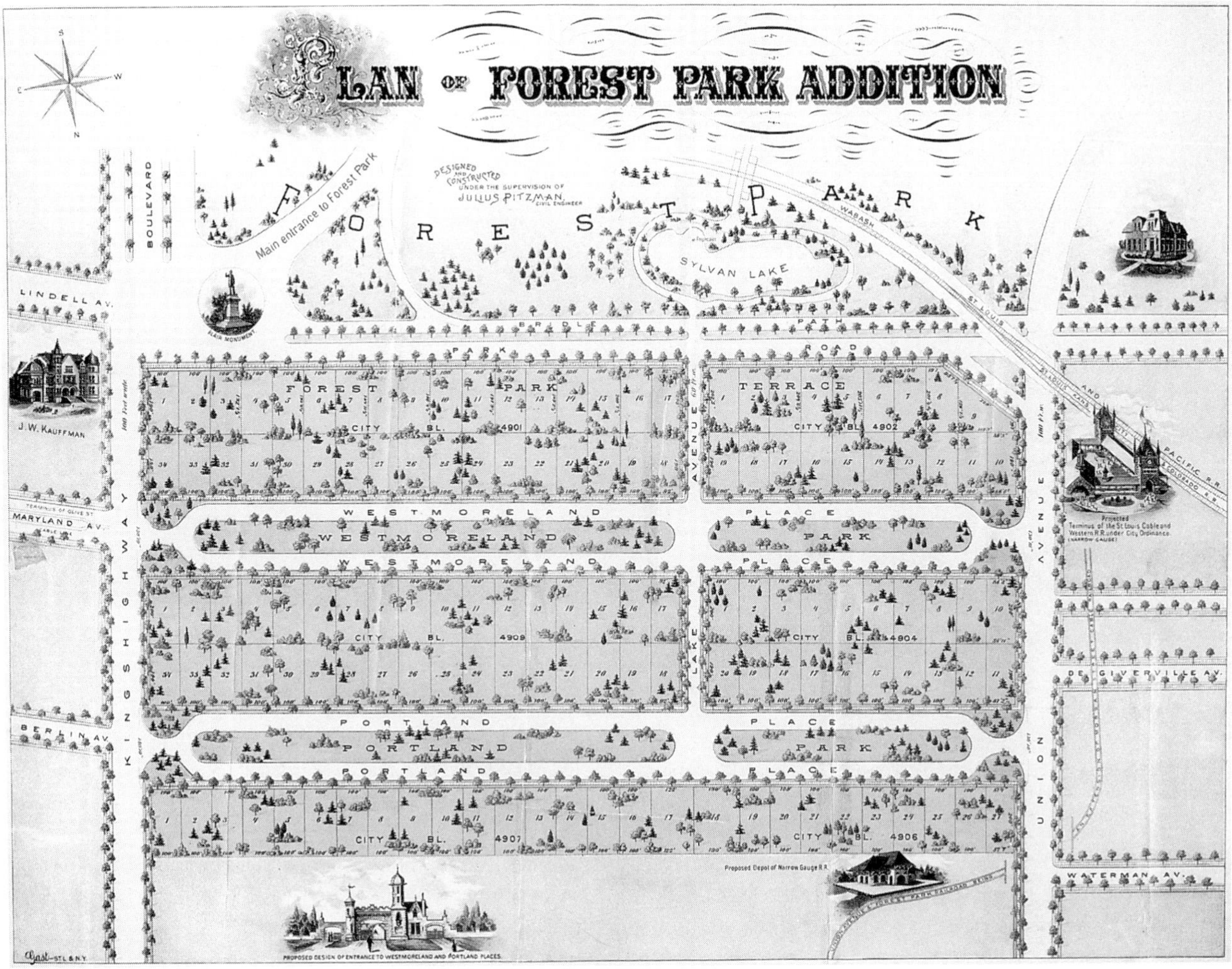

St. Louis, 1887. Prospectus plan of Forest Park additions (Westmoreland and Portland Places) showing the park islands that provided added privacy with landscaping that blocked the view of houses across the street. *(Courtesy of Special Collections, John M. Olin Library, Washington University in St. Louis)*

Pitzman. The first private places were within walking distance of the business district. As the city became an increasingly important industrial metropolis, those citizens with enough money to select among different residential locations chose to move away from downtown congestion, noise, and grime. This move was accelerated during the 1880s by the introduction of mass transit. Whereas pedestrian St. Louis had extended westward from the Mississippi River for a distance of only 1½ miles, the trolley (well known to fans of the movie *Meet Me in St. Louis*) allowed settlement to extend along radial streetcar lines for a distance of about 6 miles. Developers lost no time in creating new private places on this newly accessible, cheaper suburban land.

While several private places include curving roads that adjust to topographical conditions or political boundaries, most are extensions of the city's rectilinear street pattern. Streets that pass through them are usually divided by landscaped islands, 30 to 50 feet wide and hundreds of feet long. Residents of the houses that front on these park islands have the illusion that they live opposite a garden because the island's landscaping usually blocks the view of the houses facing their own.

St. Louis, 1987. The ornamental gate of Westmoreland Place establishes it as private property and limits through traffic. *(Alexander Garvin)*

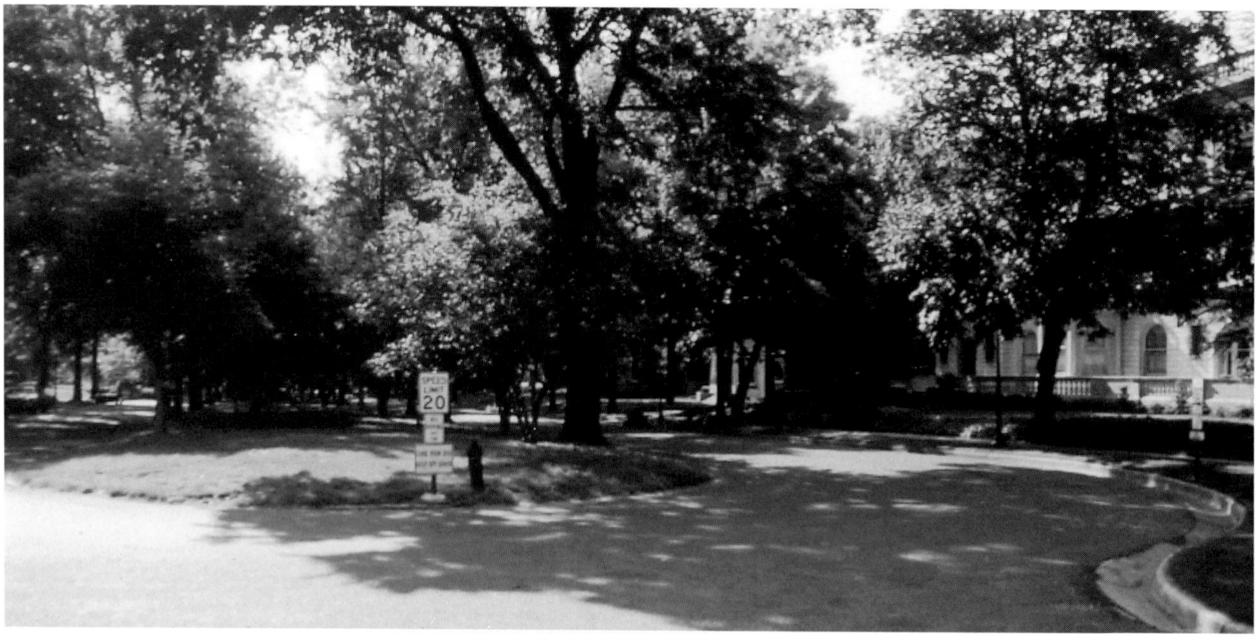

St. Louis, 1987. Trees and shrubs in the Portland Place "park island" block out the view of houses across the street and reinforce the privacy of this sylvan setting. *(Alexander Garvin)*

The most impressive of these private streets were initially conceived in 1887 when the Forest Park Improvement Association purchased a 78-acre site bordering the recently opened Forest Park (see Chapter 3). As usual Julius Pitzman was hired to create the plat. He laid out two private streets divided by park islands and connected by a cross street. The blocks were divided into large lots, 100 feet wide and 195 feet deep.

Within a year the venture was sold to a syndicate of prominent business leaders who attracted other prominent and wealthy St. Louis residents to move there. They separated the property into two entities: Westmoreland and Portland Place, each with its own street association to which all property owners had to belong and each with property restrictions to which they all had to conform. The regulations restricted land use to residential purposes (but not boarding houses), permitted only one house per lot, required all buildings to be set back 40 feet from the front lot line (verandas, balconies, etc., could extend to within 28 feet of the lot line), obliged owners to spend at least $7000 in building their houses (none was built for less than $25,000), forbade fences or walls within the front 40 feet of any lot, prohibited use of bituminous coal, and required street-association approval of all architecture. Any changes to property regulations required unanimous consent of all the lot owners.

From the beginning Westmoreland and Portland Places have been sites for some of the finest houses in St. Louis. They have retained their exclusive character because they are near Forest Park, offer an easy commute downtown, include distinctive gatehouses and landscaped park islands, are divided into unusually large lots, and observe deed restrictions to prevent intrusive development.

The only private places that have not survived are the first three. When their deed restrictions expired they were engulfed by St. Louis' rapidly expanding business district. At that time land had become more valuable for nonresidential purposes. Consequently, these properties were sold. Subsequent private places have not faced this problem because their deed restrictions are self-perpetuating, thereby preventing use for anything but one-family houses.

Boston's South End and Back Bay

The government of Boston, unlike that of Brooklyn and St. Louis, chose to withdraw the process of suburban extension from the hands of private developers. This was not because of a belief in state planning or opposition to private land development. Rather, it was because pollution had become so serious that there simply was no alternative. The city could not wait for a developer who could raise the huge sums of money and take the extraordinary risks involved in reclaiming hundreds of acres that were quickly becoming a festering swamp.[11]

During the decade between 1840 and 1850, Boston's population increased from 85,000 to 114,000. Residents were confined to a small, hilly peninsula connected to the rest of Massachusetts by a narrow neck of land that is today Washington Street. The situation was somewhat improved by leveling hills and filling in parts of the harbor. However, things became immeasurably worse during the second third of the nineteenth century when railroad lines cut off drainage in the Back Bay.

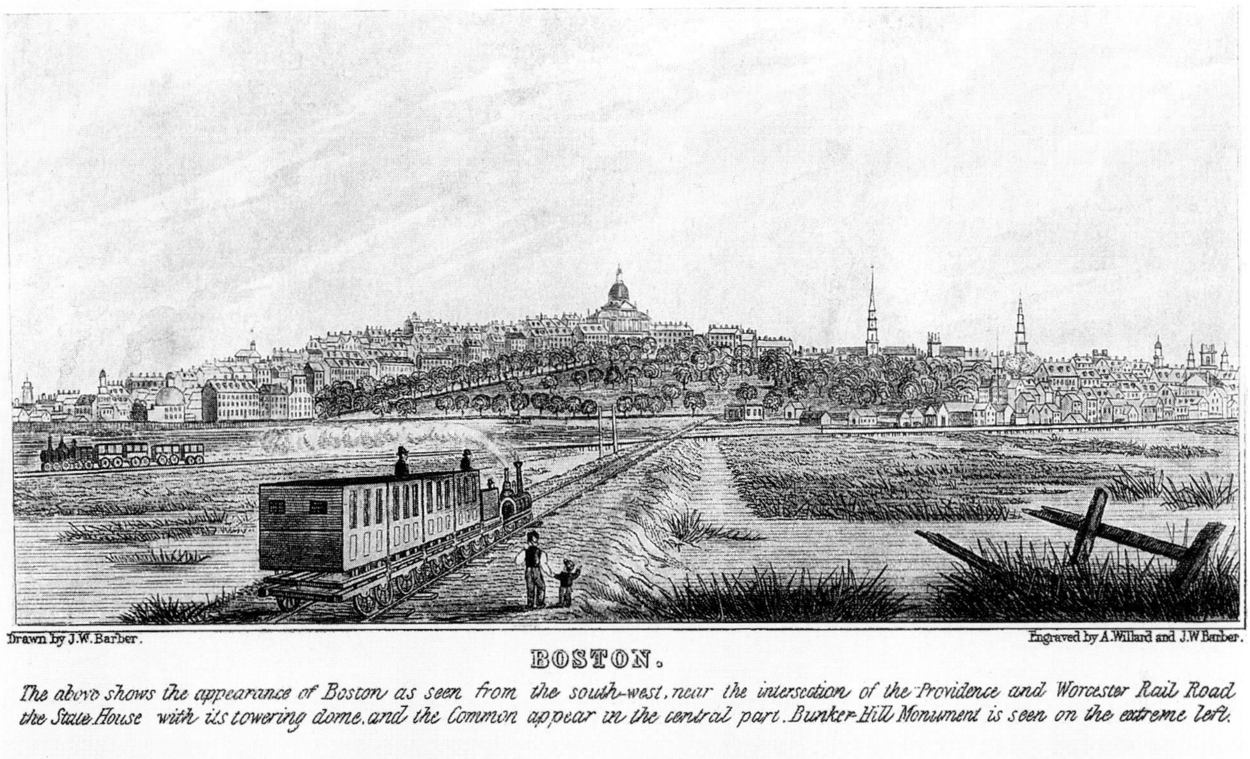

Drawn by J.W. Barber.
Engraved by A. Willard and J.W Barber.
BOSTON.
The above shows the appearance of Boston as seen from the south-west, near the intersection of the Providence and Worcester Rail Road the State House with its towering dome, and the Common appear in the central part. Bunker-Hill Monument is seen on the extreme left.

Boston, 1837. View of Boston from the Back Bay. *(Courtesy of Boston Athenaeum)*

Boston, c. 1830. View of the "Neck" (Washington Street) connecting the South End to Boston. *(Courtesy of Boston Athenaeum)*

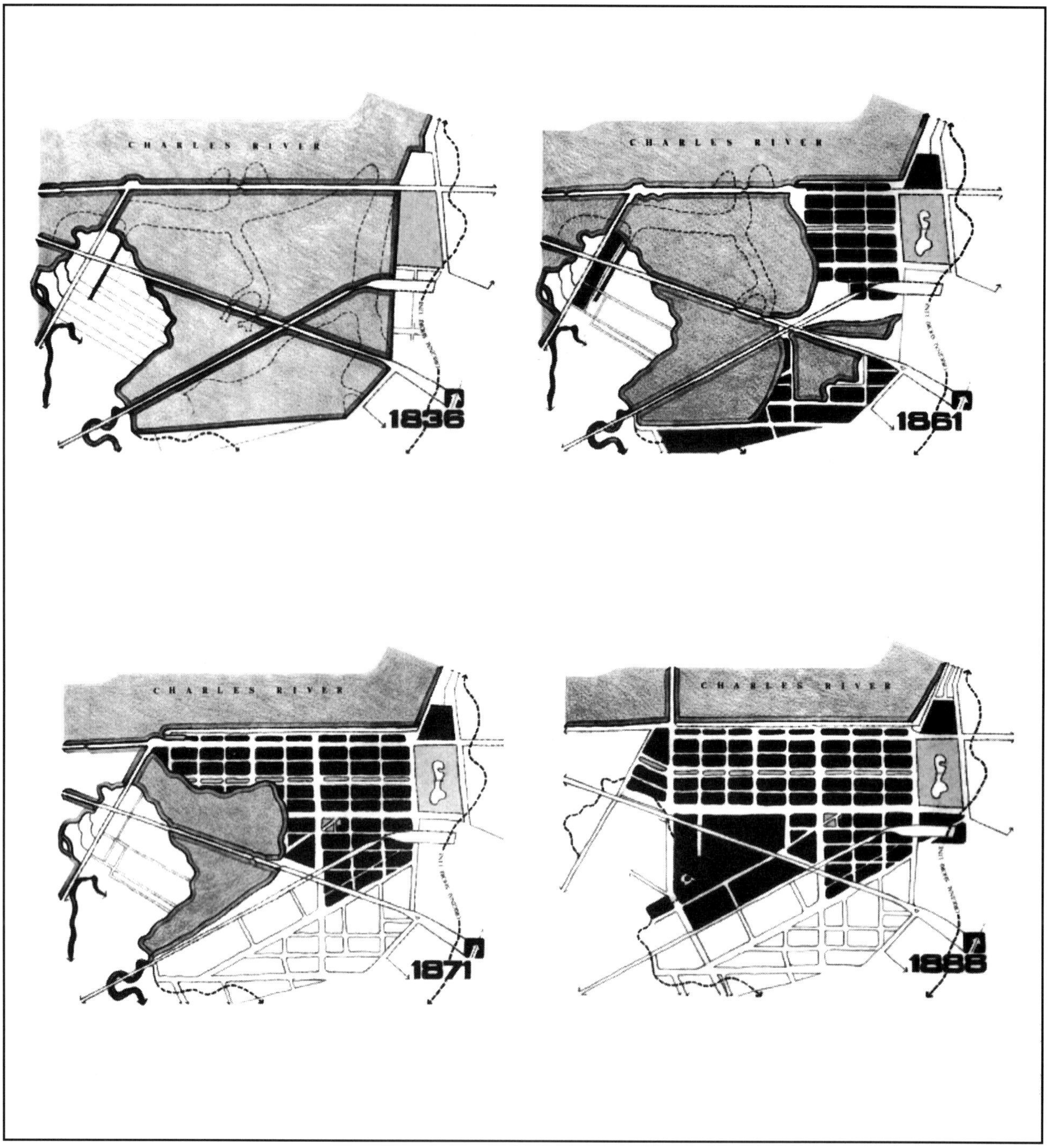

Boston, 1836–1888. Four maps showing the filling in of the Back Bay. *(Courtesy of Museum of Fine Arts, Boston)*

In 1814 the Boston and Roxbury Mill Company had been given riparian rights to more than 450 acres of the Back Bay. During high tide the area filled up with brackish water. When the tide changed, the water drained back into the Charles River.

Taking advantage of this tidal pattern, the Mill Company built a dam along the tidal Charles River. When the tide changed, power for more than 80 mills was provided.

In 1834, the Commonwealth of Massachusetts authorized the construction of two railroad causeways crossing the Back Bay. They impeded the flow of water and resulted in major litigation over the diminution in the Mill

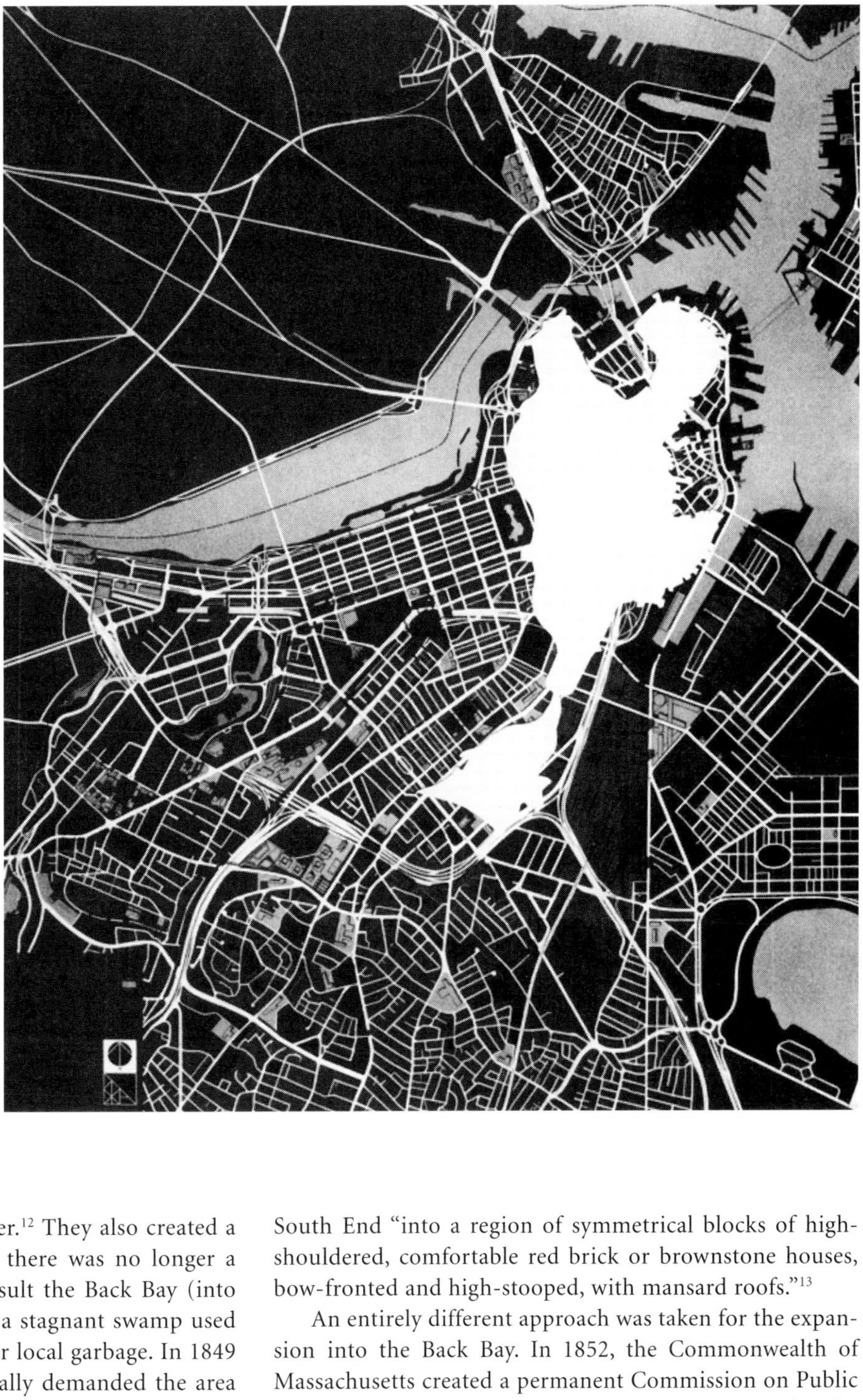

Boston, 1806 and 1969. 1806 map superimposed on a contemporary map of the City of Boston. *(Courtesy of Museum of Fine Arts, Boston)*

Company's ability to generate power.[12] They also created a significant health menace because there was no longer a way for water to flow out. As a result the Back Bay (into which city sewage flowed) became a stagnant swamp used by citizens as a dumping ground for local garbage. In 1849 the Boston Health Department finally demanded the area be filled.

At first, the only fill was for the purpose of widening the Washington Street neck leading downtown. While new streets were mapped, it was not till 1853, when horse-drawn omnibuses started to operate in the South End, that developers were able to exploit the rapidly expanding Boston market. Individual developers built row houses along the different street grids that emerged. They transformed the South End "into a region of symmetrical blocks of high-shouldered, comfortable red brick or brownstone houses, bow-fronted and high-stooped, with mansard roofs."[13]

An entirely different approach was taken for the expansion into the Back Bay. In 1852, the Commonwealth of Massachusetts created a permanent Commission on Public Lands.[14] Four years later the commission agreed to the plat that forms the Back Bay. It consists of the five east-west streets running parallel to what had been the Mill Dam and the nine perpendicular streets that divide them into blocks. Each block is, in turn, bisected by a 16-foot east-west service alley and divided into 25-foot lots. The dominant element of the Back Bay plat is its central east-west artery, Commonwealth Avenue, a 240-foot-wide boulevard with a

Boston, 1972. Row houses in the South End, one of the city's earliest suburban extensions. *(Alexander Garvin)*

landscaped central island that is broad enough to provide genuine parkland.

The commission contracted with a private company to supply fill (to an average depth of 20 feet) and to grade the site. A special railroad was built from the area to the gravel pits in Needham, 9 miles away, which, with the help of the recently invented steam shovel, supplied 3500 cartloads of fill every day. As the work was completed, each block was subdivided into lots and sold at public auction.

Building lots were not filled to street grade (17 feet above mean low tide). They stopped 5 feet lower in order to allow sewers and water mains to be installed below the service alleys. As a result the typical Back Bay house has a functional basement service area, usually including the kitchen, 5 feet below street level. Reception and dining rooms are on the main floor, and bedrooms above. The below-street-grade service level allows Back Bay houses (unlike the high-stooped buildings of the South End) to keep the number of front steps to six.

Other unusual features of Back Bay development were private deed restrictions and public laws regulating land use, building height, layout, and construction materials. They required that manufacturing uses be excluded throughout the district, commercial activity be prohibited on Commonwealth Avenue, buildings be set back not less than 20 feet from the sidewalk, structures be at least three stories high, buildings be constructed of masonry, and mansard roofs not exceed one story in height. These regulations produced a level of fire safety and structural soundness that would only be matched by twentieth-century building codes and a unity of architectural expression that has persisted despite the introduction of occasional high-rise buildings.

The project, which was completed in 1886, produced a net profit of $3.4 million. Some of this return can be attributed to demand for development sites and to a location on the edge of existing city development. The rest was the result of three factors that distinguished the Back Bay from its suburban com-

Boston, 1994. The 240-foot landscaped central island in the middle of Commonwealth Avenue is broad enough to become an integral part of the city's park system. *(Alexander Garvin)*

petition: the landscaped open space in the middle of Commonwealth Avenue; the system of sewers, service alleys, and water mains, which lowered the cost of preparing lots for development; and the building restrictions, which provided home buyers with a level of security not available in other developing areas.

Suburban Subdivisions

Despite prevalent and continuing use, the rectilinear suburban plat began to go out of fashion during the second half of the nineteenth century. Public transportation (whether rail, streetcar, or subway) and then private automobiles made possible an entirely different pattern of suburban extension: the subdivision. These new forms of transportation eliminated the need to connect new residential communities to any existing street system. Developers and commuters alike could leapfrog the edges of city development and move on to cheaper virgin land, unencumbered by previous development patterns. There they could obtain greater privacy, larger lots, and more generous landscaping, all at lower prices. Not having to graft onto existing street patterns or limit themselves to existing block dimensions, these new subdivisions could and sometimes did include elementary community facilities and landscaped open spaces.[15]

Developers could afford to pay prices that neither farmers nor country-estate owners could refuse. In between these early subdivisions and the cities from which their residents migrated, there remained farms, scruffy land uses, virgin forest, summer estates, and open territory. In time they, too, were replaced by residential subdivisions.

This leapfrog pattern of suburbanization was neither casual nor rudderless. It was methodically planned for and carefully supervised by the real estate industry and by local governments. Landowners, brokers, mortgage lenders, insurance and utility companies, contractors, lawyers, and accountants all needed procedures that guaranteed accuracy and legality of title. Government agencies needed to provide the services residents expected. Accordingly, street layouts had to be adjusted to fit into probable traffic patterns and designed to accommodate delivery vehicles and fire engines. Similarly, water, sewer, gas, and electric lines had to conform to common engineering standards if the new subdivisions were to obtain service from regional utility companies. Water mains had to be large enough to supply the area and provide sufficient pressure to permit fire fighting. In response to these needs, states enacted legislation requiring official approval and recording of all subdivisions.

California's laws regulating real estate subdivision are illustrative of the long history of government regulation and demonstrate how carefully supervised leapfrog suburbanization really is. The process of government regulation began in 1893 with a state law requiring that officially approved subdivision maps be legally recorded before anyone subdividing land could sell lots. In 1907 the state required developers to obtain approval by the local governing body of any streets dedicated for public use. Six years later local governments were given the authority to establish layout standards for all streets. The 1915 Map Act required subdivisions to be submitted to the local planning commission (if one existed) or to the city engineer for consideration of their suitability in relation to the city's development plans. In 1921 and 1923 the act was amended to also include drainage, water supply, and other engineering features.[16]

After 1934 state requirements were augmented by those of the National Housing Act of 1934. The system of FHA mortgage insurance that grew out of this legislation provided a new financial basis for the American suburb (see Chapter 8). It also established common planning and design standards for developers around the country. These standards were contained in four publications—*Subdivision Development* (1935), *Planning Neighborhoods for Small Houses* (1936), *Planning Profitable Neighborhoods* (1938), and *Successful Subdivisions* (1940)—and provided the basis for property appraisal practice in the *FHA Underwriting Manual* and thus for virtually all bank lending. They covered design and engineering recommendations for subdivisions, streets, lot layout, utility installation, and landscaping. Properties that failed to meet these standards were not eligible for FHA insurance and thus had great difficulty obtaining bank financing.[17]

Olmsted and Company

America's suburban subdivisions, like urban neighborhoods, vary in size and quality. But they look very much alike because virtually all of them are imbued with the design philosophy of one man: Frederick Law Olmsted, Sr.

Between 1857 and 1950 Olmsted's firm (first a partnership with Calvert Vaux, later with Henry Codman, Charles Eliot, and his nephew and stepson John Charles Olmsted, and eventually including his son and namesake, Frederick Law Olmsted, Jr.) was involved in planning 450 subdivisions and new communities, 47 while the senior Olmsted was still active. It actually prepared site plans for 270 communities. These suburban subdivisions, located in 29 states, Cuba, Bermuda, and the District of Columbia, along with thousands designed by former employees and students trained by its principals and tens of thousands designed by its imitators, still make up the bulk of our suburban landscape.[18]

The senior Olmsted studied agriculture at Yale in 1844–1845 and tried to support himself as a farmer until 1854. Consequently, he was intimately familiar with horticulture, and this fact surely influenced his pragmatic approach to landscape design. During 1850 he toured Europe, later publishing a fascinating account entitled *Walks and Talks of an American Farmer in England,* and probably visited some of the earliest suburban developments in England and the continent.[19]

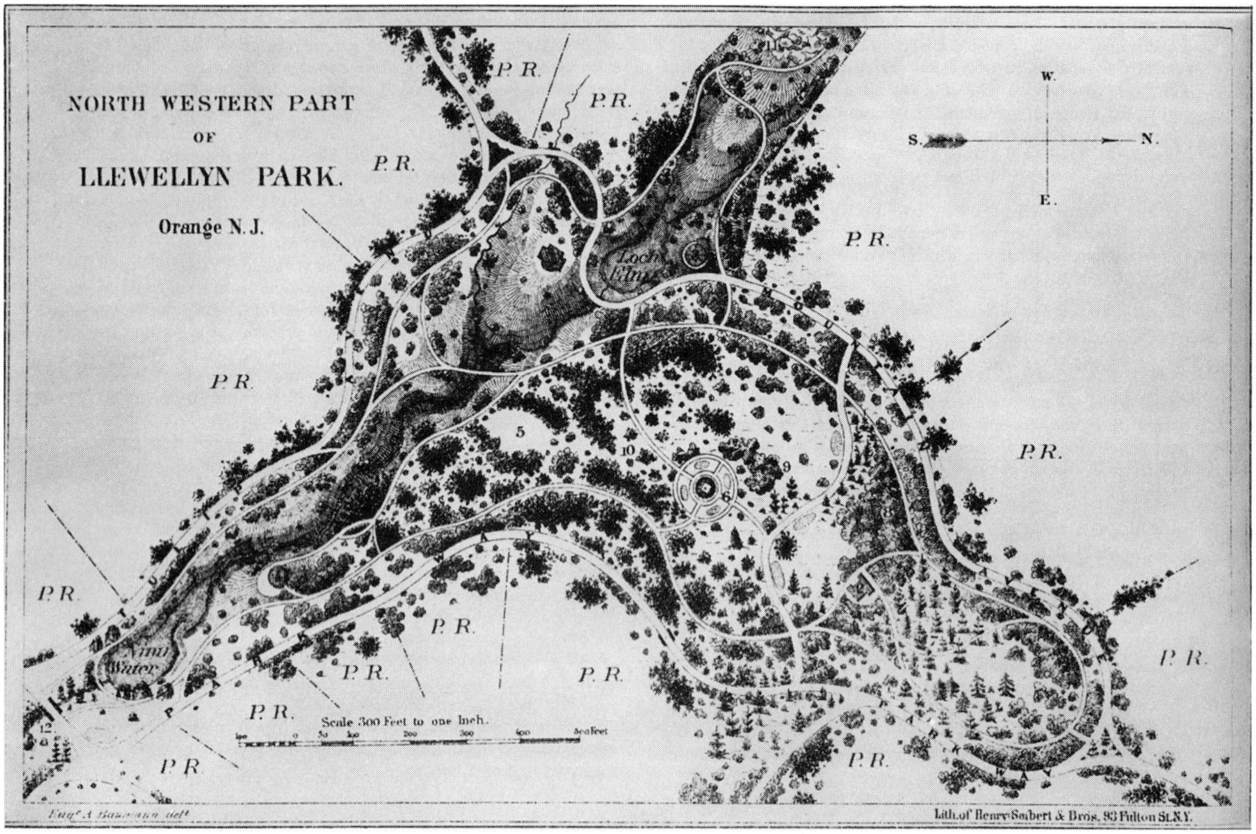

Llewellyn Park, 1859. Plan made 6 years after this community was founded by Llewellyn Haskell. *(From John W. Reps, The Making of Urban America, Copyright by Princeton University Press 1965, reproduced by permission of Princeton University Press)*

Landscape gardener Andrew Jackson Downing is usually given credit for contributing most to Olmsted's landscape design. Olmsted was an avid reader of his magazine, *Horticulturalist,* which was first published in 1846. He corresponded with Downing before getting to know him during the two years before Downing's death in 1852. He even met his future partner, Calvert Vaux, in Downing's home.[20]

Downing recommended "country villages" with "broad well-planted avenues of shade trees" and "a large central space always devoted to park or pleasure ground."[21] This park-centered approach was adopted for Llewellyn Park, New Jersey, a planned community with which Olmsted was certainly familiar. It was designed in 1853 for its founder Llewellyn Haskell (hence its name) by the architect Alexander Jackson Davis, whom Olmsted also knew. Davis was one of the friends whom he consulted in laying out his Staten Island farm.[22]

The 400 acres of Llewellyn Park were designed to be and remain an exclusive residential compound with a romantic gatehouse to screen out unwanted visitors. Its 7 miles of winding roads and 3- to 5-acre house lots are organized around a 60-acre private park. The park and roadways are managed by three successor trustees. Road maintenance and police protection are paid for by fees assessed by a board of managers elected by Llewellyn Park's wealthy residents.

The Olmsted approach to the suburban landscape was both more functionally oriented and more democratic than Downing's. It involved neither gatehouses nor large central parks. As Olmsted, Sr., explained, the principal requirements of a successful suburban community are, "good roads and walks, pleasant to the eye within themselves, and having intervals of pleasant openings and outlooks, with suggestions of refined domestic life, secluded, but not far removed from the life of the community."[23]

By good roads and walks, he meant clean, smooth surfaces and gracefully curved arteries without sharp corners, designed to accommodate several lanes of vehicular (carriage) traffic. Today this seems obvious. However, when he started designing subdivisions, paved streets were the exception. As late as 1890, not only were half the streets in America unpaved, they were used as much for dumping household garbage, industrial waste, and animal manure as for traffic.[24]

In designing suburban communities, the firm's objective was a tranquil setting with plenty of grass and trees. It introduced turf and foliage by lining roadways with trees and setting houses back a sufficient distance from the lot line to

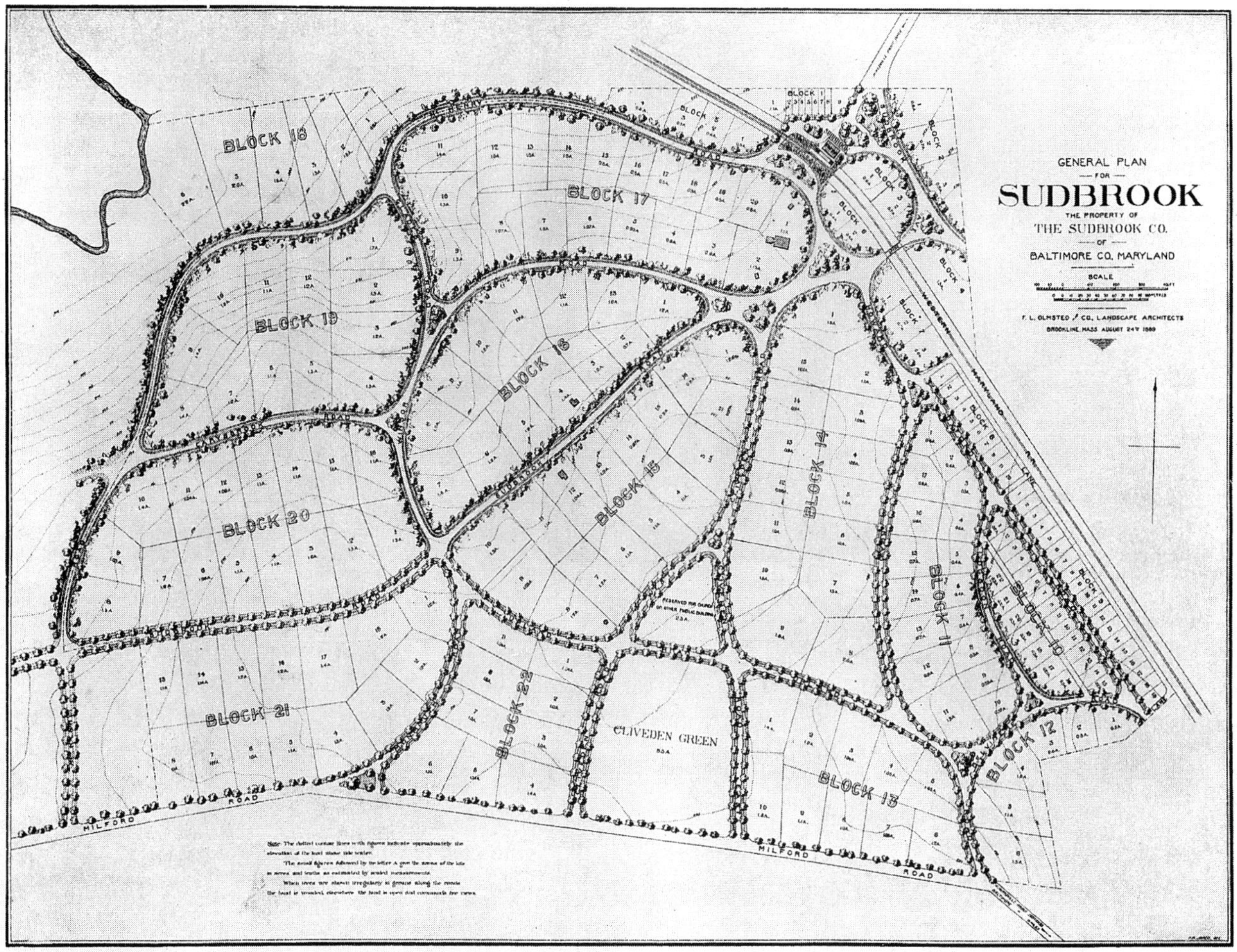

Sudbrook Park, 1889. Olmsted's general plan for Sudbrook takes advantage of the gently rolling landscape to create a charming suburban subdivision. *(Courtesy of the National Park Service, Frederick Law Olmsted National Historic Site)*

allow for broad open lawns. Trees provided the necessary seclusion for "refined domestic life." Open lawns ensured that residents would never be "far removed from the life of the community."[25]

Olmsted, Vaux, and Company designed its first suburban community, Riverside, Illinois, in 1868–1869. While Riverside has many of the characteristics of the firm's residential subdivisions, it is really a new town and is considered separately (see Chapter 15). Among the earliest subdivisions for which the firm prepared designs were Tarrytown Heights, New York (1870–1872), Parkside in Buffalo (1872–1886), and Sudbrook Park outside Baltimore (1876–1892). They all had similar features: broad, gently twisting, tree-lined streets, curvilinear blocks with large lots, and small, irregular park islands at significant intersections.

Only Sudbrook Park was executed largely as designed. It was developed by a syndicate that sought to exploit the recently opened Western Maryland Railroad station in nearby Pikesville. The syndicate purchased a 204-acre estate and commissioned the Olmsted firm to design a residential subdivision, initially for summer residents. The strategy was to rely on the railroad for commuting to Baltimore and the nearby village of Pikesville for retail shopping.[26]

The firm's design subdivided the site into 1-acre house sites. Its gracefully curving, tree-lined roadways are superimposed onto the gently rolling topography. The plan limits the number of houses within each resident's angle of vision (thereby increasing the feeling of privacy) and heightens the sensation of nature by screening out surrounding structures. The resulting design makes each house seem to be an inevitable part of a "natural" landscape.

Similar curvilinear features were used in a very different way at Fisher Hill in Brookline, Massachusetts (1884–1892). Commuter access to Fisher Hill (originally Brookline Hill) was opened up by the Newton Highlands branch of the Boston & Albany Railroad (now part of the MBTA) and the streetcar

Sudbrook Park, 1990. Olmsted's formula of houses set back from a curving, tree-lined street set the pattern for suburban development throughout the country. *(Alexander Garvin)*

lines on Beacon and Boylston Streets. The syndicate that developed Fisher Hill hired the Olmsted firm to design a modest year-round community on a steeply sloping site. Its plan consisted of lots, smaller than those at Sudbrook Park, fitted to the contours of the topography.[27]

From the street Fisher Hill has the look of other Olmsted subdivisions. It is from the rear, however, that its exceptional features are revealed. The curving roadways of Fisher Hill were laid out to hug the contours of the site so that many of the houses can open out to the view below that in most cases overlooks the nearby city of Boston.

At Druid Hills in Atlanta (1890–1908), Olmsted and Company used the usual tree-lined, curvilinear design in yet another way. Here, on a 1400-acre site, the firm proposed a broad, landscaped parkway intersected by winding roadways and landscaped waterways. The plan for Druid Hills, which was begun by the senior Olmsted and completed after his death, exploited the existing landscape. Steep slopes, ravines, and creeks were left undeveloped or became the focus of linear parks. To allow for natural drainage, roadways were located in shallow valleys and houses set back 50 to 75 feet on the slopes above. Wherever possible, the design preserved the

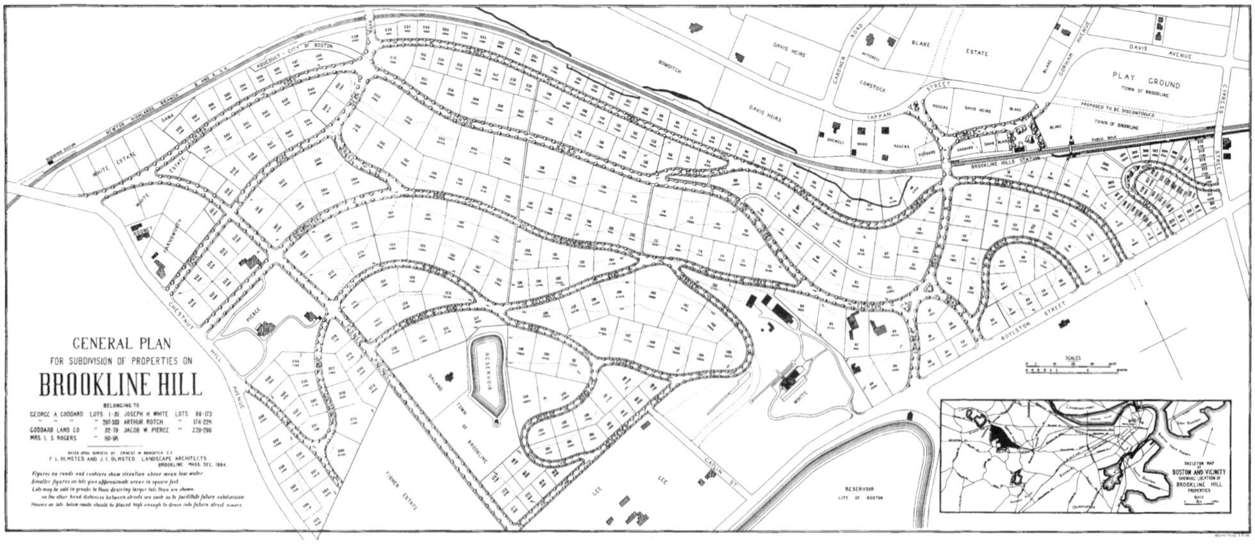

Brookline, 1984. By following hillside contours, Olmsted's plan for Brookline Hill (now Fisher Hall) minimizes steep slopes and provides many of the houses with wonderful views of Boston. *(Courtesy of the National Park Service, Frederick Law Olmsted National Historic Site)*

Brookline, 1995. The streets in Fisher Hill are located high enough above one another that the houses fronting them have views unobstructed by the roofs of their neighbors below. *(Alexander Garvin)*

Atlanta, 1991. Rolling parkland in the middle of the flanking roadways of Ponce de Leon Avenue in Druid Hills. *(Alexander Garvin)*

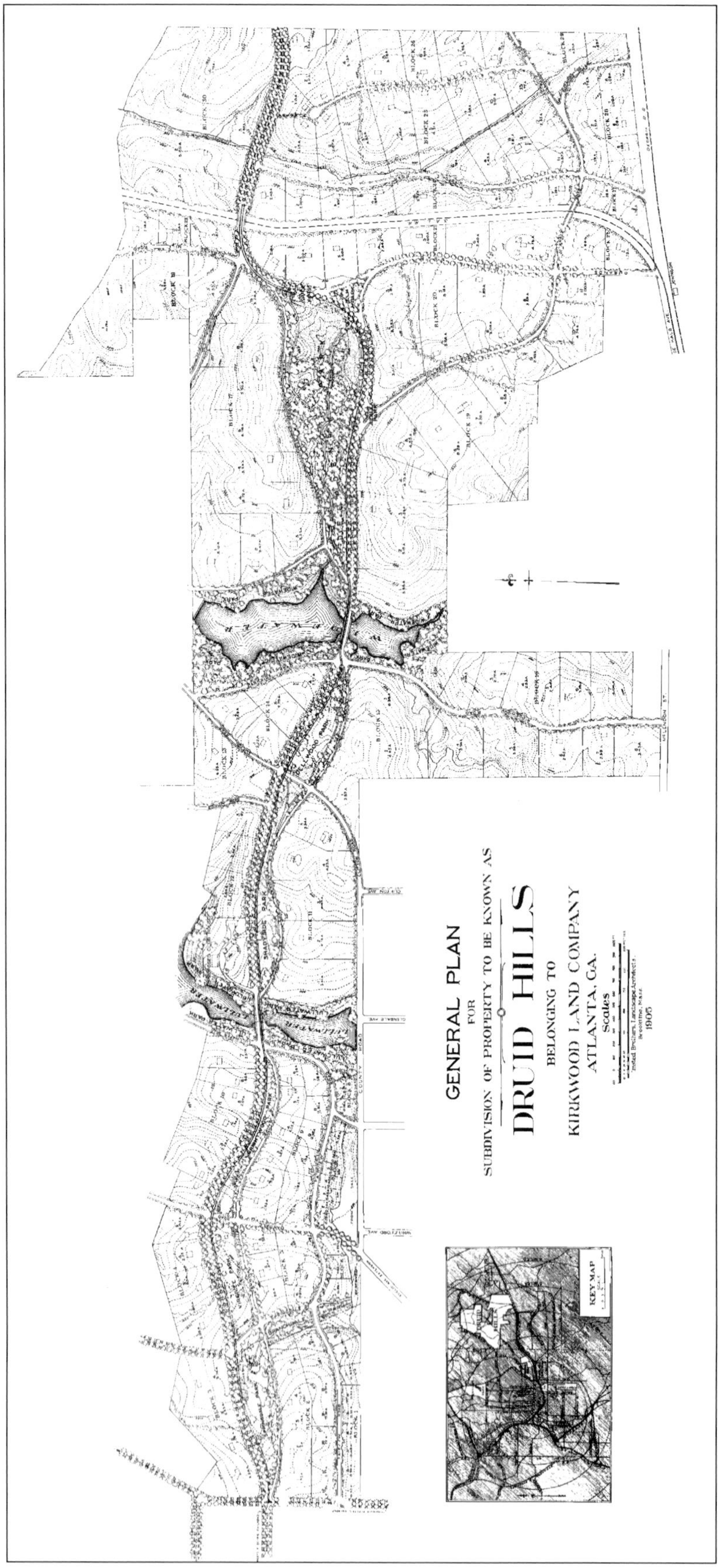

Atlanta, 1905. General plan for Druid Hills. *(Courtesy of the National Park Service, Frederick Law Olmsted National Historic Site)*

Queens, 1995. The houses at Forest Hills Gardens conform to deed restrictions that require all the buildings be set back from the street and have sloping, red clay tile roofs. *(Alexander Garvin)*

majestic Southern pines, Spanish oaks, and evergreen magnolias that gave the landscape its distinctive regional flavor.[28]

Druid Hills was developed by the Kirkwood Land Company, founded by Joel Hurt. He had already developed Inman Park, a suburban subdivision, on land that was a 5-minute trolley ride from downtown Atlanta on the Edgewood Street Railroad, which he also owned. This time Hurt wanted to extend streetcar service along Ponce de Leon Avenue. He ran into financial difficulties and had to sell the property in 1908, before the project could be completed.

While Ponce de Leon Avenue was executed pretty much as planned, the broadened creeks (Lullwater and Widewater) and hilly parks that were to feed into it were not completed. Nevertheless, enough of the original Olmsted proposal remained to ensure that the rest of Druid Hills would be completed in keeping with the firm's design. That design is largely responsible for Druid Hills becoming one of the most desirable residential sections of Atlanta.

The Olmsted firm's most famous subdivision is in Forest Hills, Queens, where, along with architect Grosvenor Atterbury, it laid out Forest Hills Gardens for the Russell Sage Foundation and later some of the surrounding area for the Cord-Meyer Development Company. Familiarity with the project is the result of the foundation's effort to portray Forest Hills as an early demonstration of the effectiveness of enlightened community planning.

The 175 acres that make up Forest Hills Gardens (1906–1911), largely designed by Frederick Law Olmsted, Jr., were not developed as a speculative real estate venture. As explained by the Russell Sage Foundation, Forest Hills Gardens was intended "to create a suburb that would combine the beauty in arrangement of grounds with attractiveness and permanency of building...and at the same time to dispose of its property at prices that will give it moderate, but fair return for the money and time invested."[29]

Like so many other subdivisions, it was planned in conjunction with public transportation, in this case the Long Island Railroad, whose station was designed to be compatible with the rest of the community. A charming square was created around the station. In addition to the station, the square includes an inn and a few retail stores. Two gently curving "greenways" radiate from the square to form the spine of the community. Lots open onto tree-lined streets that provide urbane sites for one-family homes, row houses, and apartment buildings. The structures themselves are set back from the street and conform to the requirements of their deed restrictions, most visibly to the requirement that all the buildings have sloping, red clay tile roofs.

Forest Hills Gardens is not sufficiently distinctive to warrant the special notice it usually receives. Many subdivisions have been planned in conjunction with public transportation. The few stores around the Forest Hills railroad station have trouble competing with busy retail streets on the other side of the tracks. Deed restrictions may be responsible for an admirable unity of scale, color, and design, but the landscape is not more consistent than the private places of St. Louis, or many other communities with similar restrictive covenants. The gently curving streets create an agreeable living environment, but not enough to differentiate Forest Hills Gardens from other Olmsted subdivisions or to rival the exquisite landscapes of Druid Hills or Riverside.

As a demonstration of the financial effectiveness of community planning, Forest Hills Gardens was a flop. In 1922, when the Russell Sage Foundation terminated its involvement, the loss on the investment totalled $360,800.[30] Speaking on behalf of the Foundation, Clarence Perry explained, "The cost of preparing the land, grading, electrical conduits, sewer systems, street lights, paving, and landscaping, while contributing greatly to the attractiveness of the development, was nevertheless unpredictably high."[31] There is no way of knowing whether a profit-motivated developer would have done better. However, most private developers would have been more care-

Prairie Village, Kansas City, 1994. Olmsted-inspired curvilinear, tree-lined streets with houses set back from the property line. *(Alexander Garvin)*

ful to coordinate the installation of infrastructure with the pace and price of land sales.

Visiting Forest Hills or any of the Olmsted firm's subdivisions, one wanders along the curving roads, never sure where they will end, constantly surprised and entertained by some aspect of its design. This is the result of the firm's sensitivity to the landscape, achieved sometimes by adjusting to the topography and other times by introducing new elements to enliven its uniformity. It is also caused by strategic openings along the roadways. Some openings may have been dictated by topographical features, such as waterways or steep slopes that were unsuitable for construction. Others were created by the intersections of the gracefully curving roadways.

There is nothing exotic about the elements of an Olmsted subdivision. It is basically a network of curving, tree-lined roadways bounded by houses set in the middle of open lawns. They may have become an ever-present suburban cliché, but in the hands of the Olmsted firm this combination produces places of unusual beauty. Even in watered-down form in countless suburban communities designed by mediocre imitators, it is a scheme that usually transforms suburban lemons into lemonade.

Suburban Cluster Communities

Suburban developers seek to increase the number of residences per acre because this reduces land cost per dwelling unit and allows a project to supply amenities (swimming pools, tennis courts, children's play equipment, etc.) that home owners could not otherwise afford. At the same time they do not want to sacrifice the appearance of being in the country. In 1928, architects Clarence Stein and Henry Wright devised an outstanding design solution to this problem for Radburn, New Jersey. It was decades before their ideas took hold and then only because of the growing popularity of a novel form of ownership, the condominium, and an innovative form of land use regulation, cluster zoning.

The Radburn Idea

When the senior Olmsted retired from active practice in 1895 there were five automobiles in America. In 1928, when Clarence Stein and Henry Wright started laying out Radburn, New Jersey, there were 21.3 million. During those intervening 32 years, the automobile transformed daily life and made accessible vast new areas of cheap land. However, neither developers nor their designers departed much from the Olmsted formula. Instead of driveways leading to carriage houses, they built driveways that led to garages; instead of simple roadways with a couple of traffic lanes, they built wider streets that allowed cars to park along either side.[32]

The most important subdivision to depart from the Olmsted formula was Radburn, a new form of community intended to answer the enigma: "'How to live with the auto,' or if you will, 'How to live in spite of it.'"[33] Radburn was developed by the City Housing Corporation (CHC), a limited-dividend company organized by realtor Alexander Bing. The CHC had been established for the purpose of building moderate income housing, while simultaneously producing a modest 6 percent return for its investors. Its objective at Radburn was to create housing designed to the most advanced

Sunnyside Gardens, Queens, 1990. The open space enclosed by the attached houses that line this block of Sunnyside Gardens is still owned by a homeowners' association. *(Alexander Garvin)*

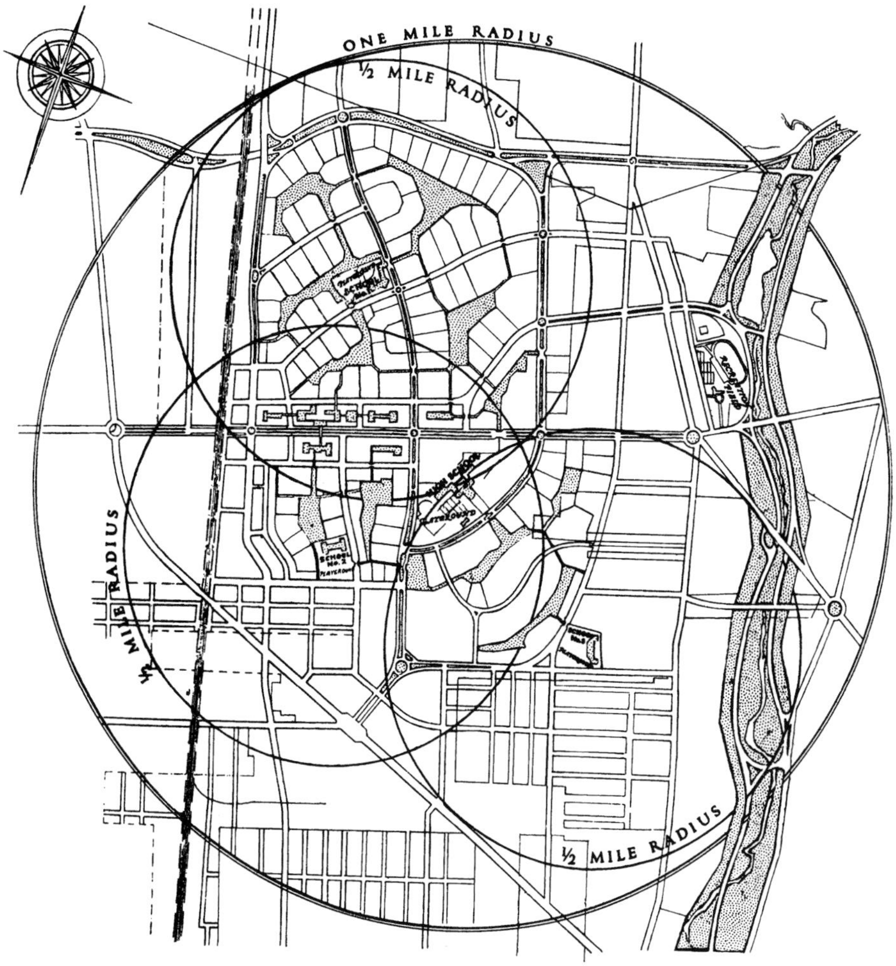

Radburn, 1929. General plan showing three school-centered neighborhoods, each $\frac{1}{2}$ mile in radius. *(From Clarence Stein, New Towns for America, 1966; courtesy of MIT Press)*

planning standards and "garden cities" based on the ideas Ebenezer Howard had been experimenting with in England (see Chapter 15).

The plan for Radburn evolved from Stein and Wright's work on Sunnyside Gardens, a community of 1202 family units that they designed for a 77-acre site in Queens that was a scant 15-minute subway ride from Times Square. Sunnyside Gardens is one of the most ingenious adaptations of the New York City 200-foot block. Each block consists of two-and-a-half-story, red-brick row houses enclosing a 120-foot-wide landscaped quadrangle.[34]

Only 28 percent of the land is used for housing. The rest is landscaped open space. Buildings are slightly set back from the street to permit small front gardens and similarly set back from the inner quadrangle to provide each house with a small, private rear yard. Each inner quadrangle was held in common ownership by the residents of the block and initially protected by deed restrictions.

Parking was provided in garage compounds on the edge of the site. Playgrounds, a baseball field, and tennis courts were provided at a $3\frac{1}{2}$-acre community-owned park. To avoid unnecessarily high initial expenditures, utility installation, street paving, and house construction were timed to meet market demand.

Sunnyside Gardens, unlike its more ambitious counterpart in Forest Hills, easily produced its projected 6 percent return and demonstrated the financial effectiveness of community planning. Upon completion in 1928, all unused land was sold for $646,000, three times its cost (initial purchase, improvements, plus carrying costs). Sunnyside Gardens' only flaw was revealed decades after completion: some of its residents preferred private gardens to common open space (see Chapter 16). "Fourteen years after the last of the original court easements expired, only 6 of the 15 center courts retain their original configuration; four are largely enclosed by fences along the property lines of the surrounding homes, though their pathways are unobstructed; three are completely enclosed."[35]

Flush with its success in Queens, the CHC decided to build a complete "garden city" for 25,000 residents. After examining 50 possible sites, it settled on 1300 acres of rolling farmland in Fair Lawn, New Jersey, a 12-mile drive from the George Washington Bridge, then under construction. The

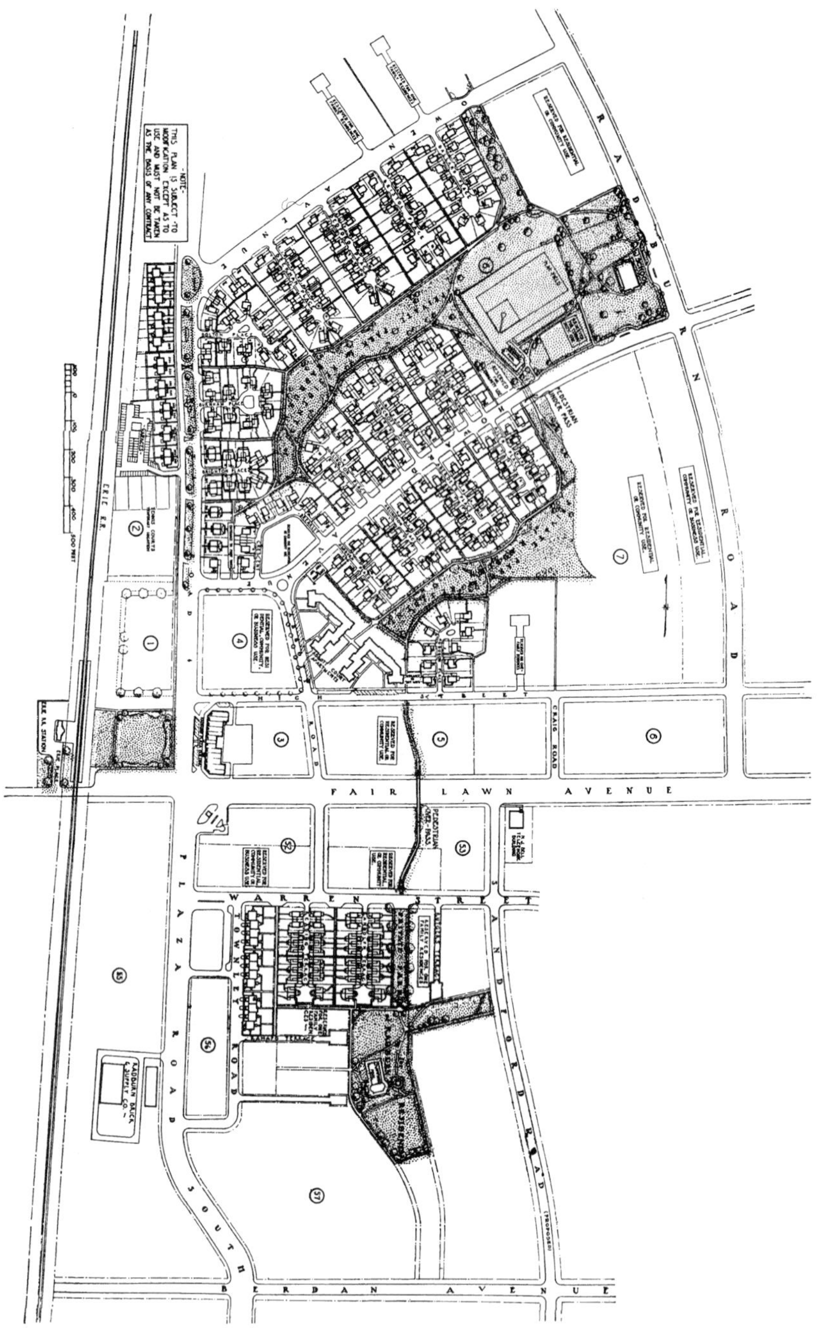

Radburn, 1930. Plan of development completed by 1930. *(From Clarence Stein, New Towns for America, 1966; courtesy of MIT Press)*

project, named Radburn, was again entrusted to Stein and Wright. Like Sunnyside Gardens, Radburn was not really a garden city such as Ebenezer Howard had envisioned. Land was subdivided and sold to individual owners, not kept in common ownership for the long-term benefit of the community. There were no industrial land uses and, thus, no opportunities for residents to both live and work in Radburn. Instead, the CHC pioneered the design of a suburban subdivision for the "motor age."

With tens of millions of cars on the road, it was natural for Radburn's planners to want to eliminate traffic accidents. They did this by removing pedestrian traffic from the street, establishing an independent pedestrian circulation system, and planning an underpass wherever this pedestrian system intersected with vehicular traffic. Stein always credited the idea to Olmsted and Vaux, who had pioneered the underpass in New York's Central Park (see Chapter 3) "almost half a century before the invention of the automobile."[36] Once Stein and Wright demonstrated its effectiveness, the underpass became the Radburn trademark and a commonly accepted symbol of "good" city planning.

It is ironic that the single underpass actually built became the Radburn trademark because other elements of the Radburn idea, especially the superblock, are so much more important. The Radburn superblock was probably conceived during what Lewis Mumford described as "the vivid interchange of ideas" that took place within the Regional Planning Association of America (RPAA).[37] As Stein explains:

> *A core of members [that included Clarence Stein, Henry Wright, Alexander Bing, Benton MacKaye, Catherine Bauer, and Lewis Mumford] met at least two or three times a week, sometimes more, for lunch or dinner...between 1923 and 1933.*[38]

In 1927, when serious work on Radburn had begun, RPAA discussions took on a special focus. Their consideration of the number of people required for "a good elementary school" was one of the discussions that helped to give shape to the Radburn superblock. The principles behind the superblock were best articulated by Clarence Perry, one of the participants in these RPAA discussions, in his presentation of "the neighborhood unit" in volume 7 of the 1929 *Regional Survey of New York and Its Environs* (conceived and published by a contemporary organization, better known by its later title, the Regional Plan Association, whose only similarity to the RPAA was its name). These principles were:

- *Size. A residential unit [should have a] population for which one elementary school is ordinarily required...*
- *Boundaries. The unit should be bounded on all sides by arterial streets, sufficiently wide to facilitate its by-passing by all through traffic.*
- *Open Spaces. A system of small parks and recreation spaces, planned to meet the needs of the particular neighborhood, should be provided.*

Radburn, 1993. Cul-de-sac. *(Alexander Garvin)*

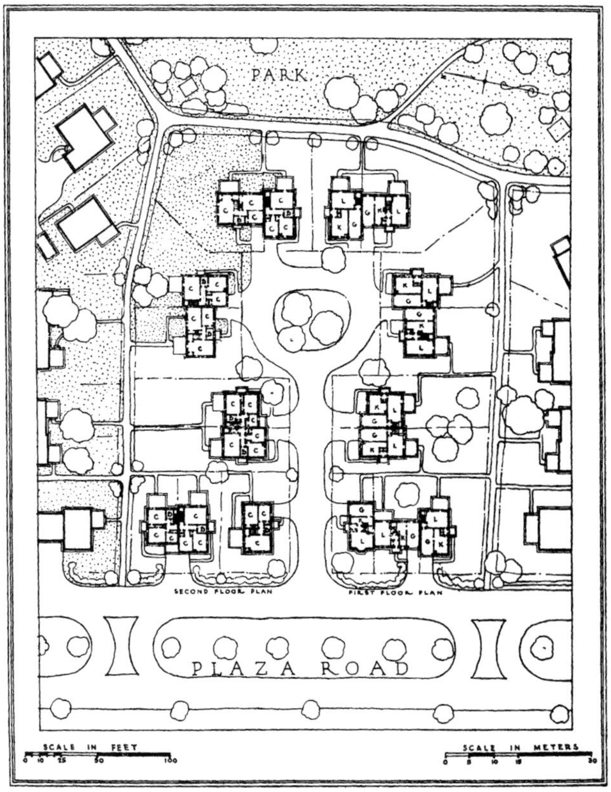

Radburn, 1929. Plan of houses grouped around a cul-de-sac (Burnham Place). *(From Clarence Stein, New Towns for America, 1966; courtesy of MIT Press)*

- *Institutional Sites. Sites for schools and other institutions having service spheres coinciding with the limits of the unit should be suitably grouped.*
- *Local Shops. One or more shopping districts adequate for the population to be served, should be laid out in the circumference of the unit...*
- *Internal Street System. The street system...[should be] designed to facilitate circulation within the unit and to discourage its use by through traffic.*[39]

Each 30 to 50 acre Radburn superblock was conceived as a fully planned neighborhood for 7500 to 10,000 residents fitted within a radius of half a mile and centered around its elementary school and playgrounds. Shopping facilities, located on the periphery, were accessible both by foot and by car.

Planning based on pedestrian-traffic separation and superblocks required unscrambling "the varied services of urban streets."[40] They were reassembled in two intersecting systems that can be better understood when thought of as interlocking combs, one gray and the other green. The spine of the gray comb is an arterial street enclosing the superblock. Its teeth are cul-de-sacs (dead-end streets), which provide vehicular access to a cluster of houses. These gray teeth alternate with green ones that provide pedestrian access to the houses and lead to the spine of the green comb, which Stein called the open-space backbone of the superblock. The diagrammatic expression of this design is quite different from what was actually created. By adjusting their diagram to the topography and carefully landscaping the resulting open space, Stein and Wright created one of America's most beautiful suburban subdivisions.

The cul-de-sac, like the underpass, was based on precedent. As Stein explains: "Henry Wright and I went to Britain, on a special investigation to study superblocks with cul-de-sacs, before we started planning Radburn."[41] Their models were the projects developed to demonstrate Ebenezer Howard's philosophy, in particular Hampstead Garden Suburb. However, unlike the conventional suburban houses fronting on the Hampstead cul-de-sac, Radburn houses were turned around to face the green pedestrian comb, thereby becoming the hinge that connected the two circulation systems. Kitchen and service rooms fronted on the vehicular cul-de-sac, while living rooms fronted onto the garden and pedestrian walkway. Stein writes that this idea "was conceived by that imaginative genius Henry Wright" and that they had both wanted to turn the houses around at Sunnyside Gardens but were dissuaded by conservative opposition.

Not only was the first Radburn superblock beautiful and practical, it was economical. Eliminating through streets reduced the required length of the utility lines and paved streets. By serving fewer houses, they also could be narrower and thus cost less. This saving covered the cost of burying utility lines, "paid for the 12 to 14 per cent of the total area that went into internal parks, [and] also covered the cost of grading and landscaping."[42]

Radburn, 1993. Houses turned around to face the pedestrian path leading to common open space. *(Alexander Garvin)*

As at Sunnyside, there were deed restrictions protecting common open space. Given the size of the landscaped areas, the amount of pavement, and the sparse services provided by government agencies in semirural Fair Lawn, there also had to be a mechanism for disposing sewage, collecting garbage, lighting streets, and maintaining park areas and recreation facilities. To provide these amenities, the CHC established the Radburn Association, "a nonprofit, nonstock corporation to fix, collect, and disburse the annual charges, to maintain the necessary public services, parks, and recreation facilities, and

Radburn, 1993. Children at play in the common open space. *(Alexander Garvin)*

to interpret and apply the protective restrictions." The Association was directed by a self-perpetuating Board of Trustees, like the one established for Llewellyn Park. Initially there were no homeowners on the board. Perhaps in reaction to this form of taxation without representation, two months after the first family moved in, residents formed a Radburn Citizens' Association. It provided a forum for community opinion but had no real power. In response to its recommendations, in 1938 the Radburn Association was reorganized to provide residents more representation and democratic control, but also more responsibility.

The City Housing Corporation started Radburn just as the Depression caused its market to collapse. The project limped along until the CHC declared bankruptcy in 1935 and reluctantly sold the remaining land back to the farmers. As Stein explains, this was inevitable: "Continuous large-scale development is essential to the financial success of a new town such as Radburn. Otherwise the carrying charges on land, main highways, and utilities will soon devour possible profit and force the operating company deeper and deeper into debt."[43]

The completed portion of Radburn covers 149 acres. It contains 430 single-family dwellings, 44 two-family houses, a 96-unit apartment complex, 90 row houses, and 23 acres of parkland. The parkland would eventually include 2 swimming pools, 4 tennis courts, 3 baseball fields, 5 outdoor basketball courts, numerous play areas, and a walkway system that led to the public school.

There is little demographic difference between Radburn and surrounding sections of Fair Lawn, largely built after World War II. However, there is a world of difference in the patterns of daily life. Radburn's children actually play in its generous park facilities, not on the street as they do in neighboring areas. As a result, during its first 20 years, there were only two traffic fatalities in Radburn, both on surrounding "main highways." Forty-seven percent of Radburn's residents shop for groceries on foot; only 8 percent of nearby residents do. One-quarter of Radburnites use bicycles for utilitarian purposes; only 8 percent of nearby residents do.[44]

Fair Lawn, N.J., 1980. Children playing in the street lined with utility poles, directly across from Radburn. *(Alexander Garvin)*

Hampstead Garden Suburb, 1981. Chatham Close, one of the cul-de-sacs that inspired Stein and Wright's design for Radburn. *(Alexander Garvin)*

Despite the obvious superiority of Radburn's planning, none of the developers in Fair Lawn chose to copy it. They created typical subdivisions with look-alike houses on streets with prominent utility poles. The overwhelming majority of America's developers have done the same. It is doubtful that 1 in 100 has even heard of Radburn. Only one component of the Radburn design crept into their work: the cul-de-sac. It reduced development costs, was endorsed by the FHA in its various publications, and became a familiar part of thousands of conventional and FHA insured subdivisions when suburban development resumed after World War II.

If Radburn is unknown to the overwhelming majority of developers, it is revered by virtually all city planners, admired by many architects, and known to housing officials around the world. It is in their work that the Radburn idea has influenced the landscape. In America it became the model for some planned new communities built after World War II. But its greatest impact was in postwar Europe, where government had a more direct role in development. There, government planners made the cul-de-sac, the superblock, and pedestrian-traffic separation familiar elements of both inner-city redevelopment and suburban new communities. This is especially true of England, where "the Radburn idea" became an important element in government-planned communities. The new town of Stevenage, outside London, for example, includes superblocks, specialized road systems, an "open space backbone," and numerous pedestrian underpasses.

Cluster Communities

Radburn may not have become the prototypical motor age suburb. However, Stein and Wright were prescient in identifying a product the suburban market would soon demand: the relatively inexpensive, automobile-oriented subdivision with common landscaped recreation space.

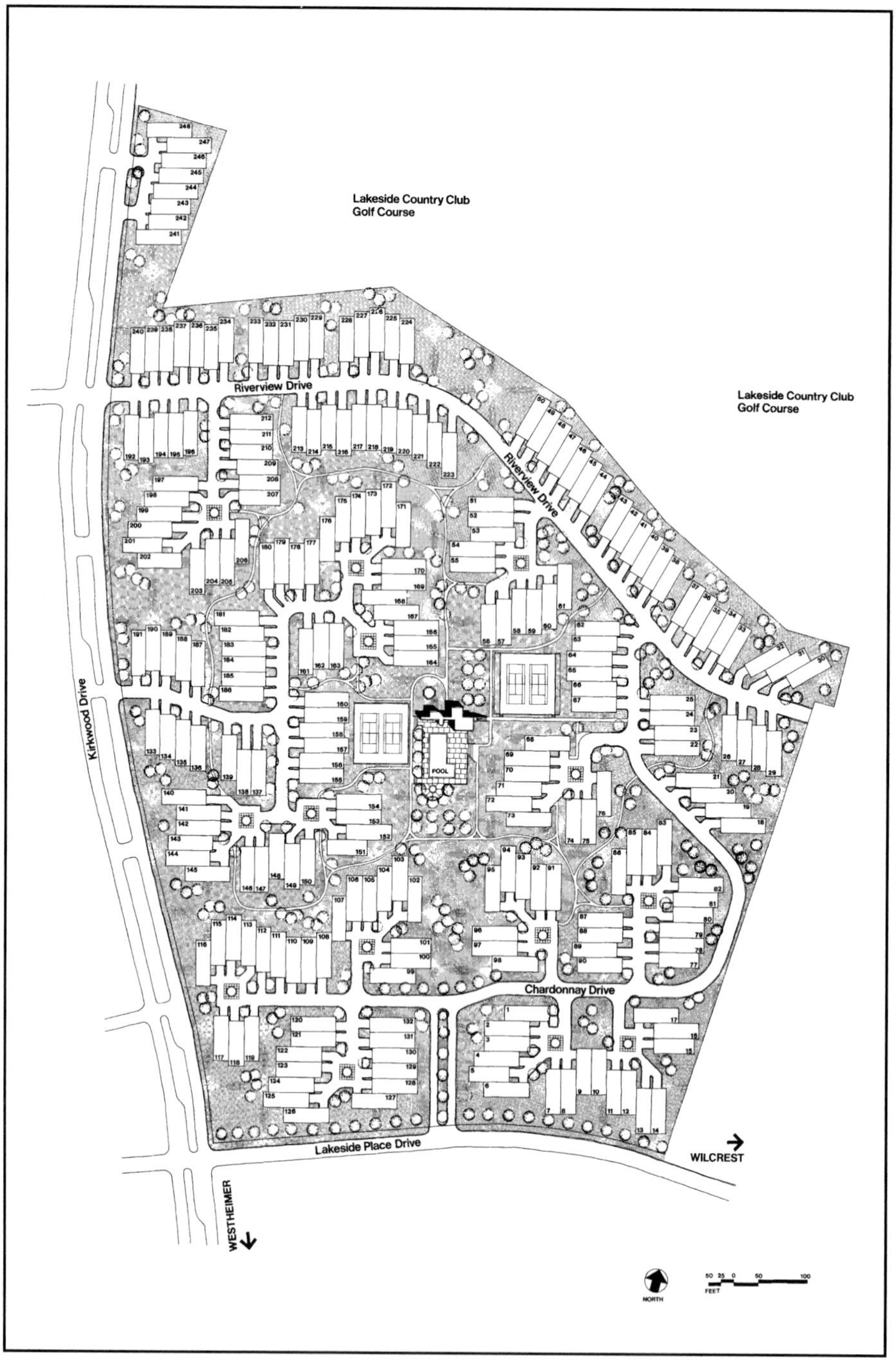

Houston, 1973. Subdivision plan for Epernay in which condominium units are grouped around cul-de-sacs and open onto greenways that lead to the swimming pool, tennis courts, and community center. *(Courtesy of Fisher-Friedman Associates)*

During the first few years after World War II, developers had no trouble supplying the seemingly limitless demand for suburban houses. FHA and VA mortgages were extended to millions of home buyers. The Federal-Aid Highway Act of 1956 provided 90 percent of the cost of interstate highways that made accessible vast areas of cheap land.

By the late 1960s, however, the cost of supplying suburban houses was climbing at a rate that exceeded the increase in consumer purchasing power. New suburban houses were becoming increasingly expensive because of the high cost of land, development, and financing. As land within reasonable automobile commuting distance of cities filled up with single-family detached houses, suitable sites for additional subdivisions became increasingly expensive. Moreover, construction costs were increasing faster than the general rate of inflation.

Mortgage interest rates, which had fluctuated between 3 and 6 percent since the 1930s, suddenly went haywire. Between 1970 and 1974, the prime rate of interest changed 65 times, reaching a high of 12 percent. During the 1981–1982 recession, it changed 77 times, reaching the all-time high of 21.5 percent.[45]

The price of a large house lot on a meandering, tree-lined street became more than many first-time home buyers could afford. Simultaneously, an alternative, cheaper product, the cluster community, appeared on the market. Cluster development reduced costs by attaching residences to one another. It reduced the land cost per unit by fitting more single-family buildings onto the same site. It lowered construction costs by the value of the unbuilt exterior surfaces. It decreased utility installation and roadway expenses by the distance they no longer had to extend.

The cluster community may have been cheaper to produce, but it faced stiff consumer resistance. A site design had to be devised that would provide each resident with easy automobile access and an acceptable amount of private, landscaped open space. There needed to be a form of common ownership for roadways and open space. Most important, this pattern of common residential occupancy had to be made acceptable to lending institutions.

The obvious site design was similar to the Radburn superblock. Residents coming by car could turn off public arteries, drive along minimal commonly owned roadways, and park in their own driveway or garage. Once there, they could use commonly owned pathways to landscaped open spaces that satisfied their desire for a little bit of nature. The designers of cluster communities may have been familiar with Radburn. But the developers and bankers that built and financed them probably had never heard of it. For them, the Radburn idea was the natural product of the economics of development.

Any complex of individually owned residences with common roadways, open space, and community structures requires a form of common ownership. It also requires a legal entity with personnel and money to operate and manage commonly held parts of the complex. Developers ignored the Radburn approach to common ownership and management. They believed a board of successor trustees would be unlikely to appeal to the mass suburban market. Instead they chose the condominium form of ownership.

The term *condominium* refers to that form of ownership in which individual title to a residence is coupled with an ownership interest in land and common areas (roads, walkways, landscaped areas, recreation facilities, etc.). The amount of this common ownership interest is determined by the ratio of square footage contained in the owner's unit to the total square footage of the project. This ratio also determines each owner's degree of control over condominium governance and the dollar amount to be paid for operating a condominium association and managing common areas within the project. The difference between a condominium association and a street association, like those established for the private places of St. Louis, or a community association, like those established for an Olmsted subdivision, lies in the form of common ownership and the specificity of the enumerated responsibilities of the condominium agreement.

Houston, 1974. Epernay housing units are grouped around a cul-de-sac with a decorative pool. *(Alexander Garvin)*

The condominium concept was so new and different that prior to 1973, the U.S. Department of Housing and Urban Development did not publish annual statistics on the number of condominium units built. In 1975, more than 85 percent of the nation's condominium units were not even 5 years old.[46] Condominium ownership may have been slow in gaining acceptance, but it increased in popularity so quickly that by 1984, condo units represented 17 percent of national housing starts.[47]

Lack of lender acceptability was one of the reasons that condominium ownership was slow in gaining acceptance. The FHA refused to insure townhouses without direct street frontage until 1961, when it approved Hartshorn Homes, a 98-unit project in Richmond, Virginia.[48] That was also the year that Congress for the first time empowered the FHA to provide mortgage insurance to condominiums. Within 2 years the FHA published *Planned Unit Development with a Homes Association,* which established condominium eligibility requirements and explained the applicability of FHA Minimum Property Standards.[49]

Appraisal practice created another financing problem. Initially the FHA, the VA, and most mortgage lenders refused to include the value of common areas and facilities in their appraisal of individual condo units. Hence, developers worried that purchasers would not be able to obtain sufficient mortgage financing. In practice this was not a serious problem. The market soon established a value that included these facilities and mortgages reflected this reality.

The quality of condominium communities is as variable as the quality of earlier one-family house subdivisions. In the hands of Olmsted and Company these subdivisions become lovely residential communities. In lesser hands they become arid settings for "little boxes made of ticky-tacky…[that] all look just the same."[50] This also is true of condominium communities. Obviously, the quality of the architecture and the landscaping is critical. However, better condominium communities can be distinguished by their success in dealing with the two critical factors identified by Stein and Wright at

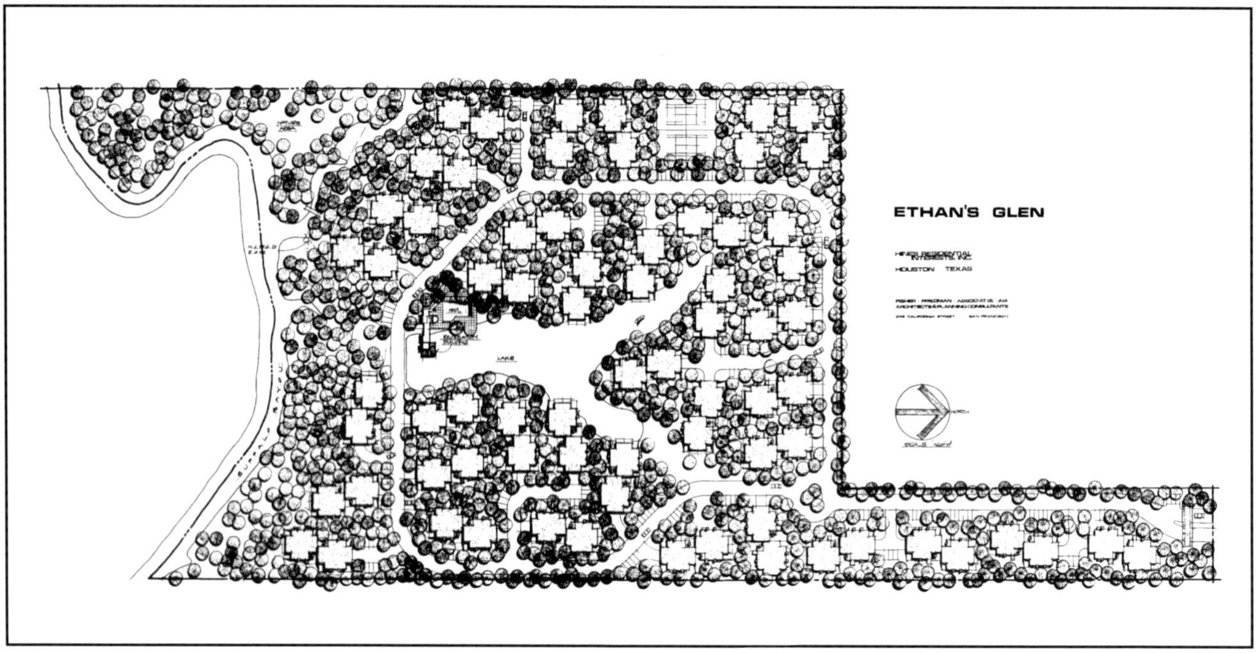

Houston, 1973. Subdivision plan for Ethan's Glen that retains the maximum number of trees by clustering 8 units into one building and locating parking for 12 cars underneath. *(Courtesy of Fisher-Friedman Associates)*

Radburn: the automobile and open space. The critical importance of these factors is beautifully illustrated by Epernay and Ethan's Glen, two Houston cluster communities.[51]

Both projects were begun in 1973 by the same team: developer GreenMark Inc. (a subsidiary of Gerald D. Hines Interests), architect Fisher-Friedman Associates, and landscape architect Sasaki-Walker Associates. Despite differences in appearance, site plan, and landscaping, these projects achieve superior results because they both include generous, landscaped common areas and skillfully incorporate the automobile into their design.[52]

Houston, 1974. Eight-plex houses at Ethan's Glen grouped around an artificial lake and community center. *(Alexander Garvin)*

Epernay is a 248-unit project built on 43.5 relatively featureless acres next to the Lakeside Country Club and Golf Course. The design, like that of Radburn, is based on pedestrian-traffic separation within a superblock in which buildings are clustered around a vehicular cul-de-sac and residences face an open-space system with generous recreation facilities (a swimming pool, clubhouse, and four tennis courts).

Epernay, however, is quite different from Radburn. It consists of clustered townhouses, not single-family residences. The buildings include small landscaped courtyards that introduce a private bit of nature into the rooms within. Radburn has no courtyard houses. Epernay separates pedestrian and vehicular traffic, but provides no underpass where they intersect. It is even more accommodating to automobiles. There are five parking spaces for each townhouse (two in resident-owned garages, two in the driveway, and one in the cul-de-sac cluster). Furthermore, each cul-de-sac provides more than just vehicular access. It is a carefully designed turn-around, specially paved to provide an urbane townhouse setting. Finally, excluding streets, 40 percent of Epernay is common open space, far more than Radburn.

Ethan's Glen is located in a 32-acre section of heavily wooded pine forest with a natural gully running through it. The site design exploits both features to produce a 288-unit condominium community distinctly different from its competitors. An earthfill dam was built in order to create the 2-acre lake and establish a base for the loop road. In an attempt to preserve as much of the forest as possible, residences are gathered together into a free-standing structure that contains 8 two-story units that are lifted half a level above grade. The half-level excavated beneath the cluster provides 12 parking spaces. As at Epernay, 40 percent of the site is common open space, including the lake, swimming pool, two tennis courts, and community center.

Epernay and Ethan's Glen may be more sensitively designed than many other cluster communities. Nevertheless, they illustrate that thoughtfully landscaped open space combined with intelligent handling of the automobile can provide suburbanites with amenities that they could not otherwise afford. This lesson was not lost on developers of rental housing. Once condominium clusters became popular, developers began creating rental communities that also integrated parking, included a swimming pool and club house, and provided common open space. The difference between rental and condo communities is essentially the market they are trying to capture. Most rental communities are aimed at singles, recently married couples, and those without sufficient savings or income to buy their residence. The condo communities are usually directed to first- or second-time home buyers.

Cluster Zoning (Planned Unit Development)

Cluster development may be a popular marketplace phenomenon, but it is even more popular with those who wish to alter

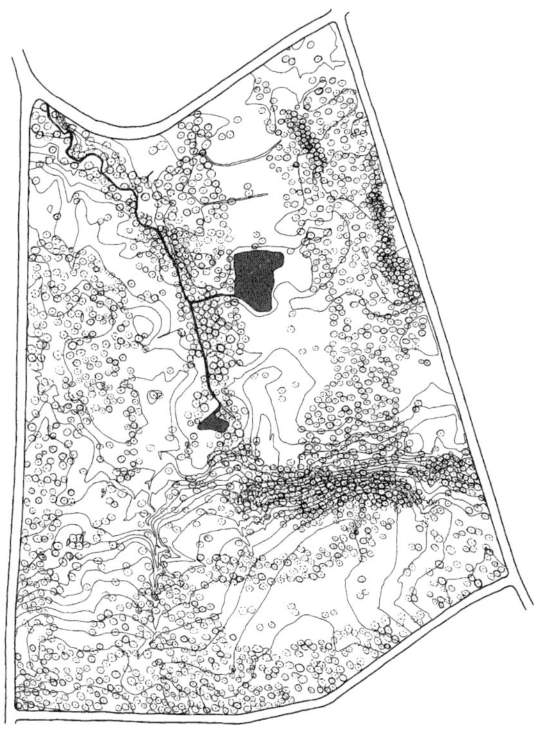

Planned unit development (PUD), 1968. Left: Contour map showing existing features (trees, ponds, creek, and bounding road) of a 205-acre undeveloped site. Top right: Site plan showing conventional street grid (with 1427 single-family house lots) that destroys the natural character of the site. Bottom right: Plan generated by using the cluster zoning approach would preserve the natural features of the site, provide for an elementary school and shopping facilities, and accommodate 1445 housing units in a range of house types (detached and semidetached houses, townhouses, and attached row houses). *(Courtesy of New York City Department of City Planning)*

marketplace desires. In the attempt to encourage this alternative to cookie-cutter suburban subdivisions they have persuaded most communities to add a cluster zoning or "planned unit development" (PUD) alternative to conventional zoning requirements.

Radburn, Epernay, and Ethan's Glen required only subdivision approval. There were no zoning regulations to comply with. In most places suburban development must comply with yard, setback, density, and a multitude of other zoning restrictions (see Chapter 16). Thus, the only way to create a cluster community with ample common open space, tailored to its site and natural features, is to do so outside traditional district-by-district zoning requirements.

Cluster zoning achieves this objective by overriding conventional lot-by-lot requirements, substituting instead general regulations that are applied to the site as a whole. It allows the same number of residences to be clustered in a manner that avoids costly construction on steep slopes or over waterways and permits attractive natural features to be retained without violating bulk, density, parking, or open-space requirements.

In its most straightforward form, cluster zoning permits density redistribution by relaxing zoning regulations for those projects that meet its requirements (e.g., minimum parcel size, minimum open space, "good" site planning). A second approach also increases density for projects that provide specified site amenities. For example, Phoenix, Arizona, allows a 1 percent increase in density for each 4 percent of unimproved common open space or each 2 percent of improved common open space.[53] New York City provides bonuses for common open space, "good" site plans, community facilities (e.g., schools, day care centers, libraries), enclosed parking, and increased room sizes.[54]

One serious problem with cluster zoning is that it is not self-executing. Furthermore, project approval is discretionary. Since requirements such as "good" site planning are matters of opinion, the approval process can be abused by the reviewing entity. As a result, poorly drafted PUD ordinances may result in bribery, political pay-offs, or extra "amenities" demanded by adjacent (opposing) community groups. From a planning perspective, the most serious result may be scaring off reputable developers. One way to counteract these abuses and encourage cluster development is to specify minimal processing requirements and impose strict time limits. When Memphis, Tennessee, for example, limited the review period for PUDs to 14 days, it experienced "a dramatic increase in the number of PUD applications."[55]

The most important benefit of PUDs is not that they produce better suburban communities. That depends on the development team (entrepreneur, architect, landscape architect, and financial institution). The real benefit of cluster zoning is that it allows greater design flexibility, permits lower production costs, and produces a landscape with greater diversity in open-space arrangement and building distribution.

The Ingredients of Success

Until now developing residential suburbs has been easy. There has been an endless stream of customers and a seemingly inexhaustible supply of land. Developers simply had to obtain the financing, package the necessary elements, and offer their product for sale. Success only required doing it more effectively than the competition.

Market

Residential suburbs attract customers by offering at lower prices a product that is equivalent to their competition, by offering amenities that are not available elsewhere, or both. Consequently, successful suburban developers are careful to keep their cost of production lower than the prevailing market price of neighboring properties or to offer a residential living environment that surpasses them.

Some developers are able to offer lower prices because the cost of land and infrastructure is spread over a large number of houses. Others find ways of lowering the cost of producing the houses themselves. The developers and designers of Sudbrook Park and Fisher Hill reduced site costs by exploiting local topography in a manner that minimized costly site work. Ethan's Glen reduced construction costs by combining eight residences into a single structure and minimizing exterior surfaces.

There are numerous ways of offering a better than average living environment. The developers of the private places of St. Louis provided enhanced privacy and landscaped islands. Sunnyside Gardens included carefully landscaped, commonly owned open space. Cluster communities add swimming pools, club houses, or other recreation facilities. Whatever the extras may be, they will help one project to outperform another.

Location

Accessibility is critical to the success of any suburban location. Boston's South End and Back Bay were sure to succeed because they were at the edge of the densely packed, rapidly expanding center city. Brooklyn Heights and Druid Hills, became desirable because their developers exploited transportation systems that improved site accessibility, underscoring that location is a matter of time, not just spatial proximity.

Too many people erroneously believe that proximity has become less important because the automobile has made distant areas more accessible. Despite widespread dependence on cars and trucks, more than 70 percent of the American population remains concentrated on 1.5 percent of the land. Since most development sites will continue to be located within commuting distance of a relatively compact existing patterns of employment, shopping, and entertainment, we must find better ways of exploiting those locations.[56]

The success of any location is tied to the character of the area itself. Druid Hills had the benefit of ravines that provided natural drainage. Fisher Hill offered splendid views of Boston. Stands of fully grown pine provided a distinctive landscape for Ethan's Glen. In each case their site plan amplified these assets.

Dull sites need something that will enliven them. Prospect Park South and Epernay were created on flat, characterless sites. Their success was dependent on skillful site planning and inventive landscaping. Too many residential suburbs fail because they offer an undistinguished location at prices that are similar to neighboring developments that offer something extra.

Design

The most common criticism of residential suburbs is their "cookie cutter" appearance. Those whose design is better are able to exploit their competitive advantage. The developers of Sunnyside Gardens, for example, offered a better arrangement of streets, sidewalks, and open space than was available in neighboring sections of Queens. Lots on Portland and Westmoreland Places in St. Louis had the benefit of more imposing gatehouses, broader park islands, and larger house lots. The Olmsteds exploited the regional character of the Southern pines and evergreen magnolias that were native to Druid Hills. In all these instances design was integral to the marketing strategy.

By altering the arrangement of lots, houses, and open space, the designers of the Back Bay and Radburn changed the pattern of daily life. The new combination of below-street-grade service alleys and broad streets in the Back Bay allowed builders to create more convenient row houses than were available elsewhere in the city. Stein and Wright accomplished a similar result in Radburn by altering the relationship between traffic arteries and houses, reorienting the service and living spaces of each house, and by relocating and connecting outdoor play areas. As a result, its open spaces were more convenient and usable than those of competing developments. More important, the site plan established a new form of suburban living that had great appeal to home buyers who chose to live in Fair Lawn.

Dimensions are particularly important in determining the marketability of residential developments. For example, the relatively compact Radburn cul-de-sac allowed Stein and Wright to increase the amount of landscaped common open space without increasing project cost. The 25-foot minimum lot width in the Back Bay guaranteed that each building could fit four relatively wide rooms on each floor, two with windows opening onto the street and two more opening onto the rear yard. Row houses in competing areas were often too narrow to fit comfortably more than one room in front and another in back.

The "look" or "build" of a residential suburb is equally important. The gatehouses at Portland and Westmoreland Places distinguish them from more modest private places in St. Louis, just as the exquisite landscaping of Druid Hills distinguishes it from more conventional Atlanta subdivisions. Some designers exploit the existing landscape to provide their project with distinctive character. The site plan for Ethan's Glen, for example, transformed existing pine trees into a design and marketing feature. On the other hand, there was nothing about the site of Forest Hills Gardens to differentiate it from the rest of Queens. Its distinctiveness was achieved by requiring all buildings to have red clay tile roofs.

Project failure is often a result of an unsightly design. In the attempt to avoid such failures, many communities adopt deed restrictions or enact subdivision regulations and zoning ordinances that determine lot size, building placement, allow able building materials, and landscaping. Unfortunately, by themselves, such controls do not guarantee a convenient or beautiful suburban landscape.

Financing

All residential suburbs encounter financing problems. Developers need capital to pay for property acquisition, planning, site development, infrastructure installation, and the expense of carrying the property till development costs have been recouped. Future residents need long-term mortgages to pay for the purchase of their house. Thus, the availability and cost of financing is critical. Joel Hurt had to sell Druid Hills to a consortium that had better access to capital. Forest Hills Gardens and Radburn both faltered on their ability to provide even a limited return during periods of meager sales. In the Back Bay the problem of development financing was eliminated by taking it out of the hands of the private sector. The Commission on Public Lands front-ended the cost of planning, filling the site, and marketing individual lots.

In 1940, 15 percent of the American population lived in suburbs. Half a century later that percentage had climbed to 46 percent.[57] Without low-interest, low-downpayment FHA and VA mortgages, this post-World-War II suburbanization would not have been possible. More important, the availability of FHA and VA mortgages ensured that new suburban development would not be reserved primarily for the upper middle class.

During the 1960s, 1970s, and 1980s, local government began to demand that developers donate land for schools, parks, and streets and even that they help pay for water and sewer pipes, bury electric wiring, and provide extra landscaping and a variety of expensive amenities. The cost of these requirements were transferred to home buyers and threatened again to limit new development to upper-middle-class consumers. The only way to reduce costs was to build row houses, apartment buildings, and condominiums. Without FHA acceptance of this form of ownership and FHA regulations establishing the requirements for condominium mortgages, such development would not have become widespread. So once again, government mortgage insurance prevented suburban development from again becoming the exclusive preserve of the upper middle class.

If we are to improve the character of our residential suburbs, we must reject national monetary policy that is dependent on roller-coaster interest rates. We must return to the relative stability of the middle third of the twentieth century when the Federal Reserve made sure that there was a stable supply of money that was large enough to finance landscaping, infrastructure, and community facilities—not just little boxes made of ticky-tacky.

Entrepreneurship

Some developers excel at coordinating the many activities and participants required to create a residential suburb. Others are better at finding innovative approaches to the development process. Public policies should make it easy for the developer to do both with minimum risk. The best way to effect this is by making it easier for developers, whether they are government agencies, limited-profit or nonprofit institutions, or private developers, to produce attractive residential suburbs.

FHA minimum property standards provide a demonstration of what intelligent government programs can achieve. Developers who depended on FHA financing were forced into producing residential suburbs that met higher standards. Once they established that minimum standard, developers of more expensive suburbs had to provide something better. Cluster zoning, for example, makes it easier for the developer to preserve natural features, provide amenities, and lower development costs.

Sometimes the cost, time, and risk involved in developing a residential suburb are too high to interest the private market. In those cases, the best option is to create and finance a public entrepreneur. Boston adopted this approach for the Back Bay. Because few areas involve such extraordinary resources or risk, the country continues to avoid public entrepreneurs and depends on the private sector.

Development by nonprofit and limited-profit institutions is often thought to be a more effective way of developing residential suburbs. Forest Hills Gardens, Sunnyside Gardens, and Radburn provide resounding evidence that they can produce projects that are more attractive than those of many contemporaneous, profit-motivated competitors. It is therefore tempting (but often wrong) to think that their projects are also less costly. Nonprofit developers still have to provide a reasonable return to their lenders. Furthermore, it is not at all clear that they spend less on personnel and overhead than their profit-oriented competition. In fact, Forest Hills Gardens was terminated because the Russell Sage Foundation could not compete with conventional developers' lower development costs.

The most serious problem with this model, though, is that only a handful of nonprofit entities are involved with real estate development. Like the City Housing Corporation, which developed Sunnyside Gardens and Radburn, they tend to go out of existence after a small number of projects. Without a large supply of experienced nonprofit developers, there is no way to sustain any serious level of production.

It is not the type of developer that is significant. It is the financial and regulatory context in which they operate that matters. Thus, the most promising route to improved suburban development are laws that are easy to understand and enforce. The certainty and predictability of such laws reduces risk. More important, they establish a regulatory environment in which developers are more likely to produce higher quality, less costly, and more appropriate residential suburbs.

Time

Some residential suburbs are designed in a manner that makes one's stay there a rich experience. The landscaping of an Olmsted subdivision, for example, enhances the experience of traveling home, spending the day on one's property, and mixing with the neighbors. Radburn provides playgrounds, swimming pools, landscaped recreation areas, and an elementary school, all gathered together in an environment free of the dangers of vehicular traffic. The promotional brochure for Epernay points out that:

> *You can enjoy relaxing around the pool or a quick game of tennis. A bicycle ride or jogging on the paths. Croquet in any one of a hundred spots in your green commonyard. Or just enjoy your neighbors—an informal chat across the backyard fence or cocktails in their patio.*[58]

Any of these examples illustrates that successful marketing of residential subdivisions requires more than a nice house at an affordable price. In addition, the trip through the project must be a pleasant experience, and living there must provide a wide range of activities 24 hours a day, 7 days a week.

The most difficult problem facing developers of residential suburbs, though, is financial security over the life of the project. Most residential suburbs require a massive investment in infrastructure and site work. The costs of carrying this investment cannot be charged to the first few lots that are sold; they must be retired by a steady stream of sales. Anything can go wrong: shortages of materials, strikes, sudden competition, unanticipated construction problems....The worst disaster is an economic downturn. If Radburn had not opened for sale just in time for the Great Depression, the City Housing Corporation might still be in business and Radburn might have become the first of many residential suburbs made up of superblocks with open-space backbones and pedestrian traffic separation.

A City Planning Strategy for the Suburban Landscape

The distinction between city and suburb withered away long ago. American cities engulf their suburbs almost as soon as they are created. Within a few decades of its inception Brooklyn Heights was already part of the city of Brooklyn. Of the suburbs discussed in this chapter, only Sudbrook Park, Maryland, and Radburn, New Jersey, are not within the political boundaries of a large city.

Even the notion of city limits has long ceased to have much meaning. H. G. Wells had it right in 1902, when he wrote that

> *"town" and "city" will be, in truth, terms as obsolete as "mail coach." For these new areas that will grow out of them we want a term, and...we may for our present purposes call these coming town provinces "urban regions."*[59]

The urban regions he foresaw have not turned out to be single-city centered. Of the 185 metropolitan statistical areas (MSA) enumerated by the U.S. Census in 1990, 71 are component primary metropolitan statistical areas (PMSA) of 20 consolidated metropolitan statistical areas (CMSA). For example, the San Francisco-Oakland-San José CMSA includes PMSAs named for those cities as well as for Santa Cruz, Santa Rosa-Petaluma, and Vallejo-Fairfield-Napa.[60]

Nor are central cities any longer the focus of life in these urban-suburban regions. As Christopher Tunnard explained in 1958, in his pioneering article, "America's Super-Cities:"

> *The family...is not beholden to any one central business district either for shopping or for employment. Travel time is the chief factor here, not distance, and it is quite possible that husband and wife may go in opposite directions to get to their jobs.*[61]

This observation has become more accurate with every passing year. The 1990 Census reported that 77.5 percent of the population lived in metropolitan areas and that, of the 29 communities that surpassed a population of 100,000 during the previous decade, 22 were not free-standing cities but political subdivisions of major metropolitan areas.[62]

Despite the complexity of these urban regions, their "suburban" residential districts are all variants of only three forms: the rectilinear plat, the curvilinear subdivision, and the cluster community. There is one significant difference between the cluster community and the other two. It is centered around common open space and therefore is as fundamentally private as is exclusive Llewellyn Park with its gatehouse and police force. The other two forms are dominated by public streets and sidewalks that, in the words of Frederick Law Olmsted, Sr., ensure their residents are not "far removed from the life of the community."

Many of the better suburban plats achieve their distinctiveness through deed restrictions that establish minimum development standards. Olmsted and Company achieved it by tailoring their subdivisions to local topography, climate, and vegetation. Developers of more recent cluster communities have done so by building in a consistent (though often heavy-handed) architectural style.

Today, virtually all development is subject to local regulations. Unfortunately, regulation is not an automatic path to lovely residential suburbs. Government cannot legislate good design. The best course is to reduce to an absolute minimum the amount of time and money spent getting public approvals and let developers spend the savings on the projects themselves.

Even if every residential suburb was beautifully laid out and distinguishable from its neighbors, it would lack a mutually reinforcing relationship with neighboring districts. The gatehouses built for the private places of St. Louis provide visible evidence that residents wish to be protected from their surroundings. Stein and Wright's attempt to include within each Radburn superblock the basic components of daily life reflects a similar desire to insulate project residents from automobile traffic. The difference is that at Radburn, Stein and Wright envisioned a system of interconnected pedestrian spines that would tie its superblocks together into a single healthy community. But even if its internal circulation system had been completed, Radburn (like virtually all residential suburbs) would still lack a mechanism with which to promote interaction with other subdivisions and with the region as a whole.

Another difficulty with the suburban landscape is that visitors and residents alike rarely have any means of orientation. Except in those regions that remained wedded to the rectilinear structure provided by the Northwest Ordinance and the Homestead Act, or that are carefully oriented to the interstate highway network, or that are shaped by prominent topographical features, it is difficult to find one's way through the accumulation of loops, cul-de-sacs, and winding roads.

Observers frequently criticize residential suburbs for failing to provide shopping, employment, entertainment, recreation, institutional, and transportation facilities. This is unfair. Our urban regions do not suffer from a lack of shopping malls, drive-in retail establishments, office parks, or industrial districts. The private sector is ready to oblige wherever it identifies a ready market for such facilities.

If there is a lack of schools, hospitals, libraries, and other public institutions, it is because the public either does not want to pay for them or is unwilling to make the tough decisions needed to locate and build them. The same is true where there is insufficient public transit or parkland.

The common prescription for correcting all these problems is regional decision making. There is a vast literature on regional planning but, as the landscape so graphically demonstrates, it has had very little impact. Nor is regional decision making likely to become more effective. The dense thicket of government jurisdictions is getting ever more crowded and the demand for local participation ever louder and more prevalent.[63]

If we are to correct the unsatisfactory nature of the suburban landscape we must deal with two different situations. On one hand, we must augment already built-up areas by providing adequate means of orientation and places in which the residents of its various plats, subdivisions, and cluster communities can interact with one another. On the other hand, we must see that developers build new residential suburbs with the framework of public places that has been missing in most existing suburbs.

An Open-Space Backbone for Existing Suburbs

There is as yet no public support for reorganizing the hodgepodge of existing suburban communities. People may think it difficult to find their way through its loops and cul-de-sacs, but they will not support public action because they think this problem can only be remedied by creating new traffic arteries. Not only would this be expensive, it also would require condemning property and dislocating large numbers of people and businesses. Besides, most suburbanites would oppose assisting strangers to intrude into secluded communities. In fact, additional roads would not be of much help. Community interaction requires places that attract large numbers of people who want to do things together, not new traffic arteries that would only increase interaction among automobiles.

Places of public interaction will not be forthcoming without changes in public opinion and political leadership. A good example is the open-space system acquired since 1967 by the City of Boulder, Colorado. When civic leaders wanted to preserve the remaining mountain backdrop and the entrances to the Boulder Valley, they did not create a regional government or publish a needs analysis; they imposed a \$.004 sales tax to be used for open-space acquisition.[64]

Boulder has acquired more than 40,000 acres. This acreage includes a system of greenways that was created out of runoff channels, drainage corridors, and streams. The money from Boulder's open-space tax allowed the city to expand, landscape, and transform these neglected corridors into bicycle/jogging trails, wildlife preserves, and recreation areas—not just storm drainage and flood channels. At the same time they connect new and old athletic fields, school yards, picnic areas, and playgrounds. Thus, Boulder's greenways perform the role of an open-space backbone that Stein and Wright had intended for Radburn.

While other communities may not have Boulder's extensive network of streams and creeks, they have other underutilized properties. These include unbuildable steep slopes, abandoned buildings (drive-in movies, isolated retail clusters, warehouses, schools, etc.), unpaved rights-of-way, once actively used roads, and empty lots. Such properties can be knitted together into a similar open-space backbone.

A different prescription is necessary for newly developing suburban areas. It, too, must be one that gratefully accepts the participation of all the economic and political factors that shape our urban-suburban marketplace. Strange as it may seem, real estate development in eighteenth-century Bath, England, provides one model for such an approach.

Bath, England

During the second and third quarters of the eighteenth century, the architect-developer-builders John Wood I and II, conceived a pattern of urbanization that consisted of an interconnected system of individual buildings, streets, and public spaces. Working in Bath, a resort which became popular during the reign of Queen Anne, they created one of the world's most beautiful urban designs.[65]

John Wood I moved to Bath in 1727 to be an agent for the 85-acre Barton Estate located on the northern edge of what was then a resort town of little more than 40 acres. He and his son went on to lease land from the Barton Estate and from other property owners; subdividing it into streets, public spaces, and building lots; specifying required building façades; preparing the necessary sublease agreements; and then either contracting with or subletting to local craftsmen, tradesmen, and builders who would execute the design. The Woods or

Colorado, 1993. Suburban sprawl prevented from spreading into Boulder by the greenbelt of parks acquired by the city of Boulder for that purpose. *(Alexander Garvin)*

Bath, 1970. Aerial photograph illustrating the sequence of park-centered housing developments created by John Wood I and II. *(Courtesy of Unichrome Ltd.)*

their lessees found the ultimate tenants, obtained their agreement to rent the proposed building for a lengthy term, and then used these agreements to obtain the necessary construction loan from a bank. There was nothing new in this process. It was the common practice in eighteenth-century England (see Chapter 3). What was different was the extent of their vision and the unity of the resulting product.

The Woods's major venture was a sequence of five projects: Queen's Square, Gay Street, King's Circus, Brock Street, and Royal Crescent. In diagrammatic form it is a square connected by a street to a circle, which, in turn, is connected by another street to a half-ellipse.[66] Each component is formed by attached row houses with interiors built to suit the occupants. The Circus, for example, appears to be a cylindrical volume of open space trisected by streets and bounded by three uniform buildings. In fact it is 33 privately owned structures which, seen from the air, appear to be a jumble of extensions from a common façade. The same is true of the 30 houses making up

Bath, 1972. Royal Crescent. *(Alexander Garvin)*

the Royal Crescent. The unity of the venture comes not from the plan alone, but from the common use of honey-colored stone, the consistent relationship of each building to the street, the similar height of the structures, the consistent Georgian style of the architecture, and the common restrictive covenants written into each lease.

The Woods were two among the many developers who, between 1725 and 1800, built the 5000 residences that formed the suburban extensions of Bath. Similar suburban extensions were built in London, Edinburgh, Brighton, and cities throughout the British Isles. The public streets and squares of Bath were built by different developers at different times. They followed no preordained regional blueprint. But they did provide the distinctive settings that differentiated one complex from another and provided a means of integrating each new addition with the preexisting whole.

An Open-Space Backbone for Developing Areas

The Bath approach has to be altered to be suitable for the American market. Here, suburban development is not controlled by great estates that benefit from whatever improvements a lessee leaves behind. Our suburbs are created by developers who purchase fee title to the land, do whatever is required to make a profit on resale, and then forget about it. Furthermore, we cannot expect our highly politicized government agencies to lavish the nurturing attention provided by long-term estate management.

Any successful planning strategy for further suburbanization must distill those practices that were successful in Bath. It must ensure that they can be understood easily by the developers that will implement them and can be sold to an increasingly choosy market at a price it can afford. Most important, these practices must be translated into government regulations that will be applied in a uniform manner by the widest variety of officials and jurisdictions.

Only one action is necessary. Local subdivision and zoning regulations must be amended to require *public* (not just private or common) open space in any subdivision or condominium community. California, for example, allows local government to create new parkland as part of the subdivision approval process. Its Subdivision Map Act authorizes cities and counties to require developers to dedicate parkland or to collect a so-called Quimby fee that will allow the jurisdiction to purchase land for parks. If every developer had to dedicate 30 percent of any site to public use and if site occupants, whether owners or renters, were legally responsible for its maintenance, our suburban landscape would begin to have the public places needed for "the refined domestic life, secluded, but not far removed from the life of the community," that Olmsted recommended.

This strategy is so simple that public officials cannot stall while they check if a development meets legal requirements; developers cannot say it is too difficult to produce; and home buyers cannot fail to be attracted by the value of its public amenities. Furthermore, it can be achieved without any appreciable increase in cost. Developers, whether building meandering subdivisions (with private open space) or condominium communities (with common open space), are already providing open space. All they need to do is locate it so that it is not separated for the exclusive use of their residents. Since most suburban developments already provide substantially more than 30 percent open space, there will be plenty of land left over to provide each resident with appropriate accessory (private or common) open space.

Whether this new, public open space takes the form of park islands, like those of the private places of St. Louis, or meandering linear parks, like those in Atlanta's Druid Hills, or some other form, it can transform noncommunities into places that are recognizably different from one another. As the landscape fills in, these new open spaces will become part of a sequence of public places that will provide a distinctive and varied setting for public activity, a connective tissue transforming independent developments into interdependent neighborhoods, and a means of orientation that can be understood and admired by residents and visitors alike.

Notes

1. James W. Rouse, "The City of Columbia, Maryland," p. 839, in *Taming Megalopolis,* vol. 2, H. Wentworth Eldredge (editor), Anchor Books, Doubleday, Garden City, N.Y., 1967.
2. Kenneth Jackson, *The Crabgrass Frontier,* Oxford University Press, New York, 1985, p. 135.
3. Pliny the Younger (c. A.D. 61–114) describing his villa at Laurentum outside Rome, quoted in: J. J. Pollitt, *The Art of Rome c. 753 B.C.–337 A.D.,* Prentice-Hall, Englewood Cliffs, N.J., 1966, pp. 171–174.
4. Address of President Hoover delivered at Constitution Hall, Washington, D.C., December 2, 1931, quoted in Charles Abrams, *The City Is the Frontier,* Harper & Row, New York, 1965, p. 254.
5. The houses fronted on streets, either 75 feet or 37.5 feet wide, and were serviced by a 22.5-foot alley.
6. I am persuaded by Christopher Tunnard and Kenneth Jackson that Brooklyn Heights is America's first planned suburb. See Tunnard, *The Modern American City,* Van Nostrand, 1968, Princeton, pp. 33–34, and Jackson, op. cit., pp. 25–32.
7. *Long Island Star,* December 24, 1823.
8. Historical and statistical information on Prospect Park is derived from New York City Landmarks Preservation Commission, *Prospect Park South Historic District Designation Report,* New York City, 1979.

9. *Prospect Park South,* prospectus, Brooklyn, 1900.
10. Historical and statistical information on the Private Places of St. Louis is derived from Charles Savage, *Architecture of the Private Streets of St. Louis,* University of Missouri Press, Columbia, 1987.
11. Historical and statistical information on the South End and the Back Bay is derived from Walter Muir Whitehill, *Boston—A Topographical History,* The Belknap Press of Harvard University Press, Cambridge, 1968, and Bainbridge Bunting, *Houses of the Back Bay,* The Belknap Press of Harvard University Press, Cambridge, 1967, especially pp. 129–139, 250–255, and 360–399.
12. For a discussion of the resulting lawsuit, see Stanley K. Schultz, *Constructing Urban Culture—American Cities and City Planning 1800–1920,* Temple University Press, Philadelphia, 1989, pp. 39–41.
13. Whitehill, op. cit., p. 122.
14. Between 1852 and 1855 the Harbor and Land Commission was known as the Commission on Boston Harbor and Back Bay Lands. After 1970 it became known as the Harbor and Land Commission.
15. Among the more interesting analyses of the impact of transportation on suburban growth are James E. Vance, Jr., *Capturing the Horizon,* The Johns Hopkins University Press, Baltimore, 1900; Sam B. Warner Jr., *Streetcar Suburbs, The Process of Growth in Boston 1870–1900,* Atheneum, New York, 1969; and David Brodsly, *L.A. Freeway,* University of California Press, Berkeley and Los Angeles, 1981 (especially pp. 61–82 and 151–160).
16. For a discussion of California's development regulations, see Marc A. Weiss, *The Rise of the Community Builders, The American Real Estate Industry and Urban Land Planning,* Columbia University Press, New York, 1987.
17. Kenneth Jackson, op. cit., pp. 203–218 and Marc A. Weiss, op. cit., pp. 141–158.
18. Historical and statistical information on the Olmsted firm is derived from Charles E. Beveridge and Carolyn F. Hoffman, *The Master List of Design Projects of the Olmsted Firm 1857–1950,* National and Massachusetts Associations for Olmsted Parks, Boston, 1987; maps, drawings, and photographs maintained at the Frederick Law Olmsted National Historic Site in Brookline, Massachusetts, by the National Park Service; Charles Capen McLaughlin and Charles E. Beveridge (editors), *The Papers of Frederick Law Olmsted,* vols. 1–6, Johns Hopkins University Press, Baltimore, 1977–1992; Laura Wood Roper, *FLO—A Biography of Frederick Law Olmsted,* Johns Hopkins University Press, Baltimore, 1973; and Elizabeth Stevenson, *Park Maker—A Life of Frederick Law Olmsted,* Macmillan, New York, 1977.
19. I am unable to determine whether Olmsted knew or visited Blaise Hamlet (1811) or Park Village West (1830), Sir John Nash's pioneering, village-inspired suburban communities.
20. Charles Capen McLaughlin and Charles E. Beveridge (editors), *The Papers of Frederick Law Olmsted, vol. 1, The Formative Years 1822–1852,* Johns Hopkins University Press, Baltimore, 1977, pp. 74–77.
21. Andrew Jackson Downing, "Our Country Villages," *Horticulturist,* 4, no. 12, New York, June 1850, pp. 537–541.
22. McLaughlin and Beveridge (editors), op. cit., p. 282.
23. Olmsted, Vaux and Company, *Preliminary Report upon the Proposed Suburban Village at Riverside, near Chicago,* originally published in 1868 and reprinted in S. B. Sutton (editor), *Civilizing American Cities,* M.I.T. Press, Cambridge, 1971, p. 299.
24. Schultz, op. cit., p. 175.
25. The idea of bringing the lawn right up to the house predates Olmsted, having been introduced during the eighteenth century by the English landscape gardener Capability Brown.
26. Most, but not all, of the streets of Sudbrook Park were completed as designed. Many of the original lots were later subdivided to accommodate smaller suburban houses. The railroad station was demolished. As a result, one can no longer see all of the community that Olmsted envisioned. Nevertheless, the bulk of Sudbrook Park remains as he designed it more than a century ago. Some sections of Parkside follow Olmsted designs. Tarrytown Heights was stillborn.
27. Historical and statistical information on Fisher Hill is derived from Cynthia Zaitzevsky, *Frederick Law Olmsted and the Boston Park System,* Harvard University Press, Cambridge, 1982, pp. 114–117.
28. Historical and statistical information on Druid Hills is derived from Elizabeth A. Lyon, "Frederick Law Olmsted and Joel Hurt: Planning for Atlanta," pp. 165–193 in Dana F. White and Victor A. Kramer (editors), *Olmsted South,* Greenwood Press, Westport, Conn., 1979, and maps, drawings, and photographs maintained at the Frederick Law Olmsted National Historic Site.
29. John M. Glenn, general director of the Russell Sage Foundation, *Statement,* dated September 4, 1911, quoted by Arthur C. Comey and Max S. Wehrly in *Urban Planning and Land Policies,* Urbanism Committee to the National Resource Committee, U.S. Government Printing Office, Washington, D.C., 1939, pp. 104–105.
30. Minutes of the Sage Foundation Homes Company, April 15, 1924, quoted by Comey and Wehrly, op. cit., p. 108.
31. Comey and Wehrly, op. cit., p. 109.
32. Statistical and historical information on Radburn is derived from Clarence Stein, *Toward New Towns for America,* M.I.T. Press, Cambridge, 1966, and Eugenie Ladner Birch, "Radburn and the American Planning Movement," pp. 122–151 in *Introduction to Planning History in the United States,* Donald A. Krueckeberg (editor), The Center for Urban Policy Research, Rutgers University, New Brunswick, 1983.
33. Stein, op. cit., p. 41.
34. Statistical and historical information on Sunnyside Gardens is derived from Stein, op. cit., and Franklin J. Havelick and Michael Kwartler, "Sunnyside Gardens—Whose Land Is It?" *New York Affairs,* vol. 7, no. 2, N.Y.U., New York, 1982, pp. 65–80.
35. Havelick and Kwartler, op. cit., p. 73.
36. Stein, op. cit., p. 44.
37. Roy Lubove, *Community Planning in the 1920s: The Contribution of the Regional Planning Association of America,* University of Pittsburgh Press, Pittsburgh, 1962.
38. Stein, op. cit., pp. 14–15.
39. Clarence Perry, *Regional Survey of New York and its Environs,* vol. 7, Committee on Regional Plan of New York and Its Environs, New York, 1929, pp. 34–35.
40. Stein, op. cit., p. 47.
41. Ibid., p. 44.
42. Ibid., p. 48.
43. Ibid., p. 68.
44. "Radburn Revisited," *Ekistics,* March 1972, p. 200.
45. Colleen Grogan Moore, *PUDs in Practice,* Urban Land Institute, Washington, D.C., 1985, p. 9.
46. Robert Engstrom and Marc Putman, *Planning and Design of Townhouses and Condominiums,* The Urban Land Institute, Washington, D.C., 1986, p. 5.
47. U.S. Bureau of the Census, *Statistical Abstract of the United States: 1989* (109th edition), Washington, D.C., 1989, p. 700.
48. Engstrom and Putman, op. cit., p. 5.
49. Moore, op. cit., p. 5.
50. Malvina Reynolds, "Little Boxes," (ASCAP).
51. Statistical and historical information on Epernay and Ethan's Glen is derived from Carla C. Sabala (editor), *Houston Today,* Urban Land Institute, Washington, D.C., 1974, pp. 94–99.
52. Common areas and facilities are not managed by a condominium association but held in trust for the benefit of the homeowners by the Texas Commerce Bank.
53. Moore, op. cit., p. 17.
54. New York City Zoning Resolution, Chapter 8, Sections 78-34 and 78-351 through 78-354.
55. Moore, op. cit., p. 19.
56. Peter Wolf, *Land in America,* Pantheon Books, New York, 1981, pp. 24–25.
57. *New York Times,* June 1, 1992.
58. GreenMark, Inc., *Epernay,* Houston.
59. H. G. Wells, *Anticipations,* quoted by Christopher Tunnard in "America's Super-Cities," in Wentworth Eldredge (editor), *Taming Megalopolis,* vol. 1, Anchor Books, Garden City, 1967, p. 6. The Tunnard article is adapted from an earlier version originally published in *Harper's Magazine,* vol. 217, issue 1299, August 1958.
60. U.S. Bureau of the Census, *Statistical Abstract of the United States: 1991,* pp. 29–31.
61. Tunnard, op. cit., p. 11.
62. Roberto Suro, "Where America Is Growing: The Suburban Cities," *New York Times,* February 23, 1991, and Edward Fiske, "U.S. Says

Most of Growth in 80's Was in Major Metropolitan Areas," *New York Times,* February 21, 1991.

63. A representative sample of this literature can be found in John Friedmann and William Alonso (editors), *Regional Development and Planning: A Reader,* M.I.T. Press, Cambridge, 1964.

64. Statistical and historical information on Boulder's open-space system is derived from Love & Associates, *Boulder's Stream Corridors—Design Guidelines,* City of Boulder Planning Dept., Boulder, 1989; City of Boulder, *Boulder's Greenways—Design Guidelines,* City of Boulder.

65. Statistical and historical information on Bath is derived from C. W. Chalklin, *The Provincial Towns of Georgian England,* Edward Arnold, London, 1974, pp. 73–80; John Summerson, *Architecture in Britain 1530–1830,* Penguin Books, Harmondsworth, Middlesex, England, pp. 386–393; and Walter Ison, *The Georgian Buildings of Bath,* Kingsmead Reprints, Bath, 1969.

66. There was to have been a second half-ellipse which would have completed John Wood II's intended coliseum-turned-inside-out.

14

New-Towns-in-Town

Manhattan, 1994. Battery Park City. *(Alexander Garvin)*

Lewis Mumford, one of the twentieth century's most ardent advocates of planned communities, presented the case to Congress in 1967, arguing that:

further increase of population in already congested centers should be met, not by intensifying the congestion in high-rise buildings, not by adding endless acres and square miles of suburbs, with ever-longer and more time-wasting journeys to work, but by building new, planned communities.[1]

No more messy, dirty, noisy, smelly, inconvenient neighborhoods! Only places that provided all necessary educational, recreational, commercial, and community facilities: "an environment so rich in human resources that no one would willingly leave it even temporarily on an astronautic vacation."[2]

To avoid adding "square miles of suburbs," new communities have to be located within existing urban areas. This allows them to capitalize on sewers, water mains, and traffic arteries that are already in place. More important, such *new-towns-in-town* can provide the critical mass necessary for a full range of facilities that could never be justified by small, scattered real estate ventures by different developers.

Mumford thought these planned communities would be like Radburn: charming, low-rise, low-density communities "for the motor age." Le Corbusier was convinced that the motor age required high-density, high-rise districts connected by super highways. Others argued for extensions of existing street grids.

Whatever its appearance, a new-town-in-town requires a site of at least 30–50 acres. Contrary to conventional wisdom, urban sites of this size can be obtained without massive clearance and relocation. They are available wherever there are underutilized country clubs, amusement parks, railroad yards, airfields, commercial waterfronts, industrial complexes, and other facilities that could profitably move to less expensive locations. Parkchester, a new-town-in-town for 12,271 families in the Bronx, replaced the Society for the Protection of Destitute Roman Catholic Children. Fresh Meadows, a new community for 3287 families in Queens, replaced a country club and golf course. At Century City, in Los Angeles, an entire regional center with shopping facilities, office towers, and condominium apartments was built on the back lot of a movie studio.

Sites that are large enough for a new-town-in-town can only be purchased for huge sums. Even more money is needed to pay for streets, sewers, water mains, housing, schools, stores, parks, and the full range of community services. Mortgage financing on this scale can be supplied by only a few titanic

The Bronx, 1994. 12,271 families live in Parkchester, a new-town-in-town with more than 100 stores, a movie theater, and even a branch of Macy's. *(Alexander Garvin)*

financial institutions, corporations, labor unions, and government agencies. For this reason many early efforts at new-towns-in-town were initiated and financed by insurance companies. Park La Brea in Los Angeles was financed by the Metropolitan Life Insurance Company; Fresh Meadows by the New York Life Insurance Company. Later new-towns-in-town were financed by large corporations and state-chartered public authorities.

Timing is the most important decision facing developers of any new-town-in-town. In order to market their project they must be able to provide prospective residents with neighborhood services as soon as they move in. This requires an enormous investment in infrastructure and community facilities. Since it will be years before all the residents will have moved in, successful developers have to schedule development so that project revenues will cover debt service on already installed infrastructure and community facilities.

At the time that Parkchester, Park La Brea, Fresh Meadows, and Century City were created, most citizens welcomed such new communities. Necessary zoning changes were relatively easy to obtain. More recent projects have resulted in lengthy environmental reviews, political opposition from neighboring residents and property owners, costly, time-consuming litigation, and even demands that developers contribute "give-backs" in exchange for the right to proceed. As a result, only those few exceptional developers who are able to orchestrate all the participants, financial arrangements, and required approvals are able to develop a new-town-in-town.

The controversy over proposed new-towns-in-town is evidence that planned new communities may not be the panacea that Lewis Mumford envisioned. Some projects are successful; others cannot be brought to completion. Some provide wonderful living environments; others are less than satisfactory. More important, some new-towns-in-town improve the surrounding city; others do damage.

There is now enough experience with new-towns-in-town to be able to determine when they will benefit surrounding communities. That experience must be codified into project requirements with which developers will have to comply. Only then will controversy die down and increasingly well-planned new communities appear within the clutter of our urban-suburban landscape.

Century City, Los Angeles

Century City takes its name from a 263-acre site that was originally the back lot of 20th Century-Fox Studios. It is strategically located in the middle of the rapidly growing western corridor between downtown Los Angeles and the Pacific Ocean. Directly to the north are the exclusive residential and commercial sections of Beverly Hills, to the west, Westwood, and to the south, the Hillcrest Country Club and the Rancho Park Golf Course.[3]

Spyros Skouras, president and chairman of the board of Fox, understood that the lot was much more valuable for real estate development than for movie production. In 1958 Skouras hired architect Welton Beckett to prepare a master plan for a complex of office towers, hotels, retail stores, and apartment buildings. He hoped to sell the concept and the property for $100 million. Since nobody could obtain the money needed to develop the site (between half a billion and a billion dollars), there were no takers.

After nearly a year, William Zeckendorf, Sr., agreed to purchase the property for $56 million, but only after he had devised a scheme which reduced the cash required; 20th Century-Fox would lease back 75 acres for $1.5 million a year in rent. As he explained, "I was actually paying only $31 million, because that $1.5 million in rent, at six-percent interest, would be worth $25 million to some insurance company."[4]

Zeckendorf had real trouble raising the money. Despite its previous policy of investing only in aluminum production or sale, he eventually persuaded the Aluminum Company of America (Alcoa) to enter into a joint venture with him. When they closed the deal in 1961, the price had been reduced to $43 million. Eventually Alcoa bought out Zeckendorf and developed the project on its own.

The site was divided by traffic arteries into superblocks, which were in turn subdivided into large individual sites. Thus, Alcoa could schedule development to meet market demand, occasionally building something themselves, but usually selling large parcels to those office, hotel, and residential developers who were able to obtain the necessary financing.

Thirty years after Alcoa began development, Century City includes more than 9 million square feet of office space, 2000 condominium and townhouse apartments, 3 major hotels, a 9-story hospital, a 17-acre shopping center, an entertainment center with one of Los Angeles' largest legitimate theaters, restaurants, and parking for thousands of cars. Half the

Los Angeles, 1993. The multiplex movie theater and food court at the shopping center in Century City. *(Alexander Garvin)*

Los Angeles, 1990. Avenue of the Stars—the main artery of Century City, a new-town-in-town that includes more than 9 million square feet of office space, 2000 condominium and townhouse apartments, 3 major hotels, a 9-story hospital, a 17-acre shopping center, multiplex movie theaters, and one of the city's largest legitimate theaters. *(Alexander Garvin)*

Los Angeles, 1991. A drive-in entrance to one of the office complexes at Century City. *(Alexander Garvin)*

superblocks are residential projects, carefully walled off from the rest of the city. The rest are commercial complexes containing high-rise buildings, decorative planting, open walkways, and "underground pedestrian tunnels [and] parking garages" that are "as confusing as they are cavernous."[5]

By the 1990s, Century City's commercial superblocks provided a glitzy setting for Los Angeles' active business world. This was not always true. When the first buildings opened during the 1960s, the place had the look of a ghost town, especially at night when the office workers drove home. But as additional buildings were completed, activity increased.

The biggest change came in 1987, when the original shopping center was renovated and expanded. It includes the Bullock's and Broadway department stores, 140 specialty stores, a "festival marketplace" with 35 different eateries, and a 14-screen AMC theater complex. This shopping center has done more than anything else to transform Century City into a 24-hour, 7-day-a-week section of Los Angeles.

In time, Century City became an identifiable destination, visible everywhere west of downtown Los Angeles, marked on tourist maps, and known to virtually all city residents. It is widely known because it is designed for the automobile. Regional traffic speeds past the project along Santa Monica, Olympic, and Pico Boulevards, turning off these arteries to breeze down Avenue of the Stars (a monumental north-south artery with a median strip for flowers, fountains, and sculpture that extends for nearly a mile) or one of the other wide boulevards. You drive directly into below-ground or hidden parking structures. From there you take an elevator or escalator up to an office, apartment, or retail destination, without ever having to emerge into the landscaped plazas, malls, and walkways that surround the buildings.

The "hard-bitten, supercommercial urbanity" of the "bland and blank, completely faceless high-rise buildings" in Century City would seem to preclude success as a new-town-in-town.[6] So it is ignored by city planners and architects alike. However, as the ever-observant architect Charles Moore noticed: "What is thoroughly puzzling…is why so many people write about it as such a success in all the other ways that matter, and why they see it as such a positive addition to the Los Angeles scene."[7] It should not be puzzling. Century City is a success, despite its mediocre architecture, because it is as much a regional employment, shopping, and entertainment destination as it is a residential community and because it is fully integrated into the traffic and land use patterns of its surroundings.

The gated residential superblocks of Century City will never develop the character and charm of a lively city neighborhood. Nor will the carefully landscaped but antiseptic business superblocks offer the variety and richness of commercial activity on Wilshire Boulevard or Rodeo Drive in nearby Beverly Hills. Century City's residential and commercial superblocks are too self-contained and too isolated from one another to generate the vibrant pedestrian activity that is key to the success of Wilshire Boulevard or Rodeo Drive. Nor will their occupants ever spill over onto neighboring streets. They would have to get back into their cars to drive there.

Century City is a notable lesson in successful real estate development. Seventy-five acres of the 280-acre property were sold back to 20th Century-Fox. Then, in 1986, Alcoa sold its remaining interest in the project for $620 million to JMB/Urban Development Company.[8] Alcoa made a fortune on this one property because the rapid transformation of Los Angeles into the nation's second-largest metropolitan area provided an unmatched market for new office, retail, and residential space. Furthermore, the site was located in the path of the city's major corridor of expansion. Alcoa did not have to

Los Angeles, 1990. One of the gated residential enclaves in Century City. *(Alexander Garvin)*

pay debt service on a mortgage covering property acquisition and development costs. More important, the company had "deep pockets" and, therefore, was able to pay real estate taxes and operating expenses without immediately having to cover these costs out of land sales. Most important, the site plan subdivided each superblock into individual parcels that could be developed whenever the market was ripe.

Arlington, 1994. A hotel, shopping mall, apartment houses, and numerous office buildings line Hayes Street at Pentagon City. *(Alexander Garvin)*

Pentagon City, Virginia

The 116-acre site of what is today Pentagon City was acquired by the Cafritz-Tompkins Group during the 1940s. It was a largely undeveloped area, notable only for its proximity to the Pentagon. In those days few developers foresaw the tremendous growth of government or the dramatic changes that growth would bring to the national capital and its metropolitan region. Furthermore, most developers expected this growth to occur in conjunction with the projected suburban beltway, not within eyeshot of the Pentagon.[9]

For years the Cafritz-Tompkins Group remained satisfied with the site's low-density industrial and commercial uses. The change came with the Washington, D.C., Metropolitan Area Transit System (METRO), which was to open in 1976. Anticipating the tremendous potential market that would accompany its opening, the site's owners hired Dewberry, Nealon, and Davis to prepare a master plan for a whole new city district. They used this master plan to persuade Arlington County to rezone the area for high-density, mixed-use devel-

Arlington, 1990. Pentagon City. *(Courtesy of Rose Associates)*

opment: 1.25 million square feet of offices; 800,000 square feet of retailing; 2000 hotel rooms; 5900 housing units; a 300-bed nursing home; 300 units of subsidized elderly housing; an 11-acre public park, and thousands of much needed parking spaces.

Cafritz-Tompkins began the project with the nursing home, 300 apartments in a low-rise apartment complex, and 600 apartments for the elderly, all at the southern end of the site. It quickly became apparent that they would not be able to proceed with a project of this scale and complexity without a skillful developer who had the ability to package the project, market the space, and attract the necessary capital. In 1977 they entered into a joint venture with Rose Associates, a major New York City-based developer, for the 99 acres that had yet to be built.

Rose Associates had been established in 1928. It already had financed and built thousands of apartments and millions of square feet of office space that it owned and managed. It also had long experience with that most complicated of politico-financial markets: New York City. Thus, there were few if any difficulties that it had not encountered and overcome.

Daniel Rose, the partner in charge of Pentagon City, devised the strategies which led both to Cafritz-Tompkins selecting his firm as the developer and to the project's financial success. The deal Rose negotiated transformed time into an asset rather than a continuing debt service liability. Instead of Rose Associates making loan payments on the ever-increasing cost of the project, Cafritz-Tompkins agreed to hold each section of the property until it was ready for development, selling it at the then market price plus a kicker (a 15 percent interest in the venture). Thus, Cafritz-Tompkins benefited by capturing the site's appreciation in value while Rose Associates benefited by avoiding any cash payment or debt service until a project was ripe for development.

Rather than allow the complexities of combining large land users to become a major stumbling block, Rose found a way to profit from their intermingling. He avoided building the retail heart of the project until the subway station had been completed, a hotel deal had been negotiated, and office space either had been occupied or preleased. This delay allowed the occupants of the office, retail, hotel, and apartment buildings to simultaneously provide customers for one another.

Arlington, 1994. The food court in the Fashion Centre Mall at Pentagon City. *(Alexander Garvin)*

Their joint effort began in 1980 with construction of 562,000 square feet of office space in two structures built to the specifications of and sold to MCI Communications. This was followed in 1985 by the sale of land to Lincoln Properties for an additional 516,000 square feet of offices. By 1984, there was enough office space to attract Melvin Simon and Associates to become a joint venture partner in the creation of an 860,000 square foot Fashion Center Mall that included Nordstrom's, Macy's, and another 150 stores; a 362-room Ritz-Carlton Hotel; a 172,000-square-foot office tower; and a 4534-car parking garage. In 1988 Rose Associates started another joint venture with the Sumitomo Corporation of America: the 16-story, 299-unit Parc Vista Apartments. It is the first of more than 5000 apartments yet to come.

Like Century City, Pentagon City demonstrates three of the ingredients of a financially successful new-town-in-town: the presence of a rapidly growing market, a location conveniently accessible to that market, and a development strategy that synchronizes capital expenditures with a dependable revenue stream. However, unlike Century City, it is more than a popular shopping facility surrounded by separate office, hotel, and residential superblocks. Thanks to the METRO station and nearby Interstate Highway 395, Pentagon City acts as a centripetal force attracting hundreds of thousands of people to a once-empty section of the Capital region. Residents from surrounding blocks filter through Pentagon City on their way to the subway and the trip to their workplace, miles away. When the subway is not used for the journey to work, it is used by people from all over the metropolitan area, who come to Pentagon City to shop, dine, and go to the movies. Thus, unlike Century City, this new-town-in-town will never be a series of separate superblocks operating independently of one another. Once the remaining apartments are completed, Pentagon City will become the pulsating heart of a dense and busy regional subcenter, generating activity along in surrounding areas.

Utopia around the Corner

One of the most common arguments for developing new-towns-in-town is that they can provide thousands of families with decent homes and healthy living environments on sites that are virtually around the corner. Unlike redevelopment projects, they can be created with little or no displacement. Unfortunately, they often turn out to be colossal housing projects rather than vibrant communities.

Park La Brea in Los Angeles, is a good example. It was built in stages, between 1941 and 1948, on a 176-acre site.

Los Angeles, 1990. Park La Brea offers 4200 families the open space and parking of Le Corbusier's "City of Tomorrow" but none of the commercial or community facilities that constitute a complete new-town-in-town. *(Alexander Garvin)*

Superficially, Park La Brea appears to be a pallid copy of Le Corbusier's City of Tomorrow. However, it has neither the vast amounts of continuous parkland nor the many community facilities that Le Corbusier envisioned. Instead, Park La Brea includes 4200 apartments and plenty of parking, but little else.

Even if projects include more than just housing, they may still fail to become lively neighborhoods. This happens when the housing is so dominant that the project becomes little more than a dormitory. Despite their very different appearance and design, Fresh Meadows and Parkchester are good examples of just such dormitory communities.

Fresh Meadows is a watered-down, mid-1940s version of one of Clarence Stein's neighborhood units. Its 170 acres include a nursery school, a clubhouse, a small professional building, a small shopping center, 141 garden apartment buildings, and two brick residential towers. Despite its essentially low-rise character, short curving streets, and rolling lawns, the 3287 apartments at Fresh Meadows never coalesced into a lively, heterogeneous new-town-in-town because the apartments occupy almost all of the site and are carefully segregated from other land uses.

Parkchester also fails to be more than an immense housing project. Begun in 1938, its 129-acre site includes a 100-store commercial center with a branch of Macy's and a 2000-seat movie theater. However, even this sizable commercial center is overwhelmed by the project's 171 elevator buildings and 12,271 apartments.

Government officials happily encourage the construction of projects like Fresh Meadows or Parkchester because they can provide so many people with decent housing, especially when they are built on predominantly vacant sites, conveniently just around the corner from already developed areas. There is an interesting history of government assistance for the development of such pseudo new-towns-in-town. The New York State Limited Dividend Housing Corporations Law of 1926, which provides real estate tax exemption to developers who limit their return on equity, is probably the earliest example of such assistance (see Chapter 11). However, it failed to deal with three major problems facing any developer of a new-town-in-town: the need for huge amounts of equity capital, the unavailability of very long term mortgage financing, and the high cost of mortgage money.

These problems were solved in the 1950s and 1960s, when state legislatures established housing finance agencies with the ability to issue tax-exempt bonds, the proceeds of which could provide housing developers with mortgage financing (see Chapter 11). These state housing finance agencies were able to extend the period of amortization for as long as 40 or 50 years. Since interest on the bonds is tax-exempt, they also were able to charge housing developers a rate of interest several percentage points lower than would be available at local banks. Finally, most housing finance agencies reduce equity requirements to an almost nominal 5 or 10 percent.

Co-op City, the Bronx

The first project to obtain benefits under the New York State Limited Dividend Housing Corporations Law of 1926 was Amalgamated Houses. This union-sponsored project involved staged construction of 1434 apartments spread over six blocks of the north Bronx.[10] It initiated a series of ever-larger planned residential communities that was brought to a halt in the early 1970s by the problems of Co-op City, still the nation's largest planned residential development (see Table 14.1).

The man behind these projects was Abraham Kazan, a union member who convinced the Amalgamated Clothing Workers of America that its members and their families should be able to obtain affordable housing. Kazan proposed raising equity capital in the form of nominal subscriber downpayments, obtaining institutional mortgage financing (in the case of Amalgamated Houses, from the Metropolitan Life Insurance Company), and then building apartments for the subscribers. When residents moved out, they had to sell their apartments back to the co-op for the amount of their original downpayment plus the accumulated mortgage amortization.[11]

The Limited Dividend Housing Corporations Law provided real estate tax exemption on all improvements for a period of 25 years, if the return on the property was limited to 5 percent (later 6 percent). Thus, occupants paid the low taxes that had been paid prior to development. Since the project was a nonprofit cooperative, the only additional payments by the occupant covered the project's operating expenses and mortgage debt service.

When the first stage of the Amalgamated Houses opened in 1927, *The New York Times* called it "the finest and largest development of low-rent (sic) housing in the entire city." For a downpayment of $500 per room and monthly payments of $11 per room per month, its occupants had a nice apartment in a modern building surrounded by trees, grass, and flowers. It was the first in a series of projects that provided more than 32,500 cooperative apartments.

By the time the final project, Co-op City, was conceived, Kazan had built up an effective development agency, known as

Table 14.1
UNION-SPONSORED COOPERATIVE HOUSING IN NEW YORK CITY[12]

Project	Borough	Number of apartments	Completion
Amalgamated Houses	Bronx	1,434	1927–1971 (in stages)
Amalgamated Dwellings	Manhattan	236	1930
Hillman Houses	Manhattan	807	1951
Corlears Hook	Manhattan	1,668	1958
Seward Park	Manhattan	1,728	1962
Penn Station South	Manhattan	2,820	1963
Warbasse Houses	Brooklyn	2,592	1965
Rochdale Village	Queens	5,860	1965
Co-op City	Bronx	15,389	1969–1972 (in stages)

the United Housing Foundation (UHF). Its only rival, in terms of number of apartments built or political influence, was the redoubtable Robert Moses. UHF projects were criticized for banal, cookie-cutter design; overpowering, almost inhuman scale; and insular planning that carefully segregated project residents from the surrounding community. But, as Roger Starr explained at the New York City Planning Commission's public hearing on Co-op City,

> *far from being inhuman, far from crushing the human spirit, far from presenting people with an inhuman environment, inhumanly scaled, [they] have actually built developments which have been subscribed and over-subscribed, in which people have now been living for many, many years, and as nearly as we can make out—have been living successfully and happily.*[13]

He also noted that they were able to live in these projects at a price that was considerably lower than comparable new, conventionally financed housing.

The original proposal for Co-op City called for the construction of 17,000 apartments on 300 acres of marshland that had previously been the site of Freedomland, an unsuccessful theme park.[14] City officials demanded and obtained changes.

The Bronx, 1994. Co-op City offers apartments at bargain prices in one of the nation's least inspiring new-towns-in-town. *(Alexander Garvin)*

The project was cut to 15,389 dwelling units, 236 of which were in the mediocre townhouses added to soften the height of the 35 apartment towers. The color of the brick was changed. Buildings could be drab gray, not just drab red. Even the site plan was altered.[15]

Co-op City appears to be the usual UHF project. There are, however, significant differences. This time, the UHF included shopping centers and a power plant that supplies residents with electricity. At city expense it also built a separate educational park including two public elementary schools, two public intermediate schools, and one public high school. There even is express-bus service to downtown Manhattan.

Despite these differences, Co-op City is still a housing project rather than a planned community for 50,000 residents. Therein lies the explanation of its failure. The rest of the Bronx lies on the other side of major highways and looks nothing like Co-op City. If, instead of arguing about brick color, the city had directed its attention to minimizing the highway barriers to surrounding communities, Co-op City's separation would not be quite as stark. If, rather than demanding token townhouses, the city had concerned itself with creating an internal street system in which residential structures, like those throughout the city, mingled with stores, schools, and other nonresidential uses, Co-op City could not be stigmatized as a project.

Kazan's conception of a working class cooperative was in sharp contrast with the reality into which the occupants of Co-op City moved. Co-op City, like Kazan's other projects, was a resident-owned cooperative in name only. Residents understood that they were temporary occupants of dwelling units whose lower cost reflected public assistance. When residents of Co-op City gave up occupancy they could only receive what they put in. Unlike owners of conventionally financed co-ops or single-family houses, they could not benefit from any appreciation in value. Their investment could never become a growing nest egg that would help finance the purchase of an even better, new residence or pay for their retirement in Florida.

From the beginning, the costs of building and operating Co-op City exceeded initial estimates. When co-op charges had to be increased, occupants refused to pay. Since they did not have any real equity interest in the project, they naturally blamed the "landlord," stopped paying "rent," and expected the government to step in. The Co-op City rent strike virtually terminated New York State's bond-financed, limited-profit housing program (see Chapter 11). A financial catastrophe was avoided only because Governor Hugh Carey in 1975 persuaded the legislature to cover debt service payments on the $390 million in bonds issued to finance Co-op City. In the end, New York State had been forced into subsidizing middle-income citizens capable of paying for their own housing.[16]

The saddest result of the "project" mentality is that $423 million had been spent without beneficial spillover elsewhere in the Bronx.[17] When Co-op City was ready for occupancy thousands of South Bronx households, especially from around the Grand Concourse, chose to move there. It can be argued that this provided a step up for both departing, primarily white residents of Co-op City and for incoming, primarily Puerto Rican and African-American residents who replaced them. On the other hand, it also can be argued that the sudden departure of thousands of stable families only weakened the neighborhoods they left behind. What cannot be challenged is that Co-op City increased the gulf between the more fortunate residents of the recently completed apartment complex and those that had to make do with the apartments they left behind.

It is also unchallengeable that Co-op City underscored the shameful lack of investment in the neighboring, primarily African-American sections of the Edenwald-Wakefield community on the other side of the highway, where streets had remained unpaved and sewers and water mains had been inadequate for decades. Had Co-op City not been separated from the rest of the city by highways, had it not been designed to function independently of everything around it, had it not been visibly different from the rest of the Bronx, there might have been some chance of its benefits spilling over into the rest of the Bronx. Instead 50,000 people moved without bringing any centrifugal impact to their surroundings.

The National Effort to Build New-Towns-in-Town

The federal government had a brief fling with new-towns-in-town. Title IV of the Housing and Urban Development Act of 1968 and Title VII of the Housing and Urban Development Act of 1970 provided a federal guarantee for up to $50 million in obligations issued by developers of approved new communities as well as up to $20 million in interest-free loans (see Chapter 15). Only two new-towns-in-town, Cedar-Riverside in Minneapolis and Roosevelt Island in New York, were approved for funding.

Minneapolis, 1992. Cedar-Riverside, one of the country's two unfinished Title-VII-financed new-towns-in-town. *(Alexander Garvin)*

Cedar-Riverside, Minneapolis

In 1968, when Congress enacted legislation to encourage the development of well-planned new communities, it contemplated projects with a mix of "homes, commercial and industrial facilities, public and community facilities, and open spaces...[and] opportunities for innovation in housing and community development technology, and in land use planning."[18]

Cedar-Riverside, in Minneapolis, was the first new-town-in-town to receive federal assistance. Architect Ralph Rapson and landscape architect Lawrence Halprin prepared an ambitious scheme that called for 12,500 apartments in six residential neighborhoods, 1.5 million square feet of commercial space, and 6 acres of cultural facilities. In the words of one of its promotional brochures, Cedar-Riverside was going to awaken a "new kind of urban life...filled with involvement. Filled with a vitality...depth, and breadth of experience."[19]

What emerged can only be called a housing project: 11 reinforced concrete buildings containing 1299 apartments organized around two quadrangles and connected by a system of walkways and pedestrian bridges. The sharp contrast between conception and reality at Cedar-Riverside was inevitable given the inexperience of its developers, the project's dependence on government financing, and the difficulties of operating within a complex political environment.

Redevelopment of Cedar-Riverside had been on the table for nearly four decades when it was approved by HUD for Title VII assistance. In 1934, the WPA thought the area was one of the most dilapidated sections in Minneapolis and called for its clearance. In 1948, the city's Housing and Redevelopment Authority (HRA) designated it as a potential renewal site. A renewal plan was finally submitted and rejected by the Minneapolis City Council in 1961.

The area started to change during the late 1950s. Two local hospitals began to expand into the area. A Lutheran seminary was transformed into a coeducational college. The HRA built 348 units of housing for the elderly. But the most significant change came when two interstate highways were built. They separated Cedar-Riverside from the rest of the city.

Despite (and perhaps also because of) this activity Cedar-Riverside's population fell from 8540 in 1940 to 4766 in 1960. The neighborhood changed from an area that consisted primarily of Scandinavian-American immigrants to one that reflected the nonconformist character of an emerging "youth" culture.

Investors, sensing the demand for housing generated by institutional expansion, began acquiring property in the area. The most important of these investors was a partnership consisting of a local doctor, his wife, and a university lecturer. By 1968, when the City Council finally approved an urban renewal plan for Cedar-Riverside, they had purchased nearly 200 parcels, had prepared a master plan for a new-town-in-town with a projected population of 30,000, had combined forces with several other local developers, and had approached HUD for funding under the recently enacted Title IV new community legislation.

Government assistance proved to be the critical element both in initiating the development of Cedar-Riverside and in bringing it to a halt. Without local designation as an urban renewal project, the area's many property owners would have withheld their parcels from the project or demanded prohibitively high prices. Without the $24 million in federal new-community loan guarantees that were approved in 1971, the project's relatively inexperienced developers could never have obtained the necessary financing. Without "new community" status they could never have obtained the set-aside of scarce federal housing subsidies (117 units of leased public housing and 552 moderate income units with FHA 236 subsidies) or the grants that helped to pay for the covered walkway system, the pedestrian bridge across Cedar Avenue, the plaza, or any of the other amenities that went into the project. In return for this government largesse, the developers had to accept complex and expensive regulations covering everything from equal employment opportunity to citizen participation.

Trouble began in 1973. First, the Nixon Administration terminated all federally assisted housing and urban development programs. Then, residents of the area successfully initiated a suit claiming the project's Environmental Impact Statement was inadequate and violated the National Environmental Policy Act of 1969 (see Chapter 16). They succeeded in obtaining an injunction against continued development. Project tenants initiated a rent strike, and the urban renewal area's citizen advisory panel called for major changes in the redevelopment plan. The project's developers had neither the financial strength nor the political skills to continue. Inevitably, Cedar-Riverside was brought to a halt.

Since Cedar-Riverside never evolved into the new-town-in-town which had been planned, there is no way of determining either the extent to which it would have awakened a "new kind of urban life" or generated a market reaction strong enough to vault over the highways to affect other Minneapolis neighborhoods. What is clear, however, is that federal grants and loan guarantees by themselves were not enough to ensure success.

Roosevelt Island, New York City

Roosevelt Island, the other new-town-in-town that received Title VII assistance, was specifically conceived to avoid the difficulties experienced by projects like Cedar-Riverside. There were no acquisition problems because the site was owned by the City of New York and no political problems because its developer, the New York State Urban Development Corporation (UDC) was a superagency with truly amazing powers.

The UDC had been Governor Nelson Rockefeller's response to the riots that erupted in cities across the country during the mid-1960s. The statute creating this superagency was enacted in 1968. As written by Edward Logue, its first president and chief executive officer, the legislation provided the UDC with powers that could overcome every difficulty he had run into, first as New Haven's Development Administrator and then as chairman of the Boston Redevelopment Authority (see Chapters 6 and 11). The UDC could condemn land, hire expert professional staff, ignore zoning and building regulations, and even issue tax-exempt bonds to finance development. Its most remarkable power was the ability to do all this without obtaining the approval of any other city, county, or state agency.

Logue needed a highly visible project with which to demonstrate UDC effectiveness. That project came in the form of a proposed new-town-in-town for an underutilized 147-acre island in the East River, directly opposite the most expensive real estate in the world: Manhattan's fashionable midtown office district and Upper East Side residential district.

Once known as Hog's Island and later Blackwell's Island, this valuable city-owned property—then called Welfare Island—was used for hospitals and nurses' residences. Over the years there had been proposals for high-density housing, parks, industrial development, even an amusement park, like Copenhagen's Tivoli Gardens. When the Transit Authority announced it would build a subway tunnel (running under the island) that would connect Manhattan with Queens, development seemed inevitable.

Mayor Lindsay appointed a blue-ribbon committee to determine the future of this underutilized asset. In 1969, based on studies prepared by David Lilienthal's Development and

New York City, 1970. Philip Johnson's unexecuted master plan for Roosevelt Island in which Main Street was interrupted every 100 feet by a 60-foot wide view of the river. *(Courtesy of Roosevelt Island Operating Corporation)*

Resources Corporation, the Welfare Island Planning and Development Committee proposed a new-town-in-town.[20]

No private developer could muster the funds necessary to execute the ambitious program they envisioned. When Logue announced that the newly created New York State Urban Development Corporation was ready to execute the plan, the mayor responded positively. Logue could get started immediately because the island had no organized community groups with whom to negotiate.

Lindsay had commitments to build thousands of subsidized housing units in urban renewal areas throughout the city. In exchange for the chance to create this model new-town-in-town, Logue agreed to build and finance a large portion of the subsidized housing that the mayor had promised (see Chapter 11). He persuaded Governor Rockefeller to obtain special set-asides of housing subsidies and other federal programs from the recently elected Nixon Administration. Thus, the island could be developed with funds that would not otherwise have been available to New York City.[21]

Logue renamed the project Roosevelt Island and hired Philip Johnson, a member of Lindsay's Welfare Island Planning and Development Committee, to prepare a master plan for the project.[22] One might have expected Johnson to produce a perfected version of the Garden City, the Radiant City, the Linear City, the Mega-City, or some other currently fashionable utopia. Instead he produced an innovative plan that responded to topography, landscape, and history.

Johnson proposed to preserve the island's historic structures. Existing hospitals (which were too expensive to move) were to continue operations. Private vehicular traffic was to be kept from the island. Cars would park at a "motor gate" from which there would be regular mini-transit service. The island's waterfront was to become a continuous 4-mile promenade accessible to the public. The buildings themselves would be gathered into high-density clusters separated by five new parks. At the core of this new-town-in-town Johnson planned an exciting town center with two large public spaces, a glass-roofed retail arcade, a 300-room hotel, and at least 200,000 square feet of office space. Altogether, there were to be 5000 apartments divided into two neighborhoods that would be built on either side of the town center.

The master plan organized these elements along a central "Main Street" spine in a unique manner intended to maximize proximity to both riverfronts. Twelve-story apartment buildings, shaped like the letter "C," were staggered so that their flat back ends defined Main Street. Pedestrians strolling along Main Street were provided river views opening every hundred feet alternately to the west and then to the east. There were also river views for building residents whose apartments faced the open ends of these C-shaped buildings and thus the waterfront beyond. In this manner, Johnson's innovative plan simultaneously defined the street, provided changing vistas of the water, and created a new, dynamic relationship between the island and the rest of the city.[23]

The UDC hired more "practical" architects (who misunderstood the master plan) to design the buildings themselves. The unique, river-oriented apartment buildings were replaced by mediocre quadrangles, one side of which blocked the water views. The 12-story height limit was ignored and the town center was eliminated.

New York City, 1976. The main and only street of Roosevelt Island became a high-density corridor unlike the lively city street envisioned in the original master plan. *(Alexander Garvin)*

While Roosevelt Island did benefit from minor grants made possible by its status as a Title VII new community, it was financed without federal guarantees. The UDC provided below-market mortgage money by issuing tax-exempt bonds. The new apartment buildings also were effectively exempt from New York City real estate taxes. These two subsidies allowed the UDC to lower rents sufficiently to attract people who otherwise would not have been able to afford living on the island. In addition, the federal government provided FHA 236 subsidies for 1003 apartments, thereby ensuring that the Roosevelt Island residents would represent a range of income levels.

Roosevelt Island did offer a few innovations. Anticipating delay in subway construction, Logue persuaded the city to subsidize construction of an aerial tramway connecting Roosevelt Island with midtown Manhattan. No other planned new community is served by a tramway or by any other form of mass transit with such spectacular views. In addition, rather than using noisy garbage trucks, all buildings were provided with the Disney World "Automated Vacuum Collection System." When the first apartments were occupied, resident children attended day-care centers and minischools mixed in with the island's housing, so that "children, parents and teachers" could "interact with each other and develop into an active community unit."[24]

Like Cedar-Riverside, development at Roosevelt Island was brought to a halt in 1973 by the Nixon moratorium. But, unlike Cedar-Riverside, the halt was temporary. The UDC had already financed and built much of the infrastructure for the rest of the project. As a government agency, it could wait until conditions changed before continuing with housing construction. However, development did not resume for more than a decade because unsubsidized rental, co-op, or condo apartments could not be produced at prices that were low enough to attract additional residents.

Enough construction has been completed to be able to judge the success of Roosevelt Island as a planned community. When tramway service began in 1976, Roosevelt Island included 2148 apartments, waterfront promenades, lawns with children tossing frisbees, glass-enclosed swimming pools, minischools, even a "Rompers Roost" preschool. Eighteen months later *The New York Times* reported:

> *The "shops, restaurants, and a range of services" that planners envisioned have not materialized yet, and as a result the "excitingly urban" Main Street mentioned in the Roosevelt Island brochure has not materialized yet either. There is no hardware store, household appliance store, shoe store, ice cream fountain, barber shop or beauty parlor...although the stationery store does sell T-shirts proclaiming that Roosevelt Island is "The Little Apple."*[25]

In 1990, when the long-promised subway station that had triggered the island's redevelopment finally opened, 3025 apartments had been completed. However, the population represented by even the projected 5000 dwellings may prove too small to support a viable retail district, especially in view of the remaining construction being planned for an area of the island ("Southtown") that is separate from the existing "Northtown." Moreover, unless additional land uses that can attract off-island visitors are included, Roosevelt Island will remain a dormitory suburb. Consequently, in 1995 the Roosevelt Island Operating Corporation, which in 1984 had replaced UDC as the island's developer, has initiated a planning process aimed at solving these problems and recapturing the long-lost spirit of innovation that had characterized the project's inception.

New York City, 1995. View of Manhattan's Upper East Side from the riverfront esplanade at Roosevelt Island. *(Alexander Garvin)*

New City Districts

The most persuasive public policy rationale for new-towns-in-town is that they can benefit the surrounding city. One way is by generating additional employment and taxes. Based on this argument, Co-op City, Cedar-Riverside, and Roosevelt Island are flops. Despite utopian rhetoric, they simply moved city residents from one part of town to another without bringing any new business to the city.

Another way in which a new-town-in-town can be of benefit is by generating further development around its periphery. The self-contained planning of many new-towns-in-town prevents this from occurring. Roosevelt Island, for example is separated from the surrounding city by the East River; Co-op City is cut off by highways. As a result, essential commercial, community, and recreational facilities had to be provided within the project, further reducing the reasons for them to spill over into surrounding neighborhoods.

New districts can also improve the character of city life if they supply services (retail stores, recreation facilities, cultural establishments, etc.) that would not otherwise be available to surrounding neighborhoods. Once again, projects like Co-op City, Cedar-Riverside, and Roosevelt Island, which have little to offer except apartments, are unlikely to attract many outsiders.

There are, however, new-towns-in-town that do provide these benefits. Battery Park City in lower Manhattan provides thousands of jobs and generates millions of dollars in taxes. RiverPlace in Portland, Oregon, includes retail and recreation facilities that attract people from the surrounding metropolitan region.

Battery Park City, Manhattan

Battery Park City, like Roosevelt Island, may have been planned, financed, and developed by a state agency, but that is the only similarity. The new-town-in-town on Roosevelt Island was created for entirely opportunistic reasons: housing without relocation and better utilization of scheduled transportation improvements. At Battery Park City, these same opportunistic consequences were the by-product of a bold urban planning strategy intended to revitalize the downtown business core.

Lower Manhattan had been losing jobs to office districts in midtown Manhattan, Connecticut, Westchester, and New Jersey since World War II. The downtown business community tried to counter this decline by encouraging construction of new office space. Its effort began with the opening of the Chase Manhattan Building in 1960, and continued under the

Manhattan, 1969. *The Lower Manhattan Plan* adapted to include the contemporary master plan for Battery Park City. *(Courtesy of New York City Department of City Planning)*

leadership of David Rockefeller (president of the Chase Manhattan Bank) when the Downtown Lower Manhattan Association pressed successfully for mapping a new interstate highway along the West Side and for construction of a World Trade Center over the railroad tracks of the Port Authority Trans-Hudson Corporation (PATH) tubes to New Jersey.

The proposed new highway offered an opportunity for restructuring business patterns throughout lower Manhattan, while the proposed Trade Center provided the excavation fill with which to extend Manhattan hundreds of feet into the Hudson River. Together, they supplied the rationale for an intelligently planned new-town-in-town on the western edge of lower Manhattan. This project, which came to be known as Battery Park City, created sites for office expansion and walk-to-work residences that could take advantage of lower Manhattan's underutilized infrastructure. What better way to improve the working environment, diversify the character of downtown business life, and enhance the city's economic and tax base?

These objectives were extended to the entire downtown business district by *The Lower Manhattan Plan* prepared for the New York City Planning Commission in 1966. This document articulated for the first time the need for carefully planned, large-scale, mixed-use development (including thousands of new apartments) along the periphery of lower Manhattan. Building in the Hudson and East Rivers guaranteed that no one would be displaced nor would existing services be interrupted. Futhermore, these riverfront projects would be able to take advantage of the tremendous existing investment in lower Manhattan infrastructure at night and on weekends when the area would otherwise be deserted.[26]

Battery Park City may have started with the compelling public policy rationale of reinforcing downtown Manhattan. However, its initial master plan, prepared at the behest of Governor Nelson Rockefeller by architect Wallace K. Harrison, promised the exact opposite: an independent entity boldly separated from downtown Manhattan. The design called for 92 acres of newly created land plus 24 acres of air rights over a depressed West Side Highway, extending 1.2 miles from the Battery on the south to Chambers Street on the north. A 32-foot-high parking structure was planned for the Hudson River side of the new interstate highway. It was to be covered with a platform that extended the entire length of the development and contained an enclosed shopping mall. The southern end of the platform was dominated by three hexagonal towers, 40-, 50-, and 60-stories high, providing 5 million square feet of office space. Marching northward two-by-two were a series of high-rise apartment slabs containing 18,000 apartments.

Manhattan, 1969. An early version of Battery Park City showing the projected multilevel parking structure, hexagonal office buildings at the southern end of the site, and waterfront promenade. *(Courtesy of New York City Department of City Planning)*

Manhattan, 1992. The World Financial Center at Battery Park City seen from the Hudson River. *(Alexander Garvin)*

In the face of enthusiastic advocacy by Governor Rockefeller and the entire downtown business establishment, the New York State Legislature voted to proceed with Battery Park City. In 1968 it created a semi-autonomous Battery Park City Authority with the power to issue the bonds necessary to finance the plan. No capital expenditures were required from the city or state, other than the cost of depressing the proposed West Side Highway, better known by its later name, Westway. (See Chapter 16.) Once the bonds were amortized, the project was expected to generate an additional $16 million per year in real estate taxes. Under the terms of the lease the authority negotiated with the city, one-third of the apartments were to be conventionally financed, one-third were to be middle-income housing, and one-third were to be low-rent housing. The necessary housing subsidies were supposed to be generated by the commercial space and conventionally financed housing or provided by the federal government.[27]

The authority issued $200 million in bonds to pay for planning, landfill, site improvements, administration, and debt service until revenues would be forthcoming. By 1976 the landfill was in place, but development was stalled by a fiscal crisis at both the city and state level. Project planning continued because bond proceeds could continue to be used for improvements, administration, and interest payments until 1980, when the first amortization payments were due. FHA insurance was obtained for a 1712-apartment complex called

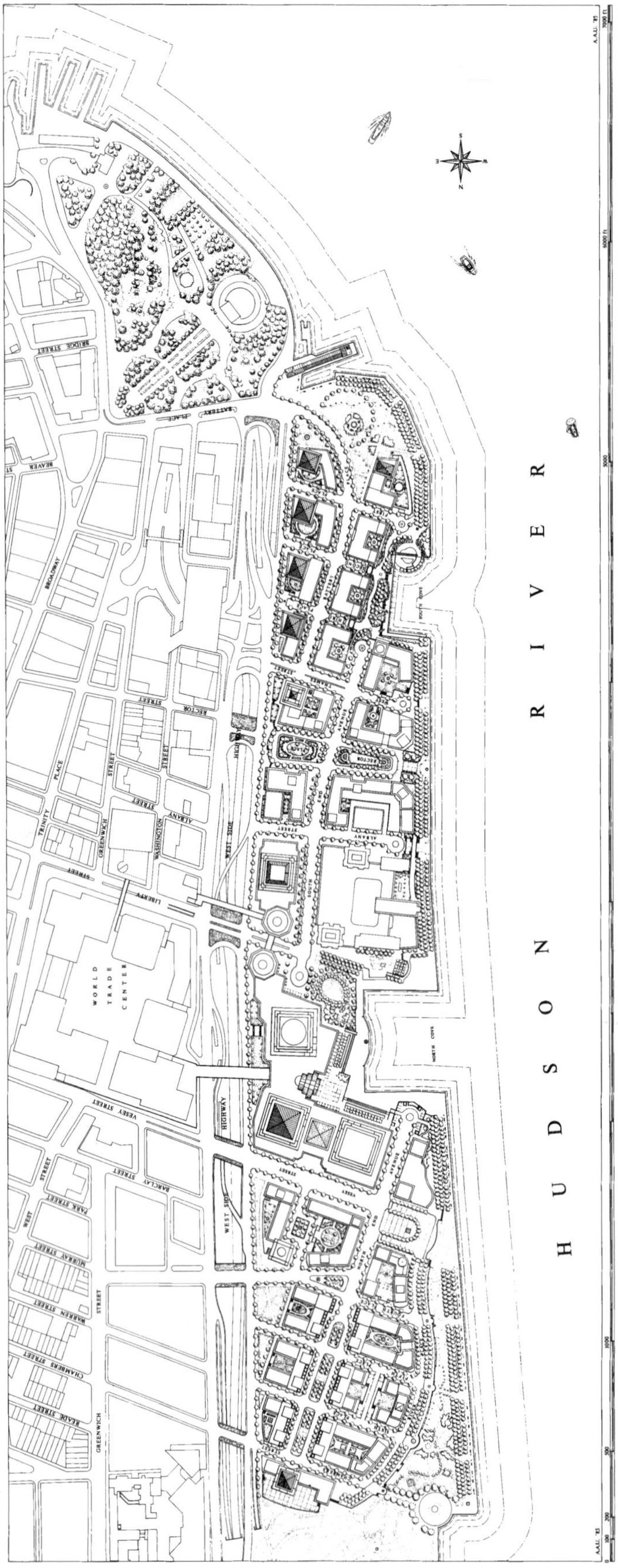

Manhattan, 1980. Cooper and Eckstut's master plan for Battery Park City. *(Alexander Cooper)*

Gateway Plaza. However, it became clear that neither Gateway Plaza nor any other revenue-producing component of Battery Park City would be completed in time to cover bond amortization requirements.[28]

The three-person Board of Directors of the Battery Park City Authority was composed of members who had been appointed for fixed terms by Governor Rockefeller. They steadfastly refused to alter the plan. When Governor Hugh Carey finally was able to replace two members in January 1979, the authority was folded into the New York State Urban Development Corporation and turned over to its president and chief executive officer, Richard Kahan, who used the possible bond default as an opportunity to prevent a planning disaster. He commissioned an entirely new master plan which Alexander Cooper and Stanton Eckstut completed within a few months.

The architects discarded everything that had been planned except Gateway Plaza, which was about to start construction, and chose instead to base their scheme on traditional New York City development patterns. As explained by Alexander Cooper, they set out to recreate "the best of New York," settling on such models as the East River esplanades at Carl Schurz Park and Brooklyn Heights, the neighborhood surrounding Gramercy Park, and the apartment houses along Central Park West. These places represented a form of urbanization that was radically different from the gigantic superblocks in Harrison's scheme.[29]

The new plan projected an eventual population of 30,000 residents and 31,000 workers. It eliminated development over the proposed highway. The remaining 92 acres of landfill were to be devoted 42 percent to residential uses (14,000 housing units); 9 percent to a commercial center relocated to be as close as possible to the subway and PATH stations at the World Trade Center; 30 percent to parks, open space, plazas, and a stunning riverfront esplanade; and 19 percent to streets and avenues. Two pedestrian bridges were planned to pass over West Street and the proposed highway.[30]

The new design reduced initial infrastructure costs. Installation of more than half a mile of trunk sewer lines, water mains, and utility conduits was avoided by moving the proposed office buildings from the southern tip of the project to the middle of the site where these lines entered the site. Elimination of the platforms saved millions more. Most important, the traditional block-by-block and lot-by-lot approach to development allowed infrastructure to be installed when dictated by market demand for building sites.

Instead of superblocks built by a few superdevelopers, Cooper and Eckstut chose to create separate neighborhoods made up of moderate-size city blocks that were in turn, divided into moderate-size building parcels that could be built at

Manhattan, 1993. South End Avenue, Battery Park City's prime residential artery. *(Alexander Garvin)*

Manhattan, 1993. The riverfront esplanade at Battery Park City. *(Alexander Garvin)*

different times by different developers. Instead of a continuous platform, 32 feet above the rest of lower Manhattan, they chose to create streets and squares that picked up the pattern of existing city streets and extended existing pedestrian views of the waterfront. Instead of separating lower Manhattan from the Hudson River, they designed a riverfront esplanade that would become a favorite downtown destination. Instead of isolating office workers away from mass transit in three towers at the southern end of the project, they proposed to create a commercial center across from a major subway interchange, right at the heart of Battery Park City. Best of all, instead of a fiscal disaster, their design made possible a financial triumph.

When Richard Kahan renegotiated the terms of a new agreement with the city, the federal government no longer offered the generous housing subsidy programs that had been available when the original plan had been approved. Thus, he was forced to eliminate all subsidized housing and establish a pay-as-you-go basis for all development. The first parcels hit the market in the early 1980s when New York City was entering a period of rapid economic growth. There was active competition for virtually every site that was initially opened for development. Bids were unexpectedly high. The success of these first projects generated additional interest in the second group of sites when they were ready for development.

Contrary to expectations, the best bid and schedule for the four separately offered office sites was from a bidder for *all* the proposed office buildings: Olympia and York, a Canadian-based real estate firm, which at that time had plenty of equity capital and ready access to secure, long-term financing. It transformed the projected 6 million square feet of office space, 280,000 square feet of retail space, the 18,500-square-foot glass-enclosed public Winter Garden, and the 3.5-acre public plaza into a single unified "World Financial Center" designed by Cesar Pelli and Associates. Thus, all the lucrative, revenue-producing commercial sites were quickly brought to completion and, in one fell swoop, guaranteed that Battery Park City would be able to meet its bond obligations on schedule. In fact, Battery Park City would generate hundreds of millions of dollars in revenues beyond these obligations—revenues that in 1986 were earmarked by the state legislature for the construction and rehabilitation of low- and moderate-income housing throughout New York City.[31]

The eventual abandonment of the Westway has left a vast right-of-way between Battery Park City and the financial district. It remains to be seen whether future planning will close this unfortunate separation from lower Manhattan. However, as more of the projected 14,000 apartments reach completion, the patina of time will set in and Battery Park City will lose its image as a new community and become another of New York's many unique, established neighborhoods.

RiverPlace, Portland, Oregon

RiverPlace, in Portland, Oregon, is another successful large-scale, mixed-use, riverfront development that evolved from a convincing public policy rationale: clearance of the blighted and underutilized warehouses and industrial buildings along the Wilamette Riverfront. There was, however, disagreement over the proper reuse of the waterfront among advocates for vehicular and rail transportation, riverfront commerce, and recreation. The controversy was resolved in 1974–1976 with the replacement of the multilane Harbor Drive by the mile-long Governor Tom McCall Park.[32]

Civic leaders were not satisfied with this beautiful swatch of green along the downtown waterfront. They wanted McCall Park to become a popular destination for residents from all over the metropolitan region. That could only be accomplished by introducing additional land uses and activities that would attract them. Accordingly, the city established the "Saturday Market" under the Burnside Bridge at the northern end of the park. The market, which operates Saturdays and Sundays, March to Christmas, brings thousands of customers

Portland, 1990. The riverfront esplanade and marina at RiverPlace. *(Alexander Garvin)*

to acquire wares from local artisans and craftspeople. At the south end of McCall Park, the city replaced a plywood mill and steam plant with RiverPlace, a 73-acre waterfront project that attracts thousands of visitors to its hotel, restaurants, shops, marina, and waterfront promenade.

The first phase of the project includes a 74-room hotel and restaurant, an athletic club, a small office building, 190 condominium apartments, a 200-boat marina and floating restaurant, 15 retail stores (mostly food service), and a single level of covered parking for 487 cars. Phase II will include another 240 to 300 rental apartments and additional parking for the popular marina and retail areas. The program for the 16½ acres of Phase III is yet to be decided.[33]

The project's first condominium apartments were completed in 1988, during a period of slack demand. Many had to be offered for rent and are only being sold on turnover. However, the hotel, restaurants, stores, and marina were an instant success. They attract astonishingly heavy use for such a modest development. Consequently, the esplanade gets quite crowded, especially in the evenings and on weekends between April and October.

The design of RiverPlace (by The Bumgardner Architects; Gaylord, Grainger, Libby, O'Brien-Smith Architects; and the Zimmer Gunsul Frasca Partnership) is appropriate to its site on the edge of downtown Portland. None of the buildings is higher than five stories. They are topped with a variety of gabled roofs that attract the attention of motorists passing across the Marquam Bridge, just to the south, and workers in the office buildings to the west. The vernacular wood construction above the first floor, while radically different from the masonry, metal, and glass buildings downtown, was selected because of its low cost and market appeal as traditional for the northwestern United States.

The best aspect of the design is its clever balance between the privacy for downtown residential developments and the busy public spaces needed for the waterfront to become an active part of the downtown. The occupants of the office, hotel, and apartment buildings enter from the city side, without having to pass through the retail portions of RiverPlace. At the same time, esplanade customers can stroll along the riverfront without disturbing the privacy of other site occupants. If these same characteristics (mixed land use with separate circulation patterns) are repeated in later phases of the project, RiverPlace will continue to provide Portland with a distinctive residential district that is simultaneously a popular destination for visitors from all over the metropolitan area.

Ingredients of Success

The success of Century City, Pentagon City, and Battery Park City is no accident. Each was able to tap huge markets because it offered an easily accessible product that its customers desired and could afford. Despite very different designs, development within each of these new-towns-in-town could be slowed (without significant financial consequences) when market demand slackened and then resumed when conditions improved. Most important, major investments in infrastructure and community facilities could be delayed until there were enough project revenues to justify the additional debt service.

Market

Some people believe that creating new-towns-in-town in rapidly expanding regions like post-World War II Los Angeles or Washington, D.C., is not difficult. However, too many planned new communities have failed for anybody to believe that success is simply a matter of selecting a site within a growing market area. The projects that succeeded did so by offering a better deal than the competition.

Some new-towns-in-town offer a better deal by marketing a good product at lower prices. Abraham Kazan's projects, for example, minimized the downpayment and lowered monthly housing expenditures. They entirely eliminated profit and received exemption from a portion of local real estate taxes. Later projects also obtained long-term, below-market-rate interest Mitchell-Lama mortgages. Cedar-Riverside tried a similar strategy. However, its lower prices depended on federal subsidies. As soon as these subsidies were no longer available, the project lost its market and came to a halt.

Projects like Pentagon City and RiverPlace attract their market by offering amenities that are not readily available elsewhere. Pentagon City includes a Metro station. RiverPlace provides a marina and a waterfront esplanade. Roosevelt Island offers its own "public" school and island-centered municipal services.

If the surrounding city is to benefit from the market attracted by a new-town-in-town, however, there must be a reason for interaction. Customers from all over metropolitan Washington, D.C., come to the Fashion Centre Mall at Pentagon City. Roosevelt Island, on the other hand, is a self-contained residential enclave with only those commercial land uses that can be supported by the residential occupants. More important, there is no way for any other section of New York City to profit from the activity it generates.

Location

New-towns-in-town often occupy leftover sites that previously were not sufficiently attractive for development or have been discarded by previous users. Thus, site characteristics rarely can be exploited for marketing purposes. In a few cases, though, they have contributed to project success. Battery Park City, RiverPlace, and Roosevelt Island, for example, all exploit the possibility of dramatic waterfront views.

If Pentagon City were far from downtown Washington, or RiverPlace far from downtown Portland, there would be less interest in living there. Mere proximity to an expanding market, however, is not sufficient. New-towns-in-town also must be easily accessible.

The pedestrian network of Battery Park City is a case in point. Until the project was redesigned, office workers would have had to hike nearly half a mile from the Path station to get to their jobs in the office towers at the southern tip of the project. Access was radically improved by relocating these buildings to a site directly across from the Path, IRT, and IND subway stations. Pedestrian bridges allow office workers to avoid the heavy vehicular traffic on West Street. These bridges also provide easy access for visitors from all over lower Manhattan who come to stroll along its traffic-free riverfront esplanade, wander among its retail stores, and make use of its restaurants during their lunch hour.

Design

The design of a new-town-in-town is largely dependent on its size, the arrangement of its components, and their relationship with the surrounding city. Roosevelt Island, for example, is separated by water from the rest of New York City. Its problems arise from a design that ignores this reality. To provide a satisfactory living environment, its design would have to adjust to that separation by providing enough residents to support a broad range of commercial and community facilities. When the "town center" that Johnson had envisioned was eliminated, the project was divided into two neighborhoods (one of which is still to be built). They are far enough from one another that neither will have enough residents to support a full range of retail stores.

Unlike Roosevelt Island, Co-op City did not have to be separate from the rest of the Bronx. Its arteries could have been connected with neighboring communities, thereby providing a critical mass of 50,000 customers able to support a wide array of services. Moreover, by creating independent shopping centers, rather than continuous shopping streets, the design deprives citizens on both sides of the highway of the safety and vitality of 24-hour activity. The result is a living environment that is as dull as the 35 drab brick towers that dominate the project.

Century City and Battery Park City, on the other hand, are mega-projects that are *not* designed to be independent districts. Not only do they include thousands of apartments, but also millions of square feet of offices. Century City and Pentagon City also include regional shopping malls with department stores. As a result, each of these new-towns-in-town has become a major city destination with people coming and going 24 hours a day.

Financing

Hundreds of new-towns-in-town never see the light of day because stable, long-term financing is unavailable. Others, like Cedar-Riverside, are terminated when money dries up. Financing for new-towns-in-town is based on the same principles that determine any real estate venture. However, because they require such huge sums, obtaining the necessary capital is no easy matter.

There are many ways to reduce the need for capital. Roosevelt Island involved no acquisition financing because it took place on government-owned land. Century City avoided major expenditures on traffic arteries and infrastructure by exploiting the existing Los Angeles street grid.

The key to a successful financing strategy, however, lies in avoiding substantial borrowing until there is an obvious source of revenue to cover debt service payments. Rose Associates deferred the cost of carrying Pentagon City until tenants had already been signed up. At Battery Park City a state authority issued tax-exempt bonds whose interest was prepaid until the project had attracted sufficient occupants. Once Olympia and York agreed to built the World Financial Center, Battery Park City was able to cover debt service and generate millions in additional revenues for other public purposes. On the other hand, the Roosevelt Island Operating Corporation has been running a deficit for two decades because it cannot recoup infrastructure and community facility costs from residents who are not yet in place.

Entrepreneurship

There are two simple models for developing new-towns-in-town. Like Park La Brea, a project can be financed and built by the same entity. This model has become less and less popular because few financial institutions are willing to risk hundreds of millions of dollars on one project or to include within their organization the necessary staff of real estate developers. Alternatively, a property owner like Zeckendorf/Alcoa can commission a plan to be filled in by individual developers in response to market demand. This model has also become more difficult to execute because there are a decreasing number of sites for new-towns-in-town that can be developed without huge up-front investments in infrastructure.

Relying on the nonprofit sector is not possible. Nonprofit developers like the United Housing Foundation require years to develop a staff with the necessary development experience. More important, they need a continuing source of revenue to support the organization. Few nonprofit organizations are able to fund such operations, and fewer still are able to sustain the necessary revenue stream. Those that engage in real estate development have the added burden of policies that try to minimize monthly housing costs for residents of their projects. Consequently, they are unwilling to charge the generous fees that will keep them in operation. As soon as anything goes wrong, as it did at Co-op City, they are unable to stay in operation. That explains why there are few nonprofit housing developers that have remained in existence for more than a decade and none (now that the United Housing Foundation is out of the development business) with the resources to develop new-towns-in-town.

Thus, the entrepreneurship needed for the creation of new-towns-in-town is most likely to come from profit-motivated developers who find ways of minimizing risk or from publicly created and financed development entities that need not consider risk.

Time

Passing through Battery Park City is a delightful experience for residents, workers, and visitors. Along the way, one can stop at a restaurant in one of the courtyards of the World Financial Center, purchase something in one of its shops, pause for a sandwich on a bench overlooking the marina, stroll along the riverfront esplanade, or wander through one of the small parks. There are no amenities like these to attract people as they pass through Park La Brea or Cedar-Riverside.

The single most important ingredient in the success of a new-town-in-town is the ability to survive over very much longer periods of time. It may take several decades to complete a planned new community. During that time the project will have to survive several economic cycles. Even a financially successful project will have to avoid development during serious economic downturns. Consequently, it must be conceived in a manner that will enable it to survive on the cash flow from already developed portions of the project. At Century City that was relatively easy. The scheme required little in the way of infrastructure. Thus, the cost of carrying the property was largely a matter of paying real estate taxes and minimal operating expenses till land sales could resume. The design of Battery Park City solved this problem by covering debt service and most other expenses out of revenues from the World Financial Center and charging residents for additional services as they became necessary when they moved in. Roosevelt Island has yet to balance project expenses with revenues.

New-Towns-in-Town as a City Planning Strategy

Lewis Mumford admired new-towns-in-town such as Fresh Meadows, believing that: "if all New York were designed on the same principles, the roads leading out of it would not carry such a weekend load of desperate people looking for a spot of green or a patch of blue or a pool of quiet—the mirage of the great metropolitan desert."[34] He was wrong, however, in believing that new-towns-in-town were the alternative to "intensifying the congestion in high-rise buildings" or endless additional "square miles of suburbs." Neither New York nor any other city is likely to grow primarily by the incremental addition of such new-towns-in-town. There is no way to mass-produce new-towns-in-town because they require too much patient capital, because too much of every metropolitan area is already filled in, and because political opposition will prevent all but a very few from reaching completion.

Mumford was right, however, in believing that new-towns-in-town can provide attractive alternative residential neighborhoods and enhance the quality of life in adjacent areas. To do so, they must be conceived as more than oversize housing projects with the minimum necessary overlay of community facilities. They must be transformed into destinations that can attract the additional users. Then they will support amenities that a city could not otherwise afford to install or continue to maintain. Most important, if considered as strategic citywide investments they can, like Battery Park City, alter the very character of city life.

Governments everywhere are faced with proposals for new-towns-in-town from private builders, public agencies, and civic organizations. Typically, once a scheme gains momentum, it causes problems for everyone. Community groups are urged to accept a plan they find unsatisfactory. Developers struggle to save their investment and commitments. Government tries to mediate, but its power to recommend alternatives is limited. The situation is neither conducive to sensible planning nor the reconciliation of differences. What government, community groups, and developers all need is a planning framework that allows desirable projects to proceed.

Any planning framework for the evaluation of new-towns-in-town must separate privately sponsored from publicly assisted projects to ensure that, at a minimum, publicly assisted projects have a public policy justification. However, since both privately sponsored and publicly developed communities will require rezoning, they should be evaluated in a similar manner and meet the same minimum standards.

New-towns-in-town will affect traffic patterns, sewage-treatment capacity, water supply and drainage systems, school loading patterns, etc. If a particular project does not have any significant negative environmental impact and does not require significant additional municipal construction or expense, there is every reason to rezone. Similarly, if the developer (private or public) is prepared to mitigate its negative impact, the site should be rezoned.

The difficulty with such simple consideration on the merits is that too often a dispute over the degree of negative impact becomes the basis of divisive political controversy and costly, time-consuming litigation. One way to avoid this is to publish standards enacted by the appropriate legislative bodies, which, if met by the project, result in automatic rezoning. These standards could include: primary and secondary processing of all sewage, a minimum level of supply of potable water per square foot of development, available school seats for every type of apartment created, a minimum number of parking spaces per square foot of office, retail, and housing, etc. Such standards should be quantifiable and measurable. A specific agency (e.g., the city planning department) would be given a specified period of time to verify that the standards had been met. Thereafter, development would be as-of-right.

A similarly straightforward approach should apply to design. The issue here is not the amount of light and air, the compatibility of land uses, or the appropriateness of the proposed density. Such matters are covered by zoning and building regulations. The issue is impact on surrounding areas. No new-town-in-town should be designed, like Co-op City, in a manner that attracts thousands of residents while draining vitality from and failing to benefit surrounding areas. These problems can be avoided if the barriers (e.g., highways, waterways, ravines) between the proposed new-town-in-town and the surrounding neighborhoods are bridged by streets and buildings, thereby tying the new district to the surrounding neighborhood; if the streets and land use patterns of the project are designed as extensions of surrounding arteries; and if the proposed new-town-in-town provides additional land uses that bring people who would not otherwise be there. As in the case of the standards for rezoning, these criteria should be specified and enacted into law so that desirable new-towns-in-town can reduce time-consuming bureaucratic review or expensive litigation.

Publicly assisted projects cannot be justified simply on the basis that they will have no negative impact on the surrounding city and will be designed in a desirable manner. There must be a defensible public-policy rationale justifying government assistance, whether it is assistance for assembling sites, or financing the prior installation of necessary infrastructure and community facilities, or providing long-term, low-cost mortgages for residential development.

Government assistance should be forthcoming only where, as at Battery Park City, it is required to stimulate investment that would not otherwise occur and where, as at RiverPlace, it will generate a desirable market reaction in adjacent areas. The problem with this simple standard is that there must be a way of separating parochial interests (whether powerful developers, domineering public agencies, or selfish community groups) from the interests of the region as a whole, without resorting to litigation.

The resolution to such controversy is to be found in the need for the massive amounts of patient capital. If a public agency believes a specific new-town-in-town is important enough to the future development of a metropolitan region to justify public financing, it should be ready to put that financing up to a vote. The vote should be on the bond issue required to finance the project, any contemplated public subsidies, and all other government approvals. Truly desirable new-towns-in-town will generate the votes needed to override parochial opposition. Once a project has been voted on, there will be many fewer opportunities for expensive, time-consuming agency processing or litigation.

So far only one city has tried to develop published standards by which to judge proposals for new-towns-in-town. That effort failed. In 1973, the New York City Planning Commission inaugurated a series of workshops and publications as part of its ongoing planning process. One of these workshops was devoted to large-scale development. It examined 20 typical sites ranging in size from 10 to 300 acres. In fact, the agency had identified more than 50 potential sites but was afraid that talking about them would generate unnecessary community opposition. Even if all the potential sites had been openly discussed, nothing would have happened because the agency abandoned the effort a few months after it had started.[35]

Many of the new-town-in-town sites identified in 1973 kept reappearing. Those that took shape as serious proposals developed into major controversies that were eventually resolved based on the political power of the participants with little or no attention to a project's impact on the city as a whole. For example, every consideration of a proposed new-town-in-town for the West Side Rail Yards in Manhattan has focused on opposition from adjacent residents, not on any intrinsic reasons for development in that location. Similarly, when a coalition of government agencies proposed a planned new community for Hunter's Point in Queens, they failed to disclose the need for well over $2 billion in public expenditures for infrastructure and community facilities, money that clearly was not available. At the same time opponents made expensive, unrealistic lists of changes and amenities they felt might mitigate the negative consequences of the proposal, without being able to focus discussion on whether the proposed project would achieve any of the city's planning and development objectives.

The course of these controversies in New York City has provided a lesson that its citizens have yet to learn: cities need clearly articulated standards and strongly presented policies by which to evaluate any proposed new-town-in-town. In their absence, every city is doomed to divisive battles and ad hoc decisions that may or may not produce healthy communities, intelligent consumption of precious, underdeveloped land, or desirable patterns of urbanization.

Notes

1. Lewis Mumford, *The Urban Prospect,* Harcourt, Brace & World, Inc., New York, 1968, p. 211.
2. Lewis Mumford, *The Highway and the City,* The New American Library, New York, 1964, p. 235.
3. Historical and statistical information on Century City is derived from Cheryl G. Cummins (program director), *Los Angeles Metropolitan Area... Today,* Urban Land Institute, Washington, D.C., 1987, pp. 110–124, and William Zeckendorf, Sr., with Edward McCreary, *Zeckendorf,* Holt, Rinehart, and Winston, New York, 1970, pp. 245–254.
4. Zeckendorf, Sr., with McCreary, op. cit., p. 247.
5. Charles Moore, Peter Backer, and Regula Campbell, *The City Observed: Los Angeles,* Vintage Books, Random House, 1984, pp. 211–212.
6. Ibid.
7. Ibid.
8. The transaction included five parcels of undeveloped land, plus half-ownership in the twin 44-story Century Plaza Towers, plus the Century Plaza Hotel and Towers.
9. Historical and statistical information on Pentagon City is derived from "Pentagon City," *Urban Land Reference File,* vol. 20, no. 4, The Urban Land Institute, Washington, D.C., 1990, and an interview with Daniel Rose, October 3, 1990.
10. Elliott Metz (project director), *Public and Publicly Aided Housing in New York City 1927–1973,* New York City Planning Commission, New York, 1974. The total of 1434 dwelling units includes 263 units subsequently demolished for Amalgamated Houses Extension.
11. Eugene Rachlis and John E. Marqusee, *The Landlords,* Random House, New York, 1963, pp. 131–163.
12. Metz, op. cit. Completion is defined as the issuance of the project's final certificate of occupancy. Tenants may have moved in earlier, upon the issuance of a temporary certificate of occupancy.
13. Roger Starr, Statement at the public hearing held by the New York City Planning Commission on April 28, 1965, as reported by the Commission's stenotypist.
14. Zeckendorf with McCreary, op. cit., pp. 291–292.
15. Ada Louise Huxtable, *Will They Ever Finish Bruckner Boulevard?,* Collier Books, New York, 1972, pp. 77–80.
16. New York State Division of Housing and Community Renewal, *Statistical Summary of Programs,* New York, March 31, 1978, p. 81.
17. Total project cost is estimated by the New York State Division of Housing and Community Renewal at $422,699,700 (excluding $46 million in construction financing for the Co-op City Educational Park).
18. *Housing & Urban Development Act of 1969,* Sec. 402.
19. Historical and statistical information on Cedar-Riverside is derived from, Judith A. Martin, *Recycling the Central City: The Development of a New-Town-in-Town,* Center for Urban and Regional Affairs, University of Minnesota, Minneapolis, 1978.
20. Welfare Island Planning and Development Committee (Benno C. Schmidt, Chairman), *Report of the Welfare Island Planning and Development Committee,* submitted to John V. Lindsay, Mayor, City of New York, February 1969.
21. In addition to Welfare Island, Logue also sought to develop a series of new-towns-in-town over the Penn Central Railroad right-of-way that extended along the Harlem River in the Bronx. Only one of them, the 1654-unit Park River Towers project, was completed. It was developed in conjunction with Roberto Clemente Park, the first state-financed park within the City of New York.
22. The idea of renaming the island after Franklin D. Roosevelt had been suggested by *The New York Times,* in an editorial dated February 15, 1969.
23. Philip Johnson and John Burgee, *The Island Nobody Knows,* New York State Urban Development Corporation, New York, October 1969.
24. New York State UDC, *Roosevelt Island Schools P.S.-I.S. 217,* undated brochure, p. 2.
25. Matthew I. Wald, "Many Roosevelt I. Shops Still Empty," *The New York Times,* December 25, 1977, section 10, p. 1.
26. Wallace, McHarg, Roberts, and Todd + Whittlesey, Conklin, and Rossant + Alan M. Voorhees & Associates, Inc., *The Lower Manhattan Plan,* New York City Planning Commission, June 1, 1966.
27. There was never any hope of generating sufficient revenues from the new office buildings and market-rate housing to subsidize so large a quantity of apartments. The proponents of Battery Park City, like so many other advocates, had cynically proposed something they were

ready to eliminate when it was proven infeasible.

28. Luckily, bond proceeds had been invested at a rate of interest that was higher than that paid to the bondholders.
29. Alexander Cooper, interview, August 1990.
30. Battery Park City Authority, *Battery Park City Vital Statistics,* undated brochure.
31. Ibid.
32. Carl Abbot, *Portland: Planning, Politics, and Growth in a Twentieth-Century City,* University of Nebraska Press, Lincoln, 1983, pp.215–216 and 224–225 and Robert Moses, *Public Works: A Dangerous Trade,* McGraw-Hill, New York, 1970, pp. 758–765.
33. Historical and statistical information on RiverPlace is derived from Urban Land Institute, *RiverPlace,* Project Reference File, vol. 18, no. 3, Washington, D.C., January–March 1988.
34. Lewis Mumford, *From the Ground Up,* Harcourt, Brace & World, New York, 1956, p. 12.
35. See New York City Department of City Planning, *Large-Scale Development in New York City,* New York City, October 1973.

15

New-Towns-in-the-Country

Seaside, 1990. *(Alexander Garvin)*

Some planned new towns, including Chestnut Hill in Philadelphia, Beverly Hills, California, and Seaside, Florida began as vacation refuge new towns. The second group, including Lake Forest, Illinois; Shaker Heights, Ohio; and Reston, Virginia, were intended to be suburban satellites of large and growing cities. Some new towns, such as Riverside, Illinois, and Palos Verdes Estates, California, are places of rare beauty. Others, such as Levittown, Long Island, and Lakewood, California, were profitable business ventures that also produced huge quantities of inexpensive houses. Still others, like the bulk of the Title VII new towns started during the Nixon Administration, were flops and are now forgotten.

Thousands of planned new towns in America may have been intended as vacation refuges or as utopian satellites of congested cities. However, from the beginning, some of their proponents have also seen them as devices for solving other pressing problems. Some argue that land is a scarce resource that, once consumed, can only be reclaimed at considerable expense and disruption. They believe that carefully planned new towns preserve this scarce resource, maximize open space available to nearby populations, and site land uses so that they interact with infrastructure and community facilities in a more efficient and economical manner.

Others argue that planned new towns are cheaper because they can be created on large properties that do not require costly, time-consuming site assemblage. Since infrastructure, community facilities, and municipal services can be provided more efficiently, the assumption is that development costs will be lower.

Some advocates even believe that there will be less crime, juvenile delinquency, and other social ills in well-planned new communities. Their rationale is not preposterous. New towns usually provide convenient access to community facilities and municipal services that are not as easily available elsewhere. Their villagelike organization may reduce conflict and increase social interaction. During the nineteenth century these ideas led to the establishment of utopian new communities by Shakers, Rappites, Icarians, Owenites, and Fourierists. Such communities continued to be founded into the twentieth century, though far less frequently.[1]

The same utopianism extends to the political rationale for new towns. Somehow, the promise of improved social interaction gets translated into a racially and economically integrated society. Orderly industrial location gets translated into living and working in the same community.

Even excluding utopian communities, company towns, and seats of government, all these claims can be demonstrated by some planned new towns. Palos Verdes Estates and Reston offer residents unusually generous open space and recreational facilities. Sea Ranch, California, preserves thousands of acres of meadowland that would otherwise have been torn up for little boxes of ticky-tacky. The design of Riverside and Shaker Heights integrates transportation and utilities in an efficient and attractive manner. Houses in Levittown and Lakewood were "a better buy" than contemporaneous, nearby, tract development. The quality of life at Seaside and Beverly Hills is more pleasant than in most suburbs. These same planned new towns can also be used to demonstrate flaws in the physical, economic, social, and political rationales propounded by their advocates. Levittown is not prettier; Shaker Heights is not more convenient; Beverly Hills is not cheaper; Palos Verdes Estates is not healthier socially; Reston is not politically more vigorous than neighboring communities.

Some new town advocates will admit the debatable nature of these rationales. They may even admit that the underlying reason for their continuing faith in planned new communities is a distaste for existing cities. Naturally, they assume that everybody feels the same way and, when provided with this much-desired alternative, will happily leave outmoded, unsatisfactory cities. Like the English social visionary and political activist Ebenezer Howard, they believe that once new towns have become sufficiently pervasive, consumers no longer will have any reason to remain behind in "obsolete" cities, which will then inevitably wither away.

Developers have been creating new-towns-in-the-country for nearly two centuries. Some of them began as vacation refuges and became self-sufficient communities that function 365 days a year. Others began as utopian satellites that are now quite independent of the cities that spawned them. Yet neither variety of new town has led people to abandon cities.

Nor are new-towns-in-the-country an exceptional phenomenon. In 1992, the Urban Land Institute issued a directory of projects that were then under way. It included 529 planned communities of more than 300 acres that contained "a substantial amount of housing units," a significant recreational amenity package," and often "significant commercial uses as well."[2]

Nevertheless, well-intentioned reformers continue to insist that the new town is the antidote to both urban blight and suburban sprawl. On three occasions they even persuaded the federal government to get into the new town building business. None of these efforts demonstrated the superiority of government-assisted new town development over more modest forms of urbanization. In fact, the loveliest of America's new-towns-in-the-country—Riverside, Palos Verdes, Sea Ranch, and Seaside—were started at different times by different developers that conceived of them as for-profit real estate ventures.

The new-town-in-the-county, like the plat, the subdivision, the cluster community, and the new-town-in-town is simply a form of urbanization. Like them, it should be allowed to flourish wherever there are developers, investors, and lenders that are willing to risk their money. Rather than saddle these new towns with responsibility for fixing our urban/suburban environment, government should insure that they do not damage it and step out of the way.

Ebenezer Howard and the Garden City

In 1871, at the age of 21, Ebenezer Howard emigrated from London to Nebraska. After a year as a farmer, he moved to Chicago and began a career as a shorthand reporter. In 1876 Howard returned to England, where he earned a living as a stenographer, worked on a series of mechanical inventions, and participated in organizations interested in land reform, urban poverty, and other public issues. His interest in social reform led, in 1898, to the publication at his own expense of *Tomorrow: A Peaceful Path To Real Reform* (revised and reissued in 1902 under its better known title, *Garden Cities of Tomorrow*).[3]

This influential book identified the problems of living in existing cities (closing out of nature, overcrowding, high rents and high prices in general, air pollution, slums, etc.) and of living in the country (lack of society, unemployment, long hours at low wages, lack of cultural and recreational facilities, etc.). Howard argued for "a third alternative, in which all the advantages of the most energetic and active town life, with all the beauty and delight of the country, may be secured in perfect combination."[4] This third alternative, which he called a "garden city," would combine beauty of nature with social opportunity, entrepreneurial opportunity with the flow of capital, accessible parks with slumless residential areas, pure air and water with plenty of things to do, etc.[5]

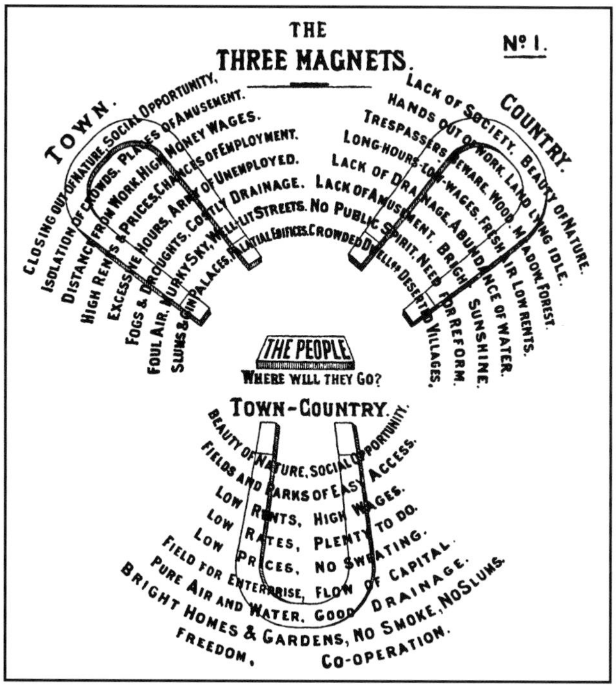

Ebenezer Howard, 1898. The best of "town and country must be married and out of the joyous union will spring a new hope, a new life, a new civilization." *(From E. Howard, Garden Cities of Tomorrow, MIT Press, Cambridge, 1965)*

The suburban utopia that Howard proposed had many of the features of English eighteenth-century suburban communities, where villas were built among open fields and groves of trees and where children could grow up sheltered from the dangers, cruelties, and immorality of the crowded, filthy streets of nearby London. However, Howard's conception went beyond withdrawing one's family from the evils of the city in order to settle in a house surrounded by trees and grass and flowers.[6]

Howard wanted to create a completely new entity. As he explained, "Town and country must be married and out of this joyous union will spring a new hope, a new life, a new civilization."[7] This attempted marriage of town and country was probably influenced by his experiences in America. During the four years that he lived in Chicago, an increasing number of city residents moved to new towns built in conjunction with suburban railroad stations. Howard must have been familiar with these Illinois communities, particularly Lake Forest and Riverside. The 1871 promotional brochure for Riverside boasts, in language very reminiscent of Ebenezer Howard's later writings, that it will "combine the conveniences peculiar to the finest modern cities, with the domestic advantages of the most charming country."[8]

Lake Forest and Riverside, Illinois

In 1856, members of Chicago's First and Second Presbyterian churches decided to found a Presbyterian school. They acquired a 2300-acre irregular, wooded site along Lake Michigan, on the recently completed Chicago and Milwaukee Railroad (later the Chicago and Northwestern Railroad.), 25 miles north of the city. The site's attractions included a lovely shoreline along Lake Michigan, a varied, rolling landscape quite different from the surrounding prairie.[9]

The Lake Forest Association, formed to develop the site, hired a landscape architect named Hotchkiss to prepare a plan for the new community. Little is known about the association's design intentions. Its business intention, however, was to auction every other lot and use the money to establish Lake Forest Academy and later Lake Forest College on a central 62-acre site.[10]

The lot sale that was held in 1857 was a success. To generate additional demand for its property, the Lake Forest Association built a resort hotel. When it opened the following summer, hundreds of wealthy Chicagoans could see for themselves the luxurious house sites that had been made available. The community's popularity spread quickly and by 1861, when Lake Forest was incorporated as a city, it was already one of "the most aristocratic of all Chicago's suburbs."[11]

The winding roads and irregular blocks of the Hotchkiss plan reflect the popular romantic, picturesque esthetic of the period (see Chapters 3 and 13). But the design itself was determined by the need to cut through thicket-covered hills and ravines to connect the railroad station on the western edge of

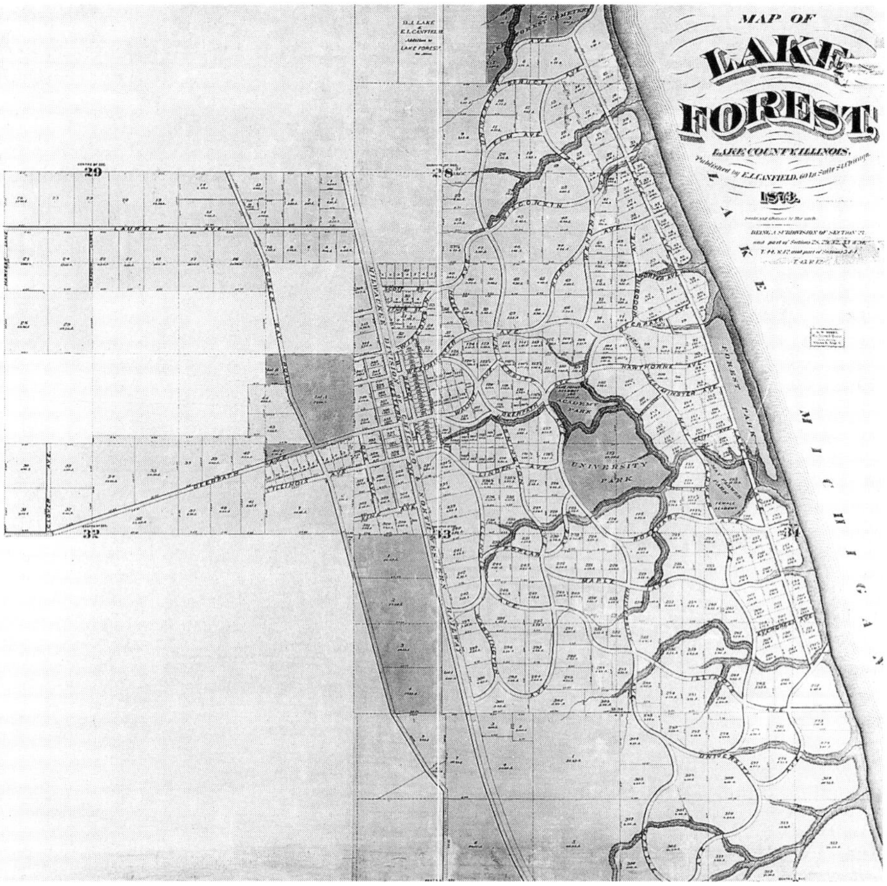

Lake Forest, 1873. Plat of Lake Forest in which the streets radiate from the railroad station to Lake Michigan, following routes that minimize topographical problems. *(Courtesy of Chicago Historical Society)*

town with the lakeshore along its eastern edge. The vehicular roadways that emerged exploit natural drainage patterns, minimize the number of ravine crossings, and radiate in an irregular manner from the railroad station and town center eastward toward the house lots stretched out along the lakeshore.[12]

As a fledgling suburb of Chicago, then only beginning to be recognized as a national center, Lake Forest would not become known outside the region for some time. Furthermore, its unique topographic features made it an unlikely model for other sites. That role would be played by Riverside, the Chicago suburb designed by Frederick Law Olmsted.[13]

Like Lake Forest, the site of Riverside was made accessible by railroad, gained popularity once its 124-room hotel opened in 1870, and soon thereafter became a fashionable upper-middle class suburb. The similarity ends there. Riverside was a business venture, not a semi-charitable land operation.[14]

Eastern entrepreneur Emery Childs understood that the Chicago, Burlington, and Quincy Railroad station that opened in the middle of the David Gage farm in 1864, greatly increased the site's proximity to downtown Chicago. He established the Riverside Improvement Company for the express purpose of acquiring this 1600-acre farm 9 miles west of Chicago, subdividing it into house lots, and offering them for sale.

The "low, flat, miry, and forlorn" site was located on the prairie, far from Lake Michigan. Its only distinguishing feature was the shallow Des Plaines River, which slowly wound its way through the farm. Childs needed a design that would attract customers to this now accessible but forlorn location.

He hired Olmsted, Vaux, and Company, whose work on Central Park in New York City and Prospect Park in Brooklyn had made its reputation as the premier landscape-architecture firm of the day. Instead of a picturesque design similar to Llewellyn Park (see Chapter 13) or Lake Forest, Olmsted proposed a scheme that could be copied (frequently quite badly) anywhere in America.

Olmsted used traffic arteries and landscaping to create an Arcadian refuge for the middle class. Seven hundred of its 1600 acres were set aside for roads, borders, walks, and parks. Houses were located about 150 feet from one another and set back at least 30 feet from the roadways. Fences were prohibited. Thus, the first impression of Riverside is one of airy expanses of open space, or what Olmsted referred to as "a sense of enlarged freedom" (see Chapter 3).

Unlike Lake Forest, where home builders had to cut through the existing landscape to open roads and clear house sites, the curvilinear streets of Riverside were intended to enliven the forlorn prairie. Olmsted designed 40 miles of carriage road and 80 miles of walks that followed curving routes with seemingly endless glimpses of what was just around the bend.

Between 1869 and 1871, the Riverside Improvement Company planted "47,000 shrubs, 7,000 evergreens, and 32,000 deciduous trees...some of them 19 inches in diameter...and 80 feet high...used 50,000 cubic yards of MacAdam stone, 20,000 cubic yards of gravel...and over 250,000 cubic yards of [excavated] earth."[15]

In the process, Olmsted demonstrated how clever landscaping could transform even the bleakest site into marketable house lots. He explained that, "We cannot judiciously attempt to control the form of the houses which men shall build, we can only, at most, take care that if they build very ugly and

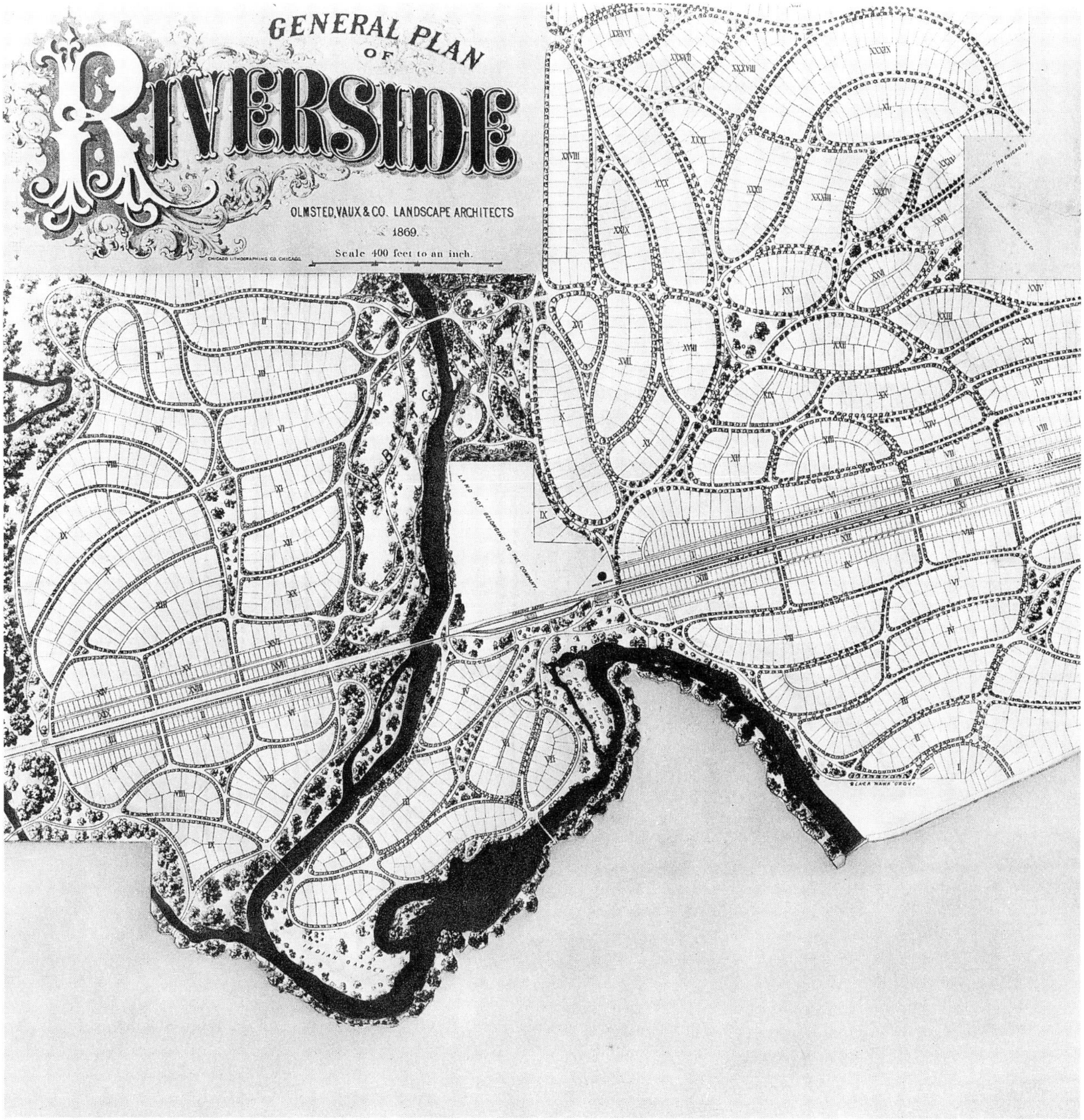

Riverside, 1969. Olmsted and Vaux's curvillinear plan was intended to enliven this flat, prairie-like site.
(Courtesy of the National Park Service, Frederick Law Olmsted National Historic Site)

Riverside, 1993. Tree-lined open lots with houses set back from the property line as a method for creating a "refined domestic life, secluded, but not far removed from the life of the community." *(Alexander Garvin)*

inappropriate houses, they shall not be allowed to force them disagreeably upon our attention."[16]

Olmsted's solution was to combine the 30-foot front yard with two trees planted between the street and the house. This combination of open front lawns, houses set back from the street, and tree-lined roadways was a cheap, easy way of ensuring privacy. It quickly became the design formula for innumerable suburban subdivisions (see Chapter 13).

Riverside, 1993. Gracefully curving arteries that are "pleasant to the eye within themselves" but also with "pleasant openings and outlooks." *(Alexander Garvin)*

The plan provided all the up-to-date conveniences of city life: paved streets and sidewalks, water and sewer mains, fireplugs, a gravity drainage system, a gas works, individual gas hookups, and street lamps. In addition to the hotel, there was a block of stores and offices near the railroad station. The only planned convenience that was not executed was Olmsted's proposed 150-foot-wide parkway extending all the way into Chicago.

The Riverside Improvement Company went bankrupt in 1873. Too much of its initial $1.5 million investment had been spent on land acquisition, infrastructure, landscaping, and operating expenses. Lot sales, while adequate at first, plummeted during the Panic of 1873. Without a revenue stream that exceeded expenditures, there was no way to pay for further improvements, to pay debt service on a mortgage that could finance them, or to repay the money that had been borrowed. Consequently, only 60 percent of the Olmsted and Vaux plan was completed as designed.

Riverside may have been established for the purpose of selling residential building lots for profit. However, what Olmsted had conceived and the Riverside Improvement Company had built was no suburban subdivision; it was an entire new town. Anything that remained to be done could be accomplished by an established government with the power to raise the money needed to pay for public services or the upkeep of the recently completed streets, utilities, and community facilities.

In 1875, only 6 years after the start of development, Riverside was incorporated as a village with a charter enabling it to provide fire, police, and other municipal services similar to those provided by the incorporated City of Chicago. This was an easy step because, unlike most residential land development projects of that era, Riverside had been established with its infrastructure already in place.

The Garden Cities Movement

Like Riverside, the garden city that Ebenezer Howard described was "to be planned as a whole, and not left to grow up in a chaotic manner." It would include every modern urban convenience: water, sewer, surface drainage, gas, power, streets, sidewalks, street lights, etc.... Houses were to stand on "their own ample grounds." Howard's description of the landscape even sounds like Olmsted: "...ample space for roads, some of which are of truly magnificent proportions, so wide and spacious that sunlight and air may freely circulate, and in which trees, shrubs, and grass give to the town a semi-rural appearance."[17]

Despite similarities, the garden city that Howard conceived was quite different from Riverside or Lake Forest. Its idealized shape was presented by Howard as circular. However, none of the new town projects with which he was involved took this form. As he later explained, "The diagrams in my book were never more than diagrams."[18]

The "new life" that Howard envisioned was to take place in 1000-acre, 30,000-person garden cities surrounded by a 5000-acre, 2000-person agricultural greenbelt. This was no dormitory suburb. Manufacturing firms located right in town would provide residents with employment. Farms located in the greenbelt would supply all the agricultural products needed by the residents.

Each garden city would own all land in perpetuity. Individual sites would be leased to their occupants at rents "based on the annual [market] value of the land."[19] Thus, as land appreciated in value, often as a result of community investment in infrastructure and public facilities, this increase accrued to the community rather than to the property's current occupant. Any earnings in excess of the cost of infrastructure and public facilities could then be used for the further benefit of the community.

Garden cities would be governed by boards of management whose activities were paid for by ground rents on municipally owned land. These boards consisted of a central council that was responsible for the planning, development, expenditures, and overall policy, and departments that were responsible for day-to-day administration. There were to be three groups of departments: Public Control (i.e., finance, assessment, law, and inspection), Engineering (i.e., roads, water, sewers, drainage, transit, light, and power), and Social Purposes (i.e., education, baths, music, libraries, and recreation). The members of the central council and the heads of the departments were to be elected from among the community's occupants.[20]

Howard's method for curing London's ills was to keep establishing new garden cities and filling them with the residents and businesses that moved from overpopulated London, until the city could be entirely abandoned. This same prescription was to be employed wherever there were obsolete, overcrowded cities.

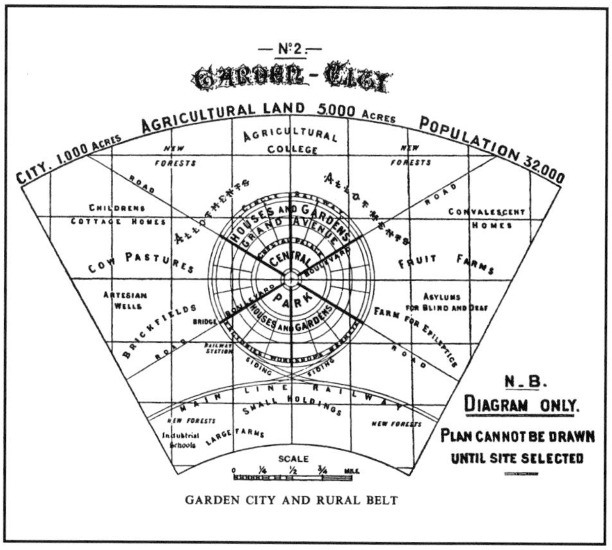

Ebenezer Howard, 1898. The *garden city* was intended to be a place "in which all the advantages of the most energetic town life" would be "secured in perfect combination with all the beauty and delight of the country." *(From E. Howard, Garden Cities of Tomorrow, MIT Press, Cambridge, 1965)*

Letchworth, 1972. A garden city that looks like many other residential sections of suburban London. *(Alexander Garvin)*

In 1899, to promote the ideas presented in his writings, Howard founded the Garden City Association (now the Town and Country Planning Association). No garden cities were forthcoming. Consequently, 4 years later he decided to demonstrate the validity of his ideas and formed a joint stock company to build the first genuine garden city: Letchworth. The company acquired a 3822-acre site, 35 miles north of London, and held a design competition that was won by architect-planners Barry Parker and Raymond Unwin.

Their scheme combined formal geometry with the more organic forms of the traditional English village. A central square was established at the highest spot on the site. Radial avenues extended from the square to provide access to the rest of the town and to the surrounding greenbelt. The only distinctive feature of the design was the use of the "close" to eliminate disturbing through traffic and reinforce a sense of community. Parker and Unwin further developed the close (better known as the cul-de-sac) at Hampstead Garden Suburb.[21]

The proposed 5–1 acreage ratio of greenbelt to garden city turned out to be too costly. Furthermore, the two-thirds of Letchworth's area that was devoted to the greenbelt, was a park, not an agricultural settlement. The notion that greenbelt residents would provide the agricultural products needed by garden-city residents turned out to be a romantic illusion.

Howard's vision of a self-contained work force also had little in common with the realities of the marketplace or the desires of garden city residents. Industrial firms did move to Letchworth. By 1949 there were 65 manufacturers, ranging in size from a handful of employees to one firm with over 1000. However, many of the workers traveled to Letchworth from surrounding areas, while many Letchworth residents worked outside the town.[22]

Neither Letchworth nor Welwyn, Howard's second garden city started in 1919, was successful in demonstrating a superiority over conventional, developer-initiated suburban development then under way on smaller sites around greater London. Neither garden city was physically different from these less-ambitious dormitory suburbs. Nor did they exhibit the lovely combination of town and country of Lake Forest, Riverside, or some of the better developer-initiated new towns in America.

Despite the failure of so many of Howard's theories, they continued to have enormous influence. During the 1920s and 1930s, reformers, intellectuals, and politicians throughout England demanded that the government institute a program of new town development as an antidote to urban overcrowding and wasteful suburbanization. In 1946, Parliament finally enacted a New Towns Act that over the next 26 years produced 22 satellite new towns and expanded countless existing towns.[23]

Howard's influence extended far beyond England. After World War II, countries throughout the world experimented with government-planned new towns. Among the most noteworthy were the new town programs of Sweden, Finland, France, and Israel.

In the United States, Howard's ideas had their greatest effect on Lewis Mumford, Clarence Stein, and the other members of the Regional Planning Association of America (see Chapter 13). But it was not Howard's philosophy that generated most American new towns. From the beginning of the nineteenth century, there was general unhappiness with city life and consumer demand for an alternative. This combination led inevitably to an attempt by profit-motivated real estate developers to supply that alternative.

The Vacation Refuge New Town

Many Americans have a profound yearning to escape the city for a healthier life in "natural" surroundings. Since most people are unable to entirely abandon the city, the next best thing is to get away as often as possible. Consequently, those families that can afford it get out of town whenever they can, sometimes moving to the country for the entire summer. During the eighteenth century there were not enough such wealthy families to warrant development activity. However, during the nineteenth century cities grew so rapidly that a large market developed and smart investors acquired attractive, country real estate.

The typical sequence began with a railroad or roadway that brought a beautiful landscape within easy access of a prosperous, growing city. Developers, often with business connections to the railroad, would seize the opportunity to profit from the newly accessible site by building a hotel for vacationing city dwellers. They also subdivided nearby property into building lots. As the area became popular, vacationers sought an alternative to the relatively short, expensive hotel stay. They bought the building lots and erected summer houses. In time many of the houses would be converted into year-round residences.

As the nearby city prospered it also expanded, frequently enveloping what turned out to be a temporary refuge. Eventually Chestnut Hill, Beverly Hills, and countless other vacation refuge new towns, which had been established to exploit the lovely countryside, ended up as distinctive sections of vast metropolitan areas. In some places the increasing demand for space and higher prices induced developers to convert larger houses into multiple dwellings. In other places they demolished and replaced them with tract houses or condo communities.

During the twentieth century, as the work week grew shorter, leisure time increased, and disposable income rose, more and more families tried to get away from the city. Increasingly inexpensive air travel and an extensive interstate highway network opened more distant sites. The communities established at these locations reflect much deeper desires for ideal living environments. As a result, Sea Ranch in California, Seaside in Florida, and other vacation refuge new towns have begun appearing in beautiful but previously untrammeled natural areas. These new communities are often more varied in character than those built closer to established cities. They also exhibit a much more obvious attempt to create an alternative to conventional city and suburban living.

Chestnut Hill, Philadelphia

Most visitors to Chestnut Hill assume it is quite separate from the city of which it has been a part for nearly a century and a half. But Chestnut Hill was not developed as a residential extension of Philadelphia or even as a speculative subdivision for commuters. It began as an alternative to spending the summer in the congested city.[24]

In 1854, when this section of northwest Philadelphia was incorporated into the city, the Reading Railroad initiated rail service connecting it with the downtown business district, 11

Philadelphia, 1986. The Wissahickon Inn (now Chestnut Hill Academy) that provided a refuge for vacationing families. *(Alexander Garvin)*

miles away. At that time Chestnut Hill was a verdant, rolling landscape dominated by the steep valleys etched by Wissahickon and Cresheim Creeks, which later became part of Fairmount Park. Prior to the railroad, the only access to the

Philadelphia, 1976. French Village in Chestnut Hill, designed in the mid-1920s by Robert McGoodwin. *(Alexander Garvin)*

city was along Germantown Avenue. The railroad opened the area to country excursions by daytrippers from Philadelphia but brought few other changes.[25]

Chestnut Hill's transformation into a summer resort began with the extension of the Pennsylvania Railroad to Chestnut Hill in 1872. Henry Howard Houston, the general (or head) freight agent of the railroad, lived in the area. He decided to profit from the new line by purchasing 3000 acres of hilly farmland overlooking the picturesque Wissahickon Valley, now only half an hour by rail from downtown Philadelphia. He hired architects G. W. and W. D. Hewitt to prepare a conventional, rectilinear plat for the area. The plan allowed him to sell lots at increasingly high prices, while building houses for rent on much of the remaining land.

The critical marketing device was the Wissahickon Inn (now Chestnut Hill Academy) built in 1884. Whole families left town for a summer stay at the Wissahickon Inn, from which fathers could easily commute to work in town. Houston also donated the land for the Philadelphia Cricket Club (a country club) and St. Martin-in-the-Fields Episcopal Church. Once the hotel, country club, and church were in place, Chestnut Hill became a fashionable resort for the Philadelphia elite. Upper-middle-class families became acquainted with the area from their visits to the Wissahickon Inn. Houston sold them sites on which they built large houses. They transformed Chestnut Hill into an elite suburb with tree-shaded streets, broad lawns, and big houses set back from the street.

After Houston died, his son-in-law, Dr. George Woodward, continued building houses for rent in Chestnut Hill. The most interesting of these are a series of charming residential developments in Norman, Cotswold, and French vernacular styles. Some are groups of one-family houses. Others are attached clusters that heighten the community's villagelike appearance.

The 30-minute train ride made Chestnut Hill too convenient. It quickly changed from a summer resort into a year-round, commuter suburb. In fact, Chestnut Hill is so convenient that during the latter decades of the twentieth century it has begun to experience second growth. Developers have been subdividing the larger estates into house lots and condo communities, sometimes even converting the larger manor houses into multiple dwellings. As a result, Chestnut Hill is slowly losing its role as an alternative to conventional city life.

Beverly Hills, California

If a tourist hotel was an effective device for marketing Chestnut Hill, it was crucial to Beverly Hills. Americans had been streaming to the West Coast by the thousands in search of their vision of Arcadia. The farmland that would become Beverly Hills was located midway between the rapidly growing city of Los Angeles and the Pacific Ocean. It was an almost perfect embodiment of that Arcadia: gentle plains, lying just below the rolling foothills of the Santa Monica Mountains, warmed by a semitropical sun, cooled by soft ocean breezes.

Land acquisition for a new community was relatively simple because initial colonization by the Spanish had divided the area into enormous ranchos, in this case, the Rancho Rodeo de las Aguas, named after the "gathering of waters" from Coldwater and Benedict Canyons during the rainy season. Easy access had been provided since 1887 by a steam railroad that ran along Santa Monica Boulevard, connecting Los Angeles and Hollywood with the Pacific Ocean. The line was electrified in 1896, sold to the Southern Pacific Railroad in 1909, and merged into the Pacific Electric interurban railway system. Despite a benign climate, picturesque landscape, strategic location, and transit service, the area spawned only unsuccessful real estate ventures. Instead of new homes, it remained occupied by lima beans.[26]

In 1900, a group led by Burton E. Green decided to drill for oil in the area. They formed the Amalgamated Oil Company and purchased what was then the 3608-acre Hammel and Denker Ranch. Instead of oil, it struck water. Green simply shifted gears and, in 1906, formed the Rodeo Land and Water Company, which purchased the site in order to resell the land as individual house lots. He hired Wilbur Cook, a New York landscape architect, to design a luxury community with broad, tree-lined streets and large, attractive house lots. The plat, officially recorded in 1907, discarded the north-south Los Angeles street system, replacing it with a gently undulating street grid of long blocks, running roughly at a 45-degree angle to Wilshire Boulevard. Green named his model community Beverly Hills, partly in memory of Beverly Farms, Massachusetts, and partly in recognition of the hilly landscape at the northern end of the site.

The new town of Beverly Hills was advertised in Los Angeles newspapers, but as one 1907 visitor explained, there was nothing there: "We got off the Pacific Electric car at the station and looked around. Very young trees, uniform in variety and spacing, had a sort of merry, hopeful look."[27] Streets were paved but sewers, gas lines, and street lights had yet to be installed. As a result, hardly anyone bought. During the next 3 years only six new residences were built north of Santa Monica Boulevard.

The situation changed dramatically in 1911, when Green decided to build the Beverly Hills Hotel. He persuaded Margaret Anderson, then manager of the popular Hotel Hollywood, to take a similar position at the Beverly Hills Hotel, but only by offering her an option to buy the hotel if it was successful. When it opened the following year, she brought her reputation, her staff, many of the furnishings, some of her clients, and, most important, instant success. Green happily sold her the hotel.

Vacationers from all over the country began coming to the Beverly Hills Hotel. Many fell in love with the area, establishing homes and businesses there. Local residents also settled in the area. By 1914, there were enough residents for Beverly Hills to become an incorporated city, quite separate from nearby Los Angeles. Within a few years, however, it had

Beverly Hills, 1915. North Crescent Drive, the newly built Beverly Hills Hotel, and the many vacant building lots that when filled-in would become one of America's most prestigious new-towns-in-the-country. *(Courtesy of Bison Archives)*

merged with the rest of the region's automobile-dominated landscape, distinguishable only because of its different street grid and more expensive houses.

The Beverly Hills Hotel had been the critical element needed to attract customers to this previously unsuccessful new community. Once there, they bought the vacant lots, built the houses, filled the empty streets, and transformed the remaining fields of lima beans into an international mecca for the rich and famous: a "fabulous clime.... Where the rain does not rain. It just drizzles champagne.... Where romance is the theme of the day... [and] everything is tremendous! titanic! stupendous!"[28]

Sea Ranch, California

Sea Ranch, the country's most dramatic vacation refuge, is a 10-mile-long stretch of splendid desolation on the Pacific coast, 100 miles north of San Francisco. Its 5200-acre site was shorn of redwood, fir, and pine forests during the 1880s and 1890s. All the loggers left behind was windswept, grassy meadowland, interrupted by an occasional logging cabin, barn, or shed. Later, Monterey cypress hedgerows were planted to act as wind breaks.[29]

The site was acquired for $2 million by Oceanic Properties, a real estate subsidiary of Castle & Cooke of Hawaii, in order to develop it as a low-density, second-home community named Sea Ranch. In 1964, it hired the landscape-architecture firm of Lawrence Halprin and Associates to prepare a master plan and the architecture firms of Joseph Esherick & Associates and Moore, Lyndon, Turnbull, & Whitaker to prepare architectural prototypes with which to begin development.

Halprin applied ecological principles to capitalize on the area's awesome, natural beauty. The idea was to design:

a place where wild nature and human habitation could interact in a kind of intense symbiosis.... We derived lessons

Sea Ranch, 1991. Wooden houses nestled into the meadows on the cliffs overlooking the Pacific. *(Alexander Garvin)*

from analyzing the wind erosion of cypress trees and studied how they were shaped into specific slopes and pitches. We realized that they were models for establishing roof slopes in buildings, which could extend their protection from the wind. We also looked carefully at drainage patterns and studied ways by which natural drainage could be channeled to maximize run-off in a non-destructive way.[30]

Soil, climate, wind, and days of sunlight were analyzed to determine which areas were appropriate for single-family houses, condominium structures, active community use, roads, and supplemental cypress windbreaks. As a result, half of Sea Ranch has been set aside as undeveloped meadows and woods that are in common ownership, deeded to a landowners' association, which is responsible for its maintenance. One-quarter is private land belonging to individual home owners. The remaining quarter is "restricted" private land that belongs to the adjoining lot owner, but cannot be built on or planted with nonindigenous vegetation.

Sea Ranch is bisected by California Highway 1. Houses in the meadows west of the highway are clustered around cul-de-sacs that tend to be perpendicular to the coast. The land in between has been left in a natural state and is overgrown with grasses and wild flowers. There are neither roads connecting the cul-de-sacs, nor sidewalks. The only concession to human activity is a trail that runs along the edge of the cliff, offering residents spectacular views of the surf and an occasional glimpse of passing whales and sea lions. The land east of the highway slopes upwards, quickly turning into forested hillsides. Here, houses are hidden in the trees or clustered into groups of condominium units.

Architectural design was subjected to the same rigorous ecological analysis that had been applied to the land. Wind studies revealed the need to shelter houses from the northwest

Sea Ranch, 1991. Houses in an open landscape owned in common by its residents. *(Alexander Garvin)*

wind. Consequently, most houses must be oriented toward the south, with gardens and parking on the leeward side. They also must have slanting roofs to direct the wind up and over adjacent open areas. All exterior finishes must be natural. Reflective surfaces and bright colors are not permitted. These requirements are embodied in a series of printed restrictions intended to generate buildings similar in size, scale, color, and material. To be absolutely sure that these restrictions have the intended effect, all construction plans must be approved by a three-person design committee.

The initial buildings by Esherick and by Moore, Lyndon, Turnbull, & Whitaker established a common architectural idiom inspired by the simple country barns and leftover logging structures that were already in place: shed roofs without overhangs for the wind to flutter, rough vertical redwood siding, and large windows placed low enough to profit from the splendid views. Virtually all of their buildings have been felicitous additions to the landscape. Later structures designed by others generally followed their example but "as the years have passed...principles have been altered by succeeding people—owners, builders, and designers...whose motivations...are less pioneering."[31]

Despite the disappointment with more conventional, later development patterns, the only real threat to Halprin's design came from government. In 1972, voters approved a referendum that established a California Coastal Zone administered by six regional commissions (see Chapter 16). Amazingly, the North Central Commission discarded Halprin's ecologically based plan because it felt the scheme did not provide the public with adequate views of or access to the ocean. The commission imposed a moratorium on further construction until Oceanic Properties, acting on their own behalf and that of the property owners in the Sea Ranch Association, agreed to establish public parking areas and public accessways to the beach, to cut down many of the Bishop pines that blocked motorists' views, and to monitor septic tank operation. The commission also demanded that the number of building lots be reduced from 5200 (an average of one house per acre) to 2329.

Most property owners objected to this form of extortion. The association tried to negotiate. Oceanic tried to litigate. Every step they took was futile. Finally, in 1980 the California State Legislature enacted compromise legislation (the Bane Bill) that exempted all of Sea Ranch from the Coastal Commission's permit process and paid $500,000 to settle all litigation and to obtain five public accessways to the beach. Development quickly resumed. By 1992, there were houses on half the building lots.

Every structure erected at Sea Ranch reduces by one more little bit the splendid desolation of its landscape. As a consequence, in a very real sense, this is an example of no-win planning. On the other hand, in comparison to what would have happened had Oceanic Properties adopted more conventional real estate practices, Halprin's ecological approach is a triumph. The master plan ensured that thousands of acres of irreplaceable meadows and woods would be set aside for future generations. It helped to make hundreds of houses (but not all) as much a part of the landscape as the hedgerows that were added decades earlier.

Despite the moratorium, Sea Ranch did not turn into a financial disaster, largely because so little had to be invested in infrastructure. Nevertheless, few developers have tried to emulate its planning. Perhaps this is because there are so few sites that are as beautiful. Perhaps it is because higher-density development generates more cash. As a result, Sea Ranch remains an appealing refuge for vacationers and weekenders that is unlikely to be replicated in more populated sections of the country.

Seaside, Florida

Seaside, Florida, the vacation refuge that is becoming a model for the new towns of the future, represents a radical rejection of previous planning theory. It is small: 80 acres, compared with 5200 acres for Sea Ranch or 3600 acres for Beverly Hills. It is proudly urban, compared with the windswept meadows at Sea Ranch or the tree-shaded lanes of Chestnut Hill. It is designed for continuous pedestrian interaction, compared with the broad vehicular boulevards of Beverly Hills or the splendid desolation of Sea Ranch. Although Seaside is so different from these profitable new communities, it has been no less financially successful.

Seaside began when architectural enthusiast Robert Davis inherited 2800 feet of Gulf of Mexico beachfront. The bulk of the site, on the Florida panhandle, between Pensacola and Panama City, was separated from the 30-foot-high dunes and broad white beach by Route 30A, a county road connecting scattered bungalows, motels, and nondescript villages. Rather than sell this undeveloped land for a few thousand dollars per acre, Davis decided to create an exclusive beach resort and sell his land by the square foot at much, much higher prices. It was a brilliant strategy. By 1990, small

Seaside, 1990. The beach. *(Alexander Garvin)*

Seaside, 1994. Aerial photo of the almost completed 80-acre beach resort for 326 houses. *(Courtesy of Alex MacLean, Landslides)*

Seaside, 1990. East Ruskin Street on axis with the pavilions at the entrance to the beach. *(Alexander Garvin)*

house lots (40 feet by 80 feet) that were the farthest from the beach, were already selling at more than $26 per square foot.[32]

In 1980 Davis hired architects Andres Duany and Elizabeth Plater-Zyberk to develop a plan for a vacation refuge that would function simultaneously as a real town. Even though this was the firm's first urban planning project, Duany and Plater-Zyberk embarked on what has become a mission to reintroduce traditional American town-planning practices into the suburban marketplace.

On paper, the Duany and Plater-Zyberk design looks more like the new town plans of the years just before and after World War I than a latter twentieth-century beach resort. Its main elements include the beach, Route 30A, which slices off an imaginary second half of the plan, a demi-octagonal central square that functions as a town center, several broad avenues radiating from the town center, residential streets with vistas that terminate in colorful public structures, picturesque beach pavilions on axis with residential streets perpendicular to Route 30A, and pedestrian paths that bisect the residential blocks and provide secondary access to all the houses.

Because of its street network, block and lot pattern, and the scale, texture, and color of the buildings, Seaside has none of the academic formalism of its geometric plan. The key feature is not the axial vista; plenty of awful streets have axial vistas. It is the reduction of every roadway, sidewalk, and path to a size that is dominated by people, *not cars.*

Seaside was planned as the first new community of a "post-motor age." Rather than standard one-way arteries with several 12-foot-wide automobile lanes mandated by every traffic engineering textbook, Duany and Plater-Zyberk designed two-way, 20-foot-wide pink brick streets. Rather than concrete sidewalks, driveways, garages, and sections of street that are carefully marked for parallel parking, they designed narrow shoulders of crushed shell that are comfortable for pedestrians and just large enough to accommodate cars.

Seaside also eliminates repetitive block and lot patterns. Most town grids have standard dimensions that are never followed. As time passes, lots are combined and recombined to fit the dimensional requirements of different buildings, built at different times for different purposes. This produces the rich texture we so admire in our oldest city neighborhoods. Duany and Plater-Zyberk achieve this from the very start by varying the widths, depths, and shapes of the building lots and by introducing diagonal streets that break the grid of blocks. This variety of lot location, orientation, size, and price naturally allows variation in household size and income that most new towns only develop decades after initial settlement.

The witty elements in Seaside's buildings are the purely decorative notes that the developer has added to the

Seaside, 1990. The houses are all pastel-colored wood-frame buildings trimmed with white or cream windowframes and porches. *(Alexander Garvin)*

streetscape: pergolas, beach pavilions, and even a water tower, brought from its former location in Norfolk, Virginia. These charming structures, which pretend to have functional attributes, fool nobody. They are there to add a note of delight to what would otherwise be a conventional streetscape.

Duany and Plater-Zyberk's most conventional (but very effective) tool for achieving Seaside's distinctive look is a set of regulations that establish eight building types and a common design vocabulary: wooden siding painted in pastel colors, white or cream-colored wood trim, vertical windows, metal gable or shed roofs (either corrugated, crimped, or standing seam), screened porches and verandas, picket fences, etc. These regulations are presented in a diagrammatic table of performance standards and in more detailed written esthetic and construction codes. To ensure that the results are consistent in character, a town architect (selected by its developer and planners) must review and approve all building plans.

A decade after Duany and Plater-Zyberk began their work, with more than half of Seaside in place, the validity of its planning is clear. The beach with its glorious dunes remains the star attraction. To it, Davis has added the colorful beach pavilions, "Per-spi-cas-ity" (an open air gift and clothing market), a popular upscale bistro, a tiny bookstore, and a sandwich shop. Even without the projected 200-room hotel, the beachfront has the panache of a much larger resort.

The plan is so effective that lot prices have climbed to amazing heights. Most purchasers come from cities in nearby Alabama, Georgia, Louisiana, and Florida. One reason purchasers are so ready to buy is that they do not have to spend every weekend at Seaside. Davis has established a successful marketing program to rent the cottages when their owners are not using them.

The central square is a long way from becoming a "town center." A decade after the project was started, it still only included three small retail establishments (a gourmet grocery, a yogurt shop, a house-garden-gift store) and a doll-sized post office. Nor will it include much more until Seaside attracts enough retail customers from other communities along Route 30A.

Even without enough customers to justify so imposing a town center, Seaside is already more than a holiday refuge. Tourists from nearby hotels and residents from nearby houses and villages do come to Seaside. The town's minimal retail outlets could not survive on just the occupants of a couple of hundred cottages. Furthermore, Seaside has attracted a rental market many times larger than its few homeowners. Thus, it is not just a successful residential development. Seaside is a chosen destination for thousands of people from all over the country because relatively inexpensive air travel has made it so accessible.

Seaside is both beautiful and profitable. Where else can one find a more charming (or nostalgic) amalgam of Cape Cod and antebellum Charleston? How many other resorts without a hotel can rent a one-bedroom suite for as much as $800 a night?[33]

Seaside demonstrates planning techniques for a "post-motor age." It has shown that we do not need to design our communities to please traffic engineers. It also has provided a way to prevent the stark uniformity of most planned development by avoiding uniform block and lot sizes. But, to judge its success as a model for the successful planning of new communities, we must know whether it will function as more than a refuge for the owners and renters of its 326 house lots.

Developers and civic leaders around the country are beginning to learn from the Seaside experience. One reason is Seaside's obvious profitability. Another is that its appearance strikes a responsive chord with virtually everybody who has seen it. As a result Duany and Plater-Zyberk have been hired by a growing number of developers and government agencies to design new zoning/building regulations and whole new communities.

It remains to be seen whether they are right in planning for a post-motor age. There can be no doubt, however, that they are right in seeking a happier balance between a community and its automobiles. More important, they have demonstrated an approach to the design of new-towns-in-the-country that promises a more humane living environment.

The Utopian Satellite New Town

Satellite new towns evolve less from the attempt to find refuge from city life than from the attempt to satisfy the demand for an ideal living environment. As early as 1871, the developers of Riverside, Illinois, were promoting it as a place with:

> *splendid improvements, found in no other suburb.... [A place where] wives and children live a more quiet and satisfactory life, and one of far greater and more varied enjoyment than can possibly be attained in any city, and can do it without sacrifice of urban conveniences.*[34]

Unlike many vacation refuge new towns, suburban utopias are intended to be and remain satellites of large cities that provide them with consumers for their land and houses, employment for their residents, and even the services without which they could not exist. Also unlike the vacation refuge new towns, these satellite communities usually do not offer stunning beaches, pine forests, a semitropical climate, or many of the other natural attractions of an alluring resort. Virtually every suburban satellite has chosen to provide its little bit of country by adopting the Olmstedian esthetic: curvilinear, tree-lined roadways and broad lawns with houses set back from the street.

Sometimes, as with Mariemont, Ohio, and Columbia, Maryland, the sites had to be assembled in bits and pieces; sometimes, as with Lakewood and Irvine, California, they already were a single property. Whatever the method of acquisition, the difference between financial success and failure has proved to be the developer's ability to carry the debt service on the investment in land, infrastructure, and facilities until cash flow from sales exceeded that debt service, operating expenses, and the other costs of carrying a huge inventory of unsold building lots.

Similarly, some satellite towns, like Levittown and Lakewood, attracted their customers by providing decent shelter at a price affordable to the vast majority of the population. Others, like Mariemont and Palos Verdes Estates did so by offering amenities not available elsewhere. But, whatever the marketing strategy, sales to customers depended on their obtaining mortgages with affordable debt-service payments.

Satellite new towns may differ in their financing and marketing strategies, but every one was established on open land that initially was far outside city limits and then was engulfed in a rapidly suburbanizing landscape. Some satellite new towns are different from these surrounding suburbs. Mariemont, Reston, and Columbia, for example, can be distinguished by substantial open space and recreation facilities. Palos Verdes Estates can be distinguished by the character of its architecture and the unusually successful integration of the built environment with the topography. Despite the utopian rhetoric, careful planning, and extra amenities, life in most satellite new towns is not very different from surrounding suburbs. Only in a very few cases can one find what Ebenezer Howard dreamed of: town and country "secured in perfect combination."

Shaker Heights, Ohio

The exclusive Cleveland suburb that is today called Shaker Heights, is the creation of two bachelor brothers: Oris and Mantis Van Sweringen. The Van Sweringens entered the real estate business in 1900. After 5 years and a few costly mistakes they bought some land in the eastern suburbs of Cleveland. The quick profits they made on the first 200 acres helped them convince investors to put up the $1 million needed to buy the rest of a 1400-acre property bordering a park.[35]

The land they purchased had been acquired in 1822 for a utopian settlement by the North Union Society of the Millenium Church of United Believers, better known as the Shakers. Their settlement was disbanded in 1889. Three years later the property was sold to a group of Cleveland businesses called the Shaker Heights Land Company, in recognition of the former settlement and the site's elevation, 400 to 600 feet above Lake Erie. Before completing the community's first roads, the company sold the land to a Buffalo syndicate that failed to sell or lease anything until 1905, when the Van Sweringens took it over.

The Van Sweringens understood that they also would be unable to sell much land until the site had ready access to downtown Cleveland. By agreeing to subsidize part of the fare, they persuaded the Cleveland Railway Company to extend its streetcar line 3 more miles to Shaker Heights. When service began in 1907, the Van Sweringens finally began to profit from lot sales. Unfortunately, the streetcar stopped at the western edge of the site. The company refused to extend service any further. As a result, the Van Sweringens went into the transit business. In 1911, they established the Cleveland and Youngstown Railroad Company, which built a profitable four-track railroad running from Cleveland, through Shaker Heights, all the way to Youngstown. The success of this project eventually led them to acquire the Nickel Plate Railroad and, in 1930, to build Terminal Tower, Cleveland's 708-foot-high combination railroad-station, retail-hotel-office center.

While the Van Sweringens were making millions in the railroad business they were also making millions in Shaker Heights real estate. The brothers assembled 4034 acres, hired the Pease Engineering Company to prepare a plan for their new town, and devised deed restrictions and design standards that specified allowable land uses, architectural styles, and construction materials. The community that emerged includes one-family houses, "English-style" apartment buildings, a colonial-style shopping complex (octagonal Shaker Square), and several private country clubs built, like the community's schools, on land donated by the Van Sweringens. There is no industry.

Shaker Heights is divided into separate residential neighborhoods by its Y-shaped system of parks, waterways, and ravines that provide natural drainage and by two major east-west boulevards with rapid transit lines running down the middle. On paper the design is a confused mixture of natural-

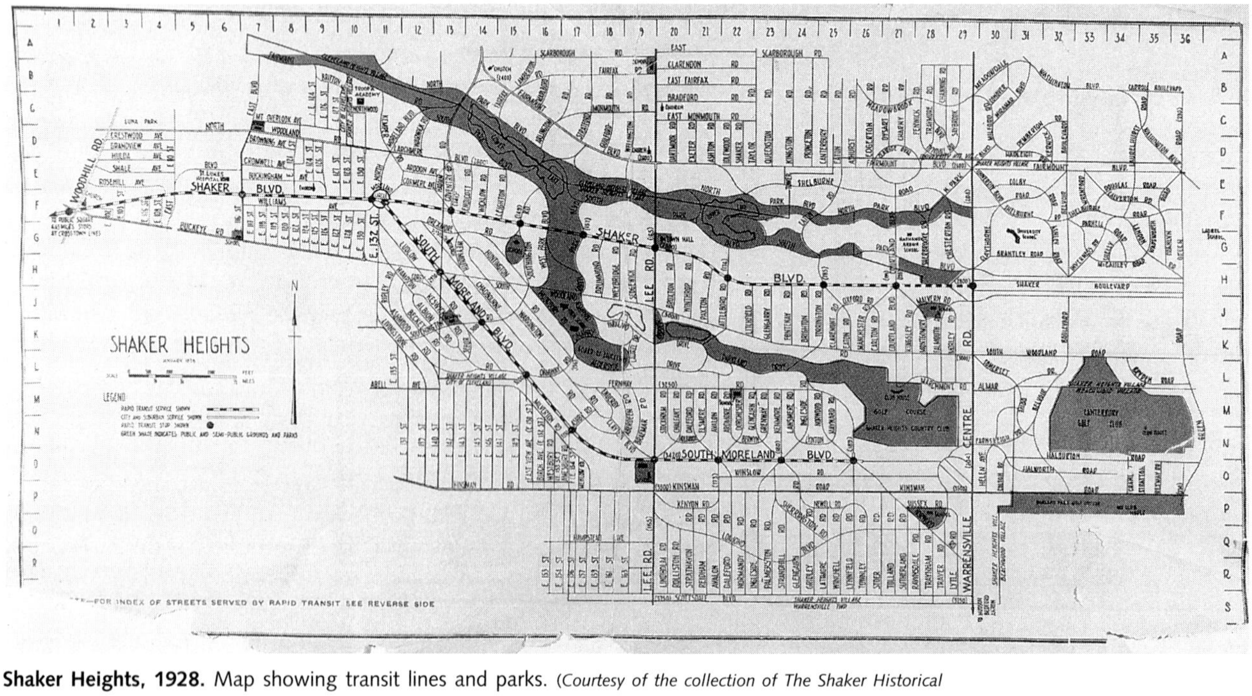

Shaker Heights, 1928. Map showing transit lines and parks. *(Courtesy of the collection of The Shaker Historical Society, Shaker Heights, Ohio)*

istic curves, parallel streets, and elliptical figures. It looks more reasonable when driving through Shaker Heights' rolling landscape because of the skillful adjustments to topographic features, the common district lot sizes, which help to differentiate the various neighborhoods, and the property restrictions, which generate a uniform look.

Many of the property restrictions are tied to lot width: the distance houses must be set back from roadways, the distance they must be set back from neighboring lots, minimum house width and depth, and even porch dimensions. Houses must be two stories high and garages, which the Van Sweringens considered unsightly, must be at the rear of the lot. Only specific periods of English, French, or Colonial architecture are allowed. The "Shaker Village Standards" even specify appropriate color schemes and materials for each of these styles.

The uniformly upper-middle class, WASP character of the Shaker Heights population began to change after World War II when, for the first time, Jews were allowed to purchase homes in the area. In 1955 an African American moved into the Ludlow section of Shaker Heights. At first there was panic and blockbusting. However, within a couple of years white and African-American residents formed the Ludlow Community Association (LCA) to stabilize the neighborhood. The LCA requested homeowners to let it handle sales. It established a second mortgage fund to help purchasers with their downpayment and organized cocktails and dinners for prospective purchasers of all ethnicities and races. Within a few years fewer houses were being sold and prices had begun to increase. By the mid-1960s, Ludlow's population had stabilized at 45 percent white. Since then, several other neighborhoods in Shaker Heights have been integrated, mostly in its southern sections, resulting in a 1980 population that was 74 percent white and 24 percent African American.[36]

Palos Verdes Estates, California

If there is one satellite new town with a truly ideal living environment it is Palos Verdes Estates. Its site is a spectacular peninsula jutting out into the Pacific Ocean. This location provides it with the only consistently pure air in the Los Angeles basin. It also provides easy access to one of the most economically successful and culturally diverse metropolitan areas in the world.

The plan of Palos Verdes Estates, by Frederick Law Olmsted, Jr., and Charles Cheney, amplifies the attractions of the site by fitting curvilinear roads to the steep topography of the peninsula, carefully nestling house lots into its slopes, and providing spectacular views of the Pacific coast. In spite of all these assets, the 26-year attempt to create a new town on the Palos Verdes Peninsula very nearly failed four times before Palos Verdes Estates was incorporated as a city in 1939.[37]

Like Beverly Hills and so many other Southern California communities, the 16,000-acre Palos Verdes peninsula belonged to a succession of ranchos until 1882, when it was acquired by Jotham Bixby, a wealthy California landowner. Bixby planted eucalyptus trees and leased some land to Japanese-American farmers, but did little with its barren hillsides and terraces, finally selling it for $1.5 million in 1913. The purchaser defaulted and the land was resold to a syndicate put together by Frank A. Vanderlip, president of the National City Bank of New York.

Vanderlip, who had never seen the site, believed its strategic location, 23 miles southwest of Los Angeles, guaranteed success. It took but one journey to Palos Verdes for him to decide how to develop its potential. As he later explained:

> *[The] first sight of Palos Verdes Ranch was... one of the most exciting experiences of my life. Before me lay a range of folded hills, miles and miles of tawny slopes patched with green, thrusting themselves abruptly from the Pacific. Above me were broad natural terraces, with here and there a little farm, backed by a range of taller hills. Wherever the road passed over a hillcrest I could see the shore-line of the ranch as a series of bold headlands spaced off by gleaming crescent beaches.... The most exciting part of my vision was that this gorgeous scene was not a piece of Italy at all but was here in America, an unspoiled sheet of paper to be written on with loving care.*[38]

Inspired by the Amalfi coast in Italy, Vanderlip decided to create his own version of a Mediterranean town. Starting in 1914, he hired a series of architects and planners to make proposals. All he built, however, was his own part-time residence.

In 1920, a real estate firm secured an option on the property, which it sold 2 years later to developer E. G. Lewis for $5 million. Lewis wanted to build a $35 million city with a regional harbor and airport and a population of 200,000. The money was to come from individual investor-partners. Although he claimed to have interested 7000 subscribers, Lewis was unable to put the pieces together. In 1923, Vanderlip stepped in for the second time, forming The Commonwealth Trust Company to take over the project. Although Lewis' investors were offered their money back, 4000 of the original backers stayed with the project. The salvaged money allowed the best located and most beautiful 3200 acres to be acquired for what came to be called the Palos Verdes Project. Vanderlip held on to the rest of the property, selling some sections and developing only small parcels, until his death in 1937.

By 1924, 6 miles of storm drains, 14 miles of gas mains, 2 miles of underground conduits, 12 miles of overhead electric lines had been installed, and more than 100,000 trees and shrubs had been planted. This was simultaneously the reason for the project's marketing success and financial problems. Subscribers were delinquent in making promised capital contributions. Land sold more slowly than had been anticipated. Consequently, expenditures on development and marketing exceeded sales revenues and capital contributions. Fortunately, the project only sold land. Had it also built houses for sale, even more capital would have been needed.

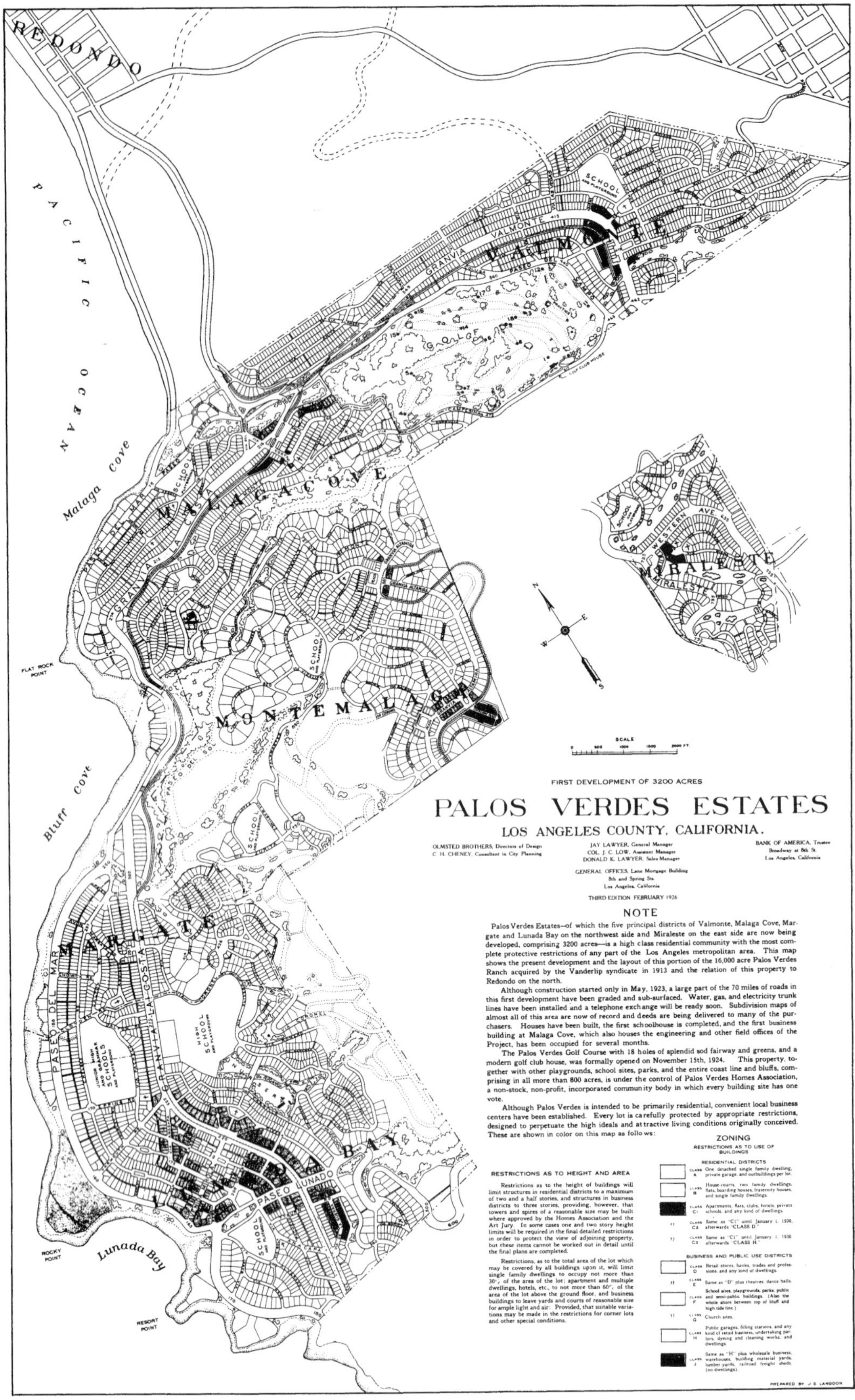

Palos Verdes, 1926. Olmsted and Cheney's plan locates streets along terraces that previously had been eroded by the Pacific Ocean. *(Courtesy of the National Park Service, Frederick Law Olmsted National Historic Site)*

Palos Verdes, 1976. Houses, with a low profile along the street, nestle into the landscape as if they were a natural feature of the topography. *(Alexander Garvin)*

To cover cash-flow requirements, the project issued $1 million in bonds. When the downturn in the real estate market at the end of the decade turned into a general collapse, the project's trustees were unable to meet interest payments and again the new company nearly failed. They precluded foreclosure by reorganizing as a corporation (Palos Verdes Estates, Inc.) and transforming the bonds into stock.

Two years after Vanderlip's death, the new town ran into trouble for yet another time. This time, the residents stepped in to save the project. From the beginning Palos Verdes Estates had been managed by its Homes Association, which maintained the street, park, water, and sewer systems, provided other municipal services, and paid Los Angeles County taxes. County taxes were particularly high because the Homes Association, which was not a government entity, was taxed on all its land, which constituted more than 25 percent of the community and included parks, playgrounds, a golf course, and 4.5 miles of seashore. The money for all these expenses came from an annual assessment collected from each property. Many of the property owners, hard hit by the Great Depression, stopped paying the assessments. By 1938, the Homes Association was $62,500 in debt, more than half of which was in the form of back taxes owed to the county.

The situation was complicated by the position of Palos Verdes Estates, Inc., which still owned more than half the undeveloped lots and was behind in both its Homes Association assessments and its county taxes. The corporation's proposed solution, in lieu of paying back taxes, was to donate large sections of shoreline (owned by both the Homes Association and Palos Verdes Estates, Inc.) to the county for use as public parks. However, residents were opposed to losing control of their most scenic lands to "the gay throngs of picnickers" and the "NOT SO GAY throngs of loafers, of prowlers, of drunkards" expected to come with them.[39] Since the Homes Association made decisions by majority vote of its 5155 lots (a large number of which were still held by Palos Verdes Estates, Inc.), the developer's proposal could very well have been accepted, despite overwhelming homeowner opposition.

When residents realized that the "solution" would still leave them with county tax bills for future years, they adopted a different strategy. First, they obtained passage of state legislation permitting establishment of a park and recreation district to which they could deed park land, and thus avoid further taxes. Then, in 1939, they voted to incorporate as the City of Palos Verdes Estates. Forever after, no matter how many

Palos Verdes, 1988. The view opening onto Santa Monica Bay and the Los Angeles Basin. *(Alexander Garvin)*

vacant lots were owned by developers, decisions affecting the community would only be made by resident voters. In part, as a result of these actions, in part as a result of the improving real estate market, Palos Verdes Estates, Inc. settled its debt to the Homes Association and, in 1940, sold its remaining property at a huge public auction.

Palos Verdes Estates had the benefit of a strategic location and a spectacular site. Its design capitalized on them to create an almost ideal version of the living environment sought by the Los Angeles market, so ideal that by 1982 the Los Angeles County Assessor valued peninsula land at $3.2 billion. Two aspects of Olmsted and Cheney's planning were responsible for creating this highly valued living environment: the street system and the building restrictions.

Palos Verdes Estates was one of the first planned communities in the Los Angeles region that did *not* depend on the Pacific Electric Railroad. In fact, it was one of the nation's first new towns that was (in words that Clarence Stein would later use in describing Radburn) designed for the motor age. The plan included a scenic circumferential roadway that not only affords drivers spectacular views, but also allows through traffic to bypass strictly residential sections. The remaining streets were all designed for easy driving and, where possible, views.[40]

Olmsted's design was entirely based on the capabilities of the site. The peninsula included 13 major terraces that had been formed by wave action and erosion. Instead of spending money to move thousands of tons of earth, he located the major traffic arteries, commercial centers, golf course, schools, and playgrounds in these generally flat areas. Canyons, steep hillsides, and shoreline cliffs were left as parkland. The remaining sloping land was made accessible by secondary roads, thereby producing choice residential sites with spectacular views. These sites allow houses to be set back from the roadway enough to accommodate driveways and garages. More important, the landscape remains dominant because many houses appear to be only one-story high, when they really are multistory structures built into the hillside so that the occupants are able to enjoy the unobstructed panorama below.

Olmsted and Cheney understood that the site plan by itself did not guarantee that Palos Verdes Estates would be built as they envisioned it. They also knew that any consumer had to "be sure when building his home there that his neighbor will have to build an equally attractive type of building."[41]

Their solution was to prepare a set of Protective Restrictions that applied to all construction. Its objectives were to preserve the views, increase the natural beauty of the landscape, and create the ideal living environment demanded by the consumer. The Protective Restrictions were enforced by a seven-member Art Jury initially appointed by the developer. It had to approve any plans for property subdivision, building construction, artwork, fences, sidewalks, and awnings.[42]

The Protective Restrictions, in a manner similar to a zoning ordinance, specified land use, height limits, setbacks, and yard requirements. Three "types" of architecture were established and mapped for specific sections of town. Type I had to have plaster or stucco walls and roofs with slopes no greater than 35 degrees that were covered with reddish-colored tiles. This meant building in the California-Mediterranean style popular at that time (see Chapter 17). Type II allowed roofs as steep as 45 degrees and greater latitude in color and appearance. Type III permitted roofs as steep as 60 degrees and darker colors and materials. Whatever the type of architecture, materials and colors had to be used "honestly, actually expressing what they are, and not imitating other materials."[43] In practice, most buildings approved by the Art Jury, even the gas station, were in a California-Mediterranean idiom.

The Protective Restrictions also included the statement that "there are the usual restrictions prohibiting negroes, Asiatics, and people of other than white or Caucasian race, except in the capacity of domestic servants."[44] Time and Supreme Court decisions have made this the only part of the Restrictions to be discarded. By 1980, 6 percent of the 14,376 people living in Palos Verdes Estates were non-Caucasian.

Frank Vanderlip's dream of building an American version of the Amalfi coast along the Palos Verdes peninsula is now reality. The stucco and red-tiled houses, which seem to grow naturally from the peninsula's terraced hillsides, give one impression of the same centuries-old partnership between man and nature that is typical of the Italian coastline. The nonresidential sections of Palos Verdes have a similarly Mediterranean look. Malaga Cove Plaza, the community's major business center completed in 1925, includes the arcades of an Italian piazza. It even has a copy of Bologna's Neptune Fountain in the middle of its parking field. Palos Verdes' fantasy Mediterranean appearance has certainly helped it to exploit its lucrative market and spectacular location. But its success was even more dependent on a patient developer with pockets deep enough to cover debt service on the money spent for land acquisition, planning, and development (i.e., streets, sewers, water mains, lighting, schools, libraries, landscaping, etc.) during the periods of slow sales.

Mariemont, Ohio

At the time Frederick Law Olmsted, Jr., was conceiving Palos Verdes, John Nolen, one of his former students at Harvard's School of Landscape Architecture, was designing a very different new town: Mariemont, Ohio. In 1903, at the age of 34, Nolen entered Harvard to begin a career as landscape architect and urban planner. He went on to complete more than 400 projects, including plans for 50 new towns.[45]

Mariemont, 1988. Affordable residences that would not be out of place in one of Ebenezer Howard's "garden cities." *(Alexander Garvin)*

Nolen was hired by Mrs. Mary Emory, a wealthy Cincinnati widow, to design Mariemont, a new town 10 miles east of the city. Mrs. Emory had become convinced that a model town for working people would "furnish better housing" and

> *illustrate intelligent and sane town planning, by following a preconceived plan along scientific lines, including proper road building, harmonious house construction and the relation of homes to industrial areas and public service facilities.*[46]

She decided to demonstrate the validity of building a model community and in so doing also establish a fitting memorial to her late husband.[47]

Between 1910 and 1920 Mrs. Emory acquired 18 farms along the Pennsylvania Railroad in an elevated area overlooking the Little Miami River. The Wooster Pike, which provided easy automobile access to downtown Cincinnati, ran right through the site. It was a perfect spot to demonstrate that good planning "could be duplicated wherever initiative, capital, and social planning could be combined to support building of new towns and suburbs."[48]

Nolen and Emory were influenced by Ebenezer Howard and the Garden Cities Movement. As a result, Mariemont was intended to be fundamentally different from such profit-motivated real estate ventures as Shaker Heights and Palos Verdes Estates. It was conceived as a small, self-contained community, very much like Letchworth, with a source of employment right in town. The plan allocated 250 of the site's 485 acres for the town: 62 acres along the railroad for industry, 32 acres for a retirement center, 59 acres for parkland, and 82 acres for playgrounds. Land and buildings were intended to remain in the hands of its philanthropic developer until the town was completed, so that its residents, like the leasehold residents of Letchworth, could enjoy its benefits without being priced out by land speculators.

Despite its aspirations, Mariemont is not very different in appearance from other residential suburbs built during the 1920s. Like so many such communities, Mariemont has a Tudor-style central square containing shops and public facilities. As at Riverside, Shaker Heights, Palos Verdes, and most other new towns planned before World War II, deed restrictions cover the type and use of structures, the cost of dwellings, setback and yard requirements, architectural approval, and racial occupancy. Its only distinguishing characteristics are the land set aside for industry, the unusually generous recreation facilities, and buried utility lines.

Mariemont's tree-lined streets are dominated by the multilane Wooster Pike, which runs right through the middle of town. It handles regional traffic and acts as the town's main thoroughfare. Local streets are laid out to fit a geometric Beaux Arts design. The resulting residential blocks enclose large, central, open areas that can be used for delivering goods, storing vehicles, or recreation. The excessive size of these open areas unnecessarily increased the amount of land allocated to each dwelling unit and the lineal distance of infrastructure installation.

When Mariemont's first buildings were ready for occupancy in 1923, all necessary utilities (including enough conduits to supply three-quarters of the building sites with steam from a central plant) were already installed. Initial infrastructure and land development expenses were too great to be recouped from revenues generated by the community's residential buildings. Before Mariemont reached one-fifth of its planned occupancy, development had to be curtailed. One-family houses were sold as private residences. Multiple dwellings were sold as conventional real estate investments. To nobody's surprise, the community that was planned for wage earners eventually gentrified.

In-town manufacturing employment proved to be as illusory as continuing community ownership of the land. As Nolen and so many other city planners have discovered, designating land uses and employment patterns is futile without market demand. That demand was never forthcoming. As a result, Mariemont's industrial land has never been occupied.

Mariemont is a noble experiment. Its tree-lined streets are not disfigured by unsightly utility lines. It provides wonderful recreation facilities. However, unlike Radburn or Sea Ranch, its design did not reduce initial infrastructure requirements. No effort was made to time its cash expenditures on infrastructure, community facilities, and landscaping with revenues from houses and stores. Thus, it does not present the argument for the superiority of planned new towns over conventional developer-built suburbs that Mary Emory and John Nolen intended.

Levittown, Long Island, and Lakewood, California

Despite the experience of Mariemont, many new towns, especially those built right after World War II, have been quite effective in providing working people with decent affordable homes. Working people constitute the largest single market in the United States. When Congress established FHA mortgage insurance and VA-guaranteed mortgages, it opened that huge market to developers (see Chapter 8). All that was necessary was a standard product that met FHA and VA requirements and a method of supplying a steady stream of those products at prices that working people could afford. Abraham, William, and Alfred Levitt were among the first builders to demonstrate how a planned new town could achieve these objectives.[49]

Levitt & Sons was established during the Great Depression. Abraham Levitt, a Brooklyn attorney, foreclosed some mortgages on Long Island property. His son, Alfred, who had formal training in architecture, designed a house for the site. His other son, William, sold it at a profit. Over the next 4 years Levitt & Sons, the company they established, built and sold another 600 houses, mostly at prices below $20,000. The company went on to create Strathmore-at-Manhasset, a 500-unit subdivision on the north shore of Long Island. Work ceased during World War II, but resumed shortly afterward with 1000 conventional, two-story plus basement and garage, five-and-a-half-room houses, selling for around $10,000. Their ambition, however, was to make a fortune selling inexpensive, mass-produced houses.[50]

They began by assembling Long Island potato fields (at $3600 an acre) into what eventually became the site of a 4700-acre new town. There, beginning in 1947, Levitt and Sons built standardized, single-story, 750-square-foot houses on 60- by 100-foot lots. The first houses were "Cape Coddages," which were identical in plan but came in five exterior variations. Inside were: a living room, two bedrooms, a bathroom, an unfinished attic, a fully equipped kitchen, and (as a marketing extra) a Bendix washing machine.

To bring sales prices down to $7990, houses were built on concrete slabs into which pipes for radiant heating were embedded. Levitt used standard, prefabricated components installed in 26 standard operations by 80 subcontractors, who paid union scale but used nonunion labor (see Chapter 9). As *Time* described:

> *Every 100 feet the trucks stopped and dumped identical bundles of lumber, pipes, bricks, shingles, and copper tubing—all as neatly packed as loaves from a bakery. Near the bundles, giant machines with an endless chain of buckets ate into the earth, taking just thirteen minutes to dig a narrow four-foot trench around a 25-by-32-foot rectangle. Then came more trucks loaded with cement and laid a four-inch foundation for a house in the rectangle. After the machines came the men. On nearby slabs already dry, they worked in crews of two and three, laying bricks, raising studs, nailing lath, painting, sheathing, shingling. Each crew did its special job, then hurried on to the next site. Under the skilled combination of men & machines, new houses rose faster than Jack ever built them; a new one was finished every 15 minutes.*[51]

Levittown, L. I., 1991. "Cape Coddages" that originally sold for $7990. *(Alexander Garvin)*

Like automobile manufacturers, Levitt & Sons made model changes every year. For 1950 it was ranch-style houses with built-in television sets. When Levittown was finished in 1951, 17,442 houses had been built.

Unlike most new towns, Levittown did not start with a completed plan. It was designed in stages that were determined by the pace of land acquisition. Nevertheless, the plan adhered to the usual Olmstedian esthetic: tree-lined, curvilinear streets with houses set back from the roadway. Perhaps because the site was not assembled when development began, Levitt and Sons built scattered neighborhood centers that included convenience retailing, a gas station, a swimming pool, a children's playground, and a community recreation building with bowling alleys and a restaurant. The firm also donated land for a variety of small neighborhood parks, two high schools, two intermediate schools, six elementary schools, six Protestant, two Catholic, and two Jewish congregations.

The stores in these centers were laid out in a shallow strip bounded on either side by streets that had been widened to allow for curbside, angle parking. At first they flourished. As Long Island's population soared, shopping malls and retail outlets were built along nearby Hempstead Turnpike. These competitors attracted customers from Levittown. Many of Levittown's retailers were unable to survive without this resident market. The vacant stores they left behind are a continuing problem for each of Levittown's community centers.

Like the Levittowns that were built later in Pennsylvania and New Jersey, Levittown, Long Island, is no longer starkly uniform in appearance or narrowly homogeneous in population. The trees have matured and the landscaping now varies from lot to lot. So do the houses, which after more than 40

Levittown, L. I., 1991. Olmsted's formula of tree-lined, curving streets, open front lawns, and houses set back from the street minimized the monotony of standardized, mass-produced "Cape Coddages." Successive improvements and remodeling give each of the houses its own personality. *(Alexander Garvin)*

Lakewood, 1990. Despite successive alterations, the flat aspect, skimpy landscaping, and rectilinear block and lot pattern continue to emphasize the uniformity in building design. *(Alexander Garvin)*

years have been remodeled, expanded, resurfaced, and repainted many times. They now sell at more than 20 times their original purchase prices. Many first-time home purchasers have retired and moved away and the predominantly lower-middle-class, white families with young children have been replaced by a community of 65,000 residents with a broader range of age, income, and race.

A year after Levitt & Sons began its first planned new town, the Lakewood Park Corporation initiated a similar venture on a 3500-acre site, 23 miles south of downtown Los Angeles. The corporation had been formed by three prominent southern-California real estate developers: Ben Weingart, Louis Boyer, and Mark Taper. Like the Levitts, they had decided that a planned new town could reduce development costs enough to offer returning veterans a dream house for no money down plus $50 a month.[52]

The site had been part of the Rancho Los Cerritos until 1866, when it was sold to a consortium including the Bixby family. They farmed portions and used the rest as grazing land for vast herds of sheep until 1897, when they sold it for $500,000 to a Montana company that used it as farmland. In 1949, it sold the property to the Lakewood Park Corporation for $8.8 million.

Developing this new town was easy. The Lakewood Park Corporation simply extended the Los Angeles north-south/east-west street grid across its level farmland. This elementary site plan was largely the work of Louis Boyer and architect Paul Duncan. It deviated from the grid by providing "landscaped parkway panels" to insulate the purely residential streets from regional traffic on wider boulevards. Several blocks were set aside for neighborhood schools and their playing fields. A 255-acre site at the center of the grid became the Lakewood Shopping Center, which for a few years after its completion in 1951 was the world's largest shopping center.

Like Levitt & Sons, the Lakewood Park Corporation standardized its product (there were only seven model homes), organized construction along assembly-line procedures, supplied marketing extras (stall showers and electric garbage-disposal units), and provided sidewalks, trees, lawns, and shrubbery. The Prudential Life Insurance Company provided the financing for both the residential and (once the May Company had agreed to sign a long-term lease for a department store) commercial development. The houses, which ranged in price from $7500 to $9000, were so popular that in 1951 *Time* reported that "on what was once an old sugar beet field...30,000 people stampeded one day last week to purchase houses in Lakewood Park."[53] By the time the project was completed, more than 17,000 houses had been built.

By 1990 Lakewood included 9½ square miles and 75,000 residents. Eighty percent of its 27,000 dwelling units are single-family homes that, like those in Levittown, have been sold and remodeled numerous times. The centrally located Lakewood Shopping Center, unlike the scattered retail strips in Levittown, has remained a busy and profitable enterprise because it is designed to serve the town's 75,000 residents *plus* customers from surrounding areas.

When the first houses in Levittown were offered for sale, critics howled that its ticky-tacky little boxes would spawn a generation of bored, alienated conformists and in very short order become the "slum of the future." Had they known about Lakewood, their howl would have been even louder and even less well founded. The residents of both Levittown and Lakewood eagerly grabbed the "best buy for the money" and went about their lives.

Both Levittown and Lakewood were initially largely populated by first-time, working-class home buyers. As time passed they became communities with a range of age profiles, household sizes, income levels, and ethnic and racial groups. They have begun to exhibit the variety and patina that only comes with age. Nevertheless, Levittown and Lakewood are difficult to distinguish from the suburban fabric of either neighboring Nassau and Suffolk Counties on Long Island or Los Angeles and Orange Counties in California. Their importance does not lie in similarity to conventional suburbs or differences from more ambitious utopian communities. It lies in their demonstration that mass-produced new communities can provide working people with affordable homes in a living environment that has the amenities that they desire.[54]

Reston, Virginia, and Columbia, Maryland

The new towns of the 1960s and 1970s were conceived in reaction to the criticism of Levittown, Lakewood, and their ilk. Rather than rows of cheap ticky-tacky, planners proposed a variety of house sizes and styles; rather than mass-produced dwelling units built by the same developer, they proposed to let different sites be built by different developers; rather than simple plats that could be built cheaply and quickly, they proposed elaborate plans that included a wide variety of open spaces, retail stores, employment centers, and community facilities. The more ambitious their proposals, the less likely that the proposed new town would be financially successful.

Of all the planned communities started during those years, Columbia, Maryland, and Reston, Virginia, seemed the

Reston, 1976. Radburn-inspired underpasses protect pedestrians using the system of open-space sinews. *(Alexander Garvin)*

Reston, 1976. An artificial lake that provides recreation facilities unknown in neighboring suburban subdivisions. *(Alexander Garvin)*

most promising. Both were located within one of the nation's fastest growing metropolitan areas, Washington, D.C. Both were initiated by enlightened developers eager to demonstrate an alternative to suburban sprawl. Both had financing from large corporations more interested in long-term appreciation of value than short-term profits. Nevertheless, both experienced financial difficulties.

Reston is named for its developer Robert E. Simon (R.E.S.ton). Simon bought 7400 acres, 23 miles northwest of downtown Washington in 1961, for $13 million. The site was a well-drained, pleasantly rolling, tree-covered landscape with a lake at the southern end of the property. It was strategically located in a portion of Fairfax County that lay astride the highway linking Washington with Dulles airport and was expected to become one of the region's major growth corridors. Building a planned new town on this site was an attractive enough investment for Simon to obtain $20 million from the Hancock Insurance Company and $27 million from the Gulf Oil Company.[55]

Simon hired A. D. Little & Company to prepare a development strategy and architects Whittlesey & Conklin to give it three-dimensional shape. The new town they devised was intended as a "serious experiment in city planning...to discover what should be done to create a quality environment."[56]

They projected a population of 75,000 living in 22,000 dwelling units of the widest variety: detached houses, townhouses, lake houses, hilltop houses, and apartment houses. The design included seven residential villages, each with accessory shopping, schools, and recreation facilities, two town centers, and a 1300-acre industrial park that was intended "to provide employment opportunities for a large portion of Reston residents."[57]

People who live in company towns often work in the same community. In Reston and most other towns, people live and work in different places. Consequently, its industrial areas do not provide employment for many Reston residents. Most of their employees come from outside Reston.

The villages are separated from one another by a system of open-space "sinews" that preserved the natural forest and ground cover as much as possible. The sinews, like Radburn's open-space system, were designed to provide pedestrians with uninterrupted access to village shopping centers, schools, and the full range of neighborhood facilities. As at Radburn, there were underpasses separating pedestrian and vehicular traffic. However, the open-space sinews were quite different in conception. The idea was to create "something of the busy life and character of a fine city street, with all of its visual and social interest, without its problems of automobile traffic."[58]

The open-space sinews make lovely bicycle paths and jogging trails that also connect Reston's villages into a single new town. But they never could provide the "busy life and character of a fine city street." Reston is built at densities that are far too low for active street life.

At the core of each village there was to be a 15-acre "center" that included housing, churches, community buildings, and restaurants, not just convenience shopping. Thus, as at Levittown, each village center was really a civic space providing a social focus for the surrounding population.

Unlike Levitt, Simon did not start with model houses from which he made sales that covered development expenses as they were incurred. His marketing strategy was to start with an 18-hole golf course; an artificial lake large enough for swimming, fishing, sailing, and all manner of water sports; and other facilities unavailable elsewhere in the Washington suburbs. This required installation of storm drainage, sewer, water supply, and road systems from the beginning. More important, it required massive amounts of cash, up front.

Residential sales always take time. At Reston they were slowed because there was no ramp connecting it to the area's only limited-access highway, which at that time ran uninterrupted from the District of Columbia to Dulles Airport. Even if everything had sold quickly, it still would have been difficult to recoup development costs from initial property sales. Simon ran out of money in 1977 and had to surrender control to his major financial partner, Gulf Oil.

Cash-flow requirements led Gulf to terminate its role as Reston's major residential builder and to increase land sales to conventional home builders. It retained much of the original planning, but abandoned Simon's commitment to architectural quality.

Columbia, 1976. Condominiums that are similar to those built in neighboring suburban subdivisions. *(Alexander Garvin)*

Columbia, 1968. Symphony Woods, part of the 20 percent of the site set aside for parks, recreation, and open space. *(Alexander Garvin)*

In 1990, when 19,000 households lived in Reston, the Mobil Land Corporation, which had acquired Gulf-Reston, began construction of a 460-acre "town center" that includes office buildings, retail space, restaurants, an 11-screen multiplex movie theater, and more than 1400 condominium and rental apartments. This town center will bring the vitality and variety that Simon hoped would make Reston a "quality environment" as different from homogenized Levittown as it is from small suburban subdivisions.

Columbia, Maryland, evolved from developer James W. Rouse's belief that building a well-planned new town was more profitable than splattering bits and pieces across the landscape. Rouse had the expertise and reputation to borrow the money he needed to prove his contention. The Baltimore-based Rouse Company, which he headed, was a successful real estate business largely devoted to shopping centers. It had financed $750 million of development and operated projects with more than $100 million in annual revenues. This record of real estate success persuaded the Connecticut General Life Insurance Company to invest $23.5 million and the Chase Manhattan Bank and the Teachers Insurance & Annuity Association of America to provide another $25 million. Debt-service payments on this money were deferred for 10 years, during which the project's limited initial cash flow was expected to help offset development and operating costs.[59]

Land acquisition began in 1962. Rouse purchased 165 farms and land parcels in 140 separate transactions. He was able to buy these 15,600 acres for the low price of $1500 per acre because he used dummy purchasers to keep the project secret. Next he persuaded officials in Howard County, Maryland, to approve the necessary rezoning and tax-exempt bonding authority and to extend the necessary roads and public utilities to the edge of the site.

The plan for Columbia was developed by Rouse and a group of professionals working under the direction of William Finley (the vice president in charge of the project) and Morton Hoppenfeld (its planning and design director). From the beginning, they worked with national experts in government, family life, health, education, psychology, sociology, housing, transportation, and recreation. These experts played a role that was similar to the one played by the Regional Planning Association of America in designing Radburn (see Chapter 13). They met twice a month over a period of 6 months, and later on an ad hoc basis, to evaluate alternative approaches to planning and development. The scheme that emerged was based on existing land features (i.e., drainage patterns, land slopes, tree masses, historic and other valued sites, vistas, etc.), water, sewer, and transportation requirements, and a retail shopping hierarchy that reflected the Rouse Company's experience in shopping-center development. The Columbia they envisioned was to have a population of 110,000 living in 30,000 residences distributed among nine villages and a town center.

Housing clusters, built by developers who did not need Rouse financing, were the plan's most elemental building block. These housing clusters were aggregated into groups of 700 to 1200 residences that could support a "neighborhood center" with a day-care center, an elementary school, a convenience store, a multipurpose meeting room, a swimming pool, and playgrounds. Four or five of these neighborhoods (about 3500 residences) would, in turn, support a "village center" that included an intermediate school, a library, and a worship center that could be shared by different religious groups, a supermarket, a drugstore, a laundry, a barber and beauty shop, a restaurant, and a few other stores.

These nine villages (about 30,000 residences) were planned to provide a sufficient market for a "town center." It had the benefit of office workers from regional branches of both Teachers and Connecticut General Life Insurance Companies. Consequently, Columbia's town center includes a 70-acre, air-conditioned shopping mall, plus office buildings and entertainment facilities.

There is a similar hierarchy for transportation: cul-de-sacs, pedestrian and bicycle paths, neighborhood streets, collector streets, and finally the widened and landscaped Columbia Pike (US 29) bisects the town. This hierarchy is also reflected in Columbia's political make-up. Residents belong to a village association that in turn provides one member of the city-wide Columbia Association.

Columbia's open-space system covers more than 20 percent of the site. It offers the widest variety of recreation options, including large areas of heavily wooded terrain and 500 acres devoted to lakes. Each "neighborhood" and "village" is visibly defined by surrounding open space. Thus, as in so many new-towns-in-the-country, the landscaping transforms scattered housing and retail centers into a distinctive new town. Approximately 1800 acres were set aside for industrial parks that attracted large employers to Columbia. As at Reston, they are romantic relics of the garden cities movement. Most Columbia residents work in other communities.

Like Reston, Columbia ran into financial difficulties. In 1973 the land sales, which had averaged $24 million per year during 1971 and 1972, suddenly dropped to $6.5 million. The decline in sales could not have come at a worse moment because the Rouse Company no longer had the benefit of 10-year, interest-free financing. The Connecticut General Life Insurance Company had no alternative but to refinance $129 million, delaying debt-service payments to 1978. By the time it sold out to the Rouse Company in 1986, Connecticut General had written off $50 million in losses.

The planning practices used at Reston and Columbia established a pattern for new town development that persists to this day: a central-place hierarchy (particularly with regard to retailing), defined business/industrial park areas, and a continuous open-space system providing a wide variety of recreation opportunities. This pattern satisfies the requirements of home builders as well as retail, office, and industrial developers. Most important, it satisfies the pervasive market demand for combining an active town life with the beauty and delight of the countryside.

Irvine, California

The largest and financially most successful new town in America is Irvine, California.[60] Its 83,000 acres occupy 17 percent of Orange County and could accommodate 26 Palos Verdes Estates, 52 Riversides, or 1038 Seasides. The project was so successful that in 1977, 17 years after development of the new town began, the Irvine Company was sold for $337 million, and then in 1983 resold for $518 million.[61]

Unlike Riverside, Palos Verdes Estates, or Seaside, Irvine is neither a serious experiment in city planning, nor a model that can be copied by other new town developers. It is too big. Moreover, the site, which was purchased by James Irvine in 1867, remained in the hands of the same family until it was sold 110 years later. Even when development began, not one cent had to be advanced to cover purchase of the property or debt service on its acquisition.

Irvine is located 40 miles southwest of Los Angeles. It stretches from the Pacific coast, just inland of Newport Beach, for 22 miles to the Santa Ana Mountains. James Irvine, Jr., inherited the property from his father in 1886. Eight years later he formed the Irvine Company, which transformed it into a sprawling, combination cattle-ranch and citrus operation. To prevent the breakup of his property after his death, James, Jr., willed 54.5 percent of the Irvine Company to a foundation controlled by handpicked life trustees. Thus, his heirs, who owned the rest, had the benefit of a luxurious income but could not sell any property.

During the 1950s, Orange County began to experience the development pressures that would soon make it one of the fastest-growing and wealthiest parts of the country. As a result, the Irvine Company faced continually increasing real estate taxes. Rather than sell property piecemeal to pay taxes, the trustees decided to go into the development business.

Architect William I. Peireira prepared Irvine's first master plan in 1960. With so much property to plan for, Peireira had the luxury of conceiving a real city, which he projected would reach its target population of 430,000 in the year 2020. It included the 1000-acre Irvine campus of the University of California plus another 560 acres for student, faculty, and staff housing. It also accommodated the San Diego Freeway, the Santa Ana Freeway, the Orange County Airport, and the U.S. Marine Corps Air Base, all of which were completely independent of the Irvine Company. Major employment centers were located at the eastern, western, and southern edges of the site. Scattered in between these huge land uses were Irvine's residential areas and the retail, recreation, and community facilities that serve them.[62]

By themselves, Irvine's industrial/business parks occupy more land than all but one of the new towns discussed in this chapter. Unlike industrial areas in these communities, those at Irvine were not romantically conceived to provide resident employment. They were intended to be self-sufficient facilities and quickly provided more jobs than there were town residents.

The 6300-acre Irvine Business Complex on the western edge is a light-industry, high-technology, and research complex. By 1987, it contained 4000 firms (one-quarter of which

Irvine, 1991. One of nonpolluting businesses attracted to the park-like setting of this carefully planned community. *(Alexander Garvin)*

Irvine, 1991. The third largest concentration of office space in California. *(Alexander Garvin)*

Irvine, 1991. Houses designed in a heavy-handed Hispanic style and painted in a Pepto-Bismol pink color indistinguishable from that of developer-built houses erected elsewhere in Orange County during the late 1980s. *(Alexander Garvin)*

were corporate headquarters) occupying 20 million square feet and employing 100,000 people. The 2200-acre Irvine Spectrum on the eastern edge is a similar facility that in 1987 contained more than 160 companies with 12,000 employees. When it is completed in the twenty-first century it is expected to provide employment for 100,000.

Newport Center, developed on Irvine land, is technically in the City of Newport Beach. By 1987, this 622-acre business center included eight office towers, a three-building medical center, three hotels, a design center, numerous low-rise buildings, and the Fashion Island shopping center (with 5 department stores, 200 retail shops, and the Irvine Ranch Farmers Market).

In 1971, to protect Irvine from annexation and additional taxes, the central portion of the site was incorporated. The resulting City of Irvine has a sphere of influence (including all areas of possible future incorporation) of 53,000 acres. Its 1985 population of 84,900, living in 28,500 residences, had a median household income of $48,900.

As at Reston or Columbia, residents live in "neighborhoods" with their own recreation center, swimming pool, and community facilities. Some have been built by independent developers, but many are Irvine Company projects. These residential areas include "village" retail shopping centers, schools, neighborhood parks, hiking and bicycle trails, and health clubs. In addition there are two lakes, four golf courses, and four major tennis clubs.

Irvine is surely not the utopian community that most new town proponents have in mind when they argue the superiority of planned new communities over conventional suburban development. It is indistinguishable in physical appearance from the rest of Orange County. With the exception of university students and staff, it is similarly indistinguishable in social composition. It is unique among planned new towns, however, in its ability to satisfy market demand, exploit its location along Southern California's busiest freeways, and benefit from the financial strength of its sponsor. Nor has any other new-town-in-the-country grown more quickly, going from a population of 62,000 in 1980 to 110,000 in 1990.[63]

National Policy Initiatives

Despite thousands of privately developed new towns, various city planners, social critics, and public officials periodically demand that government get into the new town business, often as a way of increasing housing production. They have been able to convince Congress to fund new town development three times, but in each case only in response to some crisis.[64]

The first governmental new town program provided shelter for workers involved with military-related production during World War I. It was promoted to Congress on the basis that war-production efficiency demanded sound housing and a suitable living environment for workers and their families. Since overwhelming amounts of capital were needed for the war effort, the argument went, government had to provide the funds for additional housing. The program ended with the armistice.

Another group of government-subsidized new towns were built in response to the Great Depression. This time Congress was told that the "resettlement of destitute and low-income families from rural and urban areas" required "the establishment, maintenance, and operation...of [planned new] communities in rural and urban areas." This new town program was terminated by the courts.[65]

The last group of government-supported new towns were an outgrowth of the "urban crisis" of the 1960s when angry demonstrations led Congress to seek better ways of providing "community services, job opportunities, and well-balanced neighborhoods in socially, economically, and physically attractive living environments." This time, new town proponents persuaded Congress that planned new towns would help solve virtually every aspect of the "urban crisis." New towns were oversold as devices for reducing "inefficient and wasteful use of land," preventing "destruction of irreplaceable natural and recreational resources," providing "good housing," increasing "unduly limited options for many of our people as to where they may live, and the types of housing and environment in which they may live," increasing "employment and business opportunities," supporting "vital services for all...citizens, particularly the poor and disadvantaged," reducing "separation of people within metropolitan areas by income and by race," and even increasing the "effectiveness of public and private facilities for urban transportation."[66] This effort was ended by the 1973 Nixon moratorium on housing and development programs.

Despite dubious claims for the curative effects of new town development, all three federal programs initiated valuable experiments in urban planning and created some lovely communities. More important, they also provided insights into the ingredients of successful new town development as well as its irrelevance as a device for fixing the American city.

World War I Villages

During 1917 Congress appointed three committees to examine whether full, war production depended on construction of

Camden, 1974. The Yorkship Square at Fairview. *(Alexander Garvin)*

additional housing for workers in war industries. All three had little doubt that it would be impossible for private capital to supply the necessary shelter. In response the Wilson Administration established two housing-production programs, one operated by the Emergency Fleet Corporation (EFC) of the United States Shipping Board and the other by the United States Housing Corporation (USHC) organized by the Department of Labor. Together, these two agencies helped produce 15,183 family dwellings and 14,745 accommodations for single workers.[67]

The Emergency Fleet Corporation was organized in 1917, under the Shipping Act of 1916, to acquire, maintain, and operate merchant vessels. In 1918 its authority was extended to provide housing for shipyard employees and their families. It did so by providing 10-year mortgages to realty companies incorporated by shipbuilding concerns. The mortgages covered 70 to 80 percent of the cost of development and carried an interest rate of 5 percent. However, these loans, totaling $67 million, were expected to be repaid at the end of the war, in an amount reduced by 30 percent to allow for inflated war costs.

The staff and consultants hired to run the program included some of the country's most prominent architects, housing specialists, and urban planners, among them Frederick Law Olmsted, Jr., John Nolen, and Henry Wright. Before it finished its work in 1919, the EFC had been involved with 28 projects that produced 9185 dwelling units in 15 states and 23 cities. As directed by Congress, by 1924 it had disposed of all its loans at a net loss of about $42 million.

The U.S. Housing Corporation shared the same personnel with the EFC and a similar but even more illustrious group of advisors, including Olmsted, Jr., Nolan, Grosvenor Atterbury, and Lawrence Veiller. Despite the Congressional requirement that the housing be temporary in character, they recommended construction of permanent housing in a series of industrial villages. The USHC followed that recommendation. However, instead of making loans to shipbuilding concerns it built these industrial villages itself, spending $52 million for 55 projects, finishing 27 developments in 16 states and the District of Columbia. After the war, the USHC sold off its 5998 family dwellings and 7181 single-worker units for a net loss of $26 million.

Yorkship Village (now known as Fairview) in Camden, New Jersey, is one of the largest and most interesting of these war villages. It was financed by the EFC and developed by the Fairview Realty Company, established by the New York Shipbuilding Company. Fairview was designed by architect Electus D. Litchfield in collaboration with Pliny Rogers. The project covered 225 acres. Only 90 acres were subdivided into lots for 1438 dwelling units (1021 row houses, 300 semi-detached, 56 apartments, and 61 detached houses). There were also a few stores and a theater.[68]

Yorkship Village has none of the grandeur and scale implied by its Beaux Arts design. The plan, which like Letchworth had a central square with avenues radiating from it, also includes a variety of geometrical open spaces and landscaped formal boulevards. These 48 separate squares, parks, parkway islands, and playgrounds are individually small. Together they occupy barely 36 acres. Its two-story buildings are also small.

The 78 World War I villages long ago merged into their urban or suburban surroundings. Today, they are only distinguishable by their relatively small buildings and period architecture. With the exception of Yorkship Village, which is admired by Duany and Plater-Zyberk, none of these war villages has had much impact on new town planning. However, they did allow Frederick Law Olmsted, Jr., John Nolan, Henry Wright, and others to see for themselves what new community planning and development was all about. They also provided a model for the later housing-subsidy formulas of the PWA (see Chapter 9).

The New-Deal New Towns

When the Roosevelt Administration came to office in 1933, one-third of the nation was unemployed and ready to try any prescription for relief. Among the prescriptions with which it experimented was one that promised to achieve a better world by resettling the jobless into planned new communities. The $108 million spent on this experiment produced 99 planned new communities with 10,938 dwelling units.[69]

While these planned new communities sprang from a common attempt at creating a new utopia and usually housed fewer than 100 families, they were established to serve widely different purposes. There were farm colonies, industrial settlements, colonies for stranded workers, subsistence gardens for city workers, cooperative associations, and forest homesteads. Only Greenbelt, Maryland, Greenhills, Ohio, and Greendale, Wisconsin, were genuine, planned new towns (Table 15.1). However, unlike the others that had long ago faded into obscurity, these three new towns continue to serve as object lessons in the use of public open space and community facilities to create superior living environments.

Table 15.1
THE GREENBELT TOWNS

Town	Area, acres	Dwelling units	Cost
Greenbelt, Maryland	3,600	890	$13,701,817
Greendale, Wisconsin	3,510	640	$10,638,466
Greenhills, Ohio	5,930	737	$11,860,628
Total	13,040	2,267	$36,200,901

The Greenbelt towns were the brainchild of Dr. Rexford Guy Tugwell, a member of the Columbia University economics faculty, who became a Roosevelt advisor during the presidential campaign of 1932 and Undersecretary of Agriculture in 1933. Tugwell believed that a national program established to build intelligently located and planned new towns would guarantee the efficient use of land and resources while simultaneously providing jobs, housing, and a healthy living environment for the unemployed. When Congress enacted the Emergency Relief Appropriations Act of 1935, he thought he had the necessary legislative sanction for such a program and convinced Roosevelt to sign an executive order establishing it within a newly created Resettlement Administration in the Department of Agriculture. Naturally, he was appointed its director.

Tugwell and his staff began by studying the demographic and economic trends of more than 100 cities to determine promising locations for the new towns. They selected 25 for further study. Roosevelt approved $68 million for eight new towns. The Resettlement Administration eventually settled on five, two of which were later dropped from the program.

The new towns that Tugwell envisioned were to be "demonstrations of the combined advantages of country and city life for low-income rural and industrial families."[70] He sought the best professional advice on how to create such towns, settling on Clarence Stein to provide general guidelines for the architects and planners that the Resettlement Administration hired to design them. Stein made sure that the planning reflected the principles established by Ebenezer Howard for his garden cities, by Clarence Perry for his neighborhood unit, and by Stein himself for Radburn.

The siting criteria that Stein established were intended to minimize capital expenditures and operating costs. In that way there would be enough money left over to also maximize infrastructure and community facilities. More important, as Stein explained, while the Resettlement Administration could cover initial capital costs, their "projects were to be unified, self-supporting communities in which a tenant's monthly charges must cover *all* costs."[71]

The necessary cost savings were achieved by avoiding prevalent through-streets lined with buildings and attached garages. Instead, they relied on cul-de-sacs, clustered parking, and residences that were near public open space. Stein also established criteria for house design that ensured maximum furnishability at minimum cost. This resulted in relatively compact residential plans, straightforward construction, and a common vocabulary of simple materials: brick, concrete block, stud walls, and standard double-hung windows.

Eighteen months into Tugwell's effort to pioneer a new pattern of rural-urban industrial life, the program was brought to a halt by the United States Court of Appeals in the District of Columbia. It declared Greenbrook, the fourth and largest of the Greenbelt projects, which was to have been built between New Brunswick and Princeton, New Jersey, to be unconstitutional. Dean Acheson, counsel for the surrounding township, had argued that Greenbrook would radically alter its character, unreasonably increase local expenditures without supplying a corresponding increase in its tax base, depress existing property values, and leave existing residents in danger of losing home rule. The court not only accepted these arguments, it also found the Emergency Relief Appropriations Act to be invalid. The Roosevelt Administration decided not to appeal the decision to the Supreme Court. Nevertheless, it proceeded with the three projects already under way.[72]

Greenbelt, Maryland, is 13 miles northeast of Washington, D.C., far enough away at the time to represent a serious commute. In an attempt to provide nearby employment opportunities, it was built in conjunction with the 8659-acre Department of Agriculture National Research Center. As is usually the case with employment areas designated to supply jobs for new towns, this proved to be an appealing illusion.

Greenbelt, 1990. The Radburn-inspired underpass. *(Alexander Garvin)*

Greendale, 1986. The Radburn-inspired cul-de-sac. *(Alexander Garvin)*

The employees of the Research Center commute from all over the metropolitan region, not just from Greenbelt, which is a dormitory suburb for people who work throughout the Baltimore–Washington area.

Of the 3600 acres acquired for Greenbelt, only 217 acres were used for the town; 500 acres were reserved for future expansion; 250 for parks, and the bulk of the rest for the greenbelt. As a result Greenbelt is the beneficiary of extraordinarily generous amounts of open space. Its plan consists of two parallel, crescent-shaped main roads that wrap around residential superblocks and a town center with retail stores, a school, and recreation facilities. This crescent is divided every 1000 feet into 14-acre superblocks by a series of cross streets that connect the main roads. As at Radburn, the superblocks are bounded by attached residences or garden apartment buildings and served by an internal system of pedestrian walkways. However, the similarity to Radburn is illusory. Greenbelt's open space is undefined by the surrounding residences, shabbily landscaped, and in many cases has been fenced off by its residents. The walkways are neither continuous nor provide true separation from vehicular traffic. Except in two instances where they connect to underpasses that lead to the town center, the walkways all end at the street.

Greendale, which only provided a 10-acre site for light industry, made no pretense of providing resident employment. Since it is only 7 miles southwest of Milwaukee, it is also a shorter commute. Nevertheless, Greendale, like Greenbelt, reflects the romanticism of the garden cities movement. Approximately 1830 of its 3510 acres were set aside for 13 full-time dairy farms and 53 subsistence farms, most of which have either been subsumed into the surrounding greenbelt or subdivided as suburban residences. Only 170 acres were used for its residences. As at Radburn, there are cul-de-sacs with houses turned around onto pedestrian walkways that connect to a landscaped open-space system with a creek running through it.

Greenhills also made no pretense of providing industrial employment and, being 11 miles north of Cincinnati, its 5930-acre site was even more agricultural. In fact, a great deal of the land had to be leased back to its farmers. Only 1300 acres were used for the town. The bulk of the remaining land was dedicated as public open space. As a result, Greenhills is the only one of the three new towns completely enclosed by a permanent greenbelt.

While Greenhills does have cul-de-sacs, most of the houses (primarily small, red-brick Cape Cod cottages and attached four-family residences) line its curvilinear streets. The differ-

Green Hills, 1988. Community residents can choose among a wide array of recreation facilities.
(Alexander Garvin)

Green Hills, 1988. Affordable houses in a generously landscaped setting. *(Alexander Garvin)*

ence from most suburbs is that they also back onto large, landscaped open spaces. At the heart of Greenhills are its shopping center, school, olympic-size swimming pool and recreation center, public buildings, newspaper, credit union, savings and loan, and golf course.

Better than any other of Tugwell's projects, Greenhills captures the essence of what he had in mind when he wrote:

> *I really would like to conserve all those things which I grew up to respect or love and not see them destroyed. I grew up in an American small town and I've never forgotten it. No one was very rich there, but no one was very poor either.*[73]

If any child now living in Greenhills grows up to administer another governmental new town program, he or she will have no trouble repeating these very same sentences.

Tugwell's experiment in public planning, construction, ownership, and administration of new communities was terminated in 1949 when Congress enacted Public Law 65. It required the negotiated sale of the Greenbelt towns, preferably to nonprofit organizations, cooperatives, or veterans groups. Greendale was sold to its tenants and its greenbelt largely eliminated by the Milwaukee Community Development Corporation, which had purchased it for additional housing development. Nevertheless, over 1000 acres remained in use as park and recreation facilities. Greenbelt's houses plus 708 acres suitable for development were sold to a veterans' group. Its apartment houses and shopping center were sold to separate investors. The greenbelt was transferred to the Department of the Interior. After a few years the veterans' group ran into financial trouble and sold several large undeveloped parcels to commercial developers who built the usual mediocre tract homes. The town of Greenhills plus 600 acres of vacant land were sold to a nonprofit, cooperative homeowners corporation. Some of the surrounding land went to the Cincinnati Park Service and to the Army, and the rest to a development corporation that created the more expensive subdivision of Forest Park.

The Title IV and Title VII New Towns

During the late 1960s and early 1970s, when government went into the new town business for the third time, it did so pursuant to legislation specifically designed for the purpose. The program, which evolved from Title IV of the Housing and Urban Development Act of 1968 and Title VII of the Housing and Urban Development Act of 1970, had none of the previous sense of urgency, experimental fervor, or utopian romance.[74] Everybody concerned understood and was prepared to provide for:

> *(1) the large initial capital investment required to finance sound new communities, (2) the extended period before initial returns on this type of investment can be expected, (3) the irregular pattern of cash returns characteristic of such investment.*[75]

As a result, this new town program was tailored to the requirements of the nation's financial markets. It provided federal

TABLE 15.2
TITLE IV- AND TITLE VII-ASSISTED NEW COMMUNITIES

Community	State	Developer	Type	Acres	Result
Cedar-Riverside	Minnesota	Private	In-town	100	Partial
Flower Mound	Texas	Private	Separate	6,156	Aborted
Gananda	New York	Private	Separate	5,847	Aborted
Harbison	South Carolina	Private	Separate	1,734	Revised
Jonathan	Minnesota	Private	Separate	4,884	Revised
Maumelle	Arkansas	Private	Separate	5,319	Revised
Newfields	Ohio	Private	Separate	4,032	Aborted
Park Forest South	Illinois	Private	Separate	8,136	Revised
Radisson	New York	Public	Separate	2,800	Aborted
Riverton	New York	Private	Separate	2,125	Aborted
Roosevelt Island	New York	Public	In-town	147	Under way
St. Charles	Maryland	Private	Separate	6,980	Profitable
Shenandoah	Georgia	Private	Separate	7,250	Aborted
Soul City	North Carolina	Private	Separate	5,287	Aborted
The Woodlands	Texas	Private	Separate	16,939	Profitable

guarantees of up to $50 million on bonds, notes, or other obligations issued by developers of approved new communities and 15-year, interest-free loans up to a maximum of $20 million.[76]

Government officials assumed that new town development would also utilize funding from the Urban Mass Transportation Act, Land and Water Conservation Fund Act, the Higher Education Facilities Act, and other government programs. As in the Model Cities Program, supplementary cash grants were made to state and local agencies. The grants could cover the local share of other government programs, provided they did not exceed 20 percent of project cost and the total federal share did not exceed 80 percent.

Congress wanted the new towns to reflect both national and community standards. Developers had to secure all required state and local reviews and approvals, meet areawide planning requirements, provide a substantial amount of low- and moderate-income housing, comply with all applicable civil rights laws, and adopt an affirmative-action program for equal opportunity in employment, housing, and business enterprise.

Fifteen projects were approved prior to Nixon's unilateral 1973 termination of every federal housing and renewal program. These approved projects were allegedly selected based on their compliance with HUD's performance standards that required "a financial plan or program demonstrating that the project is and will be financially sound."[77]

Despite the rhetoric, political criteria appear to have played a greater role in project selection. Soul City was to be built in a completely undeveloped part of North Carolina, by an African-American-owned company organized by civil rights leader Floyd McKissick. Roosevelt Island was approved by HUD while Nelson Rockefeller was governor. It provided supplemental funding for The New York State Urban Development Corporation. Along with Cedar Riverside, Roosevelt Island provided HUD with a chance to fund inner-city development, rather than just suburban sites (see Chapter 14).

Every project but The Woodlands and Roosevelt Island defaulted on its HUD-guaranteed obligations and only The Woodlands and St. Charles have proceeded largely according to plan (Table 15.2). Most projects had unrealistic cash-flow projections. Some were located beyond the range of serious market demand or ran into opposition from local interest groups.

The Woodlands is a project of the Mitchell Energy and Development Corporation, a *Fortune* 500 company with assets in excess of $2 billion. Its 16,939-acre site is 28 miles north of Houston. In the 1970s when development began, Houston was one of the most rapidly urbanizing sections of the country. The Woodlands was readily accessible to this large and expanding market. Property began to be assembled in 1964 by George P. Mitchell, after his firm purchased a lumber company that owned 50,000 acres of timberland in four counties north of Houston. To this, Mitchell added several large sites,

The Woodlands, 1995. Residences with access to one of the lakes so prevalent in planned new communities. *(Alexander Garvin)*

but avoided 12 holdouts in order to reduce the land cost to the relatively low price of $1688 an acre.[78]

Mitchell needed experienced consultants to deal with this essentially flat, poorly drained site with low-quality vegetation. He selected architect William Pereira, the designer of Irvine, and landscape architect Ian McHarg. The plan they arrived at, like that of Columbia and Reston, preserved the most attractive woodlands. It minimized hydrological disruption by using a natural drainage system of flood plains, small ponds, 39 lakes, and numerous ditches. As a result 3909 acres (23 percent) of the site is public open space.

The target population for The Woodlands is 150,000 people in 47,375 dwelling units (15 percent, low- and moderate-income). The residences, like those of Columbia and Reston, are grouped into 19 neighborhoods, 6 villages, and a metropolitan center that are all in turn defined and connected by the open-space system. The plan also calls for 2000 acres in industrial parks, a 335-acre commercial, conference, and leisure center; a university; trade, research and medical centers; community facilities; and public services.

Despite setbacks caused by business cycles and changing local market conditions, The Woodlands proceeded without significant difficulties. By 1980 it included 170 businesses employing 3000, 12 churches, 6 public schools, and 8800 residents in 2951 dwelling units. In 1983, HUD released the Mitchell Energy Company (which had made timely payments on its $50 million in HUD-guaranteed obligations) from its role as a Title VII new town sponsor. Development has continued throughout the decade, although somewhat retarded by the impact of the energy crisis. By 1990, more than $2 billion had been spent developing The Woodlands, whose population had passed 30,000.[79]

Ingredients of Success

Riverside, Mariemont, Reston, and every other new town that has run into financial difficulties has suffered because the initial investment in land, infrastructure, and community facilities could not be recouped from sales. Their developers and designers understood that completion would take years, but failed to adjust their planning so that the pace of development could match cash flow. Chestnut Hill, Levittown, Seaside, and the other planned communities that avoided financial difficulties, did so because development and financing could respond to periodic changes in demand.

The roles played by location, design, and entrepreneurship are equally important. Shaker Heights may have been in the path of Cleveland's expanding suburban market, but until the Van Sweringens bought a railroad and extended transit service to their property, it was not easily accessible to that market. Railroad service may have made Riverside accessible, but without Olmsted's design, this prairie location would have been far less alluring. Seaside may have had a wonderful beachfront site and a unique design, but without Robert Davis' skillful marketing, rental rates could never have justified the extremely high prices he charged for development sites.

Market

New towns succeed when people and businesses want to move there. They cannot be attracted just by designating land areas for residential, industrial, commercial, or agricultural uses. The planners who assigned land uses to specific sites at Mariemont or the Greenbelt towns confused their desires with reality.

Land uses inevitably reflect demand. Lakewood's shopping center was built because the May Company had identified a large market area without a major department store. Reston's long-promised town center became a reality when there were enough customers in the Virginia suburbs of Washington, D.C. Similarly, Seaside's town center will only be completed when there are enough tourists or residents within easy access along Route 30A.

Market income is as important as market size. Levittown would not have been successful if its customers had not been able to afford its low FHA mortgage rates. The real trick, however, is attracting customers to an affordable planned community. Burton Green built a hotel to introduce people to Beverly Hills. The Levitts attracted customers by providing appliances and landscaping not offered by the competition. Emery Childs used Olmsted's design to distinguish Riverside from other suburban communities then being built on the prairie outside Chicago. Each of them found a way to present their new town in a manner that distinguished it from its competition.

Location

Palos Verdes Estates and Sea Ranch have the benefit of stunning oceanfront locations. Other planned communities with less attractive locations have to compensate for this disadvantage. Olmsted described the site of Riverside as "low, flat, miry, and forelorn." His curvilinear, tree-lined roadways with houses set back on open lawns completely altered the site. The Woodlands avoids merging into suburban Houston by retaining critical portions of its forested landscape. At Reston, Columbia, and other recent new communities, artificial lakes perform a similar role.

Proximity is even more important than site characteristics. Lake Forest, Riverside, and Chestnut Hill were entirely dependent on the railroad; Mariemont, Palos Verdes, and Irvine on automobile access. Reston almost failed because customers were unable to use the highway to Dulles Airport. Seaside is unimaginable without the airplane.

Design

The lots, blocks, and streets of Riverside are large in order to create what Olmsted described as a feeling of seclusion that is "not far removed from the life of the community." These ample dimensions allowed Childs to market Olmsted's "sense of enlarged freedom." Similarly, the lots, blocks, and streets of Seaside are small because Duany and Plater-Zyberk were intent on restoring the dominance of residents over their cars. These small dimensions make Seaside so distinctive that Davis can sell land at prices that greatly exceed those of nearby locations along the Gulf of Mexico.

Tugwell wanted to put "houses and land and people together in such a way that...our economic and social structure will be permanently strengthened."[80] In most suburbs, churches and synagogues perform a part of that function, as do nearby ball fields, jogging trails, and swimming pools. Mariemont, Greenhills, Reston, Columbia, Irvine, and most other planned communities allocate large amounts of territory for open space and recreation that mixes "houses and land and people" in just the way Tugwell intended.

Shopping is another activity that can bring people together. Corner stores depend on high-density living patterns that are difficult to achieve in most new towns. Thus, the arrangement of retail outlets plays a critical part in determining the character of life in planned communities. At Lakewood, where a large amount of retail activity is relegated to major arterials, what social interaction there is takes place in its vast shopping mall. At Columbia and Reston, interaction is repackaged in the form of easily accessible neighborhood and village retail centers that include libraries, day-care centers, and other community facilities.

Landscaping can change the character of any planned community. As Olmsted predicted, roadside trees and houses set back on open lawns soften a Spartan design, even one as dull as Levittown. Leaving thousands of acres of meadowland untouched allows Sea Ranch to retain a feeling of splendid desolation. People drive 3 hours just to enjoy this landscape.

People who live in Palos Verdes Estates cherish the Hispano-Mediterranean buildings that emerged from its design regulations. They also benefit from the way its buildings fit into the landscape. Many houses are built on lots that are on the downside of a slope. From the street they appear to be modest, one-story structures. Many are really multistory houses that open out to the view below. Building regulations and lot patterns produce similarly distinctive but very different buildings at Sea Ranch and Seaside. Those who prefer natural materials, shed roofs, and large expanses of glass opening onto dramatic vistas will choose houses at Sea Ranch. Those who prefer front porches, painted clapboard siding, and small cozy rooms build second homes in Seaside.

Financing

The developers of Irvine and Seaside had the benefit of inherited land. They are exceptions. Most new town sites are purchased at considerable expense. Consequently, they begin with a commitment to pay a return on any equity investment and

Seagrove Beach, 1990. Bungalows across the property line from Seaside, Florida. *(Alexander Garvin)*

debt service on any borrowing. As more and more money is spent for planning, infrastructure, community facilities, and marketing, that commitment increases. This financing requirement forces new town developers to devise ways of reducing debt service, especially during the early years when development expenses are high.

Connecticut General and Teachers Life Insurance, the institutions that financed initial development at Columbia, allowed the Rouse Company 10 years of accrued debt service because they correctly assumed that during the initial years of development there would be little or no cash flow from sales. Nonetheless, neither they nor the Rouse Company expected a serious downturn in the economy to further delay payments on their loans. They should have.

The developers of Lakewood avoided extensive debt service commitments by preselling model homes and using this money on a pay-as-you-go basis. They were able to avoid large outlays because they used a simple lot and block pattern that could be extended or witheld in response to market demand. The complex designs for Reston and other more recent planned communities preclude this form of minimalist financing.

Residents also face financing problems. They need long-term mortgages with which to finance home purchases. The Levitts solved their problem by preprocessing FHA and VA mortgages on their standardized houses. But, like thousands of other developers, they had to accept FHA site-planning recommendations. Homebuilders in Irvine use a similar procedure when they market model homes. But, because the Irvine Company sells land with approved subdivision plans to different homebuilders, there is a greater variety of house designs and price levels.

Entrepreneurship

New town developers, more than most real estate entrepreneurs, must have real vision. Burton Green believed Beverly Hills could replace hundreds of acres of lima beans. Frank Vanderlip imagined his own version of the Amalfi coast built on the grasslands, farms, and cliffs of the Palos Verdes peninsula. Robert Davis envisioned an upscale community of architecturally distinguished, second homes on 80 nondescript

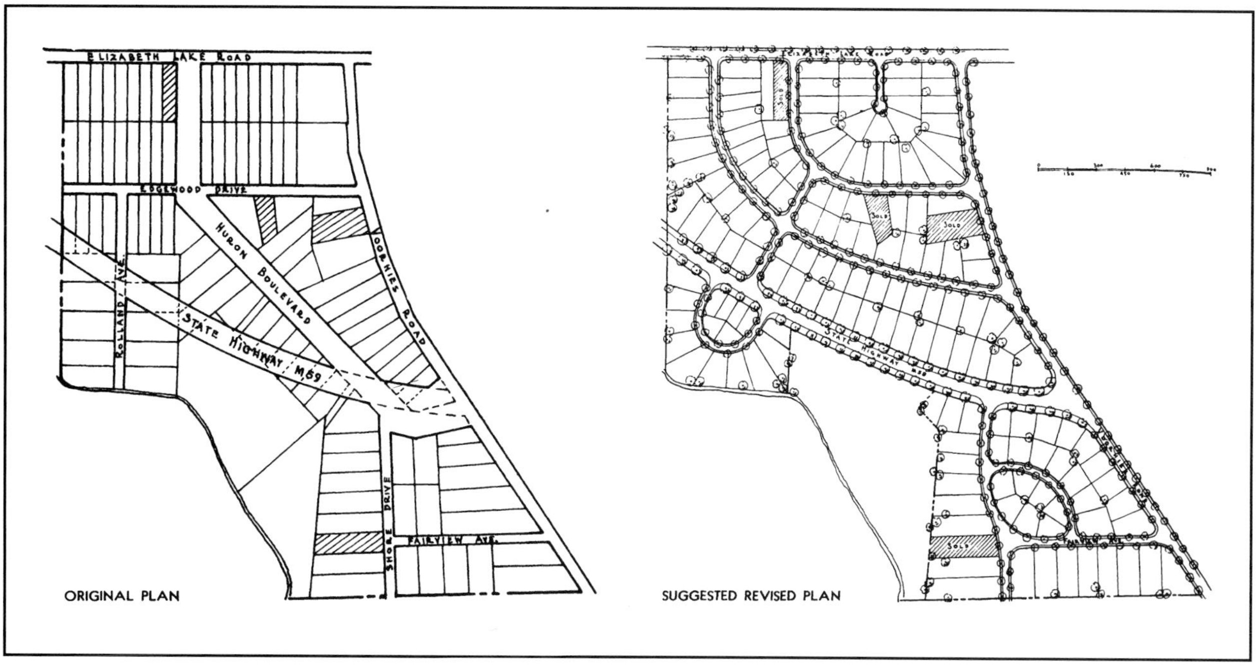

FHA, 1938. Diagram of the undesirable "original plan" and the preferred curvilinear street-pattern recommended for subdivisions receiving FHA mortgage insurance. By providing mortgages to developments that followed the government's preferred plan, institutional lenders changed the face of America's residential suburbs. *(From Federal Housing Administration, Planning Profitable Neighborhoods, Washington, D.C., 1938)*

acres along the Gulf of Mexico. Each of these men perceived a market opportunity that others had missed. Their sites would have been developed anyway, but they would have been indistinguishable from surrounding communities.

These men were willing to risk their capital. Green built a hotel when others thought he was throwing good money after bad. Every time Palos Verdes ran into financial trouble, Vanderlip put up the cash to save his vision. Davis was ready to risk his land on a venture that had never been tried before.

Coordination also pays a more important role than in other forms of real estate development. This is particularly evident in the assembly-line production techniques used by the Levitts. But it was no less important a century earlier when Childs had to coordinate the financing, design, and marketing of Riverside. Over a period of 3 years he oversaw the construction of 40 miles of carriage road, 80 miles of pedestrian walkway, a 735-foot-deep artesian well, 108-foot-high water tower, as well as the planting of 32,000 deciduous trees, 7000 evergreens, and 47,000 shrubs.

Time

The time spent passing through or finding one's destination in a planned new community can be critical to its success. Nobody driving along the major state roads that pass through Palos Verdes Estates, Sea Ranch, or Seaside can fail to notice that they are distinctive. In each case, that drive is part of its marketing strategy. Taking the roads through Chestnut Hill or Mariemont, on the other hand, gives little indication of anything special.

Suburban subdivisions rarely provide for their residents' needs and activities 24 hours a day, 7 days a week. New towns are supposed to. Whether they do or not depends on their size and density. Irvine is large enough to include an airport, three industrial/business parks, more office space than any city in California except Los Angeles and San Francisco, concert halls, theaters, shopping malls, hospitals, etc. The 80 acres of Seaside will never include anything like that, even when all 326 house lots have been filled in. Similarly, there are enough customers around Rodeo Drive in Beverly Hills to support a range of retail stores that is the envy of much of the world. Yet, even after three decades, Sea Ranch does not have a supermarket and is unlikely ever to support more than convenience retailing. Thus, Seaside and Sea Ranch cannot provide their residents with the range of living experiences one expects in completely successful new communities.

New towns usually take decades to complete. Lakewood and Levittown are among the few exceptions. Even in these cases, it has taken them decades to develop the patina of a complete community. The most serious time problem, however, is presented by the changes in market conditions that accompany business cycles. Palos Verdes Estates survived only because Frank Vanderlip had deep pockets and provided the patient capital to see the project through. Riverside, Reston, and Columbia nearly failed because they could not time the pace of cash outflows to changes in pace of sales.

The New Town as a City Planning Strategy

Writing nearly a century ago, Ebenezer Howard insisted that well-planned new towns would demonstrate how to better provide:

> *opportunities of social intercourse...beauties of nature...higher wages...reduced rents...abundant opportunities for employment...admirable sanitary conditions...beautiful homes and gardens...and co-operation...by a happy people.*[81]

Howard and other new town advocates have oversold their product. Planned new communities, even those that make creative use of the six ingredients of success, do not guarantee a better physical environment, or a social utopia, or even a more economical daily life.

The Woodlands, Sea Ranch, and many other planned new towns do preserve valuable open-space resources that would otherwise have been lost. But preplanning public open space in new towns is not the only way to provide communities with good recreation facilities. Many cities still purchase land for public parks. Minneapolis and Boulder have park systems that rival those of any planned new towns. Other communities enact land use regulations that require private developers to provide common open space.

Many new towns have buried utilities and efficient infrastructure layouts. But, as with public open space, there are alternatives. Utilities can be installed by the municipality prior to urbanization. Furthermore, subdivision regulations can be just as effective in controlling utility installation by individual home builders.

Similarly, new towns are not the only communities that make efficient use of public transportation. New York City in the 1920s and 1930s and Atlanta in the 1970s and 1980s built subways in areas that had not yet fully developed. In both cities this resulted in more effective land use patterns around the newly opened subway stations.[82]

As the Title VII new towns so graphically illustrate, carefully planned new communities may be more costly than opportunistic development of scattered sites.[83] Ironically, new town proponents were so aware that huge amounts of up-front, patient capital would be necessary that they used this as a justification for enacting the Urban Growth and New Communities Development Act of 1970.

Greenhills, Reston, and many other planned communities are visibly superior to their competition. Riverside, Palos Verdes Estates, Sea Ranch, and Seaside are oases of rare beauty in a desert of mediocrity. However, planning a large piece of land as an entire new-town-in-the-country may not produce better results than dividing it into smaller sites that are planned and built by different designers and developers.

It is understandable that architects, planners, social critics, developers, and government officials all want to create their own version of utopia and sell it to a ready public as the best alternative to our urban/suburban mess. In 1935, when Tugwell began building the New Deal new towns, he thought he had found that alternative. As he explained, "My idea is to go just outside centers of population, pick up cheap land, build a whole community and entice people into it. Then go back into the cities and tear down slums and make parks of them."[84]

Building such miniature utopias has nothing to do with fixing cities. People like Jane Jacobs even contend that new towns siphon resources and talent away from cities. She therefore concludes that they are a recipe for "undermining their economies and killing them."[85] Our great cities may be in trouble, but the nation's many new-towns-in-the-country are not responsible. For two centuries, while developers were creating planned new communities around New York, Los Angeles, Chicago, Philadelphia, and every other large American city, these cities have remained very much alive. If we are to fix our cities, we should avoid this debate, let new town developers go about what is a very difficult business, and concentrate on the many devices that will improve our troubled cities.

Notes

1. Dolores Hayden, *Seven American Utopias,* M.I.T. Press, Cambridge, 1976, and Charles Nordhoff, *The Communistic Societies of the United States,* Schocken Books, New York, 1965.
2. Urban Land Institute, *Planned Communities, New Towns, and Resort Communities in the United States and Canada,* ULI, Washington, D.C., 1992.
3. F. J. Osborn, Preface to Ebenezer Howard, *Garden Cities of Tomorrow,* M.I.T. Press, Cambridge, 1965, pp. 9–28.
4. Howard, op. cit., pp. 45–46.
5. Stanley Buder, *Visionaries and Planners—The Garden City Movement and the Modern Community,* Oxford University Press, New York, 1990.
6. Robert Fishman, *Bourgeois Utopias—The Rise and Fall of Suburbia,* Basic Books, New York, 1987, pp. 18–72.
7. Howard, op. cit., p. 48.
8. Riverside Improvement Company, *Riverside in 1871 with Description of Its Improvements Together with Some Engravings of Views and Buildings,* originally printed by D. & C. H. Blakely, Chicago, 1871, and reprinted by the Frederick Law Olmsted Society of Riverside in 1981, p. 6.
9. Historical and statistical information about Lake Forest is derived from Michael H. Ebner, *Creating Chicago's North Shore: A Suburban History,* University of Chicago Press, Chicago, 1988, especially pp. 27–35, 68–77, and 195–209.
10. Hotchkiss' first name and exact identity has yet to be discovered. See Ebner, op. cit., pp. 27–28.
11. Journalist James B. Runnion writing in 1860, quoted by Ebner, op. cit., p. 30.
12. The town was later extended to the west side of the railroad.
13. Calvert Vaux was in Europe during 1868 when Olmsted prepared the plan of Riverside.
14. Historical and statistical information about Riverside is derived from

Olmsted, Vaux and Co., "Preliminary Report upon the Proposed Suburban Village at Riverside, Near Chicago," Sutton, Browne and Company., New York, 1868, reproduced by David Schuyler and Jane Turner Censer (editors) *The Papers of Frederick Law Olmsted,* The Johns Hopkins University Press, Baltimore, 1992, pp. 273–289; Riverside Improvement Company, op. cit., Walter L. Creese, *The Crowning of the American Landscape: Eight Great Spaces and Their Buildings,* Princeton University Press, Princeton, 1985, pp. 221–240; and Ann Durkin Keating, *Building Chicago, Suburban Developers and the Creation of a Divided Metropolis,* Ohio State University Press, Columbus, 1988, pp. 61–63, 73–74, 86–87, 174, and 184.

15. Riverside Improvement Company, op. cit., pp. 17–18.
16. Olmsted, Vaux, and Company, op. cit., p. 286.
17. Howard, op. cit., pp. 54, 67, and 76–79.
18. Ebenezer Howard, "The Relation of the Ideal to the Practical," *The Garden City,* London, February 1905, pp. 15–16.
19. Howard, *Garden Cities of Tomorrow,* p. 51.
20. Ibid., p. 90.
21. Frank Jackson, *Sir Raymond Unwin—Architect, Planner and Visionary,* A. Zwemmer Ltd., London, 1985.
22. C. B. Purdom, *The Building of Satellite Towns,* J. M. Dent & Sons, London, 1949, pp. 110–118.
23. Ray Thomas and Peter Cresswell, *The New Town Idea,* The Open University Press, Milton Keynes, 1973.
24. Historical material on Chestnut Hill is derived from Willard S. Detweiler, *Chestnut Hill: An Architectural History,* Chestnut Hill Historical Society, Philadelphia, 1969, and David R. Contosta, *Suburb in the City: Chestnut Hill Philadelphia 1850–1990,* Ohio State University Press, Columbus, 1992.
25. Philadelphia City Planning Commission, *Northwest Philadelphia District Plan,* Philadelphia, 1966.
26. Historical material on Beverly Hills is derived from Fred E. Basten, *Beverly Hills: Portrait of a Fabled City,* Douglas-West Publishers, Los Angeles, 1975; Karl Stull, editor, *Beverly Hills: An Illustrated History,* Windsor Publications, Los Angeles, 1988; Pierce E. Benedict (editor), *History of Beverly Hills,* Cawston and Meier, Beverly Hills, 1934; and brochures published by the Beverly Hills Chamber of Commerce.
27. Quoted in Basten, op. cit., p. 27.
28. E. Y. Harburg (lyrics) and Jerome Kern (music), "Californ-i-ay," T. B. Harms Company, 1944.
29. Charles Moore, Gerald Allen, and Donlyn Lyndon, *The Place of Houses,* Holt, Rinehart & Winston, New York, 1974, pp. 31–48; "Ecological Architecture: Planning the Organic Environment," *Progressive Architecture,* Reinhold Publishing, Cleveland, May 1966, pp. 121–137; Richard Babcock and Charles Siemon, *The Zoning Game Revisited,* Oelgeschlager, Gunn & Hain, Boston, 1985, pp. 235–254; Donald Canty, "Sea Ranch," *Progressive Architecture,* Reinhold Publishing, Cleveland, May 1993, pp. 86–91; Lawrence Halprin, "Revisiting the Idea," *Progressive Architecture,* Reinhold Publishing, Cleveland, May 1993, pp. 92–93; Donlyn Lyndon, "Lyndon's Assessment," *Progressive Architecture,* Reinhold Publishing, Cleveland, May 1993, pp. 93–95.
30. Lawrence Halprin, op. cit., p. 92.
31. Ibid., p. 93.
32. Historical and statistical information on Seaside is derived from Urban Land Institute, *Seaside,* ULI Project Reference File, vol. 16, no. 16, October–December 1986; Beth Dunlop, "Coming of Age," *Architectural Record,* McGraw-Hill, New York, July 1989, pp. 96–103; Alex Krieger with William Lennertz, *Andres Duany and Elizabeth Plater-Zyberk: Towns and Townmaking Principles,* Harvard Graduate School of Design, Cambridge, 1991; promotional brochures printed by the Seaside Community Development Corporation; and lectures by and correspondence with Andres Duany.
33. The 1990 summer rate for a one-bedroom cottage ranges from $248 to $837 per night.
34. Riverside Improvement Company, op. cit., p. 15.
35. Historical and statistical material on Shaker Heights is derived from Ian S. Haberman, *The Van Sweringens of Cleveland,* The Western Reserve Historical Society, Cleveland, 1979; Rachlis and Marqusee, op. cit., pp. 60–86; Eric Johannesen, *Cleveland Architecture 1876–1976,* The Western Reserve Historical Society, Cleveland, 1979, pp. 57–59, 131–133, and 167–183; and Mark A. Dettlebach, "Shaker: A Suburb That Hit The Heights," unpublished, 1983.
36. Dettlebach, op. cit., pp. 23–28.
37. Historical and statistical information on Palos Verdes Estates is derived from Deland Morgan, *The Palos Verdes Story,* Review Publications Inc., Palos Verdes Estates, 1982; Augusta Fink, *Time and the Terraced Land,* Howell North Books, Berkeley, 1966; Comey and Wehrly, op. cit., pp. 85–89; and John Bacon, "Palos Verdes Estates: A Formative History," unpublished, 1982.
38. Frank A. Vanderlip, *From Farm Boy to Financier,* New York, 1935, quoted in Morgan, op. cit., p. 8.
39. Morgan, op. cit., p. 143.
40. Frederick Law Olmsted, Jr., was not only his firm's partner in charge of Palos Verdes Estates, he was also one of the first people to build himself a house there.
41. Palos Verdes Homes Association, *Protective Restrictions,* Palos Verdes, 1923, p. 1.
42. Among the first members of the Art Jury were Frederick Law Olmsted, Jr., Charles Cheney, and Myron Hunt, a prominent Los Angeles architect.
43. Palos Verdes Homes Association, *Protective Restrictions,* p. 34.
44. Ibid., p. 4.
45. John L. Hancock, "John Nolen," in *American Landscape Architecture,* William H. Tishler (editor), The Preservation Press, Washington, D.C., 1989, p. 70–73 and "John Nolen: The Background of a Pioneer Planner," in *The American Planner: Biographies and Recollections,* Donald A. Krueckeberg (editor), Metheun Inc., New York, 1983, pp. 37–57.
46. *Cincinnati Inquirer,* April 23, 1922.
47. Historical and statistical material on Mariemont is derived from Comey and Wehrly, op. cit., pp. 92–97, and Robert B. Fairbanks, *Making Better Citizens: Housing Reform and Community Development in Cincinnati, 1890–1960,* University of Illinois Press, Urbana, 1988, pp. 49–55.
48. The Mariemont Company, cited by Fairbanks, op. cit., p. 54.
49. Historical and statistical material on Levitt & Sons and its new towns in Long Island, Pennsylvania, and New Jersey is derived from Rachlis and Marqusee, op. cit., pp. 228–256; Herbert Gans, *The Levittowners,* Pantheon Books, Random House, Inc., New York, 1967; and John T. McQuiston, "If you're thinking of living in Levittown," *New York Times,* November 27, 1983.
50. A few years after Abraham Levitt died, William Levitt bought out his brother and went on to build a multimillion-dollar business.
51. *Time,* Time Inc., New York, July 3, 1950, p. 67.
52. Historical and statistical material on Lakewood is derived from Lakewood Living Corporation, *Lakewood Living: 35th Anniversary Edition,* Lakewood, 1989, and *Lakewood Service Guide,* Lakewood, 1989; Creative Network, *Lakewood 35th Anniversary Magazine,* Santa Ana Heights, 1989; and Bensel Smythe, "Lakewood Park, Lakewood Center, 'Twin Miracles' in L.A. Metropolitan Area," *Los Angeles Daily News,* November 7, 1951.
53. *Time,* Time Inc., New York, April 17, 1950, p. 99.
54. Most, but not all, residents of Levittown and Lakewood are contented with their community. What dissatisfaction there is, comes primarily from teenage, elderly, minority, and nonconformist residents. See Gans, op. cit., pp. 153–304.
55. Historical and statistical material on Reston is derived from Simon Enterprises, "Reston Virginia," May 1962, unpublished; James Bailey (editor), *New Towns in America: The Design and Development Process,* John Wiley and Sons, New York, 1973; "A Plea for Planned Communities," *Architectural Record,* McGraw-Hill, New York, December 1973; and Ann Mariano, "Reston's Town Center Soon to Be a Reality," *Washington Post,* June 30, 1990.
56. Robert E. Simon, quoted in Bailey, op. cit., p. 14.
57. Simon Enterprises, op. cit., p. 6–7.
58. Ibid., p. 3.
59. Historical and statistical material on Columbia is derived from Rouse, op. cit.; Morton Hoppenfeld, "A Sketch of the Planning-Building Process from Columbia, Maryland," *Journal of the American*

Institute of Planners, vol. 33, no. 5, November 1967, pp. 398–409; Kathy Sylvester, "Columbia Birthday," Associated Press, July 21, 1977; and Robert M. Andrews, "Developers Battle Economic Downturns, Lack of Interest; Planned Towns Face Hard Road to Success," *Los Angeles Times,* August 31, 1986.

60. Historical and statistical material on Irvine is derived from Martin J. Schiesl, "Designing the Model Community: The Irvine Company and Suburban Development," pp. 55–91, in Rob Kling, Spencer Olin, and Mark Poster (editors), *Postsuburban California,* University of California Press, Berkeley, 1991; Cheryl G. Cummins, *Los Angeles Metropolitan Area... Today 1987,* Urban Land Institute, Washington, D.C., 1987, pp. 306–333; "A Plea for Planned Communities," *Architectural Record,* McGraw-Hill, New York, December 1973, pp. 112–117; G. Christian Hill, "Real-Estate Heiress Fights to Get Control of California Empire," *Wall Street Journal,* New York, March 28, 1977; Paul Goldberger, "Coast "New Town' Has Old Familiar Look," *New York Times,* March 29, 1978; Pamela G. Hollie, "Social Patterns Are Forming As Irvine Ranch Expands," *New York Times,* May 4, 1980; and Gladwin Hill, "Big But Not Bold: Irvine Today," *Planning,* American Planning Association, Chicago, February, 1986.

61. The original deal was contested by Irvine heiress Joan Irvine Smith and resulted in a sale to a group that included Alfred Taubman, Henry Ford II, Donald Bren, and Joan Irvine Smith. In 1983 the rest of the group was bought out by Donald Bren in a sale that was also contested by Joan Irvine Smith. See Hill, op. cit.

62. Irvine also includes the campuses of (Lutheran) Christ College Irvine, (2-year) Irvine Valley College, and Rancho Santiago Community College.

63. U.S. Department of Commerce, Bureau of the Census, *Statistical Abstract of the United States, 1991,* p. 34.

64. The federal government also has built residential communities in conjunction with military installations and nuclear facilities. Among the more famous are Oak Ridge, Tennessee, Hanford, Washington, and Los Alamos, New Mexico.

65. Select Committee of the House Committee on Agriculture, "Hearings on the Farm Security Administration," 78th Congress, First Session, 1943–1944, p. 966.

66. Housing and Urban Development Act of 1970, Title VII—Urban Growth and New Community Development, Sec. 701(b).

67. Historical and statistical material on the World War I villages is derived from William J. O'Toole, "A Prototype of Public Housing Policy: The USHC," *Journal of the American Institute of Planners,* vol. 34, no. 3, May 1968, pp. 140–152, and Robert M. Fisher, "Origins of Federally Aided Public Housing," in J. Paul Mitchell, editor, op. cit., pp. 231–235.

68. Historical and statistical material on Yorkship Village is derived from Comey and Wehrly, op. cit., pp. 64–67 and 134.

69. Historical and statistical material on the Greenbelt towns is derived from Paul K. Conkin, *Tomorrow a New World: The New Deal Community Program,* Cornell University Press, Ithaca, 1959; David Myrha, "Rexford Guy Tugwell: Initiator of America's Greenbelt New Towns, 1935–1936," in Donald A. Krueckeberg (editor), op. cit., pp. 225–249; Clarence Stein, op. cit., pp. 118–187; K. C. Parsons, "Clarence Stein and the Greenbelt Towns," *Journal of the American Planning Association,* Chicago, Spring 1990, vol. 56, no. 2, pp. 161–183; and Lloyd W. Bookout, "Greenbelt, Maryland, A 'New' Town Turns 50," *Urban Land,* Urban Land Institute, Washington, D.C., August 1987, pp. 7–11.

70. U.S. Senate, *Resettlement Administration Program,* Document 213, 74th Congress, Second Session, 1936, p. 7.

71. Stein, op. cit., p. 122.

72. *Franklin Township v. Tugwell,* 85F. 2d 208 (D.C. Cir. 1936).

73. Rexford Tugwell quoted in Myrha, op. cit., p. 245.

74. This legislation is also referred to as the New Communities Act of 1968 and the Urban Growth and New Communities Development Act of 1970.

75. Housing and Community Development Act of 1968, Title IV, Sec. 403.

76. Historical and statistical material on HUD's New Communities Program is derived from *Planning New Towns: National Reports of the U.S. and the U.S.S.R.,* U.S. Department of Housing and Urban Development, Office of International Affairs, Washington, D.C., 1981; James Bailey (editor), op. cit.; and "A Plea for Planned Communities...New Towns in America—with Lessons from Europe," *Architectural Record,* McGraw-Hill, New York, December 1973, pp. 85–144.

77. Samuel C. Jackson, "Toward An Urban Growth Policy," in James Bailey (editor), op. cit., pp. 138–140.

78. Historical and statistical material on the Woodlands is derived from George T. Morgan, Jr., and John O. King, *The Woodlands: New Community Development 1964–1983,* Texas A&M University Press, College Station, 1987.

79. Urban Land Institute, *Development Trends 1991,* Urban Land Institute, Washington, D.C., 1991, p. 42.

80. Rexford Tugwell quoted in Myrha, op. cit., p. 227.

81. Howard, op. cit., pp. 48–49.

82. Edwin H. Spengler, *Land Values in New York in Relation to Transit Facilities,* (first published in 1930), AMS Press, New York, 1968, and Leon S. Eplan in "Transit and Development in Atlanta," pp. 129–144 in *New Urban Rail Transit: How Can Its Development and Growth-Shaping Potential Be Realized?,* Subcommittee on the City of the Committee on Banking, Finance, and Urban Affairs, House of Representatives, 96th Congress, First Session, U.S. Government Printing Office, Washington, D.C., 1980.

83. Richard Peiser, "Does It Pay to Plan Suburban Growth," *Journal of the American Planning Association,* Autumn 1984, American Planning Association, Chicago, pp. 419–433.

84. Rexford Tugwell (Diary, March 3, 1935), quoted in Myrha, op. cit., p. 236.

85. Jane Jacobs, *The Death and Life of Great American Cities,* p. 21.

16

Land Use Regulation

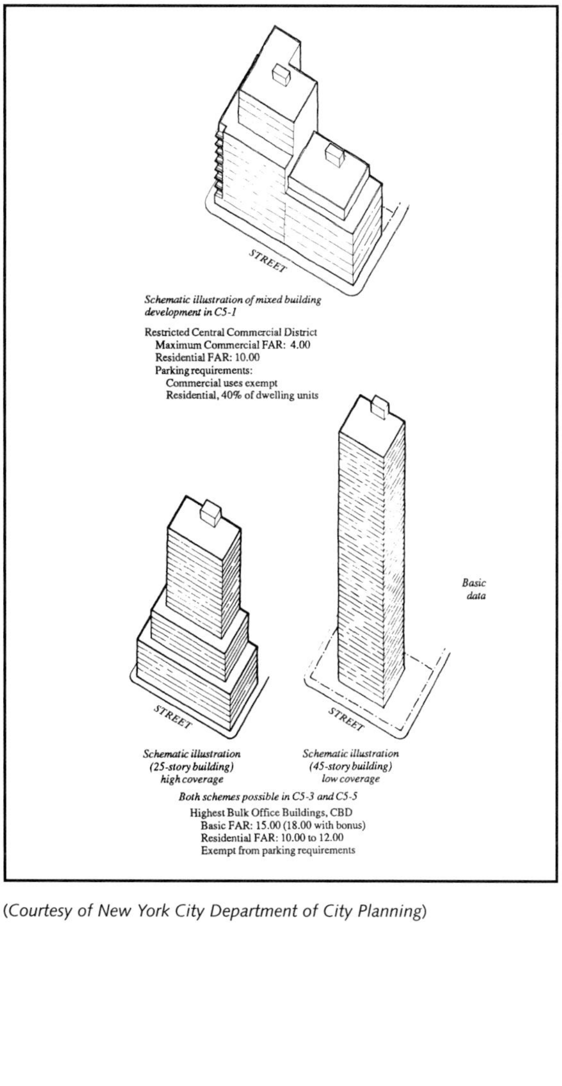

STREET
Schematic illustration of mixed building development in C5-1
Restricted Central Commercial District
Maximum Commercial FAR: 4.00
Residential FAR: 10.00
Parking requirements:
Commercial uses exempt
Residential, 40% of dwelling units
Basic data
STREET
STREET
Schematic illustration (25-story building) high coverage
Schematic illustration (45-story building) low coverage
Both schemes possible in C5-3 and C5-5
Highest Bulk Office Buildings, CBD
Basic FAR: 15.00 (18.00 with bonus)
Residential FAR: 10.00 to 12.00
Exempt from parking requirements

(Courtesy of New York City Department of City Planning)

For centuries, municipal governments have specified what property owners can and cannot do with their land. The earliest American land use regulations were scattered ordinances preventing property owners from harming other citizens or damaging their property. In 1672, for example, Boston enacted legislation that required structures to be built of such fireproof materials as brick and stone. Twenty years later, it restricted the location of slaughterhouses, stills, and tallow manufacturers. By the end of the nineteenth century every major city had similar land use statutes.[1]

A second group of regulations was modeled on the nation's first comprehensive zoning resolution, enacted by New York City in 1916. These regulations combined into a single ordinance land use, height, bulk, siting, and (later) density requirements.[2]

During the second half of the twentieth century, a third set of laws provided inducements for property owners to establish plazas, arcades, atriums, covered parking, day-care facilities, "affordable housing," and other facilities that were thought to be in the community's interest. This approach shifted the cost and responsibility for providing public space and facilities from government agencies to individual property owners.

The most recent group of laws is intended to manage growth and prevent inadvertent destruction of scenic vistas, natural habitats, unpolluted waterways, and other irreplaceable resources. These laws come in two varieties. One attempts to predetermine the location and sequence of development and avoid any unsuitable impact on the natural or human-made environment. The other avoids all planning and mandates specific review of the widest range of possible impacts that might be caused by proposed changes in land use.

The rationale behind each of these approaches is that common action can achieve results that cannot be produced by the market operating independently, or cannot be produced as inexpensively and efficiently, or cannot be produced quickly without such intervention. Economists call these situations "externalities." They may be caused by individuals acting in their own perceived self-interest, but doing so out of ignorance, short-sightedness, or lack of concern for the rest of society. The demand for intervention may also arise from society's need to provide some publicly accepted goal that can only be achieved by common action and cannot be withheld if some beneficiaries refuse to pay. But, whether the aim is to prevent the undesirable or to stimulate the beneficial, these are situations that individual citizens find difficult to deal with on their own and, therefore, require public intervention.[3]

By the end of the twentieth century, land use regulation had ceased being purely a method for preventing property owners from causing harm to their neighbors and became one of the most popular techniques for improving cities and suburbs. Many communities that employed land use regulations to achieve a broad range of goals began to apply them in a manner that was so broad in scope, specific in content, and discretionary in application that they clashed with such other societal objectives as fairness, economy, and efficiency. For example, the attempt to achieve one objective, such as protection of a lovely natural landscape, might clash with another objective, such as lowering housing cost, and cause additional problems, such as discrimination against minority groups.

In some areas, ordinances have become so complex that property owners who only employ architects and lawyers are no longer able to determine what they can and cannot do with their land. They must also employ one set of consultants (usually former municipal employees) to advise them on their initial proposal and another set of consultants (also usually former municipal employees) to expedite the processing of their requests. Inevitably, the additional time and costs are passed on to consumers, who are increasingly unable to afford the benefits. In the process, any improvement of the physical environment is seriously retarded and the cost of living escalates.

The difficulty and cost of changing existing land use regulations has now become so great that it is only tackled for major projects, developers with deep pockets, politicians with powerful connections, and civic groups with sizable constituencies. As a result, unsatisfactory and ineffective land use controls remain in place long after they can be justified.

We must clear away the existing thicket of confusing, conflicting, counterproductive statutes. There are plenty of workable regulations that are fair, inexpensive, easy to administer, and responsive to local conditions and priorities. Wherever they exist, they should remain in place. They should also be extended to those areas where they have not heretofore applied. But whatever the combination of statutes, they should be altered to harmonize with one another. Only then will we be able to protect and improve both the natural and the built environment.

Private Land Use Regulation

Private citizens can protect themselves by using deed restrictions. Such deed restrictions were common during the nineteenth century. From its inception in 1857, Boston's Back Bay was encumbered with requirements as to height, construction materials, siting, and even such appendages as steps, porches, balconies, and bay windows. In 1869, when the developer of Riverside, Illinois, began selling lots for development, the sale included deed restrictions that prohibited fences and required houses to be set back at least 30 feet from any public thoroughfare. The private places of St. Louis usually included deed restrictions that required a minimum cost of construction and design approval by the street association (see Chapters 13 and 15).

Deed restrictions have serious drawbacks. Only those properties that have restrictive covenants get the benefits of regulation. The amount of land affected thus varies with the locality. Unfortunately, traffic regulation, water supply, pollution control, and many other city planning objectives cannot be accomplished unless the entire region is included.

Another drawback is that private regulatory action is often limited in its duration and effectiveness. The minimum construction cost requirements of the private places of St. Louis, for example, were rendered irrelevant by inflation. Deed restrictions can expire. When the time is up, property owners may choose to scuttle previous decisions. Individual dwellings at Sunnyside Gardens were organized around the edges of city blocks, leaving common open space in the middle. Each block had a restrictive covenant preserving the common open space. When the covenants expired in the mid-1970s, some blocks chose to subdivide the open space, turning it into small individual back yards.[4]

Private land use regulations are often difficult, time-consuming, and expensive to enforce. Property owners have trouble preventing their neighbors from breaking the rules. Home owners in Levittown, Long Island, for example, are all required to abide by restrictive land covenants, among which are requirements that "Laundry must be hung only in the rear on a revolving portable dryer, which must be taken down when not in use" and "lawns must be mowed and weeds removed at least once a week between April 15 and November 15."

These rules may be trivial—too trivial for court action. But even if they were not, litigation still might not be practicable. Enforcing covenants is difficult, costly, and time consuming. Furthermore, the only individuals with standing to sue are property owners affected by the same covenants.

More pernicious covenants have been used to restrict occupancy to specific racial and ethnic groups. In 1948, the Supreme Court, in the case of *Shelley v. Kraemer,* ruled that the equal protection provisions of the Fourteenth Amendment precluded state courts from enforcing this form of contractual discrimination. Nevertheless, scattered cases of exclusion persist wherever the cost and complexity of proving discrimination has deterred legal action.[5]

Even the process for altering restrictions can be cumbersome and unfair. Unless otherwise specified, unanimous consent of all the affected properties is required. Even when changes can be made if agreed to by a simple majority, it usually means a majority of the lots affected. This can cause unanticipated difficulties such as were faced by the residents of Palos Verdes Estates when they sought to avoid paying county real estate taxes on commonly owned parkland (see Chapter 15).

Most localities stopped regulating land use solely by private agreement because the time, cost, and complexity of separately and individually making, amending, and rescinding these agreements proved to be too great. It seemed better to prescribe actions by legislation rather than by written agreement among the property owners affected, to make decisions by majority vote rather than by unanimous consent, and to have them enforced by administrative agencies rather than by the courts.

Houston, Texas, is the only major American city that continues to regulate land use largely by private agreement. While Houston's deed restrictions are pervasive, they have been augmented by laws that establish minimum lot sizes for areas with and without sewers and minimum setbacks for buildings on local streets and major thoroughfares and by an ordinance that allows public enforcement of private covenants. The city's attempts to combine its land use legislation into a single comprehensive zoning ordinance were rejected by referendum in 1948, 1962, and 1993.

The Police Power

The power to govern implies the power to establish suitable regulations protecting the public order, health, safety, and morals of the community, or—in nineteenth-century parlance—the power to "police." The extent to which localities can regulate land use, however, is determined by the degree to which this *police power* is circumscribed by the Constitution and specifically the Fifth and Fourteenth Amendments. The Fourteenth Amendment, approved in 1868, was intended to protect civil rights and included the prohibition against state legislation depriving "any person of life, liberty, or property without due process of law." Such language clouds the constitutionality of local property regulations because to some extent any restriction will deprive citizens of the use of their property.[6]

The degree of regulation that is justified by the police power was set forth by Justice John Marshall Harlan in the case of *Mugler v. Kansas* (1887). The case arose when Mugler, a brewery owner, challenged a Kansas law that forbade the manufacture or sale of alcohol, arguing that the law had rendered his property valueless by eliminating its use as a brewery. Justice Harlan explained that legislation that prohibits activity that is "injurious to the health, morals, or safety of the community," but "does not disturb the owner in the control or use of his property for lawful purposes nor restrict his right to dispose of it," is not a taking. It is "only a declaration by the state that its use by anyone, for certain forbidden purposes, is prejudicial to the public interests."[7]

The critical case in determining the point at which regulation becomes a "taking" in violation of the Fourteenth Amendment came in 1922 in *Pennsylvania Coal Company v. Mahon.* During the previous year, in an attempt to protect hundreds of thousands of residents of northeastern Pennsylvania from mine subsidence, the legislature had enacted the Kohler Act. The problem it was trying to solve was that land above a large number of mine shafts had subsided, leaving sags and humps in once-level streets, sometimes breaking water, sewer, and gas mains, and even opening cemeteries. The new act prohibited mining of anthracite coal in designated areas, where such mining could cause the subsidence of streets, bridges, railroads, conduits, cemeteries, public buildings, factories, stores, and private residences.[8]

Much of the land in that part of Pennsylvania had been sold by coal companies that retained mineral rights below the surface of the property. The deeds to these properties often included the stipulation that the purchaser waived future claims for property damage or personal injury due to mine subsidence against those who retained subsurface mining rights.

In September 1921, the Mahon family was notified in writing that within 10 days the Pennsylvania Coal Company would start mining operations that could cause the subsidence of their house. They started proceedings to enjoin the action as a violation of the Kohler Act. The coal company countered saying that the legislation was not an exercise of the police power by the legislature, but, rather, an unconstitutional taking of their property (the right to mine coal under the Mahon's house) without due process of law or compensation.

When the case reached the Supreme Court, Justice Oliver Wendell Holmes, writing for the majority, found that "to make it commercially impractical to mine certain coal has very nearly the same effect for constitutional purposes as appropriating or destroying it," and was therefore a taking. He further enunciated the principle that established the constitutional limits of government land use regulation: "while property may be regulated to a certain extent, if regulation goes too far it will be recognized as a taking."[9] Holmes' principle fails to answer the question: *what is too far?* It is the question that should always be paramount in the mind of anybody trying to regulate land use.[10]

The Role of Federal, State, and Local Government

The words "police power" cannot be found in the Constitution. It is among the many powers retained by the states. Nevertheless, because of a variety of other constitutionally established responsibilities, the federal government does regulate land use. For example, the Constitution gives the federal government the primary role in policing interstate commerce and thus responsibility for ensuring the navigability of the country's waterways. By implication, it must police land use along the water's edge. To better carry out these functions, Congress passed the Rivers and Harbors Act of 1899. It gave the Corps of Engineers specific authority to regulate construction of dams, dikes, piers, wharves, bulkheads, and other structures. The law also allows the Corps to establish pierhead and bulkhead lines and to regulate excavation and landfill extending into navigable waters. Another example is the Federal Water Pollution Act of 1972 that required "zero discharge" after 1985 of any refuse into U.S. waterways other than liquids flowing from streets or sewers. It allowed the federal government to establish performance standards for new industries locating along navigable waterways. The Wild and Scenic Rivers Act of 1968, Clean Air Act of 1970, and Coastal Zone Management Act of 1972, are only a few of the many other federal laws with land use implications that flow from other constitutionally authorized activity.

The most potent device in federal land use regulation does not derive directly from the Constitution, but, rather from federal expenditures. Any time Congress appropriates funds it has the right to demand that the recipient comply with specified requirements that can include anything from preventing discrimination to complying with prevailing wage rates. The most important of the funding-derived statutes that affect land use, the National Environmental Policy Act of 1969 (NEPA), does so by requiring that every major federal action as well as every federal and federally funded project prepare detailed statements concerning any major effects they could have on the quality of the environment (see the subsections "The National Environmental Policy Act" and "NEPA's Impact" that appear later in this chapter).

Local authority to "police" land use derives from state constitutions. City, county, and regional governments are considered to be "creatures" created by the states and are entitled to carry out only state-authorized functions. For this reason, when comprehensive zoning became the favored form of land use regulation, Secretary of Commerce Herbert Hoover appointed a committee to draft a model state enabling statute. The resulting Standard State Zoning Enabling Act was issued by the Government Printing Office in 1924. Within 4 years it "had been used wholly or largely in zoning laws enacted in some thirty states."[11]

Early zoning ordinances were narrow in scope. They dealt with simple questions of design and land use, ignoring such other issues as drainage, air and water quality, or noise. These first zoning laws could not have been sufficiently inclusive because the individuals who wrote them had neither the knowledge or experience to draft truly "comprehensive" regulations. Political opposition would have been so virulent that they never would have been adopted. Even if they had been adopted, no government agency could have hired the staff to enforce them because trained personnel did not exist. Equally important, they only applied in governmental jurisdictions that had adopted such ordinances. As a result, vast stretches of territory remained unregulated.

For at least half a century, large segments of the planning profession continued to duck environmental issues. The staffs of most planning and zoning commissions did not include individuals trained to consider environmental issues. The vacuum was filled by enacting environmental regulations that involved such issues as the siting of power plants, supervision of surface mining, protection of agricultural land, conservation of water resources, and the management of floodplains, wetlands, and shorelands. These regulations usually applied to property outside city limits. Proponents of such regulation were asking for the same things that had been obtained decades earlier by urban reformers demanding zoning. They were just filling the jurisdictional void caused by the absence of city governments and traditional zoning.

California's coastal-zone management is probably the best-known and surely one of the most far-reaching examples of such state land use regulation. It began as the California Coastal Zone Conservation Act of 1972, a citizen-sponsored initiative, better known as "Proposition 20." The act established six regional commissions and one state commission with the responsibility of preparing a coastal zone plan for the state's entire 1100-mile oceanfront. That plan had to include policies on land use, transportation, conservation, public access, recreation, public facilities siting, ocean minerals, living resources, maximum population densities, and educational and scientific uses.[12]

For the next 4 years, while the California Coastal Commission prepared its plan, there was a virtual moratorium on all development. The completed plan was largely rejected by the state legislature, which instead passed the California Coastal Act and State Coastal Conservancy Act of 1976. Under this new legislation local governments regained the power to adopt land use plans and zoning ordinances. However, a reconstituted Coastal Commission was responsible for approving their actions as well as virtually all new development within a broadly defined Coastal Zone, varying in width from 1000 yards to 5 miles.

These awesome responsibilities required a substantial administrative apparatus. Within 6 years, the commission had a staff of 188 and an annual budget of $10.3 million. Despite their best efforts, 15 years after passage of Proposition 20, the Coastal Commission had approved only 51 of the 103 coastal plans it was required to review.[13]

During the 1970s, Florida, Oregon, Vermont, Maine, and Wyoming took the lead in adopting statewide land use programs, which, like California's coastal-zone management program, attempted to regulate areas of critical concern as well as projects that had major regional impact. Virtually all this legislation was aimed at safeguarding the environment while simultaneously protecting such favored activities as farming, fishing, hunting, logging, and tourism. But, whether aimed at the California coastline or the Wyoming mountains, it was generated as much by unhappiness with the character of new development as by the desire to protect scarce resources that were particularly vulnerable to new development.[14]

Washington, D.C., 1981. Continuous cornice line on Connecticut Avenue established by the height limit enacted by Congress in 1899. *(Alexander Garvin)*

Land Use Regulation Strategies

Early twentieth-century urban reformers, who fought for city zoning ordinances, and latter twentieth-century environmentalists, who fought for state and federal legislation to protect the countryside, share a common distaste for entirely market-driven land use decisions. They are not willing to wait till the damage is done; till the stream has been polluted, the traffic is in gridlock, or the landmark has been demolished. Instead, they would augment the private market either with legislatively specified requirements (codes and ordinances) or with administrative review (discretionary action by a government agency). However, both the proponents of entirely market-driven land use and the proponents of government regulation are burdened with the same unrealistic expectation: that results inevitably will be satisfactory.

Land use decisions, unlike arithmetic problems, never have one and only one correct solution. Their success depends on the value systems of the people who examine them. Predominant among these values are the desire to protect private property, to encourage orderliness, and to ensure stability.

There is a continuing stream of regulations beginning with the earliest colonial settlements, all aimed at protecting private property. Prior to the twentieth century, fires that destroyed whole city districts were common. Starting with laws such as Boston's 1672 statute requiring structures to be built of fireproof materials, proponents of government land use regulation have fought for increasingly detailed construction requirements, all intended to protect property from fire. Consequently by the end of the twentieth century, construction in virtually every American city is subject to building and safety codes that minimize the possibility of property destruction in citywide conflagrations.

Orderliness (society's attempt to keep pigs out of its parlor) is another of the values behind land use regulation. In 1647, it was even put in similar terms by a New York City ordinance that attempted to avoid a "disorderly manner...in placing pig pens and privies on the public roads."[15] It was not until 1908, however, that any major American city tried to find a place for everything and put everything in its place. In that year, the Los Angeles city council enacted ordinances that established seven industrial districts, in which mills and factories were permitted, and three residential districts, from which they were excluded.[16]

In his book, *Icons and Aliens*, John Costonis identifies the desire for stability and reassurance in the face of change as one of the values behind land use regulation. He explains that the environment is "an assemblage of natural and built features, many of which have become rich in symbolic import. The 'icons' are features invested with values that confirm our sense of order and identity. The 'aliens' threaten the icons and hence our investment in the icons' values." Land use regulation, Costonis explains, can be better understood as society's attempt to preserve "icons" and exclude "aliens."[17]

The attempt to protect "icons" from the threat of "alien" intrusion is graphically illustrated by 1899 legislation in which Congress established height limits for the District of Columbia. Among the purposes of these height limits was the desire to ensure that the Capitol dome (a genuine icon) would dominate every section of the city and the city's streets and avenues would be protected from intrusive tall structures (aliens?) that would deflect attention from the Capitol.[18]

In its less attractive form, this desire for stability and reassurance becomes an excuse for ethnic and racial discrimination. A good example is San Francisco's attempt, during the latter nineteenth century, to exclude (possibly alien) public laundries from many sections of the city. This effort was directed at 240 businesses, many of which also were de facto social centers owned by (definitely alien) subjects of the Emperor of China or by Chinese Americans.[19]

In 1880, the city and county of San Francisco enacted legislation making it unlawful to operate a laundry, except in brick or stone buildings, without having first obtained the consent of the Board of Supervisors. At that time nine-tenths of San Francisco was built of wood. There were about 320 laundries in the city and county of San Francisco, of which all but 10 occupied wooden structures. Three-quarters of all laundries were Chinese-owned and -operated. Over the next 5 years more than 150 "subjects of China" were arrested on the charge of carrying on business without having consent of the board of supervisors, while all the 80 Caucasian-owned laundries remained in business, unaffected by the legislation.

In 1886, in the cases of *Yick Wo v. Hopkins,* and *Wo Lee v. Hopkins,* the Supreme Court found this legislation to be a violation of the "equal protection" guaranteed by the Fourteenth Amendment. It upheld the right of the Board of Supervisors to regulate activities "which are against good morals, contrary to public order and decency, or dangerous to public safety." But it also found that the danger of fire was no more significant in three-fourths of the territory affected (10 miles wide by 15 miles long) than in "other farming regions of the State." The court held that while there was a danger from fire in built-up portions of the city, "a fire, properly guarded, for laundry purposes, in a wooden building, is just as necessary, and no more dangerous, than a fire for cooking purposes or for warming a house." Furthermore, the court observed, "clothes washing is certainly not opposed to good morals or subversive of public order or decency."[20]

Comprehensive Zoning

Although there were a vast number of land use regulations already in effect by the beginning of the twentieth century, such regulation often is erroneously thought to start with the Zoning Resolution enacted by New York City in 1916. This law was indeed innovative. But it was not the attempt to assign specific land uses to different sections of the city that was new, it was the zoning resolution's comprehensive scope. For the first time, a land use ordinance simultaneously specified permitted land use, building height, and building placement for the entire city. It did so by providing three bulky sets of *zoning maps,* which designated the regulations that applied to every block and lot within the city limits, and a *zoning text* that explained them.

The 1916 Resolution set off a chain reaction in the rest of the country. Within 5 years of its passage, 76 communities had adopted similar statutes. By 1926 that number had grown to 564. Thus, when the Supreme Court validated the constitutionality of comprehensive zoning in the case of *Ambler Realty Company v. Village of Euclid,* the overwhelming majority of American cities had adopted comprehensive zoning patterned on the law New York had pioneered a decade earlier.[21]

The same thing happened in 1961 when New York City completely revised its resolution. At that time it eliminated height limits, replacing them with more flexible bulk regulations, and added both density controls and incentives to encourage an increase in the amount of public open space. Once again, the techniques pioneered in New York were taken up by cities across the country.

New York City Zoning Resolutions of 1916 and 1961

Although both of New York City's trail-blazing zoning resolutions tried to deal comprehensively with every section of the city, they did not emerge from a comprehensive planning process. Nor were they based on previously adopted, comprehensive city plans.[22] The 1916 resolution was enacted because a group of powerful business leaders and good-government reformers were unhappy with existing real estate activity and sought legislation to protect their property, ensure the orderly development of the districts they frequented, and establish stable land use patterns for those areas.[23]

Lord & Taylor, Saks, Tiffany, and many other fine stores objected to manufacturing firms moving to the "famous retail sections" of the city. So did the Waldorf Astoria Hotel, the University Club, the Union League, and many other exclusive establishments. In response, they started an advertising campaign that complained about "factories making clothing, cloaks, suits, furs, petticoats, etc."[24]

The intruding land uses generated pushcarts, trucks, and workers who mingled with patrons of expensive stores, hotels,

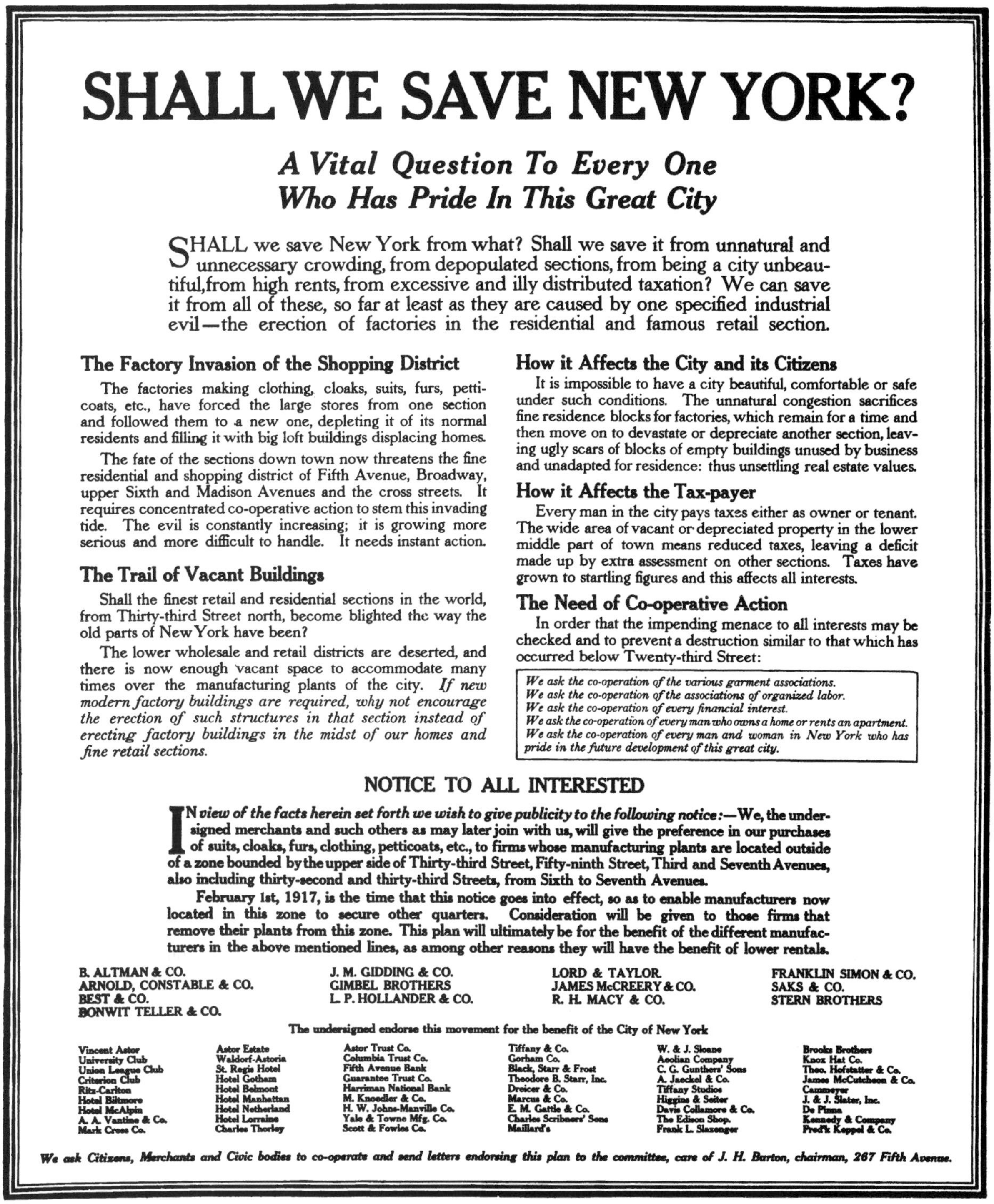

SHALL WE SAVE NEW YORK?

A Vital Question To Every One Who Has Pride In This Great City

SHALL we save New York from what? Shall we save it from unnatural and unnecessary crowding, from depopulated sections, from being a city unbeautiful,from high rents, from excessive and illy distributed taxation? We can save it from all of these, so far at least as they are caused by one specified industrial evil—the erection of factories in the residential and famous retail section.

The Factory Invasion of the Shopping District

The factories making clothing, cloaks, suits, furs, petticoats, etc., have forced the large stores from one section and followed them to a new one, depleting it of its normal residents and filling it with big loft buildings displacing homes.

The fate of the sections down town now threatens the fine residential and shopping district of Fifth Avenue, Broadway, upper Sixth and Madison Avenues and the cross streets. It requires concentrated co-operative action to stem this invading tide. The evil is constantly increasing; it is growing more serious and more difficult to handle. It needs instant action.

The Trail of Vacant Buildings

Shall the finest retail and residential sections in the world, from Thirty-third Street north, become blighted the way the old parts of New York have been?

The lower wholesale and retail districts are deserted, and there is now enough vacant space to accommodate many times over the manufacturing plants of the city. *If new modern factory buildings are required, why not encourage the erection of such structures in that section instead of erecting factory buildings in the midst of our homes and fine retail sections.*

How it Affects the City and its Citizens

It is impossible to have a city beautiful, comfortable or safe under such conditions. The unnatural congestion sacrifices fine residence blocks for factories, which remain for a time and then move on to devastate or depreciate another section, leaving ugly scars of blocks of empty buildings unused by business and unadapted for residence: thus unsettling real estate values.

How it Affects the Tax-payer

Every man in the city pays taxes either as owner or tenant. The wide area of vacant or depreciated property in the lower middle part of town means reduced taxes, leaving a deficit made up by extra assessment on other sections. Taxes have grown to startling figures and this affects all interests.

The Need of Co-operative Action

In order that the impending menace to all interests may be checked and to prevent a destruction similar to that which has occurred below Twenty-third Street:

We ask the co-operation of the various garment associations.
We ask the co-operation of the associations of organized labor.
We ask the co-operation of every financial interest.
We ask the co-operation of every man who owns a home or rents an apartment.
We ask the co-operation of every man and woman in New York who has pride in the future development of this great city.

NOTICE TO ALL INTERESTED

I*N view of the facts herein set forth we wish to give publicity to the following notice:*—We, the undersigned merchants and such others as may later join with us, will give the preference in our purchases of suits, cloaks, furs, clothing, petticoats, etc., to firms whose manufacturing plants are located outside of a zone bounded by the upper side of Thirty-third Street, Fifty-ninth Street, Third and Seventh Avenues, also including thirty-second and thirty-third Streets, from Sixth to Seventh Avenues.

February 1st, 1917, is the time that this notice goes into effect, so as to enable manufacturers now located in this zone to secure other quarters. Consideration will be given to those firms that remove their plants from this zone. This plan will ultimately be for the benefit of the different manufacturers in the above mentioned lines, as among other reasons they will have the benefit of lower rentals.

B. ALTMAN & CO.
ARNOLD, CONSTABLE & CO.
BEST & CO.
BONWIT TELLER & CO.
J. M. GIDDING & CO.
GIMBEL BROTHERS
L. P. HOLLANDER & CO.
LORD & TAYLOR.
JAMES McCREERY & CO.
R. H. MACY & CO.
FRANKLIN SIMON & CO.
SAKS & CO.
STERN BROTHERS

The undersigned endorse this movement for the benefit of the City of New York

Vincent Astor
University Club
Union League Club
Criterion Club
Ritz-Carlton
Hotel Biltmore
Hotel McAlpin
A. A. Vantine & Co.
Mark Cross Co.
Astor Estate
Waldorf-Astoria
St. Regis Hotel
Hotel Gotham
Hotel Belmont
Hotel Manhattan
Hotel Netherland
Hotel Lorraine
Charles Thorley
Astor Trust Co.
Columbia Trust Co.
Fifth Avenue Bank
Guarantee Trust Co.
Harriman National Bank
M. Knoedler & Co.
H. W. Johns-Manville Co.
Yale & Towne Mfg. Co.
Scott & Fowles Co.
Tiffany & Co.
Gorham Co.
Black, Starr & Frost
Theodore B. Starr, Inc.
Dreicer & Co.
Marcus & Co.
E. M. Gattle & Co.
Charles Scribners' Sons
Maillard's
W. & J. Sloane
Aeolian Company
C. G. Gunthers' Sons
A. Jaeckel & Co.
Tiffany Studios
Higgins & Seiter
Davis Collamore & Co.
The Edison Shop.
Frank L. Slazenger
Brooks Brothers
Knox Hat Co.
Theo. Hofstatter & Co.
James McCutcheon & Co.
Cammeyer
J. & J. Slater, Inc.
De Pinna
Kennedy & Company
Fred'k Keppel & Co.

We ask Citizens, Merchants and Civic bodies to co-operate and send letters endorsing this plan to the committee, care of J. H. Barton, chairman, 267 Fifth Avenue.

New York City, 1916. This advertisement in *The New York Times* demanding action to save the city from incompatible land uses played a major role in persuading the city to enact comprehensive zoning.

and private clubs, making it difficult for these establishments to retain customers. Consequently, the stores, hotels, and clubs were forced to move, often giving up substantial investments in properties that had lost their former value. A growing number of business leaders, led by the Fifth Avenue Association, demanded action that would alter the terms of private-market competition by keeping neighboring property owners from freely renting or selling to "incompatible" neighbors.

These activists found ready allies among good-government reformers, who had a long history with legislation that

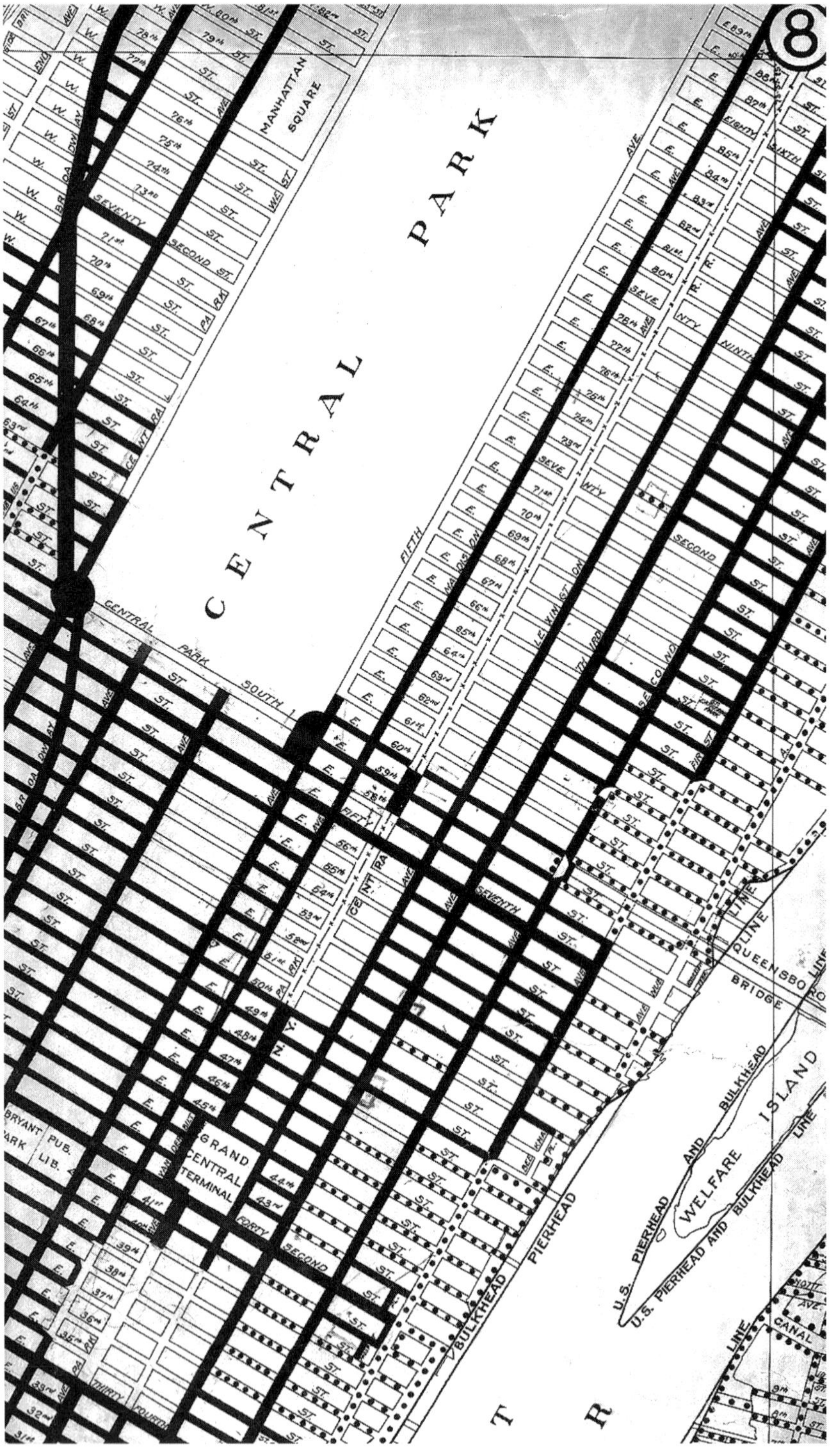

Manhattan, 1916. Land uses permitted by the Zoning Resolution of 1916. Streets and avenues left blank were zoned for residential use only. Streets and avenues marked in black were zoned for either commercial or residential use. On streets and avenues lined with black dots the zoning land use was unlimited. *(Courtesy of New York City Department of City Planning)*

guaranteed minimum levels of light and air for apartment buildings (see Chapter 10). In 1887, they had persuaded the state legislature to amend the Old Tenement Law to limit the height of all future multiple dwellings.[25] Their first twentieth-century success, the New Tenement Law of 1901, specified a height limit of one-and-one-half times the width of the widest street on which any apartment house was to be built.[26]

Spurred on by success in regulating apartment construction, reformers moved on to commercial buildings, to which the tenement laws did not apply. Perhaps in response to fires like the one that in 1911 destroyed the Triangle Shirt Waist Company and resulted in the death of 146 workers, reformers gained increasing support for regulation of commercial buildings. They allied themselves with design professionals,

Manhattan, c. 1893. Fifth Avenue north of 42nd Street was entirely residential prior to zoning. *(Courtesy of Museum of the City of New York)*

who were increasingly enamored of continuous cornice lines.[27]

In 1912, the borough president of Manhattan appointed a Heights of Buildings Commission, whose proposed height limits were never adopted. In 1914, the city's Board of Estimate appointed a Commission on Building Districts and Restrictions. But it was not until the completion in 1915 of the Equitable Building on lower Broadway that the effort to regulate commercial buildings attracted sufficient political support to obtain legislation. The 1.2-million-square-foot Equitable Building rose uninterrupted 540 feet from the sidewalk. Its floor area was almost 30 times that of the lot on which it was built. No building of such enormous bulk had ever been seen in New York, or anywhere else. Suddenly the public was in an uproar over the possibility that all of Manhattan could be covered by similar buildings that would darken sidewalks and generate serious pedestrian and vehicular traffic congestion.[28]

In 1916, the coalition of business leaders and political reformers finally obtained approval of a zoning resolution that segregated land uses by district and limited the bulk and placement of the buildings that could contain those uses. They understood that property owners would still want the highest possible return on their investments. The new law was intended to prevent them from maximizing return by erecting buildings whose occupants would be "incompatible" with their neighbors, or by building bulky behemoths blocking sun and sky.

The new zoning resolution determined the future of every part of the city in which development was to take place. Nowhere was it more effective than on Fifth Avenue. When the ordinance took effect, Fifth Avenue was lined by the mansions of the wealthy along virtually the entire stretch between 42nd and 96th Streets. The new ordinance specified that the blocks

Manhattan, 1967. Fifth Avenue north of 42nd Street became entirely commercial after it was zoned for commercial use. *(Alexander Garvin)*

opposite Central Park could be used only for residential purposes, while those south of the park could be used for either commercial or residential purposes, but not for manufacturing. Most Fifth Avenue townhouses were eventually sold to developers, who could make more money by replacing them with elevator buildings. Residential uses disappeared from the blocks below Central Park, where commercial uses were permitted, because office and retail tenants paid higher rents than apartment residents. However, opposite the park the mansions of the wealthy were replaced by apartments for the wealthy because there the zoning resolution only permitted residential land use.

The impact of height regulations was no less dramatic. Wherever buildings were erected they had to comply with the new height limits. Park Avenue between 50th and 96th Streets, for example, developed a 210-foot-high street wall because the zoning resolution forbade façades that exceeded one and one-half times the width of the avenue.

Given the speed with which the zoning resolution had been adopted and the complete lack of experience with such

Manhattan, 1898. Fifth Avenue north of 65th Street was entirely residential prior to zoning. *(Courtesy of Museum of the City of New York, The Byron Collection)*

Manhattan, 1967. Fifth Avenue north of 65th Street remained entirely residential because it was zoned exclusively for residential use. *(Alexander Garvin)*

legislation, demands for revision were inevitable. By 1961, when the 1916 Resolution was supplanted, 2500 amendments had been approved. The pressure for change was seldom directed at market-driven real estate activity. It was aimed at the regulations themselves, which were thought to be inadequate, inflexible, and unnecessarily confusing.[29]

The 1916 Resolution had been adopted without much consideration of existing or likely future development patterns. At full site utilization, it permitted a city of 55 million residents and 250 million workers. Moreover, to a great extent both the use and bulk restrictions were unrelated to what then existed. Over half the city's population inhabited districts that were not zoned exclusively for residential use. Of the areas that were zoned exclusively for residential development (largely outside Manhattan), more than half were zoned for large apartment buildings that were more appropriate to Manhattan's exclusive Upper East Side.

The regulations themselves had been developed with little concern for construction practices or enforcement procedures. Buildings were required to fit specific envelopes without regard to site, use, structure, or cost of construction. Worst of all, consulting three sets of maps and numerous written regulations was cumbersome even for the city officials with the responsibility of interpreting and enforcing them.

Despite all these deficiencies, the reform movement became effective only in 1947, when Robert F. Wagner was appointed Chairman of the City Planning Commission. He understood that zoning had to be appropriate to existing conditions. The city had changed significantly since its pioneering zoning resolution had been adopted. At that time supermarkets, chain stores, and shopping centers had been unknown. Industrial firms had not yet begun to abandon their multistory lofts for suburban locations where there was adequate land for horizontal production lines. Cars, trucks, and planes had not yet become the dominant forms of transportation.

Wagner commissioned the architectural firm of Harrison, Ballard, and Allen to prepare a new ordinance that would be appropriate to the second half of the twentieth century. Before it was completed, he was elected borough president of Manhattan, a position from which he was unable to continue his efforts for a new zoning resolution. However, when he was elected mayor in 1953, he made zoning reform a major objective of his administration.[30]

Wagner waited until there was sufficient political support before proceeding. Zoning reform would affect every business, neighborhood, and voter in New York City. For this reason, having a committed constituency was a political necessity. Conditions had ripened sufficiently in 1956 for the mayor to appoint James Felt, a successful realtor, to be chairman of the City Planning Commission. Felt led the fight for modernizing the zoning resolution. He hired a second architectural firm, Voorhees, Walker, Smith, and Smith, to draft the new resolution. In 1961, after years of consultations with architects,

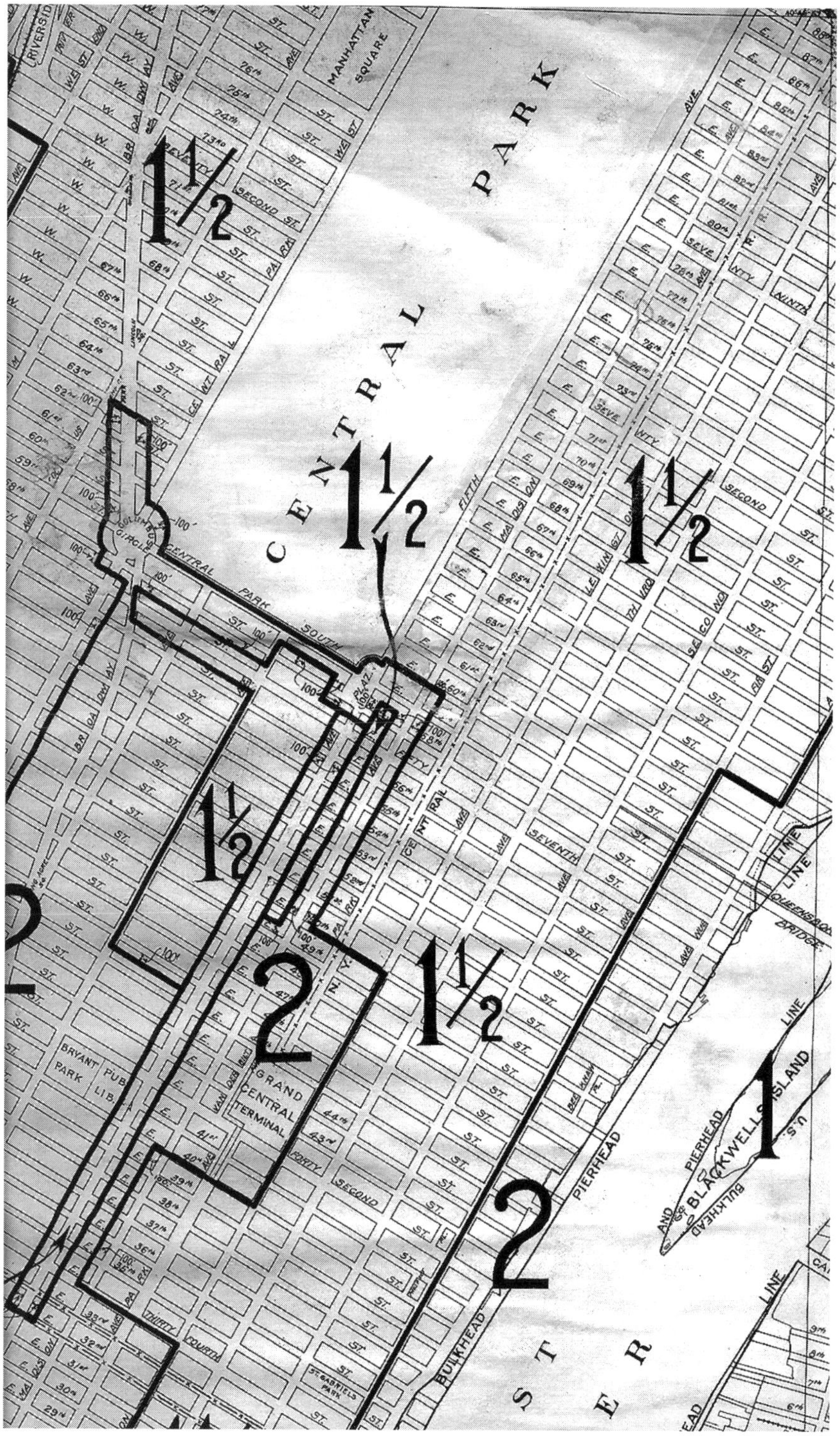

Manhattan, 1916. Height limits established by the Zoning Resolution for the blocks along Park Avenue, north of 50th Street, called for buildings 1.5 times the width of the street. *(Courtesy of New York City Department of City Planning)*

lawyers, realtors, builders, community groups, and civic organizations, after more than 850 changes to the proposed text, after dozens of formal and informal hearings, the city adopted a final version of the new zoning resolution.[31]

The 1961 Resolution consolidated the three sets of maps into a single map system. Like the 1916 Resolution, it indicated use, bulk, and building placement requirements. To these were added density and parking regulations. The text was also simplified by presenting many of the requirements in tabular form. The most important revisions, however, were in content.[32]

For the first time, the city had density controls that established the number of people likely to occupy every development site. Ostensibly, that density was related either to the existing capacity of infrastructure (i.e., water, sewer, streets,

Manhattan, 1986. The uniform height of buildings along Park Avenue is the result of the height limit imposed by the Zoning Resolution of 1916. *(Alexander Garvin)*

transit, etc.) and community facilities (i.e., schools, libraries, parks, playgrounds, etc.) or to future capacity, once planned capital construction was completed. Since New York had yet to prepare a comprehensive city plan, this was more theory than fact (see Chapter 18).

Another major change was the replacement of height limits with flexible bulk regulations that, district by district, specified the maximum allowable floor area as a multiple of lot area. Each building's shape would now depend on the regulations for that zoning district.[33] The new resolution also sought to provide additional space, light, and air for pedestrians, particularly in densely built-up areas, like lower Manhattan. In selected areas of the city, for every additional square foot of sidewalk or plaza, projects were entitled to increase the amount of floor area beyond what would otherwise be allowable.

As in 1916, New York's innovations were immediately copied. Cities everywhere adopted the single map system. They junked height limits, instead specifying a ratio of floor area to lot area. Some adopted the bonus for plazas and arcades. Many also went on to develop their own variants, thereby supplanting New York in pioneering regulatory techniques.

Cities include densely built-up areas and vacant land, highly prized districts that are not likely to change, and obsolete areas that certainly will be rebuilt, complex, heterogeneous neighborhoods, and districts whose consistency verges on the monotonous. Despite these variations, comprehensive zoning resolutions apply the same techniques to all sections of all cities, techniques that regulate allowable land uses, density, bulk, building placement, and open space.

Land Use

New York City's 1916 Zoning Resolution and all zoning ordinances patterned on it established three land use categories: exclusively *residential*, *commercial* (in which residential uses are permitted), and *unlimited* (to which manufacturing is relegated). This system recognizes that most built-up city districts include complex combinations of land uses that, when zoned *unlimited*, can coexist.

Following the precedent of New York City's 1961 Zoning Resolution, most cities dropped the unlimited category, replacing it with *manufacturing* zones (in which certain commercial, but not residential, uses are permitted). The logic behind this segregation of manufacturing is that the traffic, noise, fumes, and industrial waste that are generated are inappropriate to most residential areas. As the number of "clean" industries and businesses with fewer than 10 employees increases, though, this logic is becoming obsolescent.

Zoning ordinances usually are adopted after cities already have been built up. Thus, no matter how carefully use-categories are mapped, a substantial number of existing uses inevitably will fail to conform to the approved zoning. The idea is for these *nonconforming* uses eventually to pass away and be replaced by those that will conform with the zoning. Since after-the-fact prohibition can be considered a taking that would require compensation, nonconforming uses are usually permitted to persist, so long as the degree of nonconformity is not increased.

The disparity between actual land uses and zoning sometimes results in unfortunate situations. Occupants of a nonconforming building may find it difficult to obtain insurance, mortgage financing, or building permits for remodeling. The resulting disinvestment may spur the deterioration of the surrounding area. In fact, the very existence of nonconforming uses may render irrelevant any land use policy established by a zoning resolution, for by the time they are replaced, the zoning itself may have become obsolete.

Some critics question even the desire to separate land uses. Jane Jacobs, in her pioneering book, *The Death and Life of Great American Cities,* for example, argues for mixed land use as a way of ensuring safety and neighborhood vitality, pointing out that cities need "people who go outdoors on different schedules...for different purposes, but who are able to use many facilities in common."[34] The only way to generate activity 24 hours a day is to allow for buildings that will contain the widest variety of uses. Starting in the 1970s, more in response to entirely local situations than to Jacobs's cogent analysis, cities began redesignating zones for mixed use.

Density

The 1961 Resolution introduced regulations which, for residential construction, specified *lot area per room* and later *lot area per dwelling unit.* The intent was to establish, on a district-by-district basis, a maximum number of households that could be adequately served by local water, sewer, transportation, hospital, school, library, and park systems.[35]

There are serious flaws in the rationale for density regulations. They are applied without reference to a zoning district's demographic characteristics and remain in place although those characteristics are continually changing. Thus, the same *lot area per room* requirement applies to houses in which there are widely different occupancy characteristics and service requirements. This is difficult to justify if neighborhoods with large concentrations of low-income residents (in which the number of people per room and the amount of public services they depend on tends to be high) have the same *lot area per room* requirement as wealthy neighborhoods (in which there is a greater number of residents who belong to country clubs, own second homes, and take frequent vacations). It is also difficult to justify when the same *lot area per room* requirement remains in place long after the proportion of single-person households has changed, thereby changing loading patterns for schools, recreation facilities, and transit systems.

Density regulations reflect an implicit assumption that higher density results in greater crowding. As Jane Jacobs so eloquently points out:

> *High densities mean large numbers of dwellings per acre of land. Overcrowding means too many people in a dwelling for the number of rooms it contains...It has nothing to do with the number of dwellings on the land, just as in real life high densities have nothing to do with overcrowding.*[36]

The equation of density with crowding also results in a bias against high-density districts. As a result, zoning regulations consign lower-density districts to forever lack populations large enough to support the eating places, clothing shops, hardware stores, and other services and amenities that should be close at hand in any urban neighborhood. They also force increasing dependence on—and time lost in—automobiles.

Bulk

There are two main techniques for regulating bulk. The first, *height limits,* predates comprehensive zoning. New York City limited building height in 1887, Washington in 1899, Los Angeles in 1904. The rationale was different in each case. New York wanted to ensure adequate light and air for the occupants of apartment houses; Washington wanted a symbolic setting for the national Capitol; Los Angeles wanted to minimize damage from earthquakes. New York's 1916 Resolution consolidated height limits into five districts, in each of which maximum height was a different multiple of the width of the street on which a building was to be erected. The buildings that complied with the height limits tended to be fat and squat, cover most of their site, and leave only minimal open space.

Attitudes about building height vary. Most potential building occupants will want to be as high as possible. They recognize that the higher they are, the less they will be dis-

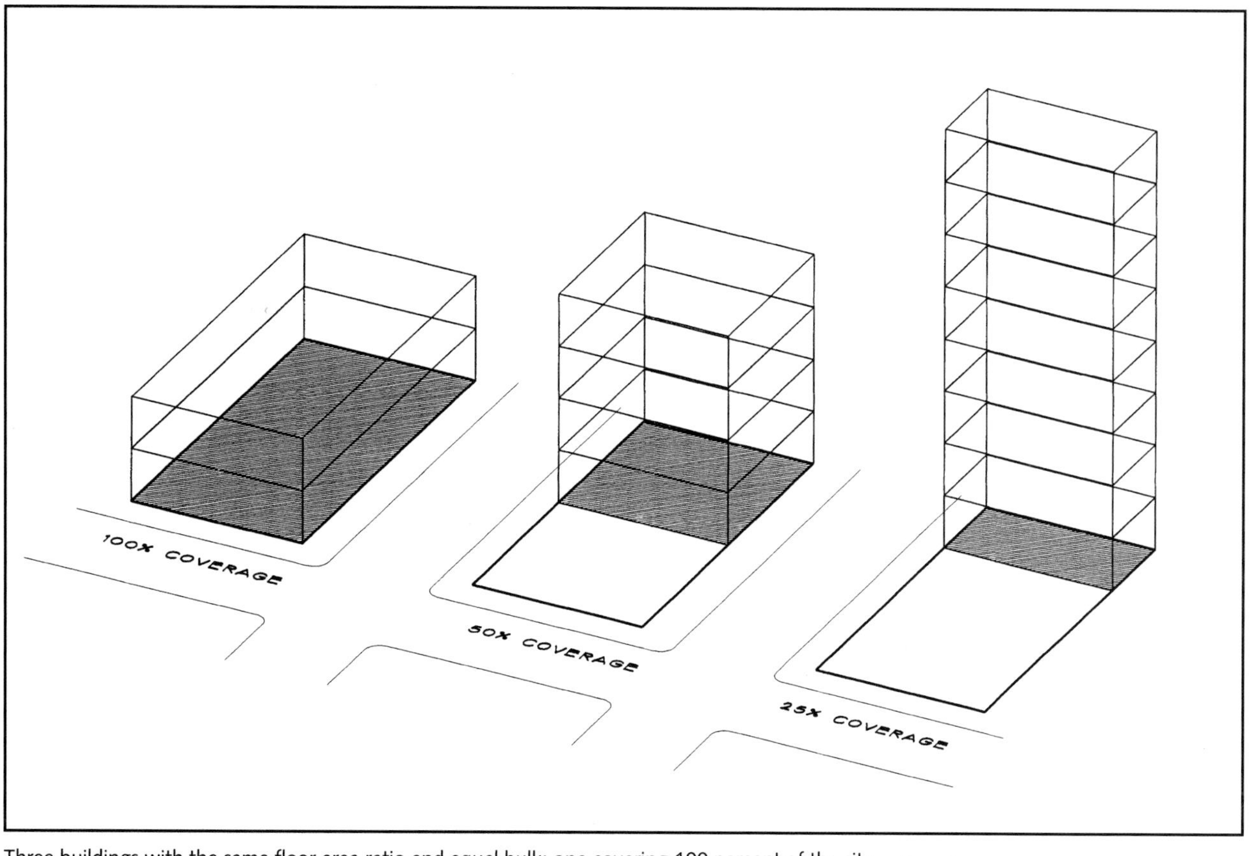

Three buildings with the same floor area ratio and equal bulk: one covering 100 percent of the site, one covering 50 percent of the site, and one covering 25 percent of the site. *(Alexander Garvin and C. Christopher Koon)*

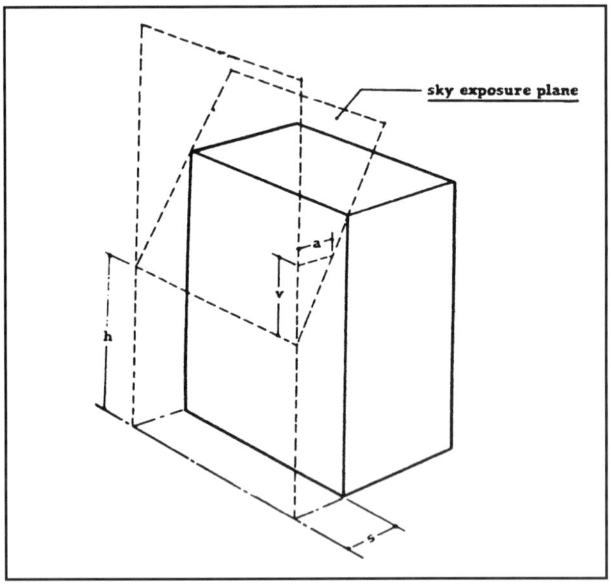

New York City, 1995. The sky exposure plane. *(Courtesy of New York City Department of City Planning)*

Manhattan, 1994. Apartment building designed to fit the sky exposure plane. *(Alexander Garvin)*

turbed by street noise and fumes, the more light and air they will get, and the better their view will be. For these reasons, both apartment dwellers and office occupants pay higher rents for higher floors, with the highest rents on the top floor. Pedestrians, on the other hand, like buildings to be as low as possible. They want to see the sky and feel the sun as they wander through the streets.

Nor do attitudes about building height remain constant. During the first half of the twentieth century communities prized skyscrapers as evidence of prosperity and technological superiority. Chicago and New York even thought it important to compete for the world's tallest building. More recently, San Francisco, Seattle, and other cities have sought to prevent further skyscraper construction.

The second device for regulating bulk is called a *floor area ratio* (FAR), relates a building's bulk to the lot on which it is to be built. It is defined as the total floor area (either already built or to be built) on a zoning lot divided by the area of that zoning lot. Thus, the allowable floor area is determined by multiplying the allowable FAR by the lot area. The maximum allowable FAR depends on city policy. New York, for example, has 10 residential districts for which the allowable FAR ranges from 0.5 to 10 or, with a bonus, 12.

The argument for a floor area ratio as opposed to a height limit is that it allows the developer and architect to select a building configuration that is less costly to produce, more marketable, more appropriate to the uses the building will contain, and less constrained to fit a particular architectural aesthetic. The allowable floor area remains the same no matter what design is selected. For example, a 5000-square-foot lot with an allowable FAR of 2 has a maximum floor area of 10,000 square feet. The building, however, can cover the entire lot and rise two stories, or cover half the lot and rise four stories, or cover one-quarter of the lot and rise eight stories, or any other combination that produces a building with no more than 10,000 square feet of floor area.

Three decades of experience with FARs have demonstrated that, while they afford greater design flexibility, they also produce a chaotic cityscape with buildings that vary in height and are set back differing distances from the property line. These setbacks can interrupt pedestrian movement, causing a decline in retail activity.

Building Placement

In addition to mapping use and height districts, ordinances that were patterned on the 1916 Resolution established "area districts." The term "area" is a misnomer since these area districts specified neither building area nor lot area, but rather the number of feet a building had to be set back from the front,

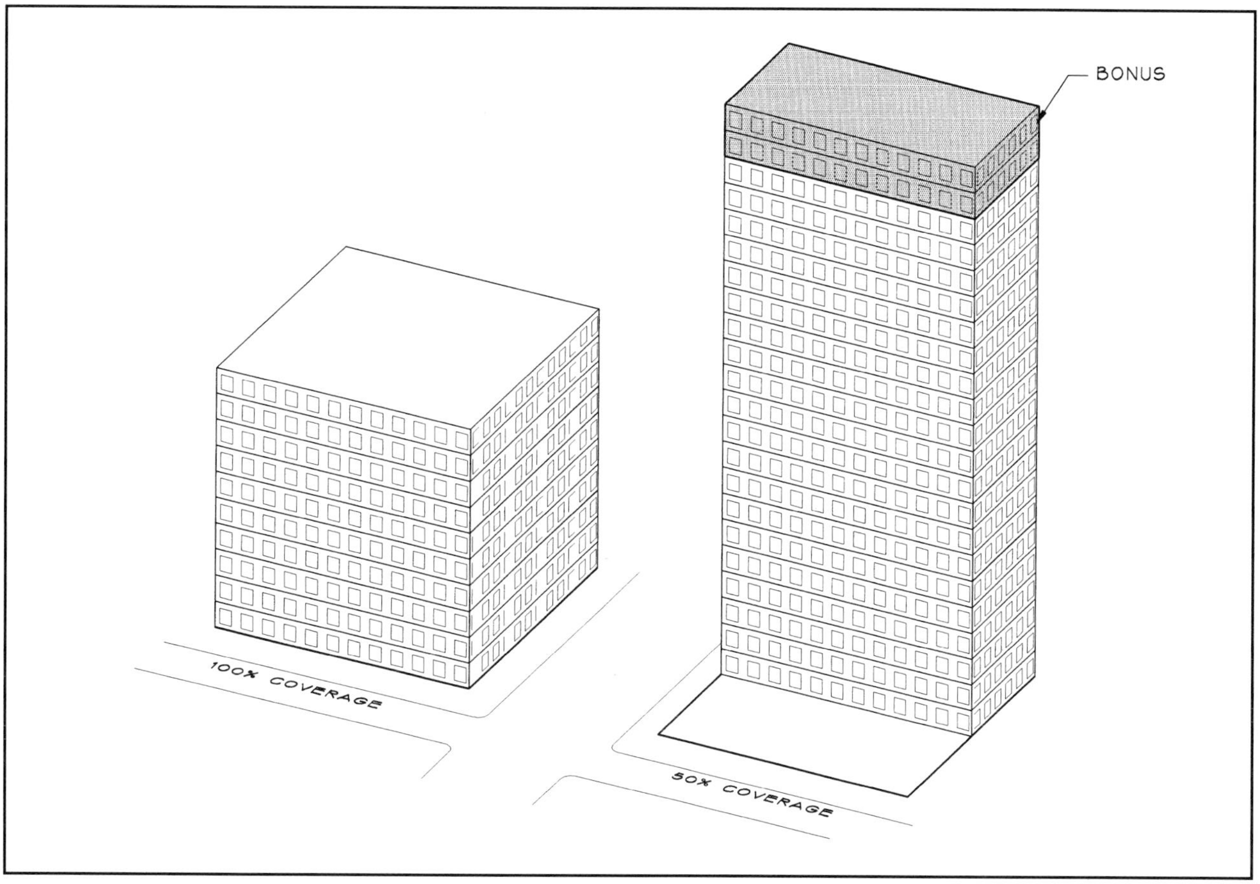

Open Space Bonus. Alternative designs for the same site. One covers 100 percent of the site, the other is able to increase rentable floor area by making use of a zoning bonus that allows 2 square feet of additional floor area for every square foot of public open space, leaving 50 percent of the site for a public plaza. *(Alexander Garvin and C. Christopher Koon)*

rear, and side lot lines. The resulting yards were intended to provide minimal levels of light, air, and privacy for building occupants (especially in detached and semi-detached houses).

Yard dimensions were unrelated to potential uses. Sometimes the leftover spaces that they produced were transformed into off-street parking spaces for automobiles or off-street loading areas for trucks. In other cases, their dimensions made them almost unusable. This was especially true of side yards. Some were so narrow that they could only be used as alleys in which to collect trash.

A second widely applied building placement technique is the *sky exposure plane.* A sky exposure plane is an imaginary inclined plane that extends from the property line. It establishes a building envelope beyond which nothing can be built. Its purpose is to guarantee adequate natural light (and frequently direct sunlight) on both street and sidewalk.

Of all the techniques of comprehensive zoning, building placement regulations have tended to have the most stultifying effect. These well-intentioned requirements tend to become a straitjacket into which architects and developers automatically fit their buildings.

Open Space

Zoning ordinances increasingly have sought to get private-property owners to set aside space for the general public. This space has taken the form of wider sidewalks, plazas, arcades, publicly accessible galleries, and even interior passages connecting streets. New York City's 1961 Resolution did so by introducing two techniques: the *open space ratio* and the *plaza bonus.*

The open space ratio (OSR) for a lot is defined as the square footage of open lot area divided by the floor area. Each zoning district includes a range of permissible OSRs, which together with other regulations determine the allowable floor area. The architect and developer select that combination of open space, building coverage, floor area, and height which best meets their needs and also complies with the zoning. However, if they wish to maximize buildable floor area, they are forced to use larger lots and erect slimmer structures that leave a high proportion of open space.

The plaza bonus is an incentive for developers to provide the public with accessible open areas around their buildings. Such plazas presumably increase pedestrian space in densely

Manhattan, 1968. In Lower Manhattan the floor area bonus for pedestrian open space reduced congestion and often allowed sunlight to reach the sidewalk. *(Alexander Garvin)*

built-up areas and sun and sky in areas with a preponderance of tall buildings. In compensation for this public benefit, developers receive a bonus of additional rentable floor area.

The 1961 Resolution established zones in which every square foot of exterior public plaza entitled the developer to an additional 2 square feet of interior floor area. This bonus "proved almost embarrassingly successful. Between 1961 and 1973 some 1.1 million square feet of new open space was created."[37] Its effectiveness, however, varied significantly. In lower Manhattan, with its narrow twisting streets and busy sidewalks, the plaza bonus produced miraculous results. It freed pedestrian traffic, provided sitting areas, opened vistas to the sky, and even allowed the sun to light up small portions of ground. But opposite parks and along wide avenues it was superfluous. In other places it produced "sterile, empty spaces not used for much of anything except walking across."[38] In 1975, in an attempt to improve the character and utility of these plazas, the New York Planning Commission adopted guidelines for seating, planting, and street furniture, but as with all such guidelines, their success is dependent on the quality of the design.

Variances

Besides the few devices discussed above, zoning resolutions have so many other provisions that they may require several volumes. Given the plethora of requirements, many structures that predate the zoning will not comply with one or more of them. Just as with nonconforming uses, *noncomplying* conditions are permitted to persist, as long as the degree of noncompliance is not increased. However, especially in the case of major renovation, this may not be possible. There also may be problems in erecting new structures that comply with the zoning. For this reason, there has to be a procedure for authorizing variances from the allowable zoning.

In a process that has parallels in all other municipalities, New York City established an appointed Board of Standards and Appeals. The board can authorize a variance, provided that (1) there are unique physical conditions, (2) these physical conditions make it impossible for the property owner to earn a reasonable return if the proposed building completely conforms to the zoning, (3) the variance, if granted, will not seriously alter the character of the surrounding neighborhood, (4) the hardships justifying the variance have not been created by the property owner, and (5) the variance granted is the minimum needed to afford relief.

While these are reasonable standards, in New York and elsewhere there are no clear, quantifiable guidelines for determining compliance with such findings. As a result, some of the individuals charged with providing quasijudicial relief from unreasonable requirements deviate from both the letter or spirit of the required findings. In the absence of either certainty that a variance will be granted or predictability of the degree of relief, property owners frequently hire attorneys who specialize in obtaining variances or appeal to "influential" friends. A few make contributions to "deserving" recipients. If they fail to obtain relief, they go to court.

Village of Euclid, Ohio v. Ambler Realty Co.

From the beginning, comprehensive zoning was attacked as an unreasonable taking of private property. It was not until 1926 that the Supreme Court, in the case of *Euclid v. Ambler*, established that citywide comprehensive zoning was a constitutional exercise of the police power. Since then disputes have centered on specific provisions of particular zoning laws.[39]

The Village of Euclid occupies 16 square miles along the coast of Lake Erie, just north of Cleveland. In 1922, when it adopted a comprehensive zoning resolution patterned on that of New York City, Euclid was a village of farms and scattered suburban houses with a population of 10,000. Two railroads and three broad arteries, including fashionable Euclid Avenue, provided easy access to a burgeoning metropolitan region.

With Shaker Heights, 6 miles to the south, already in development, Euclid seemed on the brink of change. Unlike Shaker Heights, Euclid had neither a development plan nor an owner-developer to shape its future (see Chapter 15). It chose comprehensive zoning. The specific purpose was "to keep Euclid Village as free from unsanitary conditions as possible, and to locate those unsanitary conditions in [a] segregated district."[40]

In 1911 the Ambler Realty Company began assembling an undeveloped 68-acre site between Euclid Avenue and the Nickel Plate Railroad. While its purpose in purchasing this site cannot be verified, land speculation is the obvious explanation. It also seems clear that Ambler Realty thought proximity to the railroad and to Euclid Avenue eventually would result in a sale to an industrial user ready to pay several times its value to a residential developer.

When the Village of Euclid introduced comprehensive zoning, it divided Ambler's property into three zones. The largest and northernmost strip of land that extended along the railroad was, for all practical purposes, zoned *unlimited*.[41] The southernmost strip, extending back 150 feet from Euclid Avenue, was zoned exclusively for one- and two-family houses. The 40-foot wide strip in between was zoned for apartment buildings and community facilities as well as one- and two-family houses. This strip was intended to act as a buffer between residential Euclid Avenue and the probable industrial users in the "unlimited" zone along the railroad. However, its 40-foot width and elongated configuration made construction of apartment buildings and community facilities difficult.[42]

Ambler Realty believed that, by restricting what it could do with its property, the Village of Euclid had deprived it of a significant portion of its value. It went to court claiming that property had been taken without compensation or due process of law, in violation of both the Ohio Constitution and the Fourteenth Amendment of the U.S. Constitution. United States District Judge David Courtney Westenhaver agreed. He also argued that Euclid had imposed a legislatively sanctioned but transitory idea of beauty, which was not an appropriate exercise of the police power. Worse yet, it was a subterfuge "to classify the population and segregate them according to their income or situation in life...[thereby] furthering such class tendencies."[43]

The Village of Euclid appealed the decision. By the time the appeal reached the Supreme Court, the Euclid case had taken on national significance. On the surface the issue was whether Ambler had sustained a decrease in the value of its land and whether that decrease had "gone too far" and thus was a taking. However, with similar zoning ordinances in cities across the country, Euclid became a test case for the constitutionality of this 10-year-old prescription for fixing cities.

There was incontrovertible testimony that land in Euclid would sell for higher prices if it could be used for industrial purposes than if its use was restricted to one- and two-family houses, and for still higher prices if its use was entirely unrestricted. Ambler's brief, therefore, questioned the reasonableness of the government action that reduced value. It pointed out that the most desirable land for residential use, the wooded hillsides along Lake Erie, had been zoned to exclude all but those who could "maintain the more costly establishments of single-family houses." The "men, women, and children who, for reasons of convenience or necessity, live in apartment houses or in more restricted surroundings of two-family residences" and who are "most in need of refreshing access to the lake or the better air of the wooded upland" were segregated to less desirable inland sites. Ambler further argued that by segregating industrial uses to the land around the railroads and relegating those who lived in apartment buildings and two-family houses to territory adjacent to it, zoning imposed one group's notion of order upon the entire community. It even challenged the very philosophy of zoning by arguing that no legislature could "measure, prophetically, the surging and receding tides by which business evolves and grows" and therefore could never "foresee and map exactly the appropriate uses" or "the amount necessary for each separate use."[44]

The case was argued before the Supreme Court in January, 1926. In the months that followed, the National Conference of City Planning, the National Housing Association, the Massachusetts Federation of Town Planning Boards, and a variety of other interested parties filed briefs in support of the constitutionality of comprehensive zoning. The Court scheduled a reargument for October.

In a 5 to 3 decision written by Justice George Sutherland, the Supreme Court found that comprehensive zoning in general, Euclid's ordinance in particular, and its application to Ambler's property constituted a valid exercise of the police power. In explaining the majority opinion, Sutherland wrote that:

> *the segregation of residential, business, and industrial buildings will make it easier to provide fire apparatus suitable for the character and intensity of development in each section; that it will increase the safety and security of home life; greatly tend to prevent street accidents, especially to children, by reducing the traffic and resulting confusion in residential sections; decrease noise and other conditions which produce or intensify nervous disorders; preserve a more favorable environment in which to rear children, etc.*[45]

Once the Supreme Court had spoken, every major city, except Houston, that had not yet enacted a comprehensive zoning resolution adopted one.

Incentive Zoning

When New York City included within its 1961 Zoning Resolution a floor-area bonus for developers who provided public plazas, it crossed the boundary between regulation intended to ensure minimum standards and regulation intended to induce desirable public amenities at no immediate dollar cost to government. The rationale for the plaza bonus is that while the general public benefits from additional light, air, and room for pedestrians, its chief beneficiaries are those who have to bear any additional cost (i.e., occupants, visitors, and owners of the property). While there may be extra expenses in providing this amenity, those expenses are more than offset by the additional revenues that are derived from the additional building-floor area. Most important, while the additional floor area generates additional pedestrian and vehicular traffic, increases utilization of infrastructure and community facilities, and casts longer shadows, this additional burden is offset by the benefits of the public plaza. Since property owners can build a conventional structure and are not obliged to take advantage of the bonus, the "taking issue" is eliminated.

The plaza bonus led inevitably to other forms of incentive zoning. The earliest bonuses were largely for such pedestrian-oriented amenities as arcades, through-block walkways, and small parks. Some cities went beyond pedestrian amenities, enacting bonus provisions for preservation of historic structures, cultural/entertainment facilities, public art, nurseries/day-care centers, low-income housing, and a variety of other "public benefits."[46]

Incentive zoning requires a *base FAR* and a *bonus ratio*, but not necessarily a *bonus cap* and a *FAR cap*. The base FAR establishes the bulk and density that can be accommodated in every location. Presumably, any increase in site utilization beyond this base FAR results in an additional load to the area's infrastructure and community facilities, an increase in noise and pollution, and a diminution of light and air. This negative impact, however, will be offset by the use, improvement, or facility for which there is a bonus.

The *bonus ratio* indicates the amount of additional floor area that can be obtained in exchange for providing the desired use, improvement, or facility. For example, Hartford has a *bonus ratio* of 1:4 for transient parking. Thus, for every square foot of transient parking, the developer is entitled to 4 additional square feet of rentable floor area above the base FAR.

Since there is a point at which the bonusable amenity no longer mitigates the additional burden, some zoning resolutions cap the amount of the benefit. Hartford's transient parking bonus, for example, has an FAR cap of two. Thus, no matter how much parking is provided a property's FAR base cannot be exceeded by more than two FAR. Furthermore, to ensure that the combined effect of various bonus provisions do not result in unacceptable bulk and density, some cities also cap the total possible FAR for different sections of the city.

For bonus provisions to be effective, the value of the additional floor area must be greater than the cost of providing the bonusable amenity. Otherwise, no developer will provide it. Determining a suitable bonus is quite difficult. There is no way to predict with certainty the cost of supplying the bonusable amenity. Not only do development and service costs vary, so does the ability of the developer. Nor is there an accurate means of predicting the value of the bonus. Its value will depend on regional economic conditions, citywide demand, districtwide vacancy rates, project location, site dimensions, building configuration, and even the developer's financial situation. The only predictions that can be made are that if the bonus formula is insufficiently generous, nothing will happen and if it is overly generous, the public will distrust its validity. Unhappiness with Seattle's incentive zoning, for example, became so intense that in 1989, a referendum forced substantial curtailment.

TABLE 16.1
BONUS FOR PUBLIC BENEFIT FEATURES: CITY OF SEATTLE ZONING CODE[48]

Public Benefit Feature	Bonus Ratio*	Maximum Eligible Area
Human service unit:		
new structure	7	10,000 square feet
existing structure	3.5	10,000 square feet
Day care:		
new structure	12.5	10,000 square feet
existing structure	6.5	10,000 square feet
Cinema	7	15,000 square feet
Shopping atrium	6 or 8	15,000 square feet
Shopping corridor	6 or 7.5	7,200 square feet
Retail shopping	3	0.5 times lot area (not to exceed 15,000 square feet)
Parcel park	5	7,000 square feet
Rooftop garden:		
street-accessible	2.5	20% of lot area
interior-accessible	1.5	30% of lot area
Hillclimb assist (escalator)	1.0 FAR	not applicable
Hillside terrace	5	6,000 square feet
Sidewalk widening	3	as required to meet the required sidewalk width
Overhead weather protection	3 or 4.5	10 times the lot's street frontage
Sculptured building top	1.5 square feet per square foot of reduction	30,0000 square feet
Small-lot development	2.0 FAR	not applicable
Short-term parking:		
above grade	1	200 parking spaces
below grade	2	200 parking spaces
Performing arts theater	12	subject to Public Benefit Features Rule
Museums	5	30,000 square feet
Urban plaza	5	15,000 square feet
Public atrium	6	5,500 square feet
Transit station easement	25,000 square feet	2 per lot
Transit station access:		
grade-level	25,000 square feet	2 per lot
mechanical	30,000 square feet	2 per lot
Housing	subject to Public Benefit Features Rule	maximum bonus: 7 times lot area

*Ratio of additional square feet of floor are granted per square foot of public benefit feature provided.

Seattle, the Citizens Alternative Plan (CAP)

Of all American cities, Seattle has the most sophisticated incentive zoning and the most experience with citizen opposition to its effects. The city first adopted incentive zoning in 1963, providing bonus provisions for such pedestrian amenities as plazas and arcades, but without specifying any maximum floor area ratio. As time passed, pressure mounted for zoning incentives that were more sensitive to social issues. By the late 1970s, city officials had begun work on their response: a comprehensive downtown plan and new zoning provisions for both the city's residential neighborhoods and its central business district.[47]

It was the completion in 1984 of the 76-story Columbia Seafirst Center, however, that generated enough political support for city council action. This new office tower had managed to combine enough zoning bonuses to reach an FAR of 28. To prevent further construction of truly giant office towers, the city council in 1985 adopted a *Land Use and Transportation Plan* and new downtown zoning provisions.

The 1985 rezoning divided downtown Seattle into 12 zoning districts. The density for each district was based on its

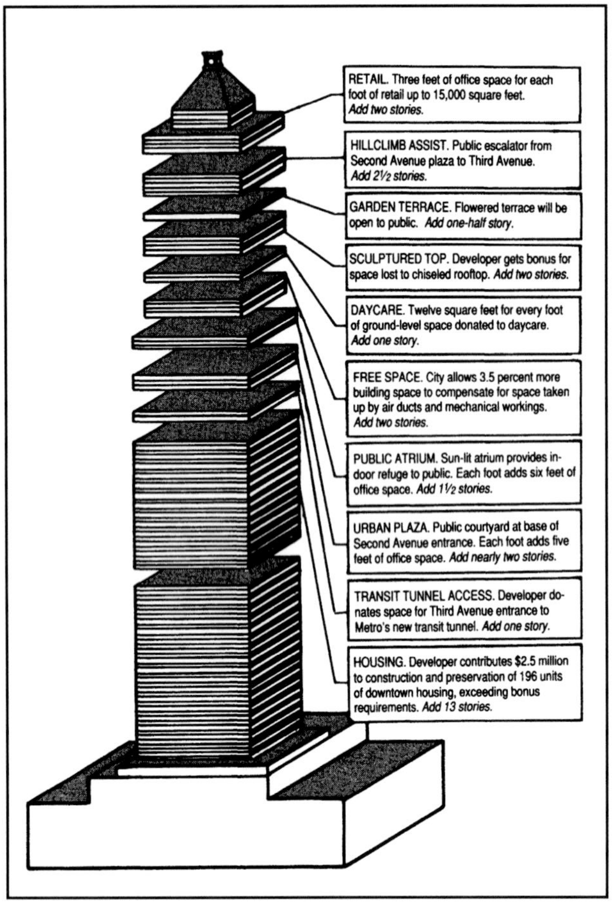

Seattle, 1985. Diagram showing additional bulk accumulated for the Washington Mutual Savings Bank Building by using FAR bonuses made available by rezoning. *(Courtesy of ULI—The Urban Land Institute)*

Seattle, 1990. The 55-story Washington Mutual Savings Bank Building (extreme left) towers over the street. *(Alexander Garvin)*

function and character as well as on projected traffic and transit capacities established by the downtown plan. The number of bonusable items was expanded from 5 to 28 (Table 16.1). This time, however, the rezoning established maximum areas that each public benefit feature could bonus as well as FAR caps for each zoning district. There were also view-corridor, setback, street wall, retail, and height requirements for each district, with a maximum height of 240 feet in the retail core and 400 feet in the office core.

Bonusable "public benefit features" included (1) *pedestrian amenities* (parks, wider sidewalks, plazas, "hillclimb assists" [a.k.a. escalators]), (2) *land use preferences* (performing arts theaters, cinemas, shopping facilities, museums), (3) *social services* (affordable housing, day-care, health, and drug-treatment facilities), and (4) *design features* (rooftop gardens, sculptured building tops, and atria). Some bonuses were directly related to a building's increased occupancy and its impact on the immediate surroundings (parking, overhead weather protection, and transit station access). Others (affordable housing, museum space, and performing-arts theaters) were intended to have citywide impact.

The bonus provisions were usable in a manner that could double the base FAR. In Seattle's most intensely developed office district, for example, a site zoned for an FAR of 10 could—with bonuses—reach an FAR of 20. One has to wonder whether the underlying base FAR was correct to begin with, if a site's bulk and density could be so easily doubled. Were the infrastructure and facilities downtown really able to support such increased utilization, either concentrated at one particular site or cumulatively, if the entire district were developed with the maximum combination of bonuses?

The citizens of Seattle soon experienced the impact of the proposed new downtown zoning because the developer of the Washington Mutual Savings Bank Building chose to comply with the zoning while it was being revised. The building that emerged combined sufficient bonuses to add 28 stories to the 27 permitted by the underlying zoning. The new 55-story tower galvanized an opposition fed up with "runaway" growth, "out-of-scale" skyscrapers, and "dangerous levels" of noise, fumes, and congestion. They were inspired by the example of San Francisco which, in 1986, had approved a voter initiative called Proposition M that capped at 950,000 square feet the maximum amount of new office construction that could be authorized during any single year.[49]

Opponents of the new downtown zoning put together a Citizens Alternative Plan (CAP), which limited new, downtown office construction to a 1/2 million square feet per year until 1995 and 1 million square feet through 1999, and lowered both the base FAR and the height limits in the city's retail and office core. CAP secured sufficient signatures to be placed on the ballot in 1989, and was approved by 62 percent of the voters. Its impact will begin to be felt when property owners have rented the millions of square feet of new office space that came on-stream simultaneously with CAP. However, one does not have to wait to discover what will happen in other cities where voters think incentive zoning has gone too far. They will also demand a "CAP" on development.

Exactions

Some communities adopt policies that make compensatory benefits a requirement of project approval. They perceive property development in terms of the additional load to infrastructure, community facilities, and public services. Rather than just tax future site occupants for this public burden in the same manner that they do current residents, they ask developers to provide "compensatory" amenities. Thus, instead of paying for amenities either with budget expenditures or with a floor area bonus, the community transfers the cost to developers, who pass it on to consumers in the form of higher prices.

Such exactions are common where property development is not as-of-right. In these cases the developer submits the proposal for approval either by agency officials or a public board. Subdivision plan approval is perhaps the most common example. The proposed block and lot layout is reviewed for its impact on traffic, drainage, sewage, waste disposal, water supply, etc. Since standards for approval are left to the discretion of the reviewing entity, there is an opportunity to negotiate for items that will mitigate prospective negative impact. Project approval then becomes contingent on relocating vehicular access, maintaining wetlands, preserving distinctive landscape features, or other changes. In this manner the desires of the reviewer supplant the printed requirements of the underlying zoning.

There is a clear police-power rationale wherever the amenities that are demanded are directly related to the added burdens caused by that particular development. For example, since factories generate truck traffic it is reasonable to require that they provide sufficient off-street loading facilities. Similarly, since shopping malls generate automobile traffic, it is reasonable to require that they provide sufficient space for off-street parking.

When an agency demands an amenity that is not clearly related to a specific development, property owners may legitimately claim it has been exacted from them only because they cannot proceed without agency approval. That is what happened when the California Coastal Commission established as its goal increasing public access to Pacific Ocean beaches and conditioned the issuance of development permits on the property owner's agreeing to provide the public with a path to the beach.

James and Marilyn Nollan applied for a permit to enlarge their beachfront house in Ventura County. The California Coastal Commission agreed to grant them a permit provided that they officially recorded a deed restriction, which established an easement for the public to pass through a portion of their property on its way to the beach. The ostensible rationale for this exaction was that the larger house would decrease the view of the ocean and prevent the public "psychologically...from realizing [that] a stretch of coastline exists nearby that they have every right to visit." The commission also stated that the house would "burden the public's ability to traverse to and along the shorefront."[50]

The case of *Nollan v. California Coastal Commission* reached the Supreme Court in 1987. In a 5 to 4 decision, it found that public access to the Pacific Ocean would not be materially affected if the Nollans built a larger residence on their property and, thus, that the purpose behind the Coastal Commission's action was "quite simply, the obtaining of an easement to serve some valid governmental purpose, but without payment of compensation." The opinion, written by Justice Antonin Scalia, went on to explain that a "legitimate state interest" justifying the exercise of the police power could only exist if there was an "essential nexus," between the regulation and the additional public burdens caused by the development. In the absence of this "essential nexus" the action of the Coastal Commission was deemed to be an unconstitutional taking of private property for public use in violation of the Fourteenth Amendment.[51]

Exactions frequently result in less development than would otherwise be permitted by the zoning, thereby diminishing rental or sales revenue. They also usually increase project cost by requiring a more expensive design, additional construction, or some other contribution. As a result, no developer can be certain that projects which comply with the requirements also will be financially feasible.

The absence of certainty that a project that complies with zoning regulations will be approved or of predictability as to what additional requirements may be exacted can lead to unintended and undesirable results. The most obvious of these is increased project cost. During the weeks or months that an agency negotiates an acceptable project, the developer is forced to spend additional sums to carry the project (i.e., debt service, taxes, maintenance, etc.). This not only increases consumer prices, it also scares away both potential developers and financial institutions. They are simply unwilling to invest time and money in situations whose outcome is unclear.

Another undesirable consequence is influence peddling by individuals who present themselves as being able to obtain necessary approvals. In addition to increasing project costs, this excludes from the development process all but those who are sufficiently well-connected to obtain project approval. The more obvious and easily dealt with problem is graft. If it can be demonstrated that project approval is contingent on payoffs, the guilty parties can and should be prosecuted.

A subtler problem is created by exactions extorted by community groups. Neither venality nor illegality is involved. Project opponents simply agree to drop their opposition in exchange for "mitigating" amenities. In the words of a committee established by the Association of the Bar of the City of New York to examine this issue, such amenities "at bottom constitute taxes, which are not levied evenhandedly on the basis of neutral principles but are required from developers on a case by case basis" and by extension "cast government in an unjust and therefore untenable role."[52]

Special Districts

There will always be districts in which conditions are sufficiently special that, without additional provisions, citywide zoning regulations are unable to accomplish the desired results. Charleston, South Carolina, was the first city to come to grips with this problem when, in 1931, it included in its zoning ordinance an "Old and Historic Charleston District," which included special safeguards for the area's unique historic structures (see Chapter 17). Other cities slowly adopted the same approach, establishing either special historic or special design districts. The use of special zoning districts for other purposes, however, only became prevalent after New York City, in 1969, established a Special Theater District.[53]

Special district zoning took New York by storm. Four years after adopting the Special Theater District, it had a dozen special districts. Twenty years later there would be 33, many of which had no impact whatsoever and one of which was even expunged from the zoning resolution. The reason for the many special districts in New York, San Francisco, Santa Monica, and other cities is that they have real appeal to public officials faced with community demands. They can demonstrate responsiveness without spending one penny, by providing special interests with special zoning districts.

The effectiveness of any special zoning districts is dependent on the appropriateness of its special regulations. This is vividly demonstrated by the provisions of two special districts intended to spur street life and retailing. The first, Manhattan's Special Yorkville–East 86th Street District was a flop. The other, Santa Monica's Third Street Mall District, has helped to revive what might otherwise have become one of the worst planning mistakes on the west coast.

New York City's Special Theater District

New York's comprehensive plan observes that:

> *The theater is a key to a whole complex of communications activities of which New York is the acknowledged center. The hotel and restaurant business also depends to a large extent on the theaters; in fact, the presence of so many legitimate theaters is a very important reason that Manhattan is a major tourist center.*[54]

For this reason, whenever the theater industry is threatened, the city government responds. Radio, talking pictures, and television had in succession threatened the market for live theatrical performances. These were threats over which city government had little control. During the 1960s, however, when New York's theater industry faced a more fundamental threat, elimination of its capital plant, the City Planning Commission responded by establishing a special zoning district.[55]

At that time, demand for new office space in Manhattan was so great and the availability of development sites so small that developers began searching outside the traditional office districts in lower and midtown Manhattan. The theater district, located west of fashionable Fifth Avenue, provided a perfect hunting ground. The Port Authority Bus Terminal was located in the southwest corner of the area. Grand Central Terminal and Pennsylvania Station were half a mile away. The many subway lines that converged around Times Square had excess capacity. For developers, though, its most attractive feature was the existence of large sites, whose buildings (i.e., theaters) used a fraction of the bulk permitted by the zoning. Moreover, these sites could generate substantially greater revenues as office buildings.

The chairman of the Planning Commission, Donald Elliott, recognized the seriousness of the situation. He wanted to find a way in which zoning could alter the probable result of market competition for land in the theater district. The Department's Urban Design Group, under the leadership of Richard Weinstein, devised a floor area bonus that would make it financially and architecturally feasible to include theaters within new office buildings at no net cost to the developer. Elliott, however, did not believe that the developers would be interested in extra floor area if it required them to go through the uncertain, time-consuming process of applying for a zoning change. More important, as an attorney he knew that any spot change to the underlying zoning would be challenged successfully in court if it provided benefits only to a few fortunate property owners.[56]

Working with agency staff, Elliott devised a solution: (1) designate the theater district as a special area, in which generic zoning was supplemented by special provisions intended to

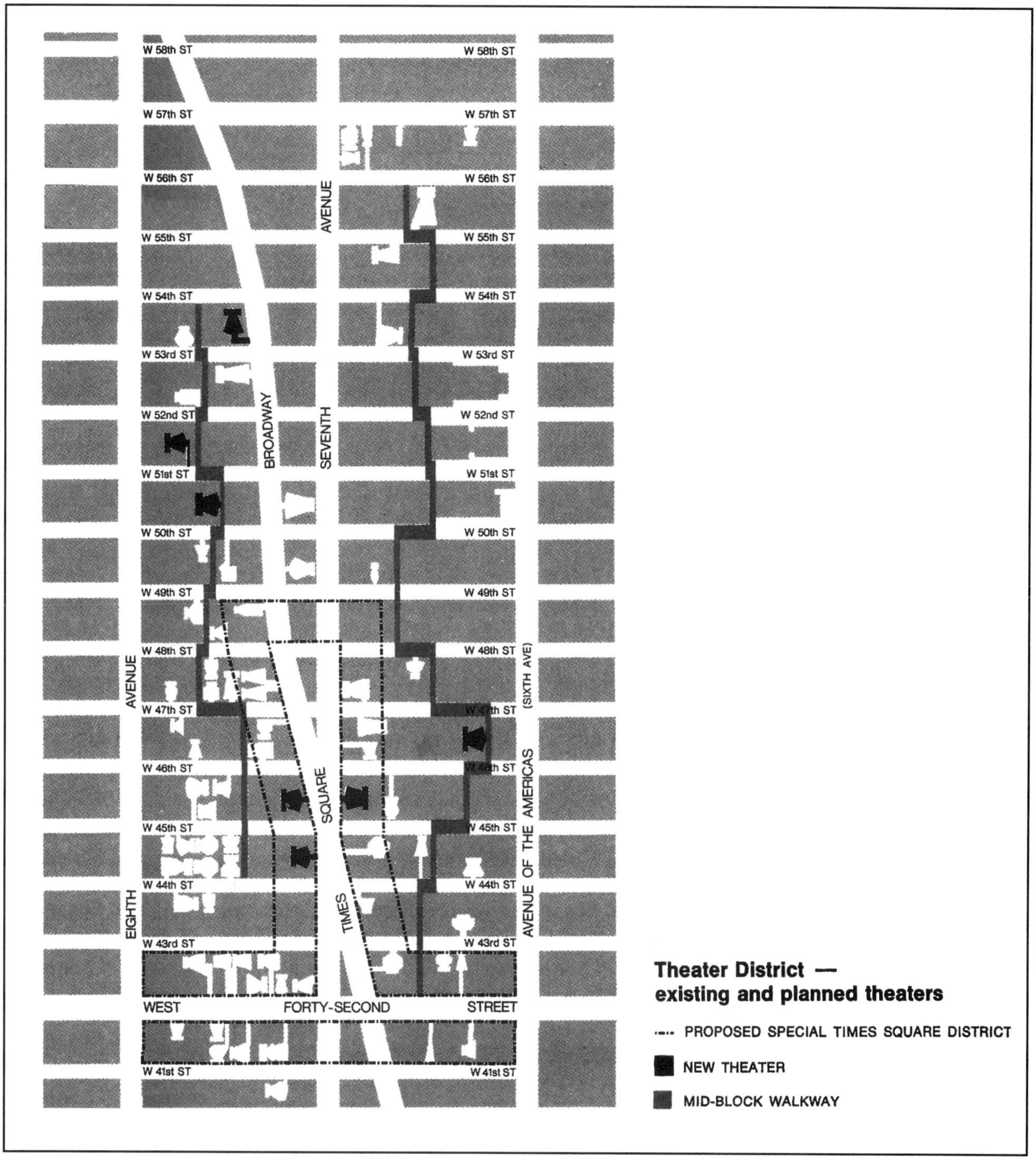

Manhattan, 1969. Map of the Theater District showing sites large enough to build modern office structures. The theaters in black were scheduled for demolition. Five of these structures were eventually built using the special zoning bonus for structures including new theaters. *(Courtesy of New York City Department of City Planning)*

support the theater industry and (2) allow all property owners in the area who were willing to include theaters within new buildings to apply for a *special permit* to erect a structure 20 percent larger than those that did not include new theaters. The proposed Special Theater District did not try to eliminate the pressures of the real estate market. In a manner similar to the generic plaza bonus, it harnessed market pressure, but to produce new theaters rather than public open space. Its bonus provisions could be obtained quickly because the City Planning Commission, having already set forth its land use policy for the

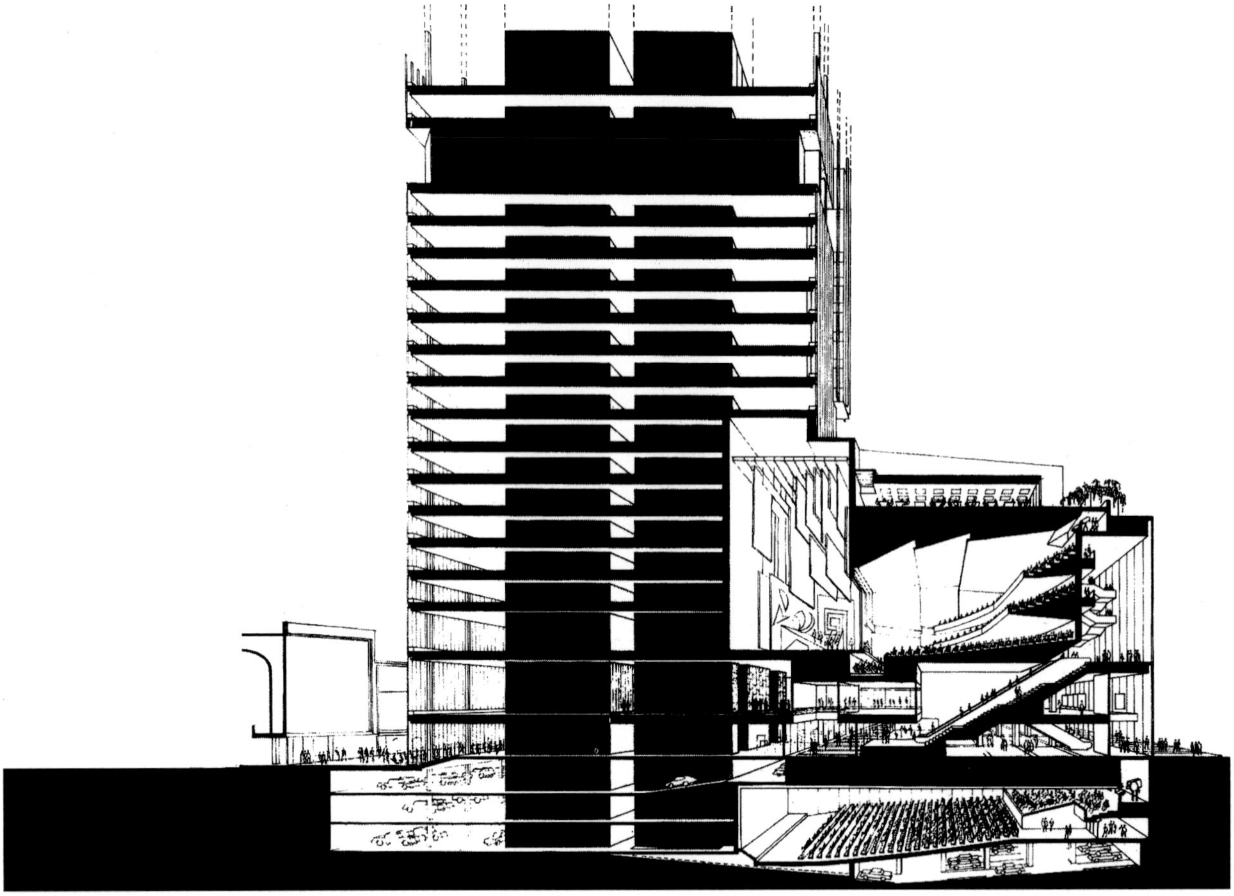

Manhattan, 1969. Illustration showing how a new theater could be included within the structure of a new office building. *(Courtesy of New York City Department of City Planning)*

Special Theater District, did not need to spend months studying each application. Since every property in the district was eligible for a theater bonus, there could be no court challenge from property owners claiming to have been denied their Fourteenth Amendment right to "equal protection of the law." Most important, by making provisions elective rather than mandatory, special-district zoning also avoided the taking issue.

The district's bonus provisions were used in building five theaters, the first since the Great Depression.[57] One of the resulting buildings, the government-subsidized Marriot-Marquis Hotel, required demolition of the Helen Hayes and Morosco Theaters. The furor caused by the loss of these theaters led the City Planning Commission, in 1982, to add a theater rehabilitation bonus, which provided benefits to projects which incorporated theater renovation.

In 1988, the commission replaced the theater construction bonus with a theater retention bonus. This provision allows developers who build within the district to purchase up to 1 FAR (but no more than 50,000 square feet of floor area) from any of the 44 existing legitimate theaters, provided that the theater owner records a deed restriction that requires proper building maintenance and use in perpetuity as a legitimate theater.[58]

The effectiveness of each of these theater incentives is dependent on market demand and processing time. Obviously, during periods in which there is little demand for new office space, developers will not be interested in erecting new buildings and, thus, there will be no market for a theater bonus. That is surely one reason that, during the real estate downturn of the early 1990s, there have been no buildings erected that utilized the theater retention bonus.

The lack of interest in the theater construction bonus during the real estate boom of the 1980s, however, was a product of the time and risk involved. Ironically, the reason for this was the special permit that Elliott devised to speed up zoning changes for the theater district. In 1977, the mayor issued an executive order establishing City Environmental Quality Review (CEQR). Among its provisions, CEQR required an environmental review prior to any discretionary act taken by the City Planning Commission. Since the issuance of a special permit was deemed to be discretionary, the theater construction bonus suddenly required CEQR analysis.[59]

The cost of a CEQR study reduced the value of the theater construction bonus, but not sufficiently to prevent its use. The more important problem was that it could take as long as 24 months to obtain agency certification that the environmental study was complete and satisfactory. At that point, the project entered the city's Uniform Land Use Review Process (ULURP). This meant another 6 months of public hearings and public controversy during which there was no certainty of ultimate approval.[60]

Even if developers had been guaranteed approval, too much time was required. Two years of additional debt service, real estate taxes, and design and processing expenses could easily exceed the value of the bonus. And even if the benefits had been worth the added costs, when the process was completed, market conditions could have changed sufficiently to make the project financially infeasible. For these reasons there were no developers willing to apply for only 20 percent more floor area than they were entitled to as-of-right.

Manhattan's Special Yorkville–East 86th Street District

The Special Yorkville–East 86th Street District, sometimes referred to as the "Anti-Gimbels District," was approved in 1974. It ostensibly arose in response to demands from the residents of Manhattan's exclusive Upper East Side to preserve the "Middle European charm" that was fast disappearing from the area. Eighty-sixth Street had long been characterized by its German-American hofbraus and konditoreis, as well as by a wide variety of small stores catering to Central European immigrants. In fact, the Special District was a response to the customers attracted by a department store and movie theater. In the words of a planner residing in the area: "When Gimbels was built and the movie theater opened in the Gimbels, replacing the old RKO...[they] attracted consumers from Harlem and the Bronx, and my wealthy neighbors objected to blacks coming into the neighborhood. And there began a real pressure to do something to keep further development of this sort from the neighborhood."[61]

The staff of the city planning department perceived the problem to be similar to the competition between theaters and office buildings. In this case, small stores were being squeezed out by chain stores, fast-food, and discount outlets that could pay higher rents. They proposed to change the terms of that competition by establishing a special district that restricted each retail establishment to a maximum frontage of 25 feet. This and other provisions were incorporated into the Special Yorkville–East 86th Street District that was approved by the Planning Commission. The only dissenting vote came from Sylvia Deutsch, who later served as the commission's chair. She predicted its failure, saying that "fast-food establishments can still flourish and small specialty stores will not come in, regardless of frontage size, unless there is a market they can serve."[62]

As she predicted, the Special District only accelerated the decline of the area's older retail establishments. They could not afford escalating rents. Fast-food outlets, high-turnover discount stores, and chain stores, however, could pay through the nose for stores of even limited frontage. Consequently, instead of preventing the demise of a gemütlich 25-foot-wide sauerbraten spot along Eighty-sixth Street, the new zoning spawned a 25-foot Burger King. In 1989, after most of the ethnic businesses had moved away, this ill-conceived Special District was finally voted out of existence.[63]

Santa Monica's Third Street Mall District

The stores along Santa Monica's Third Street Pedestrian Mall also faced competition. It came from Santa Monica Place, the city-subsidized shopping arcade that opened in 1980 (see Chapter 5). Three blocks of Third Street, bounded by Broadway and Santa Monica Place on the south and Wilshire Boulevard on the north, had been pedestrianized in 1965 at a cost of $703,000. Ninety percent of this cost was paid for by local businesses in the form of an assessment. Naturally, there was considerable unhappiness among local businesspeople when it became apparent that Santa Monica Place was attracting their customers. By the mid-1980s, the Mall had become a seedy strip of third-rate retailers, hurting for business.

In 1986, the city adopted the *Third Street Mall Specific Plan,* which set forth a cumulative mix of actions to reverse deterioration and transform Third Street into a thriving shopping street. They included: (1) establishment of the nonprofit Third Street Development Corporation to supervise the mall's revitalization, (2) redesign and reconstruction of pedestrian areas, (3) construction of additional parking, (4) implementation of peripheral street and alley improvements, (5) adoption of the Third Street Mall Zoning District, (6) creation of design guidelines to implement the new zoning, and (7) establishment of an Architectural Review Board to interpret the design guidelines. Together, these actions were intended to transform the mall into a Third Street Promenade that operated "as a unified whole rather than a series of individual shops." The new Promenade extended active use into nighttime hours and would reconfigure merchandising to "be better able to compete with the newer shopping centers which were designed as a single unit."[64]

The special zoning district includes the six blocks bounding the Third Street Promenade. It established a height limit, a base FAR of 3, a group of permitted first-floor "public inviting" uses along the Promenade, and a series of bonuses to encourage improved business conditions. The bonuses included: 0.5 FAR for hotel and mixed-use ("design-entertainment") structures that provide off-street parking, 0.5 FAR for incorporating passageways connecting the public parking garages on each of the six surrounding blocks, and 1 FAR for housing.[65]

Santa Monica, 1991. Third Street Promenade after new development that made use of the FAR bonuses of the Special Zoning District. *(Alexander Garvin)*

Since the adoption of the Third Street Plan, a large number of new buildings have been erected within the Zoning District. The most important are three multiplex movie theaters with 16 screens and mixed-used buildings on the corners of the avenues crossing the Promenade. A typical example is Janns Court, a 131,000-square-foot building that includes underground parking, 2 restaurants, 1 four-plex movie theater, 3 floors of offices, and 32 apartments.[66] The new customers these buildings have brought to the Promenade include office workers and their clients, downtown apartment dwellers, and hordes of evening revelers from all over the metropolitan area who fill its theaters, bars, and restaurants. They have also spurred the renovation of some of the older buildings along the Promenade.

The only problem that remained was the absence of anchor buildings to attract customers to the Wilshire Avenue end of the district and balance the attraction of Santa Monica Place at the other end of the Promenade. In 1995, Barnes & Noble opened a superstore which may provide this missing anchor. The rapid transformation of the Third Street Promenade is a tribute to intelligent integration of planning, design, public improvements, and specially tailored zoning.

Growth Management

Most zoning ordinances only regulate how property can be used and what can be built there. Some also try to prescribe where and when development can take place. The rationale for assigning to government control over the location and timing of development is that an unregulated marketplace can make costly mistakes. Presumably, without growth management, developers will build in areas whose infrastructure, community facilities, and public services cannot handle the impact, either because they will be overloaded or because they are not yet in place.[67]

The explanation for this market failure is that in making location and timing decisions, developers choose to minimize the additional marginal cost to themselves rather than to the community as a whole. The apparent solution is for government to determine the location and timing of development. This, proponents argue, will result in orderly development that begins where there is excess capacity and continues as government installs the necessary infastructure and facilities, until it eventually has reached service capacity and the geographic fringes of the community. In this way, government will not have to spend capital funds or incur operating expenses before there are sufficient users to pay for them.

Some observers argue that growth management by government is unnecessary because the real estate market already includes a mechanism that minimizes development in locations that are not properly serviced or are not yet ready for settlement. They contend that the consumer will pay more to live where there are good schools, adequate water and sewer capacity, good traffic conditions, etc. For that reason developers will more readily choose to build in those areas. Others criticize growth management as "gangplank" planning: once existing residents have moved in and can profit from an area's properly supplied public services, they pull up the gangplank so that others cannot move in and overload the community.

When growth management programs were first enacted by Ramapo, New York, in 1969 and Petaluma, California, in 1972, these were contentious issues. Ramapo chose to supplement its zoning with growth management based on technical analysis of the load on municipal services. Petaluma chose an annual growth cap and a political process to determine which projects would go first. Since there were no precedents for either approach, neither community was able to determine in advance if it would obtain better results than neighboring areas that depended entirely on the conventional zoning nor who would be harmed and who would benefit from such growth management. There is now sufficient experience with both approaches to evaluate the results.

Ramapo, New York

The unincorporated town of Ramapo is located west of the Hudson River, about 30 miles north of New York City. It consists of 49 square miles that are not very different from the rest of surrounding Rockland County. When the Tappan Zee Bridge was completed in 1955, the area became easily accessible to the rapidly suburbanizing population of the New York Metropolitan Area and to home builders eager to profit from this new market.[68]

Residential construction in Ramapo soared from 332 dwelling units per year in the last half of the 1950s, to 785 dwelling units per year between 1960 and 1964. The population more than doubled, rising from 20,410 in 1960 to 47,711 in 1970. In response to the sudden influx of population, the town adopted a series of planning initiatives, many of which were paid for with federal funds. They included a sewer district (1966), a master plan (1966), an official map (1967), a housing code (1968), subdivision regulations (1968), and a 6-year capital improvement program (1968). The most controversial measure, however, came in 1969, when Ramapo amended its zoning ordinance to include a section establishing a special permit procedure intended to synchronize housing construction with the availability of infrastructure, community facilities, and public services.

Ramapo established a system that assigned points for different degrees of drainage capacity and sewer service, as well as for the distance from an improved road, park or recreation facility, and firehouse. Proposed developments that could aggregate at least 15 of 23 possible points were entitled to obtain a special permit allowing them to proceed. If the town's capital improvement plan called for items that would bring the point total to 15, a project could be deferred and given a building permit for the year the necessary service would be in place. Property owners without the necessary 15 points could apply for a variance. Alternatively, they could agree to "buy out" the necessary points by providing at their own expense whatever facilities would bring their total to 15.

The impact of the growth management was dramatic. Residential construction for the period 1970 to 1974 dropped to 233 dwelling units per year, a level lower than prior to the opening of the Tappan Zee Bridge. As a result the population increased by less than 6500 people between 1970 and 1980. Ramapo had wanted to manage growth, not stunt it. Consequently, in 1983 the town voted to terminate its growth management program.

Ramapo's growth management plan clearly slowed development. It also failed to determine location and timing. This was no accidental failing. It is a fundamental flaw of all growth management plans. They have no way of predicting or adapting to economic cycles.

An equally fundamental explanation is the improbability of any community rigidly following either a comprehensive plan or a capital improvement program. Too often, such programs are wish lists—to be revised in the face of changing construction costs, changing estimates of available tax revenue, and changing demands for public expenditures. In Ramapo, the capital improvement plan had to be altered to deal with unanticipated emergencies (major damage from two hurricanes), changes in federal and state assistance programs, inflation, and unanticipated project costs. As a result, Ramapo could not offer sufficient construction sites where the requisite 15 points were available.

Another explanation is regional competition. Developers were not willing to pay for Ramapo's capital improvements when they could build in surrounding areas without adding the cost of these improvements to the cost of development. The same diversion of development activity to surrounding areas occurred in Petaluma and other cities with growth management programs.

Petaluma, 1991. Typical residential development that complies with growth management legislation. *(Alexander Garvin)*

Petaluma, California

Petaluma is located in Sonoma County, California, about 40 miles north of San Francisco. It was founded in 1833 and became a truck-farming community that was prosperous enough to generate a lively array of late nineteenth- and early twentieth-century architecture. Development pressure began to grow after the relocation and widening of Interstate Highway 101 in 1956. This improved artery significantly decreased commuting time to San Francisco and opened vast tracts of Sonoma County farmland to residential development. By the end of the decade, Petaluma had grown 37 percent, reaching a population of 14,085. Steady growth continued and by 1970 Petaluma was a city of 24,870. Suddenly the production of new housing mushroomed, soaring from an average annual increase of 346 units per year during the last half of the 1960s, to 591 in 1970, and 891 in 1971.[69]

The City of Petaluma responded in 1971 by adopting a temporary freeze on development, while it sought a suitable way to control what was thought to be runaway growth. It wished to retain its small-town character and to create a permanent greenbelt that would maintain the distinction between city and country. Petaluma also wanted to encourage filling-in of undeveloped land in central areas prior to peripheral areas that required additional municipal expenditures on community facilities and infrastructure, and to balance development among all sections of the city (recent construction had been almost exclusively east of Highway 101). After a year of public discussion and considerable controversy, the city adopted a 5-year Environmental Design Plan that capped development at 500 dwelling units per year and a Residential Development Control System that established the mechanism for determining where that development would take place.

The criteria established by the Residential Development Control System included the capacity of local water-supply, sewer, drainage, road, fire-protection, and school systems, "quality of design," and the goal of producing 8 to 12 percent low- and moderate-income dwelling units every year. These criteria were to be applied annually to all proposed development projects. A 17-member Residential Development Evaluation Board, chosen by the city council, then voted on the projects that were allowed to proceed.

After 5 years of experience Petaluma revised its Environmental Design Plan. The growth cap was changed to an annual increase of 5 percent, which by the early 1980s meant 700 dwelling units per year. In addition, infill projects of less than 5 acres, projects with fewer than 10 units, and housing for low-income, elderly, and handicapped persons were exempted from the cap. In 1981 another set of revisions replaced the appointed members of the evaluation board with the city's architectural review committee and planning commission and shifted to a rating system that operates year-round. It also increased the exemption to projects of fewer than 15 units. Including all city review and permit procedures, acceptable projects take between 6 and 18 months to obtain approval.

It can be argued that Petaluma's growth management plan has helped the city to retain its charm, architectural distinctiveness, and small-town character. However, the older sections of Petaluma had never really been threatened. It had always been cheaper for developers to build on fresh sites than to assemble lots with old houses and tear them down.

Growth management helped Petaluma to avoid leapfrog development and to grow in a fairly compact manner that minimized additional government spending for infrastructure and community facilities. Development has taken place west of Highway 101, not just on the eastern side of town. Moreover, despite the predominance of single-family house construction, some attached dwellings and cluster developments have also been built.

Petaluma, 1991. Turn-of-the-century buildings that growth management was intended to preserve. *(Alexander Garvin)*

Once Petaluma introduced growth management, virtually all new development included buried utilities, paved sidewalks, and all those good things that planners recommend. Nevertheless, there is little appreciable difference in appearance between suburban development in Petaluma and the rest of Sonoma County. The differences lie in the character of housing construction in Petaluma. The year before growth management was initiated, more than half the new houses built in Petaluma, were sold at or below $25,000 (constant 1970 dollars). At the end of the first 5-year plan only 3 percent were sold at or below $25,000 (constant 1970 dollars). During the same period in Santa Rosa, a city just to the north that had no growth management program, the number of newly built houses selling at or below $25,000 (constant 1970 dollars) remained at 37–38 percent. During that same 5-year period, the percentage of new houses of less than 1900 square feet in Petaluma dropped from 72 percent to 40 percent, while in Santa Rosa it dropped less than 4 percent, to 81 percent.

From the beginning, developers failed to fill Petaluma's annual growth quota. Even after restrictions were loosened in 1977, at least half the programmed housing construction failed to materialize. Growth management proved to be sufficiently cumbersome, time-consuming, and therefore costly, to discourage some local developers from building in Petaluma. Instead, they chose to build in more hospitable, nearby communities. Thus, given the steadily increasing demand for housing in the area, the value of Petaluma's existing dwellings increased, while the variety (in terms of cost and size) of new housing produced has been reduced.

Environmental Review

The Standard Zoning Enabling Act of 1924 and every state law based on it requires the zoning power to be exercised "in accordance with a comprehensive plan." The rationale for this is brilliantly explained by Lewis Mumford, "Zoning without city planning is a nostrum; and city planning without not merely an initial control of the land—which every municipality has in its unplanned areas—but a continuous supervision over its actual development and uses is merely a branch of oratory or mechanical drawing."[70]

Few communities maintain up-to-date comprehensive plans, capital improvement programs, or zoning ordinances that deal comprehensively with the interplay of their physical, functional, economic, social, political, cultural, and environmental issues (see Chapter 18). This absence of serious city planning leads citizens to seek legislation that will deal with issues untouched by comprehensive zoning. That is one reason that Ramapo and Petaluma enacted "growth management." It is also the reason for land use regulations independent of zoning, which protect landmarks, historic districts, and environmental quality. If zoning had been truly comprehensive there would have been no need for supplemental statutes covering historic preservation or environmental review.

The earliest efforts to supplement comprehensive zoning were those of preservationists. Charleston, which in 1931 established the nation's first historic district, chose to make preservation a component of its zoning ordinance. Preservationists, while trying to persuade other communities to create historic districts, directed their main effort at the federal government. The first step taken was the establishment during the 1930s of the Historic American Buildings Survey and the National Register of Historic Places, which listed designated national landmarks. The most important step came when Congress enacted the Historic Preservation Act of 1966. This law required an examination of the impact of actions by federal agencies or federally financed programs on landmarks listed in the National Register. It was this requirement of an impact study that in 1969 prevented the construction of a highway going through the Vieux Carre in New Orleans (see Chapter 17).

The National Environmental Policy Act of 1969

Preservationists were not alone in objecting to the narrow scope of ostensibly comprehensive zoning ordinances. Environmentalists shared their view. They also chose federal legislation as a way of introducing environmental considerations into land use regulation and adopted the impact study technique pioneered by preservationists. The National Environmental Policy Act of 1969 (NEPA) that grew out of their effort is the most significant land use regulation since the enactment of comprehensive zoning in 1916. Like the New York City Zoning Resolution, it has spawned similar statutes in about half the states of the Union.

NEPA sets forth national environmental policy and establishes the Council on Environmental Quality to supervise implementation. Its most important provision is Section 102(2)(c), which provides that:

all agencies of the Federal government shall... (c) include in every recommendation or report on proposals for legislation and other major Federal actions significantly affecting the quality of the human environment, a detailed statement by a responsible official on—

(i) the environmental impact of the proposed action,

(ii) any adverse environmental effects which cannot be avoided should the proposal be implemented,

(iii) alternatives to the proposed action,

(iv) the relationships between local short-term uses of man's environment and the maintenance and enhancement of long-term productivity, and

(v) any irreversible and irretrievable commitments of resources which would be involved in the proposed action should it be implemented.[71]

Thus, NEPA forces federal agencies considering any action whatsoever to determine whether that action is major. If it is, the agency must determine if it "significantly" affects the environment, what the alternatives are, and, if a detailed *environmental impact statement* (EIS) is required, what should be done to see that it is prepared in a procedurally and substantively correct manner.

"Major federal actions" include more than establishing an army base, erecting a post office, demolishing a landmark listed on the National Register, or other actions directly undertaken by federal agencies. The term also includes federal decisions to approve, fund, or license activities carried out by others (e.g., designating a route for inclusion in the interstate highway system, funding an urban redevelopment project, licensing utility companies to build nuclear power plants). As a result, NEPA opened a huge number of previously private activities to public review.

It is extremely difficult to establish a threshold for determining whether an action "significantly" affects the environment. As a result, agencies play it safe. Even activities that are thought to be of minor import are no longer engaged in without prior environmental review, if only to see whether it is possible to avoid producing a full EIS. Since the federal government is involved in a vast array of funding, licensing, and approval actions, NEPA has made environmental review a virtual necessity for a myriad of nonfederal activities that were not previously subject to regulation.

The guidelines for preparing and approving an EIS were established by the Council on Environmental Quality. They involve specific actions that may take years to complete. The relevant agency must decide whether an action requires an EIS. If not, it issues a *negative declaration* and proceeds with the action. When an EIS is required, the agency must first publish in the *Federal Register* a notice of intent to prepare one and, when more than one agency is involved, indicate which is the lead agency with supervisory responsibility.

The EIS must consider both direct impact and secondary effects (e.g., additional traffic congestion, air pollution, noise). In addition, it must assess all reasonable alternatives to the proposed action and their primary and secondary effects. Finally, the relevant agencies must give serious consideration to any detrimental environmental consequences caused by the proposed actions that cannot be practicably mitigated.

Once a draft EIS has been prepared, the responsible agency must publish in the *Federal Register* (and in suitable local newspapers) a notice of its availability and seek comments from the public and from other agencies with expertise or jurisdiction over the action under consideration. All these comments must be considered before the agency prepares a final EIS. This final EIS then must be published prior to any federal agency review, decision making, or course of action, no matter what environmental protection requirements are imposed as part of the approval process.

NEPA's Impact

NEPA was intended to be a method of getting federal agencies to consider the environmental consequences of their actions. While this desirable result has been achieved, too often the process becomes an elaborate, time-consuming, and extremely expensive justification of decisions that already have been made. It has also spawned a bonanza for clerical workers, testing laboratories, engineers, scientists, planners, and lawyers, all engaged in preparing, analyzing, or challenging environmental-impact statements.

Its secondary impact, providing a statutory basis for private lawsuits, is even more important. Controversial projects now can be stalled for years while opponents pursue litigation against the agency responsible for issuing an EIS. The basis for private legal action can be procedural or substantive, or both. As a result, some minor flaw can result in major delays while the relevant agency takes the necessary curative action. In the process, instead of balancing all significant interests, the agency is forced to deal with one particular concern.

The demise of New York City's Westway presents a particularly vivid example of the way in which single-function interests can dominate environmental reviews and warp the decision-making process. Westway was a 4.2-mile-long highway project planned for the western edge of lower Manhattan. It was intended to accommodate regional traffic going from Brooklyn to New Jersey as well as city traffic (especially trucks) then using New York's congested streets.[72]

Westway became part of the interstate highway system in 1970 as a result of a political compromise that included the administrations of Mayor Lindsay, Governor Rockefeller, and President Nixon. However, Westway was no ordinary highway project. In order both to maximize the flow of federal subsidies and to facilitate local approval of the highway, Westway was transformed into a giant redevelopment scheme. The crumbling, obsolete, elevated West Side Highway (which collapsed in 1973) and the 27 rotting piers along the Hudson River were to be demolished and replaced with a 226-acre redevelopment project including 178 acres of landfill. When Westway was formally unveiled in 1974, only a small portion was devoted to a new six-lane roadway, and that was relegated to a tunnel running under the land fill. Of the land to be created along the Hudson, 82 acres were to be for parks, 53 acres for manufacturing, and 35 acres for new housing.[73]

The project received formal approval in 1976. At that time its estimated cost was $1.2 billion. Not one penny was to come from the City of New York. It actually generated cash for the city. Ninety percent of project cost (acquisition, demolition of the abandoned piers, land fill, parks, new streets, etc.) was to come from the federal Highway Trust Fund. The rest would be paid for by New York State. Westway would assume responsibility for the city's Hudson River piers and pay for demolishing them. It would also pay for building a new municipal incinerator and bus garage. Better yet, the city would receive cash for its property. In 1981, President Reagan even arrived with a giant-size reproduction of the $85 million check the federal government intended to issue to pay for the right-of-way.

Almost from the beginning, city officials had to decide whether to exchange the billions of dollars that the Highway Trust Fund would pay for Westway for substitute transportation projects. Congress had authorized such trade-ins starting in 1973. Over the next decade, $6.3 billion had been paid out for trade-ins in 20 states. In 1982 Congress eliminated the

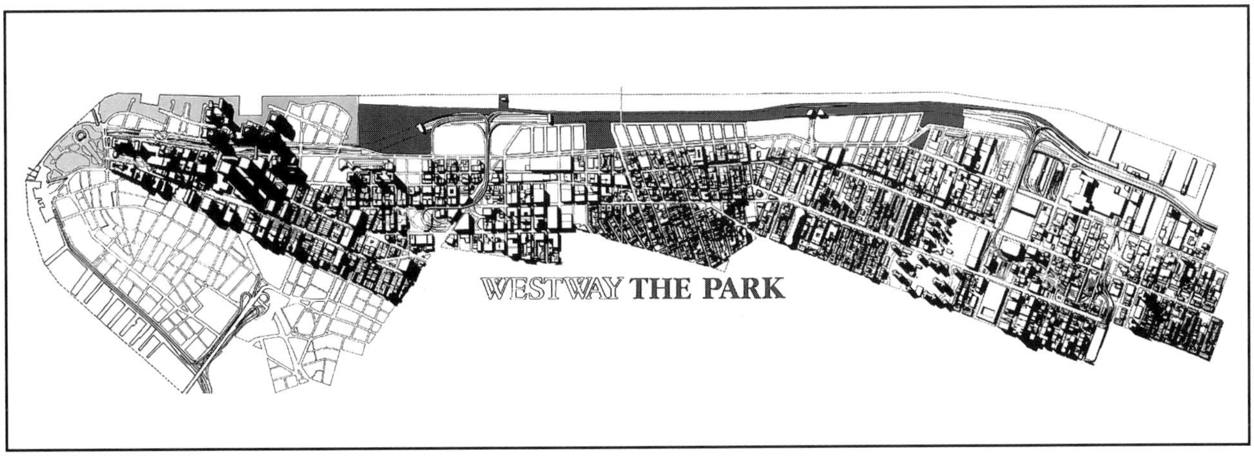

Manhattan, 1985. Plan of the defeated proposal for Westway—an underground highway and landfill project extending the West Side of Manhattan. *(Courtesy of New York City Department of Parks and Recreation)*

Manhattan, 1985. Rendering of the proposed new parkland intended to be created along with Westway.
(Courtesy of New York City Department of Parks and Recreation)

inflation escalator that previously had been applied to the estimated cost of projects from the point of trade-in. It also established a formula for the annual distribution of trade-in money. Under the formula there was no way that New York City could get anything like the annual expenditures that the development of Westway would generate. Thus, in real dollar receipts, an exchange meant less money for New York. Furthermore, nobody was sure that Congress, which had to vote on appropriations for a trade-in (but not for Westway), would agree to spend in excess of $2.4 billion (the 1981 estimated cost of Westway) in New York City, especially because the proposed roadway was so small a part of the project.

Westway raised a myriad of other issues. Should such large sums be spent on a transportation project rather than other city needs? If so, should the money be used to build a highway rather than to repair existing city arteries or to improve mass transit? How would this new roadway affect existing traffic conditions? Was the proposed plan (parks, manufacturing, housing, etc.) the right way to develop 178 acres of created land? How would so large a project affect the neighborhoods bordering Westway? What would be its impact on the city's population, employment patterns, tax base, air quality, etc.? The EIS considered these and dozens of other issues.

Ultimately, *none* of these issues played a crucial role in determining whether to proceed. Westway was brought to a halt by litigation started by a variety of environmental and community interest groups. The critical issue proved to be fish. In 1982 a federal judge invalidated the EIS on the grounds that it had not properly examined the effect on striped bass of demolishing Hudson River piers that lay in the path of Westway. Striped bass were no endangered species. They did, however, in 1980 contribute an estimated $200 million and 5600 jobs to the commercial and recreational fishing industry. Consequently, determining the effect of displacing bass from the waters under the piers, where they paused during the winter migration to the Atlantic Ocean, was no frivolous question.

Over the next 2 years the Army Corps of Engineers spent $3.1 million to catch 57,429 fish (11,415 of which were striped bass), in the words of one of the men in charge of the study, to determine "what fraction of the striped bass we are willing to displace to build the project."[74] The results were insufficiently conclusive to prevent further litigation. Accordingly, when faced with a congressionally imposed deadline for exercising the trade-in option, Mayor Koch and Governor Cuomo decided not to gamble on further environmental reviews. In 1985 they traded Westway for $1.7 billion ($690 million of which was earmarked for a replacement highway, $690 for various transit projects, and $325 million for direct assistance to the Metropolitan Transit Authority). As of 1995, the replacement highway has yet to be started.

More than $250 million was spent on Westway prior to the trade-in. Whether New York City should be building new highways, whether 10 percent of the cost of a new West Side Highway ought to be spent on planning and environmental review, whether it is necessary to transform a simple highway reconstruction project into a 226-acre package of goodies in order to obtain community approval, whether a city should be making major land use decisions on the basis of cash payments from the federal government, all can be debated. What is not debatable is that decisions of this sort and magnitude ought not to depend *primarily* on a judge's opinion about the thoroughness of a study of the spawning habits of the striped bass.

State and Local Environmental Review

Once NEPA had been signed into law, environmentalists obtained similar legislation on the state and local level. Unfortunately, they failed to perceive the fundamental difference between the situation facing the federal government and that faced by local communities. The federal government has no comprehensive mechanism for controlling land use. Local governments, on the other hand, already have land use regulations that have been in place, often for centuries.

In 1970 California became the first state to adopt legislation similar to NEPA. Four years later, 11 states had NEPA-like statutes. By 1984, 24 states had environmental-quality review laws. These statutes make it impossible to make land use decisions simply by complying with published comprehensive-zoning resolutions. Consequently, rather than make decisions based on a community's explicit land use policy, property owners in areas with NEPA-like statutes are forced to make decisions based on an assessment of the probability of lawsuits challenging the validity of environmental impact studies and the cost and time required for both preparing the studies and fighting possible lawsuits.[75]

Few state or local environmental-review laws are as rigorous as those of California. The California Environmental Quality Act of 1970 (CEQA), applies to all state agencies, boards, and commissions, to "the legislative bodies of all cities and counties," and (since 1972) to "all other local governmental agencies." In the case of *Friends of Mammoth v. Board of Supervisors*, the Supreme Court of California interpreted CEQA to apply to any agency granting or denying a permit, including permits for actions taken in compliance with local zoning resolutions and building codes. It observed that they had been enacted without the benefit of rigorous environmental-impact analysis.[76]

As a result of this decision, environmental reviews have become necessary for any action by any agency anywhere in California, except when (1) it is a purely ministerial action that involves no discretion by public officials but only the application of fixed standards and objective measurements or (2) it is specifically exempted by state legislation. Environmental review is thus required prior to the issuance of building and grading permits, sewer- and water-connection permits, franchises, leases, subdivision plans, redevelopment projects, variances, zoning changes, and a variety of other entitlements.

As in the case of NEPA, if the environmental impact is not significant, the relevant agency can issue a *negative declaration* eliminating the need for an environmental impact report (EIR). CEQA, however, is more stringent than its national progenitor. NEPA only requires that federal agencies "consider" the potential significant adverse environmental impacts presented in an EIS. The California version forbids agencies from approving projects that might have significant adverse impact when feasible alternatives or mitigating measures could lessen such impact.[77]

Unlike California, most states have adopted environmental protection statutes that are more closely patterned on NEPA. Nevertheless, the proliferation of environmental-review requirements can restrain development. This is true not only for situations in which a full EIS is required. Even when a project is entitled to a *negative declaration*, the money and time required to obtain agency action retard development and raise costs.

The chilling effect of agency processing is well illustrated by the time required by the New York City Planning Commission to make minor changes to special zoning districts. In early 1987, a property owner decided to build an apartment house in one of the city's many special districts. His site was a vacant corner that had been zoned for residential use decades before the special district had been enacted. The project was only feasible at the area's originally zoned floor area ratio. Despite the fact that the Zoning Map still displayed this FAR, special zoning district regulations permitting that bulk had lapsed 10 years earlier.[78]

The owner met with agency staff, who assured him the change was not only minor, it was also consistent with agency policy. Three months later he filed a City Environmental Quality Review statement. Over the next 18 months various city agencies requested studies whose relationship to the zoning change remains difficult to discern. They included a survey of manufacturing firms within 400 yards of the site (for which no change from its zoned residential use was requested), a compilation of all fire department permits for area gas stations, an analysis of the ethnicity of the surnames of area residents enumerated by the Census of 1850 and 1900, and a study of the site's possible archaeological resources.[79]

Eighteen months after the initial CEQR submission was received by the agency, the city issued a negative declaration; 28 months later the City Planning Commission voted unanimously for the zoning change; 30 months later the zoning change was unanimously approved by the Board of Estimate. Construction plans for a 12-story apartment house were prepared. Unfortunately, by the time they were approved by the New York City Buildings Department, market conditions had changed sufficiently that the project was no longer financially feasible.[80]

The Commmunity Board, City Planning Commission, and Board of Estimate all held public hearings and completed their work within the required statutory 6-month period. The other 24 months of review were caused by civil servants who wanted information that was of interest to them and might possibly be needed to measure or mitigate project impact. There being no specific printed requirements for CEQR submission, they had been given a hunting license to uncover anything that might have a deleterious impact. Conscientious reviewers did their best to cover every possible angle, without reference to the impact of any added cost or delay. The developer, who had to protect the project from lawsuits challenging the completeness of the environmental review, had no choice but to respond to every request for additional information, no matter how frivolous.

Nobody involved with reviewing this request for a *negative* declaration was responsible for completing that review for a specific budgeted sum of money, nor within a fixed period of time. Neither was anybody charged with determining the relative importance of any of the information requested. This is the very antithesis of comprehensive zoning, which is based on a printed document with explicit requirements. Zoning resolutions are produced by consultants and civil servants who must produce it for a specific budgeted sum and then submit it to elected officials for approval. Unlike environmental reviews, the very process by which a zoning resolution is produced and ratified guarantees that it chooses among conflicting goals and establishes priorities.

Most jurisdictions have adopted a more reasonable approach. Hudson County, New Jersey, for example, excludes entire categories of projects from review and routinely processes its few environmental assessments within a period of weeks. Nevertheless, both NEPA and NEPA-like local legislation increase the time required for, and the cost of, development. They generate direct costs (preparing reports and engaging in litigation) and indirect costs (debt service, taxes, and maintenance on a property during the period of agency review). Both increase uncertainty and thereby restrict development to those who have the time, money, and experience to obtain agency approval. There is one serious difficulty, however, that is unique to *local* environmental-quality-review statutes. They invalidate local zoning ordinances. For, if every project has to be examined individually there is no reason for communities to develop carefully considered land use policies that balance conflicting goals. Nor is there any reason for them to maintain a written set of land use regulations that predetermine what land use activity will or will not be authorized.

Ingredients of Success

During the second third of the twentieth century, communities developed and maintained standardized comprehensive zoning regulations that allowed citizens to predict the future character of any area. This reduced the risk of incompatible activity and stabilized market conditions. Once assured of a predictable future, financial institutions, real estate developers, and community residents could more confidently invest in real estate.

Market conditions began to change in the late 1960s. The primary causes were increasing rates of inflation, rising interest rates, changing income tax formulas, new banking procedures, and other factors that had little to do with land use regulation. Maintaining existing land use regulations could *not* have prevented real estate prices from rising. However, instead of maintaining existing land use regulations to help steady the investment climate, governments did precisely the opposite. Heady with the success of comprehensive zoning, they introduced incentive formulas, special zoning districts, growth management plans, and environmental-quality-review legislation. These innovative land use regulations increased the cost of complying with government regulations, the complexity of obtaining institutional financing, and the uncertainty of government approval. However, like the simpler statutes of the middle third of the twentieth century they only succeeded during periods of market demand. After all, there is nothing to regulate when nobody wants to build.

Market

There is a false notion among proponents of land use regulation that their statutes will inevitably affect the real estate market. In fact, they may be irrelevant. No matter what zoning provisions had been adopted for Manhattan's Eighty-sixth Street, for example, the number of German and other middle-European retail outlets would have declined in direct proportion with the decline in the area's immigrant population.

In many cases, land use regulation does affect the market. Improperly conceived land use regulations can stifle development pressure. Ramapo's growth management plan, for example, curtailed demand for what otherwise would have been viable development sites.

Location

There are two components of every zoning resolution—text and maps. Success lies in applying appropriate regulations (text) to the appropriate locations (map). The nation's first comprehensive zoning resolution provides a dramatic illustration of the successful combination of map and text. Its authors wanted to guarantee the city's most powerful commercial enterprises an auspicious environment in which to do business. By mapping Fifth Avenue below Central Park as a district in which manufacturing was forbidden, they successfully manipulated market pressure to a location that the business community wanted.

New York City's 1961 Zoning Resolution includes an equally dramatic illustration of the importance of location, one that failed. Its authors assumed continuing demand for manufacturing space and zoned numerous sections of the city for manufacturing, including enormous sections of lower

Manhattan. In fact, manufacturing employment in Manhattan, as in most large cities, was already declining. Between 1956 and 1989, the number of industrial jobs plummeted from 532,000 to 226,000.[81]

When the 1961 Zoning Resolution was adopted, multistory industrial lofts in many locations of lower Manhattan were already partially vacant. As demand for the uses specified by the zoning declined, so did prices. In some areas, SoHo and Tribeca in particular, the availability of cheap space attracted uses quite different from those established by the zoning. Eventually, "illegal" tenants forced the City Planning Commission to legitimize their occupancy by creating special zoning districts for SoHo and Tribeca (see Chapter 17). By continuing to zone other locations for manufacturing despite insufficient demand for such uses, public officials prescribed for these areas a future of increasingly vacant and underutilized structures.

Manhattan, 1995. Seagram Building Plaza on Park Avenue. *(Alexander Garvin)*

Design

There are a few communities, such as Santa Barbara, California, and Santa Fe, New Mexico, where appearance is crucial. These cities have nurtured sizable tourist industries by requiring all new construction to comply with an idealized regional esthetic (see Chapter 17). In most cities, however, the design component of land use regulation is not a matter of architectural style. It is an expression of land use policy. The placement of buildings along a street is a good example. If the goal is to improve pedestrian circulation, buildings should be required to set back a minimum distance from the property line, thereby obtaining wider sidewalks. On the other hand, if the goal is to increase the continuity of retail shopping, setbacks from the property line should be forbidden, thereby preventing any interruption in window shopping.

The trick is to stick with simple design requirements that will produce a suitable and consistent physical environment. Washington, D.C., provides an apt illustration. Nearly a century ago, Congress enacted height limits intended to strengthen the symbolic character of the national capital, while simultaneously ensuring plentiful light and air. These height limits were related to the width of streets and their role within the city. Neither architects nor developers could misconstrue this simple device, nor could they subvert it. It helped Washington to develop into a gracious city that is particularly consistent in appearance and in which the relative importance of each thoroughfare is reflected by the character of adjacent buildings.

Architects and developers frequently terminate the design process when they have complied with the letter of the law. This transforms minimum requirements into standardized designs that make a mockery of land use regulation. New York City's sky-exposure planes are a good example. They were intended to—and did—increase light and air for both pedestrians and building occupants. Unfortunately, too many architects and developers devised schemes that were *primarily* fitted to the relevant sky-exposure plane. As a result, New York is filled with hundreds of office and apartment buildings built in the shape of stepped pyramids that may increase the availability of light and air but contribute nothing to the functioning of the city or to the coherence of its appearance.

Public officials not only disfigure cities by allowing minimum design requirements to be transformed into standard market products. They also do so by pursuing momentary fashions rather than fundamental design principles. A good example is New York City's plaza bonus. It was adopted in an attempt to encourage development like the extraordinarily beautiful Seagram Building with its gracious public plaza on Park Avenue.

The design, by Mies van der Rohe and Philip Johnson, paid no attention to setback regulations, height limits, or sky explosure planes. In fact, it could not have been built without zoning modifications. The glorious pedestrian environment it creates is a product of the designers' concern for the way in which people walk in, out, and past the building: the approaches along Park Avenue, 52nd and 53rd Streets, the diagonal movement up steps onto to the site, the interplay of visitors on the plaza, the changing views of the city as one passes into the glass-enclosed 24-foot high elevator lobby.[82]

Dozens of buildings erected after 1961 made use of the plaza bonus. Not one creates a pedestrian environment that equals what Mies and Johnson achieved. In lower Manhattan, the additional pedestrian space has been a genuine asset. Elsewhere, the plaza bonus has resulted in some of the nation's most expensive but least necessary open space. These plazas could have been avoided if public officials had not unthinkingly adopted a fashionable design and instead only applied it to situations in which it would be beneficial.[83]

Financing

Land use regulations mandate expenditures for planning and processing, as well as specific configurations of use, bulk, and density, and public amenities that would not otherwise be provided. They all increase the cost of development, affect the availability of financing, and cause consumer prices to increase. In some cases these added costs are justifiable even to the property owner (e.g., off-street parking for retail stores, off-street loading facilities for factories, ticket-holder waiting space for movie theaters, etc.). However, too often they are adopted without any consideration of affordability.

In the case of both scattered, early, land use restrictions and later comprehensive zoning, the community as a whole carried the cost of planning. It paid these costs because individual property owners had no interest in or reason to develop city-wide policies and could not be forced to do the necessary planning. Communities also did so because they thought it only fair that these costs be shared by everybody who benefited. More recent discretionary forms of land use regulation, such as state environmental-review statutes, transfer this cost to individual property owners who, in turn, pass them on to their customers.

Discretionary reviews, such as those required by some growth-management programs, NEPA, and NEPA-like statutes, add uncertainty and the cost of litigation over the validity of decisions. Their major impact, though, comes from adding the cost of carrying the property (debt service, taxes, maintenance, and equity capital) during the review period. In the case of New York's theater-construction bonus, this was sufficient to preclude further theater construction, despite a potential 20 percent increase in buildable floor area.

The most pernicious form of increased cost is one that does not cost the consumer or the government any cash. It is paid for by degrading the environment. Such situations are caused by regulations that induce developers to pay for public facilities that elected officials are not ready to fund through normal budgetary procedures. Seattle's pre-CAP zoning provides a good example. The local government did not appropriate money to pay for sculptured building tops, skylit atriums, or escalators. Instead it offered downtown property owners added floor area as compensation for providing them. The electorate would not tolerate this prostitution of zoning and voted to CAP development.

Entrepreneurship

The beauty of comprehensive zoning is that it minimizes the time, effort, and money needed for property development. Its requirements are readily available in a published document that can be purchased by community residents, property owners, and their architects. Most important, it provides lending institutions, developers and their consumers with *certainty* that all development will comply with preestablished rules and *predictability* as to the future character of the environment. Without such government guarantees, lending institutions would be far less likely to provide the credit needed for any community to prosper.

There is a second, equally important result. The certainty and predictability of preestablished rules reduces risk. This, in turn, increases the number of people willing to get involved with real estate development. It explains why development during the middle third of the twentieth century was dominated by small real estate entrepreneurs. The resulting competition (together with New Deal banking reform, federal income-tax incentives, and highway construction) helped to keep the price of real estate reasonable and allowed the national rate of home ownership to rise from one-third to two-thirds of the population (see Chapter 8).

As the regulatory environment has grown more complex, the rules less certain, and the cost of doing business greater, the number of players in the development game has been curtailed. Increasingly, real estate has become the preserve of sophisticated, well-financed entrepreneurs, well-connected consultants with specialized knowledge of regulatory requirements, and seasoned veterans able to interpret and manipulate government operations. Sadly, the landscape they are creating is neither appreciably more convenient nor more beautiful. It is only more expensive and more likely to generate community opposition.

There is another, even less-attractive, result. The lack of certainty and predictability has increased the danger of influence peddling. Developers who require negative declarations, special permits, or any other discretionary government action are inevitably tempted to hire advocates who they believe (often erroneously) can influence the decision. They also are tempted to make deals with community organizations and special interest groups whose assistance they (also, often erroneously) believe can influence the decision.

In this increasingly discretionary environment some developers expedite favorable action by paying off government employees. No one should tolerate such graft. Those making or receiving payoffs belong in jail. Unfortunately, communities across the country unwittingly increase opportunities for corruption by increasing the number of land use regulations that require discretionary action by government officials.

Time

Time is usually the forgotten component of land use regulation. When it becomes a conscious ingredient, however, it can bring significant improvement to city life. Land use regulations affect the time in which an individual passes through an area, the 24-hour period during which people use the area, and the period of years during which the character and utilization of that area can change significantly.

The land use regulations for Santa Monica's Third Street Promenade illustrates how successful land use regulation can shape the first two periods of time. These regulations include specified ground-floor retail uses along the Promenade and FAR bonuses for projects that provide direct pedestrian access to the Promenade from public parking structures and for projects that include hotels, department stores, and design/entertainment centers. Together, they combine to shape the time spent walking from parking, past impulse-shopping facilities, on to more substantial retail destinations. They also encourage land uses that extend patronage beyond weekdays to nights and weekends. Once the Third Street Special Zoning District was enacted, developers responded by remodeling or rebuilding many of the sites along the Promenade. In short order this seedy strip of stores that used to close by 6:00 PM, became one of the Los Angeles region's liveliest shopping areas. Its movie theaters and restaurants attract crowds into the wee hours of the morning, 7 days a week.

Growth-management plans are an example of land use regulation that extends the conception of time beyond hours or days, to a period of years. Essentially, they are a form of timed zoning. When conceived to extend over several seasons, growth management can reduce the load on overburdened facilities and prevent government from spending extra sums to play catch-up. For a growth management plan to be successful, however, it must include a capital improvement program that outpaces privately financed real estate development and an annual threshold for additional construction that exceeds market demand. Petaluma's growth management strategy provides an excellent demonstration of these principles. It established a growth threshold that was double the number of housing units actually produced. As a result, Petaluma was able to minimize additional capital expenditures without unduly restraining construction.

Land Use Regulation as a Planning Strategy

We have created a crazy quilt of land use statutes and discretionary procedures that needlessly increases the price of housing, places of employment, and virtually everything else. These obsolete and often conflicting statutes disfigure the landscape with inappropriate structures, prevent large territories from being used in economically productive ways, generate angry citizen protests, and require for their operation an ever-increasing army of bureaucrats and consultants. It is time to replace this crazy quilt with a single, easy-to-understand statute that truly balances competing interests and nurtures the development of attractive, healthy, affordable communities.

There is no way for most local and regional political jurisdictions to produce, much less approve, a truly comprehensive land use statute. Only the very largest cities can afford the price. Unfortunately, the complexity of their politics and the urgency of competing demands for their money makes it unlikely that they will make the necessary budget allocation or political commitment. Even if the necessary talent, money, and commitment were forthcoming, there would be years of litigation over the adequacy of environmental impact studies.

Only the federal government can cut through this thicket and open the way for desperately needed change. The task is not as easy as it was in 1924, when Secretary of Commerce Herbert Hoover commissioned the Standard State Zoning Enabling Act. At that time, there were relatively few communities with comprehensive land use regulation, fewer court decisions defining the requirements of such regulation, and even fewer "experts" in the field. Today, the authors of any model statute would have to confront a powerful array of interests represented by existing local and state statutes. They would have to consider a huge quantity of complex and frequently conflicting objectives. (Environmental protection alone requires consideration of topography, air quality, water supply, waste disposal, soils, drainage, floods and floodplains, vegetation, natural habitats, etc.) They would have to meet the objections of lawyers, architects, engineers, city planners, and other consultants whose careers are dependent on the existing pattern of land use regulation. A task of this magnitude can only be tackled by talented individuals who can rely on the power, resources, and support of the federal government.

The Secretary of Housing and Urban Development (an agency that did not exist in 1924) should commission a Model State Land Use Act and a Model Local Land Use Act. The Model State Land Use Act would consolidate and replace existing state and regional legislation concerned with zoning, historic preservation, environmental protection, and all other land use regulation. Its provisions would apply to any property that at the time of enactment was not subject to local comprehensive zoning resolutions and within 5 years of enactment to all real property that was not subject to the Model Local Land Use Act.

The Model Local Land Use Act would establish common regulations to apply anywhere that they had been adopted. It would provide the certainty and predictability that does not now exist and without which the private market cannot properly function.

For these model land use statutes to be successful they need an intelligent text, an effective way of applying it to local conditions, an easy approach to administration, and an appropriate mechanism for continually changing both contents and application.

The objectives for their text should be clarity, simplicity, and brevity. This is no small task because any new statute would replace an increasing array of complex land use laws. This is not just a problem of substance. It is also a problem of language. Too many laws and the administrative regulations instituted to implement them consist of negatives, double negatives, exceptions, and qualifications. There is no need for any intelligent person to face a zoning resolution such as that of New York City, which is replete with language like:

> *However, no existing use shall be deemed non-conforming, nor shall non-conformity be deemed to exist solely because of... (c) The existence of conditions in violation of the provisions of either Sections 32-41 and 32-42, relating to Supplementary Use Regulations, or Sections 32-51 and 32-52 relating to Special Provisions Applying along District Boundaries, or Sections 42-41, 42-42, 42-44, and 42-45*

relating to Supplementary Use Regulations and Special Provisions Applying along District Boundaries.[84]

While the model acts would standardize land use regulations throughout the state (and, one hopes, the nation) and would enumerate criteria to be used for mapping applicable regulations, the maps that established their application to specific locations would be determined locally. As a result, local governments would have wide latitude in combining them to fit their goals and to reflect often profound differences in topography, climate, history, and social, political, economic, and cultural objectives. The model acts also would set forth standards and procedures for establishing special zoning districts for those few situations that could not be covered by the model text.

These statutes should aim for equity, efficiency, and economy of operation. The best way to achieve this aim is to eliminate all discretionary action and make the statutes self-enforcing. This can be done by transferring the permitting process from government into the hands of licensed professionals. Only professional engineers, architects, and lawyers licensed by a designated state agency would be allowed to issue building permits. For these professionals to obtain their licenses they would have to successfully complete a training program operated by the designated state agency and subsequently pass a licensing examination. Anybody licensed to issue permits who did so improperly would lose the right to issue permits, have his or her professional status revoked, and be subject to substantial fines.

Virtually all existing land use regulations suffer from a common flaw. They envisage an ideal end-state without providing for changing market conditions or changing community priorities. For this reason, the model statutes must establish triggering mechanisms for changing regulations as well as criteria for determining the character of those changes. The triggering mechanism could be a regular event (e.g., the decennial census) or a specific condition (e.g., a threshold vacancy rate). Under no circumstances, however, should it be left to the discretion of local officials. Otherwise, the quantity of land assigned to inadequately productive uses will continually increase. Similarly, the new statutes must require publication of an estimate of the impact on consumer prices of any regulatory changes. Otherwise, public officials will continually add individually desirable mandates that are ostensibly paid for by property owners without any information about their likely cost to a property's occupants or to the community as a whole.

There is no way to guarantee that suitable model land use statutes can be developed. Nor is there any guarantee that they will be widely accepted or even be successful. But if we do not try, cranes will continue to erect intrusive and unsightly new buildings; unwanted land uses will continue to disfigure otherwise delightful neighborhoods; needless actions will continue to befoul land, sea, and air—all accompanied by escalating prices and increasingly bitter political controversy.

Notes

1. Fred Bosselman, David Callies, and John Banta, *The Taking Issue,* Council on Environmental Quality, U.S. Government Printing Office, Washington, D.C., 1973, pp. 51–104.
2. Seymour I. Toll, *Zoned American,* Grossman Publishers, New York, 1969.
3. For an economist's explanation of the rationale behind government intervention into the marketplace, see Otto Eckstein, *Public Finance,* Prentice-Hall Inc., Englewood Cliffs, 1967, pp. 8–13.
4. Franklin J. Havelick and Michael Kwartler, "Sunnyside Gardens: Whose Land Is It Anyway?" *New York Affairs,* vol. 7, no. 2, New York University, New York, 1982, pp. 65–80.
5. *Shelley v. Kraemer,* 334 U.S. 1 (1948).
6. For a discussion of the police power and nineteenth-century court interpretation of its applicability, see Stanley K. Schultz, *Constructing Urban Culture, American Cities and City Planning 1800–1920,* Temple University Press, Philadelphia, 1989, pp. 33–91 and Bosselman, Callies, and Banta; op. cit., pp. 105–123.
7. *Mugler v. Kansas,* 123 U.S. 623, 8 S. Ct. 372 (1887).
8. Bosselman, Callies, and Banta; op. cit., pp. 124–138.
9. *Pennsylvania Coal Co. v. Mahon,* 260 U.S. 393 (1922).
10. Justice John Paul Stevens, writing for the majority in the case of *Keystone Bituminous Coal Association v. De Benedictus,* U.S. 107 S. Ct. 1107 (1987), took a somewhat different approach explaining that the regulation of mining rights was appropriate when it applied to all property (not just that of coal companies) and balanced the "private economic interests of the coal companies against the private interests of the surface owners."
11. Theodora Kimball Hubbard and Henry Vincent Hubbard, *Our Cities To-day and To-morrow: A Survey of Planning and Zoning Progress in the United States,* Harvard University Press, Cambridge, 1929, p. 21.
12. Elaine Moss (editor), *Land Use Controls in the United States: A Handbook on the Legal Rights of Citizens,* National Resources Defense Council, Inc., New York, 1977, pp. 117–118.
13. Robert W. Stewart and Ronald B. Taylor, "Coastal Commission—An Ideal Gone Astray," *Los Angeles Times,* September 7, 1987.
14. Hawaii is the sole exception. There, land use regulation has always been a state function. A statewide comprehensive zoning ordinance was adopted in 1961.
15. *The Records of New Amsterdam,* I, 4, quoted in James Ford, *Slums and Housing,* Harvard University Press, Cambridge, 1936, p. 28.
16. Marc A. Weiss, *The Rise of the Community Builders,* Columbia University Press, Cambridge, 1987, pp. 79–106.
17. John J. Costonis, *Icons and Aliens: Law Aesthetics, and Environmental Change,* University of Illinois, Chicago, 1989, pp. xv–xvi.
18. This explanation of height limits in the national capital does not appear in Costonis's book. It is entirely my own, as is the discussion of the Chinese laundry cases below.
19. *Yick Wo v. Hopkins* and *Wo Lee v. Hopkins,* 118 U.S. 356 (1886).
20. Ibid.
21. Hubbard and Hubbard, op. cit., pp. 162–163.
22. Some attempts at comprehensive planning had been initiated in 1914, when the city established a Committee on the City Plan. However, its report, *Development and Present Status of City Planning in New York City,* had only a tangential relationship to the 1916 Zoning Resolution. Nor did the 1961 ordinance evolve from a comprehensive plan. Although the city established a planning commission in 1938 and required it to produce a comprehensive plan, none was produced until 8 years after the 1961 Resolution had been enacted (see Chapter 18).
23. Toll, op. cit., pp. 173–183.
24. *New York Times,* advertisement, March 5 and 6, 1916.
25. The height limits were 70 feet for streets less than 60 feet wide and 80 feet for wider streets.
26. Alexander Garvin (project director), *Neighborhood Preservation in New York City,* New York City Planning Department, New York, 1973, p. 137.
27. Toll, op. cit., pp. 143–157.
28. The maximum bulk for any office building permitted by the 1961

Zoning Ordinance is 18 times the lot area on which it is erected or, with special bonuses, 21.6.
29. Harrison Ballard and Allen, *Plan for Rezoning the City of New York,* New York City Planning Commission, New York, 1950.
30. Interview with Robert F. Wagner, Jr., October 16, 1991.
31. Carter B. Horsley, "The Sixties," p. 29, in *Planning the Future of New York City,* New York City Planning Commission, New York, 1979.
32. Voorhees Walker Smith & Smith, *Zoning New York City,* New York City Planning Commission, New York, 1958.
33. The switch from height limits to a floor area ratio had been proposed by Harrison Ballard & Allen in 1950 and had already taken place in Seattle, which had adopted many of their proposals as part of its comprehensive rezoning of 1957 (Harrison Ballard & Allen, op. cit., pp. 44–45).
34. Jane Jacobs, *The Death and Life of Great American Cities,* Random House, New York, 1961, p. 152.
35. One has to wonder how this could be done in the absence of a regularly updated, comprehensive city plan and capital improvement program.
36. Jacobs, op. cit., p. 205.
37. William H. Whyte, *City,* Doubleday, New York, 1988, p. 233.
38. Ibid., p. 234.
39. *Village of Euclid v. Ambler Realty Co.,* 272 U.S. 365 (1926), and Toll, op. cit., pp. 213–253.
40. Charles X. Zimmerman, mayor of Euclid, quoted by Toll, op. cit., p. 215.
41. It was not entirely unlimited because there was a class of uses that was prohibited altogether.
42. *Village of Euclid v. Ambler Realty Co.,* 272 U.S. 365 (1926).
43. At 297 Fed. 316, quoted by Toll, op. cit., p. 215.
44. *Village of Euclid v. Ambler Realty Co.,* "Brief and Argument for Appellee," pp. 78–79 and 83, quoted by Toll, op. cit., pp. 232–233.
45. *Village of Euclid v. Ambler Realty Co.,* 272 U.S. 365 (1926).
46. Terry Jill Lassar, *Carrots and Sticks: New Zoning Downtown,* Urban Land Institute, Washington, D.C., 1989.
47. Historical and statistical material on zoning in Seattle is derived from Lassar, op. cit., especially pp. 20–25, 31–33, 81–82, 121–122; Terry Jill Lassar, "Seattle's Zoning Saga," *Urban Land,* September 1988, Urban Land Institute, Washington, D.C., pp. 34–35; T. Richard Hill, "Seattle's Voters CAP Downtown Development," *Urban Land,* August 1989, Urban Land Institute, Washington, D.C., pp. 32–33; and Robert Stevenson, "Downtown Seattle: To CAP and Beyond," 1991, unpublished.
48. Abstracted from Lassar, *Carrots and Sticks,* op. cit., p. 18.
49. Lassar, *Carrots and Sticks,* op. cit., pp. 70–76.
50. *Nollan v. Coastal Commission,* 107 S. Ct. 3141 (1987).
51. Ibid.
52. The Special Committee on the Role of Amenities in the Land Use Process: "The Role of Amenities in the Land Use Process," reprinted from vol. 43, no. 6 of *The Record,* The Association of the Bar of the City of New York, New York, 1988, p. 7.
53. Richard F. Babcock and Wendy U. Larsen, *Special Districts: The Ultimate in Neighborhood Zoning,* Lincoln Institute of Land Policy, Cambridge, Mass., 1990.
54. New York City Planning Commission, *Plan for New York City,* Department of City Planning, New York, 1969, vol. 4, p. 57.
55. Jonathan Barnett, *Urban Design As Public Policy,* Architectural Record Books, New York, 1974, pp. 17–27, and Richard Weinstein, "How New York's Zoning Was Changed to Induce the Construction of Legitimate Theaters," pp. 131–136 in *The New Zoning* (Norman Marcus and Marilyn W. Groves, editors), Praeger Publishers, New York, 1970.
56. Interview with Donald Elliott, October 17, 1991.
57. They are the American Place Theater in the Stevens Building, the Gershwin and the Circle in the Square Theaters in the Uris Building, and the Minskoff and the Marquis Theaters in buildings of the same name.
58. Interview with Con Howe (Executive Director of the City Planning Department during the period in which these changes were made), October 14, 1991.
59. Executive Order #91, August 24, 1977.
60. New York is divided into 59 community districts. Each district has a 50-person *community board* jointly appointed by the borough president and city council members that represent the affected district. The ULURP process requires public notice and hearings by the affected community board, the city planning commission, and the city council (up to September 1990 this role was taken by the Board of Estimate, which was abolished as a result of charter reform).
61. Babcock and Larsen, op. cit., pp. 99–100.
62. New York City Planning Commission, *Minutes of Meeting,* New York, April 3, 1974.
63. New York City Planning Department, *Special Yorkville–East 86th Street District: A Rezoning Proposal,* New York, 1989.
64. City of Santa Monica, *Third Street Mall Design Guidelines,* Santa Monica, undated, p. i.
65. Third Street Development Corporation, *Third Street Mall Specific Plan,* City of Santa Monica, Santa Monica, 1986, Appendix, pp. A1–A15.
66. Urban Land Institute, *Janss Court,* Project Reference File, vol. 21, no. 3, Urban Land Institute, Washington, D.C., January–March 1991.
67. Randall W. Scott (editor) with the assistance of David J. Brower and Dallas D. Miner, *Management and Control of Growth,* 3 vols., Urban Land Institute, Washington, D.C., 1975; and Douglas R. Porter (editor), *Growth Management,* Urban Land Institute, Washington, D.C., 1986.
68. Historical and statistical material on Ramapo is derived from Rockland County Planning Board, *Rockland County Data Book,* County of Rockland, New York, 1965, 1969, and 1976; *Golden v. Planning Board of Ramapo,* 285 N.E. 2nd 291 (1972); Israel Stollman, "Ramapo: An Editorial & the Ordinance as Amended," in Scott, Brower, and Miner, op. cit., pp. 5–14; Manual S. Emanual, "Ramapo's Managed Growth Program," *Planners Notebook,* vol. 4, no. 5, October 1974, Urban Land Institute, Washington, D.C.; and Robert Guenther, "Ramapo, N.Y.…is seeking to encourage growth, a sign of the economic times," *The Wall Street Journal,* August 31, 1983, New York, p. 23.
69. Historical and statistical material on Petaluma is derived from Frank B. Gray, "The City of Petaluma: Residential Development Control," in Scott, Brower, and Miner, op. cit., pp. 149–159; *Construction Industry Association of Sonoma County v. City of Petaluma,* 522 F. 2d 897 (9th Cir. 1975), *cert. denied,* 424 U.S. 934; Warren Salmons, "Petaluma's Experiment," in Porter, op. cit., pp. 9–14; and Seymour I Schwartz, David E. Hansen, and Richard Green, "The Effect of Growth Control on the Production of Moderate-Priced Housing," in Porter, op. cit., pp. 15–20.
70. Lewis Mumford, "Botched Cities," *American Mercury,* 18, New York, October 1929, p. 147.
71. 42 U.S.C. § 4331 (2) (C).
72. Historical and statistical material on Westway is derived from New York City Planning Commission, *Land Use and the West Side Highway,* New York City, 1974; U.S. Department of Transportation Federal Highway Administration and New York State Department of Transportation, *Draft Environmental Impact Statement and Section 4(f) Statement for West Side Highway,* Washington, D.C., 1974, Regina Herzlinger, "Costs, Benefits, and the West Side Highway," *The Public Interest,* no. 55, National Affairs Inc., New York, Spring 1979, pp. 77–98; and Sam Roberts, "Battle of the Westway: Bitter 10-year Saga of a Vision on Hold," *The New York Times,* June 4, 1984, p. B1, and "For Stalled Westway, a Time of Decision," *The New York Times,* June 5, 1984, p. B1, and "Bass: Why Is Hudson So Important," *The New York Times,* June 26, 1984, p. C1.
73. In its final version, Westway included 16 acres for institutional and commercial purposes, 24 acres for industry, 36 acres for the roadway, 57 acres for residential development, and 93 acres for a park. In every version the proposed industrial uses were a fantasy. Manhattan had been hemorrhaging industrial firms for decades. The allocation of land for industrial purposes was there largely to attract support from labor unions.
74. Col. Fletcher H. Griffis, Army Corps of Engineers district engineer, quoted by Sam Roberts in "For Stalled Westway, a Time of Decision," *The New York Times,* June 5, 1984, p. B1.
75. Donald G. Hagman, "NEPA's Progeny Inhabit the States—Were the Genes Defective?," in *Urban Law Annual,* vol. 7, The School of Law, Washington University, St. Louis, 1974, pp. 3–56 and Jeffrey T. Renz,

"The Coming of Age of State Environmental Policy Acts," in *Public Land Law Review,* The School of Law, University of Montana, Missoula, 1984, pp. 31–54.

76. *Friends of Mammoth v. Board of Supervisors,* 8 Cal. 3d 247, 502 P.2d 1049, 104 Cal. Rptr. 761 (1972).

77. Michaeil H. Remy, Tina A. Thomas, and James G. Moose, *Guide to the California Environmental Quality Act (CEQA),* Solano Press Books, Point Arena, Calif., 1991.

78. New York City Planning Commission, Calendar Items #53 and #54, September 20, 1989.

79. Dresdner Robin & Associates, Inc., *Project Data Statement: Special Little Italy Zoning District, Houston Street Corridor (Area B),* Jersey City, May 1987; supporting documents filed in connection with CEQR No. 87-311M; and Grossman & Associates, Inc., *An Archeological and Historical Sensitivity Evaluation of Surviving Open Areas Within the Little Italy Special Zoning District (Area B), Blocks 508, 509, and 521 (CEQR No. 87-311M),* New York, October 1988.

80. The developer was forced to spend tens of thousands of dollars for the various tests and studies required by city personnel reviewing the CEQR submission. There was only one significant additional obligation that was not already required by the zoning. The property owner agreed to remove any contaminated soil that might be found on the site. It was a gratuitous requirement for which no special environmental review was needed because every lending institution in the city would have required the same commitment in conjunction with its construction loan.

81. U.S. Department of Commerce, Bureau of the Census, *County Business Patterns,* Washington, D.C., 1958 and 1991.

82. Philip Johnson, "Whence and Whither: The Processional Element in Architecture," *Perspecta 9/10,* School of Art and Architecture of Yale University, New Haven, 1965, p. 168.

83. Whyte, op. cit., pp. 103–131.

84. New York City Planning Commission, *Zoning Resolution,* Article V, Chapter 2, Section 52-01.

17

Preserving the Past

Charleston, 1991. *(Alexander Garvin)*

Some people wish to preserve old buildings because they have a nostalgic interest in the past. Others dislike the newly built environment. During the 1960s, Christopher Tunnard, one of the pioneers of the preservation movement, proposed a more inclusive rationale for preserving the past. He believed it was society's responsibility to cultivate what he called the "cultural patrimony."[1]

Cultural patrimony means inheritance from one's ancestors. It includes places of historical significance (George Washington slept there), esthetic prominence (Frank Lloyd Wright designed it), social import (Native Americans live there), public importance (festivals take place there), and scenic distinction (guidebooks say it is worth the visit). As Tunnard conceived it, society's responsibility is not simply to preserve what we receive from our forefathers and pass it on to future generations. It is to select what is significant, nurture and enhance it, make improvements, and pass on to the next generation an environment that is richer, more fulfilling, and more beautiful.

Preserving the past can provide tremendous benefits to the surrounding city: economic benefits from the tourists it attracts, social benefits from a more heterogeneous population seeking a broader range of living environments, and cultural benefits from its enhanced setting for artistic activity. These additional benefits often offset the costs of preservation. A good example is the privately financed recreation of eighteenth-century Williamsburg, the colonial capital of the Dominion of Virginia. Tourist spending since this restoration was completed probably has generated enough money to pay for Williamsburg and a dozen other reconstruction projects around the country.

There is not enough money to create a mini-Williamsburg wherever there are properties that are worth preserving, nor are there enough tourists to visit them or curators to maintain them. Moreover, there is every reason to keep from transforming the American landscape into one continuous, institutionally owned and operated museum. Instead we should find ways to make the cultural patrimony an integral part of daily life. That means retaining landmarks without destroying their continuing utility as residences, offices, stores, warehouses, schools, police stations, etc.

When Tunnard proposed this rationale, the preservation movement was in its infancy. Federal, state, and local governments owned and maintained for public view some well-known monuments. Charleston, New Orleans, and a handful of smaller cities had public bodies with the legal authority to supervise privately owned but publicly designated landmarks and privately owned property in publicly designated historic districts. Since that time, more than 2000 communities have enacted legislation to protect landmarks and historic districts.[2]

There is now considerable experience with other preservation techniques: zoning laws that permit owners to sell development rights, revolving funds with which to purchase and resell threatened landmarks, local real estate tax benefits, and federal income tax deductions. As the use of these techniques has become more widespread, there have been increasing challenges from property owners. Sometimes they argue that local statutes impose burdens that preclude them from benefiting from the use of their property. More often, they argue that unreasonable regulations keep them from doing so. It has, therefore, become increasingly important to enact legislation that will distribute the costs and benefits of preservation more equitably.

Every preservation technique except government spending on the acquisition and restoration of historic structures depends on the existence of an active real estate market. Development rights have no value unless somebody wishes to develop a property. Revolving funds will run out of money if nobody wants to buy the buildings that have been purchased. Tax benefits have no value unless there is income from which to pay taxes. Because properties outside active market areas suffer from neglect, we also need programs that will provide property owners in these areas with the money they need to maintain and restore historic structures.

Even more serious is the continuing punishment of those who cultivate the cultural patrimony. Virtually every community increases the real estate tax on properties that are renovated. If one is unlucky enough to own a landmark, the price is even higher. Public officials invariably impose extra requirements that add to the cost of the renovation. We need to eliminate this disincentive to the ownership and restoration of historic structures.

Finally, historic preservation should not be dismissed as the enthusiasm of a privileged elite. Historic preservation cannot and should not take place in a vacuum. Cultivating the cultural patrimony also involves improving the quality of our air and water, the condition of our parks and public spaces, the safety of our streets and highways, the quality of the education we provide our children and the health care we provide the sick, the character of our entire built and natural environment. That means making tough choices among these competing demands for action. Consequently, historic-preservation activities need to be better integrated into the planning, budgeting, and governance of every community.

Preserving the Old and Historic

Whatever the stated arguments or underlying motives for preservation, the money and effort needed to restore large sections of cities exceed the financial and administrative resources of most individuals and civic groups. Occasionally, a Rockefeller will contribute the money needed to restore a historic site such as Williamsburg, Virginia. However, there are not enough fabulously wealthy philanthropists to bankroll restoration of every district and town worthy of preservation. Consequently, we look to government to safeguard our heritage.

However, government is in a poor position to maintain the cultural patrimony. The Fifth Amendment to the Constitution requires government to compensate property owners whenever it takes any land or buildings for public use. Given the multiplicity of demands for scarce municipal resources, most cities are not about to spend the extraordinary sums needed to buy all the properties suitable for preservation, much less pay for the necessary restoration. During the 1930s two cities, Charleston, South Carolina, and New Orleans, Louisiana, demonstrated that there were alternatives to massive spending for the acquisition and restoration of major historical artifacts like Williamsburg. They found a way to regulate what owners could do with the cultural patrimony.

Williamsburg, Virginia

Williamsburg was settled in 1633. Initially, it differed little from other towns in Southwestern Virginia. The first impetus for change came in 1693 when King William and Queen Mary endowed a new college that would bear their names. The second came in 1699 when Williamsburg was designated the new capital. From then till 1780, when the capital was moved to Richmond, Williamsburg remained the political, intellectual, and social center of Virginia. Thereafter it slowly slid into genteel dilapidation. By the start of the twentieth century it was little more than a seedy collection of rundown structures.

Recreating colonial Williamsburg, lot by lot, building by building, was the brainchild of the Reverend William Archer Rutherford Goodwin. He came to Williamsburg as rector of Bruton Parish in 1902. One of his first projects was the restoration of his church, the oldest Episcopal structure in constant use in America. Another was lobbying for paving Duke of Gloucester Street, Williamsburg's main thoroughfare. His real dream, though, was the complete restoration of colonial Williamsburg. Because he did not have the money, it remained a fantasy for more than two decades.[3]

After taking on a more prosperous parish in Rochester in 1909, Goodwin returned to Williamsburg in 1923 to teach religion at the College of William and Mary, to organize its endowment fund, and to resume his position at Bruton Parish. This time he found a benefactor who paid to bring his fantasy to life.

In 1926 Goodwin persuaded John D. Rockefeller, Jr., to pay for some architectural sketches of a restored Williamsburg. Together, they acquired and demolished almost 600 postcolonial structures, rehabilitated nearly 100, and reconstructed another 450. Modern stores were moved to a new business district called Merchants Square. Displaced residents were either moved back as "life tenants" when restoration was completed, provided homes in specially funded low-rent neighborhoods, or paid sufficiently high prices for their houses to allow them to purchase equivalent houses elsewhere. Utilities were buried, paving and street furniture installed, and trees, shrubs, and flowers planted. By the time the project was finished they had spent $68.5 million.[4]

Williamsburg, 1903. Wythe House prior to restoration. *(Courtesy of Alexander Purves)*

The recreation of colonial Williamsburg preserved or rebuilt structures of unusual historic, cultural, and architectural significance. More important, it became Virginia's number-one tourist attraction, bringing 3.9 million visitors during 1989.[5]

"Old and Historic" Charleston, South Carolina

Charleston was founded in 1670 on a narrow peninsula between the Cooper and Ashley Rivers. Its protected, deep-water harbor, 7 1/2 miles from an ocean sandbar, offers east-coast shipping conditions rivaled only by New York City. During the eighteenth and nineteenth centuries, prosperous Charleston merchants shipped valuable cargoes of indigo, rice, and later cotton. They provided its white population with the economic base for a life of luxury and elegance. As described by Constance McLaughlin Green, antebellum Charleston was a very special place:

> *The city was small... before 1830, numbering only about three hundred, all knew each other.... Nowhere else in America was life so truly urbane as in Charleston.... Charlestonians made gracious living their first business. The concerts of Mozart and Haydn given by the St. Cecilia society, the balls, the theater, the race course, and in 1800 the only golf links in America provided endless diversion.*[6]

The Civil War brought this prosperity to a halt. After the war other cities continued growing and changing. Charleston faded into genteel obsolescence. By 1925, DuBose Heyward in his famous novel *Porgy* could describe it as "an ancient, beautiful city that time had forgotten."[7]

It was Charleston's good luck to be a "city that time had forgotten." The wealthy planters that built it had created an environment of unequalled grace and charm. Its residential districts consisted of two- and three-story frame and brick

Charleston, 1991. Residences on Church Street in the heart of the "Old and Historic District." *(Alexander Garvin)*

houses lined with "piazzas" (arcaded galleries running the length of the structure) providing shaded outdoor living, surrounded by subtropical gardens, and enclosed in wrought-iron and brick walls. Its commercial areas retained the pedestrian scale, pastel colors, and ornamental detail of an antebellum trading center. Elsewhere, such lovely buildings would have been demolished to make way for a "higher and better use." Not only was there little demand for construction sites in Charleston, often there was not even enough money to maintain existing structures.

Neglect was not the only threat to Charleston's heritage. After World War I, the city was discovered by "a steady, but small, flow of discerning visitors.... The town found it had to protect itself from collectors of everything from ironwork to complete houses. Some of the buildings were completely taken down and carried off, from the brickwork of the basement to the timber of the roof."[8]

In 1931 Charlestonians invented a device to deal with this threat: designation of a "historic district" within the zoning ordinance. The "Old and Historic Charleston District" was a 22-block area at the tip of the peninsula that contained many, but not all, of the city's finest antebellum structures. This special district was added to the zoning ordinance to guarantee "the preservation and protection of the old historic or architecturally worthy structures and quaint neighborhoods which impart a distinct aspect of the city," assure "the continued construction of buildings in the historic styles...form, color, proportion, texture, and material" compatible with the district, "preserve property values," and "attract tourists and residents."[9]

A Board of Architectural Review was responsible for reviewing and approving construction, alteration, demolition, or removal of any structure within the district. Property owners had to apply to the board for a "certificate of appropriateness" or submit a "demolition application" in order to do anything with their property. Such strict regulation caused little hardship. During the Depression few property owners had the money to do much with their buildings.

After World War II, the exodus to the suburbs further reduced demand for development sites within the historic district. Many property owners could not charge rents high enough to cover repairs. They had little choice but to defer maintenance. Others could not find tenants. Designation as an "old and historic district" had done little to protect the area from neglect and abandonment. It did, however, prevent demolition, incompatible remodeling, and inappropriate

New Orleans, 1981. Bourbon Street in the Vieux Carre. *(Alexander Garvin)*

expansion until demand picked up in the 1960s. Thus, when tourists began coming in increasingly large numbers and residents again chose to settle in town rather than in the suburbs, the "Old and Historic Charleston District" was still there to accommodate them.

By the 1980s, neglect and abandonment were no longer a problem. Most buildings in Charleston's Historic District were finally in the hands of owners who had the wherewithal to maintain them properly. Furthermore, the Board of Architectural Review could prevent inappropriate alterations and incompatible construction.

New Orleans's Vieux Carre

In 1937 New Orleans became the second American city to designate for preservation its old and historic district, the Vieux Carre. During the previous year, Louisiana voters had approved a state constitutional amendment giving the city the power to establish a historic district and to create a commission that would regulate the actions of its property owners. The city designated a 260-acre area with over 3000 structures and the mayor appointed an eight-member Vieux Carre Commission. It had power over all exterior work within the district—everything from replacing shutters to major new construction.

The Vieux Carre is a jambalaya of Spanish, Creole, Yankee, African-American, English, and Confederate buildings. Land uses are thrown together in a colorful confusion of jazz joints, stately residences, antique shops, lodging houses, celebrated restaurants, hidden courtyards, and tourist traps. Unlike Williamsburg or Charleston, New Orleans was not faced with economic decline, nor was the Vieux Carre threatened by neglect. New Orleans had been the nation's fifth largest city for most of the nineteenth century. Its busy port had kept it a major tourist attraction for nearly two centuries. Thus, cultivating the cultural patrimony in New Orleans required a very different approach.

The Vieux Carre Commission could not create carefully scrubbed fantasies of an imagined past, like Williamsburg, nor conserve "an ancient beautiful city that time had forgotten," like Charleston. It had to maintain the noisy attractions that brought sailors, the quiet little houses that provided refuge for artists, the garish dives that spawned jam sessions, the elegant mansions that were the envy of elite visitors.

Nurturing the messy vitality of this busy urban center with a distinctive and heterogeneous past requires knowing when to step aside and when to insist upon integration with what New Orleans calls the "tout ensemble." During its first 30 years, the Vieux Carre Commission performed this task with distinction. It supervised everything from the introduction of wrought-iron gates and magnolia trees to construction of the new Royal Sonesta Hotel. Then, in the mid-1960s, the Commission faced a threat it was powerless to prevent: the Riverfront–Elysian Fields Expressway.

A riverfront highway had been proposed in 1946 by Robert Moses. He had proposed similar highways for Pittsburgh, Baltimore, Detroit, and other cities that had consulted him in his capacity as the country's leading public works planner. The Riverfront–Elysian Fields Expressway was supposed to be an elevated roadway, which, Moses explained:

> *will lift cars off the street which now interfere with service to the docks. It will facilitate modernization of the piers and give better access to them.... Decatur Street, which bounds Jackson Square, the very heart of the Vieux Carre, and separates it from the market and waterfront, would again be a local service road. Heavy traffic would pulsate along the docks. The Cathedral would still be wedded to the Mississippi, but its precincts would not be choked with needless through traffic.*

Moses intended "no violence to history or tradition." He felt that removing regional traffic from the streets and opening access to the docks would enhance the Vieux Carre as a lively tourist center.[10]

The cost of elevating the 3.4-mile section of the proposed six-lane Riverfront–Elysian Fields Expressway going past the Vieux Carre was estimated at $31 million. If it were to be depressed between Jackson Square and the Mississippi River, another $12.4 million would be required. Despite the fact that the federal government would pay 90 percent of the cost of any version of the expressway, the city council chose an even cheaper alternative: a ground-level highway that would have established a broad barrier of heavy traffic between the Vieux Carre and the Mississippi.[11]

Local designation of a historic district could not stop an interstate highway. But designation in 1965 as a historic district on the National Register of Historic Places, eventually killed the project.

The National Register had been created by the National Parks Service pursuant to the Historic Sites Act of 1935. St. Louis Cathedral, the Cabildo, the Pontalba Buildings, and many other buildings in the Vieux Carre were on the National Register. When Congress passed a comprehensive Historic Preservation Act of 1966, it provided a mechanism which would eventually save the Vieux Carre from the ravages of the proposed highway.

The Historic Preservation Act of 1966 required the newly created Advisory Council for Historic Preservation to examine the impact of actions by federal agencies or federally financed programs on landmarks listed in the National Register. When the Federal Highway Administration recommended the Riverfront–Elysian Fields Expressway, the Advisory Council for Historic Preservation entered the fray. In 1969, after a series of public meetings in Washington and 3 days of visits to the site, it recommended against construction of the expressway. The Secretary of Transportation accepted the recommendation because the Expressway would have "seriously impaired the historic quality of New Orleans' famed French Quarter."[12]

Instant Roots and Ersatz History

For a quarter of a century, Charleston and New Orleans were the only major American cities with statutes that regulated existing privately owned buildings in designated historic districts. Meanwhile, Santa Barbara, California, and Santa Fe, New Mexico, were evolving an entirely different approach to the cultivation of the cultural patrimony, one that concentrated on new construction rather than protection.

America is a country where all but a few families were once newcomers and will soon again be on the move. Wherever they go, they seek to put down roots. Civic leaders in Santa Barbara and Santa Fe understood this need. They wanted to provide instant roots for anybody coming to the area. The ersatz past that they created has a distinctive appearance that is as appealing to tourists as anything by Walt Disney. However, unlike Disneyland, Santa Barbara and Santa Fe are functioning cities filled with traffic, noise, and all the difficulties of urban living. Thus, they provide a very different model for cities interested in cultivating the cultural patrimony.

Santa Barbara

Santa Barbara was founded in 1782 as a Spanish colonial military outpost. Two years later settlers started to work on the Mission Church. Most of the structures that were built while Santa Barbara remained a Spanish and later a Mexican settlement were simple one- and two-story adobe buildings. The Anglo-Americans who emigrated during the second half of the nineteenth century had little respect for this architecture of mud and rough-hewn wood. They were used to milled lumber, manufactured nails, and plate glass. At first they rejected the more "primitive" existing building pattern and built something more like the Western towns depicted in Hollywood movies.

As the nineteenth century drew to a close, Santa Barbara, like all of California, became entranced with its Spanish colonial past. The first manifestation of this was the "Mission Revival" style (c. 1890–1915) that revived the adobe look by covering brick, hollow tile, stone, or wood walls with stucco. Other elements of this new style included arched openings, scalloped parapets, red-tile roofs, low belltowers, shaded porches, rich "Moorish" ornament, and decorative round or quatrefoil windows. Sometimes the buildings seemed more like the red-tiled villas of the French Riviera, sometimes closer

Santa Barbara, 1923. State Street in 1923, two years prior to the earthquake, when it looked like main streets throughout the country. *(Courtesy of Santa Barbara Historical Society)*

to the red-tiled houses of the Italian countryside. But all over California, one-family houses, bungalow courts, and even small, local railroad stations took on the look of this pseudo-Mediterranean fantasy.[13]

California chose to be represented by buildings of this fantasy architecture at every World's Fair from the Chicago Fair of 1893 to the Panama-California Exposition of 1915 in San Diego. In San Diego, the eastern Beaux Arts architect Bertram Goodhue provided the foundation for an even more elaborate "indigenous" architecture. His California State Building revived the highly ornamented Spanish Churrigueresque style.[14] Combined with elements of the more modest Mission style, it provided the model for the larger, monumental structures that California was then building: hotels, movie palaces, shopping centers, railroad terminals.

The resulting pastiche of Spanish, French, Italian, and Moorish components seemed just right for the state's dramatic coastal landscape and benign climate. Few Californians cared that the busy life of prosperous, urban, twentieth-century, Anglo-California would be quite different from the quiet existence in a vast natural landscape interrupted by the missions, presidios, and ranchos of the Spanish colonial past. Nor did they care that life in mass-produced bungalows along congested arteries also would be different from the quiet provincial existence in the red-tiled French and Italian villas that dotted the Mediterranean coast.

Until World War I, only a few private houses and hotels in Santa Barbara were built in this pseudo-Mediterranean style. After the war, fantasy-Mediterranean became the style of choice. In 1919, the City and County of Santa Barbara held a design competition for a combined courthouse, city hall, and veterans memorial. The winning design, in the new style, proved to be too expensive to be built. William Mooser & Company, architects of the second-place design (also fantasy-Mediterranean), together with J. Wilmer Hersey, eventually designed the building that was completed in 1929. The Santa Barbara Courthouse became the culmination of the Anglo-Californian dream of its romantic Hispano-Mediterranean past.[15]

The courthouse is the only building in Santa Barbara that took on the civic scale of Goodhue's San Diego California State Building. The rest of the city was built up in the same Hispano-Mediterranean style, but on a smaller scale. The most charming of these early buildings is El Paseo, designed by James Osborn Craig between 1921–1922. This colorful and intricate combination of courtyards, passages, small shops,

Santa Barbara, 1988. The design of El Paseo, inspired by the colorful combination of courtyards, passages, small shops, and outdoor restaurants found in the towns and villages along the Mediterranean, became an image that was copied by developers of later retail buildings throughout the city. *(Alexander Garvin)*

San Diego, 1992. Bertram Goodhue's California State Building (now the Museum of Man) erected in 1915 at the Panama-California Exhibition accelerated the state's love affair with the Hispano-Mediterranean style. *(Alexander Garvin)*

outdoor restaurants, and second-story offices was intended to recreate the narrow shopping streets and squares of the southern Mediterranean, especially Spain.

The effort to cultivate this cultural patrimony began in 1920, when the newly formed Santa Barbara Community Arts Association started to lobby for design regulations. It obtained support for the creation of a Hispano-Mediterranean public square with a new City Hall and *Daily News* building in that style. It helped to sponsor a Community Drafting Room that provided drawings illustrating how various parts of the city could be rebuilt in this style. In 1923, it hired Charles Cheney to prepare a general plan, model building and zoning codes, and design guidelines. While they were never adopted, they laid the foundation for the government regulation to come.[16]

The real impact of the Community Arts Association came after Santa Barbara was struck by a major earthquake in 1925. The association persuaded the city council to establish an Architectural Board of Review, which had to approve the exterior appearance of any structure prior to the issuance of a building permit. Simultaneously the Community Drafting Room began providing property owners with free plans for any contemplated rebuilding or renovation. Although the ordinance establishing the Architectural Board of Review was revoked the following year, in a few months it had permanently remade the city's architectural image. "At what seemed like the touch from a fairy's wand, a humdrum (it could be anywhere in the U.S.A.) city had become something special."[17]

In 1930, Santa Barbara adopted a comprehensive zoning ordinance that restricted commercial structures to four stories

Santa Barbara, 1988. City and County Courthouse erected in 1929, became the culmination of the Anglo-Californian dream of its romantic Hispano-Mediterranean past. *(Alexander Garvin)*

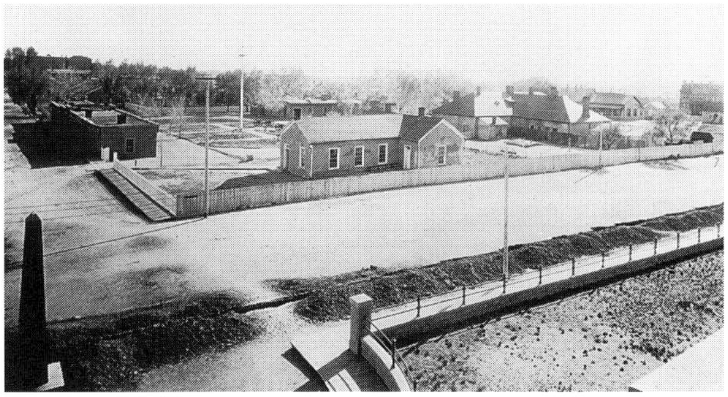

Santa Fe, 1892. The wooden Western town that preceded adoption of the "New Old" Santa Fe style. *(Negative no. 1701: Courtesy of Museum of New Mexico)*

(60 feet) and apartment houses to three stories (45 feet).[18] There was, however, no further regulation of architectural design. In 1947, the City Council established an Architectural Review Board and, 13 years later, an Advisory Landmark Committee that designated a 16-block section of downtown Santa Barbara as the "El Pueblo Viejo" District. It was named after the Spanish presidio that had occupied the site. The irony of declaring the area's charming and colorful fantasy architecture to be "historic" because it occupied the site of a long-demolished military installation seems to have escaped Santa Barbarans.

The Landmark Committee required any construction or remodeling within the district to be compatible with the area's "historical" character. In 1977, El Pueblo Viejo was expanded to include virtually the entire downtown of Santa Barbara. In doing so, the Landmark Committee guaranteed that the most important sections of Santa Barbara would continue to be rebuilt in the image established for it by civic leaders more than half a century earlier.

Like the creators of Williamsburg, Santa Barbarans had discovered the economic value of a distinctive "regional" appearance. They demonstrated that a community's desire for a "history" could be used to create a unique artificially constructed environment of considerable beauty and aesthetic significance. By so doing, they also expanded the city's attractiveness to tourists. During 1985, for example, 5 million visitors spent more than $401 million in Santa Barbara. Without an attraction like El Pueblo Viejo, there would have been fewer tourists, less tax revenues, and fewer jobs.[19]

Santa Fe

The Santa Fe style was created in a manner very similar to California's fantasy Mediterranean style. Santa Fe, like Santa Barbara, was founded as a Spanish colonial outpost in 1610. It was also built up in an adobe architecture rejected by the Anglo pioneers who settled there in the nineteenth century. At the beginning of the twentieth century, New Mexico, like California, sought to create a distinctive regional architecture. It also was presented at the California-Pacific Exposition of 1915 in San Diego. The Exposition's New Mexico State Building, designed by Isaac Hamilton Rapp, set a pattern for what was to become Santa Fe's distinctive fantasy architecture. There the similarity ended.

While the new Santa Fe style was formally inaugurated in San Diego, it had really been launched 3 years earlier by the Santa Fe Chamber of Commerce, when it sponsored New-Old Santa Fe Style Exhibition "to advertise the unique and unrivalled possibilities of the city as 'The Tourist Center of the Southwest'"[20]

While the Chamber of Commerce lobbied for the creation of an "indigenous" architecture as a way of generating tourist revenues, Santa Fe's budding colony of artists and writers lobbied for it as a way of preventing commercial exploitation. They were among the major sponsors of the Old Santa Fe Association, which was founded in 1926 to preserve the area's historic architecture and ensure that new growth would further the area's unique charm.

The new Santa Fe style was closer in appearance to an Indian pueblo than to a Spanish mission. Instead of having slanted red-tiled roofs, the buildings were flat-roofed; instead of deep arched porches and large windows, the buildings had lit-

San Diego, c. 1914. The design for the New Mexico State Building at the Panama-California Exposition later became the model for the Museum of Fine Arts in Santa Fe. *(Negative no. 13080: Courtesy of Museum of New Mexico)*

Santa Fe, 1989. Buildings erected along the Old Santa Fe Trail after the adoption of zoning regulations in 1957 that required all buildings to be in the "New Old" Santa Fe style. *(Alexander Garvin)*

tle or no roof overhang and large, flat, horizontal surfaces with few openings; instead of bright pastel or white stucco walls, the buildings were the light reddish-brown mud color of adobe.

An alliance of artists, writers, and business and civic leaders is an unbeatable combination, especially when it proposes action that will provide additional jobs and tax revenues while nurturing a community's historic identity. Over the next few decades not only were many new buildings erected in the Santa Fe style, existing buildings were remodeled to look like "Olde Santa Fe." Thus, when, in 1957, "preservationists" proposed an ordinance defining the Santa Fe Style as the only acceptable style for further construction or rehabilitation, it was easily enacted into law. The ordinance requires the city's historic style committee to deny approval to any alteration or new construction that fails to conform with the Old Santa Fe style.[21]

The fantasy world that emerged resonates with a sense of history and place. It has become just what the Chamber of Commerce wanted when it sponsored the New-Old Santa Fe Style Exhibition in 1912: "the tourist center of the southwest." In 1989, the 1.33 million tourists who visited Santa Fe spent more than $140 million.[22]

Santa Fe has also become just what the arts colony wanted in 1926 when the Old Santa Fe Association was established—one of the country's major arts centers. Its citizens took the cultural patrimony, produced new buildings with the stamp of New Mexico on them, refined the landscape in a manner respectful of its southwestern surroundings, and produced an enhanced environment of unique character and charm.

Protecting the Cultural Patrimony

During the three decades that followed creation of Charleston's historic district, fewer than 20 cities established similar districts. Because there had been little development pressure during the Depression, there was little need for preservation. During World War II, construction had come to a standstill and, thus, there was even less need for preservation. After the war, the rush to satisfy pent-up demand for new buildings decreased the likelihood of any substantial increase in the constituency for preservation.[23]

Postwar new construction changed all that. It eliminated cherished older buildings, replacing them with anonymous and unsightly structures. The preservation movement, which had long been dominated by zealous architecture buffs and Colonial Dames, started to attract ever larger numbers of angry citizens who objected to the demolition. By the 1960s, this increasingly vocal constituency was persuading legislative bodies to enact preservation laws.

Pennsylvania Station and New York City's Landmark Legislation

The event that finally transformed this angry citizenry into a powerful lobby for preservation was the demolition of New York City's renowned Pennsylvania Station. When Penn Station, designed by McKim, Mead, and White, opened in 1910, it occupied nearly 8 acres and handled a quantity of long-haul passengers, commuters, baggage, freight, and mail that still boggles the imagination. Over the years it had become a New York City icon: "a fitting gateway to the city, symbolically representing the power and position of the railroad."[24]

In 1961 the Pennsylvania Railroad announced that it could not continue to own 8 valuable acres of mid-Manhattan property that did not produce substantial revenues. Its solution was to replace the McKim, Mead, and *White* elephant with a money-making office tower and sports arena. Despite newspaper editorials and public demonstrations, the railroad was determined to proceed. Company executives insisted that it was in business to make money, not lose revenues maintaining a public monument. Demolition began in 1963. As architectural historian Vincent Scully so eloquently explains, where once one entered the city "like a god....One scuttles in now like a rat."[25]

Manhattan, c. 1930. Pennsylvania Station. *(Courtesy of Museum of the City of New York)*

In 1965, the year demolition of Penn Station was completed, the New York City Council adopted legislation that civic leaders hoped would prevent further desecration of the cultural patrimony. It established a Landmarks Commission with responsibility for designating landmark structures and historic districts. The commission was given wide latitude in determining what properties had "a special character or special historical or aesthetic interest or value" or represented "periods or styles of architecture typical of one or more eras in the history of the city." The only limitation was that a landmark had to be at least 30 years old.[26]

Landmarks and properties within historic districts that are designated by the Landmarks Commission cannot be altered without its permission. Property owners must apply for a "permit for minor work," "certificate of no effect," or "certificate of appropriateness." The commission, in turn, must act within 90 days and specify the reasons for its action. Denial neither precludes further application nor further denial.[27]

At some point, if the commission continues to deny a property owner's application, it can be challenged on grounds that it has taken the use of the property from its owner. New York City's landmarks legislation defines this point as having been reached when the property in its existing condition is unable to earn a "reasonable return" of 6 percent per year on its assessed value.[28]

If a property owner challenges the Landmarks Commission, it has 60 days to develop a plan that will provide the owner with a "reasonable return." The obvious method of achieving this is a partial or full abatement of real estate taxes. Such a plan must be approved by the City Council. If this tax relief is rejected by the owner, the Landmarks Commission can continue denying permission sought by the owner. The owner then seeks relief in court.[29]

New York City's legislation is similar to that of other cities. The only significant difference is that property values in New York tend to be so much higher. It is therefore more likely to be worth litigating landmark issues. In fact, the landmark case in this field was brought to the Supreme Court by a New York City property owner.

Grand Central Terminal

Over the objections of its owner, the Penn Central Railroad, Grand Central Terminal was designated a landmark in 1967. The building, completed in 1919, was the result of a design competition won by Reed & Stem, who were later joined by Warren & Wetmore. The scheme is an ingenious intermingling of separate traffic systems for the pedestrian, automobile, subway, and train.

Like Penn Station, Grand Central Terminal had become an icon. But, unlike Penn Station, it was at the center of the world's most expensive real estate. The right to build over the vast network of rails leading into the terminal and over the terminal itself is worth billions of dollars. From the beginning, the railroad profited from selling or leasing those rights for construction of buildings like the Yale Club of New York City, the Waldorf Astoria Hotel, and the Pan Am Building (now the Met Life Building). At the time that Grand Central was designated a landmark, the city's Zoning Resolution would have permitted additional construction of 1.7 million square feet of floor area on the site.[30]

The Penn Central Railroad opposed landmark designation because it correctly guessed that the Landmarks Commission would not allow it to continue to build over its property. Penn Central had entered into a renewable 50-year lease with Union General Properties, Ltd. (UGP) under which UGP was to build a multistory office building over the terminal. In exchange, it agreed to pay Penn Central $1 million annually during construction and at least $3 million annually thereafter.

The year after landmark designation, UGP sought permission to build over the terminal, first a 55-story building designed by Marcel Breuer and then a 53-story building. The Landmarks Preservation Commission refused saying, "To protect a landmark, one does not tear it down. To perpetuate its architectural features, one does not strip them off.... But to balance a 55-story office tower above a flamboyant Beaux-Arts façade seems nothing more than an aesthetic joke."

Since the terminal was exempt from real estate taxes, there was no way of measuring a "reasonable return" nor of using real estate tax abatement as a means of creating one. Some preservationists argued that the Penn Central was only entitled to a reasonable return from "transportation purposes." They ignored the fact that it had been earning millions from the nonrailroad-related buildings on the site. Others argued that the property's value was derived from the rights-of-way that had been granted by government or from its interrelation with the government-built and operated transit system. What the state had given, they implied, the state could take away without compensation.[31]

City officials were not sure that Penn Central was not entitled to compensation. More important, they were worried that the entire landmarks statute could be overturned as an unconstitutional taking of property. Accordingly, the City Planning Commission, in 1968, amended the Zoning Resolution to permit transfer of unused development potential.[32] The new provision permitted an owner of a landmark to transfer unused development rights to contiguous lots or to lots across a street or intersection, provided that the development potential of the receiving lot was not increased by more than 20 percent and provided that the City Planning Commission found the transfer would do nothing "to the detriment of the occupants of *buildings* on the *block* or nearby *blocks*."[33]

In 1969, the City Planning Commission and Board of Estimate approved Penn Central's sale of 4 percent of their development rights to Philip Morris for construction of their

Manhattan, c. 1968. Grand Central Terminal. *(Alexander Garvin)*

headquarters across 42nd Street from the Terminal. Despite this, Penn Central went to court against the City of New York claiming the city had taken (without paying) the 1.7 million square feet of development rights permitted by the zoning ordinance. The trial court agreed, declaring the landmarks ordinance an unconstitutional taking of private property without just compensation and a deprivation of property without due process of law.[34] It also found that allowing the transfer of development rights was insufficient compensation because only in the unlikely event that one were to demolish the Biltmore Hotel (later remodeled as the Bank of America), the Commodore Hotel (later remodeled as the Grand Hyatt Hotel), and any of the other profitable large adjacent structures, would there be enough sites to receive Penn Central's development rights. The Court of Appeals reversed the decision on the basis that the statute did not deprive Penn Central of "all reasonable beneficial use of their property." Finally, in 1978 the Supreme Court, in a 6 to 3 decision written by Justice William Brennan, upheld the constitutionality of the statute.[35]

The Grand Central Terminal case provided the constitutional foundation for landmark legislation throughout the

Manhattan, 1968. The 55-story building proposed for construction over Grand Central Terminal. *(From Exhibit 20A, Penn Central Transportation Co. v. City of New York, Supreme Court Appellate Division—First Department)*

nation. It also raised some significant issues. Local governments derive their right to regulate (the *police power*) from their responsibility for the protection of health, safety, morals, and general welfare. In the case of zoning, the rationale for regulation is easy to explain (see Chapter 16). Local government is presumed to have examined the capacity of local streets and sidewalks, the capacity of existing infrastructure and community facilities, projected capital expenditures intended to increase that capacity, and the impact of likely development in each part of the city. It is also presumed to have determined standards for providing a suitable level of light and air. Presumably, the Zoning Resolution balances these factors, determines an optimum level of development for every property, and thereby provides for the health, safety, morals, and general welfare of the community.

Protecting the cultural patrimony is an important additional way of providing for the general welfare. As Justice Brennan explained in the Penn Central case:

> *Structures with special historic, cultural, or architectural significance enhance the quality of life for all. Not only do these buildings and their workmanship represent the lessons of the past and embody precious features of our heritage, they serve as examples of quality for today...enhancing—or perhaps developing for the first time—the quality of life for the people.*[36]

Once such structures of special significance are demolished, they are forever gone. Protecting this scarce resource provides citizens with a profound connection to their culture and their history. This is the rationale for such disparate "historic" districts as those of Williamsburg, Charleston, New Orleans, Santa Barbara, and Santa Fe.

There is, however, a difference between regulating one specific property and regulating an entire area (whether a historic area or a zoning district). All the properties in the designated area are treated in a similar manner. They suffer the same intrusion into their property rights and derive the same benefits from the area's regulations.

Restricting the rights of the owners of individual properties designated as landmarks may deny them the right to use their property in the same manner as neighboring property owners, especially if landmark regulation forbids any significant further construction. Designated landmarks are probably zoned for development at the same bulk, use, and density as their neighbors. However, if landmark regulation prevents the owner from developing the property in the same manner, that regulation may be unfair.

It was this potentially unequal treatment that the New York City Planning Commission tried to rectify when it amended the zoning ordinance to permit the transfer of unused development rights to neighboring sites. At the same time, it attempted to balance positive benefits with negative impact by restricting the increase in bulk and density on any receiving site to no more than 20 percent and only permitting that increase on contiguous properties or properties across a street or intersection. Had the Planning Commission permitted development rights to be transferred to an area far from the terminal, the citizens of the receiving area (presumably only capable of accommodating the bulk, density, and use for which it was already zoned) would have been burdened by the impact of additional development (more vehicular traffic, more pedestrians, more noise, less light and air) while property owners in the vicinity of the terminal (which had the capacity to handle the added development) would have benefited (less vehicular traffic, fewer pedestrians, less noise, more light and air).[37]

The Penn Central Railroad may not be able to sell further development rights. Most eligible receiving sites are already developed up to, or close to their allowable capacity. As of 1988, the railroad had been able to make only one transfer and only of 4 percent of these rights. In 1989, it sought Planning Commission approval of a transfer of 800,000 square feet of development rights several blocks north of the terminal to 383 Madison Avenue at 46th Street. The owners of this property were prepared to pay the railroad $480 million for these development rights because it would have allowed them to build a 1.4 million-square-foot, 74-story office tower.

The Planning Commission denied approval because the office-building site would have been developed to a bulk and density 53 percent larger than permitted by the Zoning Resolution anywhere in New York City.[38] It also denied the contention that a site several blocks away from the terminal was eligible to receive development rights. The developers had argued that the necessary chain of ownership existed in the subsurface lots (used by Penn Central for its railroad tracks) between the terminal and their site. Commission Chair Sylvia Deutsch denied this logic pointing out it could conceivably establish "a link or a chain going past Yonkers."[39]

Within days of denying this development rights transfer, the Planning Commission issued a proposal that would create a Grand Central subdistrict doubling the area that could receive the terminal's development rights. The proposal restricted the permitted bulk to the same maximum level permitted elsewhere in midtown Manhattan. It was explained that the new district would provide a framework for development rights transfer "based on sound planning, rather than one based on ownership patterns."

In 1992, after considerable debate and public hearings the City Planning Commission amended the Special Midtown Zoning District to include a Grand Central Subdistrict extending from East 41st to 48th Streets, generally from the midblock west of Madison Avenue to the midblock east of Lexington Avenue, thereby increasing the number of sites eligible for transfer of development rights from landmarks. It eliminated the plaza bonus within the subdistrict and established new street-wall, height and setback, and building-entrance requirements. More important, subdistrict regulations limited the transfer of development rights to a maximum of 1 FAR(floor area ratio), and limited the total FAR on any zoning lot to the maximum permitted anywhere in the city, 21.6 FAR.

Paying for Landmark Preservation

The story of Grand Central Terminal illustrates the dilemma facing a citizenry wishing to preserve the cultural patrimony. Penn Central, like most property owners, especially those whose property has a high market value, will not willingly give up potential income in order to maintain a landmark that happens to stand on their property. Property owners are not alone in being unwilling to pay. Preservationists and local governments also would rather have somebody else pay. But if landmarks and historic districts are to be preserved the money must come from somewhere.

Several strategies have been proposed that provide funds to forestall demolition, ensure proper maintenance, and still allow owners to benefit from the market value of their property. Each requires money but is within the financial capacity of any community seriously interested in preservation. Each is a potentially useful tool but will not protect every landmark nor work in every situation.

One strategy is to establish an areawide system for the transfer of development rights. A second involves a revolving fund that provides the money to purchase threatened landmarks and then sells them with appropriate preservation covenants. The third transfers the cost of rehabilitation to local government. Property owners who pay for restoration are reimbursed annually in the form of reduced real estate tax payments. This strategy is particularly attractive to elected officials because they never have to vote to cut something from the budget or raise the revenues from a new "preservation" tax. A fourth strategy transfers the cost of preservation to the federal government. It also camouflages the price by keeping it out of the budget and spreading it over many years. In this case, the owners of a landmark pay for restoration and are reimbursed by the federal government in the form of deductions from their income tax payments.

Strategy 1: Development Rights Districts

In his book, *Space Adrift: Landmark Preservation and the Marketplace,* published in 1974, law professor John Costonis proposes the creation of "development rights transfer districts" to which and from which landmarks owners would be

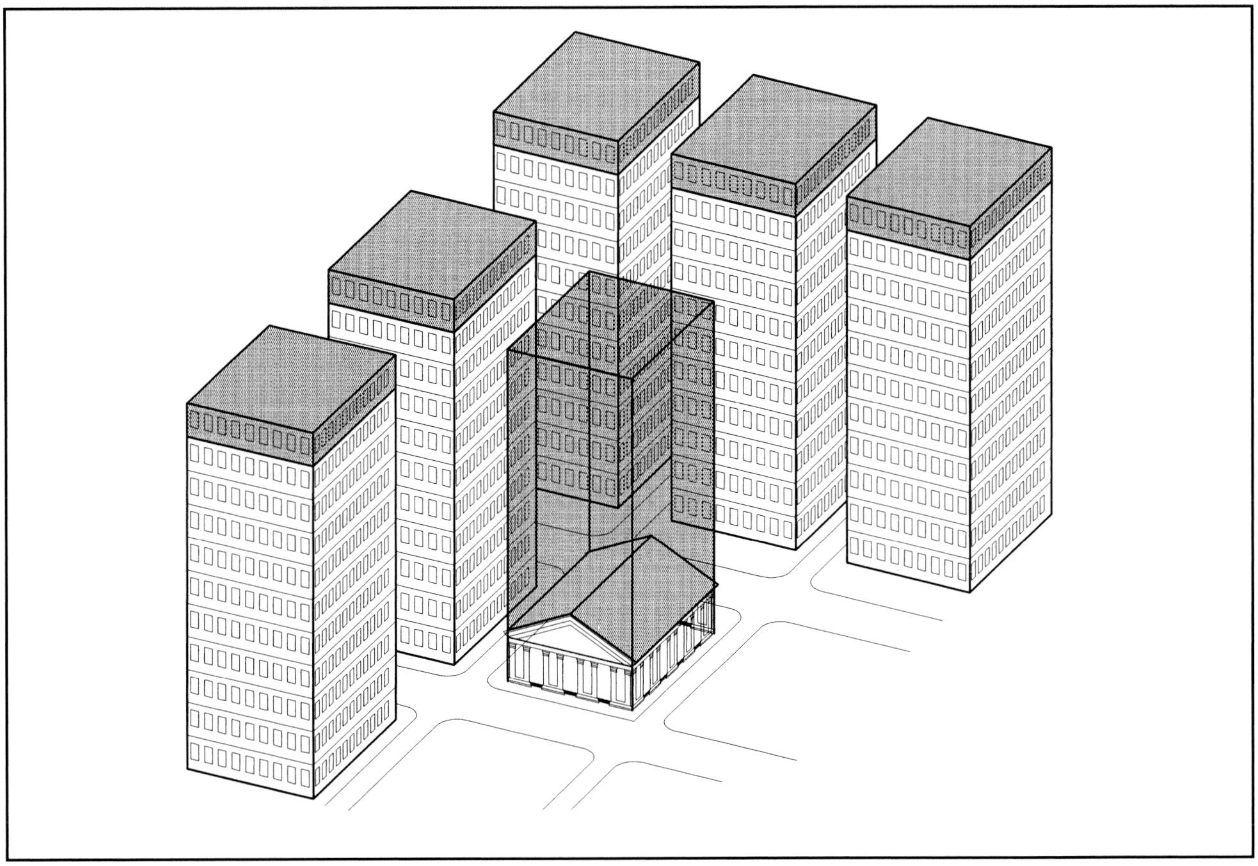

Neighboring sites to which the unused bulk over a designated landmark could be transferred. *(Alexander Garvin and C. Christopher Koon)*

Denver, 1990. The Navarre Café (currently the Museum of Western Art) was preserved because its owner was able to transfer unused development rights from this designated landmark. *(Alexander Garvin)*

entitled to convey excess development rights. The plan assumes that most sites occupied by landmarks are zoned for significantly greater bulk and density, that these sites are "concentrated into reasonably compact areas of the city, usually downtown," or in areas that are about to undergo intensive development, and that the sites which will receive additional development are located where there are plentiful public services and facilities to "absorb large numbers of people with greater efficiency."[40]

Such landmarks are threatened because they do not generate revenues that are commensurate with the property's market value. That market value is based on the development potential of the site under existing zoning. The only way to obtain the potential revenue is to demolish the landmark currently occupying the site and then to erect a building that maximizes the zoning potential.[41]

Costonis argues that demolition can be avoided by identifying and permitting the sale of the unused zoning potential of the site. He also suggests that cities establish a *development rights bank.* The bank would receive donations of development rights from philanthropic property owners and from city-owned landmarks. These rights would be sold to interested developers and the money used to fund municipal condemnation of recalcitrant landmark owners' excess development rights, whenever a landmark is threatened by demolition or neglect.

Denver's Development Rights Transfer District

Denver's "Transfer of Development Rights (TDR) Ordinance" was created at a time when millions of square feet of new office space were being built downtown, almost all on sites that had to be cleared of older buildings. When civic leaders realized that existing zoning might be preventing renovation, they decided to amend the city's land use regulations.[42]

The project that initiated this legislation was the Navarre, a landmark listed on the National Register. This four-story brick structure was originally built in 1880 to house the Brinker Collegiate Institute. Nine years later it was converted into a gambling house and bordello (known as the Richelieu Hotel). In 1914 the property was renamed the Navarre Café.[43]

The Navarre had been vacant for several years when in 1980 it was purchased for reuse as an office building. The owners of the Navarre tried to obtain a mortgage to finance the rehabilitation of their landmark. Institutional financing was available for what lenders considered the property's "highest and best use," a high-rise office building, but not for renovation. Worse yet, the banks subtracted the cost of demolishing existing buildings from the amount they would lend.

For mortgage appraisal purposes, rehabilitation was deemed to be an expense that increased the eventual cost of site preparation for a skyscraper. Banks were unwilling to lend for an activity that its appraisers believed would decrease the value of the property.

Lisa Purdy, a resourceful preservation specialist at Historic Denver Inc., went to work to reverse this bias against renovation. Taking her cue from Costonis, she proposed legislation that would transform the unused development potential of sites occupied by designated landmarks into a valuable commodity. If such legislation could be enacted, the owners of the Navarre and of other landmarks would, for the first time, have a liquid asset that could be sold without demolishing historic structures that happened to occupy their land. Moreover, they could use the proceeds from the sale of development rights to finance rehabilitation.[44]

In 1982, after a year of public review and discussion, the City Council amended the zoning ordinance to allow transfer of development rights from designated historic structures. TDR was restricted to two sections of the city: the 93-block central business district (zoned B-5) and the 15-block "Lower Downtown" (zoned B-7). In order to ensure that no receiving lot in either zone would overload the existing infrastructure, the permitted increase in floor area was restricted to 25 percent.

The business district, Denver's only B-5 zoning district, permitted commercial use at a FAR of 10. It seemed a perfect location and market for TDRs. Furthermore, the TDR legislation made no change in the area's permitted density, bulk, or land use. It simply allowed the redistribution of some of the B-5 district's bulk and density.[45]

Lower Downtown contained Denver's 1881 railroad station and the bulk of its nineteenth- and early twentieth-century warehouses, manufacturing lofts, and mercantile structures. No section of the city had a greater concentration of historic structures. Lower Downtown was Denver's only B-7 zoning district. It allowed commercial land use at a FAR of 4. The legislation only allowed the redistribution of the B-7 zone's already authorized bulk and density.[46]

To understand how Denver's TDR works, let's imagine a historic structure containing 20,000 square feet on a 10,000-square-foot lot in a B-5 zone. Since the FAR is 10, the total allowable floor area on the site is 100,000 square feet (i.e., FAR 10x10,000 square feet=100,000 square feet). The existing historic structure uses up 20,000 square feet, leaving 80,000 square feet that can be transferred. Let's also imagine that a developer has purchased a 40,000-square-foot vacant lot, 10 blocks away, also in the B-5 zone. The allowable floor area on the site is 400,000 square feet (i.e., FAR 10x40,000 square feet=400,000 square feet) and an additional 100,000 square feet, if development rights can be purchased from the owners of designated historic structures (i.e., 0.25x400,000 square feet=100,000 square feet). Any developer who purchased the site for $20 million should be willing to purchase development rights for the same $50 per square foot of floor area (i.e., $20,000,000÷400,000 square feet=$50 per square foot). The owner of the historic structure who has 80,000 square feet of available development rights should be able to sell them for $4 million (i.e., 80,000 square feet x $50 per square foot =$4,000,000). Thus the developer will be able to build a 480,000-square-foot building. To get the full 500,000 square feet, though, will require the purchase of another 20,000 square feet of TDR.

During the first dozen years in which the transfer of development rights has been possible, no new buildings in Denver made use of available TDRs. The Denver Athletic Club, did transfer 60,000 square feet of development rights to the site of the as-yet-to-be-built Midland Savings Bank, five blocks away. The D & F Tower entered into a contract to sell its development rights. These rights went unused because the energy glut and subsequent recession had brought development to a halt.

TDR legislation did result in the preservation of some historic structures. The owners of the Navarre were able to use the newly created development rights as collateral for a mortgage loan covering the cost of its renovation. When the building was sold for use as the Museum of Western Art in 1983, the previous owners kept the development rights for future sale. The owners of another building, Odd Fellows Hall built in 1889, were also able to use their TDRs as part of their collateral for a rehabilitation construction loan.

Strategy 2: The Revolving Fund

Landmarks are often owned by individuals who either do not have the money to maintain them properly, have the money to pay for ordinary upkeep but not for necessary restoration, intend to use their property in a way that would be injurious to its historic character, or are ready to sell to purchasers who would demolish what is regarded as precious. One way to avoid such situations is to acquire the property and then transfer ownership to somebody who will cherish and maintain it. This requires an entity that can act quickly. The most effective means of creating such an entity is to endow it with enough money to acquire and resell a substantial number of threatened landmarks.

The most active revolving fund is operated by the National Trust for Historic Preservation. Between 1971 and 1988, its Preservation Loan Fund provided more than $8.2 million for preservation projects in 41 states, the District of Columbia, and Puerto Rico.[47]

Most revolving funds are operated by local entities like the Historic Savannah Foundation or the Pittsburgh History and Landmarks Foundation. Once the necessary money has been raised, it is used to purchase threatened properties that are resold with protective covenants ensuring that the exterior is properly restored and then maintained. Occasionally, a revolving fund is used for necessary restoration prior to resale, for acquisition and demolition of property that is incompatible with a historic district, or for mortgage loans to purchasers unable to obtain conventional bank financing. The idea is to keep enlarging the fund, reusing sale proceeds for additional preservation activity, and always assuring that enough money is on hand to deal with emergencies.

While a revolving fund is applicable to all parts of a city, it can be particularly effective with inexpensive and neglected buildings that do not have development rights to transfer and thus cannot easily be preserved by the Costonis approach. The money is reused many times, producing many bangs for the same buck. Moreover, when a revolving fund is used as part of a strategy for a whole area, strategic renovation of a few criti-

PULASKI SQUARE - JONES STREET

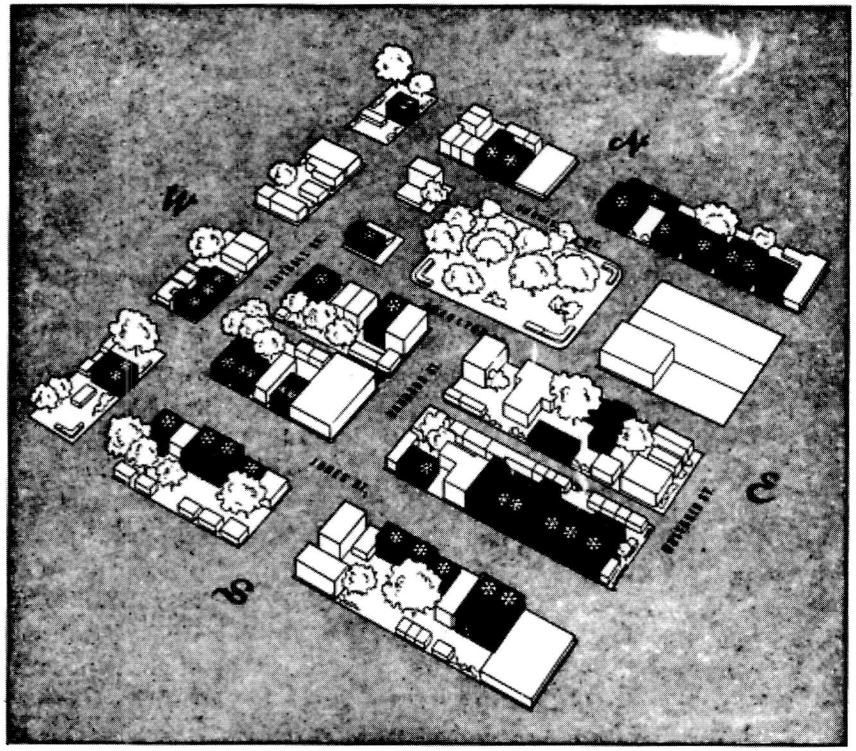

. . . . it was a 13-acre deteriorating, near-slum neighborhood. It is now being reclaimed.

46 buildings have been stabilized . . .

38 were reclaimed by Historic Savannah

28 of the 38 through direct purchase for resale

another 10 influenced by Historic Savannah's efforts since the program's inception.

■ 46 Buildings stabilized (restored or in process)

*** 38 Units reclaimed through Historic Savannah**

THIS WAS DONE IN ONLY 18 MONTHS!

Savannah, 1967. Forty-six buildings were restored or in the process of restoration within 18 months of establishing a revolving fund to purchase and resell deteriorating buildings in Pulaksi Ward. *(Courtesy of Historic Savannah Foundation)* cal buildings will bolster local self-confidence, thereby inducing neighboring property owners to make further improvements. This is what happened when a revolving fund was established for the historic wards of Savannah and Charleston.

Savannah's Historic Wards

Savannah's 26 wards provide a unique setting for the lovely eighteenth- and nineteenth-century buildings that were erected around charming public squares (see Chapter 3 and Chapter 13). By the middle of the twentieth century, many of these buildings had badly deteriorated. Two squares had been dismembered to provide additional traffic lanes. The Historic Savannah Foundation was founded to stop the further destruction of this extraordinary heritage.[48]

In 1954, when the Historic Savannah Foundation was established, there was little public interest in the city's old buildings. Savannah had neither an organization dedicated to preservation (except for a citizen group that had successfully fought cutting the squares in two with new streets) nor laws to preserve landmarks in its historic wards. Few families chose to settle downtown, where property values had been depressed for years.

In 1962 the foundation completed an inventory of historic structures that was first published 6 years later as a beautifully illustrated book entitled *Historic Savannah.* This survey provided the basis for the historic-district zoning enacted in 1972 and helped to generate increased interest in the buildings illustrated in the book. The foundation also promoted interest in historic properties by publishing a Sunday supplement in Savannah's newspaper and organizing weekend tours. In 1965, together with the Chamber of Commerce, it issued a report entitled "Savannah—A Travel Destination." The thrust of the report was that "a modest investment in the promotion and restoration effort in Savannah could bring tourist revenues of up to $100 million annually."[49]

Historic Savannah's most enterprising activity was its $200,000 revolving fund. The fund was used initially to acquire and renovate threatened landmarks in the Pulaski Square–West Jones Street Area. In just 18 months the fund saved 46 properties and generated more than $1.5 million in private investment.

During the first three decades of its existence Historic Savannah acquired and resold over 800 houses that are actively used as residences by their occupants. They have become tourist destinations for the city's 5.1 million visitors who, in 1989 alone, generated $494 million and 9400 jobs.[50]

Pittsburgh's Mexican War Streets

Pittsburgh's experience with the revolving fund was different from Savannah's, because of the city's different physical character and market conditions and because of the way in which its revolving fund operated. Pittsburgh has charming older neighborhoods with interesting nineteenth- and twentieth-century buildings. Few of them, however, are as exquisite as some of the antebellum houses of Savannah. More important, Savannah's historic preservation efforts coincided with an increasing population and expanding economy. Over the same 30-year period, Pittsburgh's population dropped from 677,000 to 370,000, and with it the demand for obsolete buildings.[51]

Despite these very different conditions, there was a similar increasing interest in historic preservation. In 1964, a group of dedicated citizens formed the Pittsburgh History and Landmarks Foundation (PHLF) to assist in meeting the city's diverse preservation needs. The PHLF issued publications on the architecture and history of the city and established a revolving fund to preserve distinctive older neighborhoods. By 1973, the revolving fund consisted of nearly $500,000, making it the largest in the nation.[52]

The neighborhood popularly referred to as the "Mexican War streets" was one of the areas selected by the PHLF for its revolving fund. Its streets had been laid out in 1848, when it was still part of Allegheny, an independent city across the river from downtown Pittsburgh. These streets were named for famous Mexican War battles and military officers. Within a few years these streets were lined with modest, two- and three-story, brick, row houses with gingerbread porches.

By the early 1960s, the Mexican War streets had become "a mixture of young and old, white and black, home owners and slum rooming house dwellers, poor to middle-income residents."[53] The buildings they occupied had deteriorated badly. In an attempt to save old and historic structures and generate further area revival, the PHLF decided to concentrate the activity of its newly established revolving fund on the Mexican War streets. The strategy was to buy out slumlords, reconvert rooming houses to family occupancy, relocate tenants "as appropriate, to public housing or other units in the area," fix up strategically located properties for continued use by low-income families, and thereby generate further investment by existing property owners and attract "new, particularly young, working residents" to the area.

During its first decade of operation, the PHLF purchased 24 Mexican War streets buildings. In order to keep housing costs at a level that was affordable to the area's existing low-income residents, the PHFL minimized rehabilitation and avoided costly replication of architectural details. When necessary, the PHLF used the revolving fund to subsidize tenants and rented the buildings at a loss. This kept poor families in the area. It also kept the buildings from being put on a sustainable economic footing and retarded further improvement.

While the revolving fund managed to save charming, inexpensive residences for households interested in living close to downtown Pittsburgh, it did not trigger much additional

Pittsburgh, 1990. Vacant and run-down buildings on Buena Vista, more than 15 years after the PHFL began acquiring and renovating buildings with its revolving fund. *(Alexander Garvin)*

investment in the neighborhood. There might have been more demand for housing in this area if Pittsburgh had not been losing population and if there had not been plenty of inexpensive housing elsewhere, often in areas with just as much charm but which were thought to be safer. The existing residents could not afford to pay for more than basic patch-up. Consequently, many buildings in the neighborhood remained run-down.[54]

Strategy 3: Real Estate Tax Benefits

If occupants cannot afford to pay more for their accommodations, if owners are unwilling to pay for "inessential" restoration that will not produce additional earnings, if purchasers are unwilling to forgo the benefits of a "higher and better use" for their property, the money for historic preservation must come from society as a whole. No community will readily provide funds to a small group of citizens simply because they own or occupy historic structures. It may, however, provide assistance if it is convinced that this money will trigger investment that would otherwise not occur and generate taxes that would otherwise not be collected. Short-term tax breaks are an effective means of doing this, provided they result in construction jobs now and additional taxes later.

While forgoing taxes does not provide money up front, the increase in a property's net cash flow may be enough to justify a bank loan to finance renovation. More than 37 states have enacted legislation enabling localities to provide tax incentives for historic preservation. Georgia, Illinois, Oregon, and other states allow cities to freeze real estate tax assessments of designated landmarks. Maryland, Rhode Island, and Wisconsin provide a state income-tax credit for the renovation of historic structures.

Some of the most effective historic preservation programs are not targeted exclusively to designated landmarks or historic districts. New York's J-51 Tax Exemption/Abatement Program, for example, provides assistance to all multiple dwellings. By exempting residential buildings from any increase in taxes due to rehabilitation and then abating a large portion of the taxes that would otherwise have had to be paid, it has made possible the preservation of thousands of historic structures (see Chapters 1 and 10).[55]

Initially J-51 was only applicable to the renovation of multiple dwellings. In 1975, the benefits were extended to conversion of nonresidential buildings into apartment buildings. In doing so, the city created a powerful instrument for the transformation of districts filled with vacant and underutilized warehouses and loft factories, many of which were significant historical structures that would otherwise have been lost. The transformation of one such area, SoHo, demonstrates how such real estate tax benefits can be used to convert major market pressure into a force for historic preservation.

Manhattan, 1980. Cast-iron buildings in SoHo. *(Alexander Garvin)*

New York City's SoHo

In 1973, 3½ years after it had held public hearings on SoHo, the New York City Landmarks Commission designated this 26-block area a historic district. The area, named SoHo because it is "South of Houston Street," contained the largest concentration of cast-iron buildings in the country.[56] These five- and six-story structures were erected during the second half of the nineteenth century. Many had ground floors with broad windows for the display of merchandise, middle floors for office work, and upper floors for storage. They were unique because of their self-supporting front walls and interior columns built of prefabricated cast-iron pieces. These cast-iron pieces were elegantly detailed components of unusual strength that permitted architects to design highly ornamented façades. Their large expanses of glass provided plenty of light to interior loft spaces supported by cast-iron columns rather than structural walls.

Today, SoHo is known throughout the world as an art center of unusual vitality, filled with trendy galleries, fashionable boutiques and restaurants, artists studios, loft apartments, and leftover manufacturing. When it was designated a historic district, the area was known for its dirty, neglected, half-empty buildings.

During the previous two decades, New York City had lost half a million industrial jobs, mostly in Manhattan. The industrial firms that remained in SoHo were marginal at best. Most healthy businesses had already left. They could not afford to operate in obsolete multistory structures built before the turn of the century.

The amazing thing was that these buildings were there at all. Robert Moses had proposed demolishing large sections of the district, first for the South Village Urban Renewal Project and then for a Lower Manhattan Expressway. Although the community had defeated both projects, they now faced a much more powerful agent of destruction—neglect and abandonment.[57]

The city's zoning precluded residential occupancy because planners mistakenly thought that they could retain manufacturing in Manhattan by restricting occupancy to industrial users. The zoning was easy to ignore. Artists with little money rented vast studio-residences in SoHo's neglected buildings at very low rates. Fortuitously, these large empty spaces with high ceilings could also accommodate huge canvases and large sculptures. Despite the occupancy restrictions, by the end of the decade there was a large community of artists living in SoHo.

In the face of such widespread illegal occupancy, the City Planning Commission altered the zoning in 1970 to permit "joint living/work quarters for artists," provided that such quarters contained less than 3600 square feet. These occupants had to be certified by the Department of Cultural Affairs as genuine "artists." The marketplace soon found ways around the restrictions. "Artists" managed to get certified for the sole purpose of converting whole floors into large unconventional apartments. Owners of buildings that were too large to qualify were happy just to get their space rented. They did not look too closely at whom they rented to. Nor did they or their tenants care whether renovation was consistent with the building's historic character or its context within the historic district.

SoHo lofts were not designed to be used as residences. Altering these buildings to meet legal safety requirements was very costly. Restoring a building's historic character added further costs to renovation. As a result, lofts were altered without reference to landmarks regulation.

Financial institutions would not provide a mortgage to pay for conversion of a structure that continued to violate the zoning ordinance, the building code, the multiple-dwelling law, and the provisions of the historic district. Even if mortgage financing had been available, conversion was not financially feasible. Because the city reassessed buildings upon renovation, new real estate taxes would have been prohibitively high.

In 1975 when J-51 Tax Exemption/Abatement was extended to include the conversion of nonresidential structures into multiple dwellings, the economics of preservation were radically altered. J-51 provided a 12-year exemption from reassessment plus an abatement of annual tax payments equal to 90 percent of the cost of rehabilitation. Banks were willing to provide mortgage commitments based on J-51 benefits. However, they insisted that any renovation be 100 percent legal. In order to obtain the necessary alteration permits, developers had to obtain certificates of appropriateness from the Landmarks Commission.

Demand for retail space on the ground floor and loft residential space upstairs became so intense that many artists could no longer afford to remain in SoHo. Lofts that had been purchased for less than $10,000 in the late 1960s, were selling for half a million dollars 20 years later. High rents even forced out the innovative retailers who had come to SoHo when there had been few customers. The J-51 program had been so successful that the City Council started cutting back benefits in the early 1980s and then terminated its use for loft conversion.

Rezoning and designation as a historic district had not been enough to guarantee the restoration of SoHo's cast-iron architecture. J-51 Tax Exemption/Abatement made available the missing ingredient: mortgage financing. Combined with the already strong market pressure to convert these buildings to residential use, the program unleashed the historic restoration that previously had been financially unattractive.[58]

Similar results were achieved in other areas (e.g., Tribeca and the West Village) that may not have had as many cast-iron structures, but had a similarly obsolete stock of warehouses and multistory manufacturing lofts. During the first 6 years in which J-51 benefits were available for the conversion of nonresidential structures, 12,000 converted apartments received J-51 benefits, many of them in these neighborhood.[59]

Critics have argued that extending J-51 benefits to nonresidential buildings squeezed out viable manufacturing firms. But it is difficult to believe that by preventing the adaptive reuse of multistory industrial lofts New York could have become the one city in America to retain manufacturing firms in congested center city locations.

Strategy 4: Income-Tax Benefits

When preservationists turn to local government for money, they must compete with others who want it spent on education, police protection, sanitation, and other worthy purposes. The easy way out is to seek the money in Washington. Most preservationists understand that the federal bureaucracy will not get the job done efficiently, economically, or in a manner that is sensitive to local concerns. Instead, they seek income-tax benefits for people who restore designated landmarks and historic districts.[60]

Congress responded to this demand for assistance with a series of changes to the Internal Revenue Code. The process began with the Tax Reform Act of 1976. As a result of this statute, owners of historic buildings who restored them could depreciate rehabilitation expenditures over a 60-month period, rather than the longer periods that applied to all other properties. This 60-month depreciation period was, in effect, a subsidy because the useful life of most rehabilitation extended far beyond 5 years.[61]

Just as the 60-month depreciation period had begun to spur interest in historic preservation, Congress provided additional tax benefits in the Revenue Act of 1978. For the first time, owners of historic properties were permitted a tax credit equal to 10 percent of the cost of rehabilitation. Unlike depreciation, which is deducted annually from property income and must be accounted for upon resale, a tax credit is a dollar-for-dollar reduction in income tax that does not have to be returned upon resale. It is a subsidy equal to 10 percent of the cost of rehabilitation, paid by the federal government in the form of uncollected income taxes.[62]

These income-tax benefits were minor compared with those provided by the Economic Recovery Tax Act of 1981. This law provided an income-tax credit equal to 25 percent of the cost of rehabilitation and also permitted full depreciation of this tax credit. For example, developers who acquired landmarks listed on the National Register for $100,000 ($20,000 allocated to land and $80,000 to the building) and spent $1 million on renovation, could take a tax credit of $250,000 (25 percent of $1 million) and still depreciate $1,080,000 ($1 million plus $80,000). Although the depreciability of the tax credit was reduced by 50 percent in 1982, it remained an extremely potent incentive.[63]

The Tax Reform Act of 1976 generated $140 million in certified rehabilitation. The Revenue Act of 1978 generated $650 million. This was small potatoes compared to the Economic Recovery Tax Act of 1981, which between 1982 and 1985 resulted in more than 10,000 restoration projects worth $7.8 billion.[64]

Congress passed the Tax Reform Act of 1986 as a means of reducing the role of tax loopholes and tax shelters and encouraging developers and lenders to make investment decisions on a market-oriented basis. The Act reduced the tax credit for the preservation of designated historic structures from 25 to 20 percent. However, the cut in this tax credit was not the primary cause of the reduction in income-tax benefits for historic preservation. The two main causes were lower tax rates and the passive loss rule.

In 1976, when the maximum tax rate had been 70 percent, any individual in the maximum tax bracket who earned $1000 paid $700 in taxes and retained $300. Thus, $1000 in after-tax income was the equivalent of $3333 in pretax cash, because the tax on $3333 would have been $2333 ($3333x.7=$2333). When the tax bracket is only 28 percent, $1000 in after-tax income is only worth $1389 in pretax cash, because the tax on $1389 is $389 ($1389x.28=$389). By reducing the value of after-tax dollars, the Tax Reform Act of 1986 reduced their impact on investment decisions. As a result, the tax credit became a less attractive incentive for historic preservation.

The impact of the passive-loss rule was no less significant. Prior to 1986, property owners and developers could sell tax benefits to passive investors who used them to shelter other income. Developers used the proceeds of the sale of tax-shelter benefits as equity or just pocketed the money. With certain exceptions, the Tax Reform Act of 1986 required that tax credits be applied only to income generated by the property. By eliminating this tax shelter, Congress effectively eliminated investor interest in historic-rehabilitation projects that did not generate the cash returns to offset the tax benefits.

Federal tax incentives are difficult to grasp in the abstract. Their impact is easier to understand by examining the evolution of a specific historic district, especially one like the West End of Dallas, which experienced little preservation activity until Congress passed the Economic Recovery Tax Act of 1981.

Dallas, 1974. West End while still in use as a warehouse district. *(Alexander Garvin)*

The West End in Dallas

When Dallas designated 30 blocks of the West End as a historic district in 1975, it was a 67.5-acre area filled with obsolete commercial structures predominantly built during the first two decades of the twentieth century. The three-to-eight-story, red-brick warehouses that filled the district had been built for businesses that depended on nearby railroad yards. These buildings were the only dense concentration of late nineteenth- and early twentieth-century commercial buildings in Dallas. But, unlike the cast-iron lofts in SoHo, few of these buildings were significant because of exceptional architectural design.[65]

Dallas did not just designate the West End as a historic district. It developed a preservation plan that included public improvements and amended the city's zoning ordinance to include specific design requirements for all renovation and new construction. They included a height limit of 100 feet and requirements for façade openings, window setbacks, parking, signs, materials, and color.[66]

Despite a booming economy, despite the example of adaptive reuse of warehouse districts throughout the country, elaborate development guidelines, and a $4.5 million streetscape improvement program, little development activity occurred prior to 1982. Then, between 1982 and 1985, more than $70 million was spent on rehabilitation in the West End.

The impetus for the adaptive reuse of the buildings of the West End came from the tax benefits provided by the Economic Recovery Tax Act of 1981. Also demand for space during the early 1980s had become sufficiently intense that smaller firms would accept secondary locations, such as the West End. The new tax credits and rapid depreciation could be sold to investors who needed tax shelters. Developers who sold them used the proceeds of this sale as equity and financed the remaining cost of renovation with institutional mortgages. Thus, the renovation of these historic structures required little or no cash from their developers.

Dallas, 1989. Market Street in the West End after several years of renovations and alterations. *(Alexander Garvin)*

The market for West End office space spilled over to the ground floor. "In 1983, only one retail/restaurant establishment existed in the West End; that restaurant produced less than $100,000 in annual sales and liquor taxes." By 1987, the area had more than 130 retail shops, 30 restaurants, and 10 nightclubs, generating $72 million in retail/restaurant sales, $5.5 million in sales taxes, and $3.3 million in city parking fees and violations. Although the West End was still experiencing a bar, restaurant, and entertainment boom at the end of the decade, development came to a halt.[67]

Designation as a historic district initially had no effect on the West End. Its preservation was guaranteed only when federal income-tax benefits became sufficiently generous to attract developers. If developers are still attracted to the West End when market pressure is restored, the income-tax benefits for historic preservation then available will determine whether they choose to demolish or renovate.

An Activist Approach

Countless landmarks have been defaced by owners legitimately trying to repair crumbling facades or leaking roofs. Anybody who has passed a once-sumptuous Victorian mansion now covered with asphalt tile or imitation flagstone knows the problem. Had the owners been aware of the historic value of their buildings or employed knowledgeable architects, society would now have a restored landmark instead of an unsightly, but watertight, monstrosity. Consequently, preservationists feel justified in demanding that government restrict a property owner's right to alter or demolish historic structures.

Denying permission to alter or demolish old buildings can be taken too far, as it was in the case of New York City's Mt. Neboh Synagogue. But, waiting for property owners to restore designated landmarks may not be a reasonable alternative either. While the preservation agency waits for owners to apply for permission to do something, important historical structures may seriously deteriorate. Consequently, more aggressive action, such as the program that brought about the restoration of Seattle's Pioneer Square, may be necessary.

Mt. Neboh Synagogue

In 1982, New York City's Landmarks Preservation Commission officially designated the former Mt. Neboh Synagogue as a landmark. Mt. Neboh was not listed in the index of architecturally noteworthy buildings of Greater New York issued by the Municipal Arts Society in 1957, nor in its successor volume *New York Landmarks,* published in 1963. It did not appear in Paul Goldberger's 1979 guide to the architecture of Manhattan, *The City Observed.* The American Institute of Architects' *AIA Guide to New York City,* first published in 1967, described it as "another West Side synagogue which has borrowed heavily from the Byzantine style." Even the chairman of the Landmarks Commission recognized that it was "not architecturally significant."[68]

This abandoned synagogue had been brought to the attention of the Landmarks Commission by a group of West Side residents who had formed a "Committee to Save Mt. Neboh."

Nashville, 1992. Two once-similar houses in the East Nashville historic district: one has been handsomely maintained, the other is the victim of ill-conceived "improvements." *(Courtesy of Old House Journal, March/April 1992, Gloucester Mass., 01930)*

They persuaded the commission to hold a public hearing on the designation of this 55-year-old building, which they argued was an example of the "synthesis of Byzantine and other Near Eastern influences." In fact, their reasons were quite different.

The synagogue had been acquired by a developer who intended to erect an apartment building. The new structure was to be as tall as neighboring buildings and just as mediocre in design. Whether opposition to this privately financed apartment house stemmed from disapproval of tall buildings, mediocre design, high-income tenants, the additional burden to community facilities, or nostalgic affection for the synagogue, continues to be debated. What cannot be debated is that neither the committee nor the Landmarks Commission had the money to acquire the property nor could they suggest any financially feasible alternative use for the structure.

The owner of Mt. Neboh had purchased the site for $2.4 million prior to any discussion of landmark status. He wanted to build market-rate housing on a site zoned for that purpose by the City Planning Commission. Landmark status kept him from proceeding. One year and $1 million later the Landmarks Commission accepted his pleas of hardship and granted a demolition permit.

By appealing to the State Supreme Court and Court of Appeals, the Committee to Save Mt. Neboh continued to stall demolition and cost the developer still more money. When the owner finally won permission to develop the site, costs had escalated to the point that he was no longer able to proceed. He sold the site to another developer who erected an undistinguished apartment house.[69]

The Landmarks Commission did not compensate the developer for the costs incurred as a result of its action. Preservation agencies have not yet had to pay for any infringement of private property rights during the period in which they consider actions proposed by property owners who, but

Manhattan, 1995. The entrance to the apartment house built on the site of Mt. Neboh Synagogue is at the third canopy from the left. *(Alexander Garvin)*

for landmarks status, could lawfully proceed without their permission. They have not had to weigh the value of potential increases in tax revenues and employment from more intensive use of such sites. Nor have they had to consider the impact of the decrease in tax revenues that may result from a drop in market value caused by landmarks designation. This may change. In 1985, the Supreme Court, in the case of *First English Evangelical Lutheran Church v. County of Los Angeles,* ruled that government has to compensate owners for such temporary taking of property. As a result, preservation agencies must now worry about potential cash damages from arbitrary or untimely actions.[70]

Pioneer Square, Seattle

Seattle was established in 1852 on Elliott Bay, a natural harbor along Puget Sound. The following year Henry Yesler built the area's first steam-powered lumber mill on the waterfront. Logs were skidded down the hill to the lumber mill, giving it the name "skid row." By 1885, the city that had grown up around the skid road included 12,000 residents, most of whom lived in wood structures. It included so many saloons, gambling joints, and other disreputable enterprises, that it provided America with the skid row label for any seedy section of town "where people not logs were on the skids."[71]

In 1889 a sudden fire destroyed the entire 25-block core of Seattle. It was rebuilt in masonry rather than wood. Since most of the buildings were built at roughly the same time, of the same material (brick), at roughly the same height (six stories), and frequently designed by the same architect (Elmer Fisher), the area took on an unusually unified character. It became known as Pioneer Square in recognition of the triangular public space at the intersection of Yesler Way ("skid row") and First Avenue.

As Seattle's business districted expanded and moved northward, Pioneer Square began a slow decline. By the 1960s the area had become little more than a hangout for drunks, derelicts, and panhandlers. Developers and planners proposed replacing its dilapidated buildings with modern office towers. Community activists objected, calling instead for restoration. In 1970, they succeeded in getting the city to declare Pioneer Square a historic district.

Seattle, 1979. First Street in the Pioneer Square District. *(Alexander Garvin)*

Seattle, 1990. Occidental Avenue was widened and relandscaped into a park that provides an attractive setting for tourists sitting at restaurant tables. *(Alexander Garvin)*

The program for restoring Pioneer Square included more than designation of the historic district. The city established an architectural review board with the power to approve any changes in exterior appearance and created the post of district manager to coordinate and supervise preservation activities. The city council appropriated $2.1 million for public improvements. Pioneer Square was relandscaped and its turn-of-the-century pergola restored. First Avenue was completely reconstructed. It became an attractive retail thoroughfare with a new median strip of trees and replicas of the area's original cast-iron light poles and drinking fountains. Occidental Avenue became a tree-lined, cobblestone, pedestrian area.[72]

In 1974, the historic district ordinance was amended to require proper maintenance of every property in the district. Should owners fail to comply within a reasonable period of time, the city superintendent of buildings has the right to make an "emergency repair" and place a lien on the property that will cover the cost of the improvements.

It took only 6 years for property owners in Pioneer Square to transform the area from a neglected skid row into a lively tourist attraction. During that time they restored more than half of the area's 150 historic structures. Numerous restaurants and retail establishments opened. Area employment jumped from 1000 to 6000 and the tax base increased 1000 percent.[73]

In the case of Pioneer Square, the carrot of public investment and the stick of threatened emergency repair sufficiently altered the market to spur building rehabilitation. This activist approach worked because downtown Seattle was expanding rapidly. Demand for secondary office space spilled over from the business district. More important, the distinctive appearance of Pioneer Square's architecture appealed to

Seattle's growing tourist business. Merchants were able to capitalize on a gussied-up image of a previous era. In areas without such market pressure, similar activism is unlikely to be successful.

Ingredients of Success

Every property owner is responsible for cultivating the cultural patrimony. Too often government inadvertently hastens the deterioration and destruction of the cultural patrimony by imposing regulations that are difficult and expensive for property owners to comply with. In those instances property owners either are dissuaded from making improvements by the added cost of complying with regulations or ignore the regulations and make less costly improvements. Such burdens prevent preservation and must be eliminated. More important, government has a more important role to play in helping property owners to cultivate the cultural patrimony through the use of strategic public investment, regulation, and incentives.

Market

Most historic preservation strategies only work when there is market demand. Without buyers for historically significant buildings, development rights, income tax credits, and real estate tax abatement will go unused and revolving funds will deplete their coffers because they cannot resell the historic properties they have acquired.

Local real estate tax benefits and state and federal income tax incentives can lower the cost of maintaining and restoring historic structures. In some cases the reduction in tax payments will be large enough to stimulate property owners to renovate old buildings. In Dallas' West End, for example, income-tax credits and rapid depreciation schedules allowed developers to offer commercial space at low enough prices to attract users of secondary office space. But tax incentives cannot do much if there are still no consumers at the lower price that these incentives make possible. That is why J-51, which had so significant an effect on the lofts and warehouses of SoHo, had so little impact on lofts and warehouses in Brooklyn and the Bronx.

Location

Historic districts begin with a significant locational advantage. The very presence of historically significant structures creates that advantage. Destroy them and the location loses its attractiveness. Thus, designation as a historic district is in the interest of most property owners. Their only concern will be the added burden of complying with regulations. If designation is accompanied by tax incentives, they may be willing to accept that additional burden.

Proximity also plays a role in determining the success or failure of a preservation strategy. Tax incentives, for example, may lower the price of space in a landmark or historic district enough to attract customers from more expensive, nearby properties. The lower prices for apartments in SoHo, for example, attracted residents who could not afford such accommodations in Greenwich Village. Similarly, once buildings in the West End had been fixed up, they were able to profit from customers who spilled over from downtown Dallas. Nor is proximity just a matter of interacting land uses. The rationale behind both historic and TDR districts is that the costs and benefits of regulation accrue in an equitable fashion to all property owners within the area.

Design

The character of each historic area is perhaps its most important design feature. Eliminate SoHo's cast-iron columns, window walls, and ornament and you eliminate its charm and attraction to an art-oriented population. Separate and reorganize into neat patterns the jumble of land uses and styles that characterize the Vieux Carre and you are likely to diminish spending by noisy tourists. Consequently, it is even more important for local preservation agencies to adopt different regulatory strategies for different districts.

The transfer of development rights presents one of the stickiest design problems. For the development rights to retain their value, the receiving property must be of similar value. Similarly, if the additional development is not to be an additional burden to the receiving area, it will have to be fairly close to the property from which these rights have been taken. Thus, the obvious purchaser becomes a neighboring site. But if all the additional bulk is concentrated on one receiving site the result will be a tower that inappropriately dwarfs its neighboring landmark. For this reason, most zoning ordinances restrict the additional bulk to a relatively small percent (e.g., 20 percent) of the receiving structure.

Preservation agencies are not the only organs of government that help to cultivate the cultural patrimony. Every historic district includes property that is publicly owned and maintained. Manipulation of the public component played a key role in the success of Pioneer Square and the West End. In both places, local agencies resurfaced traffic arteries, replaced street furniture, and planted trees. Seattle also transformed a portion of Occidental Avenue into a pedestrian precinct that, along one block, was widened to form a broad tree-shaded public square. In both cities, these changes made the ground plane more tourist-friendly. The result was an increase in street-level tourist activity and thus in tourist spending that justified increased private investment in the preservation of privately owned property.

Financing

Historic preservation often requires more money than banks are willing to lend. While there will always be wealthy property owners who will willingly pay extra for the privilege of occupying a landmark, many property owners either will not accept or cannot afford any added burden. The additional money can come from the sale of development rights, real estate tax credits, or state and federal income-tax deductions.

Banks tend to base their mortgages on the capitalized value of the net operating income of a property. They usually will agree in advance to increase that mortgage based on the capitalized value of any increased income stream produced by future tax benefits, when those tax benefits are in place. Thus, owners must pay for renovation before it is reimbursed from income-tax credits or real estate tax abatement. It is in these situations that a revolving fund can be particularly useful. Unfortunately, few preservationists have tried to exploit this interplay between a revolving fund and tax incentives.

Entrepreneurship

The Historic Savannah Foundation played the entrepreneurial role needed to acquire a significant number of historic structures and then convey these buildings to willing buyers. In SoHo, relatively poor artists supplied the ingenuity and sweat to adapt industrial lofts to other purposes. Somebody will always be needed to spark an area's preservation efforts. Thus, if we are to preserve the cultural patrimony, government has to create the conditions that will allow the widest variety of these preservationists to flourish.

Building occupants, property owners, and the institutions that finance them invest in improvements when they are sure that the money they invest in restoration will not lose its value. A location within a historic district reduces this risk. They can rely on the city's landmarks agency to approve only restorations, alterations, additions, and new construction that is consistent with the character of the district. Since they are able to predict the probable future appearance and use of the area, they are assured of relatively stable investment conditions.

Property owners also must be certain that any request for permission to make property improvements will be treated fairly and be processed expeditiously. If the application process takes too long, is too expensive, or subjects them to arbitrary demands, they will either abandon the improvements or circumvent the regulatory process. Savannah's zoning ordinance specifies building height, materials, textures, colors, and other design requirements within its historic district. Similar regulations apply in historic districts in Santa Fe, Dallas, and other cities. Owners and developers who comply with these explicit regulations can rely on timely government action and will, therefore, invest in property improvements. In other communities, where their actions are subject to discretionary review, they often defer improvements or evade the regulatory process.

The importance of low costs to poor artists renovating their SoHo lofts is easy to understand. The availability of mortgage financing is similarly critical. But even when institutional mortgages are available, there will be few takers if lenders require substantial amounts of equity capital. The federal income-tax incentives that were available during the late 1970s and early 1980s solved this problem by allowing owners of historic structures to sell future tax benefits to investors. In response to this opportunity there emerged a group of preservation entrepreneurs who used the proceeds of such tax-shelter sales as equity capital. We need to recreate a similar regulatory and financial climate if we are to attract the entrepreneurial talent needed to restore tens of thousands of historic structures that need attention.

Time

Those who advocate freezing the past are doomed to failure. No society can freeze history. Even if it had the money to acquire and embalm all buildings built prior to whatever point that it decided history ended, the remaining properties would be unable to sustain a flourishing economy. As the English architectural historian Reyner Banham so cogently explains: "If we let the paranoid preservers manoeuver us into keeping everything, we shall bring the normal life-process of decay and replacement to a halt, we shall straightjacket ourselves in embalmed cities of the past."[74] Societies that genuinely cherish their heritage never separate it from everyday life. For them, cultivating the cultural patrimony means retaining those structures that are genuinely significant, keeping them in good condition, and continually making necessary changes to ensure that they remain a vital part of the environment.

The landscapes of Tuscany and Umbria reflect this approach to cultivating the cultural patrimony. They are marked with the imprint of thousands of years of Italian history. Etruscan masonry provides a foundation for medieval walls. Architectural fragments from Roman basilicas are incorporated into Renaissance churches. Olive trees still grow along contours terraced centuries earlier. Each generation has taken the cultural patrimony, worked to enhance it, and then passed on something greater to its successors. Santa Barbara and Santa Fe are continually building and rebuilding in this same manner. In these cities, making history is a continuous process that never stops.

Preservation techniques are as subject to changing conditions as historic structures and thus need to be written so that they work in good times and bad. The regulations that apply to the buildings in Charleston's Old and Historic District were of little use during the 1930s and 1940s when there was little development pressure. They provided a predictable investment climate during the second half of the twentieth century when property values increased. Their most important role, however, came in the aftermath of hurricane Hugo in 1990. Property owners faced with the immediate need to restore damaged property had no choice but to comply with historic district regulations.

Historic Preservation as a City Planning Strategy

The effort to enrich the cultural patrimony must reflect the entire range of community values and interests. This cannot happen as long as historic preservation is treated as a special, privileged government activity. During its infancy, the preservation movement may have required such nurturing. Now that it has come of age, it is time to let the cultivation of the cultural patrimony compete on an equal footing with all the other functions of government. This means changing long-cherished government policies.

Communities must cease punishing the owners of historically significant buildings with increased tax assessments every time they invest in restoration. Designated landmarks and structures in historic districts should pay real estate taxes only on the assessed value of the land. This would eliminate the disincentive to restoration and remove the threat of demolition from all but those sites that are more valuable when used for other purposes. In such cases, local government either should appropriate the money to purchase and maintain threatened landmarks or let the organic process of urbanization take its course.

Communities must cease imposing unfunded mandates on owners of historic structures. These owners face a major burden: paying for desirable but expensive and inessential restoration that may be required by a municipal preservation agency. If it is important enough for government to require an owner to restore a slate roof rather than resurface it with less costly materials, then government should pay for the added burden. The easiest way to cover this cost is to abate real estate tax payments until the owner has taken tax credits equal to the additional cost of the mandated improvement.

The entire nation should cease treating historic preservation as a special activity unrelated to other government functions. Preservation requirements should not be separated from other land use regulations. Charleston made its Old and Historic District a part of the city's zoning ordinance. Similarly, the regulations governing the TDR District in Denver and the West End Historic District in Dallas are set forth in their zoning ordinances. By making historic preservation a significant part of citywide land use policy, subject to review and approval by the local planning agency and the local legislature, public officials will be forced to consider impact on the cultural patrimony of all land use decisions and to balance preservation objectives against other community goals.

Too many property owners either avoid improvements that require public review or make them but ignore proper procedures. Since preservation agencies are usually underfunded, they are often unaware of this activity or, if they know about it, do not have the personnel, money, or power to do much about it. Consequently, especially in poorer neighborhoods, designation as a historic district does little to enhance the cultural patrimony. We should admit reality and limit discretionary review to structures of truly major historic significance. Consequently, all other designated landmarks and historic districts should be required to comply with printed regulations and require no further review.

This combination of changes in real estate taxation and land use regulation will place historic preservation on an equal footing with other public objectives. The new real estate tax policies will remove the disincentive to investing in historic structures. Similarly, making historic preservation a part of the zoning ordinance will force public officials to consider historic preservation when they make decisions affecting land use policies. Together, they will create conditions in which cultivation of the cultural patrimony will become an easy and ongoing public responsibility.

Notes

1. Christopher Tunnard, "Preserving the Cultural Patrimony," pp. 552–567 in *Future Environments of North America*, edited by F. Fraser Darling and John P. Milton, The Natural History Press, Garden City, 1966.
2. Frank Gilbert, vice president, National Trust for Historic Preservation, personal communication.
3. Philip Kopper, *Colonial Williamsburg*, Harry N. Abrams, New York, 1986, pp. 139–233.
4. Colonial Williamsburg Incorporated, *Official Guidebook and Map*, Williamsburg, Va., 1960, p. xviii.
5. Bureau of Business Research, William and Mary College.
6. Constance McLaughlin Green, *American Cities*, Harper & Row, New York, 1965, pp. 24–25.
7. DuBose Heyward, *Porgy*, George H. Doran Company, New York, 1925, p. 11.
8. Samuel Gaillard Stoney, *This Is Charleston: A Survey of the Architectural Heritage of a Unique American City*, Carolina Art Association, Historic Charleston Foundations, and the Preservation Society of Charleston, Charleston, South Carolina, 1970 (originally published in 1944), p. 51.
9. City of Charleston, *Zoning Ordinance*, Charleston, 1973, pp. 32–33.
10. Robert Moses, *Public Works: A Dangerous Trade*, McGraw-Hill Book Company, New York, 1970, pp. 772–776.
11. Christopher Tunnard, *A World with a View*, Yale University Press, New Haven, 1978, pp. 136–141.
12. Ibid., p. 141.
13. David Gebhard, "Architectural Imagery, The Mission and California," pp. 137–145 in *The Harvard Architectural Review*, vol. I, Spring 1980, M.I.T. Press, Cambridge.
14. This architectural style was based on the work of José de Churriguera (1650–1723) who created a particularly ornate Spanish version of the Baroque.
15. Rebecca Conrad and Christopher H. Nelson, *Santa Barbara—A Guide to El Pueblo Viejo*, Capra Press, Santa Barbara, 1986, p. 132.
16. David Gebhard, Introduction, in Conrad and Nelson, op. cit., pp. 9–21

17. Ibid., p. 17.
18. The first height restrictions were enacted in 1924. They limited commercial structures to six floors and residential buildings to three floors.
19. Santa Barbara Convention and Visitors Bureau.
20. From a 1912 "flyer soliciting financial subscriptions," Carl D. Sheppard, *Creator of the Santa Fe Style—Isaac Hamilton Rapp, Architect,* University of New Mexico Press, Albuquerque, 1988, p. 75.
21. Ellen Beasley, "New Construction in Residential Historic Districts," pp. 229–256 in National Trust for Historic Preservation, *Old and New Architecture—Design Relationship,* The Preservation Press, Washington, D.C., 1980.
22. Santa Fe Visitors Bureau.
23. Christopher Tunnard and Boris Pushkarev, *Man-made America: Chaos or Control,* Yale University Press, New Haven, 1963, p. 409.
24. Leland Roth, *McKim, Mead & White, Architects,* Harper and Row, New York, 1983..
25. Vincent Scully, *American Architecture and Urbanism,* Henry Holt, New York, 1988, p. 143.
26. The New York State legislature enacted enabling legislation for the designation of landmarks and historic districts in 1956. It was not until the controversy over the demolition of Penn Station that the City Council began serious consideration of a Landmarks Preservation Law.
27. J. Lee Rankin, "Operation and Interpretation of the New York City Landmarks Preservation Law," *Law and Contemporary Problems,* vol. 36, no. 3, Durham, North Carolina, Summer 1971, pp. 366–372, and Joseph B. Rose, "Landmarks Preservation in New York," *The Public Interest,* no. 74, New York, Winter 1984, pp. 132–145.
28. New York City's procedure for establishing the assessed value of any property is notoriously imprecise and is successfully challenged by thousands of property owners every year. One can also question the notion that 6 percent of assessed value constitutes a reasonable return. No business would purchase property on the basis of a 6 percent return if it cost more to obtain the money to pay for it. Furthermore, more than three decades have passed since the prevailing rate of interest was lower than 6 percent.
29. A tax abatement plan of this sort has never been submitted for legislative approval.
30. New York City Department of City Planning, *Grand Central Area—Proposal for a Special Sub District,* New York, 1989, p. 3.
31. Richard A. Jaffe and Stephen Sherrill, "Grand Central Terminal and the New York Court of Appeals: 'Pure' Due Process, Reasonable Return, and Betterment Recovery," *Columbia Law Review,* vol. 78, no. 1, New York, January 1978, pp. 134–163.
32. Donald Elliott, Chairman of the City Planning Commission 1966–1973, interview, October 17, 1991.
33. New York City, *Zoning Resolution,* Article VII, Chapter 9, Section 74-79.
34. Norman Marcus, "Air Rights Transfers in New York City," *Law and Contemporary Problems,* vol. 36, no. 3, Durham, N.C., Summer 1971, pp. 372–379, and Madeleine A. Kleiner, "The Unconstitutionality of Transferable Development Rights," *The Yale Law Journal,* vol. 84, no. 5, New Haven, April 1975.
35. *Penn Central Transportation Company v. City of New York,* 438 U.S. 104 (1978).
36. Ibid.
37. One of the reasons that the New York State Court of Appeals, in the case of *Fred F. French Investing Co. v. City of New York* (1973), held that development rights from Tudor City could not be transferred to a vast area from 38th to 60th Streets between Third and Eighth Avenues was that this would have been an unfair allocation of the costs and burdens to uncompensated private owners.
38. The maximum floor area ratio permitted in New York City is 21.6. The transfer would have resulted in a floor area ratio of 33.1.
39. Bret Senft, "Key Players Speak Out—Air rights debate calms long enough for seminar," *Real Estate Weekly,* New York, November 1989, p. 2A.
40. John J. Costonis, *Space Adrift: Landmark Preservation and the Marketplace,* University of Illinois Press, Urbana, 1974, p. 40.
41. Ibid., pp. 28–64.
42. Lisa Purdy and Peter D. Bowes, "Denver's Transferable Development Rights Story," *Real Estate Issues,* American Society of Real Estate Counselors of the National Association of Realtors, Chicago, Spring/Summer 1982, pp. 5–8, and "An Update on Denver's TDR Ordinances," *Real Estate Issues,* American Society of Real Estate Counselors of the National Association of Realtors, Chicago, Spring/Summer 1985, pp. 1–5.
43. Helen Wadsworth, Rachelle Levitt, and Fran von Gerichen, *Denver Metropolitan Area... Today 1982,* Urban Land Institute, Washington, D.C., 1982, p. 31.
44. Lisa Purdy, interview December 21, 1989.
45. At the time the TDR ordinance was enacted, the B-5 zone included 10 locally designated landmarks with 1,362,000 square feet in available development rights, 898,000 of which were from two government-owned buildings that were unlikely to transfer development rights. There were another seven buildings that were eligible for designation as landmarks. They would generate 1,320,000 square feet in TDRs. However, 810,000 of this is from the U.S. Customs House, which was also unlikely to use its TDRs.
46. The B-7 ordinance was enacted less than a year after the B-5 ordinance and includes incentives for housing as well as historic preservation.
47. National Trust for Historic Preservation, *Financial Assistance Programs 1988 Annual Report,* National Trust for Historic Preservation, Washington, D.C., 1988.
48. Arthur P. Ziegler, Jr., Leopold Adler II, and Walter C. Kidney, *Revolving Funds for Historic Preservation: A Manual of Practice,* Ober Park Associates, Pittsburgh, 1975, pp. 26–32 and 62–75.
49. Ibid., p. 65.
50. Savannah Visitors Bureau.
51. U.S. Dept. of Commerce, Bureau of the Census, *Statistical Abstract of the United States 1978,* pp. 25–26, and *Statistical Abstract of the United States 1991,* pp. 34–36.
52. Arthur P. Ziegler, Jr., Leopold Adler II, and Walter C. Kidney, op. cit., p. 78.
53. Ibid., p. 79.
54. Some will argue that this is neighborhood improvement without gentrification that can be emulated in other areas that wish to avoid forcing out lower-income residents.
55. Lesley D. Slavitt, "State and Local Tax Incentives for Historic Preservation," New York City Citizens Housing and Planning Council, unpublished, New York, July 1992; and Richard J. Roddewig, "Preservation Law and Economics," pp. 446–456 in Christopher J. Duerksen (editor), *A Handbook on Historic Preservation Law,* The Conservation Foundation and The National Center for Preservation Law, Washington, D.C., 1983.
56. Margot Gayle and Edmund V. Gillon, Jr., *Cast-Iron Architecture in New York,* Dover Publications, New York, 1974; Margot Gayle and Robin Lynn, *A Walking Tour of Cast-Iron Architecture in SoHo,* Friends of Cast-Iron Architecture, New York, 1983; Margot Gayle, "America's Cast-Iron Heritage," in *Historic America: Buildings, Structures, and Sites,* Library of Congress, Washington, D.C., 1983, pp. 159–182.
57. Alexander Garvin, "Could Robert Moses do it in the Seventies?" *World Order,* vol. 9, no. 1, Wilmette, Ill., Fall 1974, pp. 16–28.
58. Special restoration work, even if it is required by the Landmarks Commission, is not currently eligible for J-51 benefits. However, the abatement granted for ordinary rehabilitation is usually enough to make most preservation projects financially feasible.
59. New York City Department of Housing Preservation and Development, Office of Development, Division of Financial Services.
60. John M. Fowler, "The Federal Government As Standard Bearer," pp. 33–80, in Robert E. Stipe and Antoinette J. Lee (editors), *The American Mosaic—Preserving a Nation's Heritage,* United States Committee, International Council on Monuments and Sites, Washington, D.C., 1987.
61. The benefits applied to individual landmarks listed in the National Register, buildings within historic districts listed in the National Register and certified by the secretary of the interior as contributing to the historic character of the district, buildings in locally designated historic districts which the secretary of the interior found were based

on acceptable criteria that satisfactorily protected the building. See Richard J. Roddewig, "Preservation Law and Economics: Government Incentives to Encourage For-Profit Preservation," pp. 461–464, in Christopher J. Duerksen (editor), *A Handbook on Historic Preservation Law,* The Conservation Foundation and The National Center for Preservation Law, Washington, D.C., 1983.

62. Ibid., pp. 464–466.

63. Ibid., pp. 467–471.

64. Fowler, op. cit., p. 66.

65. The area's only commercial building of national significance was the Texas School Book Depository from which it is believed that President John F. Kennedy was assassinated.

66. City of Dallas Ordinance No. 15203, June 1976.

67. Ron Emrich, "West End Historic District, Dallas Texas: Public Sector Revenue Projections," Department of Planning and Development, Dallas, 1988.

68. Alan Burnham (editor), *New York Landmarks,* Wesleyan University Press, Middletown, Conn., 1963; Norval White and Elliot Willensky, *AIA Guide to New York City,* Collier Macmillan, New York, 1978; Paul Goldberger, *The City Observed: New York,* Vintage Books, New York, 1979; and Rose, op. cit.

69. Rose, ibid., pp. 139–140

70. *First English Evangelical Lutheran Church v. County of Los Angeles,* 55 U. S. L. W. 4781 (1987).

71. Sally B. Woodbridge and Roger Montgomery, *A Guide to Architecture in Washington State,* University of Washington Press, Seattle, 1980, p.110.

72. Arthur M. Skolnik, "A History of Pioneer Square," pp. 15–19 in *Economic Benefits of Preserving Old Buildings,* The Preservation Press, National Trust for Historic Preservation, Washington, D.C., 1976.

73. Ibid., p. 19.

74. Reyner Banham, "Preserve Us from the Paranoid Preservers," p. 15, in *Observer Magazine,* London, October 21, 1973.

18

The Comprehensive Plan

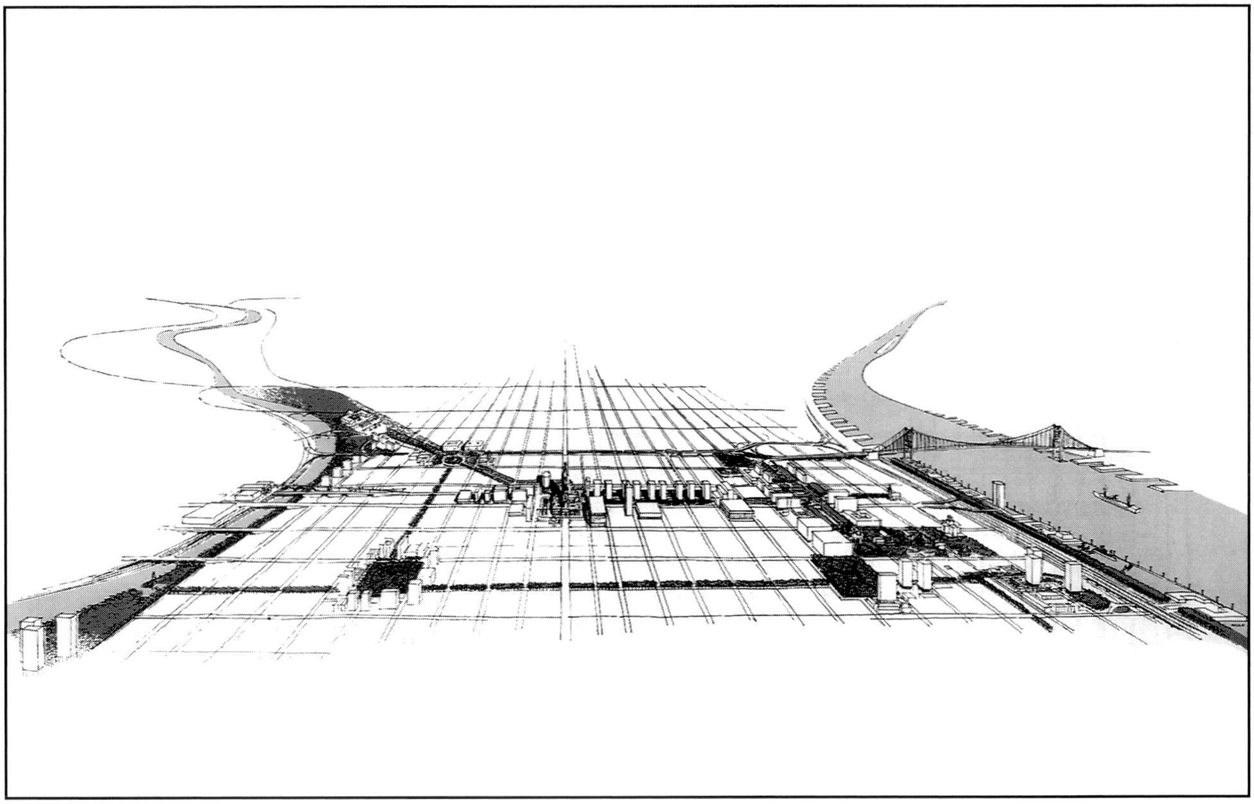

Philadelphia, 1963. Edmund Bacon's vision of the future of Center City. *(Courtesy of Department of City Planning, Philadelphia)*

The comprehensive plan is perhaps the most unfairly discredited of the many prescriptions for fixing the American city. Some have dismissed it as limited by the comprehension of the human mind. Others have ridiculed it as little more than a collection of "civic New Year's resolutions."[1] Despite these wickedly apt observations, in some instances comprehensive plans have proved to be powerful agents for change. Billions were spent executing proposals put forward in comprehensive plans for Chicago, St. Louis, Philadelphia, and New York. Billions more were spent bringing to cities across the continent the image that Victor Gruen launched in 1956 in his plan for *A Greater Fort Worth Tomorrow.* More important, Daniel Burnham's work in Chicago and Edmund Bacon's work in Philadelphia demonstrate that, like other prescriptions for fixing the city, when the comprehensive plan is based on an intelligent assessment of location and market plus an effective combination of design, financing, time, and entrepreneurship, it can be a powerful instrument for municipal improvement.

Effective comprehensive plans come in three varieties. There are those, frequently prepared by architects, that present compelling visions of the future. They crystallize the collective desires of the polity and set forth major steps that must be taken to achieve them. The authors of such plans are forced inevitably to accept the advice given by Daniel Burnham in what is the single most famous quotation about city planning:

> *Make no little plans; they have no magic to stir men's blood and will not be realized. Make big plans; aim high in hope and work, remembering that a noble, logical diagram once recorded will never die, but long after we are gone will be a living thing, asserting itself with evergrowing insistency.*[2]

This approach requires so profound an understanding of the topography, economy, social composition, and politics of a community that only a few great artists, like Daniel Burnham, have been successful with it. Such compelling visions of the future also require a level of boldness that is discouraged in our participatory form of government. Therefore, with the exception of truly extraordinary documents such as the 1909 *Plan of Chicago,* the approach is usually unsuccessful.

A second group of comprehensive plans, frequently prepared by appointed public officials, presents no vision of utopia. Instead, it attempts the strategic deployment of already agreed-upon municipal improvements. This approach was persuasively advocated in 1914 by New York City's Committee on the City Plan, which wrote:

> *City planning does not mean the invention of new schemes of public expenditure. It means getting the most out of the expenditures that are bound to be made and saving of future expense in replanning and reconstruction. With or without a comprehensive city plan, the City will probably spend hundreds of millions of dollars on public improvements during the next thirty years. In addition, during this same period property owners will spend some billions of dollars in the improvement of their holdings. To lay down the lines of city development so that these expenditures when made will in the greatest possible measure contribute to the solid and permanent upbuilding of a great and ever greater city—strong commercially, industrially, and in the comfort and health of its people—furnishes the opportunity and inspiration for city planning.*[3]

This philosophy is easy for public officials to accept and still easier for bureaucrats to implement. That is why the comprehensive plans for St. Louis in the mid-1940s and New York City in the late 1960s successfully generated so many remarkable changes to both cities.

The third approach is process-oriented. It adopts any available "good" ideas, adapting them to meet the demands of the widest variety of constituencies, altering them to fit requirements of legislation, financing, and implementing entities, adjusting them over and over again until they present a "total vision of the city" that reflects the "collective consciousness of its citizens."[4] It is best illustrated in Edmund Bacon's efforts in Philadelphia in the 1950s and 1960s, and the work of a variety of public agencies in Portland, Oregon, during the last third of the twentieth century.

While these three varieties of comprehensive planning could not be more different in philosophy and methodology, they share the same assumptions that "the formless growth of the city is neither economical nor satisfactory" and that "a plan for the well-ordered and convenient city is...indispensable."[5] They also share a similar need for gargantuan sums of money, lengthy periods of execution, and continuing acceptance by the city's political establishment.

Communities will not finance such plans unless they are deeply committed to their recommendations. Until recently, such commitment has only occurred in response to powerful proposals, such as those that emerged from the planning process in Chicago, Philadelphia, and Portland. It is now possible to base that commitment on widespread familiarity with facts. Computers can tabulate, analyze, and present information on a geographic basis. The maps and charts that they produce can alter the public dialogue in every community. Rather than respond to particular visions of a better tomorrow, citizens are now able to obtain information previously restricted to specialists and decide for themselves what actions to take and what expenditures to make. A few cities have taken steps to make such information more accessible. It is time for Congress to institutionalize this form of information-based municipal decision-making process.

Burnham and Company

America's acceptance of the effectiveness of "a plan for the well-ordered and convenient city" was launched by Daniel Burnham and the other designers of the Chicago Fair of 1893; elaborated by Burnham and his collaborators on the

McMillan Plan for Washington, D.C. (1901–1902), and the plans for Cleveland (1903), Manila (1905), and San Francisco (1904–1906); and reached maturity in 1909 with the *Plan of Chicago* (see Chapter 4). Burnham came to Chicago with his family at the age of 8 and remained there until his death in 1912. He worked as a draftsman until 1873, when he established an architectural firm in partnership with John Welborn Root. The partnership lasted until Root's death in 1891, when the firm was renamed D. H. Burnham and Company. It was responsible for some of the country's most famous buildings, including the Rookery, Monadnock, and Reliance buildings in Chicago, the Flatiron Building in New York, and Union Station in Washington, D.C. However, the firm's pioneering work in city planning, for which it did not charge a fee in the hope that this would lead to future architectural commissions, made the firm even more famous.[6]

Many talented people were involved in Burnham's city planning practice, but Charles Moore and Edward Bennett were the most important. Moore, whom he met while working on the McMillan Plan, acted largely in the role of an editor. Bennett, an English architect who began working for Burnham not long after graduating from the Ecole des Beaux Arts, became his acknowledged collaborator in developing plans for San Francisco and Chicago. After Burnham's death in 1912, Bennett went on to produce plans for Brooklyn, Minneapolis, Pasadena, and Portland, Oregon.

Paris, 1972. Avenue de l'Opera, one of the numerous new boulevards whose buildings were erected by developers who purchased surplus land that was not required for the right-of-way. *(Alexander Garvin)*

Haussmann's Influence

The single most important contribution to Burnham's city plans came from a nonparticipant: Baron Georges-Eugène Haussmann, prefect of the Seine from 1853 to 1870. Under the patronage of Emperor Napoleon III, Haussmann transformed the dirty, foul-smelling, congested clutter of medieval Paris into the city of light and air that we know today. As Burnham explained, he made it "fit to sustain the army of merchants and manufacturers which makes Paris today the center of a commerce as wide as civilization itself."[7]

Haussmann accomplished this transformation by the strategic installation of a water-distribution system, a sewer system, a street system, a park system, and a vast array of community facilities and monuments (see Chapter 3). These public improvements refashioned Paris into a city of uniform façades and axial roadways. At the intersections of these arteries, Haussmann created public squares that provided monumental settings for railroad terminals, churches, schools, theaters, government offices, the Opera, the Louvre, and other major public structures.[8]

Paris buildings rarely exceeded five or six stories because developers would not build higher than their customers would willingly climb. This practice was codified by Louis XVI in 1784 in an ordinance that set the maximum height of a cornice at 17.5 meters. From that point, buildings could rise another 4.9 meters, but they had to set back along a 45-degree angle.[9]

Even after the invention of the elevator in 1853, many Paris developers continued to build lower buildings than the permitted seven or eight stories. Elevators were too expensive. Besides, before Haussmann began his work only one of every five buildings was supplied with running water, fewer than 150 pumped it above ground level, and none could depend on a steady supply of potable water. Where pipes were not buried deep enough, winter freezes interrupted the flow. Even in good weather many conduits were inadequate to meet peak period demand, with the result that water flow often declined to a mere trickle. Worst of all, much of the water was polluted because it came from points along the Seine River that were downstream from sewers that emptied directly into the river.

Haussmann devised, financed, and supervised construction of a system that provided Paris with a dependable daily supply of 80 million gallons of unpolluted water at an even temperature during all seasons. The water came from springs and rivers east of Paris along a system of tunnels, bridges, siphons, aqueducts, and reservoirs. It was distributed through a system of underground mains that delivered it to buildings at a constant pressure, which allowed it to climb naturally to 230 feet above sea level. As a result soft, cool, fresh water could be provided to the top floor of any building in Paris, without the expense of pumping.

Haussmann's 90 miles of broad boulevards and avenues consisted of 57 miles of entirely new streets and 33 miles of existing arteries that were widened to as much as 100 feet. They provided easy access to and from new railroad stations, markets, public institutions, and parks, and thereby also pro-

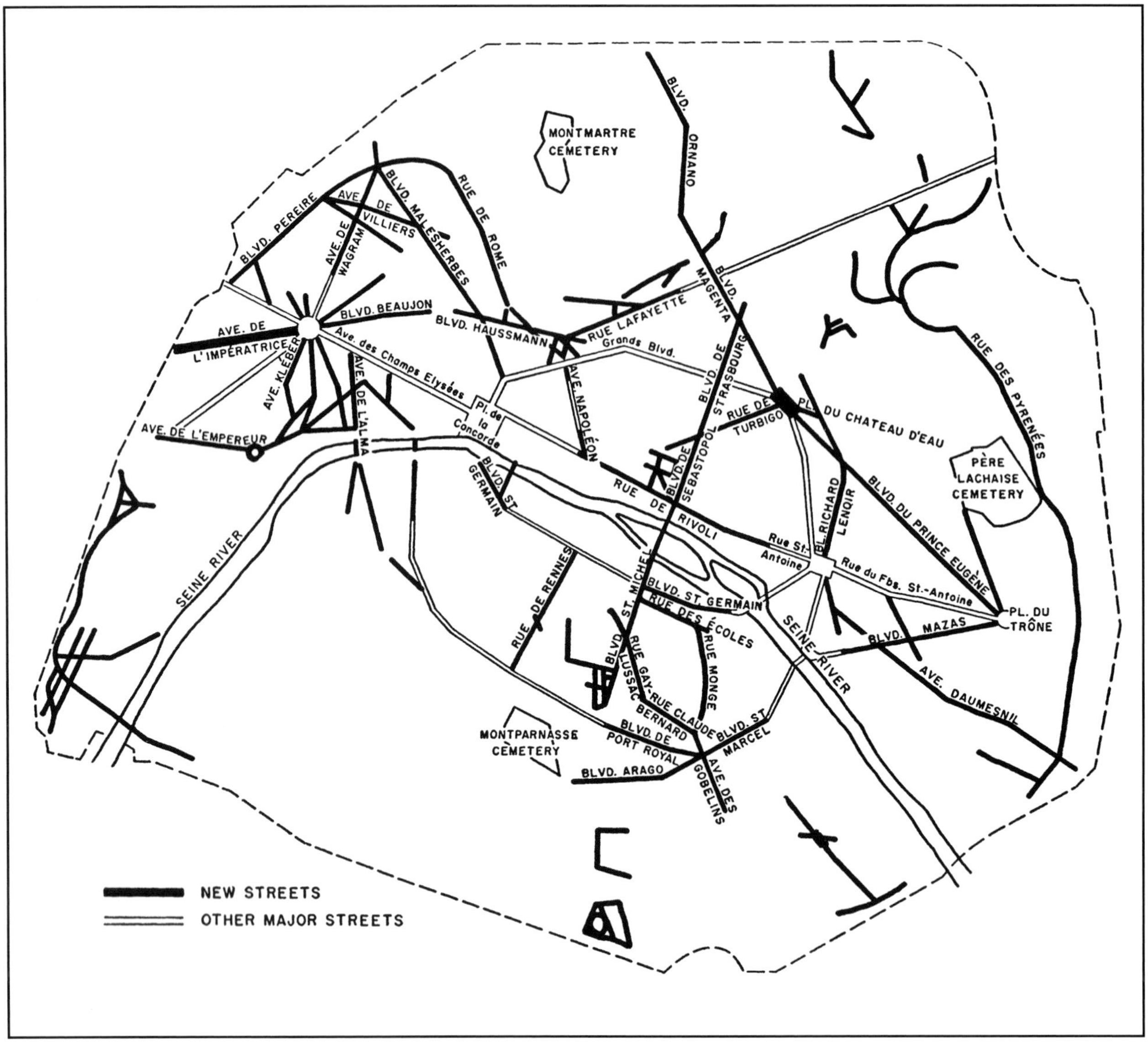

Paris, 1850–1870. Map of new streets created by Haussmann. (From *David Pinkney; Napoleon III and the Rebuilding of Paris; Princeton University Press, Princeton, 1972; reproduced by permission of Princeton University Press*)

vided for the distribution of goods and services needed by a city with a population of 2 million. To acquire the necessary rights of way, Haussmann had to condemn lots that extended beyond the projected roadways. In the process he destroyed 12,000 structures and created large attractive building sites that were easy to sell to developers. It did not take long for them to line Haussmann's new arteries with six-story buildings, supplied with running water and serviced by Haussmann's new sewer system.[10]

Impact of the Chicago Fair

When Daniel Burnham became chief of construction for the Chicago Fair, he had not seen Haussmann's transformation of Paris. His principal colleagues, Olmsted and McKim, were more than familiar with Haussmann's work. McKim had studied architecture at the Ecole des Beaux Arts in Paris between 1867 and 1870. Olmsted's travels to Paris had made him a lifelong admirer of Haussmann's parks and boulevards. These three, together with Olmsted's partner Henry Codman, conceived and built the Chicago Fair in a manner that reflected their common admiration of Haussmann's Paris (see Chapter 4, note 4).

The Fair was really a small, "well-ordered and convenient city." It had its own water, sewer, and utility systems, its own fire, police, sanitation, electric, telephone, telegraph service, and even its own elevated transit system, which pioneered the electrified third rail. Like Paris, its buildings coalesced into a consistent ensemble. However, this was the result of specific architectural decisions rather than independent private market responses to common development problems. The major

Chicago, 1893. The World's Columbia Exposition, with its own public services, utility, and transit system, became the model for the well-planned American city. *(Courtesy of Chicago Historical Society)*

buildings around the Court of Honor were built to a common cornice height of 60 feet, because the architects all agreed to that, not because developers thought that was as high as their customers would be willing to climb or because it was the maximum height to which they could pipe running water without the added expense of pumping. Major buildings, such as the Administration Building, Terminal Station, and State of Illinois Building, closed axial vistas because of the agreed-upon site plan, not because great boulevards had been cut through the fabric of an existing city to connect major destinations. The buildings were all clad in a mixture of plaster, cement, and jute fiber and painted white because this would guarantee the necessary architectural unity, not because the white cladding was the real estate industry's commonly used building material.[11]

Since the utility systems and public services were not immediately visible, architects, urban planners, and civic leaders came away from the Chicago Fair with the belief that a common building height, axial vistas, and a consistent architectural vocabulary generated "the well-ordered city." These misconstrued characteristics of Haussmann's Paris, along with clustered groups of civic structures, a central railroad station, and a regional park system, became common elements in Burnham's plans for Washington, D.C., Cleveland, Manila, San Francisco, and ultimately for scores of comprehensive plans produced by his followers.

Improvement and Adornment of San Francisco

Burnham came to San Francisco at the invitation of the city's business leaders and political reformers. Ostensibly his visit was for the purpose of speaking to the Committee for the Improvement and Adornment of San Francisco, organized by lawyer, entrepreneur, and former mayor James Phelan. The visit evolved into a pro bono effort to provide the committee with a vision of what he thought San Francisco ought to be.[12]

The project took a year, part of which was devoted to planning in the Philippines. While in San Francisco, Burnham worked from a cabin-studio atop the Twin Peaks of Diamond Heights, which provided a splendid view of the entire metropolitan region. The panoramic drawings made at the site were embodied in the *Report on a Plan for San Francisco,* produced in collaboration with Edward Bennett and Willis Polk.[13]

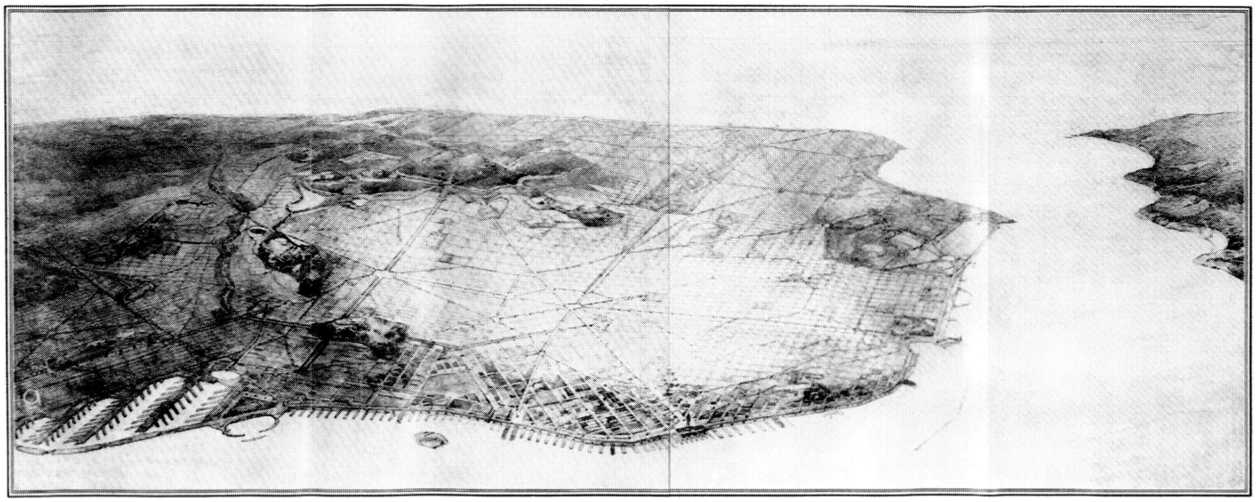

San Francisco, 1905. Bird's-eye perspective of the city from the East showing changes proposed by Daniel Burnham.
(From Burnham and Bennett, A Report on the Improvement and Adornment of San Francisco, City of San Francisco, 1905)

The *Report on a Plan for San Francisco* offered a series of proposals to transform San Francisco into an American version of Haussmann's Paris, only with hills. It proposed creating diagonal boulevards, like those Haussmann had created in Paris, that smashed through the city's street grids, connecting hills, neighborhoods, and proposed new public spaces. At their intersections, Burnham envisioned traffic circles, civic squares, and public structures such as Haussmann had created in Paris. Like Paris, the plan included a park system with 9600 acres for large regional parks, 255 acres for 12 smaller parks, and landscaped boulevard/parkways providing the connective tissue for this vast expansion of public open space.

The plan did not just copy Haussmann's Paris. It also included elements that responded to San Francisco's unique topography and thriving maritime economy. As-yet-undeveloped steep slopes and hilltops were to be preserved as public open space. The city's waterfront was set aside for maritime use, but augmented with a perimeter boulevard. A new shipping, warehousing, and manufacturing center was to be created in the Hunter's Point area. Taking a cue from the Chicago Fair, there were to be a central civic center and a rapid transit system. Finally, to be sure that all public and private development would conform with this vision of a well-ordered city, Burnham proposed an Art Commission to establish requirements for building height, street furniture, signage, statuary, paving, and street trees.

Burnham did not suppose "that all the work indicated [could] or ought to be carried out at once or in the near future." He expected it to "be executed by degrees, as the growth of the community demand[ed] and as its financial ability allow[ed]." He understood that his proposals required both further elaboration and vast expenditures. As he explained: "It is not the province of a report of this kind to indicate the exact details very closely."[14]

Burnham was very wrong in thinking that this plan interfered "as little as possible with the rectangular street system of the city." His diagonal boulevards, public spaces, and civic monuments, like Haussmann's, required massive condemnation, relocation, demolition, and reconstruction. This proved to be one of the reasons that the *Report on a Plan for San Francisco,* which was presented to the Board of Supervisors and approved in September 1905, was never implemented. The others were indirect consequences of the earthquake and fire that, in April 1906, destroyed most of the city.

Burnham and his supporters understood that a comprehensive plan of this magnitude needed a constituency, legislative sanction, a viable implementation mechanism, and lots of money. They planned a major effort to generate public support. The first step was to be distribution of the 3000 copies of the *Report* initially authorized by the Board of Supervisors. Almost all the copies were destroyed in the earthquake and fire before lobbying could begin. Suddenly, there was no way of marshaling either the necessary support or the money. Rather than take the time to consider Burnham's proposals, develop the necessary political consensus, obtain legal sanction for new traffic rights-of-way, block and lot patterns, and then acquire the necessary property, the city quite naturally devoted all its energies to quickly replacing 28,000 buildings where "now stretched a blackened wasteland of more than four square miles—512 blocks."[15]

Plan of Chicago

In his home town Daniel Burnham neither required assistance in understanding the city's topography, economic base, demographic composition, or political structure, nor in conceiving a strategy to obtain public support. But he did need powerful allies if he was to obtain the legislation, appropriations, and

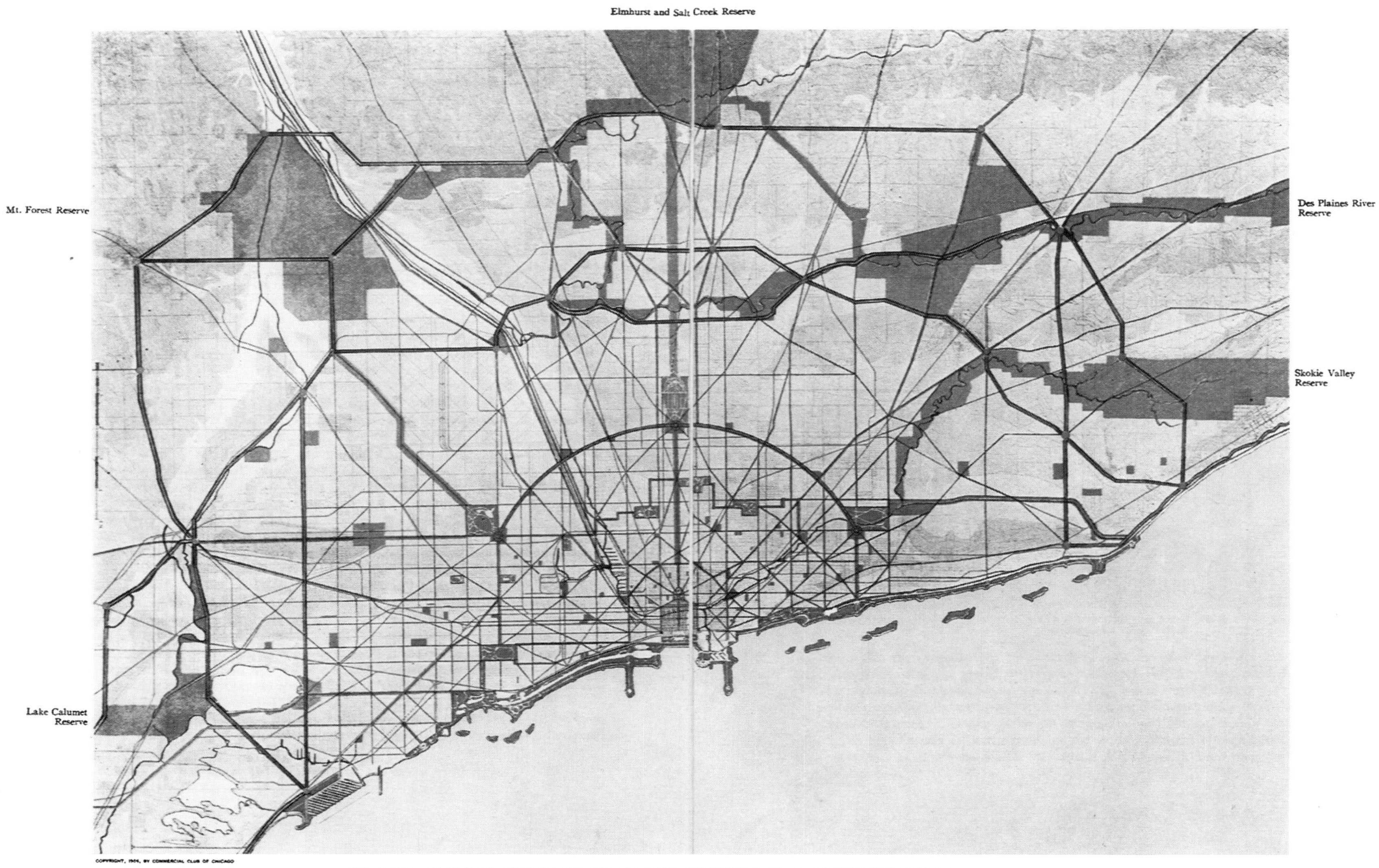

XLIV. CHICAGO. GENERAL MAP SHOWING TOPOGRAPHY, WATERWAYS, AND COMPLETE SYSTEM OF STREETS, BOULEVARDS, PARKWAYS, AND PARKS.
The parks and parkways encircle the city; they are placed in relation to the radiating arteries, and increase in area in proportion to their distance from the center (green). Also showing railroads (red), the proposed harbors at the mouths of the Chicago and Calumet rivers, and the location of outlying townships. The elevation of the ground is shown by increasing depth of color (orange), from the center of the city.

Chicago, 1909. Plan of Chicago—Map showing new system of streets, boulevards, parkways, and parks.
(From Burnham and Bennett, A Plan of Chicago, The Commercial Club, Chicago, 1909)

bureaucratic support to implement his ideas. These favorable conditions came together in 1906, when the Chicago Merchant's Club merged with the Commercial Club and established a joint committee to develop a comprehensive plan.[16] Burnham agreed to take charge of drafting their *Plan of Chicago,* donating his services free of charge with the understanding that he would "have an entirely free hand in the choice of…associates and assistants."[17]

The *Plan of Chicago* took Burnham, Bennett, Charles Moore (their editor), and a team of architects, drafters, and illustrators 3 years to produce. It is as much an introduction to "city planning in ancient and modern times" and to the history of Chicago, as it is a vision of what they wanted Chicago to become. Almost half of its pages are devoted to photos, prints, and drawings of London, Vienna, and especially Haussmann's Paris, cities that Burnham hoped the citizens of Chicago would be inspired to emulate and surpass. The most important illustrations, however, were Jules Guerin's perspective drawings rendered in watercolor and reproduced in color. They provided the magic that stirred the blood, leading generations of Chicagoans to spend billions of dollars realizing huge sections of this noble diagram.[18]

Chicago, c. 1920. View of the Chicago River prior to reconstruction. *(Courtesy of Chicago Historical Society)*

Chicago, 1909. Rendering of proposal made in the *Plan of Chicago* for straightening the Chicago River and building a double-decker drive along its edge. *(From Burnham and Bennett, A Plan of Chicago, The Commercial Club, Chicago, 1909)*

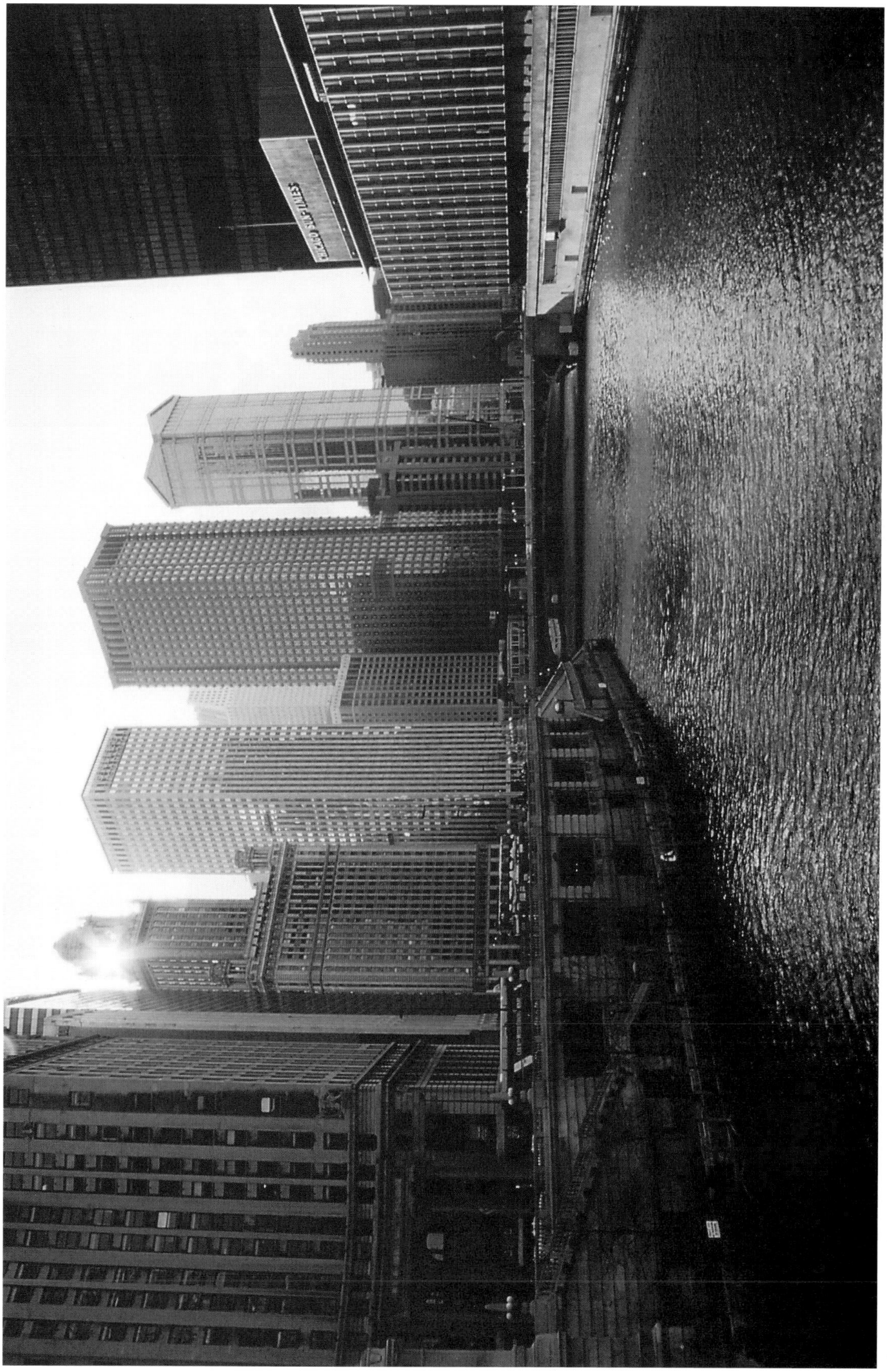

Chicago, 1993. The double-decker Wacker Drive built along the straightened Chicago River as was inspired by Burnham's *Plan of Chicago*. *(Alexander Garvin)*

Chicago, c. 1928. View through an office window of north Michigan Avenue after completion of the Michigan Avenue Bridge recommended by Burnham in the *Plan of Chicago.* *(Courtesy of Chicago Historical Society)*

It was a truly "big plan" that included: (1) more than 60,000 acres of parks, parkways, and forest preserves, (2) a regional highway system extending more than 60 miles beyond the business district, (3) a systematic rearrangement of local arteries, including new bridges and through avenues, widened streets, and landscaped boulevards, (4) 23 continuous miles of harbor, pier, lagoon, beach, park, and waterfront development along Lake Michigan, (5) a cleaned-up and straightened Chicago River, (6) a consolidated system of freight and passenger railroads, mass transit, and railway terminals, (7) a cluster of existing and new institutional buildings combined into a cultural center in an expanded Grant Park, and (8) a gigantic civic center dominated by a domed City Hall soaring to a height of more than 40 stories. Even Haussmann had not conceived of an integrated system of public works on so vast a regional scale.

The authors, like most reformers of the day, believed that government should interfere with the private sector only to provide basic government facilities and services and to ensure the health and safety of the population. Accordingly, the *Plan for Chicago* devoted its attention to infrastructure (roads, bridges, freight and passenger railway improvements, etc.) and community facilities (parks, government buildings, and cultural institutions). In doing so, Burnham and his collaborators expected to remove obstructions to circulation, improve the distribution of goods and services, encourage commerce, and provide necessary cultural, educational, and recreational facilities. They did not consider it their role to alter the distribu-

Chicago, 1984. Construction of the Michigan Avenue Bridge made possible the transformation of north Michigan Avenue into the city's premier retail street. *(Alexander Garvin)*

tion of income, the patterns of consumption, or the living conditions of any group of citizens. Less than 1 of the document's 164 pages is devoted to slums, because, as its authors explained, "the slum exists to-day only because of the failure of the city to protect itself against gross evils and known perils, all of which should be corrected by the enforcement of simple principles of sanitation."[19]

Generations of architects and historians have directed their attention to Burnham's unrealized proposals for majestic public squares and monuments, diagonal boulevards, uniform building heights, and axial vistas. It was not these inflated, academic venerations of Haussmann's Paris, however, to which Chicagoans directed their attention. It was to the inspired proposals for public improvements that Burnham persuaded them would make the city a more "efficient instrument for providing all its people with the best possible conditions of living."[20]

Once the *Plan for Chicago* had been issued, the City Council established a 328-member City Plan Commission, published and distributed 165,000 copies of a 93-page booklet entitled *Chicago's Greatest Issue—An Official Plan,* and, after two years of public debate, in 1911 formally adopted the plan. The monumental imitations of Haussmann's Paris involved too much property condemnation, relocation, and community opposition. Instead, the city proceeded with those improvements that solved commonly agreed-upon problems and exploited generally accepted opportunities.

Within a decade of the plan's publication, the city had spent $237 million on proposals put forward in it, including numerous street, railway, and park improvements and extensions (see Chapter 3). It also had acquired 14,254 acres of forest preserve. More important, the City Plan Commission proved to be "not a money-spending but a money-earning institution," generating increased property values and city revenues in the areas immediately adjacent to these improvements.[21]

By World War II, almost 40,000 acres of forest preserve had been acquired. A double-decker Wacker Drive had been constructed along a straightened Chicago River. Michigan Avenue, Roosevelt Road, and numerous other streets and viaducts had been widened and extended. The produce market had been moved 2 miles from the center of the city. Most dramatically, "over a billion dollars went into new landfill on the Lake Michigan shoreline and in constructing commercial and recreational facilities along the water's edge."[22]

Burnham's vision for Chicago was accepted because of the persuasive diagnosis he provided of its physical, functional, economic, and environmental problems and the convincing proposals he provided to solve those problems. He also explained that the radical changes he proposed in the *Plan for Chicago* "cannot possibly be realized immediately.... Therefore it is quite possible that when particular portions of the plan shall be taken up for execution, wider knowledge, longer experience, or change in local conditions may suggest a better solution."[23] That is precisely what happened as the specific design of each project was altered to meet the requirements of the time in which it was brought to completion.

The most important reason that so much of the *Plan for Chicago* was implemented, however, was effective politicking by its supporters. In the 10 years after the plan's publication, slide shows illustrating it were presented to more than 175,000 citizens. During 1912 alone, the Plan Commission "furnished Plan articles that appeared in 575 magazines, periodicals, trade and club publications...[and] permeated the catalogues and magazines of large business concerns."[24] Burnham's supporters even persuaded the Board of Education to produce 70,000 copies of a simplified version of the Plan that became the eighth-grade civics textbook in the city's public schools.[25]

Some of Burnham's proposals were commonly desired projects that might have been realized even without a comprehensive plan. The *Plan for Chicago* and lobbying effort to obtain its implementation provided many others with the push they needed to obtain public support and money. Moreover, the plan's comprehensive scope prevented the city from evolving haphazardly and provided the framework for "a well-ordered, convenient, and unified city" that inspired civic officials in Chicago and elsewhere for almost two generations.

A National Movement

During the year the *Plan for Chicago* was issued, the first national conference on city planning was held, Wisconsin became the first state to enact legislation authorizing cities to create planning commissions and prepare city plans, and Harvard became the first university to offer a course in city planning. The problem was that nobody knew what "city planning" meant. As Frederick Law Olmsted, Jr., explained in 1910 at the second national conference on city planning, "We are dealing here with the play of enormously complex forces which no one clearly understands and few pretend to; and our efforts to control them so often lead to unexpected and deplorable results that sober-minded people are often tempted to give up."[26]

One thing was certain, however—the various early planning documents produced by Charles Mulford Robinson, John Nolen, George Kessler, the Olmsted Brothers, and other fledgling city planners could not compare in scope, persuasiveness, or impact with the *Plan for Chicago.* A genuine "city planning" movement, however, would have to be based on more than the artistic genius of a single individual. There had to be a body of competent individuals trained to produce comprehensive plans, plus steady demand for their work.[27]

Despite the junior Olmsted's justifiable worry about the often unexpected and deplorable results of urban planning, there soon were plenty of self-declared professionals promising to fix our cities. Engineers, landscape architects, politicians, businesspeople, social critics, architects, lawyers, and all sorts of other professionals transformed themselves into city planners. In 1915 they banded together to form the American City Planning Association (now the American Planning Association). Harvard took the lead in 1929, creating the first separate School of City Planning to provide training for the new profession. By 1971, there would be 9 universities offering a bachelor's degree in city planning, 55 offering a master's degree, and 19 offering doctorates, representing a total enrollment of 5119 students.[28]

This growing body of city planning professionals persuaded local, state, and federal agencies to require and even pay for their services. In 1927 Secretary of Commerce Herbert Hoover appointed a nine-member committee of city planners to draft a *Standard City Planning Enabling Act.* As he explained in the foreword to the final report presenting the 1928 Act, cities required "a clearly defined permanent planning branch in local government, in the form of a commission which formulates a comprehensive plan and keeps it up to date."[29]

Municipalities everywhere accepted Hoover's recommendation because, as the size, role, and cost of government had mushroomed, public officials needed to collect and present data that provided the basis for decision making, to enumerate and coordinate the rapidly increasing array of government activities, and to compare information on the facilities and services provided to different parts of the city. By 1929, 650 cities had official planning commissions, 200 of which had been the subject of planning reports.

Local governments were happy to employ city planners, particularly when the federal government reimbursed them, which it did in conjunction with the National Industrial Recovery Act of 1933, the Federal-Aid Highway Act of 1956, the Demonstration Cities and Metropolitan Development Act of 1966, the Coastal Zone Management Act of 1972, virtually every housing act, and a continuing stream of other legislation. The extent to which this generated stable demand for city planning activities is demonstrated by Section 701 of the Housing Act of 1954, which provided assistance for:

> *(1) preparation, as a guide for long-range development, of general physical plans with respect to the pattern and intensity of land use and the provision of public facilities, together with long-range fiscal plans for such development; (2) programming of capital improvements based on a determination of relative urgency, together with definitive financing plans for the improvements to be constructed in the earlier years of the program; (3) coordination of all related plans of the departments or subdivisions of the government concerned; (4) intergovernmental coordination of all related planned activities among the state and local governmental agencies concerned; and (5) preparation of regulatory and administrative measures in support of the foregoing.*[30]

Despite the vast number of professional planners and the huge sums spent on their work, only a handful of comprehensive plans significantly affected city growth and development. The others failed when their prescriptions proved inappropriate, either because they tried to impose a design concept that had little to do with existing landscape and land use patterns, or because the city government lacked the money or the will to spend for those particular proposals, or because they would cause unacceptable disruption and, therefore, political opposition. Plans that succeeded, like those for St. Louis, Philadelphia, and Portland, did so because their authors had produced convincing diagnoses of the problems and opportunities facing those cities, prescriptions the citizenry believed could effectively solve those problems and exploit those opportunities, and implementation strategies whose costs in terms of dollars and dislocation were politically acceptable.

Visions of the Future Metropolis

Most twentieth-century comprehensive plans reflect one of two visions of the future metropolis: Daniel Burnham's amalgam of Haussmann's Paris with the Chicago Fair or Victor Gruen's amalgam of Le Corbusier's City of Tomorrow with the suburban shopping center (see Chapter 4, Chapter 6, and Chapter 7). Burnham's "noble, logical diagram" reshaped Chicago and provided the model for most city plans produced during the early part of the century. When it was exported to other cities, however, his vision of the City Beautiful only provided planning clichés (common cornice heights, diagonal boulevards, monumental civic centers, etc.) for published documents that were rarely implemented. With the exception of a handful of civic centers, it was rejected by political leaders whose constituents were unwilling to spend gargantuan sums to alter a cityscape that they felt could satisfactorily remain as is, at no cost to the taxpayer.

Victor Gruen's 1956 plan for *A Greater Fort Worth Tomorrow,* on the other hand, while rejected by the city for which it was developed, provided planning clichés (circumferential highways providing access to the business district, downtown garages accessible by highway, and pedestrian precincts) that changed the face of virtually every major American city. It was adopted by governments across the country because it responded to overwhelming local demand for an end to traffic congestion and, more important, because the federal government was ready to pay 90 percent of the bill.

While these visions could not have been more different in appearance, they were similar in other ways. Either could be superimposed on any municipality without paying much attention to its specific characteristics. Both depended on modernization of the city's infrastructure, especially its traffic arteries. Both eliminated the existing, messy mix of land uses, proposing instead to carefully segregate city life into discrete districts. Both required teams of elite professionals to orchestrate their realization and demanded such high levels of spending that they had to excite controversy.

Burnham's vision failed to be implemented outside Chicago because his followers did not have the same profound understanding of the particular city for which they were planning, or lacked the same genius for capturing the collective aspirations of its population, or could not generate the same carefully orchestrated political support. Gruen's vision, on the other hand, required neither profound understanding of a specific city nor artistic genius. It could be applied to any city with a defined central business district surrounded by deteriorating areas that could be acquired for a circumferential highway at relatively low cost without causing much dislocation or generating substantial opposition.

Implementing Burnham's Vision of the City Beautiful

The standard components of Burnham's "well-ordered city" were proposed wherever planners accepted Burnham's challenge and made "big plans." The 1910 *Report of the New Haven Civic Improvement Commission* by Cass Gilbert and Frederick Law Olmsted, Jr., included an extensive regional park system, clearance of the area between the railroad station and the central business district, and a monumental civic center. Virgil Bogue's 1911 *Plan of Seattle* prescribed demolishing whole city blocks and rebuilding entire hills to create a system of diagonal streets and highways, a grandiose civic center, a new harbor, and a vast system of parks and parkways. Carrere & Hastings' 1912 report, *A Plan of the City of Hartford,* proposed a regional park system, a reconstructed waterfront, circumferential boulevards, diagonal avenues, and elaborate outlying districts with "factory sites and workingmen's homes."

Early proponents of comprehensive planning in these and other cities had little difficulty obtaining the civic support needed to commission a comprehensive plan. Their problems began when they tried to get local governments to implement these visions of the "well-ordered, convenient, and unified city." As soon as public officials were faced with budget appropriations, bond issues, and taxes, they avoided the big plans,

Seattle, 1911. Central Avenue looking north to Central Station as proposed in the *Plan of Seattle* but never executed. *(From V. Bogue, Plan of Seattle, Lowman & Hannaford, Seattle, 1911)*

choosing as usual to implement minor projects, such as the elimination of grade crossings, or noncontroversial public actions, such as the acquisition of additional parkland in inexpensive outlying areas.

Supporters of comprehensive planning wanted to avoid such piecemeal implementation because as long as individual projects required political approval, those components of a plan that might alienate a section of the city, a large number of voters, or important economic interests would have great difficulty obtaining the necessary support. One way to avoid such parochial voter rejection was to obtain formal approval of an entire plan and make it binding. This approach was quickly tried and rejected. Virgil Bogue's *Plan of Seattle* was placed on the ballot in 1912. The vote was 14,506 in favor, 24,966 against.[31]

Bogue's attempt to copy Burnham's notion of Paris with hills was even less appropriate to Seattle than to San Francisco. Furthermore, the cost was far beyond the city's pocketbook. A contemporary opposition pamphlet placed its cost at well over $100 million, "a staggering sum in an era when land prices and construction costs were many times less than those of the end of the twentieth century."[32]

The voters also rejected this particular approach to the planning process. They were *not* offered what Burnham described as "a noble, logical diagram" that could "be executed by degrees, as the growth of the community demands and its financial ability allows." They were given an all-or-nothing proposition. In 1910 voters had been asked to approve creation of a 21-member commission to formulate a comprehensive plan, a special tax to pay for its preparation, and the requirement that "if a majority of the voters voting thereon shall favor adoption of said City Plan...it shall be adopted and shall be the plan to be followed by all City officials in the growth, evolution, and development of...Seattle, until modified, or amended at some subsequent election."[33]

They approved all three. However, two years later, when the *Plan of Seattle* was put on the ballot, the voters not only turned down its contents, they also made it very clear that they would not turn over their city to self-designated experts or give up their role in approving specific actions or let individuals that were not subject to electoral approval spend their hard earned money on grandiose schemes for municipal improvement.

Fort Worth, 1956. Aerial view of Fort Worth. *(Courtesy of Greater Fort Worth Planning Committee)*

Implementing Gruen's Vision of the Greater City

As America's leading post-World War II architect of suburban shopping centers and the designer of Southdale, the country's first climate-controlled shopping mall, Victor Gruen had an inside view of the competition facing downtown business districts (see Chapter 5). The know-how he gained developing regional retail centers provided the basis for his "counterattack against urban sprawl and anti-city chaos" and his proposals for "the revitalization of the heart of our cities."[34]

Gruen had begun his professional career with great enthusiasm for Le Corbusier's vision of the *City of Tomorrow.* But as he saw its concepts poorly translated into reality, he changed his opinion, explaining that:

> *Though [Le Corbusier] foresaw a great flood of automobiles, [he] underestimated the proportions of the deluge. The amount of traffic necessary to establish any kind of connection between the widely separated towers is indeed of such a scale that it automatically destroys part of the dream.*[35]

Fort Worth, 1956. Aerial view of Gruen's vision of A Greater Fort Worth Tomorrow. *(Courtesy of Greater Fort Worth Planning Committee)*

The automobile used too much space: 300 square feet to be kept at its point of origin, another 300 square feet when stored at its destination, another 600 square feet in roadways, and 200 square feet where it is sold, repaired, and serviced.[36]

Gruen provided an alternative model in the mid-1950s, when 20 leading citizens of Fort Worth hired him to devise a comprehensive city plan. At that time the city was suffering from ailments common to cities across the country: declining retail sales, declining building occupancy, and increasing traffic congestion. It also faced lively competition with Dallas.

In *A Greater Fort Worth Tomorrow,* he proposed: (1) a series of circumferential and radial highways providing vehicular access to Fort Worth, (2) perimeter parking terminals located along the various loop highways, (3) a central business district within the inner highway belt that was sufficiently compact to ensure no more than 3 minutes' walk to any downtown location, (4) separation of truck and automobile traffic from pedestrians within the inner highway loop, (5) construction of a new outdoor pedestrian level at the second floor of every downtown building, (6) reuse of what had been previ-

Fort Worth, 1956. Gruen's proposal for a radial highway leading to a downtown parking structure. *(Courtesy of Greater Fort Worth Planning Committee)*

ously street level (now underground) exclusively for motor vehicles, and (7) a regional mass transit system including downtown shuttle cars for those unable or unwilling to walk a few hundred feet. Gruen proposed establishment of a Central District Development Authority to administer the plan, buy, clear, and sell property, and issue bonds; a Central District Parking Authority to build and operate parking facilities; a Central District Roads Authority to coordinate federal, state, and city arterial programs; and a Central District Transit and Trucking Authority to build and operate transit facilities and basement level truck roads.[37]

A Greater Fort Worth Tomorrow quickly became the best publicized and most admired vision of a future metropolis since Le Corbusier's work of the 1920s. Even Jane Jacobs was lavish in her praise:

> *The excellent Gruen plan includes, in its street treatment, sidewalk arcades, poster columns, flags, vending kiosks, display stands, outdoor cafes, bandstands, flower beds, and special lighting effects.... It works with existing buildings and this is not just a cost-saving expedient.... This mixture is one of downtown's greatest advantages, for downtown streets need high-yield, middling-yield, low-yield, and no-yield enterprises.*[38]

One reason for the plan's appeal was that it required no specialized knowledge of Fort Worth or any other urban region. More important, the proposals could be applied everywhere.

In Fort Worth, however, it was a flop. Parking-lot operators opposed competition from a public authority. Property owners balked at losing ground-level rental income and then spending money to retrofit the second floor to accommodate lobbies and retailing. Taxpayers refused to consider the huge sums needed to create the separate vehicular and pedestrian levels.

The year Gruen published *A Greater Fort Worth Tomorrow,* Congress enacted the Federal-Aid Highway Act, which provided 90 percent of the enormous costs of land acquisition, relocation, and demolition for interstate highways penetrating directly into the city. In 1962 it approved another Highway Act that required every urban area of more than 50,000 to develop "long-range highway plans and programs which are properly coordinated with plans for improvements." It also provided the money to pay for these plans.

Gruen's vision for *A Greater Fort Worth Tomorrow* may have been stillborn but it inspired countless similar proposals. During the 1960s virtually every urban area issued federally required and funded "area transportation studies" proposing interstate-highway loops around the central business district and radial interstate highways connecting them with the suburbs. Like Fort Worth, the governments that commissioned these plans chose to ignore Gruen's radical reconstruction of the central business district. However, if there was opposition to granting such preeminence to the automobile, the local government also added a pedestrian street similar to what Gruen had proposed in 1957 for Kalamazoo (see Chapter 7). Where there was substantial momentum for housing redevelopment, a convention center, or some other prescription, these were also incorporated into the plan. But whatever the variants, they were all versions of the same noble, logical diagram asserting itself with ever growing intensity.

For the next quarter-century, Gruen's diagram remained the common vision of the future metropolis. There was a growing market of suburban residents who needed easy access to downtown jobs and an increasingly worried group of downtown merchants, property owners, and politicians who depended on their spending. There also was plenty of federal money to pay for Gruen's diagrammatic solution to their problems and little opposition from occupants of the fringe areas that needed to be acquired for the highway loops. Besides, there was no alternative diagram that better provided for vehicular traffic. Only when most of the 41,000 miles of the interstate highway system was reaching completion did Gruen's vision of the future metropolis finally lose its appeal.

Synergistic Government Expenditures

Cities continually change. Consequently, an end-state plan is of limited utility. To be effective, comprehensive planning must be ongoing. Frederick Law Olmsted, Jr., explained this in 1911 at the third national conference on city planning:

> *We must disabuse the public mind of the idea that a city plan means a fixed record upon paper of a desire by some group of individuals prescribing, out of their wisdom and authority, where and how the more important changes and improvements in the physical layout of the city are to be made.... We must cultivate... the conception of a city plan as a device or piece of administrative machinery for preparing, and keeping constantly up to date, a unified forecast and definition of all the important changes, additions and extensions of the physical equipment and arrangement of the city.*[39]

For such planning even to take place, it must be an established function of municipal government, like street maintenance or fire protection. During the first decades of the twentieth century, when Burnham, Bennett, Nolen, and the Olmsted brothers began preparing city plans, that notion seemed farfetched. At the end of the century, when municipal governments everywhere include large numbers of "planners," civic leaders still question the need for planning. Thus, whenever budget cuts are required, city planning is among the first to suffer. Nevertheless, city planning has become an important, ongoing government activity because, as New York's Committee on the City Plan explained in 1914, "it means getting the most out of the expenditures that are bound to be made." More important, the strategic deployment of these expenditures can obtain effects that are greater than would be produced if they were made independently.

Ongoing strategic deployment of municipal expenditures requires a standardized planning methodology and budget procedures that reflect that planning. Lots of cities engage in such planning without having printed city plans. Among cities that have printed comprehensive plans, two stand out because of their strategic use of government expenditures: the 1947 *Comprehensive City Plan* for St. Louis and the 1969 *Plan for New York City.* Both are based on extensive (almost atlas-like) analyses of their city's topography, infrastructure, community facilities, demography, and economy. Both demonstrate understanding and respect for past and present municipal expenditures. Yet, neither presents any vision of the future metropolis. They are snapshots of city planning at that particular time in that particular city, and their effectiveness is simply a reflection of the effectiveness of local planning activity.

Harland Bartholomew and the St. Louis Comprehensive City Plan

The 1947 *Comprehensive City Plan* for St. Louis was the work of Harland Bartholomew, who had moved to St. Louis in 1916 to become its first city planning "engineer." He remained in that position until his retirement in 1950, devoting half his time to this municipal job and the rest to establishing and administering what for decades was the country's preeminent private city planning consultant firm.[40]

Bartholomew, who was born in 1889 and died 100 years later, started his career in 1912 as a civil engineer in the New York City office of E. P. Goodrich. The just-established Newark City Plan Commission had hired Goodrich and architect George B. Ford to prepare a comprehensive city plan. Bartholomew, who like Goodrich and Ford had never worked on such a plan, was assigned to the job. Despite his inexperience and relative youth at 23, Bartholomew's role was so important that the report they produced, *City Planning for Newark,* lists him as "assistant engineer" directly beneath "expert advisors" Goodrich and Ford.[41]

Bartholomew was different from many of his pioneering colleagues because he believed effective city planning required total immersion in the locality and direct involvement with municipal government. This approach grew out of his work in Newark, where he had experienced the suspicion with which visiting "experts" are viewed by full-time civil servants. As a result, he jumped at the opportunity of becoming the City Plan Commission's engineer in 1914, when its contract with Goodrich and Ford expired. The position made him the nation's first full-time, salaried, professional planner on any municipal payroll. More important, it underscored for him the importance of being part of the bureaucracy entrusted with deciding on and then implementing any recommendations. Bartholomew moved to St. Louis two years later, before much of his work could be brought to fruition. However, the experience provided the basis for his work in St. Louis and hundreds of other cities.

Bartholomew was director of planning for St. Louis from 1916 to 1953. Three years after moving to the city he established Harland Bartholomew and Associates, a city planning consulting firm which he directed for 42 years. Because he lived in and worked out of St. Louis, he could not provide other cities that contracted for his services with the same intimate involvement. Consequently, key personnel moved to any city that retained his firm. They had to remain there for the term of the contract, usually 3 years. Once relocated, they worked with citizen advisory committees that both reviewed their work and organized political support.

Each plan was based on a standardized approach that had been devised by Bartholomew, who also was responsible for its basic strategy and contents. It usually included sections on park and recreation facilities, streets and highways, transit, water and rail transportation, sewers and water supply, city appearance, zoning, the legal and financial aspects of the city plan, and (sometimes) housing. Each of these components was also standardized. For example, the section on streets and highways included typical cross-sections illustrating the proper dimensions and layout for a range of arteries. Between 1920 and 1926 the firm produced 20 of the nation's 87 comprehensive city plans. Its foremost competitor, John Nolen, was only responsible for 12.[42]

The firm was no less successful when it came to implementing recommendations. Bartholomew was not interested in just producing documents. He wanted to institutionalize city planning as an effective component of municipal government. Thus, "if it was the wish of the contract city to retain its Bartholomew representative on a permanent basis (as it often was) and the latter was agreeable, Bartholomew acted as a kind of sponsor for the union."[43] As a result 408 cities, especially in the middle west, employed planning officials who had started their careers with Harland Bartholomew and Associates.[44]

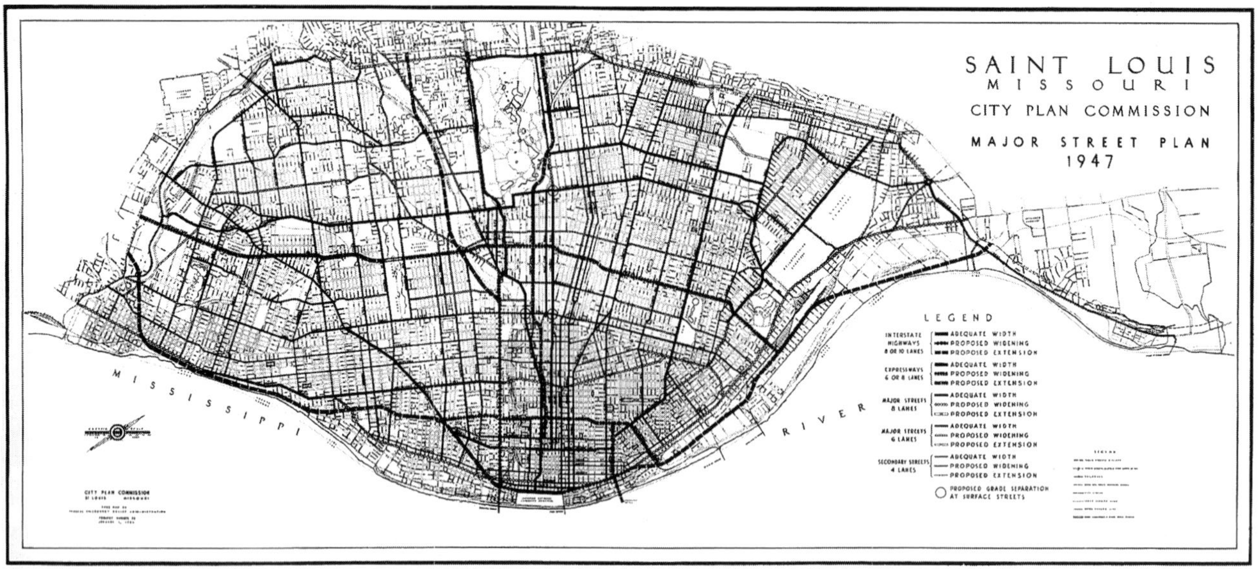

St. Louis, 1947. Highway Plan proposed by Harland Bartholomew in the Comprehensive City Plan indicates proposed widening and extensions of Interstate Highways, expressways, 8-lane major streets, 6-lane major streets, and 4-lane secondary streets. *(Courtesy of Art and Architecture Library, Yale University)*

The approach to planning espoused by Bartholomew and his followers became known as the *city efficient* or *city practical* in contrast to the *city beautiful* approach ostensibly practiced by Burnham, Bennett, and Bogue. The term may have evolved because of the many engineers attracted to the profession, or because the comprehensive plan proposals that were implemented most frequently tended to be elimination of grade crossings, installation of water and sewer systems, and street widenings, or because practicality was easier to sell politically than esthetics. It is a misnomer. All professional planners of that era were committed to clear presentation of carefully collected data, scientific analysis of this information, restructuring city government to improve its efficiency, and expansion of the bureaucracy to insure better delivery of municipal services. The city plans they produced (whether called city beautiful or city efficient) included similar proposals for park and parkway expansion, civic center development, and street improvements.

By participating in municipal government, Bartholomew ensured the entrepreneurial element needed for plan implementation. His success in St. Louis, however, came from concentrating on the money his recommendations required. Between 1916, when he prepared the first report on the city plan, and 1947, when he produced his last major plan for St. Louis, Bartholomew guided the development and expenditure of $157 million in bond issues. As a result virtually all the projects he proposed came to fruition, including the establishment, paving, and widening of streets, bridges, and viaducts; the construction and reconstruction of water and sewer systems; the creation of major public plazas, parks, and playgrounds; the removal of countless railroad grade-crossings; and the modernization, enlargement, and construction of public hospitals, firehouses, schools, garages, and even airports.[45]

By the time the 1947 *Comprehensive City Plan* was issued, Bartholomew had developed the same deep understanding of St. Louis that Burnham had of Chicago. Rather than inspire readers with European planning paradigms and gorgeous renderings of his vision of the future metropolis, Bartholomew presented quantifiable information describing St. Louis. This included graphs showing current and projected population by decade between 1800 and 1970, tables presenting the amount of land devoted to various uses by decade between 1915 and 1945, maps of existing and proposed facilities, and charts indicating existing dimensions and proposed changes to local streets, major arteries, and interstate highways. It was all intended to convince civic leaders, government employees, and voters that the recommendations made in the plan were unavoidable, given the probable course of city development.

The *Comprehensive City Plan* assumed that by 1970 the city would have grown by 10 percent and then listed the improvements needed both to accommodate this growth and to catch up with the unavoidable neglect that occurred during the Depression and World War II. Major recommendations included revision of the zoning ordinance, construction of express highways, development of extensive off-street parking facilities to eliminate downtown congestion, provision of a citywide system of neighborhood parks, playfields, and playgrounds, clearance and redevelopment of slum districts to provide decent housing for low- and moderate-income families, and creation of 35 airfields (including 3 major airports).

In fact, the population of St. Louis dropped 24 percent, from 816,000 in 1940 to 622,000 in 1970.[46] Nevertheless, most of Bartholomew's recommendations were implemented. The city continued with site assemblage and development of the Jefferson National Expansion Memorial to be created along the waterfront. It continued work on the Memorial Plaza—Civic Center (see Chapter 4). It condemned and cleared a series of "blighted areas" that became public housing and redevelopment projects. It built limited-access highways that had been recommended both along the waterfront and into the suburbs. The only major element in the plan that was ignored was its proposed 35 airfields. Bartholomew had completely misjudged the future of commercial and private aviation.

Bartholomew possessed neither Daniel Burnham's artistic genius nor his inspirational vision. However, by institutionalizing the planning function within city government, he was able to develop an equally deep involvement with his city and to persuade its citizens to spend the large sums needed to implement his proposals.

The Plan for New York City

Comparing the 1947 St. Louis *Comprehensive City Plan* with the 1969 *Plan for New York City* is like comparing a pocket dictionary with an encyclopedia. The *Plan for New York City* is a 25-pound boxed set of six oversized volumes. Unlike Bartholomew's work, it did not reflect a 30-year commitment to urban planning as an integral function of municipal government. The *Plan for New York City* was produced because the newly elected Lindsay administration decided to use the City Planning Commission to spearhead fundamental reform of city policies and programs.[47]

Although the 1938 city charter had established a City Planning Commission and required it to prepare a comprehensive city plan, none had ever been published. More important, the federal government was threatening to cut off housing and urban-renewal subsidies that, since 1959, had required such a document. The absence of a comprehensive city plan thus became the excuse for producing a document that presented the administration's policies and programs.[48]

Lindsay appointed one of his closest associates, Donald H. Elliott, to be chairman of the City Planning Commission. During the first 11 months of the administration, Elliott had been counsel to the mayor. Before that he had been director of research for the Lindsay campaign and a member of the mayor's law firm. Thus, for the first time in its history, the City Planning Commission was to be headed by an individual who had unusual rapport with the mayor and broad sanction to develop administration policy. Upon taking office Elliott rashly promised to release the much-demanded comprehensive plan. When he was given a copy of the existing draft he junked it and exploited the situation to reorganize the Department of City Planning, to refocus its activities, and to set forth publicly the planning initiatives of the new administration.[49]

Up to that time the Department of City Planning had been a small, insular agency located in one of lower Manhattan's faceless office buildings. Elliott quickly opened offices in each of the city's five boroughs, established an urban-design group to propose major planning initiatives, and added expert professional staff that worked with operating agencies on such citywide issues as housing, mass transit, economic development, and the environment. The borough offices were responsible for helping to divide the city into community planning districts, provide the forthcoming *Plan for New York City* with individual chapters on each district, and maintain ongoing liaison with these districts and their appointed community planning boards.[50]

The *Plan for New York City*, produced under the direction of Edward Robin, the administration's new director of comprehensive planning, included one volume devoted to critical issues facing the city and individual volumes on each of the city's five boroughs. The borough volumes are mini-atlases with sections on the borough as a whole, on each planning district, and on areas of special concern, such as the Model Cities neighborhoods. The district sections (which were also published separately so they could be distributed to residents) included: (1) an aerial photograph, (2) photographs of characteristic neighborhood scenes, (3) maps presenting the city's land use policy (essentially, colored zoning maps), (4) maps locating *all* community facilities, public and publicly assisted housing, transit stations, urban renewal and historic districts, and scheduled capital budget expenditures, (5) charts detailing public-school utilization and enrollment, hospital and nursing care facilities and capacity, size and apartment distribution of all public and publicly aided housing projects, scheduled capital construction projects, subway travel times, and listing virtually all other public facilities, (6) tables presenting population characteristics by age, racial composition, household size, and income, and (7) a text describing the area, its history, its population, and the planning issues it was facing. No American city government had ever before printed a document that presented such comprehensive information on all its neighborhoods. Not until 1991, when the Cleveland City Planning Commission issued its *Cleveland Civic Vision 2000 Citywide Plans* would any city government produce a document of similar scope.

The Critical Issues volume also included dozens of additional maps, graphs, charts, and photographs. It set forth the Lindsay strategy for reinforcing the city's role as the national center, increasing opportunities for self-realization, improving the city as a living environment, and making city government more responsive. William H. Whyte, doing essentially what Charles Moore had done for Daniel Burnham, was its unacknowledged editor.

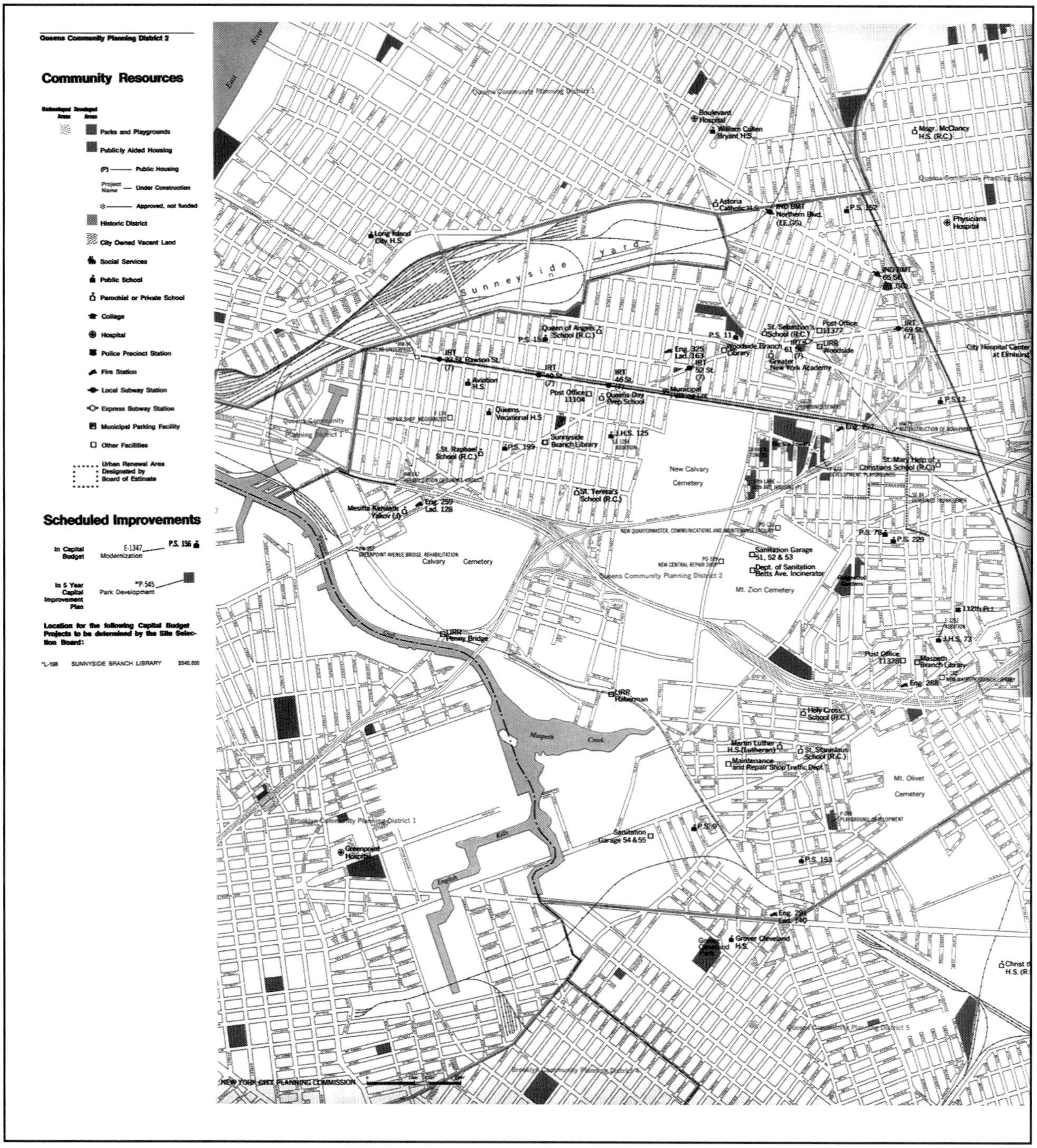

Queens, 1969. Map of community resources and scheduled capital improvements for Community Planning District 2. *(From New York City Planning Commission, Plan for New York City, vol. 5, Queens, New York, 1909)*

Comprehensive city plans had always concentrated on improving the environment. The *Plan for New York City* was different in reflecting traditional local concern for the three other critical issues: the national center, opportunity, and government. The plan concentrated on the national center because it was the engine generating the power to do everything else—*money.* By advocating programs and policies that encouraged expansion of national-center activities, the Lindsay administration hoped to generate economic expansion and, therefore, the taxes to pay for additional services in poverty areas. The focus on increasing opportunity grew out of the city's historical role in providing immigrants, minorities, and especially the poor with a chance to make better lives for themselves. Here again, by emphasizing business expan-

TABLE 18.1
SCHEDULED CAPITAL IMPROVEMENTS*[51]

Number	Description	Estimated cost, $
E-789	New West Queens High School	14,700,000
E-1265	Addition to Intermediate School 126	550,000
E-1327	Renovation to Intermediate School 126	1,289,000
F-16	New firehouse for engine company 262	567,000
HW-147	Rehabilitation of Queens tunnel viaduct	6,125,000
HW-163	Paving of Hazen Street	650,000
HW-182	Paving and repaving of 31st Avenue	715,000
L-159	New East River Branch Library	731,420
P-127	New playground at Public School 17	(lump sum item)
P-127	New playground at Public School 76	(lump sum item)
PO-106	New 114th Precinct police station	2,440,000
PW-18	Bower Bay pollution control plant, 1st and 2d stages	49,093,000
PW-133	Storehouse	
PW-186	Modernization of old county courthouse	197,000
PW-231	Rehabilitation of Queensboro Bridge	2,800,000
PW-237	Bower Bay pollution control plant, 3d stage	32,000,000
T-65	East 63rd Street–41st Street subway route	37,663,360
TF-446	New parking facility (Queensbridge Plaza)	6,125,000
TF-452	Parking field (Steinway Street and 31st Avenue)	90,000
HS-32*	New ambulatory health services station	1,289,000

*Queens Community District No. 2.

sion in Manhattan, the administration hoped to create additional employment and, thus, additional opportunity for its citizens. The attention to government reflected the administration's profound commitment to citizen participation and decentralization in the delivery of municipal services. This was not an attempt to balance the administration's commitment to the central business district. It was an attempt to alter government by an entrenched civil service, which Lindsay believed was unaccountable to its elected officials, geographically separated from the neighborhoods that it served, and thus unresponsive to its residents.

Comprehensive city plans usually presented public expenditures without offering priorities. The *Plan for New York City* proposed a strategy for selecting priorities. It separated the city into *major action areas* (essentially concentrations of poverty), where it proposed to direct 60 percent of the city's resources, *preventive renewal areas,* which could go downhill very fast without additional investment and where it proposed to concentrate 30 percent of the city's resources, and *sound areas,* which would only need 10 percent of the city's resources.

Other comprehensive city plans promised a better city once their proposals were implemented. The authors of the *Plan for New York City* made no such promise. Instead, they wrote:

> *We are…optimistic. But we are also New Yorkers. We cannot see Utopia. Even if all of [our] recommendations were carried out, if all the money were somehow raised, ten years from now all sorts of new problems will have arisen, and New Yorkers will be talking of the crisis of the City, what a hopeless place it is, and why does not somebody do something. Our hope for this Plan is that it will help give them good choices to make.*[53]

In order to avoid controversy, the *Plan for New York City* was not released until after Mayor Lindsay's reelection. The delay did not avoid a storm of criticism. The document became a lightning rod for middle-class resentment of the administration's focus on the poor, especially African Americans, Puerto Ricans, and other minorities. When the commission scheduled public hearings in each of the 62 community planning boards, it was followed from place to place by irate citizens who opposed siting public housing projects in "decent neighborhoods," civilian review of police practices, community control of ghetto schools, and a variety of other Lindsay policies presented in the document.

TABLE 18.2
PUBLIC LIBRARIES*[52]

Name and Address	Number of Books			Hours Open Weekly
	Total	Adult	Child	
Astoria: 14-01 Astoria Blvd.	26,862	14,602	12,260	40
Broadway: 20-40 Broadway	63,641	43,178	20,463	50
Queensbridge: 10-43 41st Street	13,344	6,922	6,422	30
Ravenswood: 35-32 21st Street	24,392	14,689	9,703	40
Steinway: 21-45 31st Street	34,986	22,952	12,034	47

*Queens Community District No. 2.

New York City, 1969. Major Action Areas to which the Plan of New York City proposed to direct 60 percent of the city's resources. *(Courtesy of New York City Department of City Planning)*

The plan was also opposed by the city bureaucracy, which was not at all interested in shifting its priorities or opening itself to community review. Furthermore, elected officials refused to reallocate funds (ostensibly) being spent to provide all citizens with municipal services, merely to compensate for the greater needs of poverty areas. Thus, there never was any chance of concentrating 60 percent of the city's resources in those areas the City Planning Commission designated for "major action."

Civic groups and professional organizations, impatient with the voluminous data on neighborhoods that they were not concerned with, complained that there was no vision of the future city. They wanted elaborate renderings of their favorite projects. Without these projects there was no way to obtain their support and thus no way to develop the necessary citywide constituency.

The *Plan for New York City* was quietly abandoned during the last year of the administration. Nevertheless, it has continued to have substantial, though largely unnoticed, impact. Billions of dollars have been spent on the development of Roosevelt Island, the Javits Convention Center, the North River Pollution Control Plant, the redevelopment of downtown Brooklyn, and countless housing projects, all initiated during Elliott's chairmanship and advocated by the plan. The Beame administration, in implementing the Neighborhood Preservation Program, made "preventive renewal" part of the city's housing strategy (see Chapter 12). In 1979, when the Koch administration incorporated the presentation of planning data by the community district into the annual budget process, the City Planning Department simply institutionalized techniques used in the *Plan for New York City.* Most surprising of all, a quarter-century after publication this out-of-date document is still the only comprehensive atlas of the City of New York.

Like Bartholomew's plan for St. Louis, the *Plan for New York City* was successful in shaping its city's future because it was a snapshot of ongoing planning activity that had been initiated years prior to publication and because it was the product of its authors' determined effort to institutionalize city planning as an ongoing municipal function. But also like the *Comprehensive City Plan* for St. Louis, it only influenced the city for which it was prepared and had no impact on the

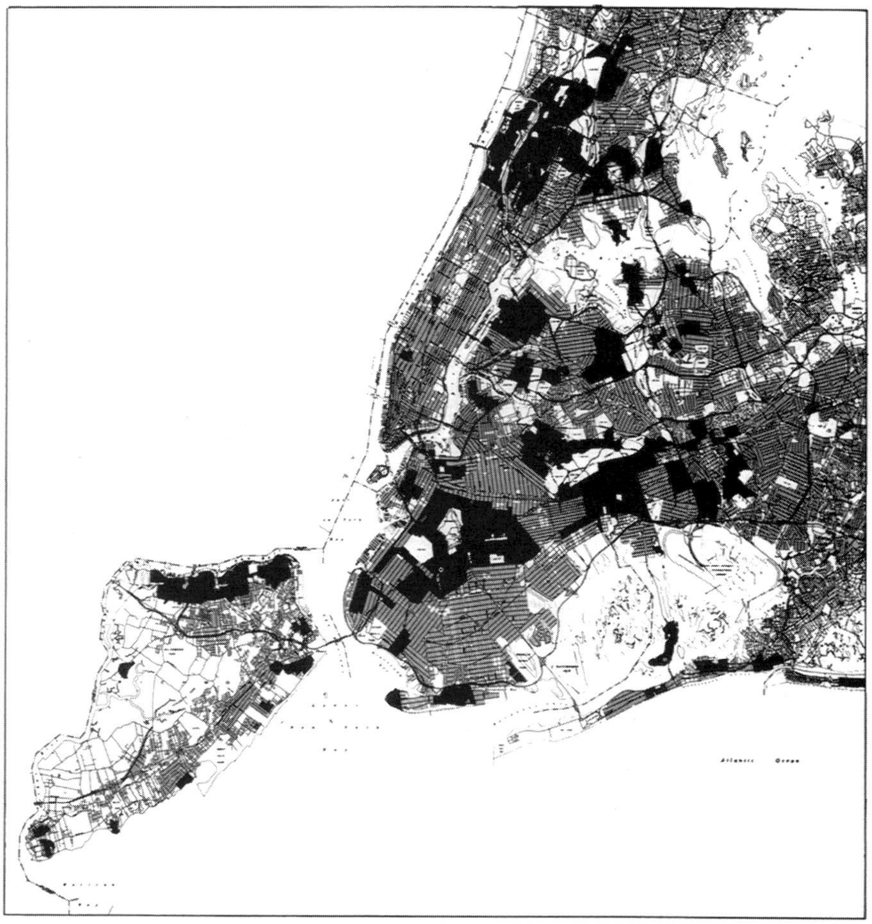

New York City, 1969. Preventive Renewal Areas to which the Plan of New York City proposed to direct 30 percent of the city's resources. *(Courtesy of New York City Department of City Planning)*

course of American city planning. A mass of data without a noble, logical diagram just does not stir the blood.

Planning as a Continuing Process

Once the World's Colombian Exposition and the *Plan of Chicago* had demonstrated the possibility of successfully planning an entire city, once virtually every municipal government had institutionalized the city planning function, civic leaders faced new and continuing demands for participation in the planning process. These demands came from developers who were unhappy with existing zoning, from neighborhood groups who wanted a role in determining the future of their communities, from architects who demanded to remake the landscape to fit their vision of a better city, from civic organizations unhappy with existing government priorities and budget allocations, from political leaders who felt they should participate in any municipal decision making, and from city residents who just wanted to improve their living conditions.

Professional planners were initially suspicious of any interference. Outside consultants hired to prepare comprehensive city plans questioned intrusion by anybody who lacked the necessary "expertise." Planners working inside government agencies were not at all eager to give up their role in determining what property owners were permitted to do with their land and buildings or their role in shaping the government's own projects. Neither group could hold out for long. People who want to solve their own problems and spend their own money usually find ways of doing so.

Every day in every city people launch proposals that did not originate within the planning profession. They sidestep strategies for municipal expenditure and visions of the good city in order to proceed with those proposals that have enough political support. This widespread citizen participation in the planning process need not produce sad results. The trick is to involve all the participants in an ongoing city planning process. This is what happened in Philadelphia in the 1940s, 1950s, and 1960s under the guidance of its planning director, Edmund Bacon and what began in Portland, Oregon, during the 1970s and 1980s.

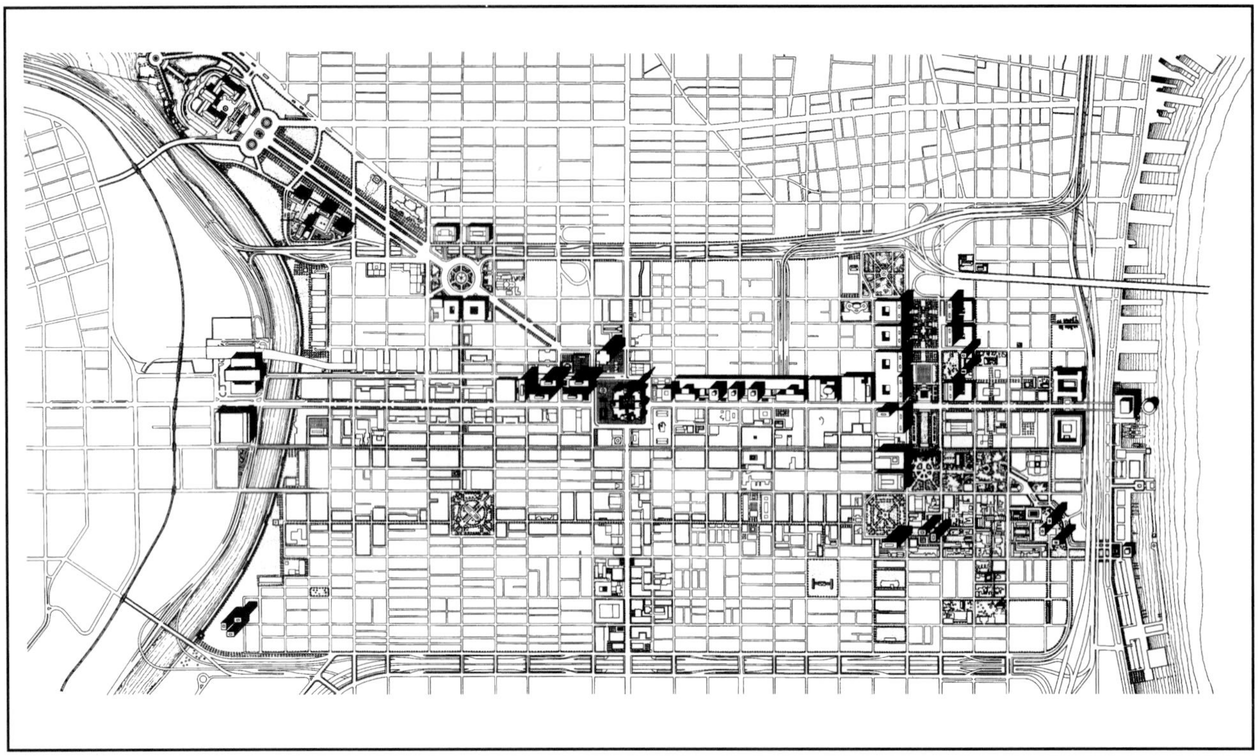

Philadelphia, 1960. Redevelopment of Center City as proposed in the comprehensive plan. *(Courtesy of Department of City Planning, Philadelphia)*

Edmund Bacon's Philadelphia

Demand for a comprehensive reconstruction of Philadelphia originated during the Great Depression. Banks, having agreed to refinance the city's debt during a period of plummeting tax collections, had imposed drastic spending restraints. Meanwhile the corrupt Republican machine that ran the city continued its outmoded, patronage-ridden, but politically profitable service delivery system. This combination of inefficient government and limited funds resulted in continuing deterioration of the city's capital plant and demands for greater levels of public investment.[54]

Planning, slum clearance, and housing reform had been dominated by the Philadelphia Housing Association since its creation in 1909. During the late 1930s a group of reformers, the "young Turks," entered the fray. This informal collection of young business leaders and professionals concentrated on charter reform and opposition to the Republican machine.

They were defeated at the polls in 1939, only to regroup as the City Policy Committee, this time concentrating on urban planning. After considerable lobbying they obtained the mayor's approval for the creation of a powerful Planning Commission, which was established by a unanimous vote of the City Council in 1942. At their suggestion the mayor appointed Robert B. Mitchell as its first director and agreed to focus the commission's efforts on demographic and topographic analysis, the condition of the city's capital plant, and mass transit.

In 1943, in order to generate additional support and monitor the new commission, reformers organized the Citizens' Council on City Planning. In 1944 the Fairmount Park Association proposed clearing the slum just north of Independence Hall and replacing it with a formal, landscaped mall. The Center City Residents' Association, formed in 1946, demanded a major effort to fight downtown housing deterioration and to prevent residential displacement by commercial land uses that were incompatible with neighboring residences.

All these demands for action came together in 1947 at the Better Philadelphia Exhibition. The show was sponsored by a blue-chip committee organized by Edward Hopkinson and Walter Philips, respectively chairmen of the Planning Commission and the Citizens' Council. They raised $400,000 to mount the show and persuaded Gimbel's Department Store to house it at no charge. The idea, as articulated in the official exhibition brochure, was "to dramatize city planning—to gain the confidence of a public made cynical by utopian futuramas and the inertia of local politicians."

During the two months that the show was open, it attracted more than 385,000 visitors, who were presented with aerial maps, drawings, cartoons, a diorama, lights that went on and off, and all manner of bells and whistles. The show, whose appearance had been conceived by architect Oscar Stonorov,

Philadelphia, c. 1950. Aerial view of the approach to the Old Broad Street Station (popularly known as the "Chinese Wall") that became the site of Penn Center. *(Courtesy of The Free Library of Philadelphia)*

was a true expression of the ideas, concerns, and interests of all the proponents of city planning in Philadelphia. The most impressive of the displays was a 30-foot-long model of downtown Philadelphia with sections that flipped over to illustrate how to achieve a better Philadelphia. It included Independence Mall, Penn Center, Society Hill, and many of the other planning projects that were to be executed over the next few decades.

One year after the exhibition closed, yet another civic organization, the Greater Philadelphia Movement, was established. Its purpose was to bring together the city's 35 most powerful business executives as a force for municipal improvement, to fight for charter reform, and to implement the projects launched at the Better Philadelphia Exhibition.

The man who would coalesce these disparate citizen groups and ideas for a better Philadelphia was Edmund Bacon. Bacon received an architecture degree from Cornell and settled in Philadelphia, where he quickly became one of the young Turks. He left to study design and planning with Eliel Saarinen at Cranbrook Academy in suburban Detroit. Then he worked for 3 years as a planner and housing expert for the city of Flint, Michigan, before returning to Philadelphia. In 1941 Bacon became managing director of the Philadelphia Housing Association. It was a position that enabled him to bridge the gulf between traditional housing reformers and the rapidly growing number of advocates for other planning activity. It was also perfect preparation for his appointment in 1949 as executive director of the Planning Commission.

The year 1949 proved critical for planning in Philadelphia. The reformers and their agenda were endorsed at the ballot box. Joseph S. Clark, Jr., was elected city controller and Richardson Dilworth was elected city treasurer. A Charter Commission was appointed. It proposed and obtained voter approval in 1951 of a strong-mayor form of government and a powerful planning commission with powers that tied together physical with fiscal planning. The new planning commission would be responsible for enacting zoning regulations, approving housing and redevelopment projects, coordinating the arterial and park development, and preparing an annual capital construction budget and a 6-year capital improvement program.

Thus, when Clark was elected mayor in 1951, he had a ready-made planning constituency, a generally-agreed-upon planning strategy, a planning commission with all the powers needed to initiate it, and a planning director who was uniquely qualified to coordinate its implementation. In an act pregnant with symbolism, Clark had City Hall scrubbed. He also had old gaslamps replaced with electric lights, regularized street cleaning, modernized garbage collection, established an $80 million sewage-treatment system, and inaugurated the $150 million capital program proposed by the planning commission.

Bacon, who was executive director of the City Planning Commission until 1970, has described his approach to urban planning as "the painful search for form." In fact, it was a continuation of a participatory process that had long been under way. Each of the projects that he worked on underwent what he called "democratic feedback." Each was forced to change, and change often, until the project satisfied the requirements of the consumer, the institutions providing the financing, the developer, neighborhood groups, citywide civic organizations, local politicians, and (if the money was coming from Washington) federal regulations. Changes to Independence Mall, for example, were made to meet the requirements of the National Park Service, which in 1952 agreed to finance the project. Changes to Penn Center were more of a reflection of real estate practices. Changes to Society Hill were a reflection of virtually all the participants (see Chapter 2 and Chapter 11).[55]

In the case of Penn Center, Clark and Bacon began by persuading the Pennsylvania Railroad to vacate its Broad Street Station, demolish its viaduct, and make the site available for construction of the commercial center that had been envisioned at the Better Philadelphia Exhibition. Bacon's 1952 design concept envisioned three similar city blocks organized around a continuous 1400-foot-long sunken concourse that was open to the sky along its 150-foot width, except where it was bridged over by the city's street grid. The concourse was intended to provide an attractive, continuous, pedestrian connection between a suburban railroad station and the center of town. Each block was to be bounded on the north and south by retail shops that opened both to the concourse level below and to the street level above. Large office slabs were to be built along the eastern edge of each block.

The scheme could not generate sufficient revenue to justify the high price wanted by the Pennsylvania Railroad. Its developer, Robert Dowling, believed the project could be made feasible by increasing rental revenues and decreasing development costs. He proposed to eliminate the underground concourse, with what he believed would be money-losing shops, and to increase revenues by substantially enlarging the floor area devoted to office space by increasing the number of office buildings, and by relocating them to the longer north and south portions of each block. These revisions required pedestrians coming from public transit facilities to cross city streets.

Mayor Clark was willing to increase the office space but forced Dowling to restore the basement-level concourse. But, without the continuous opening to the sky, the concourse became an maze of tunnels, except at those spots where small courtyards with staircases to street level provided pedestrian access and a bit of natural light. The midblock space between office slabs became a shadowed alley that could attract only minimal pedestrian activity. The compromise was poor urban design, but it allowed the project to proceed. More important, it triggered private construction of dozens of office buildings on neighboring blocks.

Philadelphia, 1976. The absence of pedestrian traffic to and from the basement-level retail concourse at Penn Center has guaranteed that the open space between its buildings remains empty and uninviting. *(Alexander Garvin)*

Society Hill required similar compromises. The original plan did not anticipate the inner expressway loop running along the Delaware River edge of the neighborhood, which the city decided to build once Congress had passed the Federal-Aid Highway Act. In 1957, the Planning Commission hired architects Larson, Stonorov, and Kling to prepare a redevelopment plan that adjusted to these new realities. The following year the plan was again revised because it did not meet the requirements of downtown homeowners for greater rehabilitation assistance. Then, when sites were offered for development, the design was changed again to meet the marketing objectives of the winning team, developer William Zeckendorf, Sr., and architect I. M. Pei.

The nation's most sophisticated and complex planning process had been under way for two decades when, in May

Philadelphia, 1994. Market Street was completely rebuilt by individual property owners once Penn Center replaced the "Chinese Wall." *(Alexander Garvin)*

1960, the City Planning Commission issued a document entitled *The Comprehensive Plan of the City of Philadelphia.* It presented an analysis of the existing conditions and desired goals in 103 pages of maps, charts, and text. There were concise discussions of the city's history, population, economy, industry, commerce, recreation, community facilities, residence, transportation, and land use. The presentation of transportation, retailing, parks, and everything else reflected a logical hierarchy stepping upward in size from the smallest neighborhood phenomenon, past the community level, the district level, the regional level, till the hierarchy came to its peak at the center city level. The plan tried to provide every citizen with at least a minimum level of service. It identified what was missing at each level and recommended action. It also proposed channeling additional growth to the center city and to major high-density corridors. Any similarity to the complex, participatory-planning process that produced Penn Center or Society Hill, however, was purely coincidental.

Over the next decade, the commission issued dozens of amplifying documents, which stated that they were "in conformity with the Comprehensive Plan." There were major District Plans (for Northwest and West Philadelphia), small but detailed Redevelopment Area Plans, and functional plans, such as the 1968 *Comprehensive Plan for Swimming Pools* (a ludicrous contradiction in terms). Perhaps these documents were needed as part of the capital programming process or to meet specific federal requirements. However, with the exception of the redevelopment-area plans, they bore little relation to the tremendous changes Edmund Bacon was bringing to the cityscape. The area around Penn Center was becoming the city's premier office district. The area around City Hall was once again a municipal asset. In an attempt to balance Penn Center, a second, combination commuter-railroad, transit, retail, office-complex was taking shape along East Market Street. Additional redevelopment projects (perhaps not as exquisite as Society Hill) were under way, and interstate highways were spreading across town.

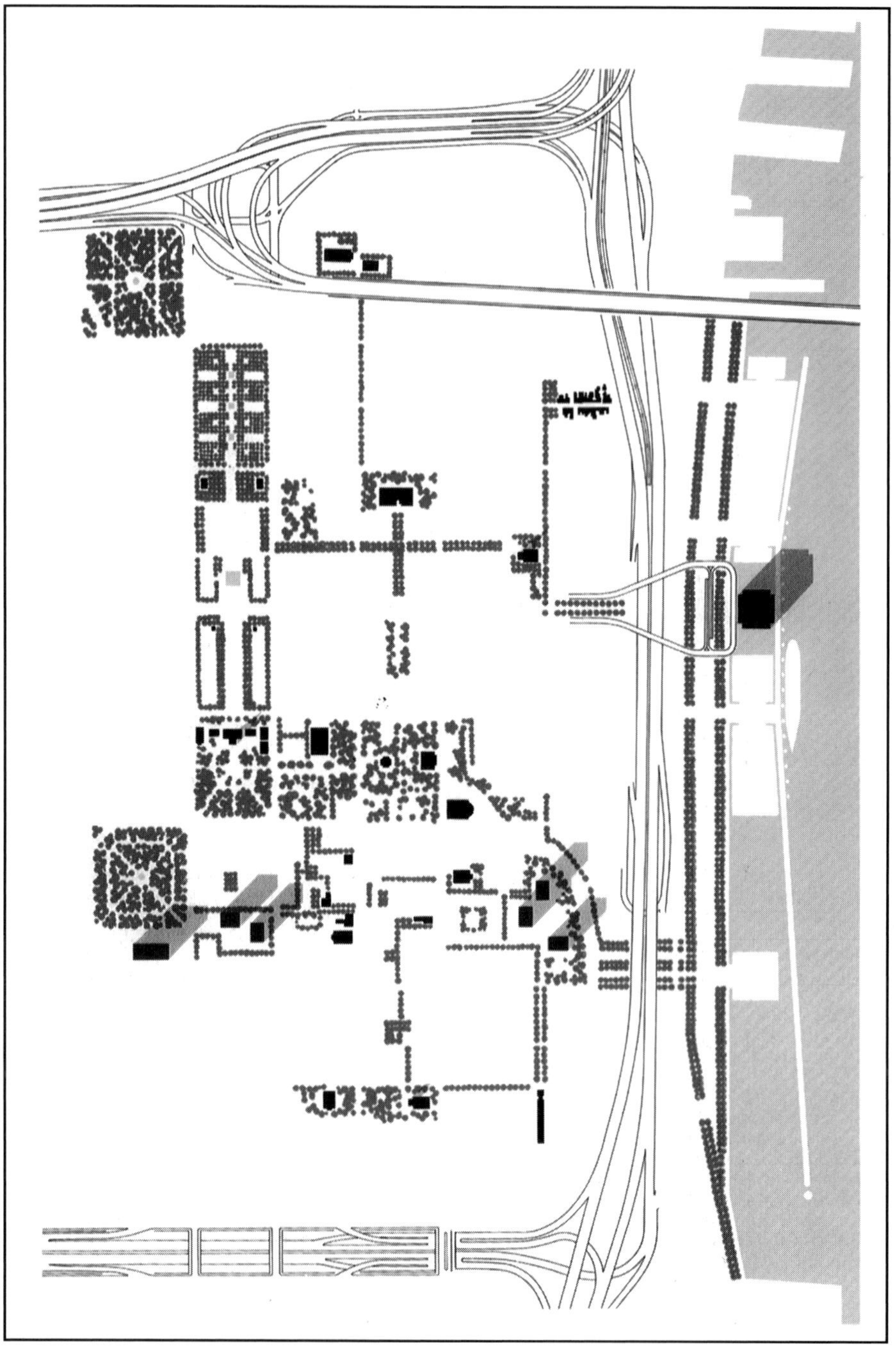

Philadelphia, 1963. Plan for Society Hill. *(Courtesy of Department of City Planning, Philadelphia)*

Only during the late 1960s, when community opposition to highway construction had become a national phenomenon, did any part of Bacon's "total vision of the city" face defeat. In 1970 the 2.8-mile South-Street link in the center-city loop highway was stopped by a coalition of environmentalists who hated highways, African Americans who feared displacement, and liberals who opposed creating a "Mason-Dixon Line" that would separate upper-middle-class whites from the African Americans living south of the proposed loop.

Edmund Bacon had greater impact on the planning and development of his hometown than any individual except Robert Moses in New York and Daniel Burnham in Chicago. Like Burnham, he had created a noble, logical diagram that had the power to stir the blood. Like Bartholomew, he had institutionalized the planning function in government and then exploited the power it brought. *The Comprehensive Plan of the City of Philadelphia* had little to do with that impact. Bacon's extraordinary effectiveness was the product of the planning process he helped to create.

By remaining an integral part of Philadelphia's planning process for three decades, Bacon himself became the focus of the city's "collective consciousness." By constantly adjusting to

Philadelphia, 1993. Society Hill continued to be one of the city's most desirable residential areas ever since the Urban Renewal Project was completed. *(Alexander Garvin)*

"democratic feedback," he met the needs of the other participants in the planning process. By seeking and employing resources from wherever they might be available, he implemented the collective "total vision of the city." This "patient search for form" had the same dramatic impact on the course of development in Philadelphia that Burnham's *Plan of Chicago* had on that city.[56]

The Transformation of Portland, Oregon

There are few more stunning examples of the effectiveness of city planning than the transformation of Portland between 1970 and 1990. At the beginning of that period Portland had been a city with a stable population but declining retail sales, deteriorating buildings, and many other symptoms of decline. At its conclusion the city's population had grown from 380,000 to 437,000. It had a port whose export tonnage was the third-largest on the Pacific Coast, a bustling retail district, plus a wide array of lively residential neighborhoods.[57]

Unlike other cities on the west coast, Portland experienced neither population growth nor economic boom after World War II. In fact, between 1946 and 1960, "the number of daily personal trips into the core business area fell from 118,500 to 105,000. The count of commuters...coming in for shopping fell by 2000, for personal business by 3000, and for recreation by 11,000."[58]

In an attempt to reverse this decline, civic leaders during the late 1950s initiated the usual combination of highway construction and slum clearance. Whether because of unhappiness with the visual character of resulting development, or the social consequences of the dislocation it caused, or just continuing economic stagnation, a new generation of activists took matters into their own hands and brought about Portland's revitalization.

The same components were used for the comprehensive replanning of Portland as were used by Burnham and Gruen—circulation, open space, and public facilities. The combination was neither spectacular nor diagrammatic. It was conceived to minimize disruption and tailored to the topography, land use, and physical development of only one city: Portland.

Circulation was the critical factor without which the other two elements would have had little impact. The necessary elements were already in place. The city's original street grid with its 200-foot by 200-foot blocks provided the framework for internal vehicular circulation. Its interstate highways provided easy access to the entire metropolitan region. Unfortunately, both systems usurped prime components of the city's public open space (its downtown streets and riverfront) and neglected the interests of anybody who was not in a car or truck.

Completion of the inner-loop highway around downtown Portland, in 1973, eliminated the need for the six-lane Harbor

Portland, 1990. Tom McCall Waterfront Park. *(Alexander Garvin)*

Portland, 1979. 6th Avenue Transit Mall. *(Alexander Garvin)*

Drive that ran along the Willamette River on the western edge of the business district. As a result Harbor Drive could be transformed into Tom McCall Waterfront Park without causing any disruption to traffic and without relocating a single resident or business.

A trade-in of interstate highway-fund reservations helped to pay for a suburban light-rail system and the two-avenue, 11-block pedestrian/transit mall that opened in 1977 (see Chapter 7). Neither the light rail nor the transitways caused much disruption because both only involved existing city streets. Moreover, the entire 300-block downtown was declared a free fare zone. As a result, by 1978, one-quarter of the trips downtown were by mass transit.

Most of the city's public open space was also largely in place. Portland, along with Savannah, is exceptional among American cities in including a substantial amount of downtown public space. The Plaza, North, and South Park Blocks provide small-scale open spaces right at the edge of the business district. The city's short blocks with sidewalks every 200 feet, allocate an unusually large proportion of downtown land to pedestrians. Prior to the city's midcentury decline, these sidewalks attracted the lively pedestrian activity that Jane Jacobs has demonstrated so persuasively is required by any healthy city.

This pedestrian activity could be revived if existing facilities (both the sidewalks and the public squares) were improved and strategic additions made to the existing system. Accordingly, the Plaza and South Park Blocks were restored and relandscaped. Fifth and Sixth Avenues were rebuilt as pedestrian/transit malls. The most important additions to the city's open space, however, were Tom McCall Waterfront Park and several new park blocks.

The first new park block was the Ira Keller Fountain, completed in 1966. This delightful place, designed by Lawrence Halprin and Associates, was created by turning an entire city block into a small, water park/amusement center. The fountain attracts children to play in its waterfalls, adults to sunbathe on nearby platforms, and tourists to gape at the lively scene.[59]

Pioneer Courthouse Square is the most important new park block (see Chapter 1). It is located at the intersection of the pedestrian/transit mall and the light rail system. The site had been occupied by McKim, Mead, and White's Portland Hotel until it was torn down for a parking garage in 1951. As the single most accessible block in downtown Portland, it had been suggested as an additional public park from the inception of the pedestrian/transit mall. In 1979, the city finally purchased and demolished the garage that occupied the site. The following year the city sponsored an international design competition that attracted 162 submissions. It was won by a team of local artists and architects that included Martin/Soderstrom/Matteson. The municipal government refused to appropriate enough money to pay for the design. Consequently, the Friends of Pioneer Square, a citizens' group formed to lobby for the project, raised an additional $750,000 by selling bricks stamped with the individual contributor's name. Pioneer Courthouse Square was completed in 1984, and quickly became the catalyst for additional development in the surrounding area.

Changes to the circulation system may have increased Portland's accessibility. A comfortable pedestrian environment may have made it an increasingly attractive destination. For the city to compete successfully for its rapidly growing regional market, however, there had to be reasons for going there. These were provided by the third element of Portland's planning: public facilities.

In an attempt to create a civic center without disrupting existing traffic or land use patterns, the city designated sites surrounding the Plaza Blocks for municipal, county, and federal buildings. The necessary central focus is provided by the Portland Building, a 15-story municipal office structure fronting on both the pedestrian/transit mall and the Plaza Blocks. This structure was considered so significant an addition to the cityscape that a design competition was held to select the architect. The winning design, by Michael Graves, was completed in 1984. Its bold design ties together nearby but very disparate civic buildings.

A few blocks away, another cluster of blocks is developing into a cultural center. It consists of facilities for the performing arts, the visual arts, and the Oregon Historical Society. The three performance halls include a remodeled 1927 movie theater converted in 1984 into the 2800-seat Arlene Schnitzer Concert Hall, and the 450- and 900-seat theaters in the Performing Arts Center, built in 1987. Visual arts facilities include the Portland Art Museum, the Pacific Northwest

Portland, 1979. Ira Keller Fountain. *(Alexander Garvin)*

College of Art, and the Northwest Film and Video Center. As in the case of the civic center, existing street, block, and lot patterns remain undisturbed.

One of the city's most unusual public facilities is "Saturday Market" at the north end of the riverfront park. There, under the Burnside Bridge, scores of artisans and craftspeople show and sell their wares. It is open every Saturday and Sunday from March to Christmas. At the other end of the park, RiverPlace attracts other tourists to its marina, waterfront esplanades, restaurants, and shops (see Chapter 14).

All these facilities draw thousands of people who would not otherwise be downtown. Together with the new and restructured public spaces and circulation systems, they have transformed Portland into one of the liveliest and most urbane of American cities. This transformation did not happen by itself. It is the result of citizen demand for something better than conventional highway and renewal projects, increasing advocacy of local interests by civil servants, and growing politicization of every aspect of city planning.

Portland has had a long history of reliance on city planning. In 1903 the Board of Park Commissioners asked John Olmsted to prepare a proposal for a major park and parkway system. After failing to attract Daniel Burnham to prepare a comprehensive plan, the Civic Improvement League hired Edward Bennett, who produced the 1911 *Greater Portland Plan.* Seven years later Charles Cheney issued a series of reports on housing and planning that provided the basis for the establishment of a Planning Commission in 1918, a Housing Code in 1919, and a Zoning Ordinance in 1924. This was followed in 1930–1932 by studies of transportation and land use by Harland Bartholomew and in 1943 by Robert Moses' 85-page plan for *Portland Improvement.*

Like Harbor Drive, much of this planning history was junked during the 1970s and 1980s. By 1970, opposition to

Portland, 1990. Pioneer Courthouse Square. *(Alexander Garvin)*

Portland, 1990. Government Center. *(Alexander Garvin)*

Portland, 1990. Broadway (performing arts center). *(Alexander Garvin)*

highways and urban renewal resulted in the election of a younger, more reform-minded city council. It included Neil Goldschmidt who, as mayor between 1972 and 1979, spearheaded the creation of the suburban light-rail system, pedestrian/transit mall, and waterfront park. The growing power of citizen action is amply demonstrated by the role played by "The Friends of Pioneer Square" in forcing the city to go ahead with this project and then raising money to pay for it.

The commitment to city planning continued, only with a very different approach. It was embodied in a series of new documents: *Planning Guidelines—Portland Downtown Plan* (1972), *Comprehensive Plan* (1980), and *Portland Center City Plan* (1988). Unlike earlier plans, these documents were prepared by municipal civil servants, not by outside experts. They were policy statements issued by the Portland Planning Commission and adopted by the City Council, not consultant reports. They were developed over several years and involved public consultation. Consequently, they reflected the opinions and desires of the city's population more accurately than earlier documents and included many more proposals that were likely to be implemented.

By the 1970s, virtually every agency in city and state governments included "city planners." There was no longer the former separation between functional agencies concerned with traffic or water supply on one hand and the city planning department on the other. More important, the thinking of the planners themselves had changed radically. Artistically determined visions of the city beautiful and carefully engineered proposals for the city efficient had been replaced by relativistic pluralism. Professional planners now saw themselves as part of an adversarial system in which they could responsibly make different proposals depending on which government agency, civic organization, or private developer they represented.

In 1967 Paul Davidoff, the most articulate spokesperson for this approach, wrote a widely read article proposing to empower citizens who were left out of the decision-making process. Government money would be appropriated to hire "advocate planners" for neighborhoods that could not afford to pay for professional services. While Davidoff's specific proposals were not implemented in Portland or anywhere else, they played a major role in shaping the character of further planning in Portland, New York, and other cities.[60]

A growing number of Portland's younger civil servants believed in widespread citizen participation, and not just because it reflected their planning philosophies. Citizen participation had become an integral part of the federal Urban Renewal, Model Cities, and Economic Opportunity Programs that paid their salaries. Consequently, they had every reason to include residents in every aspect of their work.

Community planning itself was institutionalized by Mayor Goldschmidt in 1974, when he obtained City Council approval for the creation of an Office of Neighborhood Associations (ONA). Beginning in 1975, ONA coordinated the production of "neighborhood needs reports." It became as much a part of the city budget process as the community district budgets initiated by the *Plan for New York City.* As a result of this reshaped planning process, the number of active neighborhood groups in Portland "doubled from about thirty to sixty between 1974 and 1979."[61]

Ingredients of Success

Effective comprehensive planning, like that practiced in Chicago at the beginning of the twentieth century, Philadelphia in the middle of the century, and Portland at the end of the century, provides an attractive alternative to formless growth. Few people today believe in such planning. The reason was identified in 1947 by the brochure for the Better Philadelphia Exhibition: "a public made cynical by utopian futuramas and the inertia of local politicians." We must overcome that cynicism. But that is only the first step. It must be followed by activities that generate a constituency for comprehensive planning.

Daniel Burnham clearly understood the fundamental role of a constituency for comprehensive planning when he called for big plans that stir the blood. From time to time great artists do appear. Like Burnham, they can provide the necessary "noble diagram." In those instances, the lucky city should grab this unique opportunity. As Burnham also understood, that noble diagram needs to be marketed. He worked with civic leaders to mount the single most-effective lobbying effort anywhere for the implementation of a comprehensive plan.

Artistic genius is a scarce commodity that cannot be provided to hundreds of cities at the same time. Since third-rate talent just will not provide the necessary inspiration, proponents of comprehensive planning are more likely to succeed by generating a constituency either within municipal government or from widespread participation in a public decision-making process.

An institutionalized city planning process worked for Harland Bartholomew because he simplified and standardized its components so that they could be understood and manipulated by all the participants. It also worked when it was applied to the budget process in New York City. As long as a Harland Bartholomew or a Donald Elliott is there to provide that leadership, the results are excellent. But when that process is leaderless, the results will be as chaotic as the budget and planning process in New York City during the early 1990s.

Philadelphia and Portland demonstrate that a participatory planning process also can generate support for planning. The difficulty with this approach is that its very success becomes a threat to a city's political establishment. As soon as the opportunity arises, that establishment will seek to regain its power and eviscerate the planning process. The course of planning in Philadelphia after Edmund Bacon's retirement is a very sad demonstration of this fact.

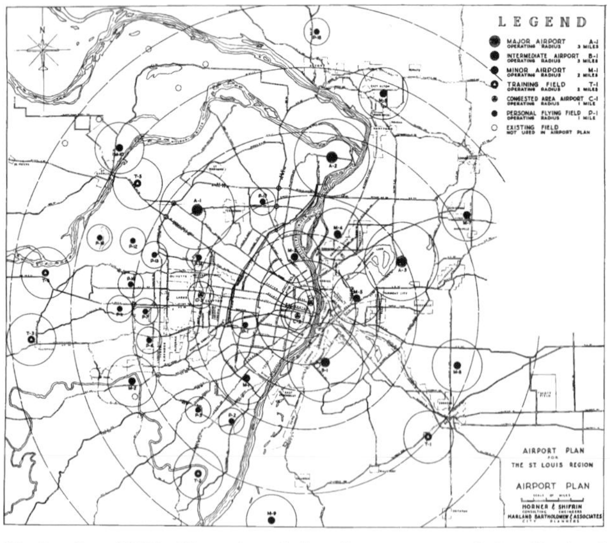

St. Louis, 1947. The airport locations proposed by Harland Bartholomew in the Comprehensive City Plan were based on the mistaken notion that air travel was a neighborhood rather than a regional service. *(Courtesy of Art and Architecture Library, Yale University)*

Market

Perhaps the least understood and most important ingredient in comprehensive planning is its market. As so many authors of Section 701 plans discovered, asserting a "need" does not mean that people will desire it enough to pay the price. Nor does portraying a "better" city mean that the electorate will support it.

Asserting a "need" and then proposing public action to satisfy that need is futile if there is no demand for it. Too often planners recommend public action without truly understanding its market context. Even as sophisticated a planner as Harland Bartholomew can misjudge the market, as he did in 1947 when he proposed 35 airfields for St. Louis. All the more reason to avoid planning that is not market-oriented.

If a market exists, intelligent planning can shape its effect on the city. For example, Edmund Bacon accurately identified demand for office space in downtown Philadelphia. He also identified some of the impediments preventing businesses from remaining there: inconvenient access from suburban areas, the blighting influence of the "Chinese Wall," and inadequate residential opportunities for a middle-class labor force that wanted to walk to work. Penn Center and Society Hill successfully eliminated some of these impediments. The marketplace did the rest.

Location

It is not enough to identify locations for transportation, recreation, housing, commerce, industry, and public facilities. Hundreds of cities have published elaborately colored maps that prescribe the correct location for every land use. Few if any of these maps have transformed the cities for which they were prepared. Those that have succeeded did so because they exploited or compensated for the characteristics of specific locations or increased proximity to desired facilities.

The *Plan of Chicago,* for example, identified Lake Michigan as a locational asset and proposed actions that would allow the city to benefit from that asset. Based on those recommendations, the city spent hundreds of millions transforming the lakefront into the location of choice for office and apartment buildings. Similarly, the plan identified the Chicago River as an obstacle to downtown commercial development and proposed straightening its course and building what became Wacker Drive. By following those suggestions, the city eliminated impediments to development along the river.

The *Comprehensive City Plan* for St. Louis proposed projects that would increase the desirability of locations throughout the city by placing public facilities near them. In the business district it concentrated on highway access and parking; for residential neighborhoods, it proposed schools and recreation-

Chicago, 1989. Billions of dollars worth of private construction was generated by the public improvements proposed by Daniel Burnham for the shore of Lake Michigan. *(Alexander Garvin)*

al facilities; for the city as a whole it advocated airports. Decentralizing airport locations may have been a mistake. But, the locational analysis of parking, schools, and recreation, however, was of real benefit in making capital-budget expenditures.

To be effective, a comprehensive plan must identify a few critical components and locate them so that they can become an interdependent combination generating more than the sum of its parts. Portland achieved this result by strategically locating improvements to its circulation system, adding open space, and building new public facilities. The interdependent combination that was created attracted a large portion of the regional market to Portland's downtown office, retail, and tourist businesses.

Design

The power of a "noble, logical diagram" lies in its clarity which, as Burnham so persuasively argues, "will be a living thing, asserting itself with ever growing insistency." This is also its liability. The entire planning profession was initially beguiled by Daniel Burnham's combination of Haussmann's Paris with the Chicago Fair. But whether it was applied to hilly San Francisco and Seattle or to relatively flat Portland and Minneapolis, this scheme proved to be stillborn. Only when Burnham himself applied it to Chicago was any part of it successful, and then only because inappropriate components were ignored.

Another approach is to tailor comprehensive planning to the topography, history, and physical development of an existing city. Edmund Bacon took this approach in planning for Philadelphia. Society Hill and Independence Mall are inapplicable to cities without significant eighteenth-century architecture; just as projects like Penn Center would be impossible in cities without suburban train stations and subway systems. Only when an inner highway ring was superimposed over existing streets, dividing long-established communities, did Bacon's plan run into opposition.

Dimensions, arrangement, and character of the components of the plan play important roles. Portland began with blocks that were 200 feet square. This frequency of streets and sidewalks allowed for greater than usual reliance on pedestrian activity. The blocks created by the 1683 plan for Philadelphia were 425 feet by 500 to 675 feet. To make them pedestrian-friendly, Bacon introduced greenways.

Bacon's scheme also rearranged the components of the city. Moving the produce market from Society Hill to South Philadelphia improved the efficiency of food distribution and removed an impediment to downtown residential development. Such rearrangement, though, is only possible when it reduces the cost of doing business. Gruen's proposal for creating a new pedestrian level for Fort Worth and banishing service vehicles to underground streets would have improved the delivery of goods and services and increased pedestrian and vehicular safety. The cost of retrofitting downtown Fort Worth, however, would have been borne by property owners. They would have had to pay to move ground floor uses to a rebuilt second level, while losing revenue from at least one story. Understandably, they scuttled his plan.

Financing

There is no way to implement comprehensive planning without money. As Burnham's *Plan of Chicago* and Bartholomew's *Comprehensive City Plan* for St. Louis both demonstrate, this is not just a matter of dollars. Cities will appropriate billions when they believe they will be getting their money's worth. Burnham's proposals for the Chicago lakeshore proved easy to finance when it became clear that private developers would follow suit by building along the lakeshore and that new construction would generate more than enough additional tax revenues to retire the bond issues that paid for the park and parkway development. Gruen's diagram was applied to cities across the country because the federal government was ready to pay 90 cents for every 10 contributed locally. Bacon's plan for Society Hill became a reality only when it became eligible for federal urban renewal assistance.

Money is available for all sorts of projects. As New York City's Committee on the City Plan wrote in 1914, comprehensive planning "means getting the most out of the expenditures that are bound to be made and saving future expense in replanning and reconstruction." Bartholomew in St. Louis and Bacon in Philadelphia, both tried to develop equitable methods for prioritizing these expenditures. Consequently, both cities made expenditures in communities that did not have their fair share of public facilities. More important, Bacon and Bartholomew also identified major projects that would have citywide impact and thereby helped to create constituencies for their implementation.

If comprehensive plans are to be effective they must, like the *Plan for New York,* specify all recommended projects, their cost, and the source of the money to pay for them.

Entrepreneurship

The entrepreneurial problem in comprehensive planning is that planners do not implement their own proposals. Burnham solved the problem by organizing a marketing effort that inspired citizens to vote for bond issues, legislators to appropriate funds, civil servants to spend this money, and private developers to build his vision for the city. Bartholomew solved the problem by placing planners within the municipal government for which he was planning, thereby generating implementation from within the bureaucracy. Bacon's genius in getting his plans realized was in adjusting his proposals until they satisfied the requirements of both private developers and government officials. Those planners who forget that they do not have the power or ability to make anything they propose happen by itself are doomed to be forever irrelevant.

Thus, if comprehensive plans are to be implemented, they must specify the actions that are necessary and who is responsible for those actions.

Time

Few comprehensive plans consider time in terms of movement through different parts of the city. Fewer still examine the quality of life, 24 hours a day throughout the year. If they did, there would be far fewer cities with areas that empty out in the morning when people go to work or are deserted at night after they have gone home.

The period of time least considered in comprehensive plans is the time it takes to implement the recommendations. So much time is required that comprehensive plans can become obsolete quite quickly. In Philadelphia, once downtown revival was under way, the constituency for further spending waned and opponents were able to defeat the downtown highway loop. In New York City, once Nixon terminated federal-housing assistance programs, the ambitious urban renewal strategy proposed in the *Plan for New York City* was no longer feasible.

Successful comprehensive plans must be both politically and financially feasible. As Burnham explained, a comprehensive plan can only "be executed by degrees, as the growth of the community demands and as its financial ability allows."[62] For this reason, he recommended not indicating the exact details too closely. The more important reason so many proposals in his *Plan of Chicago* were executed is that they could be altered to meet the demands of the political and financial context of the period in which each implementation became possible. Authors of future plans ought to follow his example.

Comprehensive Planning as a City Strategy

There is no way to force municipal governments to produce imaginative comprehensive plans like the *Plan for Chicago*. Nor is there any way to guarantee implementation. At best, one can legislate procedures that make planning issues a part of the public dialogue, provide the public with the information needed to avoid single-function decision making, and ensure that necessary personnel is in place should a municipal government decide to engage in comprehensive planning.

The significant word is *planning*, not plan. Virtually every city has produced at least one "comprehensive city plan." In most cases, these plans have lacked the vision to inspire public support and their authors have lacked the political skill and drive needed to guarantee implementation. As a result, they are only comprehensively ignored.

When citizens have ready access to information about their neighborhoods and the city as a whole, there is a better chance for a political consensus to emerge and, along with it, the demand for comprehensive planning. Inexpensive computer technology now permits both the quantitative and graphic presentation of virtually any information on an area-by-area basis. Thus, there is every reason to provide the electorate with the basis for making intelligent planning decisions about their neighborhood.[63]

Congress should enact legislation requiring and funding computerized, locally prepared, *comprehensive city information systems* that would be updated annually. These would save the federal government millions of dollars and would allow the Census Bureau to tabulate and analyze comparative data that it now has difficulty obtaining. They would also provide other federal agencies with the local information required in their decision making.

The legislation should also require cities to publish a standardized, annual *comprehensive city atlas* with both citywide and small-area information organized in tabular and map form. Small-area data would be used for presentation of neighborhood statistics in the atlas, for tabulation and analysis by the Census Bureau, and for decennial reapportionment of local, state, and federal legislative districts.

The information system and atlas would provide community groups, civic organizations, and politicians with information that is now available only on a scattered basis to selected portions of the municipal bureaucracy. Whether they choose to use this information to fight for more equitable allocation of resources or improved delivery of municipal services or comprehensive planning or anything else would depend on the locality. But at least the contents of the public dialogue would be altered forever, and the information needed for comprehensive planning would be available on an annual basis.

Most municipal governments will choose to designate their city planning department as the proper agency to maintain its comprehensive city information system and publish its comprehensive city atlas. This will simultaneously provide a clearly defined role for the city planning agency and a permanent source of funding for its activities. In the absence of other obligations, it may also relegate the agency to a bookkeeping rather than a planning function.

The best way to ensure a central role to city planning departments is to amend city charters, assigning to them an entirely new function: annual preparation of a *comprehensive city budget impact analysis* that would examine the effect of annual city expenditures on such things as property values, business investment, retail sales, employment, tax collection, housing construction and rehabilitation, and traffic flow. The budget impact analysis would be presented both on a citywide and neighborhood level and include specific proposals for future budgets. It could be paid for by allocating 1 percent of the city's annual capital expenditures to pay for agency activities. Another charter amendment would be necessary to prevent city administrations from discontinuing the activity or eliminating the money needed by the agency during periods of fiscal stringency.

Once a city government created a comprehensive city information system, published a series of city atlases and budget impact analyses, and involved community activists, elected officials, and civil servants in these ongoing comprehensive-planning activities, it would have established the necessary preconditions for production of a genuine *comprehensive plan.*

The easy availability of all this local-area information should spur private investment. For the first time, property owners, developers, investors, and financial institutions will have the data they need to predict the future of every location within the city and of government spending in those locations. The reduced level of uncertainty will make them more likely to risk their money and also more likely to make intelligent decisions.

Together, these federally and locally mandated activities will alter the public dialogue and institutionalize comprehensive planning as an ongoing municipal activity. They will improve the quality of municipal decision making and ultimately the quality of life as well. Most important, they will establish the preconditions for the realization of truly "big plans" with the magic to stir the blood.

Some cities will issue truly comprehensive plans. But whether they do or not, this planning process will make it more likely that local governments will devote increasing attention to public action that produces a sustained and widespread private market reaction.

Notes

1. Norton E. Long, *The Polity,* Rand McNally, Chicago, 1962, p. 192.
2. Despite the fact that there is no known source for this quotation it is always attributed to Daniel Burnham. It is quoted in a 1918 Christmas card from Willis Polk to Edward Bennett as a statement by Burnham made in 1907.
3. Committee on the City Plan, *Development and Present Status of City Planning in New York City,* City of New York, Board of Estimate and Apportionment, Committee on the City Plan, New York, 1914, p. 12.
4. Edmund Bacon, public comments made at a conference sponsored by the Institute for Urban Design, held in New York City, April 22, 1988.
5. Daniel H. Burnham and Edward H. Bennett, *Plan of Chicago* (first published in Chicago in 1909), Da Capo Press, New York, 1970, p. 1.
6. Historical material on the life of Daniel Burnham is derived from Thomas S. Hines, *Burnham of Chicago,* Oxford University Press, New York, 1974.
7. Burnham and Bennett, op. cit., p. 17.
8. Historical and statistical material on Haussmann's work on Paris is derived from David H. Pinkney, *Napoleon III and the Rebuilding of Paris,* Princeton University Press, New Jersey, 1958; Anthony Sutcliffe, *The Autumn of Central Paris,* Edward Arnold, London, 1970; Henri Malet, *Le Baron Haussmann et la Renovation de Paris,* Les Editions Municipales, Paris, 1973; Sigfried Giedion, *Space, Time and Architecture,* Harvard University Press, Cambridge, 1956, pp. 641–679; and François Loyer, *Paris Nineteenth Century—Architecture and Urbanism,* Abbeville Press Publishers, New York, 1988.
9. Loyer, op. cit., pp. 129, 234, and 407–408.
10. Other writers emphasize that these broad arteries provided canons with an unobstructed path of fire and, therefore, could play a major role in suppressing insurrections.
11. See Chapter 4, note 2.
12. Hines, op. cit., pp. 174–196.
13. While Edward Bennett was formally acknowledged as assisting in the preparation of the *Report on a Plan for San Francisco,* Willis Polk was not. Polk was an American architect who had spent 2 years with D. H. Burnham in Chicago before starting his own architectural practice in San Francisco. He closed his firm in order to take charge of the San Francisco office of D. H. Burnham and Company Polk's role in developing the *Report,* is presented in Richard Longstreth, *On the Edge of the World,* M.I.T. Press, Cambridge, Mass., 1989, pp. 298–304.
14. Daniel H. Burnham assisted by Edward H. Bennett, *A Report on a Plan for San Francisco, A Facsimile Reprint of the 1906 Plan,* Urban Books, Berkeley, California, 1971, p. 35.
15. Mel Scott, *The San Francisco Bay Area: A Metropolis in Perspective,* University of California Press, Berkeley, 1985, p. 109.
16. Charles Norton and Charles Wacker, chairman and vice-chairman of the Chicago Plan Committee, were to become Burnham's major allies in this endeavor. In 1909, the Chicago City Council appointed Wacker the first chairman of the City Plan Commission, a position which gave him a primary role in getting the *Plan of Chicago* adopted and then implemented. Norton, who left Chicago in 1909, became a major advocate for planning in New York City, where in 1914 he chaired the Advisory Commission that produced *Development and Present Status of City Planning in New York City,* and later spearheaded the creation of the Committee on Regional Plan, which produced the 1929 *Regional Plan and Survey of New York and its Environs.*
17. Hines, op. cit., pp. 318–322.
18. Robert Bruegmann, "Burnham, Guerin, and the City as Image," pp. 16–28 in *The Plan of Chicago: 1909–1979,* Catalogue to the Exhibition of the Burnham Library of Architecture, The Art Institute, Chicago, 1979.
19. Burnham and Bennett, *Plan of Chicago,* p. 108.
20. Ibid, p. 1.
21. Chicago Plan Commission, *Ten Years' Work of the Chicago Plan Commission 1909–1919,* Chicago Plan Commission, Chicago, 1920, pp. 2–7.
22. Harold M. Meyer and Richard C. Wade, *Chicago: Growth of a Metropolis,* University of Chicago Press, 1969.
23. Daniel H. Burnham and Edward H. Bennett, *Plan of Chicago,* p. 2.
24. Chicago Plan Commission, op. cit., p. 13.
25. Walter D. Moody, *Wacker's Manual of the Plan of Chicago,* Chicago Plan Commission, Chicago, 1916.
26. Frederick Law Olmsted, Jr., "Introductory Address on City Planning," Rochester, New York, May 2–4, 1910, reproduced in Roy Lubove, *The Urban Community,* Prentice-Hall, Englewood Cliffs, 1967, pp. 81–94. For a review of his city plans see Susan L. Klaus, "Efficiency, Economy, Beauty: The City Planning Reports of Frederick Law Olmsted, Jr., 1905–1915," *Journal of the American Planning Association,* vol. 57, no. 4, American Planning Association, Chicago, Autumn 1991, pp. 456–470.
27. Historical and statistical information on American city planning prior to 1929 is derived from Henry Vincent Hubbard, *Our Cities To-day and To-morrow: A Survey of Planning and Zoning Progress in the United States,* Harvard University Press, Cambridge, 1929. Additional material going through to 1965 can be found in Mel Scott, *American City Planning Since 1890: A History Commemorating the Fiftieth Anniversary of the American Institute of Planners,* University of California Press, Berkeley, 1969; and through 1980, in M. Christine Boyer, *Dreaming the Rational City: The Myth of American City Planning,* M.I.T. Press, Cambridge, 1983.
28. American Society of Planning Officials, *Planning: The ASPO Magazine,* American Society of Planning Officials, Chicago, September 1972, pp. 197–201.
29. Secretary of Commerce Herbert Hoover, *Standard City Planning Enabling Act,* 1928.
30. Sec. 701(d), Housing Act of 1954.
31. William H. Wilson, op. cit., pp. 213–233.
32. Ibid., p. 224.
33. Virgil G. Bogue, *Plan of Seattle,* Lowman & Hanford Co., Seattle, 1911, p.11.
34. Victor Gruen, *The Heart of Our Cities,* Simon & Schuster, New York, 1964, p. 198.

35. Ibid., p. 178.
36. Victor Gruen, "No More Offstreet Parking in Congested Areas" originally published in *The American City,* September 1959 and reprinted in George M. Smerk (editor), *Readings in Urban Transportation,* Indiana University Press, Bloomington, 1968, pp. 78–81.
37. Victor Gruen & Associates, *A Greater Fort Worth Tomorrow,* Greater Fort Worth Planning Committee, Fort Worth, 1956.
38. Jane Jacobs, "Downtown Is for People" in The Editors of Fortune, *The Exploding Metropolis,* Doubleday Anchor Books, Garden City, 1957, p. 146.
39. Frederick Law Olmsted, Jr., "President's Address of Welcome," Proceedings of the Third National Conference on City Planning, p. 12.
40. Historical and statistical information on Harland Bartholomew is derived from Bartholomew's city plans, from Eldridge Lovelace, *Harland Bartholomew: His contributions to American City Planning,* University of Illinois Office of Printing Services, Urbana, 1993, and from Norman J. Johnson; "Harland Bartholomew: Precedent for the Profession," in Donald A. Krueckeberg (editor), *The American Planner: Biographies and Recollections,* Methuen, New York, 1983, pp. 279–300.
41. E. P. Goodrich and George B. Ford, *City Planning for Newark,* L.J. Hardham Printing Co., Newark, 1913, p. iv.
42. Johnson, op. cit., p. 284.
43. Ibid., p. 287.
44. Lovelace, op. cit., pp. A-15 to A-19.
45. Harland Bartholomew, *Comprehensive City Plan, St. Louis, Missouri,* City Plan Commission, St. Louis, 1947, pp. 70–74.
46. U.S. Bureau of the Census, *Statistical Abstract of the United States: 1978,* U.S. Government Printing Office, Washington, D.C., 1978, p. 25.
47 The 1961 City Charter provided for a City Planning Commission with seven members, six appointed by the mayor for staggered eight-year terms and a Chairman who served at the pleasure of the mayor. The Charter also designated the Chairman as Director of the Department of City Planning, which was responsible for a variety of ordinary government functions (e.g., maintaining the city map, administering the zoning ordinance, preparing a 5-year capital improvement program, etc.) and for providing the mayor, the planning commission, and the city's elected officials with information and advice regarding all matters related to the development of the city.
48. The Housing Act of 1954 required every community receiving urban renewal assistance to have a *workable program* for community improvement. The workable program was required to include seven components: (1) codes and ordinances, (2) a comprehensive plan, (3) neighborhood analyses, (4) an effective administrative organization,(5) a financing plan, (6) a relocation plan, and (7) a citizen participation program. At first most communities didn't qualify. To continue receiving assistance, therefore, they had to demonstrate steady progress in completing each component. The comprehensive plan itself was required to include six components: (1) a land use plan, (2) a thoroughfare plan, (3) a community facilities plan, (4) a public improvements program, (5) a zoning ordinance, and (6) a subdivision ordinance. While New York City had long argued that all six already existed, local officials of the Department of Housing and Urban Development kept pressing for a single document which tied them together into a coherent planning strategy.
49. Donald H. Elliott, interview, April 18, 1991.
50. The 1961 City Charter required the City Planning Commission to designate community planning districts, each with an appointed planning board that advised elected officials and city agencies on planning issues. In 1968 the City Planning Commission designated 62 districts. This number was reduced to 59 pursuant to the Charter changes of 1975.
51. New York City Planning Commission, *Plan for New York City,* Department of City Planning, 1969, vol. 5, p. 25.
52. Ibid.
53. New York City Planning Commission, *Plan for New York City,* Department of City Planning, 1969, vol. 1, p. 5.
54. Historical material on city planning in Philadelphia is derived from John F. Bauman, *Public Housing Race and Renewal—Urban Planning in Philadelphia 1920–1974,* Temple University Press, Philadelphia, 1987; Jeanne R. Lowe, op. cit., pp. 313–404; Edmund Bacon, *Design of Cities,* Viking Press, New York, 1967, pp. 243–271; Robert B. Mitchell (editor), "Special Issue: Planning and Development in Philadelphia," *Journal of the American Institute of Planners,* vol. 26, no. 3, American Institute of Planners, Baltimore, August 1960, pp. 155–241; "Philadelphia Story," *Progressive Architecture,* Reinhold Publishing, Stamford, April 1976, pp. 45–83; and Michelle Osborne, "A History of the ups and downs that finally resulted in the defeat of the expressway," *Architectural Forum,* Whitney Publications, New York, October 1971, pp. 39–41.
55. Bacon, op. cit., pp. 243–271.
56. Ibid.
57. Statistical and historical material on Portland is derived from Carl Abbott, *Portland—Planning, Politics, and Growth in a Twentieth-Century City,* University of Nebraska Press, Lincoln, 1983; Gideon Bosker and Lena Lencek, *Frozen Music: A History of Portland Architecture,* Western Imprints, The Press of the Oregon Historical Society, Portland, 1985; Terence O'Donnell and Thomas Vaughan, *Portland: An Informal History and Guide,* The Oregon Historical Society, Portland, 1984; and W. Dennis Keating and Norman Krumholz, "Downtown Plans for the 1980's: The Case for More Equity in the 1990's," *Journal of the American Planning Association,* vol. 57, no. 2, American Planning Association, Chicago, Spring 1991, pp. 136–152.
58. Abbott, op. cit., p. 210.
59. The site is part of the South Auditorium Urban Renewal Area, most of which is devoted to the superblocks of Portland Center. See Chapter 6.
60. Paul Davidoff, "Advocacy and Pluralism in Planning," *Journal of the American Institute of Planners,* vol. 31, American Institute of Planners, Chicago, November 1965, pp. 186–197; Richard Bolan, "Emerging Views of Planning," *Journal of the American Institute of Planners,* vol. 33, American Institute of Planners, Chicago, July 1967, pp. 233–245; Edmund M. Burke, "Citizen Participation Strategies," *Journal of the American Institute of Planners,* vol. 34, American Institute of Planners, Chicago, September 1965, pp. 186–197.
61. Abbott, op. cit., pp. 199–202.
62. Burnham/Bennett, *A Report on a Plan for San Francisco,* p. 35.
63. For a brief explanation of the potential of geographically based computer information systems see Laura Lang, "From the Ground Up," *Planning,* vol. 57, no. 7, American Planning Association, Chicago, July 1991, pp. 30–34.

Index

· ABOUT THE AUTHOR ·

Alexander Garvin

is an architect, city planner, real estate developer and manager, educator, and public servant. For the past 28 years he has taught the introductory course on "American Cities" at Yale. He is currently a commissioner on the New York City Planning Commission and was formerly New York City's Deputy Commissioner of Housing and Director of Comprehensive Planning.